First Edition

50 Fabulous Places

to Raise Your Family

By Lee & Saralee Rosenberg

CAREER PRESS
180 Fifth Avenue
P.O. Box 34
Hawthorne, NJ 07507
1-800-CAREER-1
201-427-0229 (outside U.S.)
FAX: 201-427-2037

50 FABULOUS PLACES TO RAISE YOUR FAMILY
ISBN 1-56414-034-2, $17.95
Cover design by Dean Johnson Design, Inc.

To the best of the authors' knowledge, the information provided in this book was the most current and accurate available at the time of printing. The material is for reference purposes only and is subject to change. Readers should confirm the latest information with the appropriate sources indicated.

To order this title by mail, please include price as noted above, $2.50 handling per order, and $1.00 for each book ordered. (New Jersey residents please add 7% sales tax.) Send to: Career Press, Inc., 180 Fifth Ave., P.O. Box 34, Hawthorne, NJ 07507

Or call Toll-free 1-800-CAREER-1 (Canada: 201-427-0229) to order using VISA or MasterCard, or for further information on books from Career Press.

Library of Congress Cataloging-in-Publication Data

Rosenberg, Lee, 1952-
    50 fabulous places to raise your family / by Lee & Saralee
Rosenberg.
      p. cm.
    ISBN 1-56414-034-2 : $17.95
    1. Quality of life--United States. 2. Family life surveys--United
States. 3. Metropolitan areas--United States. 4. Social
indicators--United States. I. Rosenberg, Saralee H. II. Title.
III. Title: Fifty fabulous places to raise your family.
HN60.R65 1992
306'.0973--dc20
                                                92-39518
                                                CIP

Acknowledgments

50 Fabulous Places to Raise Your Family incorporates thousands of tiny pieces of information from what appears, according to long-distance phone bills, to have emanated from an equal number of sources. We could never have drilled this deep without a spirit of generosity. Dozens of local experts in every city endowed us with their time, expertise and willingness to say, "I don't know, but I'll find out." Our team of researchers handed in mountains of notes under the guise of, "Gee, this seems so important I hate to leave it out." Thus, we were able to share the most pertinent, current, and insightful details.

Word one could not have been keyed in without the tireless efforts of our research team: Donna Henderson, Christina Lorenzen, Eileen Maurer, Hope Newman and, especially, Mira Temkin, my devoted, older, but never a "know-it-all" sister. A special thanks to Robert Weisser and his researchers at New Day Production Company, who came in to tie up loose ends. They all persevered through eye strain, backaches, dental work and the nagging fear of epitaphs that read "Died on hold."

We are eternally grateful to the hard-working staffs at mayor's offices, chambers of commerce, economic development organizations, city manager's offices, school districts, utility companies, real estate agencies, conventions and visitors bureaus, tax departments, police departments, hospitals, and environmental causes. Without their candid assessments, our Area Profiles would be little more than trite propaganda.

Thanks also to the agencies and organizations that provided their latest data: ACCRA (American Chamber of Commerce Researchers Association), Household Goods Carrier Bureau, PHH Homequity Corp., the U.S. Census Bureau and the U.S. Department of Education.

We were especially pleased with the "sunny and never stormy" help of Bill Campbell, Director of Meteorology at The Weather Channel in Atlanta. His painstaking, accurate climate analysis of our 50 cities made *our* job a breeze! Truly, this country's only all-weather, 24-hour satellite network is a great American resource!

Ditto with Runzheimer International in Rochester, Wis. This is the leading management consulting firm for travel and living costs. Getting customized data for all 50 cities was like winning the lottery. Thank you Peter Packer, vice president of communications, for commandeering the staff on our behalf.

The "fabulous" people at Career Press came through once again—big time! The patience and support of our editor, Betsy Sheldon, kept our collective blood pressure points at operating levels. Her vision and latitude contributed immensely to a final product that reflects well on all involved. Our talented production designer, Ellen Scher, started and ended every conversation with a pleasantry (we wouldn't have blamed her if she didn't) and our publisher, Ron Fry, tried to do the same (by no means an easy feat with a perilous project of this sort).

Finally, our spirits were lifted at just the right moment by family and friends, in particular by the children, Zachary, Alexandra and Taryn. They showed their love and support by bringing down water, coffee, snacks and even words of inspiration—"You'll be finished soon, right?"

We salute you all.

To Zachary, Alexandra and Taryn

Every journey starts with a single step.

Contents

Alabama,			**New Jersey,**	
Vestavia Hills	60		Morristown	180
Arizona,			**New Mexico,**	
Fountain Hills	65		Albuquerque	185
Tucson	70		**New York,**	
Arkansas,			Huntington, L.I.	190
Arkadelphia	75		**North Carolina,**	
Fayetteville	80		Greensboro	195
California,			Raleigh	200
Sacramento	85		Wilmington	205
Valencia	90		**Ohio,**	
Vista	95		Blue Ash	210
Colorado,			**Oregon,**	
Aurora,	100		Bend	215
Florida,			Eugene	220
Coral Springs	105		Milwaukie	225
Fort Myers	110		**Pennsylvania,**	
Tampa	115		Bucks County	230
Georgia,			Mt. Lebanon	235
Roswell	120		**South Carolina,**	
Idaho,			Charleston	240
Boise	125		Columbia	245
Illinois,			Greenville	250
Buffalo Grove	130		**Tennessee,**	
Wheaton	135		Nashville	255
Indiana,			**Texas,**	
Indianapolis	140		Austin	260
Kansas,			Galveston Island	265
Overland Park	145		Plano	270
Kentucky,			**Utah,**	
Lexington	150		Provo	275
Maryland,			**Vermont,**	
Gaithersburg	155		Burlington	295
Minnesota,			**Virginia,**	
Eden Prairie	160		Chesapeake	280
Missouri,			Reston	285
Columbia	165		Richmond	290
Nevada,			**Washington,**	
Henderson	170		Kent	300
Reno	175		Spokane	305

The Grass *is* Greener On the Other Side

America's history is rich in lore about the great explorers who braved new frontiers in search of the ideal homestead. They sought out territories safe from the enemy, climates that could nurture bountiful harvests and environments where trading and commerce would thrive.

Today's "explorers" are still moving about the country in pursuit of these dreams. And they're doing so in record numbers! According to the U.S. Census Bureau, close to 43 million Americans changed residences last year alone. That represented 18 percent of the country, or one out of every 11 families. Of those, more than 6.5 million people moved to a new state.

What's interesting, the people who are picking up stakes are of the age when previous generations were comfortably settled. The majority of interstate migration today is actually greatest among those between ages 25-44. According to the latest U.S. Census Geographic Mobility Study, they account for 40.2 percent of the population shifts *between* states.

Why are so many "Baby Boomers" giving up what is secure for the great unknown? Several years ago, the American Movers Conference, a national trade association, found that 42 percent of out-of-state moves were precipitated by a career-related action. Indeed, U.S. corporations transfer a half-million employees every year. Others moved without the help of a corporate parent, but still in search of better opportunities. Another 40 percent expressed a desire for an improved lifestyle and 18 percent moved as a result of a change in economic status.

If that survey were to be taken today, we believe it would find people relocating for *all of these* reasons. With an economy in dire need of a jump-start, a depressed job market, rampant crime, and societal ills of sickening proportion, we're witnessing major social shakeups.

The "yuppies" of the '80s have been declared DOA in the '90s. There is a groundswell of support for lifestyles that nurture the family's soul rather than line its bank accounts. The quality of life they hoped was guaranteed under the "Bill of Rights" has been drastically maligned. They wonder if, when and where they'll ever be better off. Faith Popcorn, the highly regarded trend forecaster, identified this shift as a "Socioquake."

With so many of this generation "mad as hell," the frustration could possibly work as a catalyst to kick off the biggest relocation boom ever. Here's why:

We believe the backbone of our society is comprised of the 5 E's: Employment, Economy, Education, Environment and Ethics. At present, they're all in a state of jeopardy.

Employment: From June 1990 to January 1992, 2.2 million jobs were eliminated in the U.S. In fact, third quarter 1991 broke a record with 110,000 job reductions (the greatest decline since the Bureau of Labor Statistics started tracking such data in 1948). So not only has Washington failed to stem the tide, economists predict that these may be permanent pink slips. In other words, the jobs aren't coming back. As for returning to the workplace, the analysis of displaced workers found that 14 percent were still out of work after a year, 50 percent were forced to change careers and 40 percent who had found work were earning less than their previous job paid.

Reaction: Millions of people in the Northeast and West are employed, but probably have updated resumes within arm's reach. They don't fantasize about future promotions, they covet their current paycheck, hoping their employer doesn't downsize, fold, merge or relocate itself.

Economy: It started with the 1987 crash on Wall Street and ended with the realization that our country's collective debt was certifiably unmanageable. The "R" word has been on everybody's lips and one doesn't have to go any farther than the downtown district to understand the vicious cycle when empty storefronts dot the landscape.

Reaction: Consumers got caught with more "bills" than a session of Congress and they're licking their wounds to the tune of up to 21-percent interest. To compensate, spending is cautious and the urge to splurge has been replaced with the need to feed.

Education: The government spends $424.5 billion a year on education, with little corresponding improvement in student achievement. Of the U.S. population, 23 percent is still illiterate, and many innovations that could potentially reverse the slide get lost in a sea of bureaucratic lip service. Worse still, it is appalling the number of kids majoring in guns, gangs, and graffiti.

Reaction: Parents wonder if there are communities where the public schools are not only safe, but capable of turning out well-prepared students for college or vocations. They also hope the price for a quality education is not sky-high property taxes.

Environment: Many people believe that the earth is on a collision course with itself and that the task of replenishing it treacherous and costly. As for our social environment, it is possible that we've reached a point in many cities where the wilderness is safer than civilization. "There are no crack vials, no subway murders, no Scuds and no asbestos," says Ms. Popcorn.

Reaction: People are asking, "Is there any place where civility still exists, where kids can play freely outdoors without a care, and where the air and water don't shorten your life span?"

Ethics: Mention politics and ethics in the same breath and it's an unfortunate oxymoron. Respected business leaders are behind bars. Scandals, sexual harassment and date rape cases grab the headlines and much of our TV viewing time.

Reaction: One wonders, are there any places left where the governing body has high standards, integrity and vision?

These are the burning issues of our time, the Achilles heel of our generation. It all leads up to this: Surely there are families in this country that are thriving. Wonder where they live?

Alas, that was our mission. To scan the country from coast to coast and find the fabulous cities, suburbs and towns where people were not only enjoying the good life, but the *great* life! Most would be happy to find just one place that fit the bill. We found 50!

How we arrived at 50 fabulous places

The task of narrowing our list was a tremendous challenge when you consider that, there really are thousands of desirable communities across the country. So we began our search by talking to countless people. Relocation experts, realtors, state and federal government agencies, economic development organizations, school districts, chamber of commerce executives and directors at the U.S. Census who track geographic mobility.

In every case, we asked, "Where are people moving and why?"

Regardless of their reasons for relocating, there was an almost universal agreement on what the ideal community should offer: a strong local economy with growing job and business opportunities, good schools, a diversified real estate market, low taxes, great recreation and culture, low crime and an aggressive plan to preserve the environment.

Even more importantly, the best places to raise a family were ones that were passionate about kids! If there was evidence of ongoing events, programs and activities that were child-centered, parents gave their hometown rave reviews.

Finally a pattern emerged. Predictably, we heard about the great yuppie escapes of the 1980s: Denver, Portland and Seattle. We heard about the latest "hot spots" (literally): Tucson, Raleigh, N.C., Tampa, and Plano, Texas. And then we started hearing unfamiliar or what we referred to as the "you're joking!" names: Arkadelphia, Ark., Fountain Hills, Ariz., Columbia, Mo., and Buffalo Grove, Ill.

We took our list of more than 300 locations and applied our checklist of "must have's" to each. No area could be considered unless it offered a majority of 15 important criteria. Each of the cities mentioned above made the cut. Here are the criteria all 50 had to meet:

Criteria for Evaluating Communities
(In order of importance)

1. **Strong economic outlook.** Low unemployment, projected job growth and expansion, growth in new business starts, and easy access to major employment centers.
2. **Exceptional public school education and access to nearby colleges.** High student achievement levels, well-rounded curriculum, abundant programs and activities, broad range of programs for gifted and special education students.
3. **Diversified housing market.** A good mix of single family houses and multiple dwellings; wide range of housing prices/styles.
4. **Ample recreation, culture and family fun.** Plenty of quality activities and entertainment indoors and out, year-round.
5. **Abundance of community services and programs.** Progressive, local government in tune with the needs of residents, strong mix of programs, services and events that create a positive community spirit.
6. **Affordable living costs.** Access to affordable housing and higher education, reasonable utilities, services, etc.
7. **Low taxes.** Fair balance of sales, property and state income taxes.
8. **Low crime.** Where residents don't live in fear for their safety and where local law enforcement is proactive and community-minded.
9. **Quality medical care.** Access to Joint Commission Accredited hospitals and specialized care, excellent ratio of physicians to patients, well-received community outreach programs.
10. **Environmentally aware attitudes.** Where air and water quality are not in question, where communities have been recognized for aggressive environmental and recycling efforts.
11. **Religious/ethnic diversity.** Where no one race, religion or ethnic background is so dominant, it is to the exclusion of others.
12. **Fast-growing area/welcoming attitude toward newcomers.** Areas that are experiencing rapid growth and are happy about it.
13. **Scenic beauty.** Either from natural assets or manmade aesthetic improvements.
14. **Access to airports/highways.** Proximity to major roads, good transportation, relatively easy commutes, within reasonable distance to major airports.
15. **Hospitable climate.** An area was permitted one miserable (hot or cold) season, but that's it!

We don't doubt that readers will have their own priorities and wonder how the environment, let's say, would be ranked 10th in importance. Our response is that they all couldn't be first and at least it was given serious consideration.

If you peeked ahead and read the list of 50 places, you may also be jumping up and down and saying, "Hey, I've been to Reston, Va., and I know they have a commute from hell." And it's true. We did allow for some exceptions.

Huntington, Long Island (N.Y.) and Eden Prairie (Minneapolis, Minn.) have average home prices that are out-of-reach for most first-time buyers. Income and property taxes are also sky-high. Tampa and Tucson are big cities with their share of crime. And Reston is indeed the wrong place for anyone whose blood pressure rises in a traffic jam. However, each city has so much to offer in other respects (fabulous culture and recreation, booming economies, excellent schools and more), they simply couldn't be eliminated.

Then there were the cities that quickly disappeared from our list. Take Orlando, for instance (please). It is one of the fastest-growing in the country, but we found nagging problems. Being inland, the heat and humidity could be insufferable year-round. The housing market is so overbuilt that if you were unhappy and wanted to sell, the prospects would be dismal. Finally, the area is transient and there is virtually no sense of community.

We also scratched out places like Sioux Falls (S.D.), Anchorage (Alaska) and Billings (Mont.). Thanks to the "Northern Exposure" syndrome, we understand the growing curiosity about rugged, remote places like these. Perhaps in a few years they'll be added to our list. In the meantime, with limited job opportunities, limited housing, limited culture, and public schools that have some catching up to do, we declared them not ready for company.

But on to the 50 that made it. We found fabulous college towns (Fayetteville, Ark.), military towns (Charleston, S.C.), state capitals (Richmond, Va.), Little League capitals (Buffalo Grove, Ill.) and even music capitals (Nashville, of course). Why, we'll even tell you about a place where you can get all of the above (Austin, Texas)!

If your family has been fantasizing about living a particular lifestyle, but aren't sure where it exists, we'll help you find the best place. This raises the most asked question. Which place *is* the best? We don't have a clue.

What we do know is that our fabulous 50 have enough outstanding attributes to be worthy of your consideration! But since they each have their own special virtues, it hardly seemed fair to compare. It's like asking a parent, "Which of your children is the best?" The answer is "At what?" We also know that people have very different definitions of paradise.

With all due respect to the popular guides that rank and rate an assortment of lifestyle factors, throw in a year's supply of statistics and then assign each area a final score, we frankly never understood how that was valuable. Fort Myers may emerge as the top choice, but if you would be miserable in a place that had 12 months of summer, or had always dreamt of living in the mountains, would Fort Myers be *your* top choice? No way.

That's why we've provided you with the most relevant facts about each location. We've done all the homework, gotten the inside story (the good news *and* the bad) and can tell you what it would be like to live there. We've even laid out the Area Profiles in such a way that you can read them in their entirety or "cherry pick" by subjects of interest (jobs, schools, recreation, etc.) Now you can be your own judge!

Before you start your shopping expedition, however, we urge you to first read the chapters, "There's a Place For Us: How to Find a Fabulous Hometown," "Making the Grade: How to Be An Expert at Evaluating Schools," and "Moving 101: Getting Cross Country With Your Possessions and Your Sanity." These common-sense "short courses" will show you how to discover the locations that are right for your family, while offering hundreds of great ideas to save you headaches and money!

But perhaps the most important chapter of all is the one that will turn this book into an incredible investment. "Can You Afford to Relocate?: Financial Strategies for Making It Happen" has the indelible handprint of one of the foremost certified financial planners and relocation experts in the country. Lee Rosenberg shares his latest and most sophisticated strategies for managing your assets so that you can build a relocation nest egg.

You are about to embark on one of life's most fascinating journeys. Our hope is that *50 Fabulous Places to Raise Your Family* will be the vessel that takes you to your greatest destination ever. In the meantime, take heart in a wonderful discovery we made along the way.

The grass *is* greener on the other side!

## Chapter 1

"There's a Place for Us..." How to Begin the Search for a Fabulous Hometown

Here's a scene that probably takes place every day.

The alarm is ringing and you turn over. You've been tossing for hours. You sit up and look out the window. Your first thought is that it needs caulking. Next you notice your home computer. You were supposed to get up early to finish a report for the office. You shake your spouse.

Spouse (comatose): *"I'm not home."*

You (determined): *"I don't think I can take another day of this. I've had it."*

Spouse (moving slightly): *"This is a recording."*

You: *"I mean it. This pressure is making me old before my time. If my company does get taken over, I'll be out of a job. I'm tired of commuting two hours a day and I never want to hear the words wind chill factor as long as I live. I really think we should talk about moving somewhere else."*

Spouse (sits up): *"Honey, I told you I would be willing to move tomorrow if it was possible. But where would we go? And what would we say to the children? 'Hey kids, we're moving. We don't know where, we don't know anybody, and neither of us have jobs. Pretty exciting, huh?'"*

You: *"What are you saying? We're stuck here until we retire?"*

Spouse: *"I hope not (pause). All right, I'll tell you what. You name the city and if they've got a beach, I'll call the movers."*

You: *"A beach? Well, gee, that narrows it down to about 500 places on each coast. But at least it's a start. Where's my atlas?"*

Where do we begin?

Do you know why this scene is so common? Because millions of Americans are living in a place they didn't choose. It chose them. Perhaps they were born and raised in an area and never really questioned whether they liked it. It was home. Or maybe they accepted a job in another city and moved the family more for the opportunity than the locale. In many cases, people follow a friend or family member to a new city. They convince themselves that if their sister's family is happy there, they will be, too!

The problem with decisions that are made for us, particularly when it comes to something as important as where we live, is that the aftermath can leave us feeling guilty and frustrated. "How come we didn't take that job offer in another city when we had the chance?" "Why didn't we realize that the high cost of living would make things so difficult?" "How could we have been so lax about checking out employment possibilities and the schools?" Round and round the questions go until one day we might say, "Let's get out." But what then?

Some will ponder the question for years before taking action (if at all). Others will get right on the horn and start "Operation: Move." Either way, the million-dollar question is, "Where?" Where are the real opportunities in this country today? Where can a family enjoy a great quality of life?

The "where" question is undoubtedly the single biggest hurdle in getting off the dime. There are literally tens of thousands of cities, suburbs and towns in this country. How do we narrow down the prospects? Just as important, with our jobs, car pools, volunteer work, the house, the kids, doctor appointments and soccer games, who has time to do the research? By the time you figure out the "*where*," you could be of the age where you don't remember the "*why!*"

Wouldn't it be great if the selection process were like a computer dating service? "We'd like to see something attractive, fun-loving and open-minded." *Voilà*, here are your 20 choices.

We looked at a book that promised to do that. It claimed it could help people find the best place to live in the country by having them answer hundreds of questions about their likes and dislikes, needs, preferences, etc. So we gave it a whirl. And when we tabulated our scores, we looked up our perfect place to live. The problem was, it was places. It showed that one of us should be headed to Tampa, the other to Denver. When our son answered the questionnaire, we discovered he'd be happiest in Southern California. We wondered, how does a family living in three different cities spend quality time?

Next, we tried a high-tech version of the same game. We found a computer program that rated over 300 U.S. cities. All we had to do was answer another lengthy questionnaire, push enter and *poof*—up on the screen would be the cities ranked in order of preference.

With all the possible choices it could have made for us, guess what came up as our number one place to live? The place where we now live! It was a little like having a dating service fix you up with your ex-spouse.

The point is, that much as we'd like, finding the right place to live is *not* a science. There are no magic formulas. No book, no computer, no person can tell you how you'll actually *feel* about a place. You have to see the community. You have to talk to the people. The only way you will ever know if a place is right for you and your family is to experience an almost visceral reaction to it.

That's why we can't tell you the best place to live. What we will do is show you how to conduct the most effective search possible. We'll tell you the key things to contemplate, the important questions to answer and the best way to narrow down the prospects. Then we'll send you in the direction of 50 fabulous places we found to be well worth consideration. However, you first have to apply your list of personal priorities to determine if they're worthy of *your* consideration!

Two things you should know

Before you can get started, there are two very important things to keep in mind.

The first is that there is no place on earth that doesn't have its share of drawbacks. Not even the 50 we selected (we come right out and tell you what those drawbacks are)! As great as it would be to find a community or city that is perfect in every way, it is not a realistic expectation.

Instead of perfection, what you should be looking for is a community that offers you dramatic improvements in your lifestyle—greater opportunities, an easier pace, a shorter commute, better schools, a nicer home, safer neighborhoods, etc.

The second important consideration is that the only way to begin your search is with an open mind. There has probably never been a greater metamorphosis in this country than the one that took place in the go-go years of the 1980s. Billions of dollars of capital improvements permanently altered the landscapes and skylines of major metropolitan areas. Unparalleled population growth in hundreds of outlying areas catapulted suburbs into major cities and job centers unto themselves. Aggressive environmental action has converted former smokestack cities into clean, attractive places.

However, if you eliminate locations based on preconceived notions, you could end up overlooking some excellent possibilities. It's like when you're coaxing your kids to try a new food and they refuse. What's the universal parental response (all together now)? "How do you know you won't like it unless you try it?" The same can be true of places you've heard about, but have never seen.

Another example of closed-mindedness that is counterproductive was brought to light in an early press interview we did. A reporter reviewed our list of 50 and was baffled. "You picked Eugene, Oregon? When I was there, everything was practically boarded up. The town was dying." "When was that," we asked? "I guess about 1979." Then he said, "I can't believe a suburb of Pittsburgh is on this list. I choke just thinking about the place." "Have you been there since the total revitalization of downtown and the disappearance of the steel factories," we asked? "Gee, no."

The reporter's reaction helped us realize that once you record an impression or image in your mind, it can be difficult to erase. We call this "Psychosclerosis," or hardening of the attitudes! Remember, places are as apt to change and improve over the years as people are.

To prove that you can't possibly know a city until you see it with today's eyes, we've put together a short list of areas and communities featured in this book, along with the most current information. Why not test your "USA-IQ?"

Match the city/area with the proper description.

1. This city is located five minutes from the world's largest indoor shopping mall.
2. With more than 100 clubs, there is more live music performed here every night than any city in the country.
3. This town is located five minutes from the famed Mayo Clinic.
4. This city and outskirts will now have the purest, best-tasting water in the world, with the opening of its $60 million water treatment facility.
5. This city ranks second in the U.S. with the most colleges and universities.
6. 100,000 new jobs are projected to be created here by the end of the decade.
7. The city has 185 Little League teams, more than any other in the country.
8. *Fortune, Money, U.S. News & World Report, Savvy* and *Health* magazines have identified this city as one of the most livable and affordable in the country.
9. Combined annual sales of local corporations, including Hewlett Packard, Boise Cascade and Ore-Ida Foods, are $25 billion annually.
10. **Bonus Question:** Which state has more boats per capita than any other?: Florida, Arizona, Minnesota, California or Maine?

A. Nashville, Tennessee

B. Cincinnati, Ohio

C. Fort Myers (Lee County), Florida

D. Pittsburgh, Pennsylvania

E. Austin, Texas

F. Fountain Hills, Arizona

G. Eden Prairie, Minnesota

H. Coral Springs, Florida

I. Boise, Idaho

Answers: 1-G. 2-E. 3-F. (OK, this was a trick question. Fountain Hills is located five minutes from Mayo Clinic's new satellite facility in Scottsdale. The headquarter clinic is still in Rochester, Minn.). 4-B. 5-A. 6-C. 7-H. 8-D. 9-I (To make up for the trick question on the Mayo Clinic, we gave this one away). **Bonus Answer:** Arizona (there are more than 300 lakes across the state).

Although it would be an impressive feat to get several correct answers, don't worry if you didn't have a clue. What's important is that when you evaluate prospective home towns, it is only fair to base your decisions on what the city or community has to offer in the present or future, not the past!

Happily ever after?

Remember the 1937 movie classic, "Lost Horizon?" It was the story of an idyllic town on the outskirts of the Himalayas called Shangri-La "where living was not a struggle, but a lasting delight." You would come there to find a "garden spot where there's peace and security, beauty and comfort and where people are not mean and greedy."

Sounds nice, but not very realistic, at least by today's standards. So how do you find a fabulous home town? Should you look for a garden spot off I-87? A place of peace and security that's five minutes from shopping? A place of beauty and comfort that's got great schools?

While it is only natural to dream about living happily ever after in your new community, the only chance of that is if you select an area that meets your family's unique needs. Admittedly that sounds so basic and sensible, you may be thinking, "Who would be crazy enough to move to a new city that didn't have what they needed?"

Believe it or not, we interviewed hundreds of families and discovered that many of these otherwise intelligent people overlooked the important stuff when choosing a new home town. Instead of looking closely at the essentials, the tendency was to pick a place that fulfilled their fantasies!

Take the case of the Hardwicks (not their real name), a Michigan family who spent the winter daydreaming about the lucky ducks in Florida. "They get to frolic in the pool while we're sitting here freezing, sneezing and filling out medical claim forms," Jeanie told us. Then one Christmas, she and Mark treated the kids to a vacation in Orlando. The glorious sunshine, the beautiful shopping centers and lush greenery fueled a fantasy about enjoying the good life all year long. Further intrigued by no state income tax, brand-new schools and affordable homes with built-in pools, they couldn't resist the temptation to buy in one of the desirable suburbs outside the "Magic Kingdom."

Fast-forward to one year after the relocation and here's what we learned: After several months of looking for comparable-paying jobs to no avail, both Jeanie and Mark accepted lower-paying jobs for which they were overqualified. Their two boys had an easy time making friends in school ("Everybody's a new kid on the block.") but they were really bored. The curriculum was not challenging enough ("I worked on long division last year!") and the caliber of teachers was not at the level of their old school. Even worse, although the school was only a few years old, it was already over-

crowded. That meant the boys attended school at different times, creating chaos in the morning (Jeanie showed up at work a half-hour late on school days). Their new house was beautiful—bright, open and twice the size of the one back home. Unfortunately, the builder gave them several months of lip service before he could be dragged back to fix the leaky roof and cracked tiles in the master bath. And then there was the humidity, the harrowing commute along Interstate 4...

The point of this story is not to scare you (all right, maybe we do want you to feel a little unnerved), but to enlighten you as to the risks of relocating when you don't look at the big picture. Certainly you want this move to fulfill certain dreams, but, ultimately, no one can afford to choose an area that doesn't also fulfill some very basic needs.

How to get started in your search

Anyone who's ever gone on a camping trip knows to take a survival kit with food, a flashlight, first-aid equipment and other necessities. Similarly, people who move to a new city need a survival kit of sorts. We're not talking aspirin and band-aids though. We're describing the essentials your family needs to survive. These include the right environmental conditions and medical care, opportunities to earn a good living, affordable living costs and the best possible educational opportunities. These are the foundations on which to build a future!

Naturally every family will have its own personal list of needs and priorities, but at a minimum, it is important to start your search by checking out the following:

Access to the right medical care and environmental conditions. If a family member has a particular medical condition, handicap or disorder that requires a specific type of care, he or she needs to be within a reasonable distance to an appropriate medical facility. If someone has a condition affected by the weather, the family should consider areas that offer a climate that is therapeutic. For example, asthmatics and hay fever sufferers respond best to both dry desert weather and higher elevations (less mold spores, no humidity). Those with heart conditions need to avoid high elevations (the air is thinner, making it more difficult to breathe). Consult with your physician for further advice.

The right employment opportunities. Whether you plan to stay in your current occupation or profession, or use this relocation as a springboard to a new career, you need to size up the quality and quantity of local job opportunities. It is not enough to know that the area has projected tremendous job growth over the next few years. You have to find out where that growth is expected. Is it in the high-tech industries? The service sector? Manufacturing? Equally important, the nature of job opportunities needs to match your skills, qualifications and interests (what good is it if all the growth is in medical services and high-tech products, but these aren't your fields?). Other considerations are the diversity of companies (areas that are dependent on a single industry are at greatest risk for economic downturns) and the range of different-sized companies (a good mix of large corporations, medium-sized firms and small/upstart companies is important).

Acceptable living costs. Affordability is a relative thing (and if you've got rich relatives, it's all the better)! Only you know your comfort level insofar as what you can pay for housing, taxes and overall living costs. Even if a city ranks low in a national comparison of living costs, it is not a guarantee that average salaries are commensurate with expenses (Florida is a prime example. Living costs are low, but salaries are even lower). If you are fortunate enough to have a job waiting for you, or you have a good sense of pay scales for your profession, try to estimate your monthly expenses (utilities, insurance, mortgage, taxes, food, etc.). That is the only true test of affordability. Incidentally, if you are relocating to an area with higher living costs, don't assume that a higher salary will totally compensate. For example, communities surrounding the Boston, New York and San Francisco areas are not

known for bargain prices in any category. With everything costing more (medical bills, day care, entertainment, activities for the children, etc.), you should try to anticipate the impact on your budget *before* you move.

The right educational opportunities. Whether public or private schools, vocational schools or four-year universities, you can't underestimate the value of having access to the best possible education for your family. If you are happy with your current schools, at a minimum you'll want a guarantee of comparable quality. If your schools are lacking, you'll want to be assured of vast improvements. And if your child is a gifted student or requires special education, you'll want to be assured of the availability and quality of appropriate programs.

What does your family *need*?

It's time to identify your family's particular needs. We suggest you list them in the box provided on page 16, in order of importance. Rank the ones we've mentioned, if they apply, as well as adding your own. And be as specific as possible. The important thing is not to confuse this list with that of desires (we promise that's next).

For example, do you need to be in an area where there's a military base, a major university or college, or one that is suitable for a specific business opportunity? Does your profession require that you be within a short distance from an airport or major highways? Or is your priority to live in a community that offers first rate parochial-schools?

If you need some help getting started, follow our sample on the next page.

What does your family *want*?

Fantasizing about a different lifestyle is most often the engine that drives the relocation train. Some people have always dreamt of living in a mountainous area where the views are breathtaking and the opportunities for outdoor adventure are endless. Others long for a life on

[Sample]
Our Family's Survival Checklist
(List in order of importance)

1. _Jobs in accounting or financial services w/ large company_
2. _____
3. _Jobs for speech/hearing teacher, or private tutoring_
4. _____
5. _High school w/ LaCrosse so Danny can work toward scholarship_
6. _____
7. _Near major airport so Mom + Dad can visit_
8. _____
9. _Climate that won't irritate hay fever + allergies!_
10. _____

Our Family's Survival Checklist
(List in order of importance)

1. _____
2. _____
3. _____
4. _____
5. _____
6. _____
7. _____
8. _____
9. _____
10. _____

the ocean, or on the Gulf of Mexico with its warm breezes and year-round recreation. Still, others are less concerned with scenery and more interested in architecture. Perhaps they have always wanted to live in a 100-year old Victorian-style home or build a gorgeous contemporary showplace. Maybe this is the chance to finally live in a small town or a bustling city.

Whatever the fantasy, let's focus on the things that really get your collective juices flowing. This process is called internal market research or good old-fashioned soul-searching. Let's figure out what's really important to you so that when you are intrigued by an area, you can look at what you identified as your priorities and determine if there's a match. Remember, many cities are great, but if they don't have enough of the attributes you're looking for, who cares?

For instance, the Twin Cities of Minneapolis and St. Paul are absolutely terrific cities for families. Job opportunities abound, public education is excellent, crime is low and the culture and recreation are wonderful. However, if you simply can't function when the temperature dips below the freezing mark or you had your heart set on living near the mountains, it's not likely you'll ever consider this area.

In addition, should you discover that you can't agree on lifestyle choices, now is the time to discuss this. Imagine the problems when one of you goes along for the ride and then later announces, "I can't stand humidity! How did I ever let you talk me into moving to a place where the bugs are bigger than the cars?"

To start, let's see how you feel about different climates, scenery and recreation and culture. Turn to page 22 for handy charts that will help you identify your greatest desires. Fill these out as a family or make copies for everyone and compare notes).

The idea behind the charts is to create a family profile that readily identifies your priorities and desires. This is not about scores and rankings. It is about being conscious of your personal "hot buttons" so you know what to consider when weighing the merits of a new community.

Will we fit in?

Now that you are aware of your family's basic needs and wants, there is one other very important consideration before you can decide on a new hometown. It has to do with something that is less obvious. Something you can't read about in a chamber of commerce brochure. It has to do with compatibility and the sense that you fit in.

In our research, we learned that next to lack of employment opportunities, the single biggest reason families left an area was because they felt like outsiders. Maybe the local politics were completely opposite their orientation and beliefs. Maybe it was a matter of being a single parent in a sea of couples. Maybe the community was cliquish and not particularly interested in newcomers. Or perhaps it was a question of a deeper problem—bigotry and other forms of prejudice. In any case, nothing is more disconcerting than feeling ostracized, particularly in a place everyone told you was so "nice."

How can you ever be assured of fitting in? Certainly there are no guarantees, but there are a number of factors that are telltale signs, *if you pay attention.*

Families that moved away from communities because they felt like outcasts shared one consistent message. The red flags had been there all along, they just denied or ignored them. Sometimes they had no choice ("My husband already accepted the job."). Sometimes everything else seemed so perfect they didn't want to spoil the excitement ("My wife would have accused me of being negative again."). And sometimes people dismissed an instinct because they didn't want to be unfair ("We're always telling the kids not to jump to conclusions.").

Surely there are those who would say "to hell with them" and go on with their lives with apologies to no one. Others would want to avoid this type of disappointment at any price. Whatever your position, there are several things you can do *in advance* to learn about a community's true colors.

1. Look at the growth of the area. Fast-growing and/or transient communities are accustomed to newcomers and are more likely to be open to a diversity of backgrounds. Small towns and suburbs that have only seen marginal growth may be totally homogenous and more difficult to acclimate to if you're not one of the crowd.

2. Contact the county or local Board of Elections. Find out how the area voted in the last few presidential and congressional elections. If you're a staunch republican whose blood pressure would go up living among liberal democrats, let the buyer beware.

3. Contact a minister or rabbi (or two or three). Ask pointed questions about the size of the religious community with which you are now affiliated. Do they have a strong presence, if not in number than in voice? If a minority, what are recent examples that show goodwill or lack thereof? Don't rely on a realtor to give you information. Do the checking yourself.

4. Subscribe to the local newspaper. Read up on the local issues and controversies. Over a period of time, you'll recognize the news items that seem to be pervasive and those that are isolated events. This is an excellent way to scope out schools, crime, the environment, local government, business development, etc.

5. Contact a community center, a country club—any place you would expect to spend time if you actually lived there. Inquire about the cost and benefits of membership and ask yourself if the person sounded not only friendly, but interested in you. Was he or she helpful, anxious to "sell" you on the city, and happy to know of your interest in the community? Were you able to engage him or her in conversation about its merits and possible drawbacks? These are all good signs. **Caution:** Don't make a judgment call based on one or two negative conversations. Some people are just unpleasant or snobbish by nature. Or you may have approached them at a bad moment. Try to form an opinion based on your overall encounters.

What do you do with all this input?

Now that you understand the most important criteria, you're probably wondering, how does that knowledge help you find the best place to live?

Good question. For one thing, the thought process you went through did as much to help you decide on the type of places you would *never* want to live! Secondly, by being so conscious of your family's needs and desires, now you can read or inquire about a place and eliminate it without the usual hemming and hawing. No more, "I don't know. It sounds nice but I can't tell." You will know definitively the places worth considering and those that aren't.

This is the point at which you are ready for our exclusive:

5-Step Plan to Finding a Fabulous Hometown!

Step 1: Round up suspects

Begin collecting the names of cities, suburbs and towns that have always intrigued you. Places you visited on vacation or business trips. Places that friends moved to and love.

Read the 50 Area Profiles featured in this book and select places that capture your imagination. Look through an atlas and pick out cities or regions whose locations appeal to you because of the climate, scenic beauty and/or lifestyle options. Ask friends and family about places they've never forgotten. Look through books and magazines for information on fast-growing cities. Whether you come up with one name or 100 names, this is your official list of "suspect" cities.

Step 2: Put on your detective hat

It's time to gather the facts. Pick up to five cities on your list and get to work.

Note: Every Area Profile contains the information you need to contact the following offices/ organizations.

- **Contact the chambers of commerce.** If you need an address and phone number, ask your reference librarian to show you the current *World Chamber of Commerce Directory*. Then write or call to request a newcomers' package. (Ask specifically about background information on major employers). Some chambers will send this free of charge, others will ask for a nominal amount up front (we've seen prices range from $1 to $15). *Caution:* Once you are on a chamber's mailing list, you will receive literature from area realtors, insurance companies, movers and other firms that want your business. Some of this will be very valuable, the rest can be tossed.
- **Contact the convention and visitors bureaus** located in the nearest major metropolitan area (CVB's are also listed in the *Chamber of Commerce Directory*). They will gladly send you material on recreation, culture and things to do in the entire area/region.
- **Contact a relocation specialist at a local realty office.** Relocation experts are full-time professionals who have been trained to work exclusively with out-of-town buyers. Unlike part-time salespeople, they are the most qualified to advise you about all aspects of your reloca-

tion. Naturally, they would like to be your only real estate contact, but if you feel it would be in your best interest to get several different perspectives, this is your right. Get the names of local agents and/or managing brokers (licensed to manage real estate agents) from the chamber of commerce, newspaper ads, the area realty board, and from personal contacts in the area.

- **Contact the school district office.** Any local realtor can provide the address and phone. Request any available literature describing programs, facilities, curriculum, special education and gifted programs, etc. There is generally no charge for this information.
- **Subscribe to the Sunday edition of the local newspaper** for one month (the chamber of commerce will be able to provide the publication's name and address). It's the biggest paper of the week and we promise it'll be a real eye-opener! It will be packed with information on job and business opportunities, real estate, upcoming community events, local issues, etc. The subscription cost should average $10 to $15 a month.
- **Let your fingers do the walking.** If you plan to start a business and want to scope out the competition or if you are curious about the churches or synagogues, the physicians and lawyers, etc., contact your local telephone company and order a copy of the yellow pages for that area. Again, there will be a charge, but it is a terrific way to size up a place without having to first move there.

Caution: Do not investigate more than five cities at a time or you may overload. Plus, your mail carrier will be grateful if you pace yourself. Some of the newcomer packages are huge.

Step 3: Take inventory

Organization is the key to a successful search. Keep a list of your "suspect" cities and create files for the information as it arrives. Depending on the amount of material you receive, either set up the files by specific location or create state/regional files. Then when time permits, sit down in a quiet place and start your comparison shopping. You are about to turn your "suspects" into "prospects." Here's how to keep track of what you learn.

1. Create a Master Family Profile using the chart provided on page 23. Fill in the needs, desires and compatibility issues you've established as your priorities.
2. Make enough copies of the Master Profile so that there is one for every place you are investigating.
3. As you learn about various aspects of the community, check off a "Yes, They Have It," "No, They Don't," or "Not Sure" box.
4. If you find you are checking off lots of "No's" for a particular city, take the city off your "suspects" list and start the inquiry process for a new one.
5. If you find you are checking off lots of "Yes's" for a particular city, add the name to your "prospect" list—the list of cities you plan to learn much more about. Should there be several "Not Sure's" checked off, at least you know the criteria that need further investigation.

Step 4: Search and destroy

At the point that you've inquired and received sufficient information about all the cities on your "suspect" list, it's time to narrow down the possibilities. Naturally some places will have already eliminated themselves, the others will be your "prospects."

The best way to proceed is to select any two "prospects" and compare them on their merits as well as down sides. Ask yourselves, "Which one comes *closest* to what we're looking for?" If they are of equal interest, go back and compare each of them to another city and ask the question again. "Which one comes closest to what we're looking for?"

The idea is to eliminate those that don't hold up to scrutiny when compared with another location. Ultimately, you want to create a list of semi-finalists so that you can prepare for the final step and pick the winner (Isn't this beginning to sound like a Miss America pageant?).

Step 5: The on-site inspection

You can talk to people until you are blue in the face, you can read volumes about a place, you can even watch videotapes. All of this will be helpful, but by no means is it a substitute for a visit! You simply must experience the community with your own eyes and ears.

The wonderful thing about "on-site inspections" is that nobody can influence your feelings. You're on your own in the opinion department. Whatever you see or hear will effect you in a way that no brochure or pamphlet could. It's that visceral reaction we referred to earlier. You'll either be thrilled to pieces or totally turned off.

Here are two types of comments we heard repeatedly after people experienced their initial visits.

"We knew from the videos that this was a beautiful town, but we still weren't prepared for just how magnificent the views were. It's what really sold us."

"We were all set to buy in this development, just based on the tons of pictures the real estate agent had sent us. But when we went down to see it, we were shocked. It was much smaller than we expected and it was situated next to an old landfill. It smelled awful. She kept telling us it was unusual for the wind to be blowing this way and it was almost never like this. We said, if it only smells like this once in a blue moon we would never live here!"

These experiences give new meaning to the phrase, "Seeing is believing."

In preparation for your visit, we suggest the following:

1. Plan the visit around a business trip and/or vacation. Obviously for cost-efficiency purposes, try to take in as many "prospect" cities as possible.
2. Notify the real estate agent(s) you feel most comfortable with of your visit, and schedule blocks of time when they can show you around. Don't devote an entire day to house hunting. After a few hours, you'll want a change of scenery so that you can reflect on what you've seen.
3. If the children are traveling with you, schedule a fun activity in the middle of the day.
4. Put one family member in charge of the "journal"—the copious notes you take describing observations, facts, questions, comments, etc. As much as you think you'll remember everything, there will be too much going on to commit your impressions to memory.
5. Assign the best photographer in the family to take pictures and preferably videos. Nothing will be more valuable upon your return home than the visual reminders of what you saw.
6. Keep careful track of your travel expenses because if they are related to a job search, they may be tax deductible (more details in Chapter 2).

This is gonna be hard

A friend who was interested in relocating asked to read this manuscript in progress so she could get a head start on her search. When she reached this point of the chapter she said, "I hate to say this, but I'm disappointed. The steps you outlined are really logical, but I was hoping this was going to be a lot easier. I can't believe how much time and money I'm going to have to spend to do this right."

To which we replied, "If you think the search is expensive, wait until you see what it costs you to move to the wrong city!"

As we see it, if your intent is to relocate to a new city for a better quality of life, for greater opportunities and peace of mind, the expenses you incur up front to find the right place are but a small price in the end. Whatever time and money goes toward long-distance phone calls, postage, material costs and travel will hopefully come back to you in many years of happiness. Take it from the people who have relocated and been miserable. You will have to work at this as though your family's lives depend on it. Quite frankly, they do.

And the winner is...

People who have gone through this step-by-step process compare it to climbing a ladder on the high dive. At some point you have to decide to jump—or not to jump. Do you take the plunge or retreat to your old home?

The truth is, if you've really done your homework, the answer about if and where to move will be a lot easier than you think. One of two things will occur.

You'll either discover that there is no place like home and run back with open arms. Or, you'll be so incredibly excited about the place you've discovered that wild horses couldn't keep you from moving there.

Whatever the decision, take solace in the fact that neither choice is irreversible. If you went through the process and did not find a suitable place, you can always try again next year. Perhaps the underlying reasons that held you back, such as financial pressures, children experiencing difficult transitions, lack of job opportunities, etc., will be less problematic than they were a year ago.

Conversely, should you relocate and realize that it was a mistake, there is no law preventing you from moving again.

In the end, there is but one simple truth. The real key to finding the best place to raise your family is to listen to what is in your head and in your heart.

50 Fabulous Places to Raise Your Family

CRITERIA: SCENERY How would you feel about living in a place that had/was:	Would love it!	Would hate it!	Could live with it or without it.	Not sure about this.
On / near the Atlantic Ocean				
On / near the Pacific Ocean				
On / near the Gulf of Mexico				
On / near lakes, rivers and beaches				
Landlocked (not surrounded by any body of water)				
In the Southwest desert region				
In a mountainous region				
On a flat terrain (no rolling hills)				
A skyline of skyscrapers and modern architecture				
Mostly historic buildings and architecture				
A combination of old and new architecture				
Other scenic preference:				
Other scenic aversion:				

CRITERIA: CLIMATE How do you feel about a place that is / has:	Would love it!	Would hate it!	Could live with it or without it.	Not sure about this.
12 months of summer and sunshine (sub-tropical climate)				
High humidity for months on end				
Frequent thunderstorms				
Four mild seasons (never gets above 75 F)				
Desert weather — sometimes intensely hot, but always dry				
Cloudy skies and intermittent rain for weeks on end				
Four diverse seasons — cold winters, hot summers, mild spring and fall and a mixture of rain and snow				
30" or more of rain each year				
20" or more of snow each year				
Prone to hurricanes//tornadoes/earthquakes				
Other climate preference:				
Other climate aversion:				

CRITERIA: RECREATION AND CULTURE How would you feel about a community that has access to the following:	Absolutely Necessary	Very Important	Important	Not Important
Professional sports teams				
Collegiate sports teams				
Extensive art museums and galleries				
Opera, ballet and theater companies				
Extensive live entertainment (music, comedy, etc.)				
Historical sites and tourist attractions				
Ongoing local annual events (fairs, parades, races, etc.)				
State and regional parks				
Community centers, YMCAs, JCCs, etc.				
Year-round outdoor recreational activities				
Extensive community parks, playgrounds				
Other cultural/recreational preference:				
Other cultural/recreational aversion:				

Now that you've determined your priorities, consider these other essentials. Check off all those that are important to you.

Type of community
___Small town
___Rural community
___College town
___New suburb
___Older, established suburb
___Medium-sized city
___Large city

Population preference
___Under 10,000
___10,000-50,000
___50,000-250,000
___250,000 or more

Type of commute
___Length (no more than ____ minutes)
___Preferred transportation (walk, car, train, bus)

Background and beliefs
___Prefer racial/ethnic diversity within community
___Prefer large (Jewish, Black, Indian, Chinese, etc.) population_____

Environment
___Landfills, nuclear power plants, military bases, etc., have to be ____ miles away
___Water, air pollution have to be within EPA standards

MASTER FAMILY PROFILE

LOCATION NAME:_____

DATE: _____

	YES, THEY HAVE IT!	NO, THEY DON'T HAVE IT!	NOT SURE IF THEY HAVE IT
WE NEED:			
1.			
2.			
3.			
4.			
5.			
6.			
7.			
8.			
9.			
10.			
WE WANT:			
1.			
2.			
3.			
4.			
5.			
6.			
7.			
8.			
9.			
10.			
WE'LL FEEL COMFORTABLE IF THERE 'S:			
1.			
2.			
3.			
4.			
5.			

COMMENTS:

Chapter 2

Can You Afford to Relocate?
Financial Strategies for
Making It Happen

One of the greatest rewards of relocating is the promise of a clean slate. Details of financial problems, broken marriages, dead-end jobs or other "old business" can be left behind with unwanted furniture and broken toys. In fact, the prospect of starting over can be so exhilarating, many people let their impulse be their guide. Armed with a "Let's do it before we lose our nerve" attitude, tens of thousands of American families take the plunge every year, hoping that good luck is in the package delivered by the Welcome Wagon.

How does it all work out? We interviewed hundreds of families who discovered fabulous new hometowns—places that offered gainful employment, a nice home, good schools and a higher quality of life than they ever dreamt of. Their only regret was not moving sooner.

Unfortunately, happy endings have less to do with luck than with proper planning. Every year, too many families discover that the frying pan wasn't half as bad as the fire! Successful adjustments were hindered by: 1) the lack of success in finding jobs; 2) difficulty in earning decent wages (a common pitfall of living in many Southern cities); 3) feeling like outsiders no matter how hard they tried; and 4) the inability to shake off long-standing problems (runaway debts, emotional difficulties, etc.).

Nothing is more devastating than moving a family cross-country only to be no better, or perish the thought, worse off than before. In fact, from a financial perspective, a wrong move can be debilitating because the costs involved are so high.

According to PHH Homequity Corp., a Connecticut-based relocation management company, it costs corporations an average of $45,353 to transfer an employee with a family of four. But just because you may be paying for your own move doesn't mean this figure is irrelevant. Relocation costs will vary widely based on numerous circumstances (distance and time of year moved, size of the home, number of people, etc.), not by who picks up the tab. That is why it can be so helpful to understand how companies budget an out-of-state move.

On the next page is a breakout of potential costs.

In addition to these costs, there are other significant, yet forgotten expenses that can enter into the picture, including:

- Loss of one or two incomes if family relocates without firm job offers.
- Capital gains taxes if buying a home for less than the one sold (and under age 55).
- Cost of new furniture, furnishings, appliances, paint and wallpaper, etc.
- Cost of first-time consultation fees charged by doctors, lawyers, etc.
- Cost of medical insurance if unemployed/without benefits.
- Paying deductibles on new insurance policies (medical, auto, homeowners).
- Possible private school tuition.
- Cost of joining country clubs, recreation centers, health clubs plus loss of money if previous membership costs were nonrefundable before expiration.
- Possible purchase of a second or even third car (occurs when families move from big

AVERAGE COST OF RELOCATING A FAMILY OF FOUR (685 MILES)
(Based on a present home value of $137,390.)

Present Home Carrying Costs (annual): $ 3,167
Mortgage interest, insurance, property taxes,
utilities, repairs, maintenance, improvements
and miscellaneous costs.

Sale of Home Costs: $ 15,057
Resale loss, broker commission, mortgage
charges, appraisals/inspections, legal costs,
marketing costs, title expenses, transfer taxes,
buyer incentives and miscellaneous closing costs.

New Home Purchase Costs: $ 5,275
Mortgage application fee, appraisal fee, mortgage
insurance, origination fee, discount points, survey
fee, legal and title costs, recording and transfer fees,
miscellaneous fees.

Possible Interest on a Bridge Loan $ 545

Shipping Household Goods (7.7 rooms) $ 7,519
Transportation, packing and unpacking, insurance,
storage and shipment of one automobile in peak season.

Pre-Move Home Search Trips: $ 2,950
Two trips to destination city for family including
transportation, lodging, meals, car rental, childcare,
entertainment, incidentals.

Temporary Living Expenses: $ 6,095
Forty five days for one adult to rent apartment or
live in a residence-inn, including lodging, meals and
incidentals plus three trips to old home.

Final Moving Trip to New Location: $ 578
Transportation, lodging, meals.

Miscellaneous Relocation Expenses: $ 4,167
Utility hookups, cost of joining clubs, unions,
a house of worship, etc.

TOTAL $ 45,353

Source: PHH Homequity Corp.

cities with extensive transportation to suburbs with limited transportation).

- If changing climates, need for additional clothes for the family.
- New registration fees (Motor Vehicle Bureau, day-care centers, colleges, etc.).

We know what you're thinking. "Moving is so expensive, we're never going to pull this off!" But wait. Our intent is not to discourage you, but to help you see that the relocation stakes are simply too high to "wing it." Regardless of what the move costs you, you cannot go undercapitalized. If it were up to us, we'd have this message posted on moving vans:

Warning: Relocation may be hazardous to your *wealth*!

Does this mean you need $50,000 in the bank before you can tell your boss to take this job and shove it? Not exactly. It does mean you have to give yourself time to build an adequate relocation nest egg. Specifically, if you have a job in place in your new city, you'll want to have enough cash resources to cover three months of added expenses after the relocation. If you'll be job hunting after you move, you'll need enough cash resources to last at least six months.

How much will you need exactly? There is no pat answer because the amount will be dependent on several factors—whether you rent or buy, how long it takes to find comparable paying jobs, if you need medical insurance, overall living costs in the new city, etc.

The best way to gauge estimated monthly expenses is to ask a realtor's relocation specialist for help in identifying average costs—rent, mortgage payments, utilities, taxes, etc.

A national firm that provides cost-of-living information for many cities is PHH Homequity Corp. Call 800-243-1033. The destination service is free, but expect to be asked if they can put you in touch with one of 2,000 realty offices in their broker network. If are interested in an area where they have an office, the contact may be invaluable.

Another firm, Right Choice, Inc., offers customized living cost comparisons between your home town and any area you are considering.

This analysis includes cost differentials on taxes, utilities, housing and medical costs and dozens of other categories based on an extensive questionnaire you fill out. There is a one-time fee of $190, but the payout is in the ammunition you'll have when negotiating a salary and benefits package. Here will be the proof that unless you receive X amount, the relocation may result in a negative cash flow and is subsequently not a good move. Call 800-872-2294.

Financial planning basics

Now that you understand the reasons to build an adequate nest egg *in advance* of the move, you may be wondering how to go about accumulating cash when the task has eluded you under normal circumstances. Admittedly, saving money during one of the country's worst recessions is a Herculean challenge. But we didn't say it was impossible.

The most important step you can take is putting your "financial" house in order by taking a look at your investments, savings and assets—and your liabilities. This balance is the backbone of your family's existence and the best indicator of your "fiscal fitness."

Step 1: What is your net worth?

The first step in assessing your financial health is looking at what you've accumulated over the years. That's assets and liabilities, not ski equipment and gourmet cookware.

Itemizing your personal savings, home equity, pensions and investments as well as your debts—a mortgage, installment loans, etc. gives you a personal balance sheet, or net worth statement. In effect, when you subtract what you owe from what you own, you have a like-it-or-not snapshot of your personal wealth.

Here's how to prepare your personal net worth statement:

Cash reserve assets. Add up your cash or near-cash resources such as checking accounts, savings accounts and money market funds. These are your "liquid" assets because they can be "liquidated" quickly without penalties.

It's also possible to include the cash value of a life insurance policy as well as a bank Certificate of Deposit (CD). These vehicles are liquid to the extent that it's possible to tap into them in an emergency. However, doing so may result in penalties for early withdrawal, or in the case of borrowing from the cash value of a life insurance policy, trigger interest charges on the value of the loan.

Under normal circumstances, between 15 percent and 20 percent of your total assets should be liquid. Again, in preparation for a relocation, you'll need enough cash to cover your living expenses for a minimum of three to six months. If you are a young couple with minimal assets, consider that you may have to liquidate 100 percent of what you own in order to have adequate resources for this transition period.

Equity/retirement assets. Generally, the most valuable asset in your portfolio is the equity in your home. But hopefully you will also have a combination of other investment assets including stocks and options, mutual funds, taxable and tax-free bonds, T-Bills, annuities, investment property (not your residence) and/or equity in a business.

Retirement assets include IRAs/Keogh Plans, 401Ks, vested pension plans, employee savings and stock option programs. In tandem, these should represent 50 percent to 60 percent of your total assets.

Keep in mind that if you do sell off investment assets, it will more than likely trigger tax liabilities and possibly penalties for early withdrawal.

To establish the values of these assets, ask your insurance agent, accountant, stockbroker, realtor and certified financial planner for assistance. You can also refer to recent price quotes in the newspaper. Although establishing values for real estate limited partnerships is complex, it may be helpful to contact the general partner to assess current value. As for vacation time shares, for the purpose of this exercise, place the value at the price you paid.

Finally, to determine the value of your 401K or other company benefit programs, ask your employee benefits department to provide the calculations.

As for personal property—clothing, furs and jewels, cars, furniture, etc., appraise the value by estimating how much money they would generate if they were sold today (only if you intend to liquidate).

Liabilities. This represents the outstanding balances on your mortgage(s), cars, installment loans, credit cards, etc. It also includes your projected state and federal tax bill. Ideally, your liabilities should represent no more than 30 percent to 50 percent of your total assets. In preparing for a relocation, however, it is so important to carry as light a load as possible with respect to debts. They add so significantly to monthly living expenses while reducing the amounts you can be saving or investing.

In addition, the interest on car loans, credit cards and installment loans is no longer deductible. Furthermore, with banks charging anywhere from 11 percent to 21 percent interest on installment debt, but only paying 3 percent to 5 percent on savings, it doesn't take an accountant to tell you that this is a raw deal.

If you do not have a current net worth statement, please fill out the Assets chart on page 29. If you need help, consult with your financial planner and/or tax preparer.

Calling all assets. Before we move on, it is very important to review your list of assets to determine if there are any that can be converted into liquid and/or income-producing investments. As we've mentioned, there will be an unusually high level of expenses for three to six months after you relocate and you'll need access to enough cash resources to cover for these contingencies.

One possibility is to look at any nonperforming stocks that don't pay dividends. It can be highly advantageous to sell them off and purchase income-bearing government security mutual funds. These pay a predictable monthly income.

Other strategies involve selling off investment property (long-term assets) to buy bonds or dividend paying stocks. Or, when a CD paying 6 percent comes due, it can be rolled over into bonds or income mutual funds paying 8 percent or more.

ASSETS

CASH RESERVE ASSETS
Checking accounts/cash $ _____
Savings accounts   _____
Money Market funds   _____
Certificates of Deposit   _____
Life insurance (cash value)   _____

EQUITY/RETIREMENT ASSETS
Time deposits (T-bills)   _____
Stocks and options   _____
Retirement savings (IRAs/Keoghs)   _____
Annuities (surrender value)   _____
Pensions (vested interest)   _____
Profit sharing plans   _____
Collectibles   _____
House (market value)   _____
Other real estate/limited partnerships   _____
Business interests   _____
Personal property (auto, jewels, etc.)   _____
Loans owed you   _____
Other assets   _____

TOTAL ASSETS $ _____

LIABILITIES

Mortgage or rent (balance due) $ _____
Auto loan (balance due)   _____
Credit cards   _____
Installment loans   _____
Annual tax bill   _____
Business debts   _____
Student loans   _____
Brokerage margin loans   _____
Home equity loans/2nd or 3rd mortgages   _____

TOTAL LIABILITIES $ _____

TOTAL NET WORTH $ _____

Step 2: Check current cash flow

The next step in putting your financial house in order is examining your income vs. your "out-go"—what you earn compared to what you spend. It's called a cash flow analysis and believe me, this exercise generates about as much enthusiasm as stepping on the scale in January. Still, combined with your net worth statement, the cash flow analysis will be the tool you use to create a realistic family budget.

To collect the data for your analysis, you need go no further than your home office, or wherever it is you stash your checkbook register, monthly bank statements, tax returns and credit card receipts.

It's also important to dig a little deeper to try and track some of the more invisible expenditures—cash purchases. These are often the true culprits of cash flow problems because the proof of the purchase disappears into thin air...as though it never existed.

To figure out where the money goes, add up your cash withdrawals for a three-month period, multiply by four and then write down the types of things you usually pay for with cash—lunches, dry cleaning, hair and nail care, movies and videos, health and beauty aids, etc.

Provided on pages 31 and 32 are charts for recording the details.

In the ideal scenario, when you add your estimated living expenses for the year and subtract that number from your after-tax income, there should be enough left over for savings and investments. Even better is if the balance represents 7 percent to 10 percent of your net income. If it doesn't, the likely culprit is credit-card debt or overspending on nonessentials.

Step 3: Establish priorities

Cash flow analyses are ready-or-not reminders of how innocent and unimportant small purchases seem—until they're added up. They also suggest how subtly we make choices about spending. We don't deliberate about most of them; we buy now and ask questions later.

The result is that most people are very disappointed that their money never seems to buy the important things. College educations. Vacations. Investments. They attribute it to not earning enough and paying high taxes. While this is true in part, the real reason money fails to perform is that when priorities aren't established, there is a tendency for it to be spent on impulse items.

It's time to find out, what are your financial goals? We already know you are serious about relocating to another part of the country so we'll put it at the top of the list. What else is important to you and your family? Just fill in the blanks on the chart on page 33, and start talking about the future. The idea is to create a road map for your money, with you in control behind the wheel.

Step 4: The dreaded "B" word

Now you know how much you are worth and what it buys you—not enough! But you are going to change that now that you also have financial goals. As a way to make sure those goals become realities, it's time to take the most important step of all. Establishing a budget you can live with.

Some people may define a balanced budget as when the month and the money run out at the same time, but that's not what we mean. A budget is a contract you make with yourself to spend up to a certain amount per month so that you can live within your means. And with a major relocation in your plans, there is never a more critical time to take control of the money reins.

Yes, we know that in some households the mere mention of the "B" word brings out these foot-stomping, head-shaking gyrations. And that's just from the kids! Unfortunately, with today's high-priced lifestyles and unending material desires, your toughest but most important job will be rallying the troops to cooperate.

But before you start your campaign, consider this. Budgeting has received a bad rap over the years. When you strip the word bare of all the associations, the truth is a budget is a plan for spending your money. It doesn't mean you can't spend money, it means you're going to decide *in advance of spending it,* where it's going to go.

CASH FLOW ANALYSIS

INCOME

Husband's salary/bonus/commissions $ _____

Wife's salary/bonus/commissions _____

Dividends and interest _____

Child support/alimony _____

Annuities/pensions/Social Security _____

Rent, royalties, fees _____

Moonlighting/freelance work _____

Loans being paid back to you _____

TOTAL INCOME $ _____

TAXES

Combined income taxes $ _____

Social Security contributions _____

Property taxes _____

TOTAL TAXES $ _____

LIVING EXPENSES

Rent or mortgage payments $ _____

Food _____

Clothing and uniforms _____

Utilities _____

Dining out _____

Furniture/electronics _____

Vacations/recreation _____

Entertainment _____

CASH FLOW ANALYSIS (continued)

LIVING EXPENSES (continued)

Gasoline $ _____

Car payments _____

Auto repair and maintenance _____

Financial and legal services _____

Medical care/medications _____

School tuition/day care _____

Life and disability insurance _____

Car insurance _____

Health insurance _____

Property and casualty insurance _____

Pet care _____

Birthday and holiday gifts _____

Babysitting/housekeeping _____

Commutation (tolls, trains, etc.) _____

Cable TV _____

Household maintenance _____

Telephone bills _____

Religious institutions _____

Books, magazines and papers _____

Clubs, sports, hobbies _____

Dues—union and others _____

Alimony/child support _____

Parental support/nursing home _____

Personal allowances (kids, lottery, etc.) _____

Other _____

**TOTAL ANNUAL
LIVING EXPENSES** $ _____

ESTABLISHING YOUR GOALS

Goals	Not Important	Important	Very Important	Absolutely Necessary
MOVE TO _____	☐	☐	☐	☐
Chop debts	☐	☐	☐	☐
Build savings	☐	☐	☐	☐
Get more insurance protection	☐	☐	☐	☐
Buy a first house	☐	☐	☐	☐
Buy a bigger house	☐	☐	☐	☐
Buy a new/2nd car	☐	☐	☐	☐
Start a family	☐	☐	☐	☐
Save for children's education	☐	☐	☐	☐
Have a better lifestyle	☐	☐	☐	☐
Take a great vacation	☐	☐	☐	☐
Open your own business	☐	☐	☐	☐
Retire early	☐	☐	☐	☐
Retire comfortably	☐	☐	☐	☐
Other:	☐	☐	☐	☐

You've already started getting into the budgeting process by taking a good hard look at what you've got coming in and what's going out. The next step is to forecast your income and return on investments for the year so you lay the groundwork for that budget. You'll be amazed at what a big number that probably is.

In addition, don't make the mistake of waiting to see what's left over at the end of the month for savings. The secret to saving money is to pay *yourself* every month (pretend you're paying a utility bill). As long as you earmark a certain amount of your paycheck savings, the nest egg will grow.

Budget systems

The first step in creating a working budget is deciding what it will look like.

One individual set up an elaborate budget tracking system on his personal computer. He had spreadsheets and forecasting tools and year-to-date figures and analyses...and you guessed it. He never entered a single piece of information. "Takes too much time," he said.

That's an important lesson. So here are some less-complicated ideas for keeping a budget that might work for you.

Monthly reviews. Every month, add up what you spend in each category vs. what you were budgeted to spend. Compare the numbers to see where you're overdoing it, or not spending what you anticipated. After three months, look for trends and readjust the budget accordingly. While this system may not keep you from splurging, you'll be able to count on having a good sense of where the money is going...12 times a year. If things start getting out of control, just apply the brakes.

Accountant's spreadsheets. This is an extended version of the monthly review, but in this case, all the information is confined to ledger sheets, which can be found at any office supply store. The advantage of using this format is that you can put an entire year on one sheet, or "spread it out" on a quarterly basis. The other difference is that there is room on the spreadsheet to record your banking transactions, paychecks and investment income—

giving you a complete bird's-eye view of your finances at a moment's glance. If you are computer literate, you can set the system up on your PC and let the software do your year-to-date totals and projections. By the way, projections are made by comparing "actual" expenditures in a category thus far, to the amount that is budgeted for the remainder of the year. It will immediately indicate an overspending situation.

"The envelope, please." Borrowed from immigrants running cash businesses, this system is simple yet effective. It involves cashing your paychecks or other income, dividing the cash into envelopes labeled by expense categories, and paying the bills from that cash. When the envelope is empty, you stop spending in that category. Of course you can always rob Peter to pay Paul, but you get the idea. This idea is probably best for those on a fixed income whose financial needs are uncomplicated and predictable.

The bank account method. This is a more sophisticated version of the envelope method, but similar. It involves setting up three different bank accounts: a savings account for long-term goals (investments), an interest-bearing checking account or money market fund for short-term goals (tuition payments) and a checking account for bills and cash withdrawals. Budget how much is to go into each account on a monthly basis, and withdraw a certain allotment for bills. If your withdrawals exceed the budget for the month, stop taking the money out.

Truthfully, the final execution is the least relevant. What's important is that the tracking system is simple to use *on a continuing basis*.

Budget tips

Once you and your budget are comfortable with each other, here are some suggestions to keep the ball rolling.

1. As in Monopoly, pick the banker first. If the wrong person is in charge of the funds, your best intentions could be wasted. Decide which family member is the most organized, has the better memory for dates and obligations, likes working with numbers, has the most free time to handle the record-keeping, bill-paying, etc., and is preferably the saver not the spender. If both adults are equally capable or incapable of these functions, split the chores to keep each other in check.

2. Build in a reward system. There has to be both small and large payoffs for good behavior. Make sure that rewards are given as often as possible. Perhaps a family membership at a health club is a way to say thanks, or a nice vacation, dinner out...you get the idea. Keep 'em happy. Everyone deserves a break now and then.

3. Charge yourself a "check" fee. Some people find that they can save small amounts of money if they deduct $10 or $20 every time they write a check. They call it a check fee, and after a month of bill-paying, they've accumulated a few hundred dollars that can be thrown into an interest-bearing account.

4. Leave home without it. That's right. You can leave your American Express card home, along with your other credit cards, and you will survive. You'll also cut back on credit-card spending in a big way. If you use your cards, let them be for planned purchases. Also, if you're not always carrying your cards, you'll be less likely to ever report them lost or stolen.

As with anything that is experimental, you can expect the first few months of money-watching to have ups and downs. You'll discover luxuries you absolutely can't live without, expenses you overlooked, and overall bad ideas, like serving macaroni and cheese every third night. But when you do work out the glitches, you'll be thrilled at the surplus that's there at the end of the year. That's exactly what you need to prepare for a successful relocation.

A certified financial planner can help

Admittedly, the strategies we've outlined are general in nature. And yet, each of us has our own set of circumstances, financial philosophies and goals, all of which can impede our ability to do what is "textbook" simple.

This is why we strongly urge people to seek the advice of a certified financial planner. CFPs are the only experts who have gone through rigorous educational training to manage all aspects of a client's financial affairs. They do not replace your lawyer and accountant, they manage the team to insure that everyone is working toward common goals.

The greatest benefit is that financial planning is not a product, it is a process. A certified planner will meet with you, discuss your needs and goals and then develop a highly customized, detailed, financial plan which will factor in all of your personal goals and circumstances. The cost of a plan will vary with the extent of the work that needs to be done, but ultimately it won't cost you, it will *pay* you.

With a financial plan, there is the potential to save thousands of dollars every year in income tax while generating greater profits through sound investment strategies.

Check the yellow pages or call the Institute of Certified Financial Planners for a referral at 800-282-PLAN (or 7526). Another source is the International Association of Financial Planners at 800-945-IAFP (or 4237).

In the meantime...

To help you address some possible concerns, here is a list of the most frequently asked financial questions as they pertain to a major relocation.

Q. *We're concerned that in a soft real estate market, we won't be able to sell our home at the big profit we originally counted on. That would probably prevent us from buying our dream home in the city we're moving to. What are our options?*

A. If you trade up to a bigger house before you're financially able, you'll be house rich and cash poor. That will trigger a chain of events such as running up credit cards to compensate for the income that isn't there. That, in turn, will prevent you from having enough money at the end of the month to save or invest. Ultimately, your only financial security will be in that home. And with real estate no longer the hedge against inflation it once was, you really need more eggs in the basket. However, if you buy a home within your means, use some of the profits from your old home to pay off debts, you'll have the perfect opportunity to reverse this trend and get your financial affairs back on track.

Q. We've heard it is smarter to rent a place when you move to a new city, just in case you don't like it. But with such low interest rates, wouldn't it be better to buy?

A. The lowest interest rates in the past 15 years certainly make it a desirable time to buy a home. However, if you immediately buy in the new area, you lose your flexibility. What if you can't find a job, or you discover you like another community better? What if you decide you made a big mistake and want to head home? Whatever you saved on the interest will be wiped out by closing costs, real estate commissions, moving and other major expenses. We still urge newcomers to rent first and buy later. It's the best insurance policy you can buy.

Q. Can we deduct our moving expenses on our tax return and if so, what is deductible?

A. If the difference between your former residence and new job is 35 miles or more, your moving expenses are deductible (this applies to self employed individuals as well). You must also remain in the new locale as a full-time employee for 39 weeks in a year (they don't have to be consecutive or with the same employer). Moving expenses that are fully deductible include traveling costs for you and your family between the new and old locations, the total cost you paid to the moving company and up to $3,000 of moving-related expenses (house hunting expenses, temporary living quarters, etc.).

Q. Can we also deduct our job-search expenses?

A. Whether or not you relocate, job-search expenses may be tax deductible, with several qualifications. According to the IRS, you are entitled to deduct the cost of resumes, travel expenses for interviews and other related expenses if you are looking for a job in the same line of work as you are currently employed. These expenses are allowed in the Miscellaneous Deduction category, which is subject to the 2-percent AGI (adjusted gross income) floor. For example, if your adjusted gross income is $30,000, the 2-percent floor is $600. That means that the first $600 of expenses are not deductible but the balance of your expenses would be. Unfortunately, if this is your first job out of college, for example, or your first job in a new field, job-search costs are not deductible.

Q. Will I still be eligible for unemployment benefits if I relocate?

A. Yes. If you are unemployed and still receiving benefits in your present location, your eligibility status will not be changed due to a move. Notify your local unemployment office so they can arrange to transfer your records. You'll have to re-register in the new city and wait until payments resume. The waiting time will vary significantly by state and city.

The bottom line

Unfortunately, most people live in fear of their money. They worry endlessly about not having enough, when they do accumulate assets they worry that the people managing it will make bad decisions. And as they get closer to retirement, they panic that they'll outlive their money.

All of this angst is understandable, but unnecessary. At any point in the game, you can take charge of your financial affairs and look forward to a decent night's sleep. All it takes is the willingness and commitment to plan ahead, budget, save and make prudent investment decisions with the help of a trained professional.

Or as one client so aptly said, "The key to a great life is having enough money to live on, but not too much money to worry about!"

Chapter 3

Making the Grade: How to Be an Expert at Evaluating Schools

No matter how excited a family is about moving to a new part of the country, the one thing that gives parents *and* kids a serious case of the "willies" is looking for a new school. Often faced with an impossible deadline ("We have to be moved in by August.") and/or an impossible task, ("Our kids will be going to three different schools!"), the pressure to find the "right" school can seem insurmountable. The nagging concern is that the fate of a child's future rests on this very decision.

If this is your sentiment exactly, welcome to the group. Here are just some of the comments we heard from parents who recently went through the process.

"I've been transferred three times in the last 10 years so I know how stressful it is to relocate a family. The worst part is figuring out which neighborhood has the best schools. Everyone tries to be helpful, especially the real estate people and your new colleagues. But when it comes down to it—all you can really go on is your gut instincts."

"We thought that if we chose the wrong school, the kids' grades would suffer, they'd have a hard time making friends, they'd lose their self-esteem and they'd never get into good colleges. Basically they'd hate us for life. We were nervous wrecks."

"We met the principal before we bought a house in the development. She was so friendly and interested in us and asked lots of questions about the school our daughter was attending. When it was our turn, we just stared at each other. I finally said, 'I'm sorry. We don't know what we're supposed to ask.'"

Without a doubt, it is very frustrating to take a tour of a school and not have a clue what to look for, what to ask, and even what is fair game to judge. If you are told that test scores in the district are well above the national average, should you be completely satisfied? If you see brand-new, state-of-the-art computer labs and showcases full of trophies, does that suggest the school is a "winner?" If you hear that spending per student is high or the ratio of teachers to students is low, is that a guarantee of a quality education? Not necessarily.

To start, what good is a brand-new school if teachers' salaries are so low that the district can't attract experienced faculty? Who cares if the expenditures per pupil are considerably higher if the allocations are wasted on a top-heavy administration? And what about the school that boasts a high percentage of students that rank above average on standardized tests? If your child is only an average performer, will he or she be able to adjust to a "pressure cooker" environment?

With so many good news/bad news scenarios, how *does* a parent judge the merits of a school? The answer, according to today's leading educators, is to act as a consumer and comparison shop, much as you would for any major purchase. Although there is considerably more at stake when it comes to your child's education, there are similarities. You have the right to demand information before you buy, to check out the merchandise and to speak up if you are not satisfied with the product!

Before you can objectively evaluate a school, however, there are four important considerations to keep front and center.

1. **There are no perfect schools.** We've never discovered a Shangri-La Middle School or Garden of Eden High. Basically it is unrealistic to expect that any school is going to be all things to all people. Every school has its share of attributes and drawbacks. The key is to find one that has the most attributes that are important to you and your child. Remember, also, that no matter how pleased you were with your current school, it wasn't perfect either.

2. **To thine own child be true.** What *does* your child need in order to thrive? Would he or she do best in a small school setting? How would he or she handle a highly competitive academic curriculum? Does he or she show more of an inclination toward music and the arts or do you foresee a pursuit of vocational skills? Take this opportunity to assess your child's goals, needs and capabilities so that you can try to find the best possible educational arena. If you find it difficult to be objective, ask a former teacher for help.

3. **Think positively.** Understandably, parents feel overwhelmed when comparing new schools. If you move to the Pittsburgh area, for example, there are 103 different school systems to consider. But look at the bright side. If you settled into your current home town before your kids were of school age, short of choosing a private school, you had *no* choice where they went. When you relocate, you have the perfect opportunity to match your child's needs and abilities to the best possible environment.

4. **Keep an open mind.** If you feel strongly that only a brand-new school will do, consider that many older facilities are impeccably maintained and offer the latest technology. Some parents prefer the traditional elementary, junior and high schools, but may have to consider districts that segment schools (primary, elementary, middle, junior and senior high). Although each of their

children may end up attending different schools, at least they'll be in the most age-appropriate environment. Every school has something different and potentially beneficial to offer if you have an open mind.

How to evaluate a school

Now that you are being realistic, assessing your child's needs, thinking positively and with an open mind, here are some of the most important things you should ask and know when evaluating a new school.

School building

What you should ask: How old is the building? If not new, was asbestos identified as a health hazard and removed? Have any safety violations been found in the past two years and what was done to correct them? Is there an overcrowding problem and, if so, what is being done to accommodate the growth? Are there adequate funds for maintenance and repairs? Regarding facilities and support resources, what is lacking (adequate number of lockers, restrooms, computers or audio/visual equipment, etc.)?

What you should know: The ideal school is in a safe neighborhood (no major traffic, health or safety hazards in the area), is clean and well-maintained, is completely up to code and has an excellent safety record (minimal student injuries) as well as adequate financing to meet the needs of the operation.

School budget

What you should ask: How is the school financed and the budget determined? How does the latest budget compare to prior years? If there have been substantial cuts, what is being done to deal with the shortfall? What programs or materials have been affected? What is the class size policy and have class ratios been altered? How many students must there be before an aide is brought into the classroom?

What you should know: It's not the amount allocated per student that is important, it's how the school spends it! You want to see monies earmarked for technology, textbooks, supplies, resource centers, school specialists—not heavily skewed toward administration, fringe benefits, etc. Incidentally, a good ratio for primary grades is 1:15 and no more than 1:20 for upper grades, although this is more often not financially realistic. Also, every district applies its own formula for calculating ratios, so you could be comparing apples and oranges.

Faculty and administration

What you should ask: What is the average years of teaching experience? What percentage of teachers have advanced degrees? How do teacher salaries compare to the area and what is the turnover rate (sometimes a reflection of low salaries)? How long has the principal been in education? How accessible is he/she to parents and students? What are the most significant accomplishments of this administration and, conversely, what remain the biggest challenges? Also, what type of inservice and staff development is available.

What you should know: Ideally, teachers are well-trained in their fields, working toward advanced degrees and are also good managers (executives are not the only ones who should be well-versed on time management, organizational skills, people skills and creative solutions). Effective administrators should be able to clearly state the goals and objectives of the school, show strong leadership abilities and encourage staff, faculty, parents and students to work together.

Curriculum and academic performance

What you should ask: How often is the curriculum revised and who makes the decisions? What is the school's academic philosophy (whole language approach, integrated learning, hands-on programs, tracking, etc.)? What percentage of coursework is academics and what percentage music, art and special interests? How are textbooks selected? At the high school level, what percentage of students take the SATs or ACTs, and what percentage enroll in college?

What you should know: The most effective schools are strong in both core curriculum and arts/life skills. Where possible, there should also be flexibility with respect to a student's ability, maturity and interest. In addition, there should be a strong emphasis on programs for students with special needs and skills (gifted, special ed.). As for college entrance exams, the higher the percentage of students performing above average, the more competitive and rigorous the environment. Conversely, if the school or district averages are low, it may be a reflection of the number of students encouraged to take the exam, whether or not they planned to go to college. In 1992, the national combined SAT score was 899 (out of a possible 1500). The average ACT score was 20.6 (range is from 1 to 36).

Parental involvement

What you should ask: What opportunities are available to parents who wish to volunteer their time and expertise? To what extent do parents get involved in policy decisions? What functions are performed by the PTA (or counterpart) and how effective is the organization?

What you should know: Show us a school where volunteerism is the lifeblood of the operation and we'll show you a school where attendance and test scores are excellent, where teachers give 110 percent and student achievements run high at every level. If a school is unsuccessful at fostering community spirit, the apathy among students will likely be pervasive.

Extracurricular activities

What you should ask: What types of clubs and organizations are available and who pays to run them? Is there a strong emphasis on athletics? Have school teams (from debate to track) earned any state or national honors recently? What type of cultural programs are offered and have they earned any honors?

What you should know: It's a proven fact that busy, well-rounded students are the best overall performers. According to a new study from the University of Colorado, high school students who participate in sports and other extracurricular activities have a low absentee rate and have higher GPAs. The most effective schools don't just run clubs and sports, they are zealous in their efforts to recruit and reward participants.

Gut reactions

Surprisingly, there will be schools that meet your most important criteria, and yet as first impressions go, just don't "feel" right. Here are some of the common "turn-offs" that should not be ignored:

- You and/or your child were not made to feel welcome.
- The school did not appear to be well-maintained (classrooms and hallways were untidy, bathrooms needed repairs).
- Activity in the classrooms or hallways appeared chaotic and not orderly (the lunchroom doesn't count).
- The classrooms looked sterile, not bursting with creativity.
- The manner in which students and teachers were addressed was disturbing.

We urge you to explore those concerns and ask probing questions. If ultimately you are convinced that the school is the wrong fit—go with your instincts. You do have a choice!

Wave of the future

As the demands on both schools and students changes to accommodate a growing global economy in the '90s and beyond, there are other qualities that will prove to be vital. We give our highest recommendations to the schools that offer the following:

School-based management. Historically, school districts were managed through a single office where unilateral decisions were the only means of insuring equality and keeping the peace. Today, the trend is for schools to operate autonomously from the district, giving them a strong sense of ownership. Where there is school-based management, administrators, faculty, parents *and* students may have a say on hiring practices, curriculum, allocation of resources and other decisions. Schools that are held accountable for their futures are more likely to meet the needs of their "customers."

Magnet schools. When magnet schools were opened in the late '60s and early '70s, their goal was to identify at-risk, inner-city students and place them in a special setting where they'd get greater attention. Today there are an estimated 2,000 magnet schools in the U.S. that are "niche" environments for the academically gifted (particularly in math and science), artistically talented or vocational-bound. Students get a traditional education but have the chance to focus on their special areas.

Computer-assisted learning. There are an estimated 2 million computers in use at schools across the country. Some schools have computer labs, others have banks of computers in classrooms. In today's competitive world, ideally, you want your school to offer opportunities well beyond computer literacy and programming.

As you can see, evaluating a school is much more involved than comparing test scores or being razzle-dazzled by a high-tech appearance. The best way to survive the ordeal is to stay focused on the things that are most essential to you and your child, do your best to stay objective and take time to focus on the many things that will change for the positive.

Additional reading

The National PTA publishes a workbook to help evaluate schools, "Looking In On Your School." Send $1 to the National PTA, 700 N. Rush Street, Chicago, IL 60611-2571.

Chapter 4

Same Job, Different City: Conducting an Out-of-Town Job Search

Once upon a time, there was a talented but underpaid department manager who was overworked and underappreciated by a cruel employer. Yearning for a better job in the far-away city of her dreams, she mailed her resume to all the major employers there. Three of the biggest and richest companies instantly fell in love with her experience and credentials and flew her out for a series of interviews. At the end of this process, each presented her with a job offer on a silver platter.

She examined each offer carefully, and finally chose the very best company, which offered her hefty benefits, an attractive salary increase (beefed up by a yearly cost-of-living adjustment), help in buying a new home in the local community of her choice (and in selling the one she owned), full moving expenses and counseling so her spouse could find a new job.

It was a heavenly match, and naturally she accepted immediately. The company whisked her and her family across the country and they all lived happily ever after.

You've heard these relocation fairy tales. Handsome princes of employers who rescue overlooked but hard-working, loyal employees from wicked-stepmother bosses.

But enough about them. How can you increase the odds of a fairy godmother coming to your rescue?

Admittedly their job has been made difficult by an uncooperative economy. Job-hunting is a tough proposition for everyone—from entry-level workers fresh out of college to experienced career veterans dumped unceremoniously into the job market, or into a way-too-early retirement.

But all is *not* hopeless. There can be a happy ending to be had *if* you take certain key steps to make your long-distance job hunt more effective.

To begin with, it has never been more important to master the basic skills that are the foundation of good job-hunting: networking, resume-preparing, locating job opportunities, landing and conducting job-winning interviews, negotiating salary and benefits. *If you lack some or all of these skills, start by working on them.*

A wealth of material is available on all of these subjects. If you feel ill-equipped to handle a job-search, get to the bookstore or library immediately and read up on the strategies and techniques you need, whatever job you're seeking, wherever the city you're moving to.

Some of the best guides our research has uncovered: *The Smart Woman's Guide to Resumes and Job Hunting,* by Julie Adair King and Betsy Sheldon; *How to Locate Jobs and Land Interviews,* by Albert L. French; *101 Great Answers to the Toughest Interview Questions,* by Ron Fry; *Take This Job and Leave It,* by Bill Radin; *Joyce Lain Kennedy's Career Book,* by Joyce Lain Kennedy and Dr. Darryl Laramore.

Once you've mastered the basics, this chapter will give you our top 10 pointers for job-hunting from afar, identifying the trickiest problems (and their solutions) for long-distance job hunters.

Top 10 Job-Hunting Tips

1. Know what you're getting into first

Learn everything you can about the job market and economic climate of your prospective new home. It may have gorgeous ocean vistas, great air and water quality, terrific schools and affordable homes. But if there are no jobs, how are you going to enjoy all this?

That's why we've included our own detailed information in the "Earning a Living" sections of each Area Profile, which gives an overview of the area ("Economic outlook"), a detailed industry-by-industry discussion ("Where the jobs are") and the particular outlook for new businesses ("Business opportunities").

Wherever and whenever you are hoping to relocate, you must find the answers to these questions: What's the current job climate in your dream locale? Where are the majority of the jobs? Who are the key employers? Are there one or two major employers or a crop of new upstart companies? Are businesses moving into the area or fleeing as fast as the moving companies can arrive? Which companies are planning to expand? Which are downsizing? Where—specifically—is job growth expected? And is it in the areas that match your skills and career goals? Is there a diversity of industry in the area and a range of companies of various sizes? (Areas dependent on a single industry or a single large employer are at greatest risk of economic downturns.)

In addition to the information we've provided in this volume, you may want to spend the time at the library with some specific job-search reference books. Start with these:

Dun & Bradstreet Million Dollar Directory (Dun & Bradstreet Corp., Dun's Marketing Services): An annual (February) guide to 160,000 U.S. companies with a net worth of $500,000 or more. Arranged alphabetically and indexed geographic location and product.

Standard and Poor's Register of Corporations, Directors, and Executives: Published annually in January (with supplements added in April, July and October), it covers more than 50,000 U.S. corporations in Vol. 1 (including names/titles of 400,000+ officials) and biographies of 70,000 executives and directors in Vol. 2.

The Career Guide: Dun's Employment Opportunities Directory lists companies that have 1,000 or more employees. in a wide variety of industries. Entries include company name, location of headquarters, other offices and plants, training, overview of company, etc.

Ward's Business Directory of U.S. Private and Public Companies: Five-volume annual directory providing information on more than 130,000 U.S. businesses, the majority of which are privately held (and thus harder to find out about).

U.S. Directory of Manufacturers: Annual (January) guide lists more than 200,000 manufacturing companies with 10+ employees. Geographical index.

You can also contact the following for more information about earning a living in your new community:

1. Economic development organizations in the area;
2. Small business development centers;
3. Chamber of Commerce;
4. Local daily and business papers;
5. Local yellow pages;
6. Friends who live in the area;
7. Professional and civic organizations to which you belong that have chapters in the area.

2. Subscribe to the local paper

Once you have an overall idea of the job market in your chosen area(s), you can zero in on specific job opportunities. We suggest subscribing to the local paper in the area to which you want to move. While its classified ads are an obvious source for job leads, the rest of the paper will continue to "fill in" the picture of your potential new home, giving you time to learn about it before you sink your roots.

Other national publications, such as the *Wall Street Journal's National Business Employment Weekly,* may well be helpful. And while you're at the library, don't forget to ask about the availability of databases and on-line services. Depending on your particular field, you may find a specific database listing nothing but opportunities in your profession (*and* giving you the opportunity to list your own credentials for potential employers).

3. Networking with a twist

Don't depend solely on the newspapers, directories and on-line services. Most career counselors confirm that as many as 85 percent of all jobs are *never* publicized, never advertised. So unless you want to restrict your search to only 15 percent of the jobs actually available in your area, you must learn how to look for the "hidden" opportunities. That means you'll have to fine-tune your networking techniques—taking advantage of any and every contact you know—and everyone *they* know.

Your biggest contact, of course, could be the very company you're currently working for. Do they have a division, office or affiliate in or near the area to which you'd like to move? They do? There's where to start your search (presuming, of course, you like the company you're working for!).

Your neighbor knows someone at the biggest plant in your prospective city? Uncle Bob has a friend who's started his own new successful business there? What about your fellow Elks, colleagues and church-goers? Or your dentist, doctor, banker or lawyer? Once you start making a list of everyone you know—and everyone they know—you'll be amazed how quickly your network grows, and how much closer you may be to that move.

4. Let the professionals help you look

Hook up with a search firm, preferably one specializing in your career area or profession— and one with an office in the city to which you're hoping to move. If you are at a middle-management level or above, contact a respected executive search firm that specializes in your area of business in your current area

(even if they don't have an office in your new city). The good firms are in contact with businesses nationwide. Keep in mind that executive search firms are working for the employers— *not* you—so shop around, find one or several that seem to have a lot of contacts and make the most of them.

If you're looking for an administrative position or a lower-level job, you'll have your best luck with a local employment agency in your *new* city. Most employment agencies are local, not national (or even regional).

5. Consider a pilot trip

Taking an initial trip to your dream city is a good idea for many more reasons than simply to job-hunt. One to two weeks will give you the opportunity to really taste the local flavor and experience the life you're considering making yours. But make the most of your trip: Schedule meetings with employment agencies and as many interviews (informational *and* actual) as possible during your stay.

6. Tailor your resume for your search

If you're responding to an ad or sending your resume to a prospective employer in your new city, will it increase your odds of getting the job if you indicate you already live in the city? Would an employer eliminate your resume entirely because you're from out of town? Maybe, maybe not. But most experts advise that starting out under false pretenses is dangerous.

Be up-front: Put your current address on the resume *but* mention your intention of moving to that city prominently in your *cover letter*.

And don't be afraid to create two or three totally different resumes if your experience would allow you to consider two or three different jobs. Each may accentuate something different, downplay something else. (Likewise, your lack of experience may leave you wide open to *any* offer, but no employer wants someone who's career goal is "to get a job!")

7. Prepare for tricky questions

"Why do you want to move?" Your interviewer leans back in his chair, squints his eyes and glares. Message: Your answer is crucial to landing this job. If you say, "My family just decided we want to live here," will he think you're impulsive? A risk-taker? (And is that good or bad?)

You may not be able to decipher what they want to hear from you. But the safest bet is to assume that prospective employers are looking for someone who is goal-oriented, directed and clear on what he or she wants.

Answer to avoid: "I just hate Ashtabula; I'll do anything to get out of there." Another answer to avoid: "Well, I haven't really decided whether I'm moving here or to Seattle." The former is a negative response—and you want to avoid negatives during all phases of the interview process. The latter, even if it's true, reveals a complete lack of commitment to *his town*. If you're that unsure, wait until you have made a decision before going on actual interviews. Whatever your response, frame it in a positive light. For example:

> *"It's a very important goal for me to live in a community that meets our needs and wants. We've carefully explored many locations, and this city, by far, is the best location we've found—not the least because of the opportunity to work in a company like yours."*

Will your prospective employer really buy that you decided to move cross-country just for the possibility of working with his or her illustrious company? Well, they certainly don't want to hear the opposite!

Do you risk revealing something "personal" about yourself by implying your move is primarily a search for "family values"? As a rule, career experts advise you to avoid referring to issues that may bias an employer (*Hmmm... she's got kids. May not be willing to put in much overtime.*). As a rule, this is advisable, since it is illegal for the employer to *ask* about your marital status (or plans) or family (including plans).

But in this situation, you may touch on it, while still avoiding the detail that may say more than necessary about your situation: "The school has a great athletic program for the twins, the day-care programs have an excellent reputation, and the older ones like the local university."

8. Negotiating salary with all the facts

Let's fantasize: You've been offered a terrific job with a $10,000 raise in salary. Should you break out the *Dom Perignon*? Fat lot of good that raise will do if you're moving to a place where the cost of living is *twice* as high. Again, take the time to research everything about the location; know the score *before* you have to accept or decline a good job offer.

9. Consider "temping"

What if you can't find a job but want (or need) to move anyway? Or you've found a great new job but your spouse is still looking? While it's inherently risky to move without a job, if you're sufficiently committed to moving, there's no law that says you can't.

And while you're looking in your new city, why not consider working for a temporary agency? It allows you to get a feel for the work force in the area and scout around for other opportunities while you're at least earning a paycheck. Who knows? By being in the right place at the right time, you may very well end up with a job offer and a permanent place where you're currently temping.

10. Maintain a positive attitude

Job hunting in your own city wouldn't be easy, doing it long-distance requires even greater patience and perseverance. Keep in mind that the process won't happen overnight, and don't take any rejections personally. We interviewed hundreds who went through the process, and we heard repeatedly that everything tends to work out for the best.

Chapter 5

Moving 101: Getting Cross-Country With Your Possessions and Your Sanity

How can a civilization that invented microwave ovens, fax machines and computers not have a clue how to make moving a snap? Nothing would be better than relocating without packing up a household of goods and trucking them cross-country. Unfortunately, the only way to get there is the old-fashioned way, using men and their machines. To help you, we've put together a course called "Moving 101."

You'll learn how long-distance movers arrive at their estimates (let alone their destinations), the lowdown on liability coverage and making claims, great ways to keep moving costs down and how to pick a mover. Just as important, we offer our best strategies for helping your kids make it through the move, too.

What does it cost to move?

Moving to the next town can run into the thousands, so moving cross-country will certainly give one pause. It's why the first question a mover is asked is "What's this gonna cost?" The trouble is that it's like asking the price of a new car. Do you want a luxury sedan or a mini-van? What about options? The questions continue until the salesperson arrives at a number, and then the negotiating begins. So it goes with moving.

The best way to get a fix on moving costs is to be aware of all the charges that can be factored into an estimate. Three big variables include:

1. Distance. Movers will first determine the approximate mileage between your new and old homes. This is accomplished by mapping out the shortest distance between point A and point B on *highways that are usable for truck travel.* The longer the haul, the more costly the move.

2. Weight. Prices are based on every 100 pounds moved, so it's best to ask at least three movers to "guess-timate" the size of your shipment. Don't be surprised by wide variations as each mover refers to its own "Table of Weights" when working up an estimate.

3. Time of year. All movers cut prices, but how extensively depends upon the time of year. Reserving a carrier between May 15 and Sept. 30 (when 50 percent of all moves take place) almost guarantees that discounts will not be as deep. In fact, you can count on paying a 10-percent premium for moving during busy season. What's more, service is often slower because of peak demand.

Taking distance, weight and time of year into consideration, the Household Goods Carrier Bureau reports that a basic residential, long-distance move weighs 5,251 pounds (five rooms), travels 1,217 miles and costs the shipper $2,384 ($45.41 per 100 pounds). However, according to PHH Homequity Corp., a Connecticut-based cost-of-living relocation management firm, the average moving costs run significantly higher, particularly if the move takes place in peak season (May through September).

Based on PHH's 1992 survey of middle to upper middle-class families of four who relocated 685 miles (the approximate distance between Raleigh, N.C., and Tampa, Fla.), shipped 7.7 rooms (8,000 pounds) and a car (75 percent of all two-car families drive one and transport the other), the average move costs $7,519.

The following section provides a brief overview of the many services that can be factored into an estimate. As you'll see, hiring a long-distance mover is much like dining at a restaurant where everything on the menu is *à la carte*. And similar to good waiters, movers like to make tempting, but costly, suggestions. The key to negotiating a fair price is being aware of the different ways they earn their keep.

Transportation

Basic transportation includes use of the mover's truck, and use of labor to move goods out of your house, load them on the truck, drive to your destination, and reassemble everything in your new home.

If your move originates and/or terminates in a high-density area like Chicago or New York, there are additional transportation charges (ATCs). In congested locations, movers face traffic jams, construction delays, inaccessible entrances and other difficulties. To compensate for lost time, expect to pay 40 cents to $3 more per 100 pounds.

Liability insurance

By law, every interstate moving company must assume some liability against damage or loss. Unfortunately the liability they assume is at a minimum, forcing the shipper to purchase additional coverage. And even with that, the mover is protected from you almost as much as the other way around. In other words, the coverage actually limits the mover's liability if it loses or damages your shipment.

The good news is that full replacement value insurance, the maximum protection you can buy, is relatively inexpensive and worth every penny. However, before you purchase insurance from the mover, *check your home-owner's policy*. It's possible your belongings are already covered during a move, alleviating the need for additional coverage.

If you do buy liability insurance from the mover, know your rights. By law, the mover must provide you with a copy of your policy and/or a formal receipt at the time of the purchase. Without proper documentation, they can be held fully liable for any claim that is a result of their negligence.

Although there are four types of coverage, full value protection (sometimes called replacement cost coverage) is the only type we recommend. Common sense tells you that 99 percent of the contents in your home were never built to be moved cross-country. The industry reports that 25 percent of all residential moves result in claims for losses or damages, so good liability coverage is critical.

With full value protection, in the event of a loss or irreparable damage that is a result of the mover's negligence, you'll receive full replacement value. The cost of this coverage averages $8.50 per $1,000 of valuation, but can be less if you agree to take a deductible. As with any insurance policy, the higher the deductible, the lower the premium.

Packing services

Movers offer two types of packing services. The first is packing materials—dishpacks, wardrobes, cartons, etc. Say what you will about movers, they have sturdier boxes than the supermarket and liquor store. For fragile and valuable items, they are worth the money.

The second packing service is labor. You can opt to have the mover pack up your old residence and/or unpack your cartons at your new home.

There are two very important reasons to having the movers do your packing: time and money. You can avoid weeks and possibly months of standing, bending, folding, and rolling valuable breakables into newspaper when the movers are in charge.

Secondly, if the movers do the packing and there is damage, they can't blame you. Otherwise, when the boxes are marked PBO (packed by owner), it allows the mover to argue that damages were the result of a bad packing job (and they may be right).

The cost for packing services will vary according to your home county's current labor rates. On average, packing should be 10 percent of your total costs. It's worth the money!

NOTE: The mover will try to talk you into packing the house on moving day. Insist on starting a day or two before. Moving day is hectic enough and when the movers are rushed, it can lead to unnecessary loss and damage.

More extras that add to the cost

In addition to the basic cost factors, there are numerous others that can be included in your estimate. Here is a rundown:

1. From north to south. With many more people moving south than north, some movers will charge an extra 50 cents per 100 pounds to compensate for an almost certain empty van on the return trip.

2. Apartment buildings. Movers get added compensation if they have to contend with elevators, stairs, and long carries (when an apartment is far from the stairs or elevators, or the goods must be brought to a loading dock).

3. Storage. Unfortunately, storage can be a necessary evil even with the most advance planning. Often people are forced to move from their home or apartment before their new place is ready for occupancy. In other instances, unexpected delays because of illness or travel arrangements prevent people from meeting the van when it arrives. If so, the mover has the right to place the entire shipment in storage. It happens more often than you think, so build storage costs, even for a few days, into your moving budget.

4. Demand services

a. **Space reservations.** If you want to move on a specific date, you can reserve space in the van. If moving between May and September, there may be a charge.

b. **Expedited service.** If you absolutely have to be at your new home by a certain date, the mover can speed up the amount of time it takes to make the trip. Ordering an expedited service is costly, but possible.

c. **Exclusive use of a vehicle.** If you do not want your shipment moved with other shipments for fear of delays or problems associated with sharing space, you can request that your shipment be the only one on the van.

d. **Guaranteed service on or between agreed dates.** If you need to know the exact day the mover will show up on either end, you can arrange for guaranteed service, which provides that your shipment is picked up, transported and delivered on agreed-upon dates. If the mover fails to deliver as scheduled, you'll be entitled to compensation.

How to keep moving costs down

With the high cost of moving, you may already be contemplating a garage sale to end all garage sales! And no doubt you should. But now you also know that two of the three factors that drive costs through the roof are under your control: time of year and weight. Remember, the real expense is in *what* and *when* you move, not *where* you move. Here are some proven tips from the professionals:

Time of year

One of the biggest fallacies about relocating with school-age children is the assumption that the move *must* take place during summer vacation. The thinking is that it is too disruptive to yank a child from the clutches of a familiar classroom, only to throw him into a new lion's den in the middle of a school year.

"Baloney," say the relocation experts who are responsible for hundreds of thousands of corporate transfers each year. The "new think" is to move during the school year because:

1. Teachers are more sensitive and aware of a new student's needs since they will already be familiar with the other classmates. At the beginning of a new school year, teachers are so busy, they may not have time to give special attention to anyone.

2. Children who move during summer months lose out on the biggest outlet they have to meet others—school. The neighborhood kids might be away at camp or on vacation.

3. The sooner children are enrolled in a new school, the sooner they can join clubs, learn the ropes, get acclimated to new teaching methods, etc. Just think how much easier it is on them when they've had even a few months to make friends and learn their way around. It can actually be counterproductive

when a child has the entire summer to build up anxiety about a new school.

Another big advantage of moving between September and May? You may cut your moving costs by as much as 40 percent to 50 percent. Plus, with fewer moves, the process goes smoother, faster and the extent of losses and damages diminishes.

Weight

The other major cost consideration is weight. As you'll pay for every 100 pounds shipped, refer to this proven four-step method for reducing the load: *Sell it, donate it, toss it or give it away!*

Furniture... If it's old and you're tired of it, if it's not going to match your new decor, if it won't fit in the new rooms, it makes more sense to replace than to move. **Books...** Just hang on to your most treasured favorites and even inquire about shipping them UPS. **Plants...** Without oxygen and water, how would *you* look after five days? Besides, they require a certificate of inspection from your county Department of Agriculture and in some states, such as Florida, plants *are* subject to inspection upon arrival. It's better to start over. **Clothes...** If you're moving to a warm-weather climate, hang on to a few cold-weather items for return visits. Anything that's not likely to be worn again should never see the inside of the van. **Records...** 100 record albums weigh 50 lbs. Purge your collection where possible... **Toys and hobby equipment...** This is a wonderful time to teach children the meaning of charity. Toys for Tots, area hospitals and many other organizations are always looking for well-made, unbroken toys. **Miscellaneous/junk...** Every home has its own special assortment. You know where its hiding. Is it worth hundreds of dollars to have it follow you? **Rugs...** Unless they are valuable or match your new decor, clean 'em and leave 'em behind. **Artwork...** Take only what you absolutely love, is an investment or has such sentimental value it won't feel like home without it. **Musical instruments...** Pianos and organs are very expensive to move and require special handling and tuning afterward. **Chandeliers, ceiling fans, etc...** Movers add on special handling charges for these, electricians charge to disconnect and reconnect. It could be cheaper to buy new. **Appliances...** Moving major appliances is risky. They may not withstand the jostling and/or not fit in your new home (perhaps the refrigerator is too tall), plus they are very costly to ship.

The time to do the contemplating as to what goes and what stays is before you get the moving estimates. Estimates are a waste of time until you know what is an accurate reflection of the move.

Getting estimates

Movers provide two types of estimates, binding and nonbinding. A nonbinding estimate allows the mover to give you a best guess as to the cost of your move, but does not bind him to that price. Ultimately, you could pay more and in some cases less. This is because the final cost will be based on actual, not estimated weight.

If, for example, you are quoted $4,800 but are getting rid of furniture, books, etc., up until moving day, you could end up paying $4,200. Conversely, if you told the mover not to include two beds and your lawn furniture in the estimate and later change your mind, your final bill could be more than $5,000.

You would think that the problem with nonbinding estimates is that movers might "lowball" a bid to get the job. Yet a recent ICC study found that movers overestimate prices as often as they underestimate them.

With a binding estimate, the mover sizes up the job and commits to a final price based on the *estimated* weight of your shipment. Keep in mind that if the mover is going to have to live or die by this price, he's going to build enough profit into it to cover himself for certain contingencies. That could mean paying more than necessary.

Another drawback of binding estimates is lack of flexibility. For example, if you told the mover not to include the cost of shipping your piano because you were certain you could sell it, you'll have to get another estimate if that plan fails. Without a second estimate, the mover is not obligated to take the piano because according to your contract, he's not going to be paid to do so. In addition, there might not be room on the van because only a certain amount of space was allocated for you. That's a last-minute hassle you don't need.

Most people opt for nonbinding estimates because they only want to pay for what they actually ship. Regardless of which type you settle on, the estimate must be put in writing in the order for service (initial commitment) and the Bill of Lading (final contract).

Hiring a mover

Given the number of personal circumstances that can affect a move, coupled with the different services to opt for, it's vitally important to shop the competition. Prices will vary greatly, particularly off season.

However, and this is a big however, by no means is the cheapest quote necessarily the *best* quote. Movers that do "lowball" their estimates have to save money somewhere and often that somewhere is in their service. Hiring a mover is like making any other major purchase. Bargain hard but make your final decision based on price as well as other important criteria, including:

Personal recommendations... Do you know anyone who used the mover and was pleased with the service? **Overall treatment...** How were your questions and concerns addressed when you spoke with representatives of the moving company on the phone and in person? **Overall appearances...** An industry spokesman recommended making an on-site inspection of the mover's offices and warehouse to confirm they're a legitimate, seemingly well-run operation. **Better Business Bureau Reports...** It never hurts to check with your local BBB to see if there are complaints on file.

Independent vs. national carriers

People often prefer to buy brand names because a recognized company stands behind the product. It's no different with movers. When a truck is pulling off with your family's valuable possessions, there's a certain comfort level in choosing an Allied or United Van Lines over

Joe's Fast Moving Company. Also, if there are problems with an agent affiliated with a nationally known company, at least there's a home office to intervene, if necessary.

More importantly, "common carrier" agents are under contract to meet certain performance requirements. They are not intentionally going to make mistakes or jeopardize their standing.

On the down side, common carriers may not have as much price flexibility because they split their profits more ways than independent movers.

As for the independents, many have excellent reputations and can provide very personalized service. They may also be more flexible on price. The trade-off is that resolving problems can be frustrating. In a one-boss operation, recourse may be limited.

Should you decide to hire a local independent mover, an on-site inspection is very important. In addition, ask for proof that the firm is authorized by the Interstate Commerce Commission to move goods out of state. If the mover isn't licensed, your liability coverage is null and void.

Keep in mind that neither the size of the moving company nor claims that it is "bonded," "certified," or "insured" are any guarantee of reliability. However, if you see that the mover has a CMC designation, for Certified Moving Consultant, you know that at least it passed arduous tests and complies with the highest standards set by the industry.

Are your cars moving with you?

At some point before the move, it dawns on people that their cars also have to get from point A to point B. In 75 percent of the cases, one car will be driven by a family member to the new home, filled to the brim with valuables too fragile for the van. But what of the second or even third car? There are several options. If the car is older, it may not pay to ship it. Newer cars can be shipped by the mover either on the van itself or via its truck transport division. With the average car weighing 2,500 to 3,000 pounds, you might pay upwards of $1,000 for a single vehicle. A good alternative is to have an ICC-licensed auto transport company drive your car. One such company, Auto

Driveaway, has 90 offices throughout the country and moves 50,000 cars a year.

Let's say you need to get your car from Long Island to Tampa on a particular date. The company will match your request with a mature, licensed driver who has requested to drive a car from the New York area to a nearby destination in Florida. Auto Driveaway will check references and do a computer search to examine the person's driving record in all 50 states. If the driver passes muster, he or she will be photographed and fingerprinted, and will post a cash deposit (returned if the car arrives undamaged and on schedule). Incidentally, drivers are required to cover 400 miles a day.

As the car owner, you must guarantee that the car is no more than 5 years old and mechanically able to make the trip.

Auto Driveaway's standard or "casual" service, is based on the mileage between the originating and destination states. For a car going between New York and Florida, for example, the cost is $260 plus the first tank of gas. If your car is needed immediately, a paid employee can drive to your destination. The cost for "Professional Expedited Service" is based on exact mileage. For example, a trip from New York City to Ft. Lauderdale (1,267 miles) would cost $800 (63 cents a mile) plus the first tank of gas. Another option is its Truckaway division, which moves groups of cars from terminal to terminal (cost based on distance). For example, a car shipped from Atlanta to Chicago would run $391 and take 7-10 days to arrive. For more info., call 800-346-2277.

If your car is leased, find out the procedures for returning the car when the lease expires if you no longer live in the area. National leasing companies have many disposal outlets. Local leasing firms may require use of a car transport service.

Tips for a smooth moving day

Here are some important suggestions for orchestrating an uneventful, but speedy moving day.

- Read the Bill of Lading (your contract) carefully before you sign it. Keep it on your pos-

session until your shipment is delivered, charges are paid and all claims are settled. It is your only proof that the mover is working for you.

- Make sure the Bill of Lading confirms the proper liability coverage you purchased when signing the order for service.

- Join the movers as they take inventory, the process of inspecting each item being shipped. Watch to see which items they designate as scratched, dented, etc. If you disagree, argue your case right there. Once the items are on the van is no time to discover the condition report is not accurate.

- If you got a nonbinding estimate and are concerned that it may be way off, you can observe the official weighing of the van by going to the scales with the mover immediately before and after the shipment has been loaded. This will confirm or deny your suspicions.

- Make sure you have worked out payment arrangements with the mover in advance. Unloading day is the wrong time to find out that your certified check is unacceptable. You can even look into charging your move (some carriers now except credit cards).

- If your estimate was nonbinding, there's always a chance the final cost will be higher. *By law, you are only obligated to pay the estimate plus 10 percent of the remaining balance at the time of delivery.* You can usually request 15 to 30 days to pay off the balance.

- Before unloading gets into full swing, take your copy of the inventory sheets and check the condition of the items as they're pulled off the van. If you see damage, or notice something is missing, alert the mover and ask him to mark it on both your copy and the mover's copy of the inventory. This is called "taking exceptions."

Filing claims against the mover

If you can believe it, most moves are disaster-free. And the vast majority of claims only involve losses or damages of $100 or less. Nonetheless, submitting claims can be a painful process. If breakage is involved, movers will generally argue that items were improperly packed (and in lots of cases they are right). The burden of proof is your responsibility.

Remember, too, that the actual reimbursement is dependent on the type of liability coverage you bought. Still, there's no need to panic if you have a legitimate claim. Follow this checklist for getting through the process:

10 Steps for handling claims

1. It's not necessary to unpack and inspect all the cartons before signing the inventory sheet, but you should indicate any obvious damage to the carton's exteriors.

2. Concealed damage discovered at a later time can be reported. Since you'll have to offer some proof of the mover's negligence, leave the damaged items in the carton until the claims adjuster inspects the damage, or the claim can be denied.

3. Claims for loss and damage can legally be filed within nine months of delivery, but don't delay. The longer you wait, the easier it will be for the mover to claim the damage occurred after the move.

4. Movers must acknowledge claims within 30 days and settle them within 120 days.

5. Claim forms must be submitted with the Bill of Lading; keep it in a safe place.

6. All claims must be submitted in writing, but first find out if there is a special hotline number for instructions on filing claims.

7. Don't be afraid to be overly detailed in your claim report. Settlements are often delayed because more information was needed.

8. List lost and damaged items separately, along with estimates for repairs or replacement. You may be asked to justify a replacement cost. If you no longer have a receipt, check mail order catalogs or store ads for similar values.

9. If you incurred any hotel or other living expenses caused by the mover's delays or losses, add those to the claim forms.

10. Finally, understand that the actual dollar amount you receive from the mover will be determined by the representative who does the claim inspection. In anticipation of getting the kind of adjuster who assumes your furniture was shabby to begin with, it's helpful to know that you can take your case to arbitration (at no cost to you) if you are unhappy with a settlement.

Hey kids—it's your move!

With the 1,001 details that have to be worked out with the movers, realtors, banks, employers, etc., it is very easy to overlook one of the most important things you'll be moving— your kids! Before you set any wheels in motion, try using some of these simple ideas to help get them psyched for the big event.

The younger ones (ages 2-8)

- Head to the library for some great books on the subject: *Moving* by Wendy Watson (Crowell), *Moving Day* by Toby Tobias (Knopf) and *I'm Moving* by Martha Whitmore Hickman (Abington). Good choices for older children (5-8) are *I Don't Live Here!* by Pam Conrad (E.P. Dutton), *I'm Not Moving* by Penelope Jones (Bradbury) and *Moving Molly* by Shirley High (Treehouse).

- Shop for a special item to put in the child's new room—a bedspread, stuffed animal, or wall hanging.

- Give your child a new name and address directory and help write down the special friends with whom they can correspond.

- Give your child a large box for clothes, books and toys he or she wants to donate and make a special trip to drop off the items.

- Show as many snapshots (or even better, videos) of the new place and ask your child to tell you what he or she likes best. If he or she is of an age to learn the new address, create a game to encourage memorization.

- Ask your child to talk about the move with a younger sibling, close friend, a pet or even an imaginary playmate. A response is not as important as an audience of "good listeners."

The older ones (9-17)

- There are a number of good books about moving geared to preteens, such as *Lost and*

Friend by Jean Little (Viking Kestrel), *Circle of Giving* by Ellen Howard (Atheneum), *Anastasia Again* by Lois Lewry (Yearling), *Aldo Applesauce* by Johanna Hurwitz (William Morrow), and *Mildred Murphy, How Does Your Garden Grow?* by Phyllis Green (Addison-Wesley). A good choice for boys is the Alfred Slote series about Arborville's Little League teams (somebody new is always moving into town).

- Ask your local phone company to order a yellow pages directory so that the kids can check out places and businesses that appeal to them ("Hey Mom, they've got a Pizza Hut!")
- Study a local street map together and check out the locations of the school, recreation centers, shopping malls, amusement parks and other places of interest to your child.
- At any price, borrow a school yearbook so your child can pore over it. It's a great way to check out the different clubs, teams, classmates, teachers, etc.
- With the cooperation of a realtor, colleague, minister or a helpful contact in your new city, ask to be put in touch with someone in your child's grade or age who would be willing to become a pen pal (or if it's not prohibitive, a phone pal).

Psychologists will tell you that no matter the age of the child, it is essential for parents to speak positively about the move and to focus on the many things you all have to look forward to (better jobs, year-round outdoor recreation, mountain climbing or swimming in the ocean, etc.). Children are only as confident as the people leading the way.

Wrapping it all up

You don't need an expert to tell you that relocating to another part of the country will be a stressful and highly emotional period for the family. It is a time of beginnings and endings. Of intense feelings and infinite details. It's not necessarily a time to think clearly (in fact you can count on it). That's why you should be kind to yourselves by organizing a smooth, uneventful and perfectly boring move. There will be enough excitement without it!

Additional reading

Be sure to send for two very important *free* booklets. The Interstate Commerce Commission, the government agency that oversees long distance movers, publishes an excellent consumer guide, *When You Move: Your Rights and Responsibilities*. Write to the ICC at 12th & Constitution Ave., Washington, DC 20423. Or call 202-927-5500. The American Movers Conference has a thought-provoking pamphlet, *Moving and Children*. Write to American Movers Conference, 1611 Duke St., Alexandria, VA 22314-3482.

Chapter 6

How to Use the Area Profiles

Area Profiles are presented in alphabetical order by state, *then* city (from Alabama to Washington). The handy cross-reference above will help you locate them in alphabetical order by *city*.

Each Area Profile examines 17 important categories of information and more than 40 different criteria within those categories. This easy-to-use format allows you to read the entire summary, or quickly refer to the topics of greatest interest, such as schools, jobs, living costs, etc.

Before you dig into the Profiles, you might find it helpful to flip to the handy "Fast Facts" section starting on page 311. This will allow you to compare population, housing prices, household incomes and other key data of all 50 locations at a glance. It also summarizes the best reasons to live there. This is a good way to start your search.

With respect to the Profiles themselves, you'll find that most of the information is self-explanatory. However, because we have also referred to data, terminology or resources that would be unfamiliar to you, we have provided brief explanations that should provide the best possible understanding of the facts. *Explanations are listed in order of their appearance in the Area Profiles.*

Area Snapshot

Median housing price: A median housing price indicates that half the houses in the selling area are priced below the median, half are selling above it. It's a very good indicator of affordability when, for example, 50 percent of the homes sell for under $100,000. In instances where a median price was not available, we referred to *average housing prices*. Averages generally run higher than medians, but can be a better reflection of actual real estate prices.

Median household income: This figure reveals that 50 percent of the households in the area earn below the median indicated; 50 percent earn above it. This number reflects a combined family income vs. individual earnings. If a median income figure was not available, we referred to *average household income*. Again, averages generally run higher than median statistics but can be a more accurate indication of typical earnings.

What Things Cost

Runzheimer Living Cost Index: This index reveals two types of information. First, using a family of four with a household income of $50,000 as a model, it shows what they must spend annually to own a 2,000 square foot home (which carries a mortgage and incurs regular maintenance expenses) and two cars (a late model driven 14,000 miles a year and a 4-year-old model driven 6,000 miles a year, both of which incur maintenance and operating costs). It also reflects federal, state and local income tax and sales tax. In addition, a certain amount is earmarked for investments and savings each year.

What's important here is not whether your actual income is higher or lower than $50,000. Rather, it is to get a sense of how far a family's money goes in this particular area in comparison to other cities. In other words, if a family earns $50,000 but has to spend $56,000 a year

in order to cover basic expenses, this is a reflection that living costs are that much higher than a city where a family earning $50,000 only needs to spend $46,000 to cover annual expenses. The family living in the higher-cost area has two options—to earn more money so they maintain the same standard of living as other cities, or to make tradeoffs (live in a smaller home, entertain less, etc.).

The index also reveals the percentage above or below Standard City, USA. For example, a city that ranks 4.6 percent below the average, is comparatively more affordable than a city that ranks 1.3 percent above. Standard City, USA reflects an average living cost index of all 150 markets in Runzheimer's data base.

Runzheimer International, a leading management consulting firm founded in 1933, serves over 2,000 businesses, government agencies and associations worldwide. In addition to their primary data research on travel, transportation and living costs, they also publish newsletters, surveys and special reports. Call 414-534-3121.

ACCRA's national comparisons: The American Chamber of Commerce Researchers Association report (4th quarter, 1991) compares living-cost differences of 298 urban areas.

The figures are based on expenses of households with two adults (one a salaried executive) and two children. The value of this information is the ability to compare costs between areas. If, for example, housing is ranked 20 percent below average in Austin, Texas, and 19 percent above in Coral Springs, Fla., it simply indicates that housing in Austin is considerably more affordable. In effect, these comparisons reveal how much more or less consumers have to spend to purchase the same products and services in one area as opposed to another.

The Runzheimer and ACCRA data may differ because ACCRA does not calculate the tax burden (income, property or sales tax) in its living cost estimates. Runzheimer does.

Utility costs: The costs indicated are most valuable as a means of comparing relative affordability between locations, as well as to get a sense of "average rates." However, these figures are not reliable for predicting actual monthly expenses because that will vary widely based on the square footage of the home, number of people, number and energy efficiency of appliances, usage habits, etc. The same is true of **Kid care.** Actual charges for day care will vary by number and ages of children, hours used, etc.

The Tax Ax

Sales tax: This is a total figure, reflecting percentages earmarked for payment to the state, county, city, fire and police or any other source that imposes a tax on salable items.

Property tax: Our source for the latest millage and tax rates and formulas for calculating annual taxes was the local or county property tax assessor's office. "Rule of thumb" calculations were provided by area realtors and are intended to provide an easy means of estimating annual taxes. It is best to contact the property tax assessor for the most current tax rates.

State income tax: Our source for the tax rates and formula for estimating annual income tax was the state department of revenue, personal income tax division. All are located in their respective state capitals and have public information offices if you wish to contact them regarding specific questions.

Climate

The Weather Channel, the 24-hour all-weather satellite network, was our exclusive source of climatological data. They want to remind you that everything in a community is subject to change except the weather. The four seasons will prevail from year to year, so consider that if a particular type of weather is unsuitable to you now, don't count on it "improving" next year. Other weather factors that affect people are elevation (for every 1,000 feet of increased altitude, temperatures decrease by an average 3.5) and relative humidity. When high humidity is combined with high temperatures, the "misery" index jumps. For example, if the temperature is 88 and the relative humidity 78 percent, it will feel like 106 degrees. For some people, high humidity causes fatigue, can raise blood pressure, and accelerate heart rate. Finally, the most serious weather consideration is the risk of natural disaster in any location. Coastal regions are prone to flooding, high winds and hurricanes. The West Coast knows all too well about earthquakes and the Richter Scale. The Plains are at risk of tornadoes. Essentially, there is no place on earth *not* at risk at some point for an act of "Mother Nature." In selecting an area to move to, it is helpful to be aware of the calculated risks of these events and to weigh them against the overall advantages of the area.

Earning a Living

Economic outlook: Our sources for this information were area economic development organizations, local economists and business leaders, university small business development centers and chambers of commerce. Our goal was to call attention to both positive and negative influences unique to the area, as well as to share the historical perspective.

Where the jobs are: Our intent was to identify companies that have made known their expansion plans or who have announced a relocation to the area. This in no way guarantees the quantity and quality of job openings, but does indicate a strong potential for growth. Often, when books or magazines call attention to local employment opportunities, they only refer to the area's largest employers. The assumption is that the bigger the company or government agency, the greater the likelihood of expansion and/or turnover. We disagree with that premise. Generally speaking, the largest employer in an area (based on number of employees) is the government (city, county, schools, hospital, etc.). As we all know, severe budget cuts have resulted in major layoffs. The same is true with the largest private sector employers. Just because a company has 10,000 workers is no guarantee of job growth. If anything, in these lean times, it could mean it is vulnerable to massive reductions. That is why we made reference to companies, regardless of size, that were projecting growth.

Business opportunities: With the help of local experts, we have tried to call attention to the types of businesses or industries that have the greatest potential to succeed as well as fail, based on economic conditions, competition, population growth and other factors. If you are interested in sources of help for starting a business, we suggest you contact the economic development and small business development centers in the area (see *FYI* for addresses and phone numbers).

Making the Grade

Public education overview: We contacted school districts, school boards and PTAs to learn about the unique attributes of the local school system as well as to describe the major challenges. However, the only way a community could be featured in this book was if the district had an excellent reputation for academics, extracurricular programs as well as special education and gifted programs. We have also called attention to schools that recently earned national recognition, such as the Blue Ribbon School Award or *Redbook* magazine's first annual High School Report Card (April 1992). For *Redbook*, a panel of 10 judges (distinguished educators) selected the best high school in each state and the District of Columbia, as well as 89 others that have achieved excellence in one or more areas. Please note that while our intent was not to ignore private or parochial schools, we would not feature a community where the schools were so marginal, parents felt compelled to enroll their children outside the public school system.

Class size: Each district establishes a class size policy, which limits the number of students per classroom, as well as a prescribed ratio of teachers and staff to number of students. We have identified those ratios, but caution that the basis on which ratios are defined differs widely across the country. Because of the varied interpretations, we suggest that you use this piece of information as a means of comparison and as a possible indication of overcrowding.

Blue Ribbon School Awards: In 1982, the U.S. Department of Education began a program to recognize public and private schools that were meeting local, state and national goals in educating *all* students. The final selection is made by a panel of 100 educators, government leaders, press, business leaders, parents and other experts. Winners are judged according to school leadership, teaching and student environments, curriculum and instruction, student, parent and community support, student performance on standardized tests, attendance, postgraduate rates and other important criteria. An on-site inspection is required as well. Each year, either primary (elementary) or secondary (junior and senior high) schools are eligible for nomination. The following year they alternate. Secondary schools were last eligible in 1990-91; elementary schools in 1989-90. Of the nation's 110,000 schools, a total of 2,123 schools have earned Blue Ribbon awards. Only 62 schools have been recognized more than once.

Please note that Blue Ribbon Awards are one indication of excellence, but certainly not the only measure. There are several school districts cited in the book that are not recipients, but that are award-winning in many other respects.

Crime & Safety

Unfortunately in today's world, almost every local police department has had to introduce the DARE program (Drug Abuse Resistance Education). Officers speak regularly to school children about safety, self-esteem and the dangers of drug and alcohol abuse.

The Environment

We have extensively researched each area for its environmental attributes and drawbacks, but just as we were going to press, two new EPA reports came out identifying cities featured in the book. The first had to do with high levels of lead found in water systems, the other regarding cities where the new smog standards are not being met. We wanted to know more.

Cities with lead levels over EPA standards. The Environmental Protection Agency tested water in 660 water systems most likely to have high lead levels—130 were found to have levels above EPA standards (more than 15 parts per billion). Charleston and Columbia, S.C., Ft. Myers, Fla., North Fulton County, Ga. (Roswell), Chesapeake and Richmond, Va., were on the list.

The reason these cities were likely candidates was because of the disproportionately high number of older homes, most of which were built when lead plumbing, pipes and solder was considered the best available material. For the record, lead was *not* found in the water systems, but in individual homes and buildings (that's why most states outlawed lead plumbing several years ago). So the only risks are in older homes and in those cases, letting the water run for 30 seconds before use in the morning will eliminate the lead particles that accumulated overnight. Ironically, the biggest lead risk is from paint, not water.

Urban areas not meeting EPA smog standards. Another EPA report found that 56 urban areas do not yet comply with the new smog standards. Houston/Galveston, the Los Angeles Basin, San Diego County and stretches of New York/New Jersey appeared on this list. While air quality in these areas are long-standing problems and much needs to be done, it should be noted that substantial improvements have been made over a 10-year period and will continue to improve. Naturally these areas were most prone because of continual hot weather (smog is produced when hydrocarbons meet nitrus oxides/burning fuel in sunlight), the high concentration of cars and factories/refineries.

Something to keep in mind is that the urban areas listed comprise hundreds of square miles, and many communities within those areas are not as affected. Overall, while it is very important to consider air and water quality when looking at new cities, it is also important to put the statistics into perspective.

Some final notes

We have attempted to address the areas that are of greatest concern to a family considering a relocation. However, some may question what appears to be an oversight—the absence of information on race and religious diversity. In no way do we diminish their importance to family life. Certainly one of the most understandable concerns is the question of "Will we fit in?" To the best of our knowledge, the vast majority of cities and towns featured are not only racially and ethnically mixed, they are communities that take great pride in the sense of harmony that exists.

Interestingly, in a recent Lou Harris survey of children, 67 percent said they would welcome somebody of another race as a next-door neighbor, 77 percent want to go to school with someone from another country (61 percent already do). Unfortunately, the survey revealed that 68 percent felt that parents were the major source of prejudice.

With respect to religious diversity, we originally planned to identify the denominations that appeared to have the greatest number of churches or synagogues in the area. But, to our surprise, our research revealed that with the exception of Jews and Roman Catholics, many young families did not have a particular "brand loyalty" to a faith. If they were members of a church, it had more to do with convenience to their home, quality of programs, size of the church and other factors. Their choice had little to do with the faith or church their parents attended when they were growing up. For this reason, we felt it would be most helpful to list a local Interfaith Council or Clergy Alliance in the *FYI* section (if available). For those so inclined, you can contact these organizations for a list of area churches and synagogues (often the chamber of commerce will have a list as well).

Our hope is that the Area Profiles are helpful to you in two respects. The first goal is to provide you with enough in-depth information on both the attributes and drawbacks of an area so that you can decide if the area appeals to you enough to want to learn more. The second goal is to show you the many things to consider when evaluating an area so that you would be able to build your own profile when considering other areas. In either case, you will now have the necessary tools to further your exploration of fabulous places to raise your family.

Alabama	1. Vestavia Hills
Arizona	2. Fountain Hills
	3. Tucson
Arkansas	4. Arkadelphia
	5. Fayetteville
California	6. Sacramento
	7. Valencia
	8. Vista
Colorado	9. Aurora
Florida	10. Coral Springs
	11. Fort Myers
	12. Tampa
Georgia	13. Roswell
Idaho	14. Boise
Illinois	15. Buffalo Grove
	16. Wheaton
Indiana	17. Indianapolis
Kansas	18. Overland Park
Kentucky	19. Lexington
Maryland	20. Gaithersburg
Minnesota	21. Eden Prairie
Missouri	22. Columbia
Nevada	23. Henderson
	24. Reno
New Jersey	25. Morristown
New Mexico	26. Albuquerque
New York	27. Huntington, L.I.
N. Carolina	28. Greensboro
	29. Raleigh
	30. Wilmington
Ohio	31. Blue Ash
Oregon	32. Bend
	33. Eugene
	34. Milwaukie
Pennsylvania	35. Bucks County
	36. Mount Lebanon
S. Carolina	37. Charleston
	38. Columbia
	39. Greenville
Tennessee	40. Nashville
Texas	41. Austin
	42. Galveston Island
	43. Plano
Utah	44. Provo
Virginia	45. Chesapeake
	46. Reston
	47. Richmond
Vermont	48. Burlington
Washington	49. Kent
	50. Spokane

50 Fabulous Place

o Raise Your Family

EASTERN TIME ZONE

CENTRAL TIME ZONE

NORTH DAKOTA
MINNESOTA
SOUTH DAKOTA
WISCONSIN
MICHIGAN
IOWA
NEBRASKA
ILLINOIS
INDIANA
OHIO
KANSAS
MISSOURI
KENTUCKY
WEST VIRGINIA
OKLAHOMA
ARKANSAS
TENNESSEE
VIRGINIA
NORTH CAROLINA
ALABAMA
GEORGIA
SOUTH CAROLINA
MISSISSIPPI
TEXAS
LOUISIANA
FLORIDA
MAINE
VERMONT
NEW HAMPSHIRE
MASSACHUSETTS
NEW YORK
CONNECTICUT
RHODE ISLAND
PENNSYLVANIA
NEW JERSEY
DELAWARE
MARYLAND

Eden Prairie (21)
Buffalo Grove (15)
(16) **Wheaton**
Overland Park (18)
(22) **Columbia**
Indianapolis (17)
(31) **Blue Ash**
Lexington (19)
(5) **Fayetteville**
Nashville (40)
Arkadelphia (4)
(43) **Plano**
(41) **Austin**
Galveston Island (42)
Vestavia Hills (1)
(13) **Roswell**
Columbia (38)
(39) **Greenville**
Greensboro (28) (29) **Raleigh**
(30) **Wilmington**
(37) **Charleston**
Richmond (45) **Chesapeake**
(47)
Reston (46)
(20)
Gaithersburg
(36) **Mount Lebanon** **Bucks County** (35)
(25) **Morristown**
(27) **Huntington, L.I.**
Burlington (49)
Tampa (12)
Fort Myers (11) (10) **Coral Springs**

Vestavia Hills, Alabama (Birmingham)

Area Snapshot

Local population: 19,749
County: Jefferson   **Population:** 671,324
U.S. region: Southeast
Closest metro area: Birmingham (5 mi. north)
Median housing price: $105,000
Avg. household income: $54,370
Best reasons to live here: Lush, green streetscapes, outstanding public schools, access to a fast-growing job market, very low crime and pollution, great recreation and culture, easy accessibility to business and shopping, tremendous community spirit.

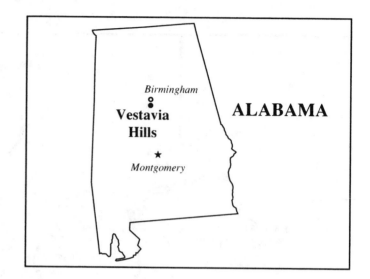

Fabulous Features

Want to hear about a best-keep secret? The Greater Birmingham area! Forget your images of the city under siege (C'mon, that was 30 years ago). Today's Birmingham and surrounding communities like Vestavia Hills offer lush rolling hills, hickory trees and neighborhoods ranging from pleasant to palatial. All are clean, green and offer stress-free access to the business districts (a 20-minute commute).

Home prices are stable ($150,000+ gives you a wide choice), because of steady streams of buyers and sellers (retirees move farther out, young execs move in). What keeps 'em coming is low crime (the stats are so low, you need fingers not computers to count), the community spirit (the Crimson Tide's Football at the University of Alabama/Birmingham spread the gospel) and most of all, the award-winning schools. Vestavia Hill High is considered one of the finest in the Southeast. *Redbook* magazine ranked it #1 in Alabama. The math team has been the national champion for four years, 90% of seniors head to college and 10% of the class was ranked as National Merit Scholars.

It's all here—the Southern charm but with progressive 1990s thinking. The region is open for business (10,000 jobs were created in 1990 and the UAB incubator program helps hundreds of startups each year), it's the high-tech and medical research capital of the state, culture flourishes (ballet, symphony and opera, galleries and museums assure you'll long for nothing) and the region's scenic beauty is the biggest surprise (the mountains and Gulf Coast beaches are great weekend getaways). Vestavia Hills and Birmingham may be one of the nicest hiding places in the Southeast. The word is out.

Possible drawbacks: Birmingham's biggest problem is still negative PR. Visitors expect to see men in white sheets and filthy smokestacks (it *used* to be the Pittsburgh of the South). Now, nothing could be further from the truth. • Great public education isn't cheap. Vestavia Hills has the highest school tax in Alabama (although it is still low compared to many other states). • Two- and three-car families are the norm. There's no public or school transportation, so the carpool is king.

"You can quote me on that"

"I think that Birmingham is the best-kept secret of the South. There's a graciousness to the people here that I think is becoming a lost art."—K.S.

Real Estate

Market overview: Thanks to a school system unparalleled in the state, a Vestavia Hills address has always meant something. Particularly to the scores of young professionals who flock here to trade up from Birmingham. Because of high turnover among corporate employees (they stay 3 years and get transferred), the market remains active but stable. The excitement is that land was just annexed for the creation of a totally planned development, Liberty Park. Commercial building is already underway and 2,000 residential homes are scheduled (garden homes at $150,000+ and spectacular custom homes up to $700,000). And, yes, children will attend Vestavia schools (otherwise realtors would be twiddling their thumbs).

What houses look like: Older homes are mostly brick ranches w/traditional layouts. Newer homes (12 years or younger) are larger 2-stories with open interiors; 2-story entries are common, as are European kitchens, master suites and decks.

Starter homes: Not really a "starter home community," but in older areas, you'll find 3BR/2BA brick ranches on rolling, tree-lined streets in the $90s-$120s.

Trade-ups: You can pay anywhere from $140,000-$300,000 for a 3-4-BR/2BA, 2-story home, with up to 1 acre, in the eastern section

Luxury homes: From $300,000-$700,000 buys a new house on 1 or more acres, 2-story, 4BR/2-3BA, all modern amenities, beautiful views (eastern section); If you're really seeking to spend, you can find homes up to $1 million in the estate section.

Rental market: Rentals are virtually nonexistent (agencies don't handle them because word of mouth gets a tenant immediately). Also, land values are so high, there are few apartments. Where available, a 2BR condo goes for $700/mo. A 3BR home might go for $900/mo.

Great neighborhoods: Mountain Vista's rolling lanes and less-expensive housing attract young families. Vesthaven (central) offers larger lots and more modern houses. Tanglewood (eastern) is a wonderful neighborhood, with many executive and professional families. Panorama and Countryridge on the east side of town are also desirable, with great views, large homes, and large lots.

Nearby areas to consider: Mountain Brook, adjacent to Vestavia, is an affluent, charming community with good schools and some spectacular estates. There's plenty in all price ranges, however. A fast-growing section to the south has ample new construction, lower prices with good-size lots and has its own school district.

What Things Cost

Runzheimer's Living Cost Index: Avg. annual costs for family of 4 with household income of $50,000: $47,378 (5.2% below avg. city).

ACCRA's national comparisons: Overall living costs are 1.2% below avg., with utilities the only category driving the numbers up (13.5% above avg.) Housing, health care and food are approximately 5% below avg. Goods and services run 1½% below avg.

Utilities: Phone: $24.56/mo. for a one party residential line. Call waiting: $3/mo. Touchtone: 90¢/mo. Hookup: $40. Electric and Gas: $65/mo. (Jan.), $75/mo. (April), $90/mo. (July), $75/mo. (Oct.).

Kid care: Day-care centers are primarily run by local churches. Costs avg. $170-$175/wk. **Pediatric visit:** $45.

The Tax Ax

Sales tax: 7%.

Property tax: Current millage rate is $92.60 per $1,000 of assessed value. To calculate, take 10% of the assessed value times the millage rate. For example, taxes on a $150,000 home could be about $1,400/yr.

State income tax: Alabama has a graduated personal income tax. Adjusted gross income over $5,000 pays a flat 5%. If you work in Birmingham, there is also a 1½% occupational tax.

Climate

Elevation 620'	Avg. High/Low	Avg. Rain (Inches)	Avg. Snow (Inches)	Avg. Days Rain	Avg. % Humidity
Jan.	54/34	4.8	.5	12	65
April	75/51	4.6	--	9	53
July	90/70	5.2	--	13	65
Oct.	76/51	2.6	--	6	65
YEAR	74/51	53	1.1	118	61
# of days 32° or below: 60			# of days 90° or above: 40		

Situated in one of the most hilly plains of north central Alabama, 300 mi. from the Gulf of Mexico, Vestavia Hills enjoys delightfully mild winters. Heavy snowfalls only occur every two years or so. Summers are another story. Heat and humidity can take their toll, causing a weekend exodus to the mountains and beaches. The good news is the area is generally safe from tropical hurricanes (heavy rains are the worst effects).

Earning a Living

Economic outlook: The area came out of recession in late 1991, continuing steady growth begun in the 1980s. Although service industries and medical technology companies lead the growth, the manufacturing sector has been strong, too. The Birmingham area added almost 10,000 jobs in 1990, more than 2,000 of them in manufacturing (at its highest level since 1981), although unemployment runs at about 6.1%. A number of local employers are upgrading their facilities, including the USX Corporation (spent almost $1 billion in the last decade creating state-of-the-art factories). Areas of growth will continue to be in advanced technology fields such as health care, telecommunications, engineering, aerospace design, computer services and electronics. The new 364,000 sq. ft. Medical Forum brings together medical supply companies from all over the country to display their products and services and educate medical conventioneers about the latest in medical technology. The new Oxmoor research park is a magnet for high-tech businesses.

Where the jobs are: UAB is the largest employer, with almost 14,000 employees. It receives more than $100 million a year in government grants, and has embarked on a $120 million expansion of its facilities. Besides the UAB Medical Center and 21 other area hospitals, there are several major health care firms: Baxter Healthcare (manufactures health care products and systems) is building new offices and warehouses, and Southern Research Institute (employs more than 600 research scientists and, along with UAB, is doing AIDS research). There are more than 10,000 engineers working at Rust International, BE&K (design and construction), Alabama Power, South Central Bell, and Southern Company Services (telecommunications) to name a few. Construction is moderately strong, with a number of commercial, civic and hotel projects underway, including the $140 million Birmingham-Jefferson Civic Center.

Business opportunities: There are several hundred business startups in the area each year. The UAB incubator—Center for the Advancement of Developing Industries—assists advanced technology firms. The Birmingham Business Assistance Network ("Bee-Ban") is an incubator for low-tech firms. Service, warehousing and distribution businesses are booming. Tourism is not a big industry here, but Birmingham is trying to acquire convention business for the Civic Center's Exhibition Hall.

Making the Grade

Public education overview: If the Vestavia Hills School District is the heartbeat of the community, then the community is in top physical condition. Consistently identified as one of the best systems in Alabama, much of its success is attributed to a well-educated community that puts its money where its mouth is. Due to the school tax, Vestavia residents pay the highest property tax in the state, but just look at the payout. *Redbook* magazine ranked the high school the best in the state. That translates to well over 92% of graduates attending college and a graduating class that received $4.2 million in scholarship money. The math team has been national champion for 4 consecutive years (the middle school math team also placed first in 1991, so it looks like the high school is a safe bet to continue its winning streak). And 10% of 1991 seniors were National Merit commendations, semi-finalists, or finalists (one graduate was named a White House Presidential Scholar). The district has added more teachers to the payroll this year in order to lower classroom ratios (it will now average 15:1). The schools recently installed state-of-art computer labs in the high school, and computers in the elementary and middle schools. Another area of accomplishment is the high school debate team, ranked top in state and national competitions for 6 straight years. There's no arguing—the Vestavia Schools have much to offer.

Class size: 15:1.

Help for working parents: There is an extended care program providing before- and after-school supervision as well as all-day summer programs.

Blue Ribbon School Awards: Vestavia Hills High School ('90-'91) was one of three in Alabama to earn the award.

School year: Runs from 3rd week in Aug. to end of May. Kindergarten students must be 5 by Sept. 2.

Special education/gifted programs: All children are kept together in the classroom as much as possible, operating under the Schoolwide Enrichment Model, a personalized approach to students (pupils will work on ability-appropriate materials within the same subjects). Learning-disabled or handicapped students have special aids in class.

Nearby colleges/universities: University of Alabama at Birmingham, (16,000+ students); Birmingham-Southern College (a small, liberal arts school); Samford University (Alabama's largest independent college); University of Montevallo; Miles College.

Medical Care

Hospitals/medical centers: The Birmingham area has 22 hospitals, led by the UAB Medical Center (ranked third-best in the nation in a 1986 study of physicians). UAB has a number of outstanding departments: Its comprehensive cancer care center and organ transplant program are both nationally recognized, and its cardiovascular care center is recognized internationally. HealthSouth Rehabilitation is headquartered in Birmingham at the HealthSouth Medical Center. Brookwood Medical Center, just outside Vestavia Hills, has a special Women's Medical Center for maternity care. Vestavia Hills operates a 24-hour Emergency Medical Service.

Specialized care: American Sports Medicine Institute, in Birmingham, sees patients from all over the world. The new $105 million Kirklin Clinic at UAB specializes in ambulatory care.

Crime & Safety

Vestavia Hills police tell us that crime is considerably lower even than in other neighboring suburbs, with burglary the biggest concern (business property theft is up 6%). There are few personal crimes, perhaps 1-2 robberies a year, and it's been 7 years since the last homicide. Police and community work as a prevention team with their "Nosy Neighbor" watch program and the Drug Awareness Task Force (teachers, parents, lawyers, police, judges, etc., brainstorm on drug education programs and other potential trouble spots).

Community Life

Vestavia Hills is a small community, and beautification is an important issue. In fact, it is known as "The City of Beautiful Homes." The Beautification Board oversees open houses and home tours. Two events that bring the Birmingham area together are University of Alabama football games. (College football is to Alabama what college basketball is to Indiana.), and the City Stages weekend in summer, featuring outdoor concerts, activities, and food in and around Linn Park.

"You can quote me on that"

"We moved from California over a year ago, but it didn't take long before this felt like home. You get a nice, small community and then 20 minutes away is a modern city with everything you could ever want or need."—W.G.

Let the Good Times Roll

Family fun: With such mild weather, outdoor recreation has no limits. Popular water sports are as close as the Cahaba and Warrior Rivers and several area lakes. Nearby Wald, Oak Mountain State and Avondale Parks offer a wide variety of camping, hiking and picnicking facilities. For a small fee, most families enjoy Wald Park, built and maintained by the city, which has extensive facilities: tennis courts, swimming pool, walking and running track, fields for baseball, soccer, and football, a Kiddie Park, and pavilion and picnic area. The Civic Center in Wald Park provides fitness and recreation classes, a fully equipped gymnasium, and an indoor track. The Temple of Sibyl, a Greek-style rotunda at the highest point in the city, is a wonderful place to enjoy the view (or get married, as many residents do). In and around Birmingham, there's the history of the iron industry traced at Sloss Furnaces National Historic Landmark. Other points of interest include the Southern Museum of Flight, the Birmingham Zoo (more than 600 animals), and the Ruffner Mountain Nature Center.

Sports: The local sports page is packed! Sports teams include the Chicago White Sox' AA affiliate, the Birmingham Barons (1991 Western Division Champions), the Birmingham Fire football team of the World League; and the Birmingham Bulls (ice hockey) of the East Coast Hockey League. There are many golf courses, and the PGA Tournament was held recently at Shoal Creek Country Club.

Arts & entertainment: Culture in and around Birmingham offers an impressive mix of the lighthearted to the serious. The city is an arts center, led by the Birmingham Museum of Art, which has up to 15 exhibits a year. Others are held around the city, at UAB Visual Arts Gallery, and more (including outdoor exhibits). The Birmingham Civic Center presents the Alabama Dance Theater, State of Alabama Ballet, and the Birmingham Creative Dance Company, The Alabama Symphony Orchestra, Birmingham Chamber Music Society, and Birmingham Opera Theater. Theaters include the Birmingham Festival Theater and the Alabama School of Fine Arts.

Annual events: Vestavia Hills' Chamber of Commerce "I Love America" Independence Day celebration (July); Vestavia Hills Dogwood Festival, a month of symphonies, pageants and tournaments (April). In Birmingham: Alabama State Fair (Oct.); Birmingham Festival of Arts (spring); Birmingham International Educational Film Festival (spring); City Stages (summer).

The Environment

Long-gone are the days of smokestack soot covering the Birmingham area, as industry has down-sized and become more high-tech and environmentally aware. In fact, Vestavia Hills and Greater Birmingham have been commended by environmentalists for air and water quality. In the 1980s, Alabama took great strides to clean up the environment in the Birmingham area, enacting laws and prosecuting companies that did not comply. Birmingham has an active Sierra Club chapter. Birmingham Water Works rates high in many national studies on water quality. Vestavia Hills is a recycling city, with curbside pickups weekly, and a special program for planting trees. There is an annual clean-up week when the entire community is assigned areas of the city to clean.

In and Around Town

Roads and interstates: I-65, I-459, U.S. 31, Route 149 (Lake Shore Drive).
Closest airports: Birmingham Airport, Shelby County Airport (approx.10 mi.).
Public transportation: None (Birmingham does have public transportation, which extends to the suburban areas).
Avg. commute: 20 min.

What Every Resident Knows

Things are really cooking in this town, with barbecue-anything the recipe to beat. Mustard-based sauces are left simmering in favor of the tomato-honey kind. Another secret-recipe contest is for Bloody Mary's. After you've tasted one in these parts, you won't bother ordering them back East. • It's not what you know, it's *who* you know. Especially here. If you need a plumber in the middle of the night, let's say, your best connection could be a guy who went to high school with your next door neighbor's brother. Just call and tell him who you know, and he'll be over in a flash. That's how it works. • In a list of the 32 best things about Birmingham, there's the great tap water, the 4th of July fireworks over Vulcan, and famous native Fannie Flagg (the Oscar-nominated screenwriter of "Fried Green Tomatoes").

FYI

Vestavia Hills Chamber of Commerce
P.O. Box 20793
Vestavia Hills, AL 35216
205-823-5011

Greater Birmingham Visitors Bureau
2200 9th Ave. N.
Birmingham, AL 35203
205-252-9825

Birmingham Post-Herald and News
P.O. Box 2553
Birmingham, AL 35282-9956
205-325-2222

Johnson-Rast & Hays Realty
1088 Montgomery Highway
Birmingham, AL 35216
205-979-6400
Lucy Baxley

First Real Estate
2534 Rocky Ridge Road
Birmingham, AL 35243
205-823-1133
Karen Anderson, Realtor

Alagasco Gas Company
20 South 20th Street
Birmingham, AL 35295
205-326-8200

Alabama Power Company
2020 Canyon Road
Vestavia Hills, AL 35216
205-252-2200

Birmingham Office of Economic Development
710 N. 20th Street
Birmingham, AL 35203
205-254-2799

South Central Bell
800-753-3320

Birmingham Chamber of Commerce Business Assistance
Hotline: 205-250-7665

School district: 205-823-0295
Property tax assessor: 205-325-5505
Welcome Wagon: 205-640-4190
National Conference of Christians and Jews: 205-322-4100
Physician's referral: 205-933-8601
Day-care referral: 205-252-1991

Fountain Hills, Arizona *(Greater Phoenix)*

Area Snapshot

Local population: 10,030; 13,000 (winter)
County: Maricopa **Population:** 2,122,101
U.S. region: Southwest U.S. (Central Arizona)
Closest metro areas: Scottsdale (10 mi. southwest), Phoenix (30 mi. southwest)
Median housing price: $115,000
Avg. household income: $45,180
Best reasons to live here: Spectacular mountain views, wonderfully diverse housing market, small, family-oriented community, abundant recreation, good schools, access to Maricopa County's booming job market, endless sunshine and clean, dry air.

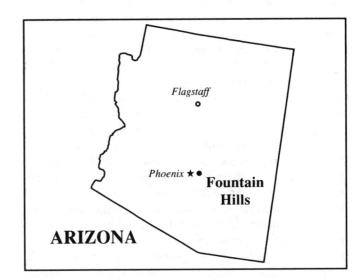

Fabulous Features

Have you ever wondered what it would be like to live on the other side of the mountain? Residents of Fountain Hills have discovered that the air is cleaner and the grass is greener. Separated by the spectacular McDowell Mountain range, the master-planned community is a short commute from three booming metropolises: Phoenix, Scottsdale and Mesa. But when you come home, it's to a mountain retreat nestled in the flora-covered Sonora Desert.

The town is small, but the scenery is on a grand scale, as with its legendary Fountain in the Park. Imported from Zurich, Switzerland, it's the world's tallest. The fountain has a jet stream that soars 560 feet (higher than the Washington Monument).

As for the environment, it is vast, with sprawling homes resting atop canyons (MCO Properties, the master developer, pales at the mention of gates or subdivisions). And yet the town is primed for change. In anticipation of the growth, it incorporated in 1989. Today it is a self-sufficient community with a surplus of close to $1 million in the general fund.

Attracted by an almost spiritual force, steady streams of people have been arriving from all over the country. Local leaders project the population could close to double by the end of the decade. Fortunately the land, the services and the low taxes are in place (no local sales *or* property taxes). Even more important is the unwavering community spirit. They're creating a dream hometown from the ground up.

Possible drawbacks: Signs should read, "Please bear with us. We've just begun." Everything is new and beautiful but *not* built-up. There are no movie theaters, Chinese restaurants or public transportation. So much for cheap dates! • Property taxes are some of the highest in Maricopa County, but still very reasonable • What's worse than a teenager? A *bored* teenager! All the major shopping and entertainment are in Scottsdale. The hope is that the presence of the new Junior/Senior High school will create activities. • Many summer days hit the 100s, so keep moving, drink water and be thankful there's no humidity and bugs.

"You can quote me on that"

"Fountain Hills is a wonderful place to live. It's got everything—a great climate, good schools, friendly community and any recreational activity a person could want."—K.H.

Real Estate

Market overview: As Fountain Hills is one of the fastest-growing communities in Maricopa County, home building is going on at a frantic pace—75% of the real estate inventory is SFHs, 15% patio homes (duplexes), and 10% are new condos. MCO Properties (the master developers) have seen to it that prices are in every range, from under $100,000 to over $1 million. Out-of-town buyers comment on breathtaking mountain views and how exquisite homes are for the money.

What houses look like: If your fantasy house is a bright expanse of arched windows and natural light with vaulted ceilings and vegas (log beams), a large gourmet kitchen, a fireplace and a huge master BR suite, Fountain Hills is calling. To think you can buy majestic mountain scenery and gorgeous contemporary homes in any price range is remarkable. Exteriors show tile, brick, stained glass and stucco in a versatile display of contemporary Southwest architecture, from Santa Fe (flat roof) to split levels to real adobes. Lot sizes vary based on terrain.

Starter homes: Smaller 3BR/2BA homes are available from the $70s, but inventory is limited. Homes ranging from the $90s-$130s (1300-1700 sq. ft.), are more popular. Many have pools, covered patios, fireplaces, split bedroom plans and 2-car garages.

Trade-ups: From the $150s-$200s buys a lavish 2000-3000 sq. ft. home (3-4BR and 2½BA) with large eat-in kitchens, lower-level dens, decks, diving pools and 3-car garages. Landscaping is uniquely Arizona: natural rock outcroppings, saguaro cacti and other dense desert vegetation.

Luxury homes: Prices start in the low $200s and don't stop until they hit seven figures. Size ranges from 2500-6000 sq. ft. Deluxe models show sunken living rooms, jacuzzi tubs, skylights, ceiling fans and Arizona rooms (screened porches).Buyers pay a premium for unobstructed views.

Rental market: Snowbirds frequently rent their furnished off-season condos to residents who want a place for company or to newcomers checking out the area. For long-term rents, SFHs start at $700/mo. Duplexes range from $500-$600/mo.

Great neighborhoods: Very few developments. Notable exceptions are Glenbrook and Cottonwoods, with lovely new houses from the $100s-$140s.

Nearby areas to consider: Scottsdale, Mesa and Tempe are very desirable areas with wide ranges of housing and prices, low taxes, jobs, wonderful recreation and culture. The biggest difference is size—Mesa's population is 280,000, Tempe's 141,000, and Scottsdales's 135,000.

What Things Cost

Runzheimer's Living Cost Index: Avg. annual costs for family of 4 with household income of $50,000: $46,784 (6.4% below avg. city).

ACCRA's national comparisons: The Phoenix/Scottsdale metro area has living costs about 4% above the national average, with residents paying 19% more for housing and 12% for health care. Grocery items are approximately 1% below avg., although the competition among the local supermarket chains is fierce. Goods and services are 4% below avg. Utilities are on par with the avg.

Utilities: Phone: $17/mo. Hookup: $47. Utilities: Avg. $90 (Jan.), $105-$110 (April), $125-$130 (July), $105-$110 (Oct.). Gas: Avg. $45 (Jan.); $15 (July). Water avg. high for the area ($40/mo.)

Kid care: Avg. day-care at a center is $165/wk. (12/hrs). At-home day-care runs $135/wk. **Pediatric visit:** Avg. $42.

The Tax Ax

Sales tax: 5.5% (prescriptions, food exempt).

Property tax: Arizona's property tax is ranked 7th lowest in the U.S. Fountain Hills taxes are 19% higher than other Maricopa County communities because there is so little commercial industry. Current rate is $14.03 per $100 of assessed value. A $100,000 home would run $1,400/yr.

State income tax: Married taxpayers filing jointly with income up to $20,000 are taxed at 3.8%; up to $50,000 taxed at 4.4% less $120; up to $100,000 taxed at 5.25% less $545. Cap is 7% for annual income above $300,000.

Climate

Elevation 1,112'	Avg. High/Low	Avg. Rain (Inches)	Avg. Snow (Inches)	Avg. Days Rain	Avg. % Humidity
Jan.	65/38	.7	--	4	30
April	84/52	.3	--	2	15
July	105/78	.8	--	4	20
Oct.	88/57	.5	--	3	22
YEAR	85/55	7.1	--	34	22
# of days 32° or below: 13			# of days 90° or above: 165		

Dry, desert climates bring 300 days of sunshine and low humidity. What takes getting used to are the high daytime temps followed by the 30° drops by evening, then seeing snow-covered mountains. At 400 ft. above Phoenix (valley floor), temperatures are moderate and smog is practically nonexistent.

Earning a Living

Economic outlook: The Greater Metropolitan Phoenix area is now ranked the 8th largest in the country in terms of population. In terms of economic health and prosperity, it could well be ranked higher because of the newly diversified business base. While tourism has traditionally been the cornerstone, today it shares the limelight with financial services, health care and especially high-tech manufacturing. Computers, computer chips, aerospace and information systems employ 150,000 people, and companies such as Motorola and Honeywell continue to expand. Just as important, new companies are coming to the area at a record clip, thanks to the high cost of doing business in Southern California. Charles Schwab (investments) is closing its computer data office in San Francisco and moving here. Same with the credit card divisions of Chase Manhattan (Tempe) and Bank of America (Mesa). The reason? Living and operating costs are low, and the availability of an educated labor force is tremendous. In fact, the combined growth of population and business could catapult the area from the 8th largest to the 5th largest by the end of the decade (projected pop. increase is 13% by 2000). In the meantime, the unemployment rate is half the national average (3.5%).

Where the jobs are: According to a recent Fountain Hills Chamber of Commerce survey, 70% of residents commute to Mesa, Tempe, Scottsdale and Phoenix. Within the region, the fastest-growing employers include Motorola, Inc., Allied-Signal Aerospace, Honeywell and McDonnell Douglas. Hewlett Packard has been laying off, but still remains a viable entity. Other major employers include the state and county government, American West Airlines Inc, U.S. Postal Service, American Express Travel Related Services, The Discover Card Services Inc., and Mayo Clinic.

Business opportunities: Entrepreneurs, listen up! Fountain Hills is crying out for certain types of businesses: men's and children's apparel, sporting goods stores, a Chinese restaurant, light manufacturing, and medical supply/research firms (the Southwest Medical Facility of Mayo Clinic borders Scottsdale and Fountain Hills). The zoning, the land and low taxes are waiting. Also the Mayor's Council for Business Growth is ready to offer expert assistance. Remember that the world's tallest fountain is a blockbuster attraction; tens of thousands visit each year. That's why tourist-related businesses are thriving as well.

Making the Grade

Public education overview: The public school system is considered progressive and well run. Many parents commented that being part of a small district has many advantages. Students get lots of individual instruction; and teachers can develop a real rapport with them. The opening of the new (and only) Junior/Senior High School will have a tremendous impact on everything from the K-12 curriculum to community spirit. Plus, kids are celebrating the end of the 14-mile bus ride to Scottsdale's Coronado High! Grades K-3 will go to McDowell Mountain Elementary while grades 4-6 attend Four Peaks Middle School. To date, reading and math test scores at all grade levels have consistently ranked well above average for the state. An estimated 75% of graduating seniors go on to college.

Class size: 18: 1 (62 faculty members serve an enrollment of 1,100, allowing for extensive individual attention).

Help for working parents: The district has instituted early drop-off and after-school latchkey programs in the elementary schools.

Blue Ribbon School Awards: Because the schools are all new (the first high school will open in fall 1993), there hasn't been a concerted effort to apply for any awards. But the potential for recognition is great. Nearly 75% of the honors earned at Scottsdale's Coronado High School came from students living in Fountain Hills.

School year: Starts immediately after Labor Day and generally ends the 2nd week in June. Children must be 5 on or before Sept. 1 to enter kindergarten (testing for early entry is possible).

Special education/gifted programs: Only students who have minor learning disabilities and can be mainstreamed have access to a special pull-out resource program for half the day. Children with more serious physical or emotional problems must look to larger school districts in Maricopa County. Gifted students also have access to a special pull-out program that offers enrichment courses and individualized instruction.

Nearby colleges/universities: Arizona State University at Tempe and Scottsdale Community College bring so much to the community in the way of culture, sports, performing arts and extensive continuing education programs, for very nominal fees.

Medical Care

Hospitals/medical centers: How's this for impressive? Fountain Hills residents are within one mile of one of the finest health care providers and facilities in the world! The Southwestern Medical Facility of Mayo Clinic borders Fountain Hills and Scottsdale and offers superior diagnostic, research and outpatient care. Here, 150 doctors cover 34 medical specialties. The facility opened five years ago, and is already expanding for the 3rd time. Additional outpatient care is available from the new Fountain Hills Family Health Center (a fully staffed satellite facility owned by Scottsdale Memorial Hospitals). It has a new cardiovascular center, a large obstetrics ward and a Level II nursery.
Specialized care: The Headache/Stress Center, Scottsdale Cardiovascular Center and Camelback Behavioral Services (Psychiatric).

Crime & Safety

Law enforcement services are contracted out with the Maricopa County Sheriff's Department, and calls from Fountain Hills are infrequent. There's an occasional burglary, but the big crime stories come out of Phoenix. What's unique to the community is the Town Marshall's Reservists, or as they're lovingly referred to, the "Posse." Comprised of local volunteers, many of whom provide their own horses, they do everything from rescue people lost in the desert to enforce town ordinances. They don't wear white hats—but they could.

Community Life

Newcomers notice immediately how active residents are in helping to run the town. What might be a municipal job in a large city is probably handled by volunteers here. That's why most people are involved in several organizations. For example, every year the Fountain Hills Great Fair and Festival of Arts and Crafts (a major event in the state) has no problem getting 200 local volunteers to man the booths. When it came time to funding a town library, volunteers organized a $25/brick fund. The Kiwanis, Rotary Club and Boy and Girl Scouts have also been instrumental in fund-raising efforts. Red Cross vans are staffed by volunteers who drive the elderly or sick to the Mayo clinic. Said one new resident, "I never joined a club in my life until I moved to Fountain Hills. Now I go to so many meetings, my kids tell people it's my job."

Let the Good Times Roll

Family fun: Forget the great job market and beautiful homes. The real reason people move here is that the vacation never ends! Within a day's drive are some of the world's most spectacular sights: the Petrified Forest, the Painted Desert and the granddaddy of 'em all—the Grand Canyon. Closer to home are more than 125 golf courses and more boats per capita than any other state—with more than 300 lakes to put them all. Adjacent to Fountain Hills is the McDowell Mountain Regional Park, perfect for horseback riding and hiking. Saguaro Lake is just miles away for boating and swimming (or come watch the multihued cliffs change colors in sunlight). The Fort McDowell Indian Community is the 25,000-acre home of the Yavapai-Mohave-Apache Indians. It's also the home of the Out of Africa Wildlife Park, an exhibit studying man cohabitating with animals. A favorite pastime is "tubing"—get your inner tube and head down the nearby Verde and Salt Rivers. Other great outings include WestWorld (an equestrian's delight with performances by world-famous contenders), hot-air ballooning, and cookouts at some of the "Old West" style restaurants. In your own front yard, you'll find Fountain Park, a central meeting place for picnics, concerts and community fun.
Sports: During spring training, local baseball fans are in heaven. The Phoenix metro area is packed with major league training camps: the San Francisco Giants, Chicago Cubs, Oakland Athletics, Milwaukee Brewers, and California Angels. Phoenix is home to the NBA's Phoenix Suns and the annual PGA Phoenix Open (actually in Scottsdale). World-class tennis tournaments are also played here.
Arts & entertainment: Newcomers marvel at the number of cultural events and programs in the area. A 40-minute ride brings you to the Phoenix Symphony, the Herberger Theater, the Museum of Fine Art and dozens of opportunities to enjoy live performing arts. Ditto in Scottsdale with the Kerr Cultural Center (jazz fests), the Gammage Center for the Performing Arts and the Lyceum Theater. With more than 100 galleries and a marvelous art school, the city is one of the preeminent art capitals in the Southwest. A tradition is the Thursday Evening Walk Arounds to view artists' works.
Annual events: Fountain Hills Great Fair (Feb.); Fountain Hills Festival of Arts & Crafts—largest in the state (Nov.); Thanksgiving Day Parade (state's only Thanksgiving Parade); Avenue Christmas Tree Lighting & Community Luminaries Display (Dec.); Sunkist Fiesta Football Bowl/Parade, Scottsdale (Dec.).

The Environment

Fountain Hills is clean from top to bottom. Air quality is excellent because of the town's higher elevations (at some peaks, Fountain Hills is 2500 ft. above the valley floor), and the McDowell Mountain Range separates the community from Phoenix's smog. Water quality is also rated very good. The town established two sources (ground wells and the Central Arizona pipeline), so it can take from the best, one at a time. As for clean streets, the Sanitation Dept. hosts the "Trash Bash" (volunteers scour the area for uncollected junk). In addition, the famous fountain is nationally recognized as an outstanding example of efficient use of recycled water (although they dye it green on St. Patrick's Day).

In and Around Town

Roads and interstates: I-17 and I-10 lead to Scottsdale, Tucson and Phoenix. Arizona 87 (Beeline Highway) takes you to Mesa and Chandler.
Closest airports: Mesa Falcon Field and Scottsdale Airport are approximately 13 mi. Phoenix Sky Harbor International is 30 mi. (40-min. ride).
Public transportation: None available.
Avg. commute: Scottsdale, Mesa and Tempe are within 20-25 min. Phoenix is 40 min.

What Every Resident Knows

With the opening of Fountain Hill High came football and basketball games. Yesss! Finally the local sports pages have something to report on other than how the men's softball team is doing (and nobody was more relieved than the men's softball team). • If you think the pets are amusing on "America's Funniest Home Videos," wait till you see Fountain Hills' Thanksgiving Day Parade. Kids dress up their pets in costumes and proudly march together. • Many couples about to exchange their vows sing "Get me to the fountain on time." Every year 30 to 40 weddings take place in front of the spectacular fountain, with ceremonies timed to the release of the jet stream. • If you feel like indulging in just one "touristy" thing after you move here, have a picture taken standing next to a 50-foot saguaro (pronounced suh-war-oh) cactus. Better ignore the suggestions to move in a bit closer, however. • There are many days when residents see spectacular rainbows from one end to the other. It's why they call Fountain Hills the town at the end of the rainbow!

FYI

Fountain Hills Chamber of Commerce
P.O. Box 17598
Fountain Hills, AZ 85269-7598
602-837-1654

Phoenix Convention/Visitor's Bureau
1 Arizona Center
400 E. Van Buren St., Suite 600
Phoenix, AZ 85004-2290
602-254-6500

Arizona Republic/Phoenix Gazette
P.O. Box 1950
Phoenix, AZ 85001
800-332-6733

Scottsdale Progress
7320 E. Earl Dr.
Scottsdale, AZ 85251
602-941-2300

Century 21 Anderson Group
13715 Fountain Hills Blvd #107
Fountain Hills, AZ 85268
602-837-1331, 800-678-3514
"Duke" and Joan Miller

U.S. West Communications
P.O. Box 29060
Phoenix, AZ 85038
602-490-2355

Salt River Project (Electric)
P.O. Box 52025
Phoenix, AZ 85012
602-236-8888

Fountain Hills LP Gas
P.O. Box 17208
Fountain Hills, AZ 85264

Mayor's Council For Business Growth
(Help for New Small Business Owners)
c/o Fountain Hills Chamber of Commerce

School district: 602-837-0690
Property tax assessor: 602-506-3386
Welcome Wagon: 602-837-7962
Interchurch ministries:
602-837-1633
Physician's referral: 602-941-4882

Tucson, Arizona

Area Snapshot

Local population: 419,100
County: Pima   **Population:** 700,500
U.S. region: Southern Arizona (Southwest U.S.)
Closest metro area: Phoenix (116 mi. northwest)
Median housing price: $80,000
Avg. household income: $41,747
Best reasons to live here: Breathtaking mountain scenery, dry, sunny climate, one of the fastest-growing job markets in the U.S., diversified housing market, abundant culture and recreation, excellent medical care, nationally recognized public schools.

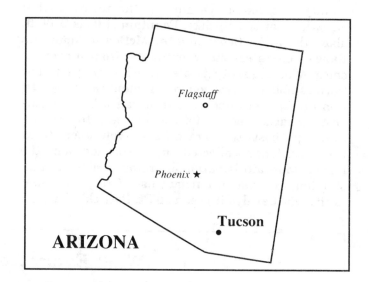

Fabulous Features

If you were to go to the drawing board to create the ideal urban environment of the '90s, you'd be wise to use Tucson as the model. It's a thriving, cosmopolitan city that hasn't run amok with glass-and-steel skylines. Surrounded by some of the world's most majestic mountains, and true to its rich Spanish, Mexican, and Anglo history, Tucson offers a unique blend of charm and contrasts. New shopping malls and crumbling adobes. Two-piece suits and bike hikes at lunch. It's a college town but not a one-horse town. While the University of Arizona is a great source of intellect and culture, Tucson has its own identity. In fact, it's considered a "you name it, we've got it" place.

After a five-year dry spell, the job market is as hot as the desert (quick—think of another big city that created over 10,000 new jobs in 1991!), and the homes are distinctly beautiful and affordable (prices range from the $50s to the $500s). The public schools are progressive and well run, the art and cultural scene is flourishing, and the pace is uncompromisingly relaxed. Perhaps it's the desert sun, or just a holdout from the days of *mañana*, but Tucson residents relish their quality of life. When work is done, they head for the hills...and the pools and the restaurants and the galleries...

Possible drawbacks: If you're moving from Nevada, the sweltering summer temps won't faze you. Everyone else—prepare to adjust! Even with the low humidity, July and August are great months to say *adiós*. • If you have fantasies about small-town living, keep looking. Tucson is spread over 500 square miles and is just starting to experience suburban sprawl. • Tucson's formation dates back 15,000 years, which critics say may have been the last time the city invested in building new roads. The highway system desperately needs updating, but older residents continue to nix bond issues to pay for improvements. Fortunately public transportation is excellent. • Arizona has the highest skin cancer rate in the country. Although 90 percent of cases are curable, newcomers must learn to protect themselves from the sun.

"You can quote me on that"

"What we've learned to love about Tucson is the large-city opportunities with a small-city friendliness. With so many wonderful neighborhoods, it's easy to get involved."—J.H.

Real Estate

Market overview: After a 5-year shutdown, a population boom (1,500 new residents a month) has given real estate sales a much-needed lift. Buyers are delighted by the tremendous diversity of housing styles, prices and neighborhoods and the fact that home appreciation has been flat. You can buy a house in Tucson for what a down payment goes for in Los Angeles (avg. monthly mortgage payment with principle and interest runs $670).

What houses look like: Home design and architecture in Tucson are some of the most original *and* reasonable in the entire Southwest. Plus, dramatic mountain vistas are free with every purchase! Landscaping is desert-style with drought-resistant plants. Inside, the newer homes show cathedral ceilings, master suites, pools and spas, split plans and Santa Fe-style rooms (high ceilings, ceramic floors). With land values soaring, 2-story homes are cropping up, but don't come looking for split levels and colonials. Homes built before 1980 are concrete and brick. Post-1980 homes are frame stucco.

Starter homes: The avg. starter home ranges from $55,000 to $60,000, which buys an older 2BR bungalow (1000-1100 sq. ft.).

Trade-ups: Expect to pay in the $135,00-$155,000 range for a 3BR/1½BA home (avg. 1600-1800 sq. ft.)

Luxury homes: Custom-built homes start at $275,000 for a 3-4BR home with 3BA, mountain views, loads of amenities, a pool and an avg. acre of land. Most are ranch-style.

Rental market: With only a 2%-4% vacancy rate year-round, apartment rentals are tight as a drum. When available, the avg. 2BR unfurnished apartments run $500/mo.; 3BR units are $600-$650/mo.

Great neighborhoods: With Tucson's growth headed in every direction, most neighborhoods are special blends of old and new—contemporary showplaces next to historic adobes. The northwest part of town is one of the fastest-growing for young families, reflecting excellent schools (Flowing Wells District), access to the major malls and a range of affordable housing. Nestled in the Catalina foothills, the north side of Tucson is *muy* desirable. Southeast Tucson, with its mountain views and proximity to IBM and other major employers, is seeing impressive growth as well.

Nearby areas to consider: Marana (23 mi. northwest), Catalina (20 mi. north), and Sahuarita (12 mi. south) are 3 small and mostly rural areas that are starting to attract young families. Housing costs and taxes are low, land is not at a premium, and the schools are good. Commutes avg. only 20 min.

What Things Cost

Runzheimer's Living Cost Index: Avg. annual costs for family of 4 with household income of $50,000: $46,105 (7.8% below avg. city).

ACCRA's national comparisons: Utility costs run 10% below the national avg., with housing and food costs about 1%-2% below. Health care costs and miscellaneous services run 5%-7% above.

Utilities: Phone: $15.92/mo. Hookup: $46.50. Electric: Avg. 3BR home $95 (Jan.), $115 (April, Oct.), $135 (July). Gas: $45/mo.

Kid care: Day-care avg. $125-$135/wk. **Pediatric visit:** Avg. $42.

The Tax Ax

Sales tax: 7% (prescriptions, food exempt).

Property tax: Arizona is ranked 7th lowest in the U.S. (0.66%; national avg. is 1.15%). Calculations vary based on school districts. A home located in Tucson School District #1 (the largest) listed at $99,970 would pay annual property taxes of $980.

State income tax: Married taxpayers filing jointly with income up to $20,000 are taxed at 3.8%; up to $50,000 taxed at 4.4% less $120; up to $100,000 taxed at 5.25% less $545. Cap is 7% for annual income above $300,000.

Climate

Elevation 2,584'	Avg. High/Low	Avg. Rain (Inches)	Avg. Snow (Inches)	Avg. Days Rain	Avg. % Humidity
Jan.	64/38	.74	--	4	50
April	81/50	.34	--	2	30
July	98/74	2.4	--	10	40
Oct.	84/56	6.6	--	3	40
YEAR	82/54	11	1.4	--	--

# of days 32° or below: 21	# of days 90° or above: 139

The advantage of a dry, desert climate is the endless sunshine. At least 40 days a year reach into the 100s. Low humidity is the saving grace. Winters (Oct.-March) are cool and comfortable.

"You can quote me on that"

"I'm so sick of people asking me how I stand the heat! After all, everything is air-conditioned! Plus we spend a lot less on doctor bills because now the kids don't come home with colds every other week."—B.L.

Earning a Living

Economic outlook: Historically, job activity revolved around government and service-oriented positions, as that represented almost half of the area's total employment. But in the past 10 years, the number of high-tech manufacturing and electronics companies doing business in Pima County has more than doubled. In fact, Tucson is projected to be in the top 10 of the fastest-growing employment centers in the U.S. over the next 5 years, growing at a projected annual rate of 2.9%. Last year 10,800 new jobs were created, making it the #1 city for job growth in the country (for cities with 750,000 or fewer workers). Unemployment stands at just under 4%. Naturally, tourism continues to be a major player in the local economy, contributing over $1.6 billion in the past year. The outlook for the next 2 years is bullish, with a strong, educated labor force expected to fuel the growth.

Where the jobs are: The University of Arizona remains the largest single employer with over 10,000 workers. Davis-Monthan Air Force Base (now the headquarters for the 12th Base because of Tucson's growing aerospace industry) has more than 7,000 military and civilian employees. Other large employers include the State of Arizona, Pima County, the Tucson Unified School District and the City of Tucson. Some of the most promising opportunities are with the Carondelet Health Care Corp., Asarco Inc.'s Ray Complex, Lockheed Aeromod, 3M Corporation, Environmental Air Products, Inc., and Burr-Brown. Major companies that have expanded or moved to the area include Sargent Controls, American Airlines Reservation Center, Sears Telecatalog Center, H.E. Microwave, the U.S. Census Bureau, United Airlines Mileage Plus and American Express Teleservices. Layoffs are still a problem for IBM, Learjet and Hughes Aircraft.

Business opportunities: Under the guise of striking while the iron's hot, Tucson is wooing New York and California companies drowning in taxes (the Muscular Dystrophy Association was one to jump ship). In the meantime, small business is a fast-growing sector of the economy, employing 60% of the work force. Of the 20,000 companies doing business in Pima County, 98% are considered small, with half of these employing 4 or fewer people. The University of Arizona's Annual Economic Outlook projects a strong rebound for tourism, falling interest rates, and many new companies relocating here—all pointing to a strong future. Contact the Chamber of Commerce for free counseling on finance, patents, marketing and other areas.

Making the Grade

Public education overview: Greater Tucson is served by 11 different school districts, with the Tucson Unified School District being the largest among them (total enrollment will be 57,000 students next year). Due in part to the highly educated labor force and the influence of the University of Arizona, Tucson public schools are excellent. The curriculum, particularly for junior and senior high schools, is very aggressive, resulting in 80% of the students going on to college. The emphasis on innovative magnet school programs and the focus on individual study and exploration account for much of the success.

Class size: 28:1.

Help for working parents: Extended-day or latchkey programs are conducted jointly with private day-care centers and the YMCA. Transportation arrangements are easily made.

Blue Ribbon School Awards: Flowing Wells High School ('86-'87, '90-'91); Walter Douglas Elementary ('89-'90); Richardson Elementary ('87-'88). Other area schools recognized by the U.S. Department of Education in the past: Amphitheater High School, Flowing Wells Junior High, Laguna Elementary, Santa Rita High School.

School year: Starts 2nd week of Aug. and ends 3rd week of May. Children must be 5 on or before Aug. 31 to enter kindergarten.

Special education/gifted programs: The Tucson Board of Education was recently cited by the National Board of Education for its exceptional special education programs. At-risk children have access to regular classrooms (for those with minor visual/hearing impairments), Pullout Resource programs (for learning disabilities), and Contained Programs for those unable to integrate (the Arizona School for the Deaf and Blind is highly respected in this area). The Gifted Enrichment Programs, found in each district's magnet schools (the number of these schools varies based on size of the district), have an excellent reputation for innovation and performance.

Nearby universities/colleges: University of Arizona at Tucson (35,000 students and home of the state's only medical school); University of Phoenix at Tucson (private university offering extensive degree programs as well as 6-month certificate programs, noncredit courses and numerous seminar programs); Pima Community College (2-year college with over 28,000 students and an excellent career skills center).

Medical Care

Hospitals/medical centers: Medical care is some of the most advanced in the Southwest. The University Medical Center, University of Arizona's teaching hospital, has achieved national recognition for its cancer, heart disease and respiratory illness research and its successful heart transplant program. The Tucson Medical Center (former Desert Sand Tuberculosis Sanitarium) is known for its arthritis and allergy clinics. St. Joseph's Hospital has the Arizona Lions Eye Bank, the Southern Arizona Bone Bank and cardiac care. Tucson General Hospital has an alcohol and chemical abuse program.

Specialized care: Charter Hospital provides private mental health services on an outpatient basis. Community outreach programs include the Carondelet Family Health Center, The Thomas Davis Birth Center and Sierra Tucson, a co-dependency residential and outpatient treatment facility.

Crime & Safety

Tucson is 65 miles from the Mexican border, which brings its share of drug traffic and related crime (burglaries and personal assaults are daily staple items in the paper). A growing homeless population is adding to the burden. However, we found the Tucson Police Department to be extremely proactive, with more programs than a TV network. Its Crime Prevention League has worked diligently to combat the 3 Gs of troubled youth: guns, gangs and graffiti. Efforts are paying off, because the crime index level is below that of the national average for a city this size. The bottom line is, residents are conscious of areas to avoid but continue to enjoy the city day or night.

Community Life

"Not words but deeds" is the attitude of Tucson residents. Over 8,000 volunteers work for 141 different local agencies throughout the year. The Volunteer Action Center, which recruits volunteers to work in all aspects of community services, and the Citizen Participation Office, which acts as a clearinghouse for neighborhood associations and chapters of national organizations, are living proof that Tucson is a city with a heart. Influential organizations include the Meals on Wheels, Casa de Los Ninos (volunteer agency caring for abused children), the Salvation Army and Prima Vera (provides services and facilities for the homeless), and Tucson Community Foundation (raises funds for a variety of worthy causes).

Let the Good Times Roll

Family fun: Here's a city with a winning combination: dry, sunny weather year-round and magnificent state parks. You'll love Gates Pass, with panoramic views, Madera Canyon's hiking trails and picnic grounds, Catalina Park (a desert park), Tohono Chul Park (fabulous nature trails and gardens), and Mt. Lemmon in the Santa Catalinas for year-round fishing, camping and picnicking. The Arizona-Sonora Desert Museum combines a zoo (rated as one of the 10 best in the U.S.), botanical gardens and Museum of Natural History. There are more than 100 parks, 28 golf courses and 300 tennis courts. Swimming pools, jogging tracks, bike paths, roller-skating and horseback riding are widely available. A favorite swimming hole is the clear pool at Seven Falls in Sabino Canyon. Reid Park, the city's largest, offers everything from a delightful zoo to a grand waterfall to the Therapeutics Clubhouse, a special facility for the handicapped. Keep in mind that Tucson is also the southernmost *ski* area in the continental U.S.

Sports: Watch great NCAA action with the University of Arizona Wildcats, the Houston Astros AAA farm team (Tucson Toros), the brand-new Denver Rockies spring training camp, greyhound racing, Northern Telecom Open (men's PGA Tournament), the Ping/Welch's LPGA Open and the Pima County Polo Club.

Arts & entertainment: New residents are thrilled to discover their new hometown is one of 14 cities in the U.S. that has a professional resident theater, opera, symphony and dance company. The city also boasts a designated Arts District, which is home to the Temple of Music and Art, the Tucson Convention Center, Leo Rich Theater and the Music Hall. The Arizona Theater Company, and the state's only opera company, Arizona Opera Company, are also based in Tucson, and continually earn national recognition. Don't miss the Tucson Ballet Company and the Southern Arizona Light Opera Company. In addition, the university also presents an exciting season of drama, music and opera. Favorite museums include the Tucson Museum of Art, The Center for Creative Photography, and now BioSphere 2, the experimental environment.

Annual events: Fiesta de los Vaceros Rodeo (Feb.); Annual Poetry Festival and Street Fair (Dec.); Mariachi Conference (April); Tucson Meet Yourself (Oct.); Copper Bowl—NCAA football on New Year's Eve.

The Environment

Water and air quality are quite good, and there are extensive efforts to preserve the environment. Tucson's Clean and Beautiful (task force) oversees a range of community programs such as "Trees for Tucson." In cooperation with the city and county, it has created 9 different curbside and drop-off recycling programs, one of the reasons the EPA and American Forests recognized the city as one of the "cool" communities in the U.S. To earn that citation, a city must excel in energy conservation. With the enormous growth, the issue of adequate water supply had to be addressed. The solution? Align with the Central Arizona Project, which recently starting bringing in Colorado River water.

In and Around Town

Roads and Interstates: I-10, I-19, I-8, U.S. 80/89, State Roads 86 and 93.
Closest airport: Tucson International Airport.
Public transportation: Sun Tran is the local intracity transit system. With routes spanning the city, it ranks among the top for a city this size.
Avg. commute: 15-25 min.

"You can quote me on that"

"We found that Tucson has so much to offer. Our kids are doing wonderfully in the schools, everyone is friendly, and even though it's a big city, there is a community feeling. The only thing that's a drawback are the long, hot summers."—J.S.

What Every Resident Knows

With Tucson being the Mexican food capital of the world, menus are like crash courses in Spanish 101. Newcomers who plan to eat well quickly learn their tamales from their tortillas. • Summer is monsoon season, bringing washes and *arroyos* (dangerous flash floods) that close roads, down power lines and otherwise wreak havoc. Then, a half-hour later, "here comes the sun." • To save money on energy, invest in a heat pump—a state-of-the-art system that pumps heat and humidity out in the summer and hot air in during winter. Call 624-PROS for more information.

FYI

Tucson Chamber of Commerce
P.O. Box 991
Tucson, AZ 85702
602-792-2250

Tucson Convention & Visitor's Bureau
130 Scott Avenue
Tucson, AZ 85701
602-624-1817

Arizona Daily Star
4850 So. Park Avenue
Tucson, AZ 85714
800-695-4492

Tucson Citizen
P.O. Box 26767
Tucson, AZ 85126
602-573-4400

First American Realty
8830 Speedway
Tucson, AZ 85710
602-296-5491
Sallie Smith, CRS

U.S. West Communications
P.O. Box 5427
Tucson, AZ 85703
602-670-2355

Tucson Electric Power
P.O. Box 711
Tucson, AZ 85702
602-623-7711

Tucson Unified School District
P.O. Box 40400
Tucson, AZ 85717
602-882-2400

SCORE (Service Corps of Retired Executives)
300 W. Congress Street
Tucson, AZ 85701
602-670-6616

Small Business Development Center
University of Arizona
602-884-6306

Property tax assessor: 602-740-8630
Welcome newcomers: 602-290-9191
Ecumenical council: 602-628-7525
Physician's referral: 602-544-2000

Arkadelphia, Arkansas

Area Snapshot

Local population: 10,018
County: Clark   **Population:** 23,400
U.S. region: West Central Arkansas (the Ouachita Mountain Region)
Closest metro areas: Hot Springs (29 mi. north), Little Rock (63 mi. north)
Median housing price: $70,000
Avg. household income: $27,000
Best reasons to live here: Small, friendly college town, great scenic beauty and natural resources, outstanding school system, growing industry, affordable housing and taxes, great recreation, very safe community.

Fabulous Features

Arkadelphia's Chamber of Commerce is accustomed to chatting with newcomers, sending out material, even showing people around. With apologies to no one, that's how things are done in this small, close-knit college town on the cusp of growth and opportunity.

In the past year, Carrier Corporation and Rohr Industries revealed plans to open state-of-the-art manufacturing plants. Dozens of small manufacturers are expanding, and former neighbor Reynolds Metal Co. has decided to return. Business leaders are projecting 1,000 new jobs and hundreds of corporate transfers by the end of 1993. Realtors are anxious to show off low-cost land for new construction and affordable homes ($70,000 buys a large 3BR house).

But the Arkadelphia school system has the ultimate show-and-tell! Its little, 2,300-student school district wins more awards (*Redbook* magazine says Arkadelphia High is #1 in the state), gets more involvement (100 percent turnout for parent/teacher conferences), and uses more old-fashioned ideas to reward performance (ice cream socials and banquets).

Situated at the foothills of the gorgeous Ouachita Mountains, Arkadelphia's glistening rivers, rolling hills and forests promise year-round recreation (fishing, golfing, hiking and camping at DeGray Lake State Park are some of the best in Arkansas). Two universities are magnets for cultural diversity and a highly educated population. For a small Southern town, the mind-set is progressive, laid-back and friendly.

Possible drawbacks: You can *have* a drink in Arkadelphia, you just can't buy it. Except for private clubs, Clark County is dry. This has put the kibosh on nightclubs and elegant restaurants. On the other hand, DWI arrests are minimal. • The good news is, local shopping sprees won't put a dent in your "plastic" collection. The bad news is, there's very little in the stores. Plan on frequent trips to Little Rock. • Summers are often hot, humid and buggy. The misery index is nothing like Florida, but most are happy when the sunny, mild autumn days reappear.

"You can quote me on that"

"I grew up in Arkadelphia and when I went away to college, everyone was excited that I was going off to greener pastures. But when it came time to raise my family, this is where I wanted to be. I think it is the best place in the country to raise children."—S.H.

Real Estate

Market overview: With an avg. of 60-100 houses on the market at one time and limited new constructions as well, buyers have to be decisive (and fast). With hundreds of corporate transfers expected, spec builders are sharpening their saws. Five new homes are already under construction north/northwest of town—not exactly the start of a development, but definitely a record! Resales are selling at their appraised values (homes are so reasonable to begin with, most out-of-towners don't haggle). Don't expect to find many townhouses or condos. SFHs are 95% of the inventory.

What houses look like: Neighborhoods are clean, green and without track housing or subdivisions. Homes are brick and vinyl siding and shake shingles. Colonials, capes and contemporaries are the most common styles, with comfortable front porches and screened back porches.

Starter homes: $25,000-$40,000 buys a small (900-1200 sq. ft.) but quaint 2-3BR/1½BA home on a nice-sized lot (60 x 100). Exteriors are part brick, part cedar or cypress shingles. Interiors are 1-2 stories with lots of walk-in closets.

Trade-ups: There is a wide range of prices for 3BR/2BA homes, depending on age and neighborhoods. Starting at $50,000-$80,000 you can get a new to "newish" (5-7 yrs.) SFH on a big lot (80 x 120). Most of the new construction is north/northwest of the city. For an avg. of $70,000, you'll get central air, wall-to-wall carpeting and major appliances.

Luxury homes: Custom-built homes avg. $150,000-$225,000 for a 4BR/2½BA (2500 sq. ft.) 2-story home on a golf course (Country Club section). Most homes are brick colonials or contemporaries on 1½- to 2-acre lots with 2-car garages or carports, large master suites and jacuzzi tubs, ample storage (built-ins), lovely front porches and backyard pools.

Rental market: College towns are notorious for tough rental markets, and Arkadelphia is no exception. Deluxe 3BR/2BA homes avg. only $425-$600/mo., but inventory is limited; 2BRs are more widely available, avg. $275-300/mo.

Great neighborhoods: There aren't any "bad" neighborhoods. Druid Hills and Leawood are convenient to schools and shopping. Country Club, North Park and Pine Hills Park are where the larger homes are being built.

Nearby areas to consider: Bismarck, halfway between Arkadelphia and Hot Springs, is starting to grow because of the convenient location (right off the interstate), incredibly beautiful landscape and inexpensive land values.

What Things Cost

Runzheimer's Living Cost Index: Avg. annual costs for family of 4 with household income of $50,000: $44,575 (11.9% below avg. city).

ACCRA's national comparisons: The closest available data is for Hot Springs. Figures show that overall living costs are approximately 2% below the national avg. The real bargains are housing (25% below avg.) and health care (19% below avg.). Utilities are 12.9% above avg., and groceries and transportation are 3% above avg.

Utilities: Phone: $18/mo. Installations: Avg. $40. Electric: $85/mo. (winter), $65 (spring), $90-$95 (summer). Gas: Avg. $35-$40/yr. (high is $85/mo. in winter, low is $15 in summer).

Kid care: Day-care center typically charge $135-$150/wk. Day-care providers charge avg. $115-$125/wk. **Pediatric visit:** $28-$35.

The Tax Ax

Sales tax: 6 1/2%.

Property tax: Home's assessed value (20% of market value) multiplied by 45.3 mills. A $50,0000 home would pay an estimated $900/yr.

State income tax: The per-capita tax burden in Arkansas is approximately 1/3 less than the national average. Net taxable income is taxed at a graduated rate of 1%-7% (the 7% cap is on income of $25,000 or more). With standard deductions, an income of $35,000 would pay $1,714/yr. Income of $40,000 would pay $2,064.

Climate

Elevation 210'	Avg. High/Low	Avg. Rain (Inches)	Avg. Snow (Inches)	Avg. Days Rain	Avg. % Humidity
Jan.	54/31	5	2.4	10	65
April	74/51	5.3	--	11	56
July	91/71	3.7	--	9	60
Oct.	77/51	3.3	--	7	61
YEAR	74/51	50	5.5	100	60
# of days 32° or below: 64			# of days 90° or above: 74		

Winters are mild, although those North American air masses can bring in sudden but short cold spells. Major snow or ice storms check in every few years. Summers are hot and humid. Precipitation is pretty evenly divided.

Earning a Living

Economic outlook: Arkadelphians know all too well about roller coaster rides. In the past 20 years, the economy reached great heights with Reynolds Metal Co., Levi Strauss and Hollywood Vassarette (among others), only to plunge when these companies pulled out. Then, in the past two years, several new industries announced their relocation here (not a moment too soon), and it looks as if the city will be riding high once again. Carrier Air Conditioning (United Technology subsidiary) is opening a plant (needing a minimum 450-500 employees), Rohr Industries (aeronautical engineering firm) is moving into the Industrial Park, and Reynolds Metal Co. is retooling its old plant to recycle aluminum byproducts (a nonpolluting process). The glue that's held the city together in lean times has been the colleges. Henderson State University and Ouachita Baptist University not only pump an average $52 million a year into the local economy, they are the magnet for culture, sports and recreation.

Where the jobs are: Equally good news on the job front is that many of the locally based firms that stuck out the tough times are thriving. Aalf's Manufacturing (makers of denim apparel) took over the old Levi Strauss factory and is now one of the city's biggest private employers (225 people). Alumacraft Boat Co., Valueline Corp. (manufacturer of hotel and office furniture), Petit Jean Poultry, General Brake, Morris Automotive and others continue to expand and diversify. In addition to manufacturing, Henderson State and Ouachita Baptist are gainful employers (350 faculty and staff). At present, Clark County's unemployment rate is 5.8% (it would be much lower if figures didn't include college students looking for summer jobs).

Business opportunities: With the introduction of several new industries in the area, this is a great time for small service businesses to provide support services. Furthermore, the city is "pro-business." Startup costs and taxes are very low, there are limited government regulations, and Arkadelphia is also very centrally located (I-30 is between Dallas and Memphis). In addition, the Arkansas Industry Training Program will provide pre-employment or on-the-job training at no cost to the business owner. Other businesses that are projected to do well include restaurants, book and specialty stores, tour companies and tourist and entertainment attractions. With the population projected to double by the year 2000, opportunities are ripe.

Making the Grade

Public education overview: With only five schools and a total enrollment of 2,300 students, this little district is a giant in the eyes of national educators! Last year alone, Arkadelphia High was recognized as a Blue Ribbon school (one of 225 in the U.S.) and as *Redbook* magazine's first-place High School in Arkansas. Students have earned state and national honors for achievements in Mock Trials (arguing court cases), Future Problem Solving (competing with students from around the world for best solutions to world problems) and Knowledge Makers (academic competition via computer). Even its band is top-rated (it's been in the Governor's Cup Conference for 20 years). Its Badgers Scholar program urges students to pledge to make a 3.5 GPA (close to half of the students make the honor roll). The Perritt Primary School (K-3) is also a Blue Ribbon winner (it is remarkable to have not one but two winners in a district this size). Aside from 100% parental involvement at parent/teacher conferences and a whole language learning approach, the school is widely praised for its special gardens, nature trails and outdoor learning center. The overall facilities are older, but impeccably maintained and state-of-the-art (the high school is 20 years old and looks 5). High school students take Japanese, Russian and honors geography via satellite, work in high-tech programs (computer drafting and design), and take courses at the two local universities for dual credit (high school and college). No wonder there's been a 20% jump in the number of students who go on to college in the past eight years (76%).

Class size: 20:1.

Help for working parents: There are no organized after-school programs for grades K-3. Nearby day-care centers coordinate early drop-off and late pick-up for older students.

Blue Ribbon School Awards: Arkadelphia High School ('90-'91), Louisa E. Perritt Primary School ('87-'88).

School year: Last week of Aug. through last week of May. Children must be 5 on or before Oct. 1 to enter kindergarten.

Special education/gifted programs: Special education students are mainstreamed where possible, with pull-out tutorials in the home school as needed. The gifted and talented programs have satellite classes (half-day devoted to enrichment programs). Advanced honors are available in high school.

Nearby colleges/universities: Ouachita Baptist University, Henderson State University.

Medical Care

Hospitals/medical centers: Immediate acute medical care is available at Baptist Medical Systems, a 57-bed facility that offers obstetrics, pediatric care, general surgery and 24-hour emergency care (including an air ambulance). St. Joseph Regional Health Center (new facility in Hot Springs) and several major hospitals in Little Rock also provide access to excellent care. These include the University Hospital of Arkansas, Doctors Hospital and Arkansas Children's Hospital.

Specialized care: The new Woodland Medical Center has 6 physicians, who provide obstetrics and gynecology, internal medicine, pediatrics and other types of care. Residents also take advantage of special facilities in Little Rock, such as the Ear and Nose Outpatient Surgery Center, the Baptist Rehabilitation Institute and the VA Medical Center.

Crime & Safety

Arkadelphia's crime rate is so low, it's practically not a rate at all. This is a town where personal property stays where you leave it, where kids play freely outside without a thought, and where locked doors may just be a habit. The police department, in cooperation with the schools, will be starting drug awareness education—not because there are problems, but to deter them from starting.

Community Life

Arkadelphians have a lot to be thankful for, so at Thanksgiving all the local congregations join together for a community service (held at a a different church each year). Young and old, white and black, whatever the religious persuasion—residents unite to celebrate the start of a joyous holiday season (said to be one of the most uplifting prayer services of the year). Other important community events are sponsored by the Joint Education Consortium, a private foundation that presents free lectures and entertainment to further the understanding of international relations. The Russian Ballet and Jimmy Carter are just some of the "ambassadors" who've met Arkadelphians.

"You can quote me on that"

"What's so great about Arkadelphia are the schools and the programs for kids. It was easy to settle in and get our roots growing. There is a sense of pride in the community that I've never quite noticed anywhere else."—A.P.

Let the Good Times Roll

Family fun: Arkadelphians don't just have fun in the sun. They have fun in the forest (a hike through the Ouachita National Forest is invigorating) and fun in the lakes, too (DeGray Lake State Park has camping, water sports, golf and hiking). This is the heart of the splendid Diamond Lakes and Ouachita Mountain regions and outdoor enthusiasts find the natural resources a pure delight. You'll find sailing, fishing and even mining for diamonds and gems at Crater of Diamonds State Park. The trout streams here are so great, no one has to lie about their catches. The city's parks and recreation department offers beautiful sports facilities and miles of hiking/biking trails throughout the city. In addition to the fabulous natural surroundings, you can head to Hot Springs for the Magic Spring Amusement Park, Mid America Museum—a "hands-on" center for kids; Duck Tours (amphibious vehicles that tour the city, then plunge into Lake Hamilton for a cruise), Hot Springs Mountain Tower (glass elevator ride), Castleberry Riding Stables, the National Park Aquarium and the famous I.Q. Zoo (for "academic" animals only).

Sports: The University of Arkansas Trojans (NCAA) and the Arkansas Travelers (AA Baseball) play in Little Rock. Thoroughbred racing is at Oaklawn Park (Hot Springs). Arkadelphia's new indoor/outdoor Tennis Center was just opened by Craig Ward, the 1991 U.S. Tennis Assoc./South Div. and Arkansas Tennis Association Pro of the Year.

Arts & entertainment: Henderson and Oauchita Universities proudly present a wide range of guest speakers, national touring companies, and their own theatrical, music, and dramatic productions. As the seat of one of the oldest counties in Arkansas, Arkadelphia is also proud of its historical antebellum homes and museums (the Barkman, Benjamin and Bozeman houses are listed in the National Register of Historic Places). A drive to Hot Springs or Little Rock opens up numerous possibilities such as the Arkansas Symphony Orchestra, The Ballet Arkansas, the Mid American Museum (largest in the state), and the Ponce de Leon Auditorium (Hot Springs Symphony). The Hot Springs Arts Center and the Gallery Walks are just the start of the flourishing arts community.

Annual events: Festival of Two Rivers (major arts and crafts festival in March); Healthfest and Mountain Valley Spring's 10K Race (Hot Springs, May); Caddo River Springfest (spring); Octoberfest (Hot Springs National Park, Oct.); That Dam Night Run (5K downhill run past DeGray Dam for 750 runners, walkers and wheelchair athletes, July).

The Environment

The Caddo and Ouachita Rivers converge in Arkadelphia, providing a clean and ample supply of drinking water (don't forget, water is Arkansas' greatest resource). Although agricultural runoff over the years has taken some of the sparkle out, this was the first city in the "Natural State" to meet new EPA standards for purity. Watch groups and action caucuses keep the waterways fit for recreational activities. Air quality is only average, with smog and haze a serious "summer factor" (the old Reynolds Metal Co. factory was a major polluter, but the new recycling plant has been updated and no longer poses a threat to the environment). Conversely, on clear days, you can see the grand Ouachita Mountains 100 miles away.

In and Around Town

Roads and interstates: Highway 7 (to Hot Springs), I-30 (to Little Rock).
Closest airports: Arkadelphia Municipal Airport recently expanded its runway to accommodate small jets (very *big* news). Little Rock Municipal Airport (65 mi.) is where to catch commercial flights.
Public transportation: Local bus service is available to seniors only. Amtrak offers service out of Arkadelphia.
Avg. commute: 5-10 min. (downtown), 35 min. to Hot Springs, 1 hr. and 15 min. to Little Rock.

What Every Resident Knows

Newcomers say they've never waved so much in their lives until they moved to Arkadelphia. Everyone waves, and naturally, it's only proper to wave back. Once people are familiar with your car, they'll wave at that, too (you don't even have to be in it). • Football fever runs high in the fall. The only place to be on a Friday night is at Arkadelphia High to watch the Badgers in action. The stands are filled no matter how the season's going. Win or lose, it's a fun night out for the family. • Arkadelphia is truly an equal opportunity employer. Group Living, Inc., a private nonprofit group, successfully trains people with developmental disabilities to be integrated into the work force. Using college students as partners (they help with shopping, life-style decisions), the program has been cited as a model for the country.

FYI

Arkadelphia Chamber of Commerce
P.O. Box 38
Arkadelphia, AR 71923
501-246-5542

Daily Siftings Herald
501-246-5525

Coldwell Banker/Tatman Realtors
107 No. 26th Street
Arkadelphia, AR 71923
501-246-4575
D. Scott Tatman, CRS

Century 21/Reader Realty
2747 Caddo Street
Arkadelphia, AR 71923
501-246-2406
Bud Reader, Broker

United National Hometown Realtors
625 Clinton Street
Arkadelphia, AR 71923
501-246-2984
Brown Hardman, Owner

Southwestern Bell
P.O. Box 5058
Hot Springs, AR 79102
501-324-4999

Arkansas-Louisiana Gas
P.O. Box 478
Arkadelphia, AR 71923
501-246-5544

Arkansas Power and Light
P.O. Box 308
Arkadelphia, AR 71923
501-246-6741

Small Business Development Center
Henderson State University
1100 Henderson Street
Arkadelphia, AR 79123
501-246-5511, ext. 3510

School district: 501-246-5564
Property tax assessor: 501-246-4431
Newcomer's Club: 501-246-3737
Ministerial Alliance: 501-246-5587
Physician's referral: 501-245-2622

Fayetteville, Arkansas

Area Snapshot

Local Population: 42,099
County: Washington   **Population:** 113,409
U.S. region: Northwest Arkansas/Southern U.S.
Closest metro area: Little Rock (192 mi. south)
Median housing price: $75,000
Avg. household income: $29,472
Best reasons to live here: Breathtaking Ozark Mountain country, delightful 4 seasons, very affordable housing and taxes, strong employment possibilities, fabulous outdoor recreation, good school system, laid-back college town.

Fabulous Features

First impressions of the Ozark Mountain region are indelible. Thanks to the unspoiled natural beauty and temperate year-round climate, residents have an invitation to spend their lives outdoors. Awaiting you are rolling hills, crystal-clear lakes, a majestic mountain backdrop and crisp, clean air.

Not that indoors is any less auspicious. The new $7 million Walton Arts Center, the legacy of late billionaire retailer Sam Walton, is northwest Arkansas' first permanent home for theater, dance and performing arts.

Now the hills are alive with the sounds of chamber orchestras, symphonies and opera. More music to your ears is the sound of people at work, to the tune of a 96% employment rate. Wal-Mart headquarters, the nation's leading retail chain, and Tyson Foods (largest poultry producer in the U.S.) are both here. Add to that low taxes (the per capita tax burden is a third the national avg.) and low living costs (a beautiful new home with all the trimmings goes for

$75,000). Employees *request* to be transferred here.

Thanks to a congestion-free commute and a laid-back attitude, Fayetteville is one of the most livable small cities in the country. Community spirit is the heartbeat of the city. (Everyone rallies behind the University of Arkansas Razorbacks.) It is why *Money* magazine, *USA Today* and other national media call it the Oasis in the Ozarks.

Possible drawbacks: Arkansas is ranked 49th in the U.S. for family household income. While living costs are somewhat commensurate, many newcomers experience "paycheck shock." • With land, interest rates and housing prices so low, everyone but students plunges into home ownership. So the rental market has very little to show. • Like to linger over the morning paper? Better keep a subscription to your hometown paper. Some say the papers here are "lightweights.".

"You can quote me on that"

"I could talk all day about living in Fayetteville. We're so happy here. For one thing, we can really stretch our dollars. When you have three kids, that matters a lot. Living here instead of California means we can have a better quality of life and we can afford it."—L.A.R.

"It was my heart's desire to own a waterfront home. Living on Long Island, I knew it was never going to happen. Now here I am overlooking Beaver Lake. It's a dream come true and I hope I never wake up!"—J.C.

Real Estate

Market overview: Here is a market where real estate agents are putting in overtime! With housing prices and property taxes going through the roof in other parts of the country, Fayetteville has been an oasis. Housing prices are 20% below the national average ($70,000 for new home), and property taxes are closer to 30% below. Home appreciation has been moderate, so many homeowners trade up every few years. It all put a strain on new construction (residential building permits were up 60% between '89-'90), creating a sellers' market.

What houses look like: "New Victorian" construction is very popular, showing wraparound porches, cathedral ceilings, sun-rooms and country kitchens. Ranches, contemporaries and Southern colonials (Georgian-style with pillars) also sell well. Exteriors are brick, native stone and masonite.

Starter homes: Handyman specials start at $45,000 (3BR/1BA), but the avg. is in the $60s-$75s range. This buys a lovely new 3BR/2BA (1400 sq. ft.) with eat-in kitchen, vaulted ceilings and 2-car garage. Brookhollow and Cedarwood are great communities.

Trade-ups: The larger new homes start at $90,000 for a spacious 3BR/2BA (2000 sq. ft.) 1- or 2-level with ceramic tile entry, fireplace, large eat-in kitchen. Lot sizes avg. 100 x 125. At the upper end, $150,000-$175,000 buys an executive 4BR/3BA (3000 sq. ft.) brick house with ceiling fans, jacuzzi tub, master suite and arched windows.

Luxury homes: Waterfront property starts at $200,000, but is only available in adjacent Springdale and Beaver Lake. Deluxe models avg. 1-5 acre lots with 9 ft. ceilings, double fireplaces, a playroom, large living rooms, and 2-3 car garage. Exteriors show pillars and Georgian-style fronts.

Rental market: With everything selling like hotcakes, SFHs are near impossible to rent. Apartments (2-3BR) go for $365-$450/mo.

Great neighborhoods: Regency Estates and North Oaks (prices in the $60s and $70s), Huntingdon, Paradise View (new development backing up to the Paradise Golf Course, with prices in the $80s to $150s), and Lovers Lane (fabulous amenities in a luxury development starting at $150 and up) are a few of the new subdivisions.

Nearby areas to consider: Springdale, Rogers and Bentonville are small, friendly communities within a short drive. Springdale's school district has won several Blue Ribbon School Awards, and home prices and property taxes are slightly lower than Fayetteville. Bentonville (Wal-Mart headquarters) is evolving into a major job center.

What Things Cost

Runzheimer's Living Cost Index: Avg. annual costs for family of 4 with household income of $50,000: $45,060 (9.9% below avg. city).

ACCRA's national comparisons: Overall living costs are about 11% *below* the national average. Health care costs are an astonishing 27% below avg., housing is about 20% below, utilities are 17% below, and goods and services run 7% below.

Utilities: Phone: $18/mo. (unlimited calling). Installation: $50-$88. Water: Avg. $40-$60/mo. Total energy costs for 3BR home run $85/mo. Newer 4BR homes with pools and central air avg. $125/mo. (winter), $200/mo. (summer). Gas: $20/mo. (summer), $150/mo. (winter).

Kid care: Day-care center costs avg. $80-$110/wk.

Pediatric visit: Avg. $35.

The Tax Ax

Sales tax: 4.5% (prescriptions, professional services exempt).

Property tax: Taxes are based on an approximate 20% of a home's assessed value. For example, an $80,000 house would owe $730/yr. A $160,000 home would owe $1,200/yr.

State income tax: Net taxable income is taxed at a graduated rate of 1%-7% (the 7% cap is on income of $25,000 or more). With standard deductions, an income of $35,000 would pay $1,714/yr. Income of $40,000 would pay $2,064.

Climate

Elevation 1,330'	Avg. High/Low	Avg. Rain (Inches)	Avg. Snow (Inches)	Avg. Days Rain	Avg. % Humidity
Jan.	48/26	2.3	5	8	62
April	70/46	4.6	.4	10	53
July	88/69	3.2	--	10	56
Oct.	74/48	3.7	--	8	56
YEAR	70/47	44.1	15.9	108	58

# of days 32° or below: 152	# of days 90° or above: 68

Daily temperature range is moderate (48°-70°). Summers are sultry with light air currents (daytime humidity is a comfortable 53%). Fall temperatures are cool and dry (wait 'til you see the magnificent foliage). Arctic air masses in winter bring 2 to 3 major snowfalls, but by spring, a flow of tropical moisture from the Gulf of Mexico brings warm weather and the year's heaviest rainfall.

Earning a Living

Economic outlook: Fayetteville is like a sleeping giant. Dormant for many years and best known as a conservative college town, it has suddenly emerged as one of the most productive business communities in the South. Eight locally based firms are Dow Jones success stories, including Wal-Mart, the single most successful retail chain in the country. Other prominent companies are Tyson Foods (sales topped the $1 billion mark in 1991), J.B. Hunt (cleanup transport firm with revenues of $10 million), Cannon Express and Hudson Foods. Job growth is an impressive 1.8% a year, and unemployment is at a low 3.7%. A benefit of being the home of retail and poultry giants is that their suppliers (IBM and Procter and Gamble, to name a few) have opened offices to serve them. Plus a new regional airport is planned, and Highway 471 will soon connect northwest Arkansas to Missouri. Both will bring jobs and opportunities to the area.

Where the jobs are: The city's largest employers are the University of Arkansas and Washington Regional Medical Center, with close to 11,000 people on the payroll. But they're not the only bosses in town. In a recent survey, 45% of local businesses said they are adding employees (K-D Tools, a multinational newcomer, expects to hire 400 workers within the next 3 years), and 42% indicated plans for expansion. Companies in the metro area that expanded facilities and/or added jobs include Campbell Soup, Cargill Processing, Tyson Foods and Rockline (Midwest Converting). The service industry, medical technology, trucking and construction are also gearing up for busy seasons, thanks to the continued residential and commercial growth.

Business opportunities: One measure of opportunity is the extent to which organizations are in place to promote and nurture fledgling enterprises. Fayetteville is doing everything short of paying for the first year of operation! Not only is there an active Small Business Development Center at the University of Arkansas (advising new small businesses on everything from financing to operations), there is a second innovative program for new science and technology firms that serves as a "business incubator." Genesis nurtures a business for 2-3 years until it is ready to go it alone (it offers low overhead, shared office space, secretarial services, access to science labs and technical support). As a result, participating companies have had an 85% survival rate. With that success rate, it was just recognized as the #1 incubator program in the U.S. for 1992-'93.

Making the Grade

Public education overview: Public education in Arkansas had nowhere to go but up, and Fayetteville's highly progressive school board has led the way. Their "list of firsts" includes being the first in Arkansas to organize a PTA, the first school system in the south to integrate, and the first to use modular scheduling. Now, even amidst budget cuts, it has only laid off noncertified staff and is still upgrading or installing computers in every classroom (Fayetteville Public Education Foundation is raising funds). Computer-assisted learning is a vital component of the curriculum starting in elementary grades, contributing to the fact that test scores in virtually every category exceed state and national levels. Fayetteville has the greatest representation at the annual Arkansas Governor's School for Gifted and Talented, where 400 students converge for an intensive 6-week program at the University of Arkansas, to study international and national issues and meet with prominent world leaders. Another successful innovation is the Apprenticeship Program for non-college-bound students (they can earn an associate degree from the Vocational Technical School by combining course work with related jobs).

Class size: 17-22: 1.

Help for working parents: Working parents can drop children off a half hour before school for an inexpensive, hot breakfast. After school, children in elementary grades are transported to one school campus for a special day-care program (free).

School year: Last week of Aug. through 2nd week of June. Children must be 5 on or before Oct. 1 to enter kindergarten.

Special education/gifted programs: Fayetteville's Gifted and Talented Program is not just for superstars but for any student showing a high aptitude (7th/8th graders excelling in math go to the university for college-level courses). High school students can take honors courses and boost their grade point average to 5.0 (a recent graduate got into Yale on a scholarship based on her 4.2 GPA but was only ranked 17th in her class). Both gifted and special education students are teamed with special coordinators who develop individual programs to meet their needs (special ed seniors are assigned job coaches to learn skills for the workplace).

Nearby colleges/universities: The University of Arkansas (14,000 students, Fayetteville campus); North Arkansas Community College (30 min.); and Northwest Vocational-Technical School (Springdale).

Medical Care

Hospitals/medical centers: In a recent survey of business leaders, 90% rated local medical services as excellent or good. This is a reflection of the highly respected Washington Regional Medical Center, a nonprofit acute-care facility with cardiac care, a trauma unit, physical therapy, hospice care, obstetrics and oncology. The new North Hills Medical Park has many privately owned specialized clinics and same-day surgery facilities.

Specialized care: Northwest Arkansas Rehabilitation Hospital specializes in the treatment of strokes, spinal cord injuries and neurological disorders. The Northwest Arkansas Radiation Therapy Institute provides excellent cancer care.

Crime & Safety

To borrow from a home plate umpire, Fayetteville is S-A-F-E! Violent crime is rare and has actually declined (in 1990 there were 21 arrests for robbery and 98 for aggravated assault; in 1991 the arrests were 14 and 73 respectively). Residents don't have to think twice about being out at night or letting their children play outdoors. There is, however, concern about the increasing number of burglaries and thefts. The Fayetteville police attribute some of this to carelessness ("New residents think they've moved to Mayberry RFD"), and the fast-growing population (the more people, the more there is to steal). Neighborhood Watch and Operation Identification programs are helping to prevent residents from being victims of opportunity.

Community Life

Why paint the town red when you can "Plant the Town Red"? That's what the local realty board asked, and answered with a great new program that donated beautiful red zinnias to each school and the local water company. Together they selected neighborhoods for planting, and now the streets are bursting with color. But not only are flowers growing, so are young minds. Thanks to the generosity of the new Walton Arts Center, there is a wonderful Arts Education Partnership Program for children in grades K-12. Special matinee performances and exhibits are presented. Each student will also receive an "Imagination Card" good for free admission to 3 shows, tuition discounts on special Imagination Workshops, and reduced ticket prices for public performances. Welcome to the neighborhood, indeed!

Let the Good Times Roll

Family fun: Who needs Disney World? The Ozark Mountain region is the ultimate magic kingdom! Start with the 500-mile shoreline of Beaver Lake, perfect for fishing, camping and boating. It's nature's playground with over 30,000 acres of sparkling water and mountains. Not to be outshone, the famed Buffalo River is one of 4 in the country identified as a national river, a coveted status due to its 95,000 acres of national parkland. White-water tubing and canoeing are just the start of the fun! Devil's Den, an exciting state park, offers spelunking, hiking and camping in the beautiful Boston Mountains. South of town is the Ozark National Forest, a hunting, hiking and picnicking playground. Trout and striped bass fishing in the White River tailwaters is an angler's dream (professional bass fishing got its start here). Lake Fayetteville and Lake Sequoyah are quick getaways for nature hikes, fishing and special events. Indoor and outdoor pools, tennis courts, and other facilities are well placed throughout the city and on the university campus. Out at Drake Airport, the Air Museum is a showcase for local aviation history.

Sports: The University of Arkansas Razorbacks, recently moved into the Southeast Conference, are leaders no matter where they play. They compete in football, basketball, baseball and track.

Arts & entertainment: Fayetteville's favorite son, the late Sam Walton, died two weeks before the opening of his dream legacy, the Walton Arts Center. Never again will residents have to travel for culture or do without. The 55,000-square-foot complex is a regional performing arts, visual arts and education center and will bring hundreds of exhibits, musical entertainment, theater, opera, dance and other performances to the area. Extensive classes and workshops will also be available. Concerts and performing arts are presented at the Chi Omega Greek Theater, an outdoor amphitheater on the University of Arkansas campus.

Annual events: War Eagle Arts & Crafts Fair (more than 100,000 people every Oct.); Hogeye Festival (April); Springfest (April); Music Festival of Arkansas (June); Washington County Fair (Aug.); Rodeo of the Ozarks—the country's top rodeo circuit (July); Old Fashioned Ice Cream Social—wear period costumes while enjoying homemade ice cream (Aug.); Prairie Grove Clothesline Fair—100,000 people come for arts, crafts and food at Battlefield Park (Sept.); Arkansas Apple Festival and Fayetteville Autumnfest (Oct.).

The Environment

Fayetteville's squeaky clean surroundings are the pride and priority of the area. Companies that want to relocate here must undergo a harrowing qualification process, and only those that don't pose a threat to air and water quality get the keys to the city. At present, water quality is excellent, thanks to a state-of-the-art treatment plant (the source water is nearby Beaver Lake). Air quality has never been an issue due to lack of smokestack industries. The biggest ecological concern is where to put the garbage when the area's landfill closes in a few years. The potential threat has stimulated enormous interest in the recycling and compost programs.

In and Around Town

Roads and interstates: U.S. Highway 71, U.S. Highway 471 and Scenic Highway 12. U.S. Highway 412 is under construction and will connect Arkansas' northwest corner to Oklahoma.

Closest airports: Drake Field (Fayetteville) and Bentonville Municipal Airport offer commuter service to major hubs (Dallas, Memphis, Kansas City and St. Louis). A proposal for a brand-new regional airport is in the works.

Public transportation: Jefferson Bus Lines provides service throughout the city.

Avg. commute: 10 min. to downtown.

What Every Resident Knows

You've heard of three blind mice? In Fayetteville the latest story is about two blind fish. When a few Ozark cave fish were discovered at the proposed sight of the new Northwest Arkansas Regional Airport, suddenly people were concerned about protecting the species. Now the hunt is on for a new location. • Where's the traffic? There isn't any, and boy, do you get spoiled fast. Heaven forbid you should have to stop for more than one light in a row! • Early birds get the worms, but in Fayetteville, they can also get your goat. The chirping and singing start at sunrise, and is it ever loud! • Speaking of animals, prepare yourself for hog country. The University of Arkansas mascot is a Razorback hog and the town is plastered with its picture. Lots of people even put hog statues in their front yard. If you can't beat 'em, join 'em. • Want the best dinner for the money? For $2.90, Ma Drake's gives you an entree, 6 different vegetables and a big piece of fresh, homemade pie (but only if you eat your vegetables)!

FYI

Fayetteville Chamber of Commerce
P. O. Box 4216
Fayetteville, AR 72702
501-521-1710

Convention & Visitor's Bureau
123 W. Mountain Street
Fayetteville, AR 72701
501-521-1710

Northwest Arkansas Times
212 N. East Ave.
Fayetteville, AR 72701
501-442-1777

Dykes Bassett Mix & Assoc., Realty
3263 North College
Fayetteville, AR 72703
501-521-5600
Mary Bassett, Broker

Southwestern Bell
114 N. East Street
Fayetteville, AR 72701
501-442-9800

Southwestern Electric Power
300 N. College Avenue
Fayetteville, AR 72701
501-521-3000

Arkansas Western Gas
Highway 471 N.
Fayetteville, AR 72703
501-521-5400

Small Business Development Center
University of Arkansas—College of Business Administration, Room 117
Fayetteville, AR 72701
501-575-5148

Genesis Business Incubator
University of Arkansas
Engineering Research Center
Fayetteville, AR 72701
501-575-7227

School district: 501-444-3000
Property tax assessor: 501-444-1506
Welcome Wagon: 501-444-9217
Interfaith Council: 501-443-3609
Physician's referral: 501-443-3377
Day-care referral: 501-521-8598

Sacramento, California

Area Snapshot

Local population: 385,127
County: Sacramento **Population:** 1,400,000
U.S. region: Western U.S./middle California
Closest metro area: San Francisco (95 mi. southwest), Reno, NV (133 mi. east)
Median housing price: $135,000
Avg. household income: $32,297
Best reasons to live here: One of California's fastest-growing and most affordable big cities, stable economy, good job growth, vast choice of housing and neighborhoods, rural, rolling hills and rivers, great recreation, pleasant Mediterranean climate, excellent transportation.

Fabulous Features

Families who've relocated to Sacramento since the '80s have a common bond with the explorers from 130 years ago. They've struck gold. OK, not the nuggets, but a gratifying, affordable lifestyle (just say the gold standard has changed).

When housing prices throughout the state were doing Olympic-style triple jumps, residents who were still "California Dreamin' " came here in record numbers (in 10 years the population increased by a whopping 34 percent). Yet the median housing price has stayed well below California's other big cities ($135,900 compared to state median of $195,000). Overall living costs don't add up here either (it costs at least 8 percent to 16 percent more to live in the other metro areas).

But bargain hunting isn't the only reason Sacramento's sizzling. In this valley of rolling foothills and winding rivers, residents enjoy small-town ambience with big-city excitement. As the state capital, home to two Air Force bases and a diversified private sector (electronics, health care, transportation and manufacturing), *Inc.* magazine rated Sacramento 5th in the U.S. for job growth between now and 1996 (Aug. 1992). Cigna and NEC are just a few corporations betting on continued growth (NEC's plant is one of the largest Japanese industrial investments in the U.S.).

As for that small-town friendliness, there are literally dozens of niche-sized communities in and around the city. From East Sacramento to Elk Grove, there is every type of architecture, price and amenity (people couldn't stop raving about their houses). With 16 school districts to choose from, you can match your child's needs to the right environment. After school, there's exciting recreation (whitewater rafting and wind-surfing) and endless events to enjoy. Sacramento is golden!

Possible drawbacks: Smog has crept into the area because of an increase in cars on the road. Still, there's no comparison to Los Angeles. • Some feel that Sacramento is like the bright, capable student who isn't living up to his full potential. *Fortune* summed it up by saying the city's pro-business attitude and labor training efforts need improving. Hopefully, it'll be by next marking period.

"You can quote me on that"

"Sacramento is ideal for a family. I have relatives in the Bay area who come here to visit and can't get over how much lower the cost of living is. I have my heart in Sacramento."—P.S.

Real Estate

Market overview: It's a buyer's market, with inventory at an all-time high. In spite of the weak economy, there has been an abundance of new construction (some of the highest levels across the state). But to sell it, builders are literally throwing in the kitchen sink (or refrigerators, washers/dryers, etc.). New homes are in the $130s, and resales in good neighborhoods start at $125,000. The diversity of neighborhoods and outlying communities are vast. Each has a unique personality, so shop carefully.

What houses look like: You'll find mostly California ranches (some Victorians), w/1 or 2 levels. Exteriors are stucco w/wood frame, though newer homes are molded siding. Almost every home has a 2-car garage. Fireplaces and pools are popular (basements nonexistent). Custom homes offer gourmet kitchens, cathedral ceilings, master BAs w/separate showers, jacuzzis or garden tubs.

Starter homes: $80,000-$120,000. At the high end, you get an older 3BR/1-2BA beds, 1100 sq. ft., 50 x 100 lot, no basement and a 1-car garage.

Trade-ups: $140,000-$200,000. For $175,000 you get an older 3-4BR/1-2BA, 1600 sq. ft., on a 70 x 100 w/2-car garage.

Luxury homes: $300,000-$500,000. The low end will buy a 4-5BR/2-3BA, larger living areas, formal living/dining room, on ¼-½ acre. For $500,000 you get 3000-5000 sq. ft., 4-5BR/3BA, on ¼-1 acre. Look at Land Park, Carmichael and Fair Oaks.

Rental market: There are plenty of apartments in Sacramento and monthly rents range from $350-$800/mo. Houses are also numerous and range between $800-$900/mo. for 3BR.

Great neighborhoods: Carmichael is a lovely area with old and new homes in the $150s. It's an older, established and affluent community that is family-oriented. Land Park is great for older homes (start at $300,000). It's very scenic and affluent. Greenhaven is ideal for families, with lots of newer homes in the $160s.

Nearby areas to consider: Roseville (20 min. northeast) is an older city with its own school system. It's convenient to shopping with lots of parks. Elk Grove (20 min. south) is a small city with good schools, lots of nice residential areas to choose from—with houses in the $170s.

"You can quote me on that"
"We love the sunny, bright California days and there's so much to do. Parents have plenty of places to play with their kids!"—K.D.

What Things Cost

Runzheimer's Living Cost Index: Avg. annual costs for family of 4 with household income of $50,000: $54,694 (9.4% above avg. city).

ACCRA's national comparisons: Not available. However, in recent studies, it appears that living costs in Sacramento are much less expensive than California's other major markets. For example, utilities cost 42% less than Los Angeles and 36% less than San Francisco. Overall costs are 7% to 15% less.

Utilities: Phone: Hookup: $35; Basic service: $12/mo. Gas: Avg. $40/mo. Electric: $80-$115/mo.

Kid care: It's difficult finding licensed day care for infants, although there seems to be adequate at-home providers. Day-care centers for ages 2+ are readily available. Avg. cost for infants is $405/mo.; $352/mo. for children 2+. **Pediatric visit:** $35-$40.

The Tax Ax

Sales tax: 7.75%.

Property tax: Established under Proposition 13 as 1% of the purchase price plus limited locally approved bonds. The total rarely exceeds 1.25%.

State income tax: The maximum rate for taxation is 9.3% for $100,000 and more. It ranges from 1% to 8% for less. In California, both earned and unearned income are taxed at these rates.

Climate

Elevation 17'	Avg. High/Low	Avg. Rain (Inches)	Avg. Snow (Inches)	Avg. Days Rain	Avg. % Humidity
Jan.	53/37	3.7	--	10	71
April	71/45	1.5	--	6	43
July	93/58	.01	--	T	28
Oct.	77/50	1	--	3	40
YEAR	73/47	17.2	--	58	46

# of days 32° or below: 17	# of days 90° or above: 77

Central California's year-round mild climate and abundant sunshine are part of what makes Sacramento a delight. The summers are remarkably dry, with comfortably warm days and pleasant nights. Winter is the rainy season, sometimes getting 30 inches between Dec. and Feb. Spring and fall are glorious—dry, sunny and mild.

Earning a Living

Economic outlook: During 1990, while economic worries caused widespread nail-biting elsewhere, Sacramento's economic vigor was reassuring. No large sectors of Sacramento's economy were in trouble. Its economy is booming, and *Forbes* magazine named it one of the top 5 American cities in which to do business (1990). The area's employment base and pay scales have grown steadily, and unemployment is at 5.5%. Industry is diverse, providing stability and an ever-growing number of employment opportunities. Growth in manufacturing and high-tech areas is promising (NEC's semi-conductor plant is one of the largest Japanese industrial investments in the U.S.). On the down side, the pro-business attitude has been criticized and labor force training is not a bright spot either (*Fortune*).

Where the jobs are: According to *Inc.* (Aug. '92), Sacramento is 5th in the U.S. for projected job growth until 1996 for cities of 500,000 or more. The government is the biggest employer. Sacramento is also the site of McClellan and Mather Air Force bases and the Sacramento Army Depot. All combine to provide about 29% of the area's jobs. In the private sector, Sacramento's economy is diverse. Service industries supply about 22% of the area's jobs, followed by retail trade at 20% and manufacturing at 7.5%. Other major employers that are expanding are Pacific Bell, Aerojet General, UC Davis Medical Center, Kaiser Permanente Medical Care Program, Sutter Health, Blue Diamond Growers, Sacramento Municipal Utility District, Raley's Inc. (supermarket and grocery chain), and Pacific Coast Building Products. The new Shriners' Children's Hospital will create primary and secondary jobs. Sacramento is also home to well-known high-tech giants: Hewlett-Packard; NEC Electronics, Inc. (largest plant outside Japan will add 500 jobs); and Cigna Corp. (one of the nation's largest insurance companies). Sacramento is a transportation hub, attracting R&D companies, manufacturing concerns, financial institutions and construction businesses.

Business opportunities: The Sacramento Metropolitan Chamber of Commerce Small Business department serves as a resource for businesses looking to expand, relocate or startup. The Sacramento Chamber of Commerce provides an excellent business start up kit that provides all the forms needed to comply with government requirements. Sacramento is very eager to encourage med-tech and high-tech businesses here. Its goal is to attract clean industry and high-paying jobs.

Making the Grade

Public education overview: Sacramento County, encompassing 16 school districts, struggles with problems of overcrowding and budget cutbacks. Many new schools have opened (the Elk Grove district has opened 11 new schools alone). And the districts come up with innovative solutions for providing quality education (providing year-round schooling, for example). Something seems to be working: 71% of graduating seniors go on to further education, and Sacramento County has one of the lowest dropout rates in the state. The Elk Grove school district is said to be the fastest-growing, serving Laguna, Elk Grove, Franklin, Florin, Valley Hi, Vineyard, Sheldon, Rancho Murieta, Wilton, Sloughouse and parts of the city of Sacramento. In 1987 Elk Grove initiated a $2 million plan to provide up-to-date technology at all grade levels. The three largest districts offer a Special Services Program for Native American students (grades K-12) who make up 1% of the student population. The San Juan district is another system with progresive programming. Its Mariloma High School offers an International Baccalaureate Program. It has also implemented a program called San Juan 2000 to achieve academic success and first rate student achievement, and encourages all community members to become involved. Sacramento City has magnet schools of choice at all levels; 11 elementary, 5 middle and 5 high schools.

Class size: 32:1 (most elementary classes have aides).

Help for working parents: Private before- and after-school programs are available at several elementary schools in the districts.

Blue Ribbon School Awards: Valley High School ('86-'87).

School year: Begins end of Aug. and ends mid-June. Children must be 5 on or before Dec. 2 to enter kindergarten.

Special education/gifted programs: Each school district provides for special education from birth to age 22. There are 3 types of placement, from mainstreaming programs to special classes. A special education school—Jessie Baker, is located in Elk Grove. Gifted programs in California are referred to as GATE—Gifted And Talented Education.

Nearby colleges/universities: California State University at Sacramento, University of California at Davis, Los Rios Community College District; American River; Cosumnes River; Sacramento City and National University. Extensions from other universities are the University of Southern California, Golden Gate University and the University of San Francisco.

Medical Care

Hospitals/medical centers: There are 18 acute care hospitals in the Greater Sacramento Area. The largest is the 438-bed U.C. Medical Center, in Davis, with comprehensive emergency services, helicopter, cardiac services, kidney/corneal transplants, oncolgy, otolaryngology, pediatrics, internal medicine and treatment of burns, poisons and psoriasis. Equipped for treating major injuries, the hospital has the only trauma center in Sacramento. Three area hospitals are run by Mercy Healthcare Sacramento, two by Sutter Health, and two by Kaiser Permanente.

Specialized care: Shriner's Children's Hospital (major research center including a 60-bed in-patient unit for medical-surgical services and a 20-bed pediatric intensive care unit focusing on orthopedic disorders, deformities, spinal cord injuries and severe burns (currently expanding); Sacramento Women's Health Care Medical Group, Inc., specializing in obstetrics and gynecology; Regional Center for Rehabilitation (American River Hospital).

Crime & Safety

Overall, the area is considered safe, although people are not naive to potential risks. During the first 6 months of 1992, crime was down from the same period in 1991. The biggest problems that face Sacramento are those that affect any city in the nation: drugs and gangs. There are many programs in place and the police department is working in conjunction with community agencies to get to the underlying problems. In the high crime areas, police are working as Neighborhood Reclamation officers, where two cops are assigned to a particular "beat." The police also have a strong presence in the schools to try to prevent drug and gang problems from escalating.

Community Life

The Volunteer Center of Sacramento has the scoop on volunteer opportunities in the area. Agencies that rely upon community volunteers are Meals on Wheels, Sacramento Children's Home, Stanford Home Settlement, the Big Brother/Big Sister Program, Red Cross, and many others. There are also cultural volunteer opportunities with the opera, symphony and Sacramento History Museum. Because Sacramento is the state capital, there are hundreds of charitable and fund-raising events here. MADD (Mothers Against Drunk Driving) was started in Sacramento.

Let the Good Times Roll

Family fun: With both the American and Sacramento Rivers, there are 1,000 miles of waterways intertwined through Sacramento, and water recreation tops the list for outdoor activities. Salmon and steelhead fishing, river rafting, and boating are just a few. The riverfront offers sightseeing by excursion boats or steam trains. Waterworld USA Family Waterpark is home to the largest wave pool in northern California and the highest slides in the West. Sutter's Fort offers a historical perspective of the area. Children enjoy Visionarium, a hands-on children's museum, Sacramento Children's Museum, as well as the Sacramento Zoo and Fairytale Town. Funderland and Scandia Family Fun Center are popular amusement parks and The Wooz is America's largest human maze and family amusement park. Sacramento also offers a 26-mile bicycle trail, which winds along the American River. Just a short drive away are exciting sightseeing and recreational opportunities in the Napa Valley wine county, San Francisco and Tahoe.

Sports: Major league sports are represented by the NBA's Sacramento Kings at Arco Arena, and the Sacramento Surge (World Football League) at Hornet Stadium. There are several semi-pro baseball teams that currently play at Renfree Park, and it is no secret that the city would like to see a professional baseball team represent Sacramento. College sports are also very popular, and volleyball games are big at Sacramento State, American River College, and Cosumnes River College. Sacramento City College also has a very good softball team.

Arts & entertainment: There are five major arts organizations in the Greater Sacramento Area: the Crocker Art Museum, the Sacramento Ballet Company, the Sacramento Theater Company, the Sacramento Opera Association and the Sacramento Symphony. There are more than 150 other organizations that provide cultural and artistic entertainment in dance, music, literature and theater. Sacramento is home to numerous museums including Crocker Art Museum, State Indian Museum, Towe Ford Museum, Silver Wings Aviation Museum, Folsom History Museum, the California State Railroad Museum, and Sacramento History Museum. For those who love shopping, Old Sacramento has many shops that sell antiques and collectibles.

Annual events: Camellia Festival (March); Sacramento Jazz Jubilee (May); International Youth Soccer Festival (Aug.); California State Fair (Sept.); California International Marathon (Dec.); Folsom Rodeo (July).

The Environment

Sacramento is concerned both about its air and land environment. Air quality is continuously monitored for traces of carbon monoxide, nitrogen dioxide, ozone, sulfur dioxide, sulfates and particulates. Recycling is encouraged, with regular pick-ups. Flood control and water supply are interrelated issues that local, state and federal agencies are struggling to solve. A huge deluge in 1986 resulted in a so-called "100-year flood" that pushed Sacramento's levees to the limit and reminded residents that the valley is also a flood plain. A key to solving the problem appears to be construction of a dam at Auburn. The big question remaining is whether Auburn Dam should be only for flood control, or if it should be a large multipurpose structure with water storage and hydroelectric generation.

In and Around Town

Roads and interstates: I-5 (north-south), I-80 (east-west), State Highway 99 (parallels I-5 up and down the state) and State Highway 50 (parallels I-80).

Closest airports: Sacramento Metro Airport (12 mi. northwest of downtown); Sacramento Executive Airport (private planes).

Public transportation: Regional Transit has a fleet of more than 200 buses that criss-cross Sacramento County on some 70 routes. The bus service dovetails with RT Metro, an 18.3 mile light-rail system that links the eastern and northeastern suburbs with downtown Sacramento.

Avg. commute: 30-45 min.

What Every Resident Knows

Sacramento and Paris are similar in one respect. There are more trees per capita here than other city in the world—even Paris. • Is there really gold up in them thar hills? You betcha! Or at least there was back in 1848 when gold was discovered 30 miles east of Sacramento, marking the beginning of the Gold Rush. • Residents are accustomed to their hometown nickname, "Sacratomato," a reference to the fact that so many people grow their own. Never again will you settle for canned tomato soup. • Like to mingle with folks from around the world? Stick around Memorial Day weekend for the annual Sacramento Traditional Jazz Jubilee. It attracts so many people, hotels are booked a year in advance.

FYI

Sacramento Metropolitan Chamber of Commerce
917 7th Street
Sacramento, CA 95812
916-552-6800

Sacramento Convention & Visitor's Bureau
1421 K Street
Sacramento, CA 95814
916-264-7777

The Sacramento Bee
2100 Q Street
Sacramento, CA 95816
916-321-1111

The Sacramento Union
301 Capitol Mall
Sacramento, CA 95814
916-442-2222

Century 21 Nolan Inc.
1506 W. El Camino Avenue
Sacramento, CA 95833
916-927-6666
Charles Gray, Relocation Dir.

Sacramento Municipal Utility District
6201 S Street
Sacramento, CA 95817
916-452-7811

Pacific Gas & Electric
5555 Florin-Perkins Road
Sacramento, CA 95826
916-383-2323

Pacific Bell
4111 Marconi Avenue
Sacramento, CA 95821
916-593-2525

California Dept. of Commerce Office of Small Business
1231 I Street
Sacramento, CA 95814
916-324-1295

California Assoc. of Economic Development
1022 G Street
Sacramento, CA 95814
916-448-8252

School district: 916-366-2591
Property tax assessor:
916-440-5271
Physician's referral: 800-258-1640
Day-care referral: 916-366-4661

Valencia, California

Area Snapshot

Local population: 160,000
County: North Los Angeles
Population: 686,000
U.S. region: Southern California
Closest metro area: Los Angeles (60 mi. south)
Median housing price: $230,000
Avg. household income: $46,361
Best reasons to live here: Gorgeous master-planned community, one of the best commutes to Los Angeles, low crime, ample recreation, choice homes and schools, great climate without the smog, wonderful mountain views.

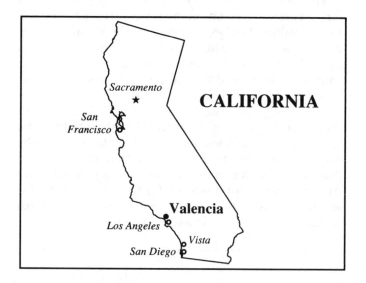

Fabulous Features

Building a town from the ground up is like giving birth. Just ask proud parents like the Newhall Land and Farming Company. For the past 25 years, they've conceived and nurtured the master-planned community of Valencia. Situated in the dynamic Santa Clarita Valley, less than an hour from Los Angeles, is this family mecca complete with exquisite neighborhoods, carefully planned commercial properties and awesome recreational possibilities (parks, pools, golf courses and other facilities are impeccably maintained).

But the star of the show is the 10-miles of *paseos*, a lush network of pathways, bridges and tunnels that lets joggers, bikers and school-bound children travel without traffic. Even better, the trip to school is worth it. Valencia sends to three of the most respected districts in the state (Hart High's participation in state and national academic competition is legendary). There are also several community colleges, including the Disney-endowed California Institute of the Arts (the only fully accredited performing arts university in the country).

But this is no Micky Mouse town. Since 1991, there have been many exciting commercial developments. For Christmas, residents got to open Valencia Town Center, a magnificent regional shopping mall (110 stores and a 10-plex theater were as welcomed as a drink in the desert). The new state-of-the-art Valencia Commerce Center, the Valencia Hilton and several corporate relocation announcements (U.S. Borax and Kaiser Permanente) resulted in one of the most productive periods ever.

Real estate is also busy, thanks to a steady inventory of buyers who are snatching up super-looking single family and attached houses at very un-California prices (much to choose from under $200,000). Bet the Newhall Company is so proud of its prodigy, they carry pictures in case anyone asks about offspring.

Possible drawbacks: California's golden glow has been tarnished by fiscal and natural disasters. For the first time, more people are moving out than in. Valenica may be an oasis, but it is not an island! • Local unemployment is up; many firms are fleeing to cheaper states.

"You can quote me on that"

"Few people realize that Valencia is not a 'city.' It's a community within the valley. We're part of a city but rural at the same time. We have the tranquility with the benefit of city jobs. The best of both worlds!"—K.H.

Real Estate

Market overview: It's basically a buyer's market with the most activity in the lower-priced homes. First time buyers are taking advantage of the low interest rates. Sellers must come down in order to make their sale. New construction is low and not expected to pick up, but resale inventory is increasing. A reasonably priced house in good condition can sell in 2-3 days but the avg. time is 80-90 days.

What houses look like: Mediterraneans, California missions and modified Tudors are predominant. Stucco exteriors w/tile roofs are all over. There are some California ranches w/wood siding. Most homes are 2-story. Huge, vaulted areas in the family room, skylights, gourmet kitchens and white appliances and fixtures are in demand. Houses under 10 years may have garden tubs. Separate showers and BAs are common.

Starter homes: $130,000-$225,000. Condos are the least expensive buy, at $130,000-$175,000. Living space ranges from 900-1300 sq. ft. $180,000 buys 2-3BR/1-2BA home, 900-1200 sq. ft., and 2-car garage. $225,000 buys 3BR/2BA, 2-car garage, fireplace, central air and heat, 1300-1500 sq. ft. on a 60 x 100 lot.

Trade-ups: $230,000-$375,000. At the low end, you get a 2-story 3-4BR/2-2½BA, w/fireplace, pool, vaulted ceilings, gourmet kitchen, playroom, 1700-1800 sq. ft., 60 x 100 lot. For $350,000 you can find a 5-6 yr. home w/4BR/3BA, family room, fireplace, gourmet kitchen, 2200-2300 sq. ft., 60 x 100 lot.

Luxury homes: $350,000-$700,000. At the high end, you can get a house with a view, 5BR/3-4BA, 6000-8000 sq. ft. on an 80 x 100 lot, 3-car garage, pool and contemporary features.

Rental market: Townhouses are limited and avg. $800/mo. and up. Apts. are limited for $800/mo. and up, SFHs are scarce and avg. $1,100/mo. and up. Condos are available and run $850/mo. and up.

Great neighborhoods: San Canyon is a very elite neighborhood where the houses are newer, with more land. There are also elegant older homes with beautiful views. It offers a rural feel, w/nearby horseback riding, but is 15 min. from shopping and conveniences. The Summit offers homes for $250,000-$600,000, an 80-acre park w/riding trails, 4 recreation centers, pools, tennis, and shopping.

Nearby areas to consider: Newhall offers a mix of old and luxurious homes, close to shopping, excellent school system (one of the top 10 in the state), scenic with lots of recreation, 45 min. from the beaches. Grenada Hills (10-15 min.), is part of the L.A. school system, an older, developed area, with affordable houses.

What Things Cost

Runzheimer's Living Cost Index: Avg. annual costs for family of 4 with household income of $50,000: $65,354 (30.7% above avg. city).

ACCRA's national comparisons: Overall living costs in the Los Angeles area are 26.9% above the avg. city. Housing prices, at 94.6% above avg. make home ownership near impossible for many, though costs are much less in the Santa Clarita valley. Health care is another budget buster, with costs 34.9% above avg. Utilities are the only break, at 13% below. Food is an estimated 6.7% above.

Utilities: Phone: Hookup: $34.75; Measured service: $4.45/mo. Unlimited local service: $8.35/mo. Gas: Avg. $100/mo. Electric: Avg. $200-$225/mo.

Kid care: Day care costs $544/mo. for infants and $350/mo. for older children. Childcare is readily available. **Pediatric visit:** $50.

The Tax Ax

Sales tax: 7.5% (groceries and medical supplies exempt).

Property tax: Property taxes are established under Proposition 13 as 1% of the purchase price plus limited locally approved bonds. The total rarely exceeds 1.25%.

State income tax: The maximum rate for taxation is 9.3% for $100,000 and more. For less, rates range from 2% to 8%. In California, both earned and unearned income are taxed at these rates.

Climate

Elevation 1,300'	Avg. High/Low	Avg. Rain (Inches)	Avg. Snow (Inches)	Avg. Days Rain	Avg. % Humidity
Jan.	64/40	4	4	6	52
April	72/45	2	.5	4	51
July	91/57	.02	--	1	45
Oct.	80/52	.8	--	2	50
YEAR	76/48	21.52	1	37	48

# of days 32° or below: 15	# of days 90° or above: 43

A higher elevation allows Valencia to escape the stifling summer heat and smog found in the Los Angeles basin. Summers are warm and dry. Winters are rainy season, with occasional polar air masses sweeping through. There's even rare snowfall (disappears in a day or so). Year-round, the skies are sunny, and temperatures are delightfully warm and pleasant.

Earning a Living

Economic outlook: Business continues to be rosy for the Santa Clarita Valley. The services sector leads the way, comprising 28% of the total employment. Manufacturing comes next, at 25%, and retail trade at 14.6%. The labor force is a highly skilled pool, with the majority of the population employed in the private sector in management, professional, technical or administrative positions. While employment in Los Angeles County is projected to increase by 33% by the year 2010, projections for the Santa Clarita Valley show an increase of 257% over the same period.

Where the jobs are: Santa Clarita's strong continued consumer demand, generated by its rapid population growth, has already drawn more than 5,000 retail businesses to the area and produced a considerable upward curve in retail sales. The Valley's businesses are diverse, ranging from small, family-owned shops and boutiques to numerous franchise outlets to shopping center anchors. New arrivals include an increasing number of franchise stores and restaurants, which have opened in recently developed retail centers. The Valencia Industrial Center exists as the Southland's 4th-largest industrial park, with more than 300 firms and 10,000 employees. Included are such major corporations as Sun Oil, Sperry Univac, Lockheed, and H.R. Textron. In addition, the Valencia Corporate Center offers prestigious corporate space, with sites that range from 2-20 acres. Baxter Pharmaseal locates its headquarters here. Future industrial developments providing hundreds of new jobs are: the Valencia Town Center, a $180 million project including a 2-level, enclosed mall, and expected to house 160 shops; Valencia Commercial Center, a high-tech industrial center on a 1,600 industrial acre site, expected to provide 25,000 new jobs; The Magic Mountain Resort Complex on an 800-acre site, planned as a destination resort/business complex. In addition, the U.S. Postal Service recently broke ground on a $50 million mail-sorting building that should bring 2,000 jobs to Valencia and the Santa Clarita Valley. The film and television industry does an extensive amount of production work in the Valley. A new $10 million dollar, 6-stage film studio is now being built. In addition, construction is underway on a new $25 million company headquarters for U.S. Borax and Chemical Corporation, in Valencia Corporate Center.

Business opportunities: The Chamber of Commerce and SCORE. provide assistance and information for new entrepreneurs and small businesses.

Making the Grade

Public education overview: The Newhall school district has a lot to brag about: 5 California Distinguished School awards, 1 Nationally Distinguished School Award, Administrator of the Year for the last 6 years in the elementary schools, a daily attendance of 95.3%, to name a few. The salaries for administrators and teachers are 10.5% above the state avg. for districts of 100 or more children. Schools are crowded and the need for new schools is a concern. At the William S. Hart High School, 83% of graduating seniors go on to college. On SAT scores, seniors in the class of '92 scored above the national mean in both verbal and mathematics. Hart High students also consistently score in the top percentile in 4 academic honor competitions that are either statewide or national competitions: Sports championships are numerous for both boys and girls athletic programs. There is a program with local community colleges where students can earn college credit. Some students in the Valencia area participate in an Independent Study Program. **Class size:** 30:1.

Help for working parents: The YMCA in Valencia offers before- and after-school childcare in at 4 elementary schools within the Newhall school district.

School year: Starts after Labor Day, ends 2nd wk. of June. Children must be 5 on or before Dec. 2 to enter kindergarten.

Special education/gifted programs: GATE, the Gifted and Talented Education program, is for grades 4-12, its focus primarily on language arts and math. GATE children receive instruction beyond the core curriculum. The high school has an advanced placement program allowing students to earn college credit in computer science, composition, biology, French and Spanish. Special Education within the Newhall district is provided by the department of Special Services for grades K-6. There are a number of programs available for children with various learning disabilities. Los Angeles County Special Education Division handles the severely handicapped.

Nearby colleges/universities: In Santa Clarita Valley: College of the Canyons, a 2-yr. community college; California Institute of the Arts, the nation's only full accredited visual and performing arts university established by Walt Disney; The Master's College, a Christian-oriented, 4-yr. school. There are also top-rated colleges and universities located in the Los Angeles area.

Medical Care

Hospitals/medical centers: Henry Mayo Newhall Memorial Hospital and Medical Center includes a 24-hour emergency center, trauma center, ambulatory center, and helicopter ambulance service. A cancer center, emergency outpatient surgery, women's health, and adult day care are also provided. Newhall Community Hospital/Tan Medical Clinic offers full laboratory services, physical and respiratory therapy and outpatient and inpatient surgery. Holy Cross Hospital is an acute care facility with a chemical dependency and trauma center.

Specialized care: SCV Mental Health Services; KARES Aux/Spec. Children Center; Valencia Surgical Center, an outpatient surgery facility with laser surgery and sports surgery; SCV Occupation Center handles work injuries, physicals for employment and corporate drug testing.

Crime & Safety

An involved police force and lots of safety awareness programs help make for a safe community. DARE (K-5) and BE COOL (7-8) are two drug prevention programs in the schools. A neighborhood watch program has 9,000 participants, who receive the quarterly Crime Stoppers bulletin. Personal safety programs include rape prevention, senior safety, bicycle safety, CAT (Combat Auto Theft), an auto safety program, child fingerprinting, bank robbery prevention, employee theft prevention, bomb threat program, graffiti removal. There are hotlines where citizens can call anonymously to report gang activity, narcotics, etc. Plans in the works include a crime prevention program on local cable TV.

Community Life

Valencia is very community-oriented. Volunteer organizations include the Association to Aid Victims of Domestic Violence, Lions Club, ZONTA, and Rotary. The city has Pride Weeks where residents clean up neighborhoods. The SECURE program (Santa Clarita Educated Communities United in Response to Emergencies) works with local volunteers that prepare neighborhoods for natural disasters. The Santa Clarita Boys and Girls Club is a nonprofit guidance, educational, and recreational center with a membership of 1,100 children and is staffed by community volunteers. This spring, the Police Department sponsored the first annual Block Party where all Emergency Response Personnel were invited.

Let the Good Times Roll

Family fun: Six Flag's Magic Mountain is a popular amusement park in the area, with 260 acres of attractions. It includes more than 100 rides, including Colossus which is the world's largest roller coaster according to *The Guiness Book of World Records.* Just 10 miles away is Lake Castaic, a popular place to go boating and fishing. There are four additional lakes within a short drive. The Pacific Ocean and gorgeous beaches are just 40 miles away. Saugus Speedway, a former rodeo stadium, hosts stock car races. Placerita Park and Nature Center is built at the site of California's first gold rush. The spectacular Vasquez Rocks in Agua Duce is a popular television and film location and is great for climbing, hiking, and picnicking. William S. Hart Park in Newhall is the home of the former silent screen star, and has been enlarged to include picnic grounds, a barnyard zoo and hiking trails. Old Orchard Park, Canyon Country Park and Newhall Park offer pools, playgrounds and softball fields as well as baseball fields. Edwards Arena and Mann Theatre are ideal for concerts, live shows and plays. Great skiing is just an hour's drive away. Two golf courses, numerous pools, tennis courts, and the unique *paseo* system, which is 10 miles of landscaped walkways spread throughout the city, all contribute to the healthy, active lifestyle.

Sports: High school sports are popular with residents. For professional sports, spectators travel to Los Angeles, 40 miles away. There you can watch the L.A. Dodgers and California Angels (baseball), Raiders and Rams (football), and Lakers and Clippers (basketball). AYSO Soccer and Little League are popular in the community.

Arts & entertainment: The California Institute of Arts sponsors events including exhibits, dances and musical concerts. The "Performing Arts Summer Series" is a free concert series offered each Sunday at different parks. The Saugus Train Depot was built in 1887 and has a large collection of old locomotives and fire engines. The Los Angeles area offers unlimited opportunities for museum-going, concerts, galleries, theaters, and other activities.

Annual events: (Dec) Tree Lighting Ceremony and Tour of Homes (Dec.); Frontier Days (Oct.); Business Expo (Oct.); Miss Santa Clarita Pageant.

The Environment

Valencia's water quality is excellent, but air quality is not. Even with its high desert locale, ocean breezes and mountains, smog is a way of life. On the bright side, recycling and conservation are strong. Valencia has recently instituted a city-wide curbside recycling program. Santa Clarita Valley's motto is "Reduce, Reuse, and Recycle!" City efforts also include telephone and Christmas tree recycling, special environmental fairs, and a public information campaign.

In and Around Town

Roads and interstates: I-5 (north-south); Highway 126 runs through the northern part of the Valley, west to the Pacific Ocean; Highway 14 runs north-south into L.A. (south) and Lancaster/Palmdale (north).

Closest airport: Los Angeles International Airport (40-60 min.).

Public transportation: Santa Clarita Valley Transit provides bus service. New subway and rail transit commuter lines for the Santa Clarita Valley are in the works.

Avg. commute: 60-75 min. to Los Angeles. Commuter traffic can be hellish.

What Every Resident Knows

If you think you heard someone shout "action," you're probably not imagining things. There are three active movie studios in the Santa Clarita Valley. And in fact, so much filming is done in the Newhall area, it's often called "Newhallywood!" • Get your credit cards handy. With more than 5,000 stores and service businesses in the Valley, there's no need to trudge to the big city for anything. There's even a Santa Clarita Savings Club, which offer discounts for patronizing neighborhood merchants. • You'll go round in circles here, but not to worry. It's because of the magnificent carousel being built in the Rotunda of Valencia's new Town Center. The custom-designed merry-go-round's animals and music will depict images of the Claude Beatty Circus that wintered here for 20 years starting in the 1930s.

FYI

Santa Clarita Valley Chamber of Commerce
23920 Valencia Blvd.
Santa Clarita, CA 91355
805-259-4787

Greater Los Angeles Convention and Visitors Bureau
515 S. Figueroa Street
Los Angeles, CA 90071
213-624-9746

The Signal
24000 Creekside Road
Valencia, CA 91355
805-259-1234

The Daily News
24800 Rockefeller Avenue
Valencia, CA 91355
805-257-5200

Los Angeles Times
23920 Valencia Blvd., Suite 245
Valencia, CA 91355
805-259-5035

Vista Realty of Valencia
24330 McBean Parkway
Valencia, CA 91355
800-400-4620
Bob Lieffring

Southern California Edison Co.
25625 West Rye Canyon Road
Valencia, CA 91355
805-257-8291

Southern California Gas Co.
800-660-4495 (in state only)

Pacific Bell
800-339-6622 (out of state); 811-6660 (in-state, no area code needed)

Santa Clarita Valley Small Business Center
26455 N. Rockwell Canyon Road
Santa Clarita, CA 91355
805-253-0100

School district: 805-259-5440
Property tax assessor:
805-254-9550
Welcome Wagon: 805-254-0479
Physician's referral: 805-253-8888
Day-care referral: 805-255-2474

Vista, California

Area Snapshot

Local population: 76,000
County: San Diego   **Population:** 2,500,000
U.S. region: Southern California
Closest metro areas: San Diego (35 mi. south), Orange County (65 mi. north), Los Angeles (90 mi. north).
Median housing price: $186,000
Avg. household income: $32,500
Best reasons to live here: Absolute perfect climate, dynamic job and business growth, rated best high school in California, wonderful recreation and fun, solid community spirit, best of San Diego 45 minutes away.

Fabulous Features

A beauty contestant's worst nightmare is the gal who's a gorgeous honor student and also a sure bet to win Miss Congeniality. That's how most small cities would feel competing with Vista. This dyanmic beauty, seven miles from the Pacific Ocean shores has it all in the bag. Why else would the population have nearly tripled in the past 20 years (three of five people looking in San Diego end up in North County)? Who wouldn't want to be in the "climactic wonderland of the United States" (average daily temperature is 74 degrees), the community that had the best high school in the state (*Redbook*, April 1992) and that also had six times the national average number of parks within its 18 sq. miles?

As for job growth, Vista has been minding its own business! More than 400 companies have started here since 1986, the 15 million sq. ft. Business and Research Park opened in 1990 (within the first year, 1,000 jobs were created) and corporate expansions and relocations are still making headlines (Vans sneakers chose Vista over 30 sites, creating 600 jobs).

And so as not to let success spoil her good looks, strict zoning laws have kept the rolling hills and pleasant rural surroundings intact. It's why neighborhoods are so attractive, in looks *and* price. There is abundant inventory in the $150,000-$200,000 range and with the open, airy home designs (skylights are common as light switches) and the lush California vegetation, it's picture-perfect. So are the days when you can head to gorgeous state parks, beaches, world-famous San Diego Zoo and even the shops in Mexico (an hour away). And now that many of the schools are year-round, every third month is a vacation, giving plenty of time to take it all in. If you're lucky, there will be a Vista on your horizon.

Possible drawbacks: All roads lead to Vista, but with accessibility also comes major traffic and congestion. Although Highway 78 was recently widened, commuters to San Diego are still putting in plenty of overtime on the roads. • Vista's new redevelopment plan will rebuild downtown, but will eventually result in higher property assessments and taxes.

"You can quote me on that"

"We've been here for three years and Vista is as close to perfection as you can get. The scenery, the climate and the nice people make you forget your problems."—P.B.

Real Estate

Market overview: Vista is indeed a buyer's market with interest rates low and inventory high. A fairly priced home sells within 60 days. Prices in the $150s are attracting a lot of first-time buyers and new residents to the community. New construction is minimal, but a lot of resales are available.

What houses look like: What a variety! Ranches, capes, splits and Victorians can all be found, and many with great views. Homes tend to have unusual layouts, some w/driveways on a different level, some 1-stories appearing as 2-stories. Most have 2-3-car garages. Pools are common. Houses are mostly stucco though there's some brick and stone. Gourmet and island kitchens are in demand. Master suites w/separate showers are very popular. Basements are rare. Popular features are skylights, cathedral ceilings, and tile floors.

Starter homes: $140,000-$175,000 For the low end, you get 3BR/2BA, 1500 sq. ft., ½ acre, 2-car garage and fireplace in a fairly new home in an area such as Shadow Ridge or Ulta Vista.

Trade-ups: $200,000-$300,000. $250,000 buys a 3-5BR/2-3BA, ½-1 acre (horse property) and 2-3 car garage in Shadow Ridge or Ulta Vista.

Luxury homes: $400,000-$1.5 million. $500,000 buys a great view, 4-5BR, 2-3 acres, pool, jacuzzi, gated entry, spiraling driveway, tile work in kitchen and BAs, 4000 sq. ft., den and family room and 2-3 fireplaces. Elevado is the place to look.

Rental market: SFHs are easily found; 3BR/2BA is $875-$1,000/mo. Condos & townhouses, 2BR/2BA, are $650-$675/mo. Apts. are plentiful but 3BRs are very limited—a 2BR/2BA is $550-$650/mo.

Great neighborhoods: Shadow Ridge offers new houses (oldest are 4-5 yrs.), new schools and new shopping. Homeowner fees are the rule. Any neighborhood in the hilly southeastern area offers a mix of old and new homes, with great schools and convenient shopping. Shadow Ridge has condos and single family homes and could be considered a planned community with golf courses, tennis courts and more.

Nearby areas to consider: Escondido offers nice residential areas with a hot climate for those who love the heat. This is a very fast-growing community with good schools, conveniences and lots of recreation. San Marcos is a planned community next door to Vista with a variety of communities, its own lake, docks for boating, convenient shopping and great schools. San Marcos is known for Restaurant Row, a stretch with every kind of restaurant imaginable featuring seafood to pizza.

What Things Cost

Runzheimer's Living Cost Index (San Diego metro area): Avg. annual costs for family of 4 with household income of $50,000: $60,786 (21.6% above avg. city).

ACCRA's national comparisons: Not available.

Utilities: Phone: Hookup: $40; Basic service: $13/mo. Electric: $100-$275/mo. Gas: $60-$85/mo. Water: $55/mo.

Kid care: Though difficult to find, infant care avg. is $100/wk.; 18 mo. and older is $88/wk. **Pediatric visit:** $35.

The Tax Ax

Sales tax: 7.75%.

Property tax: Property taxes are established under Proposition 13 as 1% of the purchase price plus limited locally approved bonds. The total rarely exceeds 1.25%.

State income tax: The maximum rate for taxation is 9.3% for $100,000 and more. For lower income, rates range from 1%-8%. In California, both earned and unearned income are taxed at these rates.

Climate

Elevation 331'	Avg. High/Low	Avg. Rain (Inches)	Avg. Snow (Inches)	Avg. Days Rain	Avg. % Humidity
Jan.	67/42	2.8	--	6	53
April	71/49	1.4	--	5	56
July	82/59	.01	--	T	64
Oct.	77/52	.9	--	2	59
YEAR	74/50	17.21	--	41	59

# of days 32° or below: 1	# of days 90° or above: 18

Located 7 miles inland from the Pacific Ocean, Vista enjoys cool summers and warm winters compared to other cities at the same latitude. Although freezing temperatures are rare, hot weather may be delivered by easterly "Santa Ana" winds (particularly in fall). Low clouds hang over the coastal valleys in the morning, but afternoons are generally sunny and clear.

> **"You can quote me on that"**
> *"It scares me to think we almost moved someplace else. Vista was the ideal choice. It's beautiful and safe."*—G.H.

Earning a Living

Economic outlook: Growth and diversity are two words used frequently to describe Vista's economic situation. The master-planned Vista Business and Research park includes 15.5 million sq. ft. of floor space devoted to and designated for specific corporate, research and industrial uses—it's seen more than 400 new businesses move in since 1986. In 1992, 1,000 new jobs were created in the industrial park, and 1 new business a week has moved in. A $44 million dollar bond issue for public improvements was passed after 2 area banks did a 20-year analysis and found that the city was growing at *twice* the rate of California and 50% faster than San Diego. Unemployment stood at a below national average of 6% as of April, 1991. In addition to a civilian labor force of more than 1 million, North County benefits from the proximity of Camp Pendleton Marine Corps Base, one of the largest military bases on the West Coast.

Where the jobs are: Non-manufacturing companies that are expanding include: Vista Unified School District; City of Vista; Tri-City Medical Center; and San Diego Regional Justice District. Manufacturing companies continuing to expand: XenteK electronics; Stikees (window decals); Doorway Sales (carpentry); P.I. Industries (furniture); Cade Grayson (importer). In addition, Vans, Inc., the popular manufacturer of sneakers, announced in spring of 1992 that it will open a 90,000 sq. ft. plant that will employ 600. Home-Base, a large home-improvement store, announced it will open a 100,000 sq. ft. production facility and add 80 new jobs to its employment roster. Pennysaver is expected to contribute employment opportunities by moving its corporate headquarters here. Drawn by Vista's large industrial parks, other companies to relocate recently are Joseph Webb Foods, Inc., Directed Electronics, Inc. and Armor Safe Corp. Procare Products of San Marcos announced it will construct a facility for the manufacture of orthopedic products in 1993, which will employ 220 workers. Other companies opening new facilities include Frito-Lay, Kaiser Permanente and Secure Horizons.

Business opportunities: There is a need for retail since residents go outside the community for major shopping. No shortage of groceries, video stores, gas stations, convenience stores and fast-food places though. Sit-down restaurants would be welcome. The Vista Economic Development Association (VEDA) develops and supports new industrial, commercial and retail centers, and assists new businesses.

Making the Grade

Public education overview: Despite the challenges facing the district (budget cuts, changing demographic make-up and skyrocketing numbers of new students), the Vista school system has achieved many successes. The Rancho Bueno Vista High School was named by *Redbook* as the best in California. But both comprehensive high schools have received national recognition for the last three years as "schools of excellence" from the federal government. Both high schools participate in the International Baccalaureate, headquartered in Geneva, Switzerland. An average of 20 Vista students per year graduate from this program. Vista schools were the first schools in California to implement a year-round program—students are in school two months, out one, which allows the system to utilize resources more efficiently. Kids and teachers love this program, though childcare is often a problem with parents. There are special magnet schools for K-5 for visual and performing arts and science/technology. An estimated 50% of Vista high school students go on to college.

Class size: 30:1 (elementary), 30-32:1 (middle and high school).

Help for working parents: Childcare programs are available at elementary schools as early as 6:30 a.m. and as late as 6 p.m. Tutorial programs and sports programs are also available after school at the middle school level and a full range of high school athletic programs.

Blue Ribbon School Awards: Rancho Buena Vista High School ('90-'91), Vista High School ('88-'89).

School year: Beginning in July 1990, Vista placed 14,000 students, grades K-8 on a year-round calendar in 12 of 13 elementary schools and 3 middle schools. (2 months in school, 1 month on vacation).

Special education/gifted programs: The Learning Center is a classroom program for the disabled and learning-disabled. However, children are mainstreamed whenever possible. For severe orthopedic or other handicaps, there is the California Avenue School, a special facility for children who cannot be mainstreamed and need full-time special attention. For gifted students the GATE program (grades 9-12) is offered.

Nearby colleges/universities: There are two junior colleges: Palomar (25,000 students); and Miracosta (15,000 students). California State at San Marcos State University is a 4-year university 10 min. from Vista.

Medical Care

Hospitals/medical centers: Tri-City Medical Center (5 min. from downtown) is a modern, state-of-the-art facility offering comprehensive health care services. And San Diego is known world over for medical research, and emergency/trauma services. University of California at San Diego Medical Center has highly respected cancer care and organ transplant programs. Scripps Memorial Hospital, part of the famous Scrips Institute, offers the Whittier Institute for Diabetes and the Cardiovascular Institute.

Specialized care: University of San Diego Rehabilitation and Children's Centers; Continental Hospital (rehabilitation); San Diego Regional Center (for developmentally disabled children); Children's Convalescent Hospital (up to age 15); Southwood Psychiatric Hospital (in children).

Crime & Safety

For a city its size, crime is low. Vista was reported to have the 5th-lowest crime rate per capita in the county (1991), and the city has few homicides and property crimes. This is attributed to the excellent way the sherrif's department is managed—treating the community more like a small town. Because of the growing population, however, crime is on the rise, particularly in the areas of drug and gang activity and homeless problems. The city and sheriffs department has responded with a Street Narcotic Unit. Vista has added a specialized gang unit and a Transient Deputy to combat gangs and the homeless respectively. The DARE program in the schools, a traffic crime prevention program, neighborhood watch, and a McGruff program are just a few of the ways the community addresses problems.

Community Life

Vista residents take a very active role in community life. Rotary, Soroptimist, and Elks organizations are very popular, and the Women's Club has more than 300 members. The Vista Town Center Association (VTCA) is a nonprofit organization leading the "Revitalization of Downtown." A new Senior Center was recently built, and depends upon volunteers for programs such as the Senior Feeding Program. place to volunteer is The Boys and Girls Clubs. Citizens here are very willing to speak up— and the local government listens! In fact, the mayor is very accessible Friends of the Library has gotten a $3 million grant and a new library will be built by 1994, which is quite an accomplishment in these hard economic times.

Let the Good Times Roll

Family fun: Vista is 1 hour from Disneyland. The Pacific Ocean is only 7 miles away. What more could a family ask for in recreational and leisure activities? How about an ideal climate, a community that offers lots of sports programs for kids and adults, and an opportunity to visit another country just an hour away? There's more: Vista is surrounded by state parks that offer hiking, biking, camping and horseback riding. There's is breathtaking scenery and fascinating wildlife to explore— such as the Anza-Borrego Desert. In Vista, the Community Services Department coordinates more than 30 adult and youth recreation programs year-round, including adult co-ed softball and senior softball. Nearby San Diego offers a multitude of recreational opportunities including the San Diego Zoo and Wild Animal Park. Day trips to Palomar Observatory are also popular. Wildwood Park is small children's park with picnic areas. And for a change of pace, Breezdale Park is rustic with lots of hiking trails and baseball fields. Major ski resorts are within driving distance for winter recreation.

Sports: Sports fans travel 40 minutes to San Diego to watch professional games. And just 90 minutes away is Los Angeles with additional opportunities to enjoy spectator sports. More than 20 public and private golf courses are located within a 45-minute radius, including the world-famous La Costa Resort and Golf Course.

Arts & entertainment: Vista's Moonlight Amphitheater is located in Brengle Terrace Park and presents 5 productions each summer. Winter theater productions take place at Rancho Buena Vista High School Auditorium. Rancho Buena Vista Adobe is an original land grant Mexican ranch, which offers a historical perspective of the area and is open for guided tours, special events, or can be rented for parties. The Antique Gas & Steam Engine Museum located in Vista gives a history of trains. Gallery Vista and Rancho Buena Vista Adobe are 2 art galleries that offer guided tours. There are no dance companies or theaters in Vista.

Annual events: Western Regional Chili Cook-off (Sept.); Rod Run, a car race (Aug.); Weekly Street Fairs and Farmer's Markets (Thursday nights in summer); Moonlight Amphitheatre outdoor concerts (summer); Japan Festival, featuring dancers, food, and art at the Buddhist Temple in Vista (spring).

The Environment

The major environmental factor affecting Vista? Landfill is at capacity. Bcause other areas don't want to share their landfills, when the Vista landfill can no longer be used, the cost of refuge collection may rise sharply if the refuse must be carted far away. Currently, environmentalists are battling this issue in court. Vista has a very aggressive recycling program, with a weekly pickup, in three separate categories—general refuse, recyclable materials (glass, aluminum, tin and plastics); and yard waste pickup. Vista is part of a regional cooperative instituting the Clean Water Act. It participates on the Regional Quality Board, in implementing a program to monitor the pollution level of Buena Vista Creek. Since Vista is a light-industry or nonpolluting community, it is not as concerned about water contamination or toxic waste.

In and Around Town

Roads and interstates: I-5 (north-south), I-15 (north-south), State Highway 78 (east-west), State Highway 76 (east-west).

Closest airport: San Diego International Airport (37 mi. south); John Wayne Airport in Irvine (45 mi. north); Los Angeles International Airport (93 mi. north). Palomar Airport and Oceanside Municipal Airport handle small planes.

Public transportation: The North County Transit District provides bus service in Vista.

Avg. commute: 45-60 min. to San Diego during rush hour (40 min. non-rush hour).

What Every Resident Knows

Bumper stickers everywhere proclaim that Vista is the country's "Climactic Wonderland" and "Vista and proud of it." But don't worry about the hype. With an average year-round temperature of 74 and an abundance of community spirit, there has yet to be any complaints of false advertising. • Make sure your Bowling Night isn't Thursday. You wouldn't want to miss the weekly Farmers Market on Vista Way. Fresh fruits, vegetables, pecans, macademias, kiwis and pumpkins and the prized strawberries (purported to be the best in California) are all for sale. And don't think it's only farmers selling. Some of the choice stands are manned by lawyers, accountants and teachers.

FYI

Vista Chamber of Commerce
201 Washington Street
Vista, CA 92084
619-726-1122

Vista City Hall
P.O. Box 1988
Vista, CA 92085
619-726-1340

Vista Press
425 West Vista Way
Vista, CA 92083
619-724-7161

San Diego Union Tribune
220 W. Second Avenue
Escondido, CA 92025
800-533-8830

Century 21/Gieseler & Assoc.
890 E. Vista Way
Vista, CA 92084
619-724-7141
Peggy Cole

Pacific Telephone
800-310-8899 (in-state)
714-339-5111 (Call collect)

S.D. Gas & Electric
P.O. Box 1831
San Diego, CA 92112
619-743-3222

Vista Economic Development Association
600 Eucalyptus Avenue
Vista, CA 92085
619-726-1340, Ext. 3560

School district: 619-726-2170
Property tax assessor:
619-531-5399
Welcome Wagon: 619-224-3586
North County Interfaith Council: 619-489-6380
Physician's referral: 619-724-8411
Day-care referral: Contact the Chamber of Commerce.

Aurora, Colorado (Denver)

Area Snapshot

Local population: 222,000
County: Arapahoe, Adams
Population: Adams-265,000; Arapahoe-392,000
U.S. region: Rocky Mountains/Western U.S.
Closest metro area: Denver (5 mi. west)
Median housing price: $85,932
Avg. household income: $32,549
Best reasons to live here: 300 days of sunshine and an equally bright economic outlook, phenomenal recreation and family fun, top-rated Cherry Creek school district, excellent medical care, great neighborhoods, new airport and major league baseball team creating positive momentum.

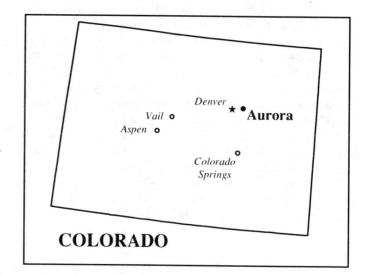

Fabulous Features

Denver is indeed the "Mile High City." And it's no exaggeration to say it is head and shoulders above many other cities. Not just for altitude, but for *attitude*! Denver has gone to great heights to make a mid-course correction after the economy nose-dived in the mid-'80s (100,000-plus arrivals were greeted with news that thousands of energy, banking and real estate jobs were departing).

Now look again. The Denver metro of the '90s has lots of golden eggs in the basket (cable TV, telecommunications, high-tech manufacturing, agriculture). It also has enough "openings" on the calendar to make ribbon-cutting a cottage industry: a 43,000-seat big-league baseball stadium for the brand-new Colorado Rockies, Denver International Airport (the world's largest), the first light rail system and a new location for the beloved Elitch Gardens amusement park.

And just to the east of Denver is one of the area's fastest-growing communities, Aurora. Families from around the world have settled here (53 languages are spoken) to take advantage of the fine schools (local districts are recognized nationally for superior academics), the first-rate parks and recreation facilities and variety of housing (from $75,000-$350,000).

But no matter where you land, you're within minutes of skiing, mountain-climbing, camping and endless year-round recreation, sports action (the Broncos, Nuggets and Rockies) and the culture (Denver's Performing Arts complex is the second-biggest in the country). Name it, it's here and that's no pie in the sky!

Possible drawbacks: If you love driving, there's ample opportunity to be behind the wheel. Bus service is spotty (the metro area grew in such a way that direct routes to and from outlying areas were difficult to connect). Hopefully, residents will support the light rail system coming next year, which should alleviate some of the car dependence. • You can sing in the sunshine (75 percent of the year), but it may be in between coughs. With the high altitudes, winter air inversions and the distance from the ocean, air quality is undesirable on many days. The area should be in compliance with EPA standards by 1995.

"You can quote me on that"

"I love Aurora! The Cherry Creek schools are excellent and offer my son so many athletic programs, he's really involved. The neighborhoods are also quiet and family-oriented."—V.M.

Real Estate

Market overview: Heard the expression, "A day late and a dollar short"? That's how buyers feel here. With the lowest interest rates in 13 years and high buyer demand, homeowners are getting their prices and then some (home prices up 7%-10% a year). Also inventory is more limited than anyone can remember (1,400 listings, down from 2,000+ in the late '80s). New construction is up. Overall, the drawing cards for the area are the great Cherry Creek schools and the wide range of prices (from $50,000-$350,000).

What houses look like: 2-stories and 4-levels (split-levels w/BAs on one floor, the living and dining rooms and kitchen on another, a family room on the 3rd, and basement on a 4th) are most popular. With high land values, it's more efficient to build up. Most exteriors are frame and brick. New homes show vaulted ceilings, master suites, open kitchens and oak *everything*.

Starter homes: Homes start at $50,000, but get very presentable at $75,000-$80,000. That buys a 15-year-old 3BR/2BA, (900-1600 sq. ft.) with 1-2 car garage. Most are frame split-levels and ranches. Look at Aurora Central and Aurora South.

Trade-ups: $125,000-$160,000 buys a 2000-2800 sq. ft. frame and brick home, usually a 2-story or bi-level ranch. Some have 3-car garages, extra BAs and energy-efficient, open-floor plans. Skylights and solar systems are trends. Consider Aurora South and Littleton.

Luxury homes: New luxury homes are in the $200,000-$350,000 range for a 2500-5000 sq. ft. for a showplace. Brick exteriors w/stained woodwork interiors, rounded stairways, master suites in separate quarters are hot. Most are 2-story contemporaries or Spanish-style (stucco, tile roofs, curved archways). Look at Parker and Highlands Ranch.

Rental market: Because of the big influx of Californians and limited multi-family dwellings, the rental market is dry as the desert. 2BR apartments go for $400-$450/mo. Single family homes rent for $700/mo. where available.

Great neighborhoods: Cherry Creek school district neighborhoods are the first requests (south Aurora). Look at Seven Lakes, Hampton Hills, Tollgate, Smoky Ridge, Piny Creek and Chinnengo (listed from lowest to highest housing prices).

Nearby areas to consider: Highlands Ranch (15 mi. southwest), Mission Viejo and Smoky Hill are all desirable with upscale buyers. Aurora Highlands, Kingsborough, and Dam East are communities with good schools and affordable prices for first-time buyers.

What Things Cost

Runzheimer's Living Cost Index: Avg. annual costs for family of 4 with household income of $50,000: $47,770 (4.5% below avg. city).

ACCRA's national comparisons: Overall living costs in metro area are 2.5% above the national avg. The trouble spot is heath care costs (18.8% above). Housing and transportation are an estimated 5%-7% above. Groceries and utilities are 3%-4% below.

Utilities: Phone: $35 hookup; $14.48/mo. basic service. Water: No hookup charge unless building a home; there may be a $5,830 "tap fee." Gas/electric: Avg. $75-$80/mo.

Kid care: Licensed day care is at a premium, so inquire ASAP. In Adams County, costs range from $50/wk. for before-/after-school care to $80-$90/wk. for preschool care. In Arapahoe County (south Aurora), costs start at $45/wk. for before-/after-school to $145/wk. for all-day. **Pediatric visit:** $50.

The Tax Ax

Sales tax: 7.3% for most items (groceries, prescriptions exempt). Also a 2% "tourism tax" on meals & drinks for immediate consumption, rental cars, etc.

Property tax: In Aurora, assessments are 14.34% of home's present value (reassessed every 2 years). Multiply the assessed value by the district mill levy. A $100,000 house is assessed at $14,340. If the millage rate is 152.786 (avg. levy), property taxes would run $2,190/yr.

State income tax: 5% of modified federal taxable income.

Climate

Elevation 5,280'	Avg. High/Low	Avg. Rain (Inches)	Avg. Snow (Inches)	Avg. Days Rain	Avg. % Humidity
Jan.	44/16	.2	8	4	48
April	61/34	1	9	6	34
July	87/59	1.8	--	9	36
Oct.	67/37	.7	4	4	36
YEAR	64/36	11	61	70	40
# of days 32° or below: 164		# of days 90° or above: 32			

Aurora enjoys the mild, sunny, semi-arid climate of the Central Rocky Mountains. Wind is cut by the mountains. Hot and cold extremes are rare and when they do occur, are short-lived. A long distance from sources of moisture, humidity is low with relatively little precipitation—300 days a year are sunny and mild or warm.

Earning a Living

Economic outlook: No wonder *Fortune* magazine said the Denver metro was the 7th best American city for business. Things are looking up, no small thanks to the new Denver International Airport (east of Aurora), 50 sq. mi. in size. Just recently, United Air Lines announced construction of a $246 million line maintenance operation. Overall, the outlook is excellent because 1993 will be the 6th straight year of expansion. With the exception of mining and manufacturing, there's been job growth in every sector. Part of the success has been extensive business relocations and expansions including: Metropolitan Life; Merrill Lynch; Charles Schwab, Oppenheimer, Janus and other mutual fund companies and financial services; Southern Pacific Railway; GeoVision, a firm that does computerized mapping; and thanks to Nobel prize-winner Dr. Cech (University of Colorado at Bolder), many biotech and biomedical have been successfully launched here. Denver is headquarters to the largest cable operations in the country and is considered the birthplace of this fast-growing industry. The housing market, commercial development, retail and service sectors here are growing like crazy. The unemployment rate in Aurora is 4.2%, with 2%-3% annual job growth expected.

Where the jobs are: Denver's major employers include Lockheed, TRW, AT&T, U.S. West Communications, IBM, Adolf Coors and United Airlines. Recent business expansions and relocations include: Kaiser Permanente's $32 million construction of a medical specialty building; J.D. Edwards (integrated software systems); StorageTek computer hardware; American Express (adding 700 jobs to its Integrated Payment Systems group); Neodata Services, a magazine subscription marketing firm; Industrial Compliance Inc. (environmental cleanups) expects to grow from 165 to 600 by 1995; Sykes Enterprises Inc. (computer consulting) is adding 100 people to its Denver office; MCI is adding 450 new people to its telemarketing office; Lockheed Corp is establishing a computer operations headquarters, which will employ 200.

Business opportunities: High-tech, aviation and service industries are growing rapidly in anticipation of serving the new airport. In Aurora, businesses that appeal to young families are doing well (the median age is 31). The National Renewable Energy Laboratory has broken ground there on a $20 million facility that will research alternative energy sources. This will support companies in this area and will create spinoff need for services for alternative energy research.

Making the Grade

Public education overview: Aurora is divided into 2 districts: Aurora Public Schools and Cherry Creek. Aurora Public Schools boasts an ethnically diverse student population. Of the 25,000 total enrollment, more than 2,000 students come from homes where English is a second language. (Spanish, Korean and Vietnamese comprise more than half of the 53 language groups in the community.) There are 4 comprehensive high schools, an accredited alternative high school, a prize-winning technical center and 3 year-round elementary schools. Cherry Creek is perhaps the better known of the districts (includes part of Arapahoe County as well), having received frequent national recognition. Because curriculum decisions are made by the school administration, it meets community desires. Here, 85% of high school students take college entrance exams, graduation rate is 90.1%, and 75% of graduates go on to higher education. There's a School/Business Partnership Program, pairing various companies with schools and allowing them to work together creatively.

Class size: 25:1 in both districts.

Help for working parents: Before- and after-school care is provided in some schools from 7 a.m.-6 p.m. ($8-$14/day).

Blue Ribbon School Awards: Smoky Hill High School/Cherry Creek ('90-'91), Indian Ridge Elementary ('89-'90).

School year: Starts last wk. of Aug.to 1st wk. in June. Children must be 5 on or before Sept. 15 to enter kindergarten.

Special education/gifted programs: Aurora P.S.: Aurora Gifted and Talented Experience (AGATE) program for grades 3-5; approx. 3% participate in this program. Special programs and services are available for handicapped students 4-21 years. Cherry Creek: Special curriculum at elementary/middle levels, but no pull-out programs. Advanced placement and honors classes are offered in high school.

Nearby colleges/universities: In the area are: University of Colorado at Boulder; University of Colorado Springs; Colorado State University in Fort Collins; Colorado School of Mines (known for engineering) in Golden; University of Denver; and University of Colorado at Denver; Community College of Aurora (fastest-growing community college in the state); Columbia College of Aurora; Pickens Vocational Training Center; and Arapahoe Community College.

Medical Care

Hospitals/medical centers: The Denver area offers a wide range of top-quality medical care. Humana Hospital-Aurora is a full-service acute-care facility including a comprehensive cardio-vascular program, the Colorado Spine Center, the Diabetes Center of Excellence and the Women's Health Education network. Aurora Presbyterian Hospital is a full-service nonprofit medical center with cancer support services, a rehabilitation/fitness center, women's health, and emergency medicine and occupational health services. Major hospitals in Denver include Rose Medical Center, Denver General, St. Joseph's and University Hospital. University of Colorado Medical Center (Denver) is a teaching/research hospital that offers comprehensive inpatient and outpatient services, and a well-known cancer center, AIDS Clinical Trial Group and specialties in allergies and immunology.

Specialized care: Aurora Community Mental Health Center; Children's Hospital; Center at Porter Memorial Hospital (chemical dependency treatment; Mercy Medical Center (alcohol and drug abuse treatment); Aurora Center for Treatment (outpatient drug and alcohol program); The National Jewish Center for Immunology and Respiratory Medicine (the only hospital in the country dedicated exclusively to treating respiratory, allergic, and immunologic diseases).

Crime & Safety

The Aurora Police Dept. provides home security checks and sponsors neighborhood watch programs. Although gangs have been in the area for awhile, they've only recently been in the limelight because the department started a gang intervention unit (it keeps files on all known gang members). The result is that violent crimes such as homicide, assault, and rape are down, as the penalties for such crimes are much stiffer than for nonviolent crimes.

Community Life

People in Aurora get involved in a number of ways. First, there is great support for youth sports. Performers in the community theater, choral group, and orchestra are local citizens, not professionals. These organizations perform at the Aurora Fox Arts Center. Several hundred people volunteer at the Senior Center, providing meals and programs. Residents get involved in beautification, planting flowers and shrubs in local parks. A program called "Rent-a-Teen," lets residents and businesses call a central number to hire teenagers to do odd jobs.

Let the Good Times Roll

Family fun: Colorado's outdoor action is unsurpassed. Start with some of the best skiing in the world. Nearby ski areas include Arrowhead, Beaver Creek, Keystone/North Peak, Loveland Basin and Valley, Vail, Aspen and Breckenridge. Aurora's proximity to the Rocky Mountains and too many state parks, forests and recreational areas to count offers a whole lot more than just winter action. In warmer months, take a short drive for horseback riding, hiking, river running, fishing, sailing, hunting, mountain-climbing or rockhounding. Rocky Mountain National Park is Colorado's largest, with 78 peaks more than 12,000 feet high. Aurora has more than 50 local parks with amenities such as indoor swimming, bicycle paths, and tennis courts. Area attractons include the U.S. Mint, Denver Museum of Natural History, Denver Botanic Gardens, Denver Zoo, Museum of Western Art, Buffalo Bill Memorial Museum, and Colorado Science Center. Also, there's Elitch Gardens amusement park, Big Fun (an indoor high-tech playground), and Celebrity Sports Center, built by Walt Disney, with water slides, pools, bowling and arcades.

Sports: Watch the Nuggets (NBA) at the Denver Coliseum, the Broncos (NFL) at Mile High Stadium; and, starting in 1993, the Rockies (expansion National League baseball team) in the new Coors Stadium. Collegiate sports action is offered by Colorado University, Colorado College, University of Denver and Colorado State. There's minor-league baseball with the AAA Denver Zephyrs.

Arts & entertainment: The country's 2nd-largest performing arts center is the Denver Center for the Performing Arts, featuring the Denver Symphony Orchestra, the Colorado Ballet, the Denver Opera, Young Artists Orchestra, Children's Chorale, Denver Center Theater, Festival Ballet and Colorado Contemporary Dance. In addition, there are numerous theatrical companies, opera and musical performances throughout the city. The Aurora Fox Arts Center is home to the Aurora Singers and the Aurora Symphony Orchestra. The Denver Art Museum has Native American art, modern art, and art from around the world. Other museums include the Black American West Museum, the Colorado History Museum, and the Museum of Western Art.

Annual events: Taste of Colorado, food fair (Aug.); People's Fair, crafts and entertainment, (Mem. Day wknd.); Octoberfest (Sept.); Cinquo de Mayo, Mexican and Hispanic celebration (May); National Western Stock Show (Jan.); Gateway to the Rockies parade (Sept.); Fourth of July celebration; Aurora Memorial 5K Run/Walk (Nov.).

The Environment

Aurora's water is excellent—in 1990 it was rated #1 in a Denver-area taste test—and is well within environmental guidelines for pollutants. Air quality is usually good, although the metro area is not in compliance with federal standards for carbon monoxide. It is close to compliance, and should be by 1995. The area also experiences inversions in winter, causing smog. On high-pollution days, residents are advised not to use woodburning stoves. The electric utility has upgraded its coal-fired generators to reduce emissions; drivers are advised to use gasoline with high oxygen content. Closer to Aurora, there is a Superfund site, within the Lowry landfill, that is being studied for a clean-up that should take place in the next 2 years.

In and Around Town

Roads and interstates: I-70, I-25, I-76; U.S. 6, 36, 40, 85, 87, 285, 287.
Closest airports: Stapleton International Airport, just north of Aurora; new Denver International Airport (opening late 1993), just east of Aurora
Public transportation: Regional Transportation District (Denver) operates bus lines to Aurora from its downtown Denver terminals, and also several lines within Aurora itself. Basic fare is 50¢ to $1. Express bus service to downtown Denver is $1.50; intercity service (for example, to Boulder) is $2.50.
Avg. commute: 25-40 min. from Aurora to downtown Denver in rush hour.

What Every Resident Knows

With all the tourist attractions in the area, nearby Boulder is still one of the most popular. For the thirtysomething crowd, the appeal is a throwback to the purist years. Supermarket aisles are devoted to tofu and bulk grains, there are metaphysical book stores, palm readers and vegetarian restaurants. Forget local interests, here you get a take on the entire universe. • Don't party too hearty at first. Even experienced drinkers can be affected by alcohol contents at this altitude. Talk about Rocky Mountain High! Cooks must also allow for the altitude. The lower air pressure means that water boils at a lower temperature—which means you have to cook things longer. If the directions on the box say cook for 8 minutes, make it 15!

FYI

Aurora Chamber of Commerce
3131 S. Vaughn Way, Suite 622
Aurora, CO 80014
303-755-5000

Denver Metro Convention & Visitors Bureau
225 W. Colfax Avenue
Denver, CO 80202
303-892-1112

Denver Post
1560 Broadway
Denver, CO 80202
303-832-3232

Aurora Sentinel (Weekly)
1730 S. Abilene, #203
Aurora, CO 80012
303-750-7555

Re/Max Brokers
13770 East Rice Place
Aurora, CO 80015
303-693-6666
Gary Brockway, Sales Associate

Re/Max 3000
3091 S. Jamaica Ct., Suite 100
Aurora, CO 80014
800-336-3555
Marilyn Kanne

Public Service Company
9722 East 16th Avenue
Aurora, CO 80231
303-623-1234

U.S. West Communications
303-896-1111 (Call collect)

Economic Development Council
15701 E 1st Avenue, Suite 206
Aurora, CO 80011
303-340-2101

Small Business Assistance Center
9915 E. Colfax Avenue
Aurora, CO 80010
303-361-0847

School districts: Cherry Creek Schools 303-773-1184; Aurora Schools 303-344-8060
Property tax assessor: Arapahoe County 303-795-4600; Adams County 303-654-6038
Newcomer's Club: 303-751-9523
Interfaith Council: 303-940-8439
Physician's referral: 303-695-2607
Day-care referral: 303-534-2625

Coral Springs, Florida

Area Snapshot

Local population: 83,000
County: Broward   **Population:** 1,278,384
U.S. region: Southeast Florida/Lower Gold Coast
Closest metro areas: Ft. Lauderdale (10 mi. southeast), Miami (23 mi. south)
Median housing price: $105,100
Avg. household income: $43,200
Best reasons to live here: One of the most successful planned communities in the U.S., fabulous neighborhoods, award-winning parks, endless family recreation and events, best public schools in the county, no state income tax.

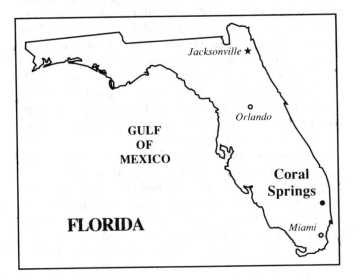

Fabulous Features

Just as with a fine wine, some places get better with age. Coral Springs, a thriving planned city, is owned by Westinghouse Electric Corp. (it was originally conceived as a showcase for the company's technological innovations). When it opened in 1963, homes sold out immediately, but not because of self-cleaning pools or lights that turned on with a wave of a hand.

The "brightest" idea Westinghouse had was their choice of location. Situated midway between Miami and West Palm Beach, Coral Springs turned out to be at the epicenter of Florida's growth. Since 1980, its population has increased by an overwhelming 166% (yes, you read correctly)! Today the community is young (median age is 34), active (there are 600 organized teams playing every competitive sport), and a safe place to live (crime is the lowest of any city in the state with the same population).

The ocean is 30 minutes by car, the same as the commute to Ft. Lauderdale. As a master-planned community, everything is at your doorstep: the impressive Coral Springs Medical Center, shopping malls, parks and recreational programs, and award-winning public schools (a rarity in Florida). Although real estate prices are higher than other parts of the state (expect to spend $175,000-$250,000), the homes range from moderate to magnificent.

Possible drawbacks: The past two years have been rough ones for the ABCs of south Florida's economy—airlines, banking and construction. Layoffs have resulted in an 8% unemployment rate. Ironically, companies are relocating here because of high levels of unemployed and *under*employed (it's a gold mine for labor-hungry companies). • Living in a planned community may remind you of living under your parent's roof. If you don't abide by their laws, trouble ensues. Coral Ridge Properties is a no-nonsense authority figure. Some claim the developer goes overboard with protective covenants, but you can't knock their success • Florida summers are hot, humid and rainy. Adjustment periods vary, but the first year is the worst year (remember—subtropical climates offer little change).

"You can quote me on that"

"Everybody tells you how bad the schools are in Florida, but it's not true here. My youngest is doing work in 1st grade that my older kids didn't touch until 3rd grade in New York. The only bad thing about Coral Springs is that it's getting to be expensive. Our property taxes are almost what we used to pay on Long Island. But believe me, it's worth it. We have a very nice life."—B.D.

Real Estate

Market overview: The Coral Springs real estate market is like Wall Street—buyers and sellers are never in short supply. Thanks to the tremendous volume of new construction, the buyer is boss. Homes are so attractive, people get caught up in the "Grab it 'cause there's not another one like it" syndrome. Nothing could be further from the truth! More than 50 independent builders have been approved by Coral Ridge Properties, and that creates an abundant supply of housing.

What houses look like: Out-of-town buyers are thrilled with the "Florida" look: new, clean and bright. Most homes are ranch-style, although some new models offer traditional 2-story layouts. Models show high, flat ceilings, master suites, Florida rooms, European-style kitchens and screened-in pools. The most popular layouts are stacked (BRs on one side of the house) or splits (master BR on one side). Exteriors are concrete block with stucco.

Starter homes: New home prices range from $130,000-$150,000 and buy a 4BR/2BA house (1800-2200 sq. ft.) including 2-car garages, eating area off the kitchen, and sliders off several rooms leading to the pool (add $18,000 for patio, pool and cage). Lot sizes avg. 75 x 125.

Trade-ups: For $175-$250,000 you can buy new 4BR/2½-3½BA homes in Kensington and other developments. Homes are spacious (2300-3000 sq. ft.), and layouts show high ceilings, large sliders off the master suite and a full bath separating the children's bedrooms. Brookside and North Springs have many homes in this price range.

Luxury homes: Custom-built homes from $250,000 to $1 million are unlimited. Often situated on canals and/or cul-de-sacs, these 3000-5000 sq. ft. showplaces have 4-5BR/3-4BA layouts complete with covered courtyards, cabana baths, European-style kitchens and breakfast rooms off the pool area. Look at Eagle Trace, Fairway South and Lake Coral Springs (with its first phase, The Isles).

Rental market: Single-family home rentals are limited and expensive, with avg. rent at $1,200-$1,500/mo. Apartments and condos (2BR) are in much greater supply, with avg. rent $450-$500/mo.

Great neighborhoods: Brookside Court, Westview Village and Kensington are just some developments showing homes in all price ranges.

Nearby areas to consider: Parkland, adjacent to Coral Springs, is a small (pop. 6,000), peaceful community known for its horse farms and trails. The Landings, Coral Ridge Properties latest development, offers larger lots and quiet surroundings. Home prices start at $200,000.

What Things Cost

Runzheimer's Living Cost Index: Avg. annual costs for family of 4 with household income of $50,000: $50,633 (1.3% above avg. city).

ACCRA's national comparisons: The closest metro area ranked is West Palm Beach/Boca Raton (16 mi). Total living costs are 10.5% above the national average. Food and transportation are below (3%-5%), while utilities and housing are well above (34% and 19% respectively). Health care is 13.5% above.

Utilities: Phone: $14/mo. Installations range from $44-$75. Avg. monthly utilities run $90 (Jan.), $110 (April) and $275 (July-Aug.).

Kid care: There are 30 family/licensed day-care centers in the city. The avg. cost is $80/wk. for preschoolers (infant care avg. $95/wk.) There is also a licensed drop-off baby-sitting service for days, evenings and weekends (Avg. cost is $4/hr.). **Pediatric visit:** Avg. $50-$57.

The Tax Ax

Sales tax: 6% (food, medicine and professional services exempt).

Property tax: Florida offers a $25,000 homestead exemption for permanent residents whose principle home is in the state. Property taxes are based on millage rates (the current rate in Coral Springs is 24.53). A rule of thumb is to calculate 2% of the home's market value. For example, a home valued at $200,000 would pay approximately $4,000/yr.

State income tax: None.

Climate

Elevation 5'	Avg. High/Low	Avg. Rain (Inches)	Avg. Snow (Inches)	Avg. Days Rain	Avg. % Humidity
Jan.	76/59	2.2	--	7	59
April	83/67	3.6	--	6	52
July	89/76	7	--	16	63
Oct.	85/71	8.2	--	15	63
YEAR	83/68	59.8	--	129	59
# of days 32° or below: 0			# of days 90° or above: 31		

People have a love/hate relationship with Florida weather. When friends up north complain about windchill factors, it's great! When the temperature *and* humidity reach 98, you wonder why you stay. Although ocean breezes moderate the heat, they also make the area prone to hurricanes. Afternoon showers are frequent, short and predictable.

Earning a Living

Economic outlook: Several factors have temporarily taken the wind out of South Florida's sails. The collapse of Eastern and Braniff airlines put thousands of people out of work. The savings and loans debacle hit hard, resulting in bank closings, consolidations and layoffs. Finally, the construction business fell apart with the slowdown in newcomers. The bottom line is an 8% unemployment rate. But there are plenty of bright spots, and one reason is, believe it or not, high unemployment. With so many qualified people out of work or underemployed, businesses are relocating to take advantage of the educated labor force. Kemper Insurance will be moving a 200-person office into a new 100,000 sq. ft. office in Plantation and hiring 800 more to fill it. NA Banco, a credit card clearing agency (Sunrise), will be hiring several hundred workers, Humana Hospital's data processing operation (Miramar) will be hiring 500 people, and a division of a major biomedical conglomerate will be employing 300 people (Weston). The biggest fish in these waters, however, is Florida's first major league baseball team. Starting in 1993, the Florida Marlins are projected to pump $100 million into the economy (jobs, tickets, concessions, parking, etc.). That could well be the impetus that turns the tide.

Where the jobs are: Because of the close proximity to Latin America, locally based international trading companies are affecting the economy. Recently Basic Food International (Broward County) was named the top international business in Florida. As for employment opportunities, there is a demand for paralegals, banking/credit card employees, medical technicians, suppliers and computer/high-tech workers. Although Jordan Marsh is gone, business at Mervyns, Biz Mart, Target, Cosco, Home Depot and Sam's Warehouses is promising.

Business opportunities: Import/export companies, high-tech manufacturing, biomedical companies and computer-related services are perfect for the area. Restaurants, small retail and marine products are experiencing high failure rates.

"You can quote me on that"

"My wife would never come to Florida, even for a vacation. She hated the weather. But when a business opportunity came up, she agreed to try it for a year. That was three years ago, and now she'd never leave. I come home at 6:30 and I've got the whole evening to play tennis, swim, or just be with my family."—L.L.

Making the Grade

Public education overview: Florida takes a lot of "heat" for the dismal state of public education, but in Coral Springs, children attend first-rate schools. Although class sizes are large, top honors, awards, and recognition are constant. When Coral Ridge Realty published a booklet about the schools, it took 40 pages to list all the citations and success stories (see FYI). For example, the high schools have produced 10 Westinghouse Science Talent Search winners as well as a consistently large number of graduates who enter Ivy League schools. Overall, 85% of high school grads go on to college, and test scores remain above county and national averages. Recently Coral Spring Middle School was identified as one of the 10 best in the country (Department of Education)! Success is attributed to a tremendous level of parental involvement, highly progressive curriculum and salaries (teachers are the second highest paid in the state). Team Teaching and Project Read (older children teach younger ones) are examples of "group thinking" that have been instrumental in the district's success.

Class size: Kindergarten-25:1; grades 1-5, 28:1 (28 or more requires an aide); grades 6-8, 32:1.

Help for working parents: Coral Springs operates under "school-based management." Each school develops programs to address its particular needs. Some have programs offering everything from computer games to homework help. Others open at 7 a.m. and serve breakfast.

Blue Ribbon School Awards: Coral Springs Middle School ('90-'91), J.P. Taravella High School ('88-'89).

School year: Last week of Aug. through mid-June. Children must be 5 on or before Sept. 1 to enter kindergarten.

Special education/gifted programs: A teleconferencing network links challenging math instruction classes from Tallahassee. Field and laboratory experiences match students and teachers to enhance skills. Children with auditory, language and learning disabilities have access to a unique curriculum that eliminates typical barriers. There are also "niche" programs for at-risk students.

Nearby colleges/universities: There are 17 institutions within commuting distance. Nova University at Coral Springs offers programs for postgraduates and is widely respected for its master's degree programs at the Friedt School of Business and Entrepreneurship and the Center for Psychological studies. Other colleges include Broward Community College North, Florida Atlantic University and Atlantic Vocational-Technical Center.

Medical Care

Hospitals/medical centers: North Broward's 4 public hospitals are Joint Commission Accredited and have Chest Pain Emergency Units. The newest hospital (and only one in Coral Springs) is the Coral Springs Medical Center, which has state-of-the-art surgical services and family care (it delivers 1,000 babies each year). It offers a Level II neonatal intensive care unit, fully equipped maternity suites and a highly respected pediatric pavilion. It will soon have an Emergency Trauma Unit and helipad. In addition, there are 10 private hospitals in the area.

Specialized care: In Ft. Lauderdale, there's The Children's Diagnostic and Treatment Center, MED-WORK (occupational, industrial medicine for Broward County employees), and the Broward General Heart Institute. The Cleveland Clinic opened a satellite office for outstanding diagnostic care (soon to open a large hospital).

Crime & Safety

Coral Springs has the lowest crime rate in Florida for a city this size. Of course, it has its share of trouble spots. Burglaries and vandalism are the most predominant problems, and as of late, the police are coping with child abuse cases and even gang violence. The answer is increased visibility. Police have a presence in every school (for drug awareness programs and to monitor activities). In addition, officers who live in the city can take their patrol cars home so they can intervene in incidents occuring while off duty as well as providing a sense of protection in their neighborhoods. Residents spoke of feeling safe in the community and having confidence in the police.

Community Life

What's wonderful about new communities is that residents move there by choice and feel a vested interest, insuring that the city maintains a high quality of life. Coral Springs epitomizes this community spirit. It started in 1963 with the creation of the Volunteer Fire Department. Today a group of 100 trained fire fighters responds to an average of 1,200 calls a year (response time is 4.5 min.). Other large-scale volunteer efforts include the thousands of parents who manage the 600 organized sports teams. There's even a new program called Adopt-A-Mile, in which residents pick one mile in the city to monitor for violations, repairs, and any other problems the city should be aware of.

Let the Good Times Roll

Family fun: Coral Springs *is* Kids' Town, USA. Everything is geared toward kids' enjoyment and interests. How else can you account for the fact that parents have organized 280 Little League teams? There is a total of 600 organized teams playing every major competitive sport. That's 6,000 games a year at Mullins and Cypress Parks. The city provides the fields, but parents do everything else. Fortunately the city's parks are winners, too! The Coral Springs Parks and Recreation Department has received ample national recognition, such as the Amateur Athletic Union Department of the Year award and the National Park Maintenance Award. The brand-new Aquatic/Fitness Complex has a 50-meter competition pool, a beautiful gymnasium and exercise area, and professional trainers.

Sports: Professional sports in south Florida is now covering all the bases! The Miami Dolphins (NFL) were the first to arrive. Last year they were joined by the Miami Heat (NBA), and now there is tremendous excitement since major league baseball awarded the first Florida franchise to the National League's Florida Marlins (they'll play in Miami). The Atlanta Braves and Montreal Expos have spring training camps in Palm Beach. Throughout the year there are numerous events at Coral Springs parks, including the International Invitational Soccer Tournament and the AAU Men's Masters Basketball National Championship.

Arts & entertainment: The brand-new City Center has already brought great family entertainment to town. Comedienne Paula Poundstone, singer Bobby Rydell and actress Lynn Redgrave are just a few of the stars who have graced the 1,500-seat theater. There are also an amphitheater and dance studio. The Coral Springs Cultural Center presents everything from children's musicals to dance workshops to delightful plays as well as the Coral Springs Pops (25 live performances a year). For road tours of Broadway shows, take a short ride to the Broward Center of Performing Arts in Ft. Lauderdale. In nearby Boca, there are so many cultural events, call 800-ARTSLINE to find out what's coming to the area.

Annual events: Our Town Festival (attracts hundreds of thousands to Coral Springs—in the fall); Hollywood Jazz Festival (fall); Jaycees River Raft Race (Ft. Lauderdale, fall); Orange Bowl (Miami, winter); Riverwalk Art Festival (Ft. Lauderdale, winter); Broward County Winterfest and the Annual Holiday Boat Parades (Ft. Lauderdale and Pompano Beach).

The Environment

Coral Springs' environment gets a clean bill of health. There are no landfills (garbage is disposed of through nonpolluting incineration), days aren't placed under smog alerts, and water quality meets all EPA requirements (chlorinated and fluoridated). There are strict preservation ordinances to preserve the woodlands (Broward County borders the Everglades National Park) and in fact, a Coral Springs High School biology class recently created an organization called "Save What's Left." It was instrumental in having ordinances passed guaranteeing further protection of wooded sites. There has been a 90% response rate to the curbside and drop-off recycling centers programs. During a 5-month period, the city recycles enough newspaper to save 20,000 trees.

In and Around Town

Roads and interstates: I-95, Florida Tpk., Federal Highway (U.S. 1), State Road 7, A1A, and the Sawgrass Expressway (23-mi. road connecting 17 northern communities to Dade County).
Closest airport(s): The Palm Beach, Ft. Lauderdale and Miami International Airports are all within 30-45 min.
Public transportation: Commuting has improved considerably since the recent introduction of the Tri-Rail Monorail System. Trains travel from Palm Beach to Metro Dade (Miami) in approximately 25 min. One way fare is $1.
Avg. commute: 15-30 min. to Ft. Lauderdale and other areas in Broward County; 30-45 min. to Miami.

What Every Resident Knows

Why does everyone in Coral Springs look familiar? Because they came from the same place you did! With such a large number of people moving from New York, the most popular expression is "Hey, look who's here from Massapequa!" • Batter up! There are more Little League teams here than anywhere else in the country. Parents have organized 280 different teams, about 50 more than they have in Houston, the 2nd highest-ranked city. • "Hot town, summer in the city" means farewell to jackets and ties. Office attire, even among executives, gets very casual. • When in Florida, do as the Floridians do. Buy a boat, grab a fishing pole or learn how to waterski. Between here and the Keys are some of the world's most glorious natural resources.

FYI

Coral Springs Chamber of Commerce
9801 West Sample Road
Coral Springs, FL 33065
305-752-4242

Southern Bell
800-753-0710

Fort Lauderdale Sun-Sentinel
800-548-NEWS (6397)

Broward Review
800-777-7300

*Coral Ridge Realty, Inc.
9335 West Sample Road
Coral Springs, FL 33065
800-633-4038, 305-752-1100
Ann Hamels

Florida Power & Light Co.
1982 N. State Rd. 7
Margate, FL 33063
305-797-5000

Century 21/Tenace Realty
1835 University Drive
Coral Springs, FL 33071
305-755-2100
Jean Blair

Coldwell Banker Residential Real Estate
2868 University Drive
Coral Springs, FL 33065
305-752-3000
Brenda Ghibaudy

Commerce & Economic Development Department
9551 West Sample Road
Coral Springs, FL 33075
305-344-1075

Welcome Wagon: 305-739-1674
School district: 305-765-6285
Parochial school: 305-753-1280, 305-752-2870
Property tax assessor: 305-765-4630
**Interfaith council: None
Physicians referral: 305-739-2305
Childcare connection: (Broward County) 305-486-3900
Jobline: 305-344-5920

*Contact them for their "Education: Learning and Progressing," an in-depth look at Coral Springs public and private schools (free).

**For a list of churches and synagogues, contact the Citizens Service Department at 305-344-1001.

Fort Myers, Florida

Area Snapshot

Local population: 45,206
County: Lee **Population:** 335,113
U.S. region: Southwest Florida
Closest metro areas: Tampa (119 mi. north),
Fort Lauderdale (97 mi. southeast)
Median housing price: $70,100
Avg. household income: $35,686
Best reasons to live here: Subtropical climate and one of the "hottest" job markets in the country, real estate in all price ranges, greatly improved school system, gorgeous Gulf Coast beaches, no state income tax.

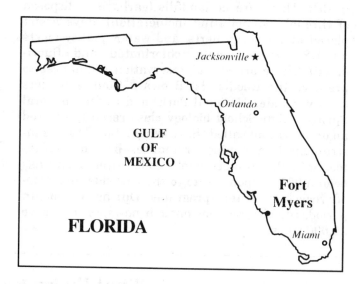

Fabulous Features

Thomas Edison made more than one great discovery when he settled in Fort Myers back in 1855. What a "bright" idea to live on the dazzling Gulf of Mexico! It still is, which explains the area's population explosion since 1980—an overwhelming 63.2 percent! If moving to a fast-growing area is a top priority, you might as well head to the one place projected to lead the country in job, income and population growth by the year 2000.

If you're under the impression it's only retirees coming down, think again. The median age in Fort Myers is 32.2. What do these people know that you don't? For starters, with no state income tax, reasonable real estate costs (the median housing prices are the lowest of all Florida's major metro areas), and abundant job and business opportunities (medical care, financial services and data processing fields are booming), this city can cure what ails you!

Speaking of which, the most unique medical center in the country just opened here. Health Park Florida, a cross between a glitzy indoor mall and a luxury hotel, is actually an acute-care hospital and physicians' office complex.

As for schools, a new superintendent has turned the Lee County district upside down, paving the way for seven innovative magnet schools, more new schools, and the need for an additional 250-350 teachers a year. Adding to the excitement is the area's crown jewel, the quartz sand beaches and sunny, sub-tropical climate. Newcomers ask, "Is it always this beautiful?" The answer? Only 99% of the time.

Possible drawbacks: You're not crazy about summer heat and humidity? Or lightning and thunderstorms you can set your watch to? Better check out another city. • While jobs are here for the asking, wages and salary levels are shockingly low. They're 9% below the state average, and Florida never broke any records for high pay to begin with! The salvation is lower overall living costs, but paychecks for experienced workers can be comparable to starting salaries elsewhere. • Property taxes and land values have soared, and it's hard to predict how high is up. Some are concerned about eventually being priced out of the market altogether.

"You can quote me on that"

"We moved from Virginia to pursue careers in real estate. It's very competitive, but we love our life-style. The weather is fantastic and there's so much to do, there's even more an hour away."—M.P.

Real Estate

Market overview: Fort Myers experienced a ripple effect from poor real estate sales up north. Inventory sat and prices dropped 2%-4% since last year. Now, with lower interest rates, it's a great time to buy! New construction has leveled off, but there are ample new and nearly new homes on the market. Sellers still get their price for waterfront properties. Comparison shop 'til you drop. The homes are so gorgeous, people are easily enticed before they really know what they're looking at.

What houses look like: The typical Florida home is a 1-story concrete block with stucco (anything less sturdy couldn't withstand the climate). Most new interiors show the split plan (master BR opposite from other BRs), vaulted ceilings, carports or garages, large island kitchens and lanais (screened porches), and caged pools. Distinctive landscape design, huge master BAs and ceiling fans are Florida trademarks.

Starter homes: Modest 2BR/2BA home resales (20-30 years old) range from $60,000-$70,000. Fort Myers Villas and San Carlos Park are popular with young families. Most are 1000-1200 sq. ft. homes on 80 x 100 lots with carports.

Trade-ups: 3BR/2BA homes (1400-2000 sq. ft) are in the $100,000-$140,000 range (80 x 110 lots). Beautiful entries with arched widows and gardens greet you. Most are Mediterraneans with caged pools, 2-car garages and bright, airy rooms. Look at Caloosa Trace, Tanglewood and Brookshire (racquetball and junior Olympic-sized pool).

Luxury homes: For $175,000 to $225,000 are 3-4BR/2-3BA homes (1600-1800 sq. ft.) with high entryways (pillars and canopies), multilevel roof lines, designer island kitchens, huge master suites, marble jacuzzi tubs and tremendous walk-in closets. Waterfront property avg. is $275,000+. Town and River, Iona/McGregor and Palmetto Park are exquisite communities.

Rental market: Due to heavy tourist trade, rental homes are near impossible to find, not to mention costly. In season, a 2-3BR beachfront home goes for $1,200/wk. Off season, rents range from $650 to $1,200/mo. 2BR/2BA condos are $450-$800/mo (higher prices are furnished units).

Great neighborhoods: Gateway, Whiskey Creek, The Forest, Fiddlesticks and Eagle Ridge.

Nearby areas to consider: Cape Coral is a big bedroom community (pop. 75,000) perfect for young families. Homes are less costly, schools are excellent (several Blue Ribbon schools), and a second dual-span bridge makes commuting to Fort Myers easier than ever (avg. 15 min.).

What Things Cost

Runzheimer's Living Cost Index: Avg. annual costs for family of 4 with household income of $50,000: $47,774 (4.5% below avg. city).

ACCRA's national comparisons: Not available. But according to the latest Florida Price Level Index, Lee County is neither below nor above avg. for overall living costs.

Utilities: Avg. electric (no gas available) is $80/mo. except for summers (expect bills to double). Phone: $20/mo. with a $30 line activation charge. Water and sewer charges avg. $29/mo. Residents also pay an avg. $225/yr. for trash collection.

Kid care: Most licensed day-care centers charge $25-$35 registration fees. **Pediatric visit:** $40.

The Tax Ax

Sales tax: 6% (food, medicine and some professional services exempt).

Property tax: Florida offers a $25,000 homestead exemption for permanent residents whose principle home is in the state. Property taxes are based on millage rates (the total tax rate for homes in Fort Myers is 18.1614). A quick rule of thumb is taxes average 1 1/4% of a home's appraised value. For example, a $100,000 home would run approximately $1,250/yr.

State income tax: None. However, there is an intangibles tax on stocks, bonds and other securities at the rate of $1 per $1,000 of valuation.

Climate

Elevation 10'	Avg. High/Low	Avg. Rain (Inches)	Avg. Snow (Inches)	Avg. Days Rain	Avg. % Humidity
Jan.	75/52	1.6	--	5	57
April	85/62	2	--	5	48
July	91/74	8.9	--	18	60
Oct.	85/68	4.4	--	8	57
YEAR	84/64	54	--	113	56
# of days 32° or below: 1			# of days 90° or above: 121		

Situated on the sparkling Gulf of Mexico, Fort Myers' subtropical climate brings 12 months of warm to hot days and cool, comfortable evenings. Humidity is the bad news, reaching an avg. 80% in the day. May through Sept. brings frequent if not daily thunderstorms. The hurricane watch lasts May through Nov. Winters are delightfully mild.

Earning a Living

Economic outlook: Forget that *retirees* used to be the city's biggest import. Today the city just wakes up in the morning and it's earned another stripe for growth or achievement! It is one of the fastest-growing headquarters in the U.S. of high-tech manufacturing, medical services, warehousing and distribution, and financial services (trade and service jobs grew 28% and 32% respectively since 1980). Although still reeling from bank failures and mergers (the merger of NCNB and C&S/Sovran could lay off up to 500 people), the mortgage market is more than holding its own (the Lomas "Hotness" index rates FortMyers/Cape Coral as third in the nation for the ratio of residential building permits to population). At present, unemployment is 4.4% (well below state and national levels). Education remains the county's largest employer and will continue to be, with the recent announcement of Florida's newest 4-year university, scheduled to open in 1996. Several health care manufacturers from the East are soon expected to announce their relocation to the area.

Where the jobs are: Lee County has been ranked the fastest-growing job market in the U.S., with more than 100,000 new jobs to be created by the end of the decade. Medical care is one of the fastest-growing segments of southwest Florida's burgeoning economy (combined investment of new/expanded health care facilities is $175 million), and brings the promise of thousands of jobs. For example, Health Park Florida (see Medical Care) will continue to expand until it reaches its 10-story, 400-physician office capacity. Nursing care, technicians and staff openings will be substantial. Some of the largest and/or newest employers to move here include the U.S. Postal Service (regional processing center will employ 500+, but expect them to periodically expand and contract), Intertech Resources and Sussex Electronics (medical manufacturing), GE Client Business Services (accounting, payroll), and Garrity Industries (second-largest maker of flashlights is opening a large distribution center).

Business opportunities: Based on job growth, number of business starts and the percentage of young, "hot" companies, *Inc.* magazine consistently identifies Fort Myers/Cape Coral to be among the top 20 cites for entrepreneurs to relocate or start a business. *Kiplinger's Personal Finance* magazine also identified Fort Myers as one of 15 "supercities"—the best places to look for a job, launch or relocate a business. Lee County has targeted data processing and financial services as its number one recruitment priority.

Making the Grade

Public education overview: A new superintendant is making things happen! After a one-year trial, there will be 7 magnet schools in Fort Myers, including the Edison Park Creative-Expressive Arts School and the Franklin Park Science-Technology Environment (they were huge successes in terms of record attendance, intensive parental involvement and high energy levels among teachers and students). Other positive improvements include use of school-based management, the start of technology-based classes in all schools, and dramatic curriculum changes. The most tangible result is the district's SAT scores. It finally ranked above the state average (it shot up 16 points!). Also, in Florida's Student Assessment Tests, Lee County students beat Dade, Hillsborough (Tampa), and Orange County (Orlando) scores, demonstrating the greatest percentage mastery over basic skills (grades 3-8). Voluntary desegregation has also been a top priority. Lee County is under federal court order to move toward equitable distribution of resources, and with the creation of more magnet schools, it'll soon reach its goal. Now for the downside. Class size is too high (budget cuts are the cause), parental involvement is shameful (parents blame lack of communication from schools), and state funding cuts continue. With the tremendous growth rate, the district has a full plate of challenges, but rest assured, no previous administration has ever shown more courage or determination in moving forward.

Class size: 30:1.

Help for working parents: The YMCA and the Parks and Recreation Department offer many educational and recreational programs after school.

Blue Ribbon School Awards: Fort Myers Middle School ('90-'91), Fort Myers High School ('84-'85). Cape Coral has four Blue Ribbon schools (Caloosa Middle School is most recent).

School year: Last week of Aug. to mid-June. Children must be 5 on or before Sept. 1 to enter kindergarten.

Special education/gifted programs: Handicapped students attend special classes within the schools and will eventually be mainstreamed. The severely physically and emotionally handicapped attend special centers.

Nearby colleges/universities: Edison Community College and University of South Florida (branch campus in Fort Myers). A new 4-year state university is scheduled to open in Lee County in 1996 (unofficially named Florida Gulf University).

Medical Care

Hospitals/medical centers: Southwest Florida is fast emerging as the "medical mecca" of the Southeast with its profusion of state-of-the-art facilities. Gulf Coast Hospital is a general medical/surgical facility that will soon be the only teaching hospital south of Tampa. It is the only acute-care hospital in the county that has dual accreditation (JCAH and American Osteopathic Association). An obstetrical unit and pediatric unit are planned. Its Basic Card program allows anyone with health insurance to reduce their hospital bills. Lee Memorial Hospital has a diabetes center, the George M. Cox Cancer Center and an excellent cardiac unit. Both hospitals also offer physical therapy services. Southwest Florida Regional Medical Center offers dialysis.

Specialized care: The new Health Park Florida has 200 beds, 60 doctors' offices, with a nursing home and child development center in the works. Fort Myers also has The Eye Center, one of 10 sites in the U.S. to experiment with laser surgery to correct nearsightedness.

Crime & Safety

Many told us without hesitation that, despite increased drug-related crime, Fort Myers was a safe place to live. Last year there were 8 murders and a lower per-capita crime rate compared to the rest of the state. Auto theft shot up 60%, but there's still less than a 3% chance a car will be stolen. City police and county sheriff's departments run programs for at-risk children—the "A-Team" (officers help 6th-8th graders with academics and share community service projects) and "Grandpa Cops" (retired officers teach grade school students about stranger danger and more). STARS (Success Through Academic and Recreational Support) is a youth facility you must "earn" membership in. It all contributes to a low per-capita crime rate.

Community Life

The Fort Myers annual Edison Festival of Light is a month-long festival and culminates with the Pageant Parade. It is such a "can't miss" event, people put out chairs or tape off sections of a block a month in advance to be sure of a good view! Other efforts that get tremendous support are Jimmy Carter's Habitat for Humanity effort (several hundred residents build homes for the needy) and "Paint Your Heart Out," a "Keep Lee County Beautiful" program in which volunteers paint the homes of elderly or low-income residents.

Let the Good Times Roll

Family fun: The expansive 38-mile shoreline is all the invitation you need to enjoy water recreation year-round. Between the intoxicating Gulf of Mexico, the Caloosahatchee River and Pine Island Sound, you can swim, sail and fish to your heart's content (tarpon fishing is best from Boca Grande and Pine Island). If shelling is more your style, welcome to the world's "Seashell Capital" (don't forget your plastic bag for collecting sand dollars). Back on land are beautiful parks (Lakes Park is great for paddleboating), nature trails and the Everglades Wonder Garden (exotic wildlife). There are 4 National Wildlife Refuges in the area (the J.N. "Ding" Darling on Sanibel Island is a 5,000-acre sanctuary). Get into the swing of things at the more than 25 private and public golf courses in the area. Famous golf architects like Fazio and Hills have built enough double doglegs and Cape Cod bunkers to challenge the pros. Residents are also delighted with the new Lee County Sports Complex, which has soccer and softball fields, jogging trails and a fishing lake.

Sports: Speaking of the Lee County Sports Complex, that's where you'll batter up with the world Champion Minnesota Twins (their new training camp and 7,500-seat stadium is a beaut). Coming in January 1993 is the great American Bo Sox (Boston Red Sox) spring training camp (their new 7,000-seat stadium is in downtown Fort Myers).

Arts & entertainment: From Bach to rock, the Barbara B. Mann Performing Arts Hall of the University of South Florida brings year-round shows, concerts and entertainment. Fort Myers is also home to the Southwest Florida Symphony, the Nature Center and Planetarium, and the Fort Myers Historical Museum. Lee County Civic Center brings in great family entertainment such as the circus, Disney on Ice, etc. Welcome additions to the community are the new $1.5 million Lee County Alliance of the Arts Cultural Arts Center (exciting indoor and outdoor theatrical performances, dance recitals and string quartets) and the restored Arcade Theater (they discovered an orchestra pit during renovations). It will also offer an exhibit gallery, a library and exciting art education program. A great outing is to the Henry Ford and Edison winter homes (the tour of Edison's laboratory and experimental gardens is unforgettable).

Annual events: Edison Pageant of Light (Feb.); Arts Festival (Jan.); Caloosa Catch & Release Tournament (June); Taste of the Cape (Sept.); Munich in Cape Coral (Oct.); Pine Island Seafood Festival (March); Arts in the Air (Nov.).

113

The Environment

Lee County meets or exceeds the EPA's Clean Air Act, which insures that air quality is good to above average (Dade County is still working at it). Drinking water is frequently tested for bacteria and is of excellent quality. A brand-new state-of-the-art water supply system will further improve the supply (however, with iron and calcium carbonate in the water, many newcomers dislike the taste). Recycling efforts are quite innovative, with Goodwill Industries running the city's program. It earns money from the sales, hires otherwise unemployable people, and donates usable items. To help educate students, schools will have their own recycling efforts and take field trips to landfills.

In and Around Town

Roads and interstates: I-75 (now merges with "Alligator Alley"), U.S. 41, State Road 80 (to the ocean), State Road 78 and State Road 31. When I-75 is complete, Miami and Tampa will only be a 2½-hr. drive.

Closest airport: Southwest Florida Regional Airport (RSW). Its $567 million expansion plan will allow for international flights (great for passenger travel and international trade).

Public transportation: LeeTran provides bus service throughout the county.

Avg. commute: 15-20 min. With new and improved roads, many people can easily commute to Naples (40-min. south).

What Every Resident Knows

It's great to be at one with Mother Nature, but don't feed the animals. Wild raccoons openly beg food in picnic areas and will bite if irritated or startled. Also, the coral snakes (poisonous) and king snakes (harmless) look a lot alike, with alternating rings of coral, black and gold. Remember this rhyme: "Head of red, go ahead. Head of black, stay back." • "Yankee Traffic" strikes from December to March. Then out come the bumper stickers that say, "When I get old I'm going to go up north and drive real slow." • Come New Years Day, black eyed peas are practically black market items. Age old superstitions here say that eating the peas on Jan. 1 brings good luck. Nobody much cares for them, but down the hatch they go.

FYI

The Greater Fort Myers Chamber of Commerce
P.O. Box 9289
Fort Myers, FL 33902
800-366-3622

Fort Myers News Press
800-468-0233

Century 21 Accent Realty, Inc.
7101-28 Cypress Lake Drive
Fort Myers, FL 33907
813-481-2222
Barry L. Musser, Relocation Dir.

Lee County Utilities
2178 McGregor Blvd.
Fort Myers, FL 33901
813-335-2800

United Telephone Company of Florida
813-335-3111 (Call collect)

Florida Power & Light
1926 Victoria Avenue
Fort Myers, FL 33901
813-332-2627

Small Business Development Center
College of Business Administration
University of South Florida
Fort Myers, FL 33907
813-489-4140

Business Development Corporation of Southwest Florida
12800 University Drive, Suite 650
Fort Myers, FL 33907
813-481-2131

School district: 813-337-8386
Property tax assessor: 813-335-2294
Welcome Center: 813-542-3721
Interfaith council: None (Contact Chamber of Commerce)
Physician's referral: 813-768-8414 (Gulf Coast Hospital), 813-939-8414 (SW Florida Regional Hospital)
Day-care referral: 813-278-4114
Lee Cares (County Govt. Info. Hotline): 813-335-2462

Tampa, Florida

Area Snapshot

Local population: 288,565
County: Hillsborough **Population:** 842,031
U.S. region: Southern U.S./Florida's Gulf Coast
Closest metro areas: St. Petersburg (21 mi. south), Orlando (82 mi. northeast)
Median housing price: $72,500
Avg. household income: $26,626
Best reasons to live here: Semi-tropical climate, fabulous recreation on the Gulf of Mexico, vast corporate relocations and expansions, low living costs, no state income tax, good schools and health care, affordable housing.

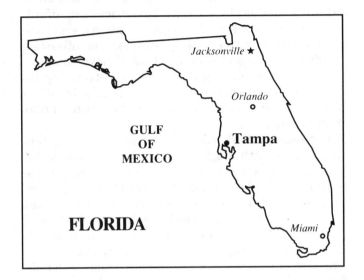

Fabulous Features

If living on the Gulf of Mexico isn't enough incentive to relocate to the Tampa Bay area, you've never seen the spectacular sunsets. Or maybe you're unaware of the progressive business climate (it's as hot as the mid-day sun). What if we throw in outstanding parks and recreation, vast cultural offerings, miles of powdery beaches, state-of-the-art educational opportunities, exciting housing choices, no state income tax, the Tampa Bay Buccaneers—even the most aromatic cigars north of Cuba?

Interested? If not, step aside for the more than 175,000 new residents expected by the year 2000 (almost 200,000 relocated between 1981-1991). What's the rush? The "J" word! This is one of the top three regions in the U.S. for immediate job growth. Almost 200,000 are expected to be created between 1990 and 1995. Why? Dozens of firms like Salomon Brothers, Time Warner, Metropolitan Life and STRAK TWO (a consortium of corporations) scoured the U.S. for relocation sites and chose Tampa.

Two things always close the deal. Time and money. There's time for a leisurely life because it's 20 minutes in any direction (downtown, the beaches, the new Performing Arts Center, pro sporting events). Even better, the cost to live and do business won't rob you blind. The under $100,000 housing market is astounding.

Top grades are given out for Hillsborough County Public Schools, too. Last year, 750 seniors earned more than $10 million in college scholarships and this is the only district in the state to have 100 percent Red Carpet Schools (Florida's top education award). All around, Tampa Bay is a first-class place!

Possible drawbacks: Everyone knows that salaries are lower but think, "My experience warrants higher pay." Tampa is overflowing with highly educated, experienced people. "Paycheck shock" is a reality. Comparable jobs may pay 20 percent less. The trade-offs are no state income tax and affordable housing. • Summers are oppressively hot and humid. Round-the-clock air conditioning and daily dips in the pool help. • The daily papers are filled with crime stories. Drug-related crimes are as frequent and gruesome as in the biggest cities.

"You can quote me on that"

"We love that the neighborhood is not only friendly but so family-oriented. It's easy to relate to neighbors who, like us, are concerned with our children's environment. As far as recreation goes, we've joined a country club right in the area and there's everything from picnics to formal dances."—M.A.

Real Estate

Market overview: Tampa is a stable (prices show little fluctuation) buyer's market. Prices are affordable and there's a wide range of options, from exclusive communities with golf courses to suburban neighborhoods to city living. Lots of new construction as well as desirable resales are attracting incoming residents and transfers, especially first-time buyers. Choose carefully: Selling is much harder than buying!

What houses look like: Newer homes are Florida ranch-style with huge bay windows and a light, open feel. New construction offers contemporaries, even traditional colonials (2-story). Other styles are Spanish, Mediterranean and Caribbean with stucco roofs. In-ground, screened pools, gourmet and island kitchens, master suites, spas, jacuzzis and 2-car garages are popular. Basements are rare.

Starter homes: Homes range from $75,000-$90,000. The low end buys a new or older 3BR/2BA on a 60 x 90 lot, sometimes 80 x 100, w/garage. The higher end shows 3-4BR/2BA, pool, garage, on a 80 x 100 lot. Town & Country and Brandon are great.

Trade-ups: $100,000 buys a 4BR/2BA, w/pool, garage, 80 x 100 lot, formal living/dining room, and eat-in kitchen. At $120,000, you can buy an "executive" home, a new 3-4BR/2BA, formal living/dining room, pool, fireplace and layouts ideal for privacy and entertaining. Northwest communities like Carrollwood, are where to look.

Luxury homes: Homes range from $200,000-$500,000. For $200,000, you can buy a 4BR/2 1/2BA "executive" home, w/home office (or 5th BR), 2000 sq. ft., pool, fireplace, gourmet kitchen, formal living/dining room. A little more money buys waterfront. At the higher end, you'll get a 4500-5000 sq. ft., 5BR/3BA, custom-built with all amenities. Exclusive neighborhoods include Cheval, Tampa Palms and Avila.

Rental market: SFHs are tough to find because they sell so fast. Rentals in Town & Country or Brandon avg. $550-$650/mo. for 3BR/2BA. Carrollwood offers 4BR homes for $1,000-plus/mo. Condos in Temple Terrace area are comparable to SFHs.

Great neighborhoods: Carrollwood is a professional suburban area with loads of young families. It's in the middle of everything, with a metro feel.

Nearby areas to consider: City of Brandon (20 min. east), has excellent schools and lower prices. It offers a country feel and a 30-min. commute to downtown Tampa. Temple Terrace (near University of South Florida), is an older, established area. Prominent builders are showing affordable new homes with a country feel.

What Things Cost

Runzheimer's Living Cost Index: Avg. annual costs for family of 4 with household income of $50,000: $49,862 (.3% below avg.).

ACCRA's national comparisons: Overall living costs are 1% below the national avg., not the bargain people expect. While housing costs are 4.5% below avg., utilities are that much above avg. (4.8%). Health care and goods and services are a fraction below avg.

Utilities: Phone: Hook-up is $53.25. Gas: Avg. $65-$105/mo. Electric: Avg. $90-$165/mo. and deposit is waived with a letter of good reference from past utility company. Water: Avg. $30-$50/mo. and includes sewage.

Kid care: Day care in Tampa runs roughly $80/wk. for infants, $65/wk. for 2+. Recently, Florida law mandated a higher ratio of caregivers to infants (1:4). Day-care services are in hot demand, so it's important to get on the waiting list early.

Pediatric visit: $35-$40.

The Tax Ax

Sales tax: 6.5% with some food items, professional services and prescriptions exempt.

Property tax: Florida offers a $25,000 homestead exemption for permanent residents whose principle home is in the state. Property taxes are based on millage rates (avg. millage rate in Tampa ranges from 23-28.8). As a rule of thumb, the avg. $100,000 home would run $1,987 (26.5 millage)/yr.

State income tax: None.

Climate

Elevation 19'	Avg. High/Low	Avg. Rain (Inches)	Avg. Snow (Inches)	Avg. Days Rain	Avg. % Humidity
Jan.	71/50	2.3	--	6	59
April	82/62	2.1	--	5	49
July	90/74	8.4	--	16	63
Oct.	84/66	2.5	--	7	56
YEAR	82/63	49.4	--	107	57
# of days 32° or below: 4			# of days 90° or above: 85		

Twelve months of summer with endless sunshine and cool breezes best describe Florida's Gulf Coast. Comfort levels vary by season, with summer bringing high humidity, an average temperature of 91, and severe thunderstorms. However, frequent precipitation cools things off (temps drop from the 90s to the 70s). June to Oct. is hurricane season.

Earning a Living

Economic outlook: The sun isn't the only thing sizzling in Tampa. It's a major industrial, distribution and trade center of Florida and one of the most desirable cities for corporate relocation. The number of new businesses has increased by more than 46% in the past decade. The varied industries and continued economic growth have kept unemployment to 4.9%. In fact, employment in the Southeast is projected to grow at a faster rate than the national average through the year 2000. Tampa has been ranked by economists as the nation's eighth among 25 metropolitan employment growth centers. The area's leading industries are construction, printing and publishing, transportation, tourism, shipping, commercial fishing and shrimping and the wholesale, retail and service industries.

Where the jobs are: Florida is projected to have the greatest increase in employment of all the eight Southeastern states, with the Tampa area leading the state in the formation of new jobs through the turn of the century. Hillsborough County School Board continues to be the largest employer with more than 15,000 employees, followed by Hillsborough County (8,600) MacDill Air Force Base (8,600), Tampa International Airport (5,000) and GTE Florida (4,800). Tourism is an ever-growing factor in economic growth, with the recent construction of the Tampa Convention Center (a $62 million impact on the economy). Recent newcomers include USAA, GTE, ITT, Southern Bell, Price Waterhouse, Travelers Insurance, Anchor Glass, Aetna, Eastman Kodak, Delta Airlines, Xerox, Cigna, Citicorp, Chase, Blue Cross, IBM, Unisys AT&T and MetLife's Southeast Head Office (joined last year by the company's employee financial services division).

Business opportunities: Everything from advertising firms to print shops to day-care services are needed to support the expanding business community and population growth. Opportunities exist for light and high-tech industries and support services for the Tampa Convention Center's business and trade meetings. But research ideas carefully. Competition is tough and only the strong survive.

"You can quote me on that"

"I'm still finding my way around here. Our neighbors have gone out of their way to make us feel at home. Not only is it much more affordable, but we have the luxury of living right on the water."—H.J.

Making the Grade

Public education overview: Education is a shared commitment and top priority. Public schools have established 2,500 business partnerships through the Hillsborough Educational Partnership Foundation, Inc. (and raised $1.5 million for the schools). Hillsborough County, one of the largest public systems in the nation, is the first school district to have 100% Red Carpet Schools (Florida's top education awards). Some schools will offer year-round classes. The school system is also implementing in 1992 a middle school program. Of district high school graduates, 74% go to college or advanced training. Its dropout rate (3.5%), is the lowest in the state for large districts. Hillsborough High, one of the country's oldest schools, helps college-bound students by offering dual enrollment at Hillsborough Community College, and the school board has approved 12 new magnet programs. Hillsborough County has led the state for 6 years in the number of students recognized as Florida Academic Scholars; (in 1991 seniors won more than $10.7 million in scholarships). In the elementary schools, there are numerous programs to increase knowledge in math, science, art and more. Two unique programs include Nature's Classroom and the Environmental Studies Center Program.

Class size: 27:1 (elementary); 30:1 (middle).

Help for working parents: YMCA offers after-school day care at 51 elementary school sites (serves 2,500 children). They provide games, arts and crafts, snacks and homework time. Cost is based on family income.

Blue Ribbon School Awards: H.B. Plant High School ('90-'91).

School year: Starts 3rd wk. of Aug. and ends 1st wk. of June. Children must be 5 on or before Sept. 1 to enter kindergarten.

Special education/gifted programs: Exceptional Child Education encompasses comprehensive programs at all grade levels for students who are physically, mentally or emotionally handicapped or who have learning disabilities. Programs are provided in every school, and/or in special centers. Hillsborough County's summer program for gifted students is the largest in the nation. The Academically Gifted Program (grades 3-6) stresses math and science/health. Enrichment programs are offered at all secondary schools.

Nearby colleges/universities: University of South Florida (headquartered in Tampa); University of Tampa; Hillsborough Community College; Tampa College; Florida College.

Medical Care

Hospitals/medical centers: Tampa, known as the medical center of Southwest Florida, has 16 major general, specialty and military hospitals, with more than 2,000 doctors and 15,000 nurses. Tampa General Hospital (TGH) has an international reputation for quality health care, and its specialties are laser cardiac angioplasty surgery, advanced burn treatment, open-heart surgery, and transplant and rehabilitation technologies. St. Joseph's Hospital and Health Care Center is the only hospital in Central Florida equipped with Positron Emission Tomography, used in the treatment of mental health and Alzheimer's diseases. St. Joseph's also offers a "Careflight" helicopter, diabetes center, and cancer and heart institutes. Humana Women's Hospital in Tampa has sophisticated neonatal intensive care and infertility clinics.

Specialized care: H. Lee Moffitt Cancer Center; USF Psychiatry Center; James A Haley Veteran's Hospital; and Shriners Hospital for Crippled Children.

Crime & Safety

Florida's crime rate is high, and Hillsborough County's is slightly higher than the national average. Of this, 80% is drug-related. (Tampa's coastal location plays a part). However, recent reports show that the crime rate has dropped 1% from '91-'92, and the year before that, it dropped 11.6% (robberies are down 2% and rapes dropped by 6%). Police attribute the drop to the QUAD Squad. Residents now have beepers and notify police if they think a crime is being committed. There are also police patrols, golf cart patrols, and active neighborhood watch programs.

Community Life

Each April, nearly 3,000 Tampa neighbors participate in "Paint Your Heart Out Tampa." They help paint the homes of the elderly, but don't stop there: Some volunteer teams adopt a house for a year, help with exterior and interior repairs, and have even chipped in to buy TVs. Other volunteer activities are the annual River Clean Up (brings 1,500 girl scouts, boy scouts, environmentalists and concerned citizens out to the river banks to clean up the Hillsborough River). A big picnic celebrates the clean-up afterward. Say No To Drugs is an annual walk sponsored by the police department that draws thousands of participants.

Let the Good Times Roll

Family fun: Situated on the semi-tropical Gulf Coast, Tampa offers everything from lazy days on the beach to action-packed recreation. The question is, what to do first? Sailing or water-skiing? An exciting dinner cruise or on-the-beach camping? A short drive takes you to rural Hillsborough County, past cattle ranches and farms. Drive 90 minutes and you're in the amusement capital of the country. Visit Disney World, Epcot Center, MGM Studios Theme Park, Universal Studios and more. Or stay home and visit Cypress Gardens, or Busch Gardens—you'll feel you've flown the family to Africa when you explore the acres of natural habitat and wildlife. There's the Children's Museum of Tampa, a realistic outdoor miniature village and indoor hands-on exhibits. For golf lovers, there are 36 courses. And *Tennis* magazine rates Tampa among the top 10 tennis cities—there are more than 1,000 public and private courses.

Sports: Sports fanatics are in luck! The Tampa Bay Buccaneers, the Tampa Bay Lightning (hockey), and the spring football team, Tampa Bay Storm, play at Tampa stadium. Tampa Jai-Alai has one of the fastest (150 mph) games with hundreds of winners every performance. There's also thoroughbred dog racing, and polo at Tampa Bay Polo Club (the only polo facility on Florida's West Coast).

Arts & entertainment: The Tampa Museum of Art is a premier cultural facility downtown, with changing visual arts exhibitions from around the world and its own permanent collection. The Tampa Bay Performing Arts Center is the largest performing arts complex south of the Kennedy Center, with 23 theaters and world-class entertainment. Many shows feature pre-performance buffets or champagne brunches. Tampa Theatre is a restored 1926 movie palace, which features films, concerts and special events. Ybor City State Museum is housed in a century-old bakery building, and captures political, social and cultural influences that shaped Tampa's Latin Quarter. The Museum of African-American Art is home to the 50-plus-year-old Barnett-Aden collection, which was chartered in Washington, D.C., in 1943. This is Florida's only African-American art museum. Historical Ybor City is fascinating for walking tours.

Annual events: Florida State Fair hosts more than 800,000 visitors to see horse shows, armadillo racing, alligator wrestling and more (Feb.); Strawberry Festival in Plant City draws top country stars (March); Gasparilla Festival is a month-long celebration, with pirates kidnapping the mayor (Feb.).

The Environment

Hillsborough County has one of the most vigorous local environmental programs in Florida and the Southeast. Its environmental concerns and efforts are considered by the EPA to be preeminent in the state as well as the nation. It boasts one of the model programs for clean air and water in the state. There is a strong water quality monitoring effort, and the passage of the Clean Air Act in 1990 has helped maintain good air quality. The county is involved in all aspects of environmentalism, from recycling to wetland protection to solid waste management. There is a recycling pick-up once a month, and recycling baskets are placed around the community. Tampa is also very protective of its waterways and beaches, since it is so reliant on the tourist industry.

In and Around Town

Roads and interstates: I-4, I-75, I-275, U.S. 41, U.S. 92, U.S. 301, SR 60, SR 674, SR 580, SR 640.
Closest airports: Tampa International Airport. Facilities for private planes are maintained at Peter O. Knight Airport, MacDill Air Force Base, Vandenberg, and Plant City Municipal.
Public transportation: Urban transportation is provided by Hillsborough Area Transit Authority (HART Line). There are 192 buses, 50 routes and 15 Park-and-Ride Lots.
Avg. commute: 20-30 min.

What Every Resident Knows

Residents love to visit Ybor City, once the world's cigar-making capital, with its jazz and ethnic clubs, featuring appearances of Cuban and Spanish singers as well as flamenco dancers. • Each spring, Tampa turns out to see "the boys of summer." The Cincinnati Reds and a New York Yankees minor league team play near Tampa Stadium. Seven spring training sites are within 45 minutes from downtown. • Weekly regatta sails, with more than 100 boats on parade, lure visitors to the beaches every Thursday night during the summer.

FYI

Tampa Bay Chamber of Commerce
801 East Kennedy Boulevard
Tampa, FL 33602
813-228-7777

Tampa/Hillsborough Convention and Visitors Association
111 Madison Street, Suite 1010
Tampa, FL 33602-4706
813-223-1111

Tampa Tribune
202 South Parker Street
Tampa, FL 33606
813-272-7422

Century 21—Geiger
9250 N. 56th Street
Tampa, FL 33617
813-681-4465
Julie Yonan, Relocation Director

Tam-Bay Realtors
4901 W. Cypress Street, Suite 200
Tampa, FL 33607
813-289-6600
Jana Coleman, Corp. Relocation Dir.

Unique Property Managemente (Rentals)
4214 West Kennedy Blvd.
Tampa, FL 33609
813-286-7549

People's Gas System
1200 North 13th Street
Tampa, FL 33605
813-228-9743

Tampa Electric Co.
702 N. Franklin Street
Tampa, FL 33602
813-228-4111

General Telephone Co. of Florida
519 Zack Street, Box 110
Tampa, FL 33601
800-458-1217; 800-483-2762 (Fla.)

Small Business Development Center
College of Business Administration
University of South Florida
E. Fowler Ave., BSN 3403
Tampa, FL 33620
813-974-4274

Committee of Economic Development
801 East Kennedy Blvd.
Tampa, FL 33602
813-228-0606

School district: 813-272-4000
Property tax assessor: 813-272-6100
Welcome Wagon: 813-877-0927
Physician's referral: 813-754-4444 or 813-254-3484
Day-care referral: 813-876-1763

Roswell, Georgia (Atlanta)

Area Snapshot

Local population: 47,923
County: North Fulton   **Population:** 90,400
U.S. region: North Central Georgia
Closest metro area: Atlanta (23 mi. south)
Median housing price: $148,000
Avg. household income: $55,646
Best reasons to live here: Vibrant regional economy, historic, fast-growing community, great neighborhoods and schools, award-winning parks, wonderful year-round climate, fantastic diversions for kids, excellent transportation.

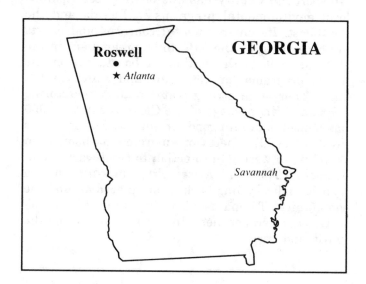

Fabulous Features

If Georgia's on your mind, it's with good reason. Peaches aren't the only thing in blossom, particularly in North Fulton County. The $64,000 question is, why have 64,000 newcomers settled here in the past 10 years? Could be because the comfortable climate, the rolling hills and old magnolias are the welcome mat they dreamt of. Could be the booming economy, with its "Golden Corridor." AT&T, American Honda, Digital Equipment, Kimberly Clark and Ciba Vision are some who are "reaching out." Could be that Roswell is part of the desirable Atlanta metro.

It's all of the above, plus something even more compelling: a rich, rewarding lifestyle. Take the master-planned community, Roswell, for example. This charming, historic city on the banks of the Chattahoochee River is setting the standard for what's important to families. Great schools (gifted and special ed. programs just earned top honors, and a $243 million renovation program will result in 11 state-of-the-art facilities), great recreation (the Parks Dept. is an award-winner), great neighborhoods (doz-ens of stunning developments offer new, affordable homes and unbelievable amenities) and a city government with vision (it built a $13.6 million municipal complex, with a 600-seat auditorium, library and city hall).

But Roswell also has what money can't buy—pride in its heritage. This former 1800s mill town restored its 540-acre historic district. Of course, residents also have their eye on the future. Atlanta will be the area to watch in 1994 (the Super Bowl is coming) and again in 1996 (site of the Summer Olympics). Keep your eye on the ball and even better, keep your eye on Roswell.

Possible drawbacks: Many new residents express a "close the doors after I get in" attitude, especially after they see how population growth has affected traffic. During rush hour, a routine 20-minute trip can turn into an hour ride. • People are just as concerned that growth will have a negative impact on the cherished small town, "know everybody" environment. On the other hand, that very growth has resulted in millions of dollars worth of improvements.

"You can quote me on that"

"We weren't sure we'd like the South, but Atlanta is more a melting pot. We learned a lesson from our kids about making friends and making an effort. They made us see what a special community Roswell is. Now we love it. Our only regret is that there are no beaches."—D.T.

Real Estate

Market overview: Currently a buyer's market, the metro area was ranked the country's 7th-best real estate market, reflecting affordable prices, a 14% jump in housing starts in a year and a healthy business climate—40%-50% of all homes sales are from relocating families. A mix of housing prices is found in most areas, even within a block or so of each other. Younger families tend to live in the newer northside subdivisions. Virtually all newer construction (last 10 yrs.) is subdivisions.

What houses look like: All styles are here, from small brick ranches to stucco Southern-style mansions. More than 90% of the homes are traditional. But, modern interiors are seen in newer construction. Most lots are ½-1 acre. Planned communities often have shared amenities such as clubhouses, pools and tennis courts.

Starter homes: For $80,000-$100,000, you can buy a 1500-1800 sq. ft., 2-3BR/1-2BA, split-level or 2-story, large windows, large bathtubs, fireplace and deck, but no basement. Exteriors are wood frame, with brick fronts and stucco. Check out Barrington Farms, Berkshire Manor, and Long Indian Creek.

Trade-ups: For $125,000-$170,00, homes are larger, 2000-3,000 sq. ft., with 3-4BR/2BA, gourmet kitchens, recreation rooms, pools, saunas, jacuzzis, skylights and, almost always, full basements. Exteriors range from brick front, to combination stucco and brick, to stacked stone. Look at Barrington Farms and Park Bridge.

Luxury homes: For $200,000+, you can get 12,000 sq. ft., 4+BR/2+BA, w/solarium, high ceilings, extra fireplaces, tennis court, location on a golf course, private lake, or in a luxury planned community. The most exclusive neighborhood may be the Country Club South, a Jack Nicklaus community.

Rental market: The only rentals are homes that haven't sold yet. Home rentals range from $1,000-$3,000/mo. There are very few apartments in the area.

Great neighborhoods: Barrington Farms (east), 6-10 year olds, attracts lots of young families. Homes range from $80,000-$110,000. Park Bridge, a smaller subdivision, offers attractive older homes as well as new homes (less than 6 yrs.) for $110,000-$120,000. Roswell Farms (west) offers older homes (frame with brick fronts for $80,000-$100,000) in a small, family-oriented neighborhood.

Nearby areas to consider: Alpharetta (north) is a new community, with affluent areas as well as more affordable neighborhoods. A planned community, Alpharetta is considered "horse country," and homes offer a lot of acreage.

What Things Cost

Runzheimer's Living Cost Index: Avg. annual costs for family of 4 with household income of $50,000: $51,428 (2.9% above avg. city).

ACCRA's national comparisons: Overall living costs for the Atlanta metro are .4% above the national avg. Health care and utilities are the main offenders (21.8% and 14.4% above avg. respectively). Food, housing and transportation are slightly below avg. (1%-2%).

Utilities: Phone: $20/mo. Installations are $43. Electric: $65/mo. with $18hook-up. Gas: $40/mo. Hookup: $15 for previously occupied homes, $25 for new residences.

Kid care: There are 20 centers providing day care. Availability for infants is limited to waiting lists, easier for 2 years and older. Infant care (6 wks.-18 mo.): $90-100/wk. Age 2+ $85/wk. **Pediatric visit:** $45-$60.

The Tax Ax

Sales tax: 6%.

Property tax: Homes are appraised at 40% of fair market value times a millage rate of approximately $50 per $1,000. Deduct $2,000 for a homestead exemption. A $100,000 home would run about $2,000/yr.

State income tax: Georgia taxable income is taxed at $320 for the first $10,000 and 6% thereafter. Standard deductions are: $3,000 for married filing jointly, $2,300 single head of household, $1,500 per dependent.

Climate

Elevation 1,200'	Avg. High/Low	Avg. Rain (Inches)	Avg. Snow (Inches)	Avg. Days Rain	Avg. % Humidity
Jan.	51/32	4.2	.7	12	61
April	71/50	4.6	--	9	52
July	87/68	4.9	--	12	64
Oct.	73/52	2.5	--	6	53
YEAR	70/50	48.3	1.6	116	57
# of days 32° or below: 58			# of days 90° or above: 19		

Roswell weather conditions take their cue from the mountain ranges, the Gulf of Mexico and the Atlantic Ocean. In short, the climate is glorious all year long. Winters are mild (it snows 1-2 times a decade), summers are warm but not unbearable (hot spells don't last). Severe thunderstorms occur between March and May.

Earning a Living

Economic outlook: The North Fulton County economy continues its sustained growth. The 6% unemployment rate is slightly below the country's, reflecting a highly skilled labor force, and a strong transportation and distribution center. The quality of life, lower operating costs, progressive infrastructure, low-cost land and stimulus of the Georgia Route 400 "Golden Corridor" (45 companies employing nearly 5,500 people) have enticed major corporations such as AT&T, Herman Miller, Kimberly Clark Corp., Digital Equipment Corporation, Equifax, G.E. Capital, Hitachi, Digital Communication and Siemens Energy & Automation to establish operations here. Major employers and home-grown businesses, combined with the support of state and local governments, maintain a thriving retail and business climate. Roswell's annual growth rate has been a steady 1.54%. There's been some recent economic downturn, mostly in construction. Two of the Fortune 100's fastest-growing companies are here—First Financial Management (holding company) and Knowledgeware (Fran Tarkenton's software concern) are ranked 31st and 37th respectively.

Where the jobs are: In addition to the many major corporations here, the large new Alpharetta shopping mall and Northside Hospital are also big employers. Atlanta, known as the "Capital of the South," is a regional center for banking, politics and transportation, and home to many national and international firms. Communications and high-tech areas are growing the fastest, fueled by county attempts to attract more warehouse and light, clean manufacturing industries. In addition, the Atlanta airport has been supporting a growing number of industries such as air cargo. Many companies have been moving into the Fulton County area from California and the Northeast. UPS has recently relocated, bringing in an estimated 250-400 jobs, and GE Capital is expected to create 250 jobs. The pro-business climate has been further supported by the prospects of additional growth brought on by the summer Olympics.

Business opportunities: The climate for small business is good. In addition to high-tech, service industries in general, especially those aimed toward upscale market, should do well. The Roswell Chamber of Commerce and the Fulton County Economic Development Division-Dept. of Planning and Economic Development are extremely helpful to start-up and small businesses. The organizations provide financial and location services. Of late, there are a number of restaurant openings.

Making the Grade

Public education overview: After years of lagging behind in funding and test scores, public education in Fulton County today bears no resemblance to its former self. And given the tremendous disparity among families in the Fulton County district (44,000 students come from underprivileged minority families to highly affluent homes), administrators are doing a respectable job of meeting a variety of needs. The high schools offer three study tracks—general, vocational and college prep as well as alternative high schools with flexible schedules. Both the special education and gifted programs just received top honors in the state (Gifted Program of the Year, 1990-1991, and the Promising Practices Award-Special Education). Kindergarten is now full-day with a strong emphasis on math and science. And a $243 million renovation program to be completed in 1993 will result in 11 new schools and 40 renovated schools. Students in the Roswell schools are performing at the highest levels in the district (90% of the students take the SATs, compared to 40% nationally). SAT scores are also the highest in the county and well above the national avg. Critics argue that Atlanta's schools aren't the caliber of the Northeast, but many districts up north are facing budget cuts while schools here are benefiting from tremendous population growth and subsequently a larger tax base for funding.

Class size: 24:1 (avg.).

Help for working parents: The YMCA runs Prime Time, an after-school enrichment program in all elementary schools. Fees are based on a sliding scale. All schools open early for breakfast.

Blue Ribbon School Awards: Crabapple Middle School ('87-'88).

School year: Starts week before Labor Day and runs through first week in June. Children must be 5 on or before Sept. 1 to enter kindergarten. Exceptions may be made for children moving into the area.

Special education/gifted programs: Fulton County offers special resource or full-day special education classes for handicapped, learning disabled or emotionally disturbed children. Talented and Gifted (TAG) students are in pull-out programs with trained teachers.

Nearby colleges/universities: Atlanta is home to several fine public and private colleges including Emory University, Morehouse College, Georgia State University, Clark University and Georgia Tech. Kennesaw State College is in Marietta.

Medical Care

Hospitals/medical centers: North Fulton Regional Hospital is Roswell's full-service facility, with close to 400 physicians on staff. It offers a Women's Health Promenade and neonatal intensive care unit, a Level II trauma/emergency center and a brand-new Outpatient Center with extensive diagnostic and laser surgery services. Northside Hospital (Atlanta) is building a new medical center and cancer center in nearby Alpharetta. Its maternity care and women's services are rated as some of the best in the country. St. Joseph's and Northside Hospitals are large Atlanta-based hospitals.

Specialized care: Scottish Rite Children's Medical Center (Atlanta) specializes in pediatric Level II trauma, orthopedics and oncology. The Renaissance Rehabilitation Center (affiliated with North Fulton Regional) is widely known for its care of stroke and brain-injured patients.

Crime & Safety

Even with a growing population in Roswell, property crime, the biggest crime problem, is on the decline. Most of the crimes—auto theft, car break-ins, burglaries—are committed by juveniles. In 1991 there were no murders, and since 1987, there've been no more than one murder per year. In Roswell, 75%-80% of the city participates in a neighborhood watch program. The police department is well-staffed. The chief of police makes his home phone number available to residents to call about any problems. Streets are well-lit and residents feel safe to walk at night. Roswell is safe because the police and community work together.

Community Life

Call Roswell fanatical about preserving its city's history and no one will take insult. The people are truly committed to preserving historical sites and buildings and perpetuating the era of Southern charm and gentility. Youth Day (a 30-year tradition) brings the community together to honor youth with a big parade. There's a strong PTA, and organizations relating to schools and sports. The city government has about six different boards and commissions that are run by volunteers. Area churches and businesses got together and formed the county of North Fulton Community Charities, which provides assistance to needy families. Many community volunteers help run the program.

Let the Good Times Roll

Family fun: Roswell's Recreation & Parks Department is a five-time winner of the Georgia Recreation & Parks Association Agency of the Year Award. City parks offer an unlimited menu of outdoor and indoor recreation, with an avg. 4,000 visitors a day. The New Visual Arts Center and Gymnastics Center have classes for all ages and abilities. Wills Park in nearby Alpharetta has major equestrian shows. The Chattahoochee Nature Center is 60 acres of ponds, canoeing, nature trails, exhibits and environmental seminars. Vickery Creek trail features a ruined mill and a spectacular old stone mill dam. And nearby Chattahoochee River National Recreation Area has beautiful hiking trails. Other family draws, in Roswell and nearby, are: the Roswell Mill, with a wonderful model railroad and puppet shows; Roswell Fire Museum; Maudlin Doll Museum, CNN Studio Tour, Telephone Museum, American Adventures, SCITREK, the newly opened Teaching Museum, White Water Park, and Six Flags over Georgia

Sports: If you like poring over the morning sports page, local action promises plenty of great reading. There's the always exciting Atlanta Braves (Ted Turner's National League team), the Atlanta Falcons (NFC Football), the Atlanta Hawks (NBA), two NCAA teams and now comes the ultimate news of the century—the 1994 Super Bowl *and* the 1996 Summer Olympics!

Arts & entertainment: The Old Roswell Mill (restored 1838 mill) is a marketplace overlooking Vickery creek, with upscale shops, an arts pavilion, and American and international restaurants. The 540-acre Roswell Historic District features antebellum homes, antique stores and excellent restaurants. The Chattahoochee Theatre Co. performs a wide variety of classic plays and musicals, and the children's theater offers workshops. The $13.5 million Municipal Complex, on 17 acres in a park-like setting, is a cultural center with a 600-seat theater, library and museum. A new regional theater company has just opened there. Bulloch Hall, listed in National Register of Historic Places, is a cultural center and gallery; featuring demonstrations and story-telling for kids.

Annual events: Colors of North Fulton Community Celebration (a tennis tournament and Magnolia Ball in April); Youth Days Festival (Aug.); Summer Concert Series at the Roswell Mill; Heritage Days Festival (Sept.); Roswell Arts & Crafts Festival (Sept.); and Oktoberfest at Roswell Mill.

The Environment

Roswell's new state-of-the-art recycling center and curbside programs are making a clean sweep. The Adopt-a-Stream program, winner of an environmental award, involves kids and adults in preserving water quality. They test the water, clean the streams and banks, and seek out sources of pollution. The Chattahoochee River is a valued resource, and water quality is excellent; it's used for fishing, swimming and other recreation. Roswell Clean & Beautiful program is a certified program of Keep America Clean & Beautiful (nationwide program). It has been all volunteer for 6 years. There are no hazardous waste sites in the city.

In and Around Town

Roads and interstates: I-285, Highway 400.
Closest airport: Hartsfield Atlanta International Airport (1 hr.).
Public transportation: MARTA (Metro Atlanta Rapid Transit) has a 32-mile rail system and 775 buses covering the area. There are eight bus stops in Roswell. The Brookside train station is the closest train stop for Roswell/Alpharetta residents (to downtown Atlanta, the airport, Fulton County Stadium and other major stops). A new Park and Ride parking lot for residents has just opened.
Avg. commute: 45 min. to Atlanta via Turner McDonald Parkway (Highway 400).

What Every Resident Knows

People can barely stand the excitement since Atlanta was chosen as the site for the 1996 Summer Olympics. But already there's a big brouhaha over the state flag. Seems the confederate battle flag symbol has never been removed. Civil rights leaders claim it's a major embarrassment. Opponents say, "Hey, it's part of our history." Nobody is quite sure how it will all fly in the end. • If you like having ample choices when flying in or out of the Atlanta Airport, you'll be thrilled that it is one of the biggest and busiest in the country. Of course, when catching a flight requires taking an underground train that connects the four domestic concourses and 132 gates, you might say, "Who do they think I am? O.J. Simpson?" • Growth has brought tremendous change to Roswell with one exception. Mayor W.L. "Pug" Mabry has been in office for 26 years and is running unopposed in the next election. He's been called the quintessential good guy and story-telling master.

FYI

Greater North Fulton Chamber of Commerce
1025 Old Roswell Road
Roswell, GA 30076
404-993-8806

Atlanta Gas Light Co.
89 Annex
Atlanta, GA 30389
404-522-1150

Alpharetta-Roswell Revue
301 North Main Street
Alpharetta, GA 30201
404-442-3278

Atlanta Journal-Constitution
P.O. Box 4689
Atlanta, GA 30302
404-526-5151

Jenny Pruitt & Associates Real Estate
1730 Mount Vernon Road
Atlanta, GA 30338
404-394-3130
Samantha Ashbacher/Sam Zittrower

Northside Realty
10915 Highway 9
Roswell, GA 30076
404-993-1020
Don Cherry

Prudential Atlanta Realty
863 Holcomb Br. Road
Roswell, GA 30076
404-992-4100
Carl Erbesfield

Georgia Power Company
96 Annex
Atlanta, GA 30396
404-325-4001

Southern Bell
800-356-3094

Planning & Economic Development
141 Pryor Street SW
Atlanta, GA 30303
404-730-8000

Georgia State University
Small Business Development Center
30 Pryor Street, Suite 900
Atlanta, GA 30303
404-651-3550

New Neighbors League:
404-399-5377
Interfaith Council: Contact Mayor's office: 404-641-3727
Physician's referral: 404-751-2600
Day-care referral: 404-885-1585

Boise, Idaho

Area Snapshot

Local population: 125,738
County: Ada   **Population:** 206,775
U.S. region: Western U.S./Southwest Idaho
Closest metro area: Salt Lake City (336 mi. southeast)
Median housing price: $92,896
Avg. household income: $27,774
Best reasons to live here: Sparkling clean mountain town, some of the best recreation in the West, very diversified business base, affordable housing and taxes, friendly people and low crime.

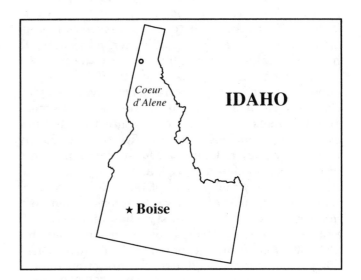

Fabulous Features

The Boise Chamber of Commerce hears from about 500 people a week who inquire about the good life. What Boise offers is a taste of the *great* life! In this City of Trees, where the majestic Rocky Mountains converge with the Boise River, residents know the inspirational powers of natural resources.

But since scenery doesn't pay the rent, fortunately opportunities are also bountiful! Hewlett-Packard, Albertsons, and Morrison Knudson are just a few firms in expansion modes, and in keeping with the pioneer spirit, entrepreneurs are coming in caravans: Dodge Caravans, RVs, etc. (there were close to 1,400 new business starts last year).

Boise is Idaho's state capital, the largest city in the state and a land of contrasts. On the high end are culture (Shakespeare under the stars), outdoor recreation (alpine skiing), and educational outlets (Boise State University's influence is tremendous). On the low end are crime, taxes and housing prices. The real estate market is breaking records, but not at the expense of fairly priced, wonderfully dramatic houses (a great selection under $100,000).

If Boise were a movie, they'd call it, "Spirit of the Wild West Meets the Star Wars Generation" (some of today's most innovative computer technology was invented at BSU). But it's not the movies, it's real adventure, 1990s style!

Possible drawbacks: There may be 100,000 trees in Boise, but don't expect to find jobs growing on them! Job satisfaction is so great, turnover is minimal (less than three percent a year). However, entrepreneurs catering to Hewlett-Packard and other "big boys" are thriving. • Boise never expected so much company (for every 100 who move out, 163 move in). Schools are getting crowded, there's rush-hour traffic, and housing prices have been steadily creeping up. • San Francisco is only an hour from here...by plane. By car, the closest big metro area (Salt Lake City, Utah) is a five-hour drive!

"You can quote me on that"

"The biggest surprise for us was moving to a city this size and discovering there's no crime. We really don't have to lock our doors. The other nice thing is that everyone is so friendly. We had no difficulty meeting people. The bad news is finding out how little Idaho spends per student. They're ranked 43rd in the country. So far we're very happy with the schools, but it makes you wonder how it will eventually affect your kids' education."—K.T.

Real Estate

Market overview: The economy is strong, big corporations have recruited top talent, and real estate is hot! There are close to 1,600 residential properties listed for sale and 1,200 licensed realtors to help you make up your mind. In just the past 2½ years, homes have appreciated 10-17%. Attractive homes, priced right, sell in days. Avg. carrying charges on a SFH (principal/interest) are $714/mo.

What houses look like: Boise neighborhoods show everything from 100-year-old Victorians to lovely new 3BR ramblers (ranches). Most older homes are brick, newer models are brick and wood frame (local timber industry makes sure of that). New construction shows dramatic dormers, wraparound porches, master baths and Victorian-style bay windows.

Starter homes: Modest older homes sell for $35,000-$45,000 on the north end of town. These 30-year-old 2BR/1BA (800 sq. ft.) are often handyman specials. Homes in the $50,000-$60,000 range are limited but available.

Trade-ups: For $80,000-$90,000, buyers get new 3BR/2BA homes (1350 sq. ft.) southeast of town. Amenities pick up in the $115,000-$124,000 range, buying a 3BR/2BA home (1800 sq. ft.) on a 80 x 100 lot with 3-car garage. Ramblers are most popular. Coventry Manor is a beautiful subdivision with homes under $100,000.

Luxury Home: $250,000 buys a gorgeous new home on 1+ acres. Avg. prices range from $300s-$800s for lavish 4-6BR/3BA homes (2600-6000 sq. ft.) with master BR suite, 3-4 car garage, and a gourmet kitchen. Magnificent older homes are in the historic district (Warm Springs Ave.)

Rental market: With such demand for SFHs, rental inventory has dried up and prices are as high as mortgages ($600-$800/mo.). There are a lot of apartments, duplexes and triplexes; 3BRs go for $575-$650; 2BR condos rent for $490-$600.

Great neighborhoods: On the west end of town, farmhouses surround contemporary subdivisions. The Bench area (a prestigious address) has both new apartments and lovely, older homes and is centrally located. Most of the new SFH construction is south and southeast. Columbia Village, Boise's first planned community, is a development with shopping, recreation and moderately priced homes.

Nearby areas to consider: Eagle (pop. 4,000 and 10 mi. northwest of Boise) is small-town living in a country setting (lots of horse farms). Prices of homes range from $70,000-$270,000. Meridian (pop. 15,000) is a fast-growing bedroom community 10 mi. southwest with award-winning schools and great housing values (homes under $100,000).

What Things Cost

Runzheimer's Living Cost Index: Avg. annual costs for family of 4 with household income of $50,000: $45,538 (8.9% below avg. city).

ACCRA's national comparisons: Overall living costs are ½% less than the national avg., but utilities are at 25% below. Food and transportation costs are 5-7% below, with housing prices approximately 10% *above* avg. Health care costs rank 8% above (the quality is top-notch).

Utilities: Phone: $16/mo. Installation: $42. Gas: Avg. $48/mo. Electric: Avg. $58/mo. Water: Avg. $20/mo.

Kid care: 365 licensed childcare providers charge avg. $60-$80/wk. for infants and toddlers. **Pediatric visit:** Avg. $35.

The Tax Ax

Sales tax: 5% (gasoline, utilities exempt).

Property tax: Compared to other major cities in Idaho, Boise has the lowest property tax rate in the state. Estimated annual taxes are 1½-2% of a home's market value. A $150,000 home would run about $3,000/yr. A major plus is the state exemption for owner-occupied properties, which allows for a 50% deduction up to $50,000 of the home's value.

State income tax: Based on a graduated rate of 2% to 8.2%. Net taxable income of $20,000 or more owes $1,387.50 plus 8.2% for the amount over $20,000.

Climate

Elevation 2,838'	Avg. High/Low	Avg. Rain (Inches)	Avg. Snow (Inches)	Avg. Days Rain	Avg. % Humidity
Jan.	37/21	.7	8	9	71
April	61/37	1	1	8	36
July	91/59	.2	--	2	21
Oct.	65/39	--	.1	7	41
YEAR	63/39	9.4	21	82	44

# of days 32° or below: 124 # of days 90° or above: 43

Situated in a river valley surrounded by foothills and mountains, Boise has a definite change of seasons, but no extreme temperatures or conditions. Cold air masses from the Pacific peter out before they arrive, so winters are mild, cloudy and rainy. Summers are dry, warm and comfortable (the sun shines an avg. 250 days a year). Tornadoes and severe thunderstorms are rare.

Earning a Living

Economic outlook: The local business base is so diversified, the "R" word here is not *recession*, it's *results*! As headquarters to some of the most widely recognized national and international corporations, Boise profits from its combined annual sales of $25 billion! Attracted by favorable living costs, low taxes and low utility costs, companies calling Boise home are Albertsons (the sixth largest food chain in the country), Boise Cascade Corp., Hewlett-Packard Co. (this is one of its largest plants, with close to 4,000 employees), Micron Technology, Morrison Knudsen Co., and Ore-Ida Foods (Div. of H.J. Heinz), to name a few. In addition, Boise is the "capital" for government, banking (every bank in the state is headquartered here), medical services (Boise is the closest regional medical hub within 5 hours), and education (Boise State University has the biggest college enrollment in Idaho). Still vital are agriculture, mining and timber, which gave the local economy its first legs to stand on. Current unemployment rate is 4%-4½%. With the opening of Town Center (large mall) and other retail operations, revenues climbed to $1.5 billion. Boise certainly has wonderful things in store!

Where the jobs are: The good news is the high rate of job satisfaction in Boise. Commutes are short (a *lot* of people get to work on two wheels), many companies offer flextime, and when the whistle blows, anything goes. The bad news is that few people ever quit. Hewlett Packard has a 3% turnover (other employers report smaller than that). In addition, even companies in expansion modes are paring down staffs. Boise Cascade and Morrison Knudsen (engineering/construction firm responsible for much of the rebuilding in Kuwait) only have entry-level positions. Possible employers to contact are West One Bank, Idaho Power, Boise School District and the Saint Alphonsus Regional Medical Center or St. Luke's Regional Medical Center.

Business opportunities: Joe Albertson, J.R. Simplot, the Parkinson Twins (founded Micron Technology), and other successful entrepreneurs have been putting Boise on the map for generations. The mountains inspire people to think big. Must be why so many come to follow in their footsteps. Last year alone, there were an estimated 1,400 new business starts—98.7% were small businesses (under 100 employees), which employ more than 55% of the work force (350 major companies, government and schools employ the rest). The small companies taking off are primarily in electronics and high-technology services.

Making the Grade

Public education overview: Boise schools are often the target of criticism from many who feel that lack of state funding makes it difficult to maintain high standards. Still, the district has made tremendous strides, and while it's not perfect (60% of graduates are college-bound and there's a consistent 12%-16% dropout rate), it is competitive. One indication is the latest annual report, which included 25 pages of national, state and local awards or citations earned by students and staff. In addition, voters overwhelmingly approved a $22.6 million bond issue, which will greatly improve/add facilities. Two new elementary schools (2 others opened in 1990), a junior high and renovations to the high schools are planned. There is a high level of parental involvement (they conduct everything from vocational courses to AIDS education). The caliber of teachers is also excellent (60% have master's degrees or higher, and turnover is low). And now with site-based management, they help schools establish special goals. The staying power of teachers has allowed changes to be made without sacrificing the quality of what exists (i.e., Japanese and Russian were added to an already excellent Spanish, German, Latin and French curriculum).

Class size: 21:1 (elementary grades), 25:1 (junior high), and 30:1 (high school). Use of aides and portable classrooms eases the crunch of 600-800 new students until two new schools open.

Help for working parents: A pilot program between 2 elementary schools and the 4-H Club started recently, providing supervision at 7 a.m. and after-school activities until 6 p.m. Up until recently, the demand for care was limited because a high percentage of mothers stay home.

Blue Ribbon School Awards: Frontier School (Meridian School District, '90-'91).

School year: Last week of Aug. through the first week of June. Children must be 5 on or before Aug. 15 to enter kindergarten.

Special education/gifted programs: Boise schools provide special instruction for mentally retarded, emotionally disturbed, learning disabled, visually or hearing-impaired and orthopedically handicapped children. Students are mainstreamed where possible. Boise's advanced placement efforts have been recognized by the American Placement Service (1/3 of all AP tests taken in the state are written by Boise students).

Nearby colleges/universities: Boise State University (14,000 students) has a new College of Technology; College of Idaho (oldest in the state) is a private 4-year institute in Caldwell (20 mi.).

Medical Care

Hospitals/medical centers: According to the American Hospital Association, Idaho has less hospitalization than most other states (cancer rate is 13th lowest of 100 top metro areas). It helps that therapeutic and diagnostic facilities are state-of-the-art. Saint Alphonsus Regional Medical Center is the designated Trauma Center (it has the Life Flight air ambulance) and has specialists in neurosurgery, ophthalmology, orthopedics and psychiatric care. A new 5-story addition is planned. St. Luke's Regional Medical Center is the largest regional facility and is undergoing a 7-year expansion. Neo-natal intensive care will be enhanced. It currently provides excellent maternal-pediatric services, comprehensive cardiac care (including open-heart surgery), a sleep disorders lab and a regional epilepsy center.

Specialized care: Mountain State Tumor Institute (affiliated with St. Luke's) is a well-known cancer care facility. Other hospitals include CPC Intermountain Hospital (a private psychiatric facility), Mountain States Surgery Center (outpatient), Northwest Passages Adolescent Hospital (psychiatric), and the Veterans Administration Hospital.

Crime & Safety

Of the 111 largest U.S. metro areas, Boise has one of the lowest homicide rates and the second-lowest robbery rate. Violent crime here is 31% below the national avg. The biggest problems are property crimes (burglaries and auto theft). The police are stepping up their prevention programs. A unique program in cooperation with the schools and police department is called "block homes." People designate their homes as safe spots for children who might feel threatened to or from school.

Community Life

Volunteerism is the lifeblood of the city. One of the best examples is the annual "Paint the Town" program. For the past 10 years, area residents, realtors and business leaders have painted homes owned by elderly citizens who can no longer maintain them. Another wonderful effort is the Boise Schools' "Neighbors Helping Neighbors." Each school identifies a neighborhood facility, group or organization that needs assistance and uses creative ways to provide the help. In turn, local businesses fund programs and materials for schools that aren't in the budget. Business leaders and professionals put on programs on creative thinking and resourcefulness.

Let the Good Times Roll

Family fun: Name the sport and if can't be done in Boise, it may not be legal! Skiing, hiking, hunting, boating, fishing, mountain climbing and spelunking are just some of the ways to take to the outdoors. Residents also cherish their Greenbelt, a spectacular 25-mile network of city parks that parallels the Boise River. The Julia Davis Park (a 90-acre wonder) houses Zoo Boise, the Idaho Historical Museum and the Boise Art Museum. Barber Park is where you "float the river" (bring a tube, a raft or your own invention). Veterans Memorial State Park (a popular fishing hole) and Eagle Island State Park (there's a natural swimming hole off the Boise River) are great places to spend the day. For fabulous skiing (water and snow), sailing and fishing, the Lucky Peak Recreation Area is a year-round wonderland. If you love the fast track, there's horse racing (Les Bois Park has thoroughbred and quarterhorse races), auto racing (Firebird Raceway has championship drag racing), and rodeos (the Snake River Stampede is world-famous)! For exciting skiing, the Bogus Basin Ski Area (16 miles) has 2,000 acres of Nordic, alpine and cross-country trails (night skiing is outstanding).

Sports: Yes, you can root, root, root for the home team. The Boise Hawks, a semiprofessional baseball team, play at Memorial Stadium June-Sept. In the fall, Boise goes bonkers over championship Boise State football.

Arts & entertainment: Families never tire of the Discovery Center of Idaho (one of Boise's most unique attractions), the science and industry facility with hands-on learning. Culture, concerts and performing arts also fill up the calendar. BSU's Morrison Center for the Performing Arts is home to the Boise Philharmonic Orchestra, The Boise Master Chorale, the Boise Opera Company and the American Festival Ballet. When the kids get out of hand, take them to the Old Idaho Penitentiary (circa 1870). It was home to some of the Wild West's most dangerous desperadoes (it closed in 1973, but don't tell the kids).

Annual events: The new Boise River Festival (started in 1991, but already touted as one of country's 100 best family events) has 100 different happenings including a hot-air balloon rally, jazz concert and a Nite-Lite River parade (June); Idaho Shakespeare Festival (June-Aug.); National Old-Time Fiddler's Contest (300 contestants and thousands of fans converge in June); Western Idaho Fair (old-fashioned country fair in Aug.); Art in the Park (Sept.).

The Environment

Situated upstream at the start of the Boise River, the city gets first crack at the groundwater supply. Thanks to stringent bans and conservation, the quality and quantity of the supply are excellent. Air quality, however, is another story. Because of the valley's high elevation, Boise contends with a natural phenomenon called air inversions. In winter, woodsmoke and other residual discharges don't blow over. To avoid unacceptable levels of pollution, the city has imposed stiff ordinances. It helps that there are no active waste sites in the county. In addition, curbside recycling and "Recycle the Fall" (residents make compost heaps from leaves and grass clippings) help maintain a clean environment.

In and Around Town

Roads and interstates: I-84, and the 184 connector (to downtown), U.S. 95 and U.S. 55.
Closest Airport: Boise Air Terminal (10 min. from downtown), served by United, Delta and 5 regional carriers.
Public transportation: Boise Urban Stages provides bus service throughout the city (one-way fare is 75¢).
Avg. commute: 10-20 min. to downtown from outskirts.

What Every Resident Knows

Competition between Idaho cities is fierce, with Boise the target of jealous rivals. Legislation favoring the city is often voted down because "Boise already gets too much funding." It's like your kid brother complaining you always get the bigger piece. The only hope is to wait until everyone grows up! • Endear yourself to residents and pronounce the name of the city correctly. It's Boy-see, not Boy-zee (this isn't Joisey). • Everyone knows J.R. Simplot, or "Mr. Spud" as his license plate so aptly reads. He was McDonald's original supplier when it started buying Idaho potatoes in bulk. Now he's one hot potato himself! • Want to overlook Boise at a breathtaking spot? Head up 4½ miles to Table Rock. There's a 35-foot neon cross (lit every night of the year) and an unforgettable view.

FYI

Boise Chamber of Commerce
300 N. 6th Street
Boise, ID 83702
208-344-5515

Boise Convention and Visitor's Bureau
168 N. 9th Street, Suite 200
Boise, ID 83707
800-635-5240

The Idaho Statesman (daily)
P.O Box 40
Boise, ID 83707
800-635-8934

Idaho Power
P.O. Box 70
Boise, ID 83707
208-383-2000

Intermountain Gas Co.
P.O. Box 64
Boise, ID 83732
208-377-6840

U.S. West Communications
P.O. Box 7888
Boise, ID 83723
208-333-8440

House of Brokers Realty
1310 Vista Avenue
Boise, ID 83705
800-828-9667
Glen Stephens

RE/MAX of Boise
7201 Franklin Road
Boise, ID 83709
800-574-4013
Bernadette Bonaminio

Boise Area Economic Development Council
P.O. Box 2368
Boise, ID 83701
208-344-5515, ext. 315

Idaho Small Business Development Center
Boise State University
College of Business
1910 University Drive
Boise, ID 83725
208-385-3875

School district: 208-338-3400
Property tax assessor: 208-383-4433
Interfaith Council: 208-338-1227
Physician's referral: 208-386-3080
Day-care referral: 208-343-5437

Buffalo Grove, Illinois *(Greater Chicago)*

Area Snapshot

Local population: 36,427
Counties: Lake, Cook   **Population:** 516,418
U.S. region: Midwest
Closest metro area: Chicago (35 miles southeast)
Median housing price: $160,023
Avg. household income: $57,508
Best reasons to live here: Impressive school districts, excellent parks and recreation system, all "young family" neighborhoods, convenient access to the "golden career corridor," major shopping in every direction, low crime.

Fabulous Features

Many places develop such unique personalities, they're described in human terms—charming, laid-back, perhaps snobbish. The village of Buffalo Grove might best be characterized as the young, athletic type. It's in great physical shape (neighborhoods are clean and beautiful), it's team-spirited (hundreds of professionals serve on 12 civic committees), and it's very aggressive (Village Hall has a real can-do spirit)!

Over the past 20 years, families gravitated here like "herds of buffalo" in search of a suburban panacea (from 1980 to 1990, the population increased by 63.7 percent). Word got out about big new houses with manageable property taxes, award-winning school and park districts, and access to one of the fastest-growing suburban career corridors in the country (over a dozen major business parks and some of the largest pharmaceutical companies are here).

Growth has slowed somewhat (the recession didn't ignore Chicago, it simply left it for last), but like a lean, mean suburban machine, Buffalo Grove keeps the ball in play. It finally has its own post office, bike paths and sidewalks are springing up like wildflowers, and its snow removal efforts are so fast, it should be allowed to compete in the winter Olympics!

And then there's the community's true pride and joy—kids! Its high school, Adlai Stevenson High (Lake County), has one of the strongest academic achievement records in Illinois. As for extracurricular activities and park district programs, the list is so long (and so terrific), it could be the subject of its own book!

Possible drawbacks: Over the river and through the woods may be the only shortcut during rush hour when heavy traffic is a way of life. A proposed overpass raising Lake Cook Rd. over Milwaukee Ave. and the widening of State Highway 83 should help. • New school buildings and additions are in the works to ease overcrowding, but already high property taxes are the source of funding. Lake County residents pay some of the highest taxes in Illinois. • While shopping centers/strips are in great supply, there's a shortage of hangouts for teens. Movie theaters, water parks and mini-golf centers are too far to bike to (translation: "Mom, can you drive us to Northbrook?").

"You can quote me on that"

"We moved here five years ago from Ohio and love it. It was a big plus moving to an area that was well established but still had lots of new people. What I like best is that we're close enough to enjoy all the wonderful things to do in Chicago, but far enough so that we don't have to deal with big-city problems."—K.H.

Real Estate

Market overview: Housing prices and appreciation have stabilized in the past two years—fewer people trading up, and Buffalo Grove's land is almost completely developed. That's great news for buyers, especially those in the market for luxury homes ($200,000-$300,000). Avg. monthly carrying charges for a SFH are $1,500-$2,000.

What houses look like: Newer homes (2-7 yrs.) offer high-tech cabinets, custom-designed fireplaces, bathroom suites (vanity, shower & tub in separate spaces), and decks with screened-in porches. Two-level foyers and family rooms are also popular. Out-of-town buyers comment on the quality of construction and tremendous square footage.

Starter homes: Older 3BR/2BA ranches (avg. 1400 sq. ft.) are priced between $135,000-$140,000. Exteriors are frame and brick, and avg. lot size is ¼ acre (bigger than for most new homes). Interiors are roomy, and most have nice-sized yards. Look at the Strathmore section (20-year old Levitt development) north of Lake Cook Rd.

Trade-ups: In the $200,000-$250,000 range, buyers get 4BR/2½BA colonials or 2-story contemporaries with large family rooms, basement, cathedral ceilings, skylights and closets the size of studio apartments. Exteriors are brick and aluminum. Check out Vintage, Old Farm Village and Woodlands of Fiore (SFH & huge townhouses right on the golf course) in north Buffalo Grove. New developments in Cook County Buffalo Grove are Windsor Ridge and Williamsburg Estates.

Luxury homes: Newer 4BR/3BA homes (3000 sq. ft. homes on 1/3-½-acre lots) offer family room, den, large eat-in kitchens, master BR suites w/jacuzzis, 3-car garage. Prices range from $300,000-$700,000. Exteriors are brick and cedar. Churchill and Sterling Green are very exclusive developments.

Rental market: SFHs (3BR/2BA) are very limited (they're gone in two days). Where available, rents are steep ($1,100-$1,500/mo.). Condos (2-3BR) are also limited and costly ($600-$700/mo.). There's a good availability in apartment complexes, with rents avg. $800-$900/mo.

Great neighborhoods: Canterbury Fields is a gorgeous new development in the luxury end of the market. Strathmore Grove East and Highland Grove offer great resale values. Cherbourg is a lovely townhouse development.

Nearby areas to consider: Grayslake (15 mi. north) has lots of new construction under $200,000. Vernon Hills (10 mi. north) offers moderate housing prices and great schools and parks (a gorgeous new teen center is in the works).

What Things Cost

Runzheimer's Living Cost Index: Avg. annual costs for family of 4 with household income of $50,000: $56,783 (13.6% above avg. city).

ACCRA's national comparisons: Not available.

Utilities: Phone: Avg. $14/mo. Installations: $55. Electric: Avg. $58/mo. fall/winter, double in summer. Garbage and recycling: $14/mo.

Kid care: Licensed childcare is widely available, with several new centers being built. The park district's program is also excellent. Avg. cost in the area is $104/wk for preschoolers ($136 for infants). Before- and after-school care is also available (avg. $67/wk.). **Pediatric visit:** Avg. $45.

The Tax Ax

Sales tax: 7% (food, medicine taxed at 1.25%).

Property tax: Buffalo Grove covers both Cook and Lake counties, with Lake County taxes substantially higher (70% of Lake's property taxes pay for education). The rule of thumb is 2% of sale price for new construction, slightly less for resales. A new $200,000 home would pay $4,000. A $200,000 resale would pay $3,100.

State income tax: Flat 3% of federally adjusted gross income minus $1,000 exemption per taxpayer and dependent.

Climate

Elevation 600'	Avg. High/Low	Avg. Rain (Inches)	Avg. Snow (Inches)	Avg. Days Rain	Avg. % Humidity
Jan.	31/15	.8	11	8	68
April	58/38	3.6	2	13	55
July	83/61	4.1	--	9	57
Oct.	66/42	2.6	.4	8	55
YEAR	59/39	30.4	40	111	60
# of days 32° or below: 131			# of days 90° or above: 31		

The Chicago region's reputation as the "windy city" may have more to do with long-winded politicians than the Lake Michigan breezes. Still, winter wind chill factors and 40-inch snowfalls are a way of life. Summer heat and humidity can be oppressive for days at a time, but the continental climate is highly changeable. Modified by Lake Michigan, wind shifts eventually bring relief from both cold and heat. (Buffalo Grove's proximity to the lake does offer a few degrees of protection).

Earning a Living

Economic outlook: With convenient access to air, rail and highway transportation and tremendous availability of improved land, Lake County has continued to experience unprecedented commercial development (between 1989 and 1991, 1,120 new firms opened or expanded here). It was recently identified as the 12th fastest-growing county in the U.S. (*City & State Magazine*, July 1990). Developed as a high-tech or "golden career" corridor (23 major development parks), this area has attracted hundreds of Fortune 500 companies, including Federal Express, Zenith Data Systems, Konami, Ciba-Geigy, Kitchens of Sara Lee and Toshiba. Lake County is home to Abbott Labs, a leading multinational health care company (soon to be 10,000+ employees), Baxter International, the world's largest manufacturer and marketer of health care products, systems and services (employs 8,000), and the Kemper Group (billion-dollar mutual insurance group). Although some companies are downsizing, it appears that Lake County's economy will be among the first to rebound from what was a short dance with the devil.

Where the jobs are: Not only does opportunity knock here, it practically blows the door down. To start, the unemployment rate is 2.5% in Buffalo Grove (compare that to Lake County's 5.1% and the national 7%+ figures). But what really contributes to the high quality of life is how easy it is to live and work in Buffalo Grove or the immediate area (70% of people who live in Lake County, work in Lake County). The list of Buffalo Grove companies that are new or have recently expanded is phenomenal—Motorola Lighting, Liberty Mutual, Metropolitan Life Insurance, Airborne Freight, Hitachi America, Owens-Corning Fiberglass, Exxon Chemicals, GE Consulting, Zenith Data Systems Corp., Landis Gyr (major heating/air conditioning firm), among others.

Business opportunities: Buffalo Grove residents would willingly name a street after any entrepreneur or company who brought quality family entertainment and restaurants to town. With a young, affluent and growing population, and *no* competition, this is an open invitation!

"You can quote me on that"
"Before we moved here from New Jersey, we researched all of the Chicago suburbs. We chose Buffalo Grove because of the schools and the relatively easy commute. We haven't been disappointed."—J.H.

Making the Grade

Public education overview: Lake County schools are not only maintaining top-quality standards, they're breaking records in academic achievements (Adlai E. Stevenson High is the first and only Illinois public high school to have received two Blue Ribbon School Awards). Students in every grade score above average in reading, language and math (they rank #1 when compared to all the other northwest suburban districts), but the magnet that pulls people into Buffalo Grove is Stevenson High. It is one of the top-rated in the state, with a long lists of awards and citations, and one of 25 U.S. schools recognized for its fine arts program. Of the 2,200 public/private high schools in 13 Midwestern states, it also ranked in the top 1% for students who earn honors grades on the College Board's Advanced Placement program. Of its graduates, 95% enroll in college or in postgraduate training. At present, they are developing the Stevenson Academy for Interdisciplinary Learning (SAIL), the first program in the country modeled after the European "school within a school" approach. In it, 80-100 freshmen will have the same teachers for 3 years to foster continuity of learning in a familiar setting. Note: Parts of Buffalo Grove send students to Cook County schools.

Class size: 23:1 (primary); 24:1 (junior high).

Help for working parents: The Buffalo Grove Park District, in cooperation with 7 elementary schools offer the "Clubhouse," a before- and after-school program with educational and recreational activities. Charges range from $25-$172/mo.

Blue Ribbon School Awards: Adlai E. Stevenson High School ('86-'87, '90-'91).

School year: Last week of Aug. to mid-June. Children must be 5 on or before Sept. 1 to enter kindergarten.

Special education/gifted programs: District #96 participates in SEDOL (Special Education District of Lake County.) where learning disabled students attend special resource classes within the district. Pull-out enrichment programs for gifted students are offered in grades 3-5. Gifted 6th-8th graders are grouped together.

Nearby colleges/universities: The College of Lake County (Grayslake) and William Rainey Harper College (Palatine and Wheeling) offer vocational training. Chicago's Roosevelt University has a branch in Arlington Heights. Other colleges include: Northwestern University (Evanston), the University of Chicago, Illinois Institute of Technology, Loyola University and DePaul University.

Medical Care

Hospitals/medical centers: Top-quality medical care centers practically trip over one another. In Buffalo Grove alone, Northwest Community Hospital and Condell Hospital have 24-hour immediate care facilities. Accredited acute-care hospitals include Highland Park Hospital, Lutheran General Hospital (Park Ridge), Northwest Community Hospital (Arlington Heights), and Condell Memorial Hospital (Libertyville). Chicago is widely known for its outstanding medical care at Northwestern Hospital, the University of Chicago Hospital, St. Luke's and Children's Memorial Hospital.

Specialized care: There are 20 public and private mental health facilities in Lake County as well as numerous services and programs for substance abuse and physical disabilities. There are almost 250 listings for health and family services in just the northwest suburbs alone.

Crime & Safety

Buffalo Grove boasts one of the lowest crime rates in the northwest suburbs. Most criminal activity stems from residential and vehicle burglaries, with violent crimes rare (avg. 12/yr.). Overall crime statistics show a decline from 1990-1991, especially arrests for criminal damage and DWI). Success is attributed to a highly visible city-operated police force (other communities rely on the county sheriff's department). Prevention and awareness programs are widespread (their DARE and Omni Youth Services programs have been very effective).

Community Life

New residents are always welcome, particularly if they come to the neighborhood willing to share their skills and expertise. Buffalo Grove's Board of Trustees depends exclusively on municipal volunteers to review and investigate city needs. It appoints volunteers to 12 important commissions, including transportation, health, blood donor and emergency services.

"You can quote me on that"

"We lived in Buffalo Grove for seven years, moved to the San Francisco area, then got transferred back. We couldn't believe how much the area had grown in just two years. There are so many new developments and new shopping, like Town Center. We're thrilled to be back."—L.S.

Let the Good Times Roll

Family fun: Buffalo Grove's park district offers phenomenal programs and facilities, including 43 summer camps (parents can't stop raving), 30 parks, the Aquadome (a newly renovated indoor pool), and more than 384 acres of parkland (6 playgrounds are scheduled for expansions or improvements). It also has one of the most active Little League programs around, with 2,100 children competing in 185 different leagues! Parents must volunteer in some capacity or pay $25 plus registration. During the summer, thousands of residents also come out for the free concert series, "Lawnchair Lyrics," Buffalo Grove Community Theater presentations, and the new Thursday concerts in Town Center. For thrills and chills, Six Flags Great America, Gurnee, Ill. (May-Oct.), boasts the new "Batman" ride (which, fortunately, is shorter than the 20-minute ride it takes to drive to the park). Gurnee Mills, one of the world's largest discount shopping malls, is right across the street. It features two miles of stores, food and fun. For excellent children's theater, there's the Marriott Resort (Lincolnshire). For a day in the past, the Long Grove Historic Village has more than 80 shops, an authentic covered bridge, cider mill, ice cream parlor and antiques.

Sports: The "C" in Chicago stands for "crazy" about those teams. Sports are so important that if you can't talk baseball, basketball and football, you can't talk! Here's who you'll be watching: Two-time world champion Chicago Bulls, Chicago Cubs and White Sox (major league baseball), Chicago Bears (NFL) and the Chicago Blackhawks (NHL).

Arts & entertainment: Chicago's cultural offerings are extraordinary, with some of the finest art, music and theater in the world. It's home to the internationally renowned Art Institute of Chicago, the Chicago Symphony Orchestra, Lyric Opera of Chicago and Goodman Theater. Second City, the offbeat improvisational theater that has launched many Hollywood careers (John Belushi, Bill Murray), is here. Music lovers look forward to one of the nicest waterfront music festivals in the country—the Ravinia Festival "Concert Under the Stars" in nearby Highland Park (lawn tickets are very inexpensive), a 12-week season of jazz, rock and classical concerts.

Annual events: Buffalo Grove Days (parade, fireworks, carnival, Taste of Buffalo Grove and family entertainment—Labor Day wknd.); Wheeling Family Fest (rides, games and a Taste of Wheeling—July 4th wknd.); Lake County Marathon (April).

The Environment

Compared to other small cities, Buffalo Grove has zoned 3 times as much land for open space (15%). They are so passionate about greenery, they encourage people to honor loved ones by planting trees through their Living Memorial Tree Program. In addition, the city now has a great bike/jogging path system. Water is considered excellent (purity and quality) now that their source is Lake Michigan. Air quality has been declining because of increased traffic and congestion. They are attempting to change traffic patterns and improve the road system to reduce exhaust levels.

In and Around Town

Roads and interstates: Route 53, I-94 (Edens Expressway) and I-294 (Northwest Tollway).
Closest airports: O'Hare International (12 mi.); Palwaukee Airport (5 mi.). Some drive to Milwaukee's newly renovated Mitchell Field (35 min.) to avoid the congestion at O'Hare.
Public transportation: PACE and Nortran Buses connect with Northwestern Railroad at Arlington Heights (closest stop for commute downtown). A site in Buffalo Grove has been selected in anticipation of getting commuter rail service through Wisconsin Central Railroad.
Avg. commute: 30 min. downtown (train), 45 min.-1 hr. (car), 15-20 min. to other outlying suburbs.

What Every Resident Knows

There are only two seasons in Chicago...1) winter and 2) construction! • If Buffalo Grove were restaurant row, it would be a *very* short row. There are so few, when Wendy's opened, there was talk of a parade! • They're not the White Sox or the Bears, but Buffalo Grove Little League baseball and Bills football (training leagues) generate the same excitement (maybe more) as pro ball. The 185 teams have totally filled rosters, games are well attended, and in season, there is probably more fast food consumed per capita than anywhere else (games and practices are so long, the dinner hour is dead). • Who says you can't fish in the suburbs? Greenlakes Park is a great spot, although on occasion the catch of the day is an old tire.

FYI

Buffalo Grove Chamber of Commerce
P.O. Box 7124
Buffalo Grove, IL 60089
708-541-7799

Lake County Convention & Visitor's Bureau
P.O. Box 888
Waukegan, IL 60079-0888
800-525-3669

Chicago Tribune
800-874-2863

Buffalo Grove Countryside
200 James Street
Barrington, IL 60010
708-381-9200

Red Carpet Leiberman Realty
314 McHenry Road
Buffalo Grove, IL
708-541-5000
Shula Elbaz-Cohen, Agent

RE/MAX Experts
1125 Weiland Road
Buffalo Grove, IL 600
708-634-6200
Andy Ackerson, Agent

Lake County Department of Planning
18 N. County St., Rm. A-803
Waukegan, IL 60085
708-360-6350

Commonwealth Edison
800-334-7661

Illinois Bell Telephone
800-244-4444

North Shore Gas Co.
P.O. Box 0
Chicago, IL 60690-3991
708-945-1200

Northern Illinois Gas Co.
P.O. Box 190
Aurora, IL 60507
708-490-8900

Small Business Development Center
College of Lake County
19351 W. Washington
Grayslake, IL 60030
708-223-3633

School district: 708-459-4260 (#96), 708-634-1358 (#102)
Property tax assessor: 708-360-6363
Newcomer's club: 708-541-5492
Interfaith Council: Call Village Hall for churches/synagogues: 708-459-2500
Physician's referral: 708-362-2905, ext. 5610

Wheaton, Illinois *(Greater Chicago)*

Area Snapshot

Local population: 51,464
County: DuPage   **Population:** 781,666
U.S. region: Midwest
Closest metro area: Chicago (23 mi. east)
Median housing price: $148,700
Median family income: $54,920
Best reasons to live here: Historic community with traditional values, one of the fastest-growing regions in Illinois, outstanding schools and local universities, beautiful neighborhoods in parklike settings, convenient commute to booming Research and Development Corridor, phenomenal shopping, low crime.

Fabulous Features

Everything old is new again in Wheaton. The recent multi-million-dollar restoration of the downtown district, with its shiny cobblestone streets and historic architecture, sends a clear message. Old-fashioned values never went out of style. An outgrowth of strong religious ties (37 churches and Billy Graham's own Wheaton College used to rule the roost), today's city fathers and mothers are more likely to transcend their fervor into community life.

The park district alone is testimony to that fact. There's a gorgeous new water park *and* a spectacular new community center, complete with a 6000-square-foot fitness center, theater and children's museum. The school system is superior, with cutting-edge innovations (computer labs and whole language/literacy programs have grade school children outreading and outtesting most other schools in the state), and Wheaton is deeply committed to the environment (recycling is serious business now that residents pay per bag for trash pick-up). The neighborhoods are impeccably maintained (the lush, tree-lined "streetscape" is right out of a magazine).

But Wheaton is more than a peaceful bedroom community. It's a vibrant city situated in the heart of one of the fastest-growing counties in the state (DuPage County's population soared by almost 20% in the 1980s). With so much

commercial/retail development and the new East-West Research and Development Corridor in nearby Naperville, DuPage was recently ranked 13th in the country for number of available jobs based on population.

As for real estate, you'll find a choice selection of Victorians and colonials ranging from $170,000 to $300,000+. But it's not the houses that are selling Wheaton (you can buy one anywhere), it's the harmony. There is a humble, albeit powerful, movement to nurture family life. That's the investment in which residents get the greatest dividends!

Possible drawbacks: Liberal democrats who love warm weather should look elsewhere. Wheaton is a conservative, Republican stronghold big on protective bans and short on flexibility. • Although restrictions pale compared to previous decades, there are still curfews for minors, limited liquor licenses (or any packaged liquor stores), and strong parental involvement in the school curriculum. Just this year, parents of elementary school children tried to ban a reading series, claiming it taught about the occult and devil worship. Ultimately the courts threw out the case, but the controversy wages. • Chicagoland weather turns ordinary people into expert meteorologists. In no time they speak fluently about windchill factors, humidity and freezing temperatures.

Real Estate

Market overview: Of the top 100 U.S. markets where homeowners fare best, the Chicago area was ranked first (*U.S. News & World Report*, 4/92), thanks to extensive job growth coupled with slow-growth appreciation (prices rose less than 7% in the 1980s). In Wheaton, pricey new construction drove resale prices up, and buyers looked elsewhere. That led to greater inventory. The avg. home price is $170,000 (typically 8-10 years old), and the avg. monthly carrying charges are $1,067/mo. New construction is mostly south, convenient to I-88 and the Research Corridor, the Town Center (a fabulous new shopping area) and the new park facilities.

What houses look like: Older homes are Victorians and Tudors on large lots (avg. 1/3-1/2 acre). Split levels, colonials and Georgian manors are also popular. Most have brick fronts with cedar or aluminum siding. Interiors of new homes show hardwood floors, elaborate woodworking and large, open staircases.

Starter homes: Prices range from $100,000-$150,000 for 3BR/2BA split levels or colonials (2200 sq. ft.). Most are 20-30 years old with 1-car garage and quiet, well-manicured neighborhoods.

Trade-ups: For $180,000-$250,000 you'll buy a 3-4BR/2½BA split or traditional 2-story colonial (2600 sq. ft.) on a 60 x 150 lot. Most show updated kitchens, beautiful landscaping and large rooms.

Luxury homes: New homes are traditional 2-story colonial or split level (3000 sq. ft.) with 3-car garage, European-style kitchens, grand entrances with hardwood floors, large, luxurious BAs, king-size BRs and master suites. Prices avg. $275,000-$400,000.

Rental market: Apartment rentals are strong, with an estimated 4,500 units on the market; 3BRs are $700+/mo. Inventory of SFH's is very limited, but where available, rent for an avg. $1,200/mo.

Great neighborhoods: Wheaton Ridge and St. James Place, on the northern tip, have many large, older homes in the $300,000 range. Smaller starter homes in the Arrowhead section are south (homes avg. 10 years). South of downtown are Stonehenge, Academy Highlands and Danada (very posh). And so many young families have moved in, they call it "Big Wheels" territory.

Nearby areas to consider: Carol Stream (pop. 31,000), north of Wheaton, is a young community with great schools and lower housing prices (avg. $140,000-$150,000). Naperville (pop. 73,000) is DuPage County's largest city. Excellent employment, shopping and schools, plus a huge inventory of homes. Prices range from $110,000-$400,000+.

What Things Cost

Runzheimer's Living Cost Index: Avg. annual costs for family of 4 with household income of $50,000: $56,078 (12.2% above avg. city).
ACCRA's national comparisons: Not available.
Utilities: Phone: Avg. $13/mo. Hookup: Avg. $55. Electric: Avg. $85/mo. Gas: Avg. $50/mo.
Kid care: Day-care centers charge $100-150/wk. Private day-care for school-age children avg. $65/wk. **Pediatric visit:** Avg. $40.

The Tax Ax

Sales tax: 6.75% (food, medicine taxed at 1.25%).
Property tax: Wheaton's tax rates are among the lowest in DuPage County. Property tax works out to 1/3 the market value. Tax on a $150,000 home would avg. $3,000. Luxury homes ($300,000+) pay an estimated $8,000/yr.
State income tax: Flat 3% of federally adjusted gross income minus $1,000 exemption per taxpayer and dependent.

Climate

Elevation 600'	Avg. High/Low	Avg. Rain (Inches)	Avg. Snow (Inches)	Avg. Days Rain	Avg. % Humidity
Jan.	31/15	.8	11	8	68
April	58/38	3.6	2	13	55
July	83/61	4.1	--	9	57
Oct.	66/42	2.6	.4	8	55
YEAR	59/39	30.4	40	111	60

# of days 32° or below: 131   # of days 90° or above: 31

Although the Chicago region has earned its reputation as the "windy city," it may have more to do with long-winded politicians. Still, winter wind chill factors and 40-inch snowfalls are a way of life. Summer heat and humidity can be oppressive, but the continental climate is highly changeable. Modified by Lake Michigan, wind shifts eventually bring relief from both cold and heat.

"You can quote me on that"
"When my husband was relocated here, I had my doubts. I honestly did not have a good first impression of Wheaton. But now I love it. A few months ago there was talk of a promotion and relocating south. I was so depressed. I would hate to leave."—B.F.

Earning a Living

Economic outlook: Although Wheaton and surrounding DuPage County have experienced a slowdown in job growth in the past year (unemployment climbed to 5.7% after years at the 4.5% level), area businesses seem to be riding the recession storm, confident they only caught the tail wind. Retail has been the star of the show, with a revitalized downtown (virtually all the commercial space is rented) and the opening of a brand-new concept in shopping, the Town Square. Built as the first prototype in the country, this totally outdoor mall has no anchor department stores, only first-class specialty shops (Williams Sonoma, Ann Taylor and more). It's centered around a "town square," used for family entertainment and exciting shows (ice sculptures were on display at the grand opening). In addition, Target Stores have also recently announced the opening of a superstore in Wheaton, and competing Wal-Mart recently opened in Naperville. Construction is moving along at a good pace, showing a 9% increase in residential and commercial building permits in the past year.

Where the jobs are: An estimated 25% of Wheaton residents commute to downtown Chicago, another 25%-35% work in outlying suburbs, and the balance work or own businesses right here. The highly successful East-West Research and Development Corridor in Naperville, a quick 15-minute commute, is home to AT&T (employs more than 10,000 people in its Bell Labs Software Center, but recently announced cutbacks), Amoco Research Center, General Motors Regional Headquarters and Nalco Chemical Company. Other Naperville operations include *The Wall Street Journal* Midwest printing plant (printing and publishing jobs grew by 8% last year), Nabisco Brands manufacturing and Amurol Products (Div. of Wrigley). Two federally funded research labs, Argonne National Labs (4,300 employees) and Fermi National Accelerator Labs (2,380 employees), are also here. As Wheaton is the DuPage County seat, city and county government are the major local employers.

Business opportunities: Estimates show that within driving distance to Wheaton, close to 300 new businesses open each year (200 in Wheaton alone). Because there is no more available land in Wheaton for industrial development, all are retail or service-related (last year, 150,000 square feet of retail space was constructed and leased). Now, however, it appears that growth has peaked and any additional growth will take place in the suburbs west of Wheaton (adjacent Kane County is starting to boom).

Making the Grade

Public education overview: Amidst $5 million dollars in budget cuts, Wheaton's School District #200 continues to be a testimony to a cutting-edge curriculum. The innovative district is inundated with teacher applicants attracted by respectable salaries ($38,793: well above the state avg.), career ladder programs (tenured teachers can get money to travel), and most of all, the ability to teach creatively. There's no prescribed curriculum. The approach is holistic—look at the big picture, not the parts. At the elementary level, hands-on science projects and the "Math Their Way" program were developed after studying how children learned naturally. Their literacy/whole language program has the average first grader reading 200+ words. Expenditures per pupil are now under $5,000, but district test scores continue to outpace state and national averages (ACT scores are among the highest in Illinois). Better than 85% of students are college-bound, and 20% of seniors were identified as State Scholars. The "New 200 Foundation," a private funding drive, is a "creative" approach to meeting the needs of 12,000 students without hitting up taxpayers. Writing labs, technology centers and visiting science programs are a few of the programs developed.

Class size: 23:1 (grades 9-12 are slightly higher).

Help for working parents: Three elementary schools will be participating in a new "before and after" school program (nominal fees to be charged).

Blue Ribbon School Awards: Franklin Middle School ('87-'88).

School year: Last week of Aug. to mid-June. Children must be 5 by Sept. 1 to enter kindergarten.

Special education/gifted programs: The district's special education program mainstreams children with the assistance of an aide. More than 8% of students are in gifted programs. Starting from first grade, qualified students attend accelerated and enrichment courses. Both high schools offer extensive advanced placement classes.

Nearby colleges/universities: Wheaton College, one of the most renowned Christian liberal arts schools, was identified as one of the "10 Best Colleges for the Money" (*U.S. News and World Report*). The College of DuPage (Glen Ellyn) is the largest community college in Illinois. New to the area is the Daniel F. and Ada L. Rice Campus, (affiliated with Illinois Institute of Technology). Next year the National Louis University, a college of education, will open. Within commuting distance are the University of Chicago, Northwestern University and the University of Illinois at Chicago.

Medical Care

Hospitals/medical centers: Central DuPage Hospital, an acute-care hospital in nearby Winfield, is one of the top surgical centers in the state. Its Neurospine Center is one of the few in the country. The hospital offers a Level II Trauma Center and specialties in orthopedics, ophthalmology, gastrointestinal disorders, and adult and adolescent psychology. With an emphasis on "wellness" programs, it conducts more than 3,300 screenings a year and hosts classes and "reach-out" programs. Immediate-care facilities are in Wheaton, Naperville and Bloomingdale. Six other hospitals are located within DuPage County.

Specialized care: Linden Oaks Hospital (Naperville) is a full-service psychiatric facility. The Alcoholism Treatment Center (family-centered recovery process) and Marklund Children's Home (care for the developmentally disabled) are affiliated with Central DuPage Hospital. The hospital also runs a 24-hour mental health crisis unit.

Crime & Safety

Wheaton crime stories would bore television audiences, but they make for good press in the city. The area is viewed as extremely safe, with vandalism and burglaries the major (albeit limited) source of police work. The police department offers a full-time Crime Prevention Unit to help educate residents about reducing the odds of being a victim and also runs an aggressive DARE program in the local elementary schools. Crisis intervention and counseling are also available.

Community Life

Civic organizations and local churches are the benefactors of Wheaton residents' commitment and generosity. The Chamber of Commerce alone has a group of 500 volunteers. There's a city-operated Volunteer Services Department that matches up people's talent and skills with organizations and services needing assistance. The Sister City Commission promotes cultural exchanges between Wheaton and Karlskoga, Sweden; 60 "ambassadors" from the town recently visited.

"You can quote me on that"

We have lived all over the country. But there was something about the values and the emphasis on family that was missing in the other places. There is a great emphasis on morality and caring. Everyone reaches out."—M.M.

Let the Good Times Roll

Family fun: Chicago's lakefront is one of the most beautiful in the country, offering biking, boating and fishing on Lake Michigan and surrounding shores. In Wheaton, the park district is fabulous, with more than 40 parks, a petting zoo, and a 27-hole golf course. A tremendous asset to the city is the gorgeous, new 13-acre Community Center, complete with a children's museum, 600-seat theater and an exciting 6000-square-foot fitness facility. Rice Pool and Water Park is another new and beautifully maintained city-owned facility. Wheaton is also "in the path" of a unique nature trail, the Illinois Prairie Path. It's a 55-mile trail for jogging, hiking, biking and equestrians. Spring Lake Forest Preserve and West DuPage Park Forest Preserve are nearby for boating and cross-country skiing.

Sports: If you don't follow sports in Chicago, you'll have the city to yourself when there's a big game in town. Here's who you'll be watching: Two-time world champion Chicago Bulls (it's perfectly acceptable to name your firstborn after Michael Jordan), Chicago Cubs and White Sox (major league baseball), Chicago Bears (NFL), and the Chicago Blackhawks (NHL).

Arts & entertainment: Some of the finest art, music and theater in the world are here. Chicago is home to the internationally renowned Art Institute of Chicago, the Chicago Symphony Orchestra, Lyric Opera of Chicago, Goodman Theater and Second City, the offbeat improvisational theater. Back in Wheaton, the Park District's "Entertainment in the Park" summer programs bring family entertainment to the Memorial Park Bandshell. The Wheaton Municipal Band (one of the best community bands in the country) also performs here. DuPage County has more than 15 museums, including the award-winning Adams Memorial Library (it is one of Wheaton's 4 buildings listed on the National Register of Historic Places). Wheaton is also home to The Billy Graham Center (one of the largest collections of evangelistic history).

Annual events: Autumn Fest (Tommy Dorsey Orchestra kicks it off) attracts 10,000 area residents; Cream of Wheaton (arts and crafts fair each June); Wheaton Criterium (exciting professional bike race through downtown in Aug.); Farmers' Market (fresh flowers, produce, throughout Wheaton from June-Oct.); Spirit of Christmas Walk, Kris Kringle Day, candle-lighting parade (Nov.-Dec.).

The Environment

For the 5th consecutive year, the National Arbor Foundation identified Wheaton as a "Tree City USA" (communities with strong urban forestry programs are cited). Last year the city planted 225 trees along the parkway as well as in the central business district. As for water quality, Wheaton is now tapping into Lake Michigan water, which improved quality and taste. Air quality is good to excellent. Aggressive recycling and solid waste collection are in place, with households being charged for the amount of garbage they dispose of (their pay-per-bag system has made Wheaton the recycling leader in DuPage County). An active Environmental Improvement Commission sponsors ongoing recognition programs for residents, students and businesses.

In and Around Town

Roads and interstates: East-West Tollway (I-88), Eisenhower Expressway (I-290).
Closest airports: Chicago's O'Hare Field and Midway Airport (1 hr.).
Public transportation: Northwestern commuter train to Chicago's Loop (downtown). PACE is the city bus service.
Avg. commute: Drive to the Loop: 60 min. (45 min. by train). East-West Research and Development Corridor (Naperville) 15-20 min.

What Every Resident Knows

DuPage County has one of the highest rates of wealth per capita in the country, surely the reason some of the most abundant shopping opportunities in the country are strategically placed here. Wheaton alone has 6 major shopping areas plus nearby Oakbrook Center (Nordstroms, Saks Fifth Ave, Neiman-Marcus, etc.). A frequently seen bumper sticker sums it up: "I Shop London, Paris, Rome, Wheaton." • Here's one thing you could see on a bumper sticker, but probably never will: "Wheaton...The Protestant Vatican." There's a church or a religious organization on almost every corner, a testimony to the strong values that are the backbone of the community.

FYI

Wheaton Chamber of Commerce
331 W. Wesley
Wheaton, IL 60187
708-668-2739

DuPage Convention & Visitor's Bureau
2001 Butterfield Rd., Ste. 320
Downers Grove, IL 60515
708-241-0002

Chicago Tribune
800-874-2863

Wheaton Daily Herald/DuPage County
4300 W. Commerce Ct.
Lisle, IL 60532
708-955-3500

RE/MAX Suburban West
1417 N. Main Street
Wheaton, IL 60187
708-653-1900
Lynn Bertrand, Agent

Century 21/Auble Real Estate, Inc.
534 W. Roosevelt Rd.
Wheaton, IL 60187
708-668-2900
Glen Auble, Broker

Northern Illinois Gas
P.O. Box 190
Aurora, IL 60507
708-629-4000

Commonwealth Edison Electric
P.O. Box 278
Lombard, IL 60148
800-334-7661

Illinois Bell/Centrex
800-451-2761

Wheaton Economic Development
303 W. Wesley Street
Wheaton, IL 60187-0727
708-260-2018

School district: 708-682-2000
Property tax assessor:
708-682-7040
Welcome Wagon: 708-469-8470
Interfaith Council: None
Physician's referral: 708-260-2685

Indianapolis, Indiana

Area Snapshot

Local population: 741,952
County: Marion   **Population:** 797,159
U.S. region: Midwest/central Indiana
Closest metro area: Louisville, Ky. (114 mi. south)
Median housing price: $84,100
Avg. household income: $36,530
Best reasons to live here: Rapidly growing economy, good job prospects, affordable housing and living costs, outstanding medical, clean environment, low crime, great sports, recreation, culture, innovative schools, exceptional higher education, very family-oriented.

Fabulous Features

What does one do when they hail from a great city that commands as much respect as Rodney Dangerfield? For years it was referred to as India-No-Place, but now, Indianapolis is running circles around cities twice its size. Whether it's business opportunities, schools, health care, sports (*especially* sports), there's excitement at every turn.

The city was just ranked the 5th best place in the country for job growth by *Inc.* magazine, having grown 12,000 jobs last year alone. And airports everywhere went after this trophy: the United Airlines $1 billion maintenance facility (opening in 1994). Over a dozen other major expansion and relocation announcements have been made by leading firms in the past two years. A $4 billion dollar gift from the Lily Foundation for renewal added to the close to $2 billion spent on the infrastructure during the '80, whipping this city into a major contender for even more corporate relocations.

Selling this city is easy. Low living costs, low taxes and a tempting housing market (annual appreciation is around 4%-5%) speak for themselves. Housing prices average $20,000 less than other cities, and the charming, tree-lined neighborhoods are the finishing touch. The award-winning schools are innovative, health care is outstanding (the I.U. Medical Center is one of the top research and health providers in the U.S.), and sports action is simply unparalleled (this really *is* the amateur sports capital in the world). Between the Pacers (NBA), the Indy 500 and hundreds of exciting events each year, the sports pages are as big as some local newspapers.

Possible drawbacks: Good thing Christopher Columbus didn't try to sail the ocean blue in Indianapolis. The area is landlocked and level as a pancake. From here, he might have surmised the world was indeed flat. • Summertime humidity has residents sweating like the Pacers at halftime. • The big new City Circle Mall, part of the downtown revitalization, is on hold pending more financing. With the two major department stores now closed, this wasn't the news people wanted to hear.

"You can quote me on that"

"If you like having a big-city environment with a small-town coziness, you'll love Indianapolis. It's really easy to get around and there are so many great things to do."—S.B.

Real Estate

Market overview: This is an active market, but with a large inventory (15,000-20,000 listings at any time), houses sales aren't zooming. Buyers appreciate the choice of quality resales (appreciation at 4%-5% a year) and prices that average $20,000 below the rest of the country (according to National Association of Realtors). New construction is mostly north/northeast in Geist and Carmel and offers excellent schools and easy commutes.

What houses look like: Oldies but goodies are everywhere. The 2-3-story colonials on Meridian Street date back to the 1800s. Ranches and capes are post-World War II. Newish construction (20 years or less) offers all of the above on winding streets or quiet cul-de-sacs. Most are brick, shingle and vinyl siding. New homes show cathedral ceilings, decks, master suites and large eat-in kitchens doubling as entertaining areas.

Starter homes: Small 2BR/1BA ranches (1000 sq. ft.) on 50 x 120 lots start in the $50s-$60s. These are generally 40+ yrs., well-constructed but needing work. Look at Broad Ripple, Pike Township and Wayne Township.

Trade-ups: In the $100,000-$160,000 range you'll find nice 3BR/2BA (1800 sq. ft.) 2-story homes. Newer editions are in Castleton and Pike Township. Older homes (60-80 years) are in Washington Township. Many have large master BAs with separate dressing area ("garden bath"), fireplace and 2-car garage.

Luxury homes: $175,000-$350,000 buys a beautiful 4-5BR/2-3BA home (2500+ sq. ft) on ½ or larger acre. Amenities include 1-2 fireplaces, finished basement, den, 2-3-car garage, deck, and updated kitchens and BAs. Look at Carmel, Geist, Greenwood and, for those with an inheritance, at the mansions on Meridian (prices up to $750,000).

Rental market: Apartment rentals are wide open with avg. rents for 2BR at $550-$650/mo. 3BRs go up to $750/mo. SFH rentals are scarce and can go for $800/mo.+ where available.

Great neighborhoods: Most new developments are north of the city (Geist, Carmel) or west (Eagle Creek). Eagle Creek is adjacent to one of the largest municipal parks in the U.S. Wayne, Lawrence and Warren Townships are nice for moderate-priced homes and good schools. Broad Ripple is a colorful neighborhood with lots of parks and nightlife.

Nearby areas to consider: Rural communities with good land values are Brownsburg (10 mi. west) and Franklin (25 mi. south). Zionsville (4 mi. northwest) in Boone County has good schools, easy access to downtown (30-40 min.) and affordable prices.

What Things Cost

Runzheimer's Living Cost Index: Avg. annual costs for family of 4 with household income of $50,000: $48,830 (2.3% below avg. city).

ACCRA's national comparisons: Overall living costs are 3.2% below avg., with utilities about 10% below avg. Groceries, housing, transportation and health care are all 2-3% below avg. Goods and services are 1% below.

Utilities: Phone: Basic budget w/unlimited calling: $19/mo.; Hookup: Avg. $47. Electric: Avg. $100-$110 (Jan.); $85 (April); $95 (July); $85 (Oct.). Gas: Avg. $95 high (Jan.); $15 low (July). Year avg. is $42-$45/mo.

Kid care: By state law, day-care homes cannot watch more than 12 children at a time. Avg. costs are $60-65/wk. Day-care centers charge $50-$100/wk. and availability is good. **Pediatric visit:** $50-$65.

The Tax Ax

Sales tax: 5% (prescription drugs and food are exempt). Extra 1% on restaurant food/beverages.

Property tax: Ranges from $4.95 to $13.85 per $100 assessed value (assessed value is 1/3 cash value of property). To estimate, take 1/3 of the homes value, divide by 100 and multiply times tax rate. There is a 5% homestead credit and credits for solar energy. Taxes on a $100,000 home in Lawrence Township would pay $2,900/yr. ($11.06 rate).

State income tax: 3.4% of income after exemptions. Federal income taxes not deductible. County Option Income Tax is extra (.5% in Marion County). It's applied if you live and/or work there.

Climate

Elevation 792'	Avg. High/Low	Avg. Rain (Inches)	Avg. Snow (Inches)	Avg. Days Rain	Avg. % Humidity
Jan.	36/20	2.3	6	9	69
April	63/42	3.9	.5	12	55
July	85/65	3.7	--	9	60
Oct.	67/44	2.5	T	8	57
YEAR	62/42	36.5	22	116	62
# of days 32° or below: 120			# of days 90° or above: 15		

The continental climate brings 4 varied seasons, with occasional wide temperature swings in a short period. Late spring and fall are pleasant (sunny and dry). Summers get humid and muggy and winters see 2-3 major snowfalls each season.

Earning a Living

Economic outlook: Motor Speedway isn't the only place where things have been revving up! Indianapolis' business district is breaking records, too. *Inc.* magazine said it was among the best cities to grow a business. *Newsweek* called it a boom town. *USA Today* said was at the top of "the new big cities on the block." Ernst and Young reported that Indianapolis is its first choice in the Midwest for distribution facilities. And in a brand-new report, *Inc.* said it was ranked 5th in the nation for job growth ('90-'91). In a 12-month period, 12,600 jobs were created. The outlook is so promising because of a well-educated labor force, low utility costs, abundance of affordable office space, advanced telecommunications, proximity to major interstates and a low tax burden. But equally important is the diversity of industry. With a solid manufacturing base, there is also strong activity in retail, government (it's the state capital), transportation, health care, distribution, finance, insurance and back-office telecommunications. Another important catalyst has been the $4 billion that the Lily Endowment (pharmaceutical giant Eli Lily & Co. started here) committed to development and renewal. Newcomers include the Electronics Manufacturing Productivity Facility (a $7 million navy research and development center), United Airlines (building a new $1 billion aircraft maintenance facility), and the U.S. Postal Service (the site for its $62 million Eagle Air Hub). In addition, Thomson Consumer Electronics (manufactures for RCA, GE, and others) is opening its North American headquarters here. As the amateur sports capital of the world, conventions and the hotel industry are in full swing.

Where the jobs are: In addition to the expansions and relocations, two industries experiencing substantial growth are health and hospitals (gained over 9,000 jobs in 10 years) and entry-level data processing (more openings than applicants). Jobs in medical technology, government, engineering and research are also available. Companies hiring are Charles Schwab, Dayton Hudson, Firestone and United Airlines (will employ 6,300 by the year 2004). Significant downsizing has occurred at AT&T, Borden, Unisys, and L.S. Ayres (unemployment rate is around 5.1%.).

Business opportunities: Indianapolis had a net gain of 800 businesses from 1987-1991 (an annual growth rate of 4%). There is abundant office and factory space and suburban office rental rates are some of the lowest in the nation. Government services and permits are streamlined, making it easy to get started.

Making the Grade

Public education overview: The "I" in Indianapolis Public Schools stands for innovation. The largest system in the state (85 schools and close to 50,000 students) has virtually customized curriculums. For 13 years, its "Programs of Choice" have been a tremendous success. Elementary students apply to be in an option program, including Basics, Montessori, and Key (based on Harvard theory of multiple intelligence). Magnet schools for junior and senior high students focus on everything from performing arts to foreign language to business and health careers to an academic academy. However, most of the growth in the area has been in outlying communities such as Pike, Washington, Lawrence and Carmel townships, all of which have their own excellent school districts, low teacher-student ratios, new facilities and strong college prep programs. All of Carmel schools have received national excellence awards. Pike schools are known for gifted and talented and special education programs. Schools in Washington Township have earned the Indiana 2000 Awards among others. The Lawrence District (includes Geist) has 5 schools earning national excellence awards and last year had 22 National Merit semi-finalists.

Class size: 16:1.

Help for working parents: YMCA Before and After School/Child Care Program, and At-Your-School Child Services are available on site.

Blue Ribbon School Awards: 15 area schools have earned Blue Ribbon Awards. The most recent are: Mary Evelyn Castle Elementary ('87-'88), Eastbrook and Indian Creek elementary schools ('89-'90), Southport Middle School ('88-'89), Winchester Village Elementary ('87-'88).

School year: Last wk. of Aug. through 1st week of June. A child must be 5 by June 1 to attend kindergarten, although attendance is not mandatory under Indiana law.

Special education/gifted programs: IPS offers the School for the Blind, School for the Deaf and the Marion County Association for Retarded Children. Therapy and counseling are also provided. Gifted grade school students are in the Academically Talented Elementary Program.

Nearby colleges/universities: Indiana University-Purdue University at Indianapolis (28,000 students, 160+ degree programs); Butler University (4-year); University of Indianapolis; Marion College; Indiana Vocational Technical College; Franklin College; Indiana University at Bloomington (4-year) and DePauw University.

Medical Care

Hospitals/medical centers: Indiana University Medical Center operates 5 major hospitals and numerous clinics and is one of the largest, most respected health care facilities in the country. It's known for its work in cardiology, testicular carcinoma, endocrinology, pediatrics, and alcohol-related disorders. St. Vincent Hospital offers the Indiana Heart Institute, a consortium of cardiologists and cardiovascular surgeons. Methodist Hospital offers the Joslin Diabetic Clinic and performs organ and tissue transplants. Indianapolis has 33 doctors per 100,000 residents.

Specialized care: Riley Hospital for Children is one of the country's most widely regarded for the diagnosis and treatment of birth defects, blood disorders, and heart ailments. Humana Women's Center is known for its care of high risk pregnancies.

Crime & Safety

The good news is Indianapolis has the fourth lowest crime rate of the 50 largest U.S. cities and ties with Louisville for having the lowest violent crime in the Midwest (FBI). The bad news is that criminals are gaining on 'em. Figures show that in a one-year period ('90-'91), there were increases in every category, presumably due to a growing population and a higher-than-ever number of events attracting visitors. In response, neighborhood crime watch programs are beefing up their presence and Mayor Goldsmith has instituted a Neighborhood Policing Campaign. More officers are walking their beats instead of "drive by" patrolling. It's helping. The 1992 stats show slight declines in overall crime.

Community Life

According to a recent Indiana University survey, 52% of Indianapolis residents respond to "Help wanted" messages during the year. That's the call for volunteering, not jobs. Whether it's for the Children's Museum, where youngsters volunteer and grow up to become unpaid supervisors, or the Indianapolis U.S. Men's Tennis Championships (volunteers do everything from chase tennis balls to make social arrangements), people think nothing of giving their time. And now the 5-year old neighborhood Clean City Committee really has people cleaning up their act. It's been successful setting up recycling centers, keeping downtown clean and establishing the successful Earth Day celebration. The local Sierra Club is eternally grateful.

Let the Good Times Roll

Family fun: If your family's not having fun in Indianapolis, you can't be trying too hard. Start with the 5,100-acre Eagle Creek Park and Reservoir. This the largest municipal park in the U.S., perfect for boating, hiking, cross-country skiing and nature walks. Within a 2-hour drive are 18 state parks, 11 major recreation sites, 8 state forests and 15 fish and wildlife areas. One of the most beloved is Brown County State Park (basking in the fall foliage eating hot roasted nuts is a dream day). In the city is the White River State Park, home of the Indianapolis Zoo (this $64 million zoo has 2,000 animals in simulated natural habitats), the National Institute for Fitness and Sport and the Eiteljorg Museum. It is also the site of the $1.3 million ½-mile River Promenade and the statewide mini-Olympics. The Children's Museum (said to be the nation's largest) has a wonderful planetarium and exciting year-round programs. The City Market is a restored historical area with 90 shops, and the Conner Prairie Pioneer Settlement is a recreated version of Indianapolis dating back to the 1800s. *U.S. News and World Report* gave it its highest rating for authenticity and entertainment.

Sports: Indianapolis wins the championship as the world's amateur sports capital. The granddaddy of all events is the annual Indy 500 Race, the largest one-day sporting event (350,000+ spectators). The festivities last a month, with Memorial Day weekend as the finish line. $168 million has been invested in world-class sports facilities including Market Square Arena (home of the NBA Pacers), the Hoosier Dome (home of the NFL Colts), the Indiana/World Skating Academy at Pan Am Plaza, the Indianapolis Sports Center (tennis) and the Hoosier Horse Park.

Arts & entertainment: Cultural life is also a winner. The Indianapolis Museum of Art is internationally acclaimed. Other popular museums are the Eiteljorg Museum of American Indian and Western Art, the Children's Museum, Indiana State Museum, Hook's Historical Drugstore & Pharmacy Museum and the Motor Speedway Museum. The Indianapolis Symphony Orchestra offers a full calendar of shows and concerts. Other offerings are the Indiana Repertory Theater, the Indianapolis Ballet Theater and Indianapolis Opera Company. More than 230 not-for-profit arts groups are here.

Annual events: Indianapolis 500 (the most exciting racing spectacle in the world: Memorial Day weekend); Indiana State Fair (Aug.); Earth Day Celebration (April); Balloon Classic (hot-air balloon race: May); Penrod Arts Fair (Sept.)

The Environment

What a difference 10 years makes! Since then, several state-of-the-art municipal wastewater treatment plants were built that improved water quality significantly. Stringent surface water standards are also in effect. The biggest sign of improvement is that there are fish swimming in the county waterways again. 95% of municipal water comes from reservoirs (but an estimated 1/3 of Marion County residents have private wells. Water is hard and since carbon filters are not used, water may have a faint smell. Air quality is good, meeting the EPA pollution attainments. One problem remains. The antiquated sewer system overflows during heavy rainstorms, releasing sewage into local streams. No immediate solution is in the works.

In and Around Town

Roads and interstates: Indianapolis is called the "Crossroads of America" because it is the most centrally located of the country's top 100 cities. Rapid travel around the city is possible with 4 expressways extending into downtown, intersecting the I-465 loop. I-65, I-74, I-70,I-69, I-67 are U.S. Highways that also feed into the city.
Closest airports: Indianapolis International Airport (12 min. from downtown). Eagle Creek Airport handles 100,000 general aviation flights a year.
Public transportation: The Indianapolis Metro bus system covers downtown and suburban areas with 53 routes. Metro also has several express routes, 43 park-and-ride locations and a weekday trolley service.
Avg. commute: 15-25 min. to downtown.

What Every Resident Knows

Bet you'd love to know what a "Hoosier" is. So would we, but with more than 30 theories on where the name originated, it's anyone's guess. Was it from early settlers who answered the door, "Who's yere?" Was it from "hushers" who settled squabbles by banging fists on tables? The debate continues. • Nearby Carmel, Indiana is pronounced like the candy, not like Carmel, California, the city famous for breathtaking drives. • Speaking of exciting driving, 16th and Georgetown Road during Memorial Day weekend doesn't get any more so. That's the site of the Indianapolis 500 at Motor Speedway. Ironically, the rest of the city is business as usual because many of the 350,000 spectators are from out-of-town! • Long for Greenwich Village? Then take the kids shopping at Broad Ripple Village. They can feed the ducks in Broad Ripple Canal while you enjoy the art galleries, second-hand clothing shops, sidewalk cafes, even a feminist bookstore.

FYI

Indianapolis Chamber of Commerce
320 N. Meridian Street, Suite 928
Indianapolis, IN 46204
317-464-2238

Indianapolis Visitors Bureau
One Hoosier Dome, Suite 100
Indianapolis, IN 46225
317-639-4282

**Indianapolis Star and
Indianapolis News**
307 N. Pennsylvania
Indianapolis, IN 46204
317-633-9211

Century 21 Gold Key Realtors
8200 Haverstick Road, Suite 100
Indianapolis, IN 46260
800-533-3446 / James Pearsall

Indianapolis Power & Light
25 Monument Circle
Indianapolis, IN 46204
317-261-8222

Citizens Gas & Coke Utility
2020 N. Meridian Street
Indianapolis, IN 46202
317-924-3311

Indiana Bell
240 N. Meridian Street
Indianapolis, IN 46204
317-556-4200

**Indianapolis Economic
Development Corporation**
320 N. Meridian, Suite 906
Indianapolis, IN 46204
317-236-6262

**Indiana Small Business
Development Center**
One N. Capital Street, Suite 1275
Indianapolis, IN 46204
317-264-2820

School district: 317-226-4411
Property tax assessor:
317-327-4907
Newcomer's Club: 317-252-3482
Interfaith Council: 317-926-5371
Physician's referral: 317-351-7800
Day-care referral: 317-232-0948

Overland Park, Kansas (Kansas City)

Area Snapshot

Local population: 111,790
County: Johnson **Population:** 355,000
U.S. region: Midwest/Northeastern Kansas
Closest metro areas: Kansas City, Miss (8 mi. east)
Median housing price: $125,700
Median household income: $44,246
Best reasons to live here: Fastest-growing county in Kansas, stable economy, low unemployment, superb public schools, affordable housing and beautiful new subdivisions, excellent health care, great roads/transportation.

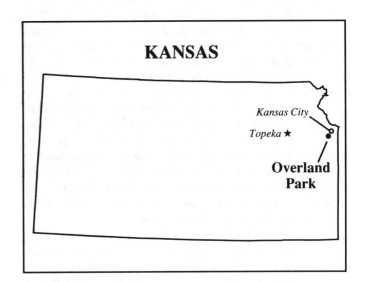

Fabulous Features

To borrow from a familiar theme, "There's no place like Kansas," and definitely no place like Overland Park. Situated on the rolling plains of the Kansas/Missouri state line (yes, there are actually hills), here is both a kinder, gentler city for children as well as a community where parents can prosper. With an outstanding parks and recreation department (12,000 children participate in ongoing programs), three of the finest nationally recognized school districts in the country, and an extraordinarily low crime rate, children get off to the best possible start. As Johnson County is one of the fastest-growing and most affluent counties in the state, Mom and Dad have access to exciting career opportunities in the service sector. Jobs doubled in the past 10 years, and unemployment is a low 2.4%.

But what really gets the heart pounding are the high incomes and low living costs. Overland Park has the highest per-capita income in the metro area, while real estate prices and taxes are very reasonable, particularly in the luxury market. Out-of-town transferees marvel that

for $200,000, they can live in a palatial new home on a lake and a golf course, pay $2,400 in taxes *and* be 10 minutes from the office (30 percent of residents work in Overland Park).

You can kiss the "commute from hell" goodbye and say hello to the good life. Professional sports, ample recreation, and the theater are waiting. With a 35-percent increase in population in the past 10 years, that's a lot of people who have discovered that Overland Park is as nice as any place over the rainbow.

Possible drawbacks: Kansas is inextricably landlocked. The only thing that comes from the Gulf is the humidity. If you've dreamt of life on the waterfront, you'd better like manmade lakes. • Cultural diversity is lacking. While the array of offerings has improved significantly, most of the "openings" will be on your calendar. • Overland Park is very transient because of a high level of corporate transfers. This makes it difficult to establish a real sense of community. However, we heard that companies are having a harder time convincing people to leave, so perhaps stability is on the way.

"You can quote me on that"

"I wasn't so sure we could make an easy transition from Pennsylvania. I guess we expected this to be a hick town. It's not! People are extremely well educated and very caring. You hear about Southern hospitality, but it doesn't hold a candle to Midwest neighborliness. This is a wonderful, friendly community."—L.L.

Real Estate

Market overview: Lower interest rates and pent-up demand for "trading up" made the first half of 1992 the best sales period since 1987. New home sales are strong; resales are, too, a reflection of only modest appreciation in the past 10 years (avg. sale price is $110,000-$125,000 for a super 4BR Tudor). What's unique is that homes in each subdivision are in the same price range, which helps hold resale values. Overall, starting prices are in the $70s and $80s, and homes are spacious and well-constructed. Most inventory is SFHs (80%), but there has been a surge of new condo developments (from $50,000-$150,000). With ample inventory in all price ranges and a steady stream of customers, buyers *and* sellers are happy to be in the market.

What houses look like: Older homes show 4BR split levels, ranches and bi-levels (raised ranches). Most have basements and double garages. Popular in new construction are 2-story Tudors (all BRs on 2nd level) or 1½-stories (master suite on 1st level). New exteriors show stone, stucco and brick. Interiors have media rooms, nurseries attached to master suites and study lofts.

Starter homes: Resale starters (6-20 years old) go for $70,000-$80,000 for a small 3BR/1½BA ranch, but the avg. price is between $90,000-$110,000. This buys a 4BR split level with 2-car garage.

Trade-ups: In the $125,000-$150,000 range, buyers get a new 4BR, 1½- or 2-story in Scenic Woods, Amber Meadows or other subdivisions.

Luxury homes: Starting from $240,000, new 4BR/3½BA homes (2900-3900 sq. ft.) are selling faster than any segment of the market. Most have all bedrooms with adjoining BAs, 2 fireplaces (perhaps one in the kitchen), 3-car garages, large European-style kitchens and nice-sized lots (80 x 150). Most high-end subdivisions have a pool and tennis association.

Rental market: The rental market for SFHs is very tight. A 3-4BR home selling for $100,000 would rent for $850/mo. if you could find one; 2-3BR condos are easier to find (and quite nice). Rents start at $450/mo. and go up to $1,000/mo.

Great neighborhoods: Oak Park is a very nice development for resales (prices in the $135,000 range). Deer Creek (on a golf course), Nottingham Forest South and Hallbrook are gorgeous new developments with homes from $200,000+.

Nearby areas to consider: Olathe, south, offers moderately priced homes ($80,000-$90,000), and the schools are fantastic. Lenexa and Leawood also have ample new construction, and children attend top-rated Shawnee Mission schools.

What Things Cost

Runzheimer's Living Cost Index: Avg. annual costs for family of 4 with household income of $50,000: $47,309 (5.4% below avg.)

ACCRA's national comparisons: (For Kansas City.) Overall costs are 3.7% below avg. Utilities are 9.2% below avg., food is 6.2% below, and housing is 2.2% below. Health care is the only above avg. cost (2.1%).

Utilities: Phone: Avg. $16/mo. Installations: Avg. $39. Electric is highest in Jan. (avg. $90/mo.) and July (avg. $98/mo.). Spring and fall bills avg. $70. Gas: Avg. $42/mo. (Jan. bill can run as high as $95).

Kid care: Licensed day-care centers charge $165-175/wk. At-home day-care avg. $125-$135/wk. **Pediatric visit:** $35-$40.

The Tax Ax

Sales tax: 6.5%.

Property tax: Property taxes are an estimated 12% of a home's appraised value multiplied by the local mill levy. Overland Park's current levy is $100. For example, a $125,000 home would run $1,200/yr. A $200,000 home would run $2,400/yr.

State income tax: Federal adjusted gross income minus Kansas taxable income (personal deductions) is taxed at graduated rates. For married filing jointly, the first $30,000 of income is taxed at 3.5%. The next $30,000 is taxed at a rate of 6.25%. All taxable income over $60,000 is taxed at 6.45 (the cap).

Climate

Elevation 1,014'	Avg. High/Low	Avg. Rain (Inches)	Avg. Snow (Inches)	Avg. Days Rain	Avg. % Humidity
Jan.	36/19	.7	6	7	67
April	65/45	3.5	.7	9	53
July	88/70	4.4	--	5	46
Oct.	69/48	3.2	--	6	58
YEAR	64/45	35	20	98	60
# of days 32° or below: 102			# of days 90° or above: 38		

Located in the geographical center of the U.S., Overland Park experiences all kinds of weather extremes. Early spring is fickle, jumping from last-minute winter storms to flash floods and thunderstorms. Winter temps are not severe, but there can be snowfall from Oct. to March. Summers are warm and humid, and the fall is mild and sunny.

Earning a Living

Economic outlook: Overland Park is an "edge city"—a former bedroom community that is now also a major business community. In the past 10 years, it experienced a phenomenal growth spurt, with employment nearly doubling (from 34,000-69,500 jobs). In that same period, more than $2 billion was poured into new construction (residential and commercial office space), and retail sales close to tripled (from $694 million to nearly $1.71 billion). Now you know why it's one of only 12 U.S. cities that has earned its 5th consecutive AAA bond rating (Moody's) and its 4th from Standard and Poors. At present, the local unemployment rate is 2.4% (it's consistently been less than half the national avg.). Even better, close to half of all residents work in Johnson County (30% of those jobs are in Overland Park). Although the service and financial/insurance/real estate sectors are prominent (the Kansas City metro area has traditionally been the Midwest hub for national companies), the most dynamic growth has been in wholesale trade (a 600% increase in jobs between 1969-1989). J.C. Penney has a huge distribution center here, as does Yellow Freight. Commercial development also continues to break records ($237 million in new construction in a year). With dozens of new residential subdivisions already built, the largest luxury development in the city has just been announced (Lions Gate plans a 1,000-unit community on a golf course). Given the projected population increase of 14,000 by the mid '90s, there is no end in sight to the growth.

Where the jobs are: In the past 7 years, O.P. has stood for Office Park more than Overland Park, with a 48% to 142% increase in insurance, professional communications and transportation offices built. Among the city's largest and expanding employers are Farmers Insurance Group, Yellow Freight Systems, Travelers Insurance, Black & Veatch (internationally known architectural engineering firm), United Telephone, Humana Hospital, CNA Insurance and United Telecommunications. U.S. Sprint recently announced plans to expand its national headquarters into a 247-acre office project. The NCAA recently relocated here.

Business opportunities: With Overland Park's desirable demographics (disposable income is the highest in the state), thousands of major and minor (niche) retailers are based here. Restaurants are also in great supply. Manufacturing is nonexistent, and the city is not looking for that to change (it's happy leasing its 7 million square feet of office space).

Making the Grade

Public education overview: Overland Park students attend Shawnee Mission, Blue Valley or Olathe Schools. Average scores on national tests place students in the top 10% of all public schools in the country. Shawnee's motto is "Today's students, tomorrow's global leaders." It opened a Center for International Studies (its International Marketplace has elementary students learning currencies, cooking recipes, and having festivals for different countries). In 1991, 31 of the county's 45 National Merit finalists were Shawnee Mission students. Blue Valley High School was named best in the state by *Redbook* magazine (April 1992); 85% of this district's graduates attend college, and parental involvement is marvelous. At Back-to-School Night, 1,800 parents attend—not bad for an enrollment of 1,400. The district is best noted for its award-winning library media program and commitment to technology (every elementary class has a computer). Olathe South High School was one of 42 schools in the U.S. rated for overall excellence by *Redbook*. The common goals of Overland Park educators are to broaden students' horizons outside the classroom and make the schools the pride of the community. They succeed, big time!

Class size: 21:1 (Blue Valley); 20:1 (Shawnee Mission); 17:1 (Olathe).

Help for working parents: After-school latchkey programs are in most elementary schools. Programs are supervised by the YMCA or other agencies.

Blue Ribbon School Awards: Blue Valley District: Blue Valley Middle School, Blue Valley North High, Valley Park Elementary and Morse Elementary. **Shawnee Mission District:** Brookridge Elementary, Hocker Grove Middle School, Meadowbrook Junior High, Shawnee Mission South High and Shawnee Mission West High. **Olathe District:** Oregon Trail Junior High, Santa Fe Trail Junior High, Tomahawk Elementary.

School year: Last week of Aug. to the first week of June. Children must be 5 on or by Sept. 1 to enter kindergarten.

Special education/gifted programs: Mainstreaming and "class-within-a-class" programs with the help of a trained aide are used in the districts. Children with severe or multiple handicaps are assigned to the Catherine Carpenter School. Gifted students attend pull-out programs at 8 schools.

Nearby colleges/universities: There are 30 institutes of higher learning in the metro area, including Johnson County Community College, University of Kansas Regents Center, Ottawa University, and Baker University in Kansas City.

Medical Care

Hospitals/medical centers: Humana Hospitals/ Overland Park, Shawnee Mission Medical Center and St. Joseph Health Center have 24-hour emergency centers and wellness programs for the community. Humana Hospital has a state-of-the-art cardiology division, nationally acclaimed infertility services and the Diabetes Center of Excellence. Other area hospitals include Saint Lukes Hospital (excellent maternity services), Olathe Medical Center (coronary care has Space Labs, the latest monitoring available), University of Kansas Medical Center (nationally acclaimed burn center), Menorah Medical Center, and Children's Mercy Specialty Center.

Specialized care: Johnson County Mental Health Center, Johnson County Mental Retardation Center, the Adolescent Center for Treatment (intermediate-care inpatient alcohol/drug treatment facility), and Crittendon (range of mental health programs for children and families).

Crime & Safety

Overland Park Police are the first to admit the city is vulnerable to crime. It is accessible by major roadways, and nonresidents come every day to shop and patronize the restaurants. And yet, the overall crime rate is extremely low. The homicide, burglary and auto theft rates are a fraction of the Kansas City metro area. It stays this way because the police have strong financial support from the city (the equipment and resources are the latest available), they're super-tough on DUI (10% of the force work on reducing traffic offenses), and they're highly visible in the community (they're constantly on the lecture circuit talking about crime prevention).

Community Life

Anyplace that has a New Arrivals Greeting Service, a Welcome Wagon and a New Neighbors League, and the theme "Welcome home to Overland Park," will no doubt be happy to see you when you move in. Friendliness and generosity are the hallmarks of this city, with hundreds of volunteer opportunities coordinated through the Volunteer Center of Johnson County. Its Christmas Bureau shares food, clothing and gifts with 3,400 people. When Johnson County Community College cried, "Help," city businesses responded with "Broadway on the Boulevard," raising $100,000 for scholarships. Close to $500,000 was raised at the American Cancer Society's annual gala.

Let the Good Times Roll

Family fun: Overland Park maintains more than 1,600 acres of green space (not to mention that only 60% of the city is developed) with 60 beautifully maintained parks, a children's petting farm, and Indian Creek, a gorgeous 10-mile bike and hike trail, which will eventually connect with adjacent communities. Residents also have access to an ample number of playing fields, two 18-hole golf courses and 6 municipal pools. The latest addition is the new outdoor Aquatic Center, complete with lush landscaping, exciting water slides and other recreation. The city also owns 2 large indoor recreation centers. The Johnson County Park and Recreation District operates more than 4,600 acres of parkland, including the Oakridge Farm Stables and the innovative Streamway Parks system (when complete, it will run parks and trails through 8 stream corridors). Park facilities also allow for canoeing, sailing, fishing and other outdoor activities. A favorite exhibit is the Deanna Rose Farmstead, a miniature replica of a turn-of-the-century farm, created for children. Residents can even reserve plots to grow their own garden. Great fun awaits on the Missouri side of Kansas City at the Worlds of Fun (an amusement park with international delights) and Oceans of Fun (world's largest water park).

Sports: Professional sports enthusiasts head to Kansas City for year-round action. The Kansas City Royals (major league baseball), the Chiefs (NFL), and the Attacks (indoor soccer) are here. Collegiate sports fans were delighted when the NCAA moved its national headquarters to Overland Park.

Arts & entertainment: Johnson County's Theater in the Park draws more than 90,000 people a year, making it one of the biggest performing arts attractions in the metro area. The Theater for Young America, a year-round professional troupe, presents wonderful family shows. In 1990 the Cultural Education Center opened at the Johnson Community College, which has brought wonderful programs and exhibits to the community. Kansas City offers Broadway touring companies, the Kansas City Symphony and Ballet as well as the Nelso-Atkins Museum of Fine Art (received international acclaim for its Oriental collection), the Harry S Truman Library and Museum, and the Center for Performing Arts at the University of Missouri. A new dinner theater has also recently opened.

Annual events: Arts and Crafts Fair (Sept.); Art in the Woods (May); Corporate Woods Jazz Festival (June); 4th of July Celebration (first one in 8 years, was a big success).

The Environment

Overland Park is green and clean. For the 13th consecutive year, it has been recognized as a Tree City USA. And with no manufacturing plants, Overland Park's air quality has always been excellent. It's also helpful that the Kansas City metro area is the largest in the country to have met the strict standards of the EPA's Clean Air Act. Water quality is also good with respect to abundance and purity (Missouri and Kansas Rivers meet or exceed all state and national regulations). The streets are immaculate, too. Approximately 22,000 households participate in curbside recycling and composting yard waste. The city has also asked the state for funds for a permanent facility for household hazardous waste.

In and Around Town

Roads and interstates: I-35 (to downtown), I-435 (to north Kansas City), Highway 169, and I-635 (to Kansas City International Airport), and Highway 56 (Shawnee Mission Parkway) through Johnson County.

Closest airports: Kansas City International Airport (40 min.), plus 2 business/commuter airports within 20 min. (Johnson County Executive Airport and Johnson County Industrial Airport).

Public transportation: Johnson County Transit provides 12 bus routes (including express service to downtown). Commuters are encouraged to join the regional Rideshare program. KCI Express provides direct service to the airport.

Avg. commute: 25-30 min.

What Every Resident Knows

Kansas' Governor Joan Finney, Senator Nancy Landon Kassenbaum, State Representative Jan Meyers and State Treasurer Sally Thompson are proving what women have always known. Their place is in the house...*and* the Senate (the Overland Park Chamber of Commerce even hired a woman president—its first!). • Speaking of elected officials, here's a place where "honest politician" is not a contradiction in terms. City government has earned the faith of residents by properly planning for growth. Proof is in the fact that virtually all the bond issues and ballots get passed by large majorities. • KCK is not a new type of chicken, it's the local's nickname for Kansas City, Kansas. Guess what they call Kansas City, Missouri. Right... • People perceive Kansas to be the plains state, flat as a pancake. But in the northeast part, it's hilly, lush and green. Out-of-town buyers all sound the same. "This is Kansas?" Yes, Dorothy, it is!

FYI

Overland Park Chamber of Commerce
P.O. Box 12125
Overland Park, KS 66212
913-491-3600

Kansas City Star (daily)
1729 Grand Avenue
Kansas City, MO 64108
816-234-4141

Sun Publications (biweekly)
7373 W 107th Street
Overland Park, KS 66212
913-381-1010

REMAX/Realty Suburban
11900 W. 87th Street
Shawnee Mission, KS 66215
800-825-0240
Darrell Wallingford, agent

Angel Berry Realtors, Inc.
7050 W. 107th Street
Overland Park, KS 66212
913-341-4441
Angel Berry, Pres.

Southwestern Bell
800-574-4000

Kansas City Power & Light Co.
P.O. Box 419330
Kansas City, MO 64141
816-471-5275 (KCPL)

KPL Gas Service
P.O. Box 419981
Kansas City, MO 64194
816-221-4600

Overland Park Economic Development
P.O. Box 12125
Overland Park, KS 66212
913-491-3600

School districts: 913-681-4000 (Blue Valley), 913-831-1900 (Shawnee Mission), 913-780-7000 (Olathe)
Property tax assessor: 913-371-7350
New Neighbor's League: 913-681-5103
Interfaith Council: Chamber of Commerce has a list of houses of worship.
Physician's referral: 913-541-5200
Day-care referral: 913-341-6200

Lexington, Kentucky

Area Snapshot

Local/county population: 225,366
County: Fayette   **Population:** 348,428
U.S. region: Central Kentucky (Bluegrass region)/Southern U.S.
Closest metro areas: Louisville (73 mi. west), Cincinnati, Ohio (82 mi. north)
Median housing price: $73,900
Median household income: $28,056
Best reasons to live here: Beautiful horse farm country, delightful year-round climate, historic college town, low crime, range of housing options, strong public school system, abundant recreation, low unemployment, taxes.

Fabulous Features

The past is present in splendid Kentucky Bluegrass country. Amid internationally acclaimed horse farms, antique street cars and stately Victorian homes, here's a fast-growing region with forward-thinking ideas. The city and county merged their governments 18 years ago to insure smooth operation (the only red tape in Lexington is at the horse tracks)!

Population growth has been steady (10.4% increase since 1980), with projections for another 20,000+ by 2000. Real estate development is burgeoning south of the city. Ironically, realtors apologize for high prices (compared to other parts of Kentucky), but they obviously haven't shopped other states! From $65,000 on up, there's a broad inventory of traditional, elegant homes in rural, suburban and city neighborhoods.

Of course, once you own the house, don't plan to spend time indoors. Families can't wait to head for the festivals, historic sites, recreation and sports (this is the thoroughbred capital of the U.S., and home of thousands of basketball fans)! The delightful year-round climate (warm, sunny days with low humidity) means you can swing a racket from April to December.

As Lexington is a bustling college town (14 in all), educational and employment opportunities are vast. The public school system is light-years ahead of other Kentucky districts. The Toyota plant keeps growing, and Clark Equipment Co. is returning home with 200 jobs. Lexington is in the winner's circle.

Possible drawbacks: The Fayette County School System took a big financial hit with the enactment of the Kentucky Education Reform Act. Programs are intact, but every dollar spent on operations is subject to scrutiny. • The geographic dispersion of horse farms had always landlocked neighborhoods. But with many farms closing and the population growing, developments are cropping up where privacy once was. • Two things make the world go round here—horses and basketball. If you don't absolutely love one or the other (or both), you might not make a party host's "A list."

"You can quote me on that"

"I lived in Florida, North Carolina and Hawaii before moving to Lexington, and this is one of the most pleasant places there is. It's not very big and people are so friendly. I like the community spirit, too. I'm a single parent and am very comfortable raising my children in this environment."—M.G.

Real Estate

Market overview: The market's been up, down and around in the past two years, with the most recent trend showing a 10%-15% drop in prices. This has stimulated a lot of activity, particularly in the under-$100,000 market (they go faster than a thoroughbred). The luxury market is also strong (Fayette County is one of the wealthiest in Kentucky). And don't worry that you'll only see "Old Kentucky homes"—gorgeous new homes are widely available.

What houses look like: They're some of the most well-built homes we've seen. Colonial-style, ranches or capes with brick and/or frame construction are very popular. Many new homes have contemporary interiors, with open space, great rooms and exquisite master BAs. Homes in the $80,000+ range offer a basement and garage. Buyers marvel at the beautiful cabinetry (generations of craftsmen are here).

Starter homes: Prices range from $50,000-$80,000 for a 3-4BR/1½-2BA townhouse (very popular) or SFH (1000-1200 sq. ft.). Houses are on 50 x 100 lots, with capes and ranches widely available. Avg. age is 30-35 years. Look at Blue Ridge Acres and Kenawood (northeast).

Trade-ups: For $90,000-$130,000, choose between old homes (50+ years) in Ashland Park and Chevy Chase or "newish" homes (15 years) in Landsdowne Merrick. Older homes are 1½-story capes (1BR/1BA on the 1st floor, 2BR/2BA on the 2nd floor) with ceiling fans and screened porches.

Luxury homes: From $160,000 to a half a million buys a stately, traditional showplace. Large foyers with tile flooring, big family kitchens with breakfast areas, and tremendous formal living and dining rooms are the trademarks.

Rental market: With almost half the city's population under 34, rentals are big business. A 2BR townhouse avg. $525/mo. For SFHs, expect annual rents to be about 10% of a home's value.

Great neighborhoods: Chevy Chase, Landsdowne Merrick and Ashland Park are older, prestigious addresses. Hartland, Andover and Palomar are beautiful new developments in all price ranges. Waterford and Cumberland have very affordable new homes to show.

Nearby areas to consider: Versailles (pronounced Ver-sales) in adjacent Woodford County offers scenic country roads and grand Victorian architecture. Access to 4 parkways makes it a quick hop downtown. Other nice communities are Georgetown (Scott County), Nicholasville (Jessamine County), and Paris (Bourban County—which, surprisingly, is a dry county).

What Things Cost

Runzheimer's Living Cost Index: Avg. annual costs for family of 4 with household income of $50,000: $47,689 (4.6% below avg.).

ACCRA's national comparisons: Overall living costs are approx. 2% below the national avg. Utilities are 18% below, health care is 3% below. Housing and food are avg.

Utilities: Electric: Avg. $35/mo. Gas: Avg. $48/mo. Phone: $26/mo.

Kid care: Day-care avg. $65-$85/wk. After-school programs are $30-$40/wk. **Pediatric visit:** $40.

The Tax Ax

Sales tax: 6% (food, prescriptions, medical aids and some utilities exempt).

Property tax: Homeowners pay an *ad valorem* tax based on services provided in their area. Rates range from 71¢-92¢ per $100/valuation. A rule of thumb is 1% of the assessed value. For example, a $100,000 home would owe $1,000/yr.

State income tax: Up to $3,000 of taxable net income is 2%; next $1,000 or portion is 3%; next $1,000 or portion is $1,000; next $3,000 or portion is 5%; balance in excess of $8,000 is 6%. Federal income tax not deductible. Note: Fayette County also imposes a local gross income tax of 2%.

Climate

Elevation 966'	Avg. High/Low	Avg. Rain (Inches)	Avg. Snow (Inches)	Avg. Days Rain	Avg. % Humidity
Jan.	41/25	3.4	.6	11	67
April	66/45	3	.2	13	55
July	86/66	4.8	--	11	58
Oct.	69/47	2.1	--	8	55
YEAR	65/45	42.8	17	126	59
# of days 32° or below: 95			# of days 90° or above: 17		

Lexington's mild year-round climate is a breeze to adjust to. The sun is never directly overhead, and humidity is always low. Light breezes keep days cool and comfortable. Fall is sunny, and winters are short and sweet.

"You can quote me on that"
"We always wanted to raise our kids in a college town. Everyone thinks and acts young. I think we heard that half the population is under 34."—S.F.

Earning a Living

Economic outlook: In 1985 Lexington was in the race of its life. Its IBM plant was breaking records for growth and expansion, and Toyota announced plans to move in (an $800 million investment decision). Along with growing agricultural, manufacturing and health care industries, no one could say this was just a one-horse town! Then it experienced the loss of IBM and the beginning of hard times for the Japanese automotive industry. Although the local Georgetown plant produces the hot-selling Camry, business leaders were concerned that if Toyota was vulnerable, so was Lexington. The region is now holding its own. Lexmark International took over the IBM plant, and Toyota announced a $90 million expansion (adding 200 jobs by 1994). An important byproduct has been the 50+ companies that opened to serve Toyota (employing 9,000 people). Clark Equipment (a Fortune 500 company) just announced it was bringing 200 manufacturing jobs back from Korea. ("We'll prove we can still be globally competitive!") Another industry that has come full circle is Kentucky's bourbon distillers. A 200-year tradition was threatened by lack of "spirit" in the U.S. for hard whiskey, but global marketing exported six million cases in 1991. With marked progress in a variety of industries, particularly health care and education, personal income shot up by 126% in the past 10 years.

Where the jobs are: Despite a steady job growth (27,000 new jobs in the past 10 years) and low unemployment (currently at 4%), the economy is not totally out of the woods. Education remains the largest employer, with both the Fayette County Schools and a dozen major universities and colleges in the area. Other notable employers include GTE Products, Square D Company, General Electric, Hart Schaffner & Marx, United Parcel Service, Rand McNally, Rockwell International and seven regional hospitals (Central Baptist is the biggest). Ashland Oil recently expanded its Valvoline Oil headquarters to make room for its Superamerica subsidiary. Hughes Display Products (subsidiary of General Motors) occupied a new 130,000 sq. ft. facility, employing 250.

Business opportunities: Two years ago, *Inc.* magazine ranked Lexington 29th of 192 communities for its entrepreneurial opportunities (it cited the number of new business startups and percentage of high-growth companies). Numerous resources, including the Community Ventures Corporation (CVC) and the Bluegrass Microenterprise Fund (offers first-time loans up to $25,000), assist business owners.

Making the Grade

Public education overview: Parents of Fayette County's 32,000 schoolchildren were holding their collective breath when the Kentucky Education Reform Act was passed. Knowing it meant a substantial blow to the school budget (in the millions), they were less certain about the impact in the classroom. Although the adjustment period isn't over, there are signs that many programs have actually been strengthened. Foreign language programs start in first grade. In primary grades, children are in dual-age classes (for example, second and third graders are together) to encourage working at their own pace without stigma of failing. And students will now participate in performance-based assessments tests (at grades 4, 8 & 12). In addition to conventional testing, writing and thinking skills will be evaluated. At present, test scores are well above state and national levels. On the extracurricular side, Lexington schools consistently rank at the top in many state and national competitions (especially debate teams and orchestras). As for faculty, there has always been a long waiting list for teaching jobs. The draw is the salary level (at $33,687, it's one of the highest in Kentucky) and that teachers work only in their accredited subjects.

Class size: 16:1.

Help for working parents: The Creative Activity Program (CAP), an after-school program, is available for grades K-5 for $5/day plus $1/day if transportation is needed. Teachers are on duty for early drop-off (cost is $7.50/wk.).

Blue Ribbon School Awards: Southern Elementary School ('89-'90).

School year: Third week in Aug. through the first week of June. Children must be 5 on or before Oct. 1 to enter kindergarten.

Special education/gifted programs: The district's Early Start program is an important step in getting at-risk 3- and 4-year-olds off to the best start. Special education programs are tailored for each child. Gifted programs are widely available along with magnet middle and high schools. A special mathematics, science, and technology center at the new Paul Laurence Dunbar High School offers advanced curricula for college-bound students.

Nearby colleges/universities: Lexington is "college country," with a wide range of schools including the University of Kentucky (55,000 students), Transylvania University (1,000 students), Eastern Kentucky University, Kentucky State University (liberal arts), and several junior and vocational-technical colleges.

Medical Care

Hospitals/medical centers: Lexington/Fayette is the medical hub of Central/Eastern Kentucky, with 7 major hospitals: St. Joseph (offers a heart institute and oncology center), University of Kentucky's Chandler Medical Center, Good Samaritan (known for its vascular and breast care centers), Central Baptist, Humana-Lexington and two Veterans Administration Medical Centers. Chandler has implemented the only bone marrow transplant program in Kentucky, has the first nonprototype nuclear magnetic resonance (NMR) diagnostic imaging system in the world, and has pioneered PASAR, a new type of pacemaker for the treatment of severe cardiac arrhythmias.

Specialized care: Cardinal Hill Hospital specializes in rehabilitation, Charter Ridge Hospital and Eastern State Hospital offer psychiatric services, and Shriner's Hospital for Crippled Children specializes in pediatric orthopedics.

Crime & Safety

Lexington police not only talk tough on crime ("We have zero tolerance for criminal activity"), they *act* tough. When drug dealers became the "landlords" of the federal housing projects, police moved in. They built a PAL facility for the kids and now have an ongoing presence (crime is way down, and sanity is way up). Overall, Lexington is a quiet, safe community with a very low per-capita crime rate. A blessing in disguise was the merging of the city/county governments. Now there aren't jurisdiction battles. Public schools and the two universities also have security forces, and there is a feeling that police protection is everywhere. The department built "Safety City," a mock town where children can learn highway, pedestrian and bike safety.

Community Life

With horse farms the lifeblood of Bluegrass country, imagine the horror when internationally renowned Calumet Farms was headed for the auction block (as had been the fate of many other farms). Rumors were flying that this national landmark might become a shopping mall (the city was diagnosed as clinically depressed). But a Polish-born industrialist (a virtual stranger to residents) flew down and saved the day with a check for $17 million. Today Calumet Farms is being preserved down to the last miles of white fences and may even become a world-class training center. Ask any Lexington resident who their hero is and you'll hear the name Henryk de Kwiatkowski.

Let the Good Times Roll

Family fun: Did you know that Lexington is the "Thoroughbred Capital of the Nation"? The 400 area farms produce one third of all stakes winners in North America. But what everyone wants to know is, can you ride those gorgeous horses? You betcha! At the Kentucky Horse Park on Iron Works Park, there's a campground, riding instruction, the International Museum of the Horse and more than 1,000 acres of land and attractions. Kids love watching the workouts at Keeneland Race Course and the Red Mile Harness Track (as the Kentucky Derby approaches, families are out at the crack of dawn). There are 80 neighborhood parks, and the Raven Run Nature Sanctuary (300 acres of wildflowers, streams and hiking trails). The Kentucky River, Lake Herrington and the Dix River are ideal for boating and fishing. Outdoor concerts at the park and those famous Kentucky crafts fairs are joyous ways to spend the days and nights.

Sports: The University of Kentucky Wildcats (and its "sister" team, the Lady Kats) and the University of Transylvania Pioneers keep ticket takers busy in season. Or head to Cincinnati and enjoy the Bengals (NFL) and the Reds (National League Champs) at Riverfront Stadium.

Arts & entertainment: You'd expect a city called the "Athens of the West" to deliver a thriving cultural scene. And it does! The local Art League and Arts and Cultural Council work tirelessly to support area theater, music and dance groups. Now with the magnificently restored Lexington Opera House and the University of Kentucky's Singletary Center for the Arts, there are permanent homes for Lexington's own philharmonic orchestra, ballet, children's theater, youth symphony orchestra and modern dance troupe (there's a major emphasis on exposing children to the arts). Also, there are the Children's Museum, the Living Arts and Science Center and the University of Kentucky Art Museum. There are numerous others, along with the dozens of historic sites (a favorite is the Mary Todd Lincoln House). Adding to the fun, the old Kentucky Theater (a glamorous Italian Renaissance style movie house) has been totally restored.

Annual events: Kentucky Horse Park Steeplechase (April); Midsummer Night's 5K Run (Aug.); the Bluegrass 10,000 (kicks off 4th of July celebrations); Roots and Heritage Festival (celebrating Afro-American art and music in Sept.); University of Kentucky Bluegrass State Games (July); Equi-Festival of Kentucky (races, parades and entertainment in Oct.); Lexington Christmas Parade.

The Environment

The attitude toward preservation of the environment and the horse farms is "whatever it takes." Fayette is the most heavily ordinanced county in Kentucky. For example, developers must provide ample new street trees or they can't build (no doubt the reason Lexington has been a Tree City USA since 1988). With no heavy industry, a new $120 million upgraded sewage treatment plant and aggressive recycling efforts (soon to be mandatory), air and water quality are quite good. To maintain the wide-open spaces, builders are confined to a 75-square-mile service area. Anything outside of it is designated for horse farms or 10-acre lots (a big help in controlling police and fire protection, too).

In and Around Town

Roads and interstates: I-75, I-64, Bluegrass Parkway, Mountain Parkway.
Closest airport: Blue Grass Airport (4 mi. west of downtown); with 50 daily commercial departures.
Public transportation: LexTran bus service has 18 routes throughout the city. Dial-A-Ride offers additional transportation to the Camelot and Walnut areas. Trolleys serve the downtown loop during business hours.
Avg. commute: 15-20 min. (that also takes you from one side of town to the other).

What Every Resident Knows

OK, the grass is not really blue. It's green like everywhere else, but when a sea of bluish-purplish buds spring up, it sure looks blue! • Everyone (and we do mean everyone) follows Big Blue Basketball (University of Kentucky Wildcats). Some nights there are more than 10,000 people in the stands to watch preseason workouts. What's the big deal? They practice at midnight! • Lexington is full of fast talkers. You'll hear the typical Southern drawls, but at lightning speed (maybe the horses are doubled-parked). • Watching the waistline is near impossible with that great Kentucky cooking. Who can get tired of sampling blue-ribbon pies, country ham and biscuits or delectable French cuisine? • Lexington is proud of a phenomenon that is common among local executives. When offered a promotion outside the area, the typical response is, "Thanks, but no thanks."

FYI

Greater Lexington Chamber of Commerce
P.O. Box 781
Lexington, KY 40507
606-254-4447

Lexington Convention & Visitor's Bureau
800-84LEXKY

Lexington Herald-Leader
100 Midland Avenue
Lexington, KY 40508
606-231-3100

Rector-Hayden Realtors
2100 Nicholas Road
Lexington, KY 40503
800-228-9025
Keith Rector

Turf Town Properties, Inc.
2560 Richmond Rd., Suite 200
Lexington, KY 40509-1521
606-268-4663
Edith Dillon, Partner

Kentucky Utilities Company
One Quality Street
Lexington, KY 40507
606-255-1461

Columbia Gas of Kentucky
P.O. Box 241
Lexington, KY 40584
606-255-3612

GTE South
318 E. Main Street
Lexington, KY 40507
606-223-9422

Bluegrass Area Economic Development
3220 Nicholasville Road
South Park, KY 40503
606-272-6656

Central Kentucky Small Business Development Center
University of Kentucky
Rm. 11, Porter Building
Lexington, KY 40506-0205
606-257-7666

School district: 606-281-0100
Property tax assessor: 606-254-2722
Newcomer's Club: 606-273-2901
Kentucky Council of Churches: 606-253-3027
Physician's referral: 606-278-3444 (Ask-A-Nurse)
Childcare Council: 606-254-9176

Gaithersburg, Maryland *(Washington, D.C.)*

Area Snapshot

Local population: 43,732 (+35,000 in Montgomery Village)
County: Montgomery **Population:** 757,027
U.S. region: Mid-Atlantic, Eastern Seaboard
Closest metro area: Washington, D.C. (17 mi. south)
Median housing price: $155,000
Avg. household income: $60,586
Best reasons to live here: Good schools, growing business base, low crime, relatively affordable housing, abundant recreation facilities, beautiful planned community, residents have strong voice in city government.

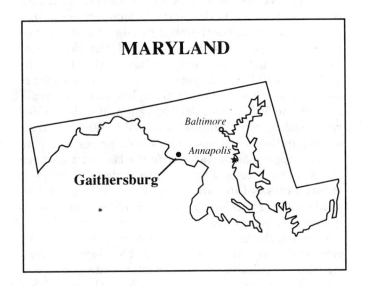

Fabulous Features

"Best of both worlds" often describes suburbia, but its particularly appropriate when referring to Gaithersburg. It's a gavel's throw from our nation's capital so you can enjoy or work in Washington, D.C., without having to live there (if the high rent doesn't get you, the high crime will)! This small, historic community (it's a "Maryland Main Street" city) thinks residents are customers whose needs are top priorities.

Another key to success has been its "pay-as-we-go" philosophy (Maryland does the same and is the only state with an AAA bond rating). But, you get what you pay for! The city offers award-winning parks and recreation programs, beautifully maintained green space (it's been a Tree City USA for three consecutive years), and some of the most affordable homes in the Washington area.

Adjacent to the city limits is Montgomery Village, an attractive, 250-acre planned community with fabulous recreation programs and smartly designed neighborhoods. New construction and resales start at $70,000 and go up to $500,000 (with plenty in the $200,000 range).

The best news is that children in both Gaithersburg and Montgomery Village attend Montgomery County schools, one of the top districts in the country (expenditures per pupil are close to $6,500, well above the national average). They have more successful programs than a TV network.

Access to Maryland's burgeoning service industry and the I-270 High Technology Corridor is another major incentive—60% of firms added personnel between 1988-1990, contributing to the under 4 percent unemployment rate. If you're looking for big-city opportunities with a small-town lifestyle, the best of both worlds is Gaithersburg.

Possible drawbacks: Snow storms, no matter that they happen every season, invariably throw the metropolitan highway departments for a loop. The good news is Gaithersburg is the quickest "picker-upper" in the county. • Are you always late? Move here and you'll have the perfect excuse. You were stuck at one, or if really late, both train crossings. Traffic does come to a screeching halt several times a day.

"You can quote me on that"

"When we moved here last year, we kept seeing bumper stickers that said, "Gaithersburg is great" and thought, "How hokey can you get?" Now we understand the pride. This is a very caring and safe community."—W.G.

Real Estate

Market overview: It's a buyer's market with new building down 30%-40% and the local economy in a holding pattern. Gaithersburg's edge has been fair prices. Compared to Rockville and Potomac (Beverly Hills east), you couldn't buy a closet for the $80,000-$130,000 that gets you a luxury townhouse here. New construction, although slowed, is available in the $250,000-$350,000 range. Resales priced right and in good condition can sell in 60 days. With an expanding business base, stable prices and continued appreciation (only a few cities in this area can say that), sellers may regain some of the edge.

What houses look like: Architecture is quite versatile (2-story colonials are favorites). In Montgomery Village, buyers can also choose from Southwestern-style townhouses to California contemporaries. Newer homes show hardwood floors, imported tiles, fireplaces, elegant master suites, designer kitchens, his and hers everything, decks and 2-car garages (basements also common). Frame construction with brick fronts and vinyl siding are popular.

Starter homes: $80,000-$130,000 buys a small townhouse (1-2BR) or an SFH with 3BR/1BA (900-1200 sq. ft.). For $150,000, you'll see 3BR/2BA homes (1600-1800 sq. ft.) w/fireplace and garage. Check out Audubon Square, Observatory Heights and Deer Park. In Montgomery Village, there's West Deer Park, Town Crest and Hamlet North.

Trade-ups: $185,000-$250,000 gets a larger home in a lovely subdivision. On the lower end are 3BR/2½BA in town. In the outlying areas are newer, 4-5BR/3BA homes w/fireplace, 2-car garage on 1/4 acre lots. Look at Pheasant Run, Amberfield, Woodland Hills and North Potomac (outside city limits).

Luxury homes: Homes for $300,000-$1 million are more likely to be Kentlands, Washingtonian Woods or Potomac addresses. Old English Tudors or grand colonials with 4BR/4+BA (2200+ sq. ft) are standard. Stone driveways and fireplaces, gourmet kitchens with separate eating areas are common.

Rental market: Rentals are plentiful (currently 20,000 listings). 1BR condos are $495+, townhouses $750-$950/mo., and SFH for up to $1,200/mo.

Great neighborhoods: Montgomery Village is a planned community with pools, a lake, a $1.7 million gymnasium and recreational programs. Condos start at $70,000. Avg. home is about $200,000. On Gaithersburg's west side is Kentlands, a new community w/homes from $160,000-$400,000+.

Nearby areas to consider: Olney and Laytonsville are smaller, rural communities attracting young families. Laytonsville children attend Gaithersburg schools.

What Things Cost

Runzheimer's Living Cost Index: Avg. annual costs for family of 4 with household income of $50,000: $56,618 (13.2% above avg. city).

ACCRA's national comparisons: Overall living costs in the D.C./Maryland/Virginia metro area are 11% above avg. Housing costs are an estimated 35% above, utilities and health care 12-13% above. Goods and services are slightly below (2.8%).

Utilities: Phone: $20/mo. (unlimited) plus $17/mo. for unlimited calls to northern Virginia/Prince Georges County (Md.). $125 deposit required ($75 credited on first bill, $50 applied to installation). Electric: Avg. $77/mo. w/low of $35; high of $89. Gas: Avg. $79/mo. ($120/mo. in winter).

Kid care: Avg. $103/wk. for toddlers and $195 for children under 18 mos. Day care is widely available (even for infants) at convenient locations throughout the city. **Pediatric visit:** Avg. $47.

The Tax Ax

Sales tax: 5% (groceries, medical supplies exempt).

Property tax: Property is appraised at 100% of market value and assessed at 40% of the appraisal. To determine annual taxes, take 40% of the home's value, divide by 100 and multiply by the current millage rate (ranges from $2.466 to $3.573 per $100 of assessed value). A $200,000 home would be $2,500/yr.

State income tax: Net taxable income over $3,000 and under $100,000 is taxed at 5%, plus $90 for the first $3,000. You'll pay a Montgomery County income tax equal to 60% of your state income tax bill. All Maryland counties assess a tax at varying rates.

Climate

Elevation 10'	Avg. High/Low	Avg. Rain (Inches)	Avg. Snow (Inches)	Avg. Days Rain	Avg. % Humidity
Jan.	44/28	2.1	5	9	54
April	67/46	2.9	--	10	48
July	88/69	4.1	--	10	52
Oct.	70/50	2.7	--	7	51
YEAR	67/48	37.2	17	107	52
# of days 32° or below: 74			# of days 90° or above: 37		

With the Blue Ridge mountains to the west and the Chesapeake Bay to the east, climate is consistently mild. Spring and autumn are sunny and dry. Winters are mild and major snow accumulation (10" or more) is rare. Summers are of warm and humid with sudden heavy rain and thunderstorms.

Earning a Living

Economic outlook: Say what you will about the federal government, it's supporting a lot of families in these parts. Government employees represent 11.4% share of total employment in the county and close to half of all the high-tech firms are working with revenues from federal contracts and grants. Couple that with the impact of the impressive high-tech I-270 corridor, and the low 3.9% unemployment rate makes sense. Although the recession stung (real estate values plunged in many outlying areas) and companies retreated more out of fear than necessity, Montgomery County looks like a sure winner in the coming years. Per-capita income is the highest in the state (median household income is $60,586). In addition, IBM, National Geographic Society, Bechtel Power Corp. and the National Institute of Standards and Technologies are here along with a growing number of other research/technology firms. In fact, there are so many, they coined the phrase "Beltway Bandits," a reference to the private firms with government contracts that have moved here from the I-495 beltway.

Where the jobs are: The service industry dominates, representing close to 33% of all jobs in Montgomery County. Contributing to that has been the development of the I-270 corridor. While specialties are diverse, the majority of companies are in information technology (67%) and biotechnology (19%). It has also recently expanded to international business (18%) and nearly half of all the companies have introduced a new product or service within the past year—60% added employees between 1988 and 1990. Corporations with the fastest growth record over the last few years are C & P Telephone, Marriott Corp., Vitro Corp., Bechtel Power Corp., Geico Insurance, Atlantic Research Corp. and CAE-Link Tactical Simulation Div. (military support services). At present, hiring remains static, as the bigger corporations are taking a cautious view (employing temporary help vs. new hires). Ironically, its the smaller firms doing most of the expanding, including American Express Health Systems Group, Applied Management Sciences (government contractors); Automatic Data Processing, Bell Atlanticom Systems, CNA Insurance, Century Technology Inc., and Data Measurement Corp.

Business opportunities: In Gaithersburg as in the county, the high-tech service businesses are the most coveted. Information and assistance for entrepreneurs is available from the Small Business Development Center and the Gaithersburg Chamber of Commerce's Economic Development group (*see FYI*).

Making the Grade

Public education overview: Montgomery County public schools have a longstanding reputation for offering significant programs and for supporting schools with solid financing. Despite recent budget cuts, expenditures per pupil are $6,143 (compared to the national avg. of $5,261) and teachers are some of the highest-paid in the state. With a multicultural student body of 15,000 (representing 127 different countries and speaking over 97 different languages) the focus is on global education and language (foreign-language programs in grade schools too). The past graduating classes have averaged 993 on the SATs (national avg. is 899) with 89% going to college. The class of '92 had 44 National Merit Scholars. Some of the successful programs include Maryland Tomorrow (drop-out prevention), the Edison Career Center (vocational training, career education and biotechnology programs), Adopt-A-School (businesses offer instruction and hands-on experience) and the Connection Resource Bank (teachers call any of 4,000 local businesses in the data bank to get speakers). At present, Gaithersburg schools (10 elementary, 2 junior high and 3 high schools) are undergoing extensive reorganization. Although budget cuts were the initial stimulus, layoffs are not anticipated and administrators feel the schools will be even better primed for the growth and the increasing demands for technology training.

Class size: 28:1.

Help for working parents: Several day-care providers are contracted to service Gaithersburg's 6 elementary schools. All have early drop-offs (7 a.m.) and are open to 6 p.m. Avg. cost: $250/mo.

Blue Ribbon School Awards: Gaithersburg Elementary ('89-'90), Diamond Elementary ('89-'90), Whetstone Elementary ('87-'88).

School year: Starts after Labor Day through mid-June. A child must be 5 on or before Dec. 31 to enter kindergarten.

Special education/gifted programs: Where possible, special ed. students attend regular classes—80% of schools offer self-contained resource programs for severe learning disabilities. Two county schools have programs for the severly handicapped (busing available). Pull-out enrichment classes are offered for gifted students.

Nearby colleges/universities: Montgomery College (2-yr. junior college and one of the top 10 in the country); University of Maryland (College Park), Hood College (Frederick); Georgetown University, American University; and Howard University (Washington, D.C.).

Medical Care

Hospitals/medical centers: The greater Washington, D.C., area offers among the most technologically advanced medical care in the world. Johns Hopkins University Medical Center in Baltimore and Bethesda Naval Hospital in Maryland have internationally renowned reputations. In nearby Rockville is Shady Grove Adventist Hospital offering 24-hour emergency service and a wide range of medical specialties, including complete maternity care and a child health center, laser surgery, cardiology, dialysis, coronary care as well as a hyperbaric burn treatment center.

Specialized care: TLC (Treatment & Learning Centers) in Rockville specializes in physical and occupational therapy and head injuries, among other disabilities. The Psychiatric Institute offers inpatient and outpatient care for chemical dependency for adults and adolescents. The Montgomery Hospice in Rockville assists terminal patients at home.

Crime & Safety

The Gaithersburg and Montgomery police work in tandem, providing excellent patrol and preventive programs. Violent crime is negligible and residential burglaries have remained consistently low. To promote "Drug-Free Gaithersburg," officers are assigned to the drug task force or DARE. They even have an Adopt-A-School program (officers assigned to each school) to promote ongoing communications between students and law enforcement. It's working. Often times, the county's 24-hour referral and assistance hot line will hear from concerned kids about upcoming parties. That's "Team Gaithersburg" in action.

Community Life

One of the most wonderful charity efforts we heard of was Gaithersburg's Holiday Cheer for Children. Every year, groups organize six different events such as the Nutcracker, Winter Wonderland, Holiday Village of Lights, etc. The admission fee? A gift for a child. Events chairpersons select a different charity to which all the gifts will be donated. Gaithersburg HELP, Boys & Girls Home of Maryland, Greentree Shelter and Howard University Hospital have been some recipients. Gaithersburg HELP has an all-volunteer staff that provides food and toys to the needy throughout the year. Each year when the Parker Playhouse comes to town from Ocean City, the admission for a special performance is canned goods, which go to Gaithersburg HELP.

Let the Good Times Roll

Family fun: Gaithersburg's Parks and Recreation Dept. is a national gold-medal award winner, thanks to its fabulous facilities and exhaustive list of programs (it even runs birthday parties). The new Casey Community Center, a multi-purpose facility, offers recreation for all ages, indoor flea markets, even a Mom's Morning Out program. The Gaithersburg Sports Association organizes dozens of sports leagues for kids and adults. You'll love the laps at the Gaithersburg Aquatic Center (large indoor pool and sun deck) and at Summit Hall Farm Park Pool. There's a whole summer of good times at this 57-acre city-owned park, complete with the three P's of summer fun: ponds, a playground and three unbelievable pools. The little ones make great friends with the giant frog slide and other creatures in the splash pool. Family entertainment is as close as Gaithersburg High's Newman Auditorium, acoustically equipped for comedies, musicals and concerts. During the summer, the city sponsors "Noon Tunes," free concerts at Olde Towne Park. The National Chamber Orchestra (in Rockville) often performs here. Cabin John (Bethesda) and Pershing Park Ice Rink in Washington are favorite winter wonderlands. Adjacent to the city is Seneca State Park with great year-round activities.

Sports: The Baltimore Orioles (American League) and the Washington Redskins (NFL) keep local sports fans guessing, "Will this be our year?" Other action includes the Washington Bullets (NBA), the Washington Capitals (NHL) and the Frederick Keys (Orioles' Class A Farm team).

Arts & entertainment: Returning residents to the Washington, D.C., area claim there is no more exciting city in the world for sightseeing, culture, museums and the arts. Where else can you find the world-renowned Smithsonian Museum (actually 18 museums including 2 underground art museums), Union Station Park and National Arboretum Park, the Kennedy Center for Performing Arts, the Washington Ballet, the National Gallery of Art, the National Zoological Park, the National Symphony Orchestra and the Washington Chamber Symphony? Back home, the city brings in nationally known entertainers (like Alvin Ailey dancers) while the City Council for the Arts showcases local performers, concerts and theater at Newman Auditorium. City Hall features exhibits by area artists (Gaithersburg High).

Annual events: Montgomery County Fair (largest on East Coast in Aug.); Olde Towne Gaithersburg Day (food, fireworks and train museum exhibits in Sept.); Gaithersburg Ethnic Festival (food, costumes and entertainment in May).

The Environment

Ten years ago, the Gaithersburg Beautification Program planted trees and flowers and set up Program Tree-rific (committee assists homeowners associations with plantings for subdivisions and pays 50% of the cost). The result? For the past three years, it has been recognized as a Tree City USA by the National Arbor Day Foundation. Every spring, the committee also runs a week-long Environmental Awareness Week. The city's Environmental Affairs Committee coordinates present and future recycling programs. Its pilot Multi-Material Drop Off Recycling Program (Saturday drop-offs at City Hall) is working well, and plans for curbside collection will go into effect with the completion of a county processing facility. The city's recycling mascot, "Mary Bee," will educate children about the environment.

In and Around Town

Roads and interstates: I-270 to I-495 (the famed Beltway).
Closest airports: Baltimore-Washington International Airport, Dulles International and Washington National are all within an hour's drive. Private aircraft are served by the Montgomery County Airpark, north of Gaithersburg.
Public transportation: Gaithersburg has the MARC service to Union Station (to D.C. in 43 min.). the Metrorail Red Line (Shady Grove stop arrives in D.C. in 30 min.) and the Metrobus service. Montgomery County bus service feeds into the Metrobus and rail system for convenient coverage.
Avg. commute: 50-55 min. to Washington D.C. and Baltimore.

What Every Resident Knows

After hours of househunting, stop in at Roy's Place, a great sandwich shop with 100 different varieties, all named for local celebrities like Doug Llewlyn (People's Court) and Arch Campbell (NBC movie critic).• Night driving on the interstates takes practice. Deer are known to dart out, causing everything from a major scare to a major accident if you're not prepared. • Local historians will delight in telling you about the Forest Oak Tree and how it shaded George Washington and General Braddock on their way to Ft. Duquesne. It's 200 years old, alive and well at the intersection of 355 and the B&O Railroad, and most important, it's the symbol of Gaithersburg.

FYI

Greater Gaithersburg Chamber of Commerce
9 Park Avenue
Gaithersburg, MD 20877
301-840-1400

Washington D.C. Convention & Visitor's Bureau
1212 New York Ave. NW, Suite 600
Washington, DC 20005
202-789-7000

City of Gaithersburg
31 S. Summit Avenue
Gaithersburg, MD 20877
301-258-6300

Montgomery Journal (daily)
#2 Research Court
Rockville, MD 20850
301-670-1400

Gaithersburg Gazette (weekly)
18705 N. Frederick Road
Gaithersburg, MD 20879
301-948-3120

Century 21 Carr
4 Professional Drive, Suite 111
Gaithersburg, MD 20879
301-330-5900
Bill Carr, Juanita Boglen

Montgomery Village Foundation (Homeowners Association)
P.O. Box 2130
Montgomery Village, MD 20886
301-948-0110

C&P Telephone
P.O. Box 227D
Beltsville, MD 20705
301-851-8000

PEPCO (Electric)
1900 Pennsylvania Avenue NW
Washington, D.C. 20068
202-833-7500

Maryland Natural Gas
800-752-7520

Economic Development
101 Monroe Street, Suite 1500
Rockville, MD 20850
301-217-2345

Small Business Development Center
900 Hungerford Drive
Rockville, MD 20850
301-251-7940

School district: 301-353-0815
Property tax assessor: 301-279-1355
Physician's referral: 301-598-9815
Day-care referral: 301-774-0001

Eden Prairie, Minnesota *(Minneapolis)*

Area Snapshot

Local population: 39,311
County: Hennepin   **Population**: 1,032,431
U.S. region: Upper Midwest
Closest metro area: Minneapolis/St. Paul (10 mi. northeast)
Avg. household income: $60,872
Median housing price: $142,000
Best reasons to live here: Beautiful lakefront city, low crime, outstanding health care and public schools, very committed to family recreation and the arts, stable job market, phenomenal shopping, friendly people.

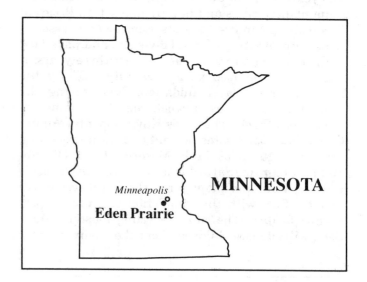

Fabulous Features

Residents of Minneapolis and St. Paul take a lot of heat for their Siberian winters. But life in the Twin Cities is so easy and the opportunities for advancement so great, you simply can't judge this book by its snow cover. In the largely European-influenced communities, the unwritten bylaws are to educate, employ and enjoy. That's why the school systems and avenues for higher learning are extraordinary (half of all state revenues are earmarked for education).

As for the hard-work ethic, hundreds of major companies have quietly forged ahead, paving the way for a stable economy and job market (medical, manufacturing and computers/high-tech fields are preeminent forces). The number one company on "Fortune's Fast 100" list is St. Paul's own Zeos International, a maker of PCs.

And then there's the part about enjoyment. Against a glimmering backdrop of lakes and rolling hills, residents have a voracious appetite for sporting events and outdoor recreation. The variety of performing arts and culture is astounding.

A burgeoning community to the southwest of Minneapolis (20 years ago there were only 6,900 people and an equal number of cattle), Eden Prairie offers smartly designed homes, award-winning schools and easy access to the major job centers. It's even a snowball's throw from the new Mall of America, a mega shopping center so vast, patrons rent cellular phones and golf carts. This is one fun place!

Possible drawbacks: Many newcomers experience the "Goldilocks Syndrome." They cry, "This day is too hot and this day is too cold..." The subzero temps can last from November to March. And summer humidity and bugs are no picnic either. Still, conditions can't be that intolerable—75 percent of residents never move out of state. • Between sales, personal income and property tax, Minnesota ranks in the top 10 states for overall tax burdens. • While it's no match for Los Angeles, commuters on I-35 are quickly learning about rush-hour traffic.

"You can quote me on that"

"Minneapolis is what I would call a 'boomerang' city. You move away and then eventually end up coming back. For a major metropolitan area, we have this small-town attitude. And as long as they don't start griping about the weather, new people will feel at home right away."—J.M.

Real Estate

Market overview: Home prices in Eden Prairie can be out of reach for first-time buyers, but once you own, there's excellent value for the money. Houses are well built, properties are a good size, and neighborhoods are beautifully maintained. Inventory of new homes and resales is plentiful, and the rate of appreciation hasn't deviated much (a steady 1%-2% a year). The appeal of suburbs like Eden Prairie is the large percentage of land allocated exclusively for parks and green space. Avg. carrying charges on an SFH (principal and interest) here are estimated at $800/mo.

What houses look like: New homes are "soft" contemporary (part traditional, part modern). Most are wood frame construction, 3BR/2BA on ¼- to ½-acre lots. Resales are 10-20 years old and exceptionally well maintained.

Starter homes: Prices start at $100,000 for an older 3BR/2BA with basement. Most are ramblers (ranch style) or traditional 2-story. Many are on ½ acre with lovely landscaping.

Trade-ups: Avg.-price homes are in the $120s-$140s range for larger 3BR/2BA. Most have family rooms, 2-car garage and updated interiors.

Luxury homes: Most deluxe models are new construction starting at $175,000 but avg. $200,000 and up. Interiors are 1800-2200 sq. ft. with master BAs and 2-story vaulted ceilings. Another trend is 3-car garages (for the boat, snowmobile and 4 seasons worth of toys)!

Rental market: Minnesota offers numerous tax credits to homeowners, so inventory of rental homes is limited. Where available, a typical 3BR/2BA rents for $800/mo. Condos are limited (2BR/2BA between $600-$800/mo.), but apartment rentals are readily available (2BR/2BA for $550-$750/mo.).

Great neighborhoods: The Preserve, a wonderful development for families on Neill Lakes, offers new and resale homes in all price ranges. The Mitchell Lake area is lovely and has many good corporate homes (houses bought by companies whose employees relocate). They're in move-in condition and priced to sell ($200s). Cardinal Creek and Olympic Hills (on a golf course) are communities priced on the high end ($300s).

Nearby areas to consider: Older established suburbs are southwest: Edina (fairly exclusive), St. Louis Park (large Jewish community), and Minnetonka (fabulous schools). The nicest suburbs with new construction are Bloomington (home of the new Mall of America), Roseville and Plymouth. In St. Paul, look at Eagan, Woodbury and Shoreview.

What Things Cost

Runzheimer's Living Cost Index: Avg. annual costs for family of 4 with household income of $50,000: $52,724 (5.4% above avg. city).

ACCRA's national comparisons: Overall costs are 2.3% above avg., with housing (17%) and health care (15.8%) the major culprits. Food is 9% below avg., utilities and goods and services 7% below.

Utilities: Phone: $20/mo. Connection charge: $32. Gas: Avg. $136/mo. (winter). $20-$44/mo. (summer). Electric: Avg. $50/mo. in spring/fall and $80 in winter/summer.

Kid care: Day-care centers charge $86/wk. After-school family centers avg. $65/wk. The Twin Cities were ranked the #1 metro area in the U.S. for working mothers because of strong day-care regulations and liberal parental-leave laws (*Working Mother*, 3/90). **Pediatric visit:** Avg. $43.

The Tax Ax

Sales tax: 7% (food, clothing, prescriptions exempt). Add 3% for lodging, entertainment, liquor and restaurants.

Property tax: The first $72,000 of value is taxed at 1%; values between $72,000-$115,000 at 2%, and values of $115+ at 2.5%. A $150,000 home would run approximately $2,500/yr.; 50% of taxes are earmarked for education.

State income tax: Based on federal deductions on taxable income, ranging from 6%-8½%. Net federal income between $14,000-$47,000 is taxed at 8%. Income above that is taxed at 8½%. Homeowners with combined income under $60,000 are eligible for a property tax refund. There's a separate income tax refund for homeowners whose property taxes jumped by more than 10% in a single year.

Climate

Elevation 830'	Avg. High/Low	Avg. Rain (Inches)	Avg. Snow (Inches)	Avg. Days Rain	Avg. % Humidity
Jan.	21/3	--	9	--	67
April	56/35	1.1	3	9	54
July	82/61	3.7	--	10	54
Oct.	61/39	1.8	.4	8	59
YEAR	54/34	21.2	47	99	61
# of days 32° or below: 158			# of days 90° or above: 14		

In a year, temperatures fluctuate from -20° to 100°. Summer humidity has residents longing for Labor Day and the start of chilly nights.

Earning a Living

Economic outlook: Thanks to a long-standing and diversified business base, the economic climate remains vibrant. There are 31 Fortune 500 companies headquartered in the Twin Cities, including 3M, Honeywell, Pillsbury, Dayton Hudson, General Mills, Hormel, Land O'Lakes and Control Data Corp. Northwest Airlines is also headquartered here (although tough going in the airline industry spells potentially large layoffs). Barring any unforseen economic shifts, the unemployment rate should remain at a low 4.2% while job growth is projected at a healthy 7% between 1989 and 1996. The growth will come from the smaller upstart companies that are devoted to niche marketing—80% of the world's supercomputers and cardiac pacemakers are produced here. And unlike major job centers in the South where newcomers experience "paycheck shock," salaries are commensurate with living costs. All of this contributed to the selection of suburban Bloomington as the sight for the largest shopping center in the U.S., the Mall of America. Expected to employ 10,000 people, the mall has projected that first-year revenues could reach $650 million (twice the budget of St. Paul). Local businesses are gearing up for the overflow, an estimated 40 million visitors in the first 3 years of operation.

Where the jobs are: Minnesota's famed "Medical Alley" includes hundreds of large corporations such as Cardiac Pacemakers and an equal number of fast-growing small firms developing technologically advanced diagnostic and rehabilitative equipment. With continued diversification in the high-tech, food services and medical fields, coupled with the opening of the Mall of America, employment opportunities in the next few years will be brisk. At present, there is a widespread shortage of medical personnel (particularly nurses). Major employers in Eden Prairie are all high-tech: Magnetic Peripherals, Rosemount Engineering and CPT are a few.

Business opportunities: Computer high-tech firms, printing and publishing, and wood products are some of the fast-growing local industries. Fueled by a highly educated work force and an excellent transportation infrastructure (air, river, rail and highway systems get products in and out, hassle-free), Minnesota has been ranked in the top 20% for strong economic development. Shopping by Canadian neighbors helps to fuel retail sales (mall stores report year-to-date gains of 17%-30%).

Making the Grade

Public education overview: Minnesota is so deeply committed to education, it is one of the few states to offer open enrollment (choose the school of your choice) and to allocate 50% of the entire state budget to education (more than $5,000 per student, one of the highest per-student expenditures in the U.S.). No wonder they have the highest graduation rate in the country (90%). Statewide test scores and scholastic honors also rank among the highest. Eden Prairie schools offer a highly competitive curriculum and are one of 16 educational institutions in the country eligible to vie for the famed Malcolm Baldridge Quality Award. The goal is to become the "J.C. Penney" of schools, insuring customer satisfaction among students (the superintendent is the "CEO," and parents are one of many "suppliers"). Other attributes include a unique Kindergarten Center and comprehensive foreign language programs starting at 5th grade (high school students can take Russian and Chinese by interactive TV). All students K-12 learn computer literacy and can compete in 16 different competitive sports. Wait until you see Eden Prairie High School, complete with a new athletic stadium. There are also 50 private schools in the Twin Cities (costs are comparable to college tuition).

Class size: 17:1.

Help for working parents: Eden Prairie elementary schools, in cooperation with the YMCA, have a latch key program for before and after school (primarily childcare). A second option is the After School Connection program for grades 1-4 offering recreation and enrichment activities. Costs range from $17-$33/wk.

Blue Ribbon School Awards: Minneapolis offers open enrollment, and without exception, every district has earned state and/or national recognition. In the Greater Minneapolis/St. Paul area, 25 schools have earned Blue Ribbon School Awards since they were established in 1982.

School year: Minnesota schools open after Labor Day and run through mid-June. Children must be 5 on or before Sept. 1 to enter kindergarten.

Special education/gifted programs: Children with learning and behavior problems, mild mental handicaps, and speech and language needs have access to special programs in each school. The district's KEY program groups gifted students in cluster classrooms from 1st grade on.

Nearby colleges/universities: There are two public universities (University of Minnesota and Metropolitan State University), and 10 private 4-year and junior colleges.

Medical Care

Hospitals/medical centers: When a state can boast of having the second-highest average life expectancy in the country, it's a safe bet the quality of health care is exceptional. The internationally acclaimed Mayo Clinic in Rochester (75 mi.) and the University of Minnesota Hospital and Clinic have some of the finest facilities, diagnostic programs, medical research and physician care available. The University Hospital is considered the transplant capital (the first open-heart surgery was performed here almost 30 years ago). The concept of HMOs (prepayment for services) was born here, and close to 1 million residents are enrolled in such a program. In the 7-county metro area, there are 32 full-service hospitals.

Specialized care: Minneapolis Children's Medical Center, Shriner's Hospital for Crippled Children, and VA's Medical Center. Several nationally recognized treatment centers for alcoholism and chemical dependency (such as the Hazelden Foundation) as well as the Courage Center (a United Way rehabilitation center) are here.

Crime & Safety

With a crime index of 24% below the national average, Minnesota's statistics bear out what residents already know—it's one of the safest places to live in the U.S. Some speculate that climate is a contributing factor (it's either too hot or too cold to be out there mugging and marauding). Regardless, less than 7% of all crimes committed are violent (that's an average of 50% lower than the rest of the country).

Community Life

When you say, "Put your hands up" in this town, no one bats an eye. They know it's not a robbery in action, it's a call for volunteers. And people respond! Through Minnesota's Keystone Program, more than 100 companies contribute 2%-5% of their pretax earnings to local charities. United Way programs raise an annual $20 million, and Taste of the Nation just raised more than $120,000.

"You can quote me on that"
"You can't appreciate what a wonderful city this is until you live here. The crime rate is low. Everyone has a job or goes to school. I don't know of another place where the quality of life for families is so high."—A.L.

Let the Good Times Roll

Family fun: The Twin Cities are situated on 1,000 lakes, but alas, there are only 500 fish. Anglers confront the challenge while everyone else enjoys the fabulous recreation. There are 6,300 acres of land and water to enjoy. The 4 state parks (William O'Brien, Fort Snelling, Afton and Minnesota Valley Trail) and 1,000 locally owned parks are where to head for downhill and cross-country skiing, swimming, boating, golf and tennis. In Eden Prairie, the parks and preserves are vast and beautiful, offering everything from bike trails to beaches. The Eden Prairie Community Center has an indoor pool and ice-skating rink, racquetball and other facilities. Great family fun is at Como Zoo (St. Paul's answer to one great time), or go south to the Minneapolis Zoo in Apple Valley and the ValleyFair Amusement Park in Shakopee (the largest theme park in the upper Midwest).

Sports: "Tickets" is Minneapolis's middle name. Spectator sports include the major league champion Minnesota Twins, the Minnesota Vikings (NFL), Minnesota Timberwolves (NBA), Minnesota North Stars (NHL), plus all the Big 10 action at the University of Minnesota. And guess where the Vikings' new training camp is? Eden Prarie!

Arts & entertainment: You've heard of the Big Apple? Minneapolis is the Big Cheese. With more than 90 performing arts organizations, it is second only to New York City in terms of the number and diversity of cultural offerings. Theater, ballet, dance and opera tickets are affordable and available. Ordway Music Theater, Orchestra Hall, the Guthrie Theater and Walker Arts Center are just a few places to enjoy the Minnesota Orchestra, the St. Paul Chamber Orchestra (formerly under the direction of Pinchas Zuckerman), and the Minnesota Opera. Wonderful museums and galleries include the planetarium (in the Minneapolis Public Library). Also for families are 2 resident children's theater groups, the Children's Museum and the hands-on Science Museum of Minnesota (3M's Omnitheater thrills viewers with the world's largest film projector).

Annual events: Twin Cities Marathon (Oct.); Minneapolis Aquatennial (the country's oldest summer festival, July); St. Paul Winter Carnival (the world-famous ice sculptures in Rice Park will take your breath away, Jan.-Feb.); Summerfest at Orchestra Hall (July); Festival of Nations (Aug.-Sept.); Wayzata Chilly Open (charity golf tournament on a frozen Lake Minnetonka, Feb.).

The Environment

Minnesota was one of the first states to ban smoking in public places (no doubt the influence behind Minneapolis-based Northwest Airlines being the first airline to prohibit smoking on domestic flights). A pox on the house has been the polluted Mississippi River, a direct result of abuses by the City Water Works (high levels of metal were found). The City Council recently surrendered, agreeing to pay $3.4 million for upgrades and cleanup. At present, air quality is excellent.

In and Around Town

Roads and interstates: I-94, I-35, Highway 62 (crosstown artery).
Closest airport: Minneapolis/St. Paul International Airport (approx. 15-20 min.).
Public transportation: Metro Transit Commission covers the entire metro area. Minnesota Rideshare offers incentives for carpools.
Avg. commute: From downtown Minneapolis to suburbs is under 30 min.; 17 min. to Bloomington or other adjacent suburbs.

What Every Resident Knows

Between months of ice and snow or intense heat and rain and the highest traffic volume in the city's history, you probably wouldn't envy workers at the Roads Department. But that's where you'll find some of the smartest transportation experts in the country. Their latest invention has timed lights at entrance ramps to stagger the number of cars on the roads. Things may slow down, but they rarely stop. • To dispel a myth, not *all* Minnesotans have blond hair and blue eyes. OK, so close to 70% have German or Norwegian ancestry. But in the past decade, there has been more ethnic diversity than at any time in the state's history. • Famous musical Minnesotans include Prince, Bob Dylan and Judy Garland.

FYI

Eden Prairie Chamber of Commerce
250 Prairie Center Drive
Eden Prairie, MN 55344
612-934-2830

Convention & Visitor's Bureau: 612-348-4313

Minneapolis Star Tribune
425 Portland Ave. South
Minneapolis, MN 55488
612-673-4343

*Edina Realty
1400 S. Highway 100, Suite 200
Minneapolis, MN 55416
800-328-4344
Peggy Hempel, Reloc. Dir.

RE/MAX Results
11095 Viking Drive, Suite 100
Eden Prairie, MN 55344
612-829-2900
Mike Best

Coldwell Banker Elite Homes
7110 France Ave., South
Edina, MN 55435
612-920-1224
Donald R. Harff, CRS

Northern States Power
3115 Center Point Drive
Roseville, MN 55113
612-639-1234

Minnegasco
201 S. 7th Street
Minneapolis, MN 55402
612-372-4727

U.S. West Communications
612-293-0665

Eden Prairie School District #272
8100 School Road
Eden Prairie, MN 55344
612-937-1650

Central Placement and Assessment Center
612-627-2918

Minneapolis Dept. of Trade & Economic Development
900 American Center Bldg.
150 E. Kellogg Blvd.
St. Paul, MN
612-296-8285

Small Business Development Center
University of St. Thomas
23 Empire Drive
St. Paul, MN 55103
612-223-8663

Property tax assessor: 612-348-3046
Welcome Wagon: 612-332-6231
Council of churches: 612-870-3660
Hillel Foundation: 612-379-4026
Day-care referral:
612-823-7237, 612-341-2066
Physician's referral: 612-623-9555
Renter's Hotline: 612-927-8600

*Edina Realty has a *free* publication for children, "What I Like Best About Living in the Twin Cities."

Columbia, Missouri

Area Snapshot

Local population: 68,600
County: Boone   **Population:** 108,800
U.S. region: Midwest/Central Missouri
Closest metro areas: Kansas City (130 mi. west); St. Louis (127 mi. east).
Median housing price: $80,900
Avg. household income: $22,059
Best reasons to live here: One of the nicest small metro areas in the country, highly educated population, award-winning schools, outstanding medical care, affordable housing, abundant green space, booming job market, great college town.

Fabulous Features

Mid-Missouri may seem an unlikely place to discover gold, but deep in the heart of the "Show Me" state is a city with the Midas Touch. Columbia is an unpretentious place that stacks up state and national awards at a record pace. School District #93 is consistently identified as one of the most progressive in the country (this year *Redbook* magazine and SchoolMatch USA gave it their highest honors). The hospitals and medical centers are continually cited for important research and state-of-the-art care. And to walk through the vast, scenic nature trails is to understand the national recognition earned by the parks department.

At every turn, this quiet city forges ahead. Businesses are thriving (more than 2,000 jobs were created last year), and as home to the University of Missouri, it offers a vitality as natural as the rolling hills. An unexpected present? Exceptional home values. For under $100,000 you get the keys to a spacious new house with fabulous country views. Property taxes, state income taxes and overall living costs are also very modest (10%-25% below the national average). That's what attracts people. What makes them stay is how clean, green and accessible the city is. It operates like a well-oiled machine (only if the oil is good for the environment), and community spirit borders on embarrassing (save Friday nights for Tiger pep rallies). Columbia is like the little city that could. Pitch in or get out of the way.

Possible drawbacks: It's a bird, it's a plane, but it's not landing in Columbia. Air service from the regional airport via a major carrier is limited, and you'll choose between two evils—a two-hour drive to the bigger airports or a quick but costly air shuttle. • For a city overflowing with hospital beds and doctors, appointments are booked weeks in advance. As the closest medical hub for Missouri's nonmetro areas, patients come great distances. Doctors and clinics are as busy as Macy's at Christmas.

"You can quote me on that"

"We were one of those yuppie couples who wanted out. We looked at a lot of places but always got cold feet. Columbia was different. We couldn't believe how inexpensive the houses were, but they're beautiful. I used to commute an hour; now it takes me 8 minutes. There's time to enjoy things like volunteering. The only things we don't like are the nutty weather and the lack of gourmet restaurants."—T.T.

Real Estate

Market overview: Out-of-town and first-time buyers are elated with how far their housing dollars go. Sellers are pleased at getting fair prices. A boom in new construction (more than 1,400 residential homes were built last year) and the fact that Columbia is a darling of the media sends buyers from even California and New Jersey. Avg. monthly payment (principal/interest) runs $604, and homes are appreciating at a rate of 2% annually.

What houses look like: Most new homes are brick; older homes are part brick and masonite or vinyl. Interiors show split foyers, split levels or ranch-style layouts. Avg. lot size is ½ acre or larger (buy gorgeous views and they throw in the house). Many developments offer community facilities.

Starter homes: Prices range from $50,000-$70,000 for a 2-3BR/1½ BA (1200-1500 sq. ft.) home that is 10-15 years old. Many have garages (no basement), large kitchens and a great room (combined living room/den). Look north of town.

Trade-ups: Prices range from $80,000-$120,000 for a 3BR/2BA home (avg. 2000 sq. ft). Large master baths are popular, as are basements and fireplaces. Choose from new construction to 50-year-old homes. Ranches, Cape Cods and traditional 2-stories south and southwest of town sell fast.

Luxury homes: Most new luxury models range from $150,000-$250,000 (some in the $300,000 range) and are beautiful 2-story or ranch-style, 3000+ sq. ft. homes with 4-5BR/2-3BA, brick exteriors, full basements, large island kitchens, skylights, arches and 2-3 car garages. Southwest Columbia is where to shop.

Rental market: Expect limited availability of SFHs because home prices and mortgage rates are so low. Homes (3BR/2BA), where available, start at $450 and go up to $700/mo. Duplexes, condos and apartment rentals range from $350-$650/mo.

Great neighborhoods: Excellent values are in northside neighborhoods, such as Valley View, Parkade and Blue Ridge (homes priced between $60,000-$80,000). New construction is in the southeast (check out Southridge homes from $70,000-$90,000) and the southwest (anything adjacent to the Country Club of Missouri is *the* place to buy). Other desirable areas are the Highlands, Green Meadows, Hillshire, Stony Brook and Johnson Farms.

Nearby areas to consider: Ashland (12 mi. south) is halfway between Columbia and Jefferson City (state capital). It's ideal for working couples with jobs in both cities. Housing values are excellent, school districts are small, and the airport is nearby.

What Things Cost

Runzheimer's Living Cost Index: Avg. annual costs for family of 4 with household income of $50,000: $44,917 (10.2% below avg. city).

ACCRA's national comparisons: Overall living costs are almost 10% below the national avg., with utility costs 25% below (the benefits of a city-owned water and electric company). Housing costs are almost 15% below avg., and food items 8% below. The only costs above avg. are health care at 6%.

Utilities: Phone: $12/mo. Installation: $25. Electric/Water: Avg. $50/mo. Total energy costs (including gas) avg. $83.

Kid care: Over 50 registered/licensed day-care facilities in town. Avg. weekly cost is $75. Some charge less, depending on income. **Pediatric visit:** New patient avg. $44. Checkups avg. $18-$33.

The Tax Ax

Sales tax: 6.5%.

Property tax: The formula is complex but as a rule, property taxes run between 1% and 1.25% of a home's sale price. A house sold for $112,000 would run $1,120 annually (estimate).

State income tax: Missouri has one of the lowest personal income tax rates in the U.S. The calculation starts with the taxpayer's federal adjusted gross income and allows for individual, dependent exemptions as well as exempting 100% of your federal income tax deduction. The first $9,000 is taxed at $315, balance taxed at a rate of 1.5%-6%.

Climate

Elevation 758'	Avg. High/Low	Avg. Rain (Inches)	Avg. Snow (Inches)	Avg. Days Rain	Avg. % Humidity
Jan.	38/21	1.0	6	6	67
April	65/45	3.7	1	11	55
July	87/67	3.9	--	8	54
Oct.	69/47	3.4	--	9	56
YEAR	64/45	35	23	106	60

# of days 32° or below: 108	# of days 90° or above: 37

Temperatures can vary widely in a short period, especially in winter. One day can be frigid (below zero), the next warm and balmy (in the 50s and 60s). Hot, mildly humid summer days are followed by chilly, dry nights. Most rain occurs in spring and early summer, with thunderstorms and tornado watches starting in August. Fall is lovely with its lush foliage and comfortably warm days.

Earning a Living

Economic outlook: With a surprisingly low unemployment level of 3%, Columbia is practically recession-proof, as declared by business leaders. In fact, the metro area had a net gain of 2,021 new jobs last year from a very diverse group of industries. The reason? Columbia's economy is dependent on insurance, education and health care—the three things that people buy, no matter how tight the economy.

Where the jobs are: Columbia is the regional headquarters of State Farm Insurance, the national headquarters for Shelter Insurance, the Midwest office of Colonial Insurance (just recently moved here), and the national headquarters for Datastorm Technologies (a leading computer software company started by local university students that is now one of the fastest-growing in the country). Textron (auto parts manufacturer) recently broke ground for a new plant that will employ 150 people. IBM, 3M, Oscar Mayer and Toastmaster also have plants here. More than 5,000 employees work for the 7 hospitals and twice as many clinics and health-related services. The University of Missouri, Stephens College and Columbia College employ over 13,000 people.

Business opportunities: Missouri has one of the most favorable corporate tax structures in the country (less than 5% of revenue comes from corporate income tax, and inventories are exempt from property tax). Couple that with the steady population growth (1%-1.5% annual increases) and the reasonably priced office/commercial space, and you'll understand why Columbia is a viable place for new small businesses. There is currently a need for more light and medium manufacturing as well as a cry for 4-star gourmet restaurants. Columbia is an eat-out town, but most of the restaurants are family style or fast food.

"You can quote me on that"

"We moved from Chicago so my wife and daughter could start college together. The one big change for us is that we're not so stressed out, because we don't waste hours commuting. My younger son, who practically had to be revived when told we were moving, has adjusted beautifully. He likes school, has made friends, and even signed up for sports."—A.G.

Making the Grade

Public education overview: With an enrollment of only 13,000 students, an annual budget of $72.4 million and school bond issues that pass by a margin of 80%, Columbia's school district has repeatedly earned the most prestigious state and national awards. It's produced 9 Presidential Scholars, the National Governor's Conference has cited it as one of 16 model districts, and the Department of Education has given Blue Ribbon honors (the highest recognition) to 5 of its schools. Last spring, *Redbook* magazine cited Hickman High as the best in Missouri due to an outstanding media center, a first-place chamber choir, access to faculty tutors on the hour and lots of parent volunteers. The elementary schools boast student achievement levels consistently ranking in the upper 15% nationally (they're very high-tech). The district is equally proud of its commitment to students at risk of dropping out. Its Secondary Learning Center (an alternative environment) has successfully graduated 50% of the enrollment. A new middle school is scheduled to open Sept. 1994.

Class size: 23:1 (primary grades 21:1).

Help for working parents: In cooperation with the University Extension Program and 4H, 10 elementary schools have after-school programs. The cost is on a sliding scale. A fabulous summer enrichment program is also available.

Blue Ribbon School Awards: Oakland Junior High School ('88-'89), Rock Bridge Senior High ('86-'87), John Ridgeway Elementary, Fairview Elementary ('85-'86). David E. Hickman High has also been recognized in past years. Midway Heights School was a 1991 Missouri Gold Star winner (only 10 of the state's 1,100 elementary schools achieved this).

School year: First week of Sept. to second week in June. Children must be 5 on or before July 1 to enter kindergarten (those born between July-Sept. can be tested for early entry).

Special education/gifted programs: Five percent of students are involved in gifted classes, and the curriculum is so successful, it is used as a model throughout Missouri. The Special Education program works with more than 1,600 children (its annual budget is $5.5 million.)

Nearby colleges/universities: Columbia is home to three excellent schools: The University of Missouri (noted alumni are the late Sam Walton, Wal-Mart Founder, and Debbye Turner, 1990 Miss America); Columbia College (4-year college, recently went coed); and Stephens College (the second oldest women's college in the U.S.). There are 7 other vocational and career-training colleges.

Medical Care

Hospitals/medical centers: The University Hospital and Clinics has just completed a $7.7 million renovation that helped open 12 new operating rooms (it anticipates performing 7,000 surgical procedures a year). It offers a state-of-the-art Level III newborn intensive care and Level I trauma center The burn center has received national attention for use of hyperbaric oxygen therapy. Columbia Regional Hospital is known for outstanding orthopedic facilities and sports medicine; Boone Hospital Center (going through a $12 million expansion program) offers excellent outpatient services; Truman Veterans Hospital, the only VA hospital in the Midwest, offers comprehensive cardiac care.

Specialized care: The Ellis Fischel Cancer Center, The Cancer Research Center, and Health South, one of the largest independent providers of rehabilitation services in the U.S., are also here. Rusk Rehabilitation Center specializes in head injuries. Charter Hospital is a private psychiatric facility with adolescent drug dependency programs.

Crime & Safety

Everyone knows of the powerful Colombia drug cartel, which, fortunately, has no ties to the Missouri town of the same name. Brace yourself, however, for we did hear rumblings about drug use here. As with many university towns, drugs are available, although the basis for the whisper campaign is probably that *any* illegal activity is big news here. Thanks to a proactive police department and the cooperation of the 230 Neighborhood Watch programs, there is a very low occurrence of drug-related crime. Burglaries are down significantly (almost 50%) in the past 5 years. The combination of an aware community and educated police force (90% are college grads) allows for a place where kids play outdoors, and grown-ups don't fear for their safety.

Community Life

With such a diverse, growing population, it's intriguing how deeply committed people are to the city's future. Bonds and referendums get passed by overwhelming majorities (school bond issues pass by 80%-90%, and a recent vote to invest in alternative wastewater treatments passed by 94%.) Leaders attribute the support to the fact that a majority of residents are transplants and will do anything, even pay higher taxes, to assure this city doesn't become like the place they left.

Let the Good Times Roll

Family fun: Couch potatoes beware. Columbians are weekend warriors, thanks to the abundance of outdoor recreational parks and trails (the parks and recreation areas have been nationally recognized). The newest kid in town is the fabulous M-K-T Nature and Fitness Trail, 4.7 miles of stream beds, wooded passages, and 20 fitness stations. When completed, it will offer a 200-mile hiking biking and handicapped-use trail. Other Columbia Cosmopolitan Recreation Areas include Bear Creek Park, cross-country ski trails, and the Grindstone Nature Area (a national archaeological site). For spelunking buffs, Missouri is also the "Cave State." Check out Rock Bridge State Park and Boone Cave (formed 275 million years ago). Finger Lakes State Park and Three Creeks State Forest are other popular recreation havens. Less than 2 hours away is the magnificent Lake of the Ozarks recreation area.

Sports: Columbia is Tiger Country—the whole city is wild about Mizzou's (MU's) Big Eight football and basketballs teams. Friday nights in football season are Tiger Nights (the whole town turns out for the granddaddy of pep rallies). Professional sports fans head to St. Louis and Kansas City for NBA, NFL and major league baseball action.

Arts & entertainment: The Columbia Entertainment Company and Maplewood Barn Theater (a fabulous old outdoor arena with a petting zoo) put on musical and theatrical productions for children. Columbia and Mizzou offer a tremendous range of art, culture, museums, live theater, music and big-name entertainment. The University Concert Series brings international ballet and performing artists to the stage. Hearnes Center is where you'll see everything from rock concerts to the circus; Rhynsburger Theater and Stephens College present stage productions all year long; and the Performing Arts Center holds a wonderful summer festival featuring well-known classical musicians. The Museum of Art and Archaeology, the Columbia Art League Gallery and Macklanburg Art Gallery are just a few of the great cultural finds in town.

Annual events: The Show Me State Games (18,000 amateur athletes converge for the final rounds of Olympic-style competitions the last 2 weekends of July); Art in the Park art fair (a 34-year tradition every June); Soap Box Derby (June); Memorial Day Parade and Air Show, Mizzou's Homecoming Celebration (100-year-old tradition—the oldest in the nation); and the Holiday Parade and Lighting (Nov.).

The Environment

Columbia has one of the most progressive, environmentally sensitive city governments in the Midwest, contributing to excellent air and water quality. Curbside recycling programs, stringent bans on land disturbance and burning, billboard control and deposits on cans (the only U.S. city to impose one) show the commitment. It's also a no-smoking city. The most compelling effort of a commitment to the environment is the new wastewater system. When completed, it will convert solid waste to wetlands.

In and Around Town

Roads and interstates: I-70, U.S. 63.
Closest airport: Columbia Regional Airport offers direct service to St. Louis 19 times each weekday via Transworld Express (TWA) (weekend flights also available).
Public transportation: Columbia Area Transit System has more than 10 intercity routes. Adult fares are 50¢, children 25¢, and transfers are free. School cards cost $2.50/wk.
Avg. commute: 10 min.

What Every Resident Knows

The "tree huggers" and environmentalists have a strong presence on the City Council, which is wonderful for conservation and a "thorn" in the side, say some business owners and developers. Interestingly, this has been going on for decades, long before most cities woke up to preservation and the ecology. • There is a certain amount of snob appeal to living here compared to Jefferson City (the state capital). Seems with such a large surplus of "smarty pants" (medical professionals, university professors and other experts), some are of the opinion that Columbia is the brains of the Missouri family. • Columbia has more journalists per capita than even Washington, D.C. You can't sneeze in this town without a pack of reporters covering the "blow-by-blow" descriptions. • The "Show Me" attitude is alive and well. Nothing happens in this state unless proven necessary.

FYI

Columbia Chamber of Commerce
P.O. Box 1016
Columbia, MO 65205
314-874-1132

Convention & Visitor's Bureau
P.O. Box N
Columbia, MO 65205
314-875-1231

Columbia Daily Tribune
P.O. Box 798
Columbia, MO 65205
314-449-3811

The Columbian Missourian
P.O. Box 917
Columbia, MO 65205
314-442-3161

REMAX/Boone Realty
33 E. Broadway
Columbia, MO 65203
314-442-6121
Sharon Kinden, Vicky Miserez

Buyer's Agent Real Estate, Inc.
103 Buckner Street
Columbia, MO 65203
800-283-2205
Reba Jett, Karl Burpo or Karen Hamilton

Hawthorne Management Co. (Rentals)
205 E. Forest, Suite B
Columbia, MO 65203
314-442-3831
Diana Groshong

Columbia Water and Light Dept.
City-County Building
701 E. Broadway
Columbia, MO 65201
314-874-7380

GTE-North, Inc.
625 E. Cherry Street
Columbia, MO 65201
314-876-3656

Columbia Public Schools
1818 W. Worley Street
Columbia, MO 65203
314-886-2100

Regional Economic Development, Inc.
P. O. Box N
Columbia, MO 65205
314-442-8303

Small Business Development Center
1800 University Place
Columbia, MO 65211
314-882-7096

Property tax assessor: 314-874-7587
Interfaith Council: 314-442-3606 or 314-449-5674
Physician's referral: 314-874-8985 (Boone County Medical Society)
Day-care referral: 314-874-7488

Henderson, Nevada (Las Vegas)

Area Snapshot

Local population: 83,913
County: Clark   **Population:** 805,000
U.S. region: Western U.S./southern Nevada
Closest metro area: Las Vegas (12 mi. north-west)
Median housing price: $100,700
Avg. household income: $52,425
Best reasons to live here: Fastest-growing city in Nevada, excellent job prospects, breathtaking mountain scenery, fabulous culture and recreation, dry desert climate, no state income tax, beautiful new homes, first-rate medical care, central to the "Best of the West."

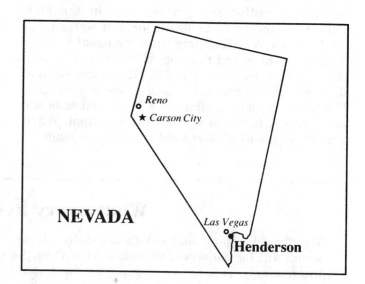

Fabulous Features

Las Vegas holds the winning hand when it comes to exciting cities. Not since the California gold diggers has there a more successful merging of God-given natural assets with man-made momentum. Surrounded by mountain ranges and vast desert terrain, the Las Vegas area has a lot to boast about: a growth rate of 3,000-5,000 newcomers a month, the number-one business climate in the U.S. (*Inc.* magazine), and it's led the country in employment for four years (30,000 new jobs anually).

Las Vegas is close to great recreation (Lake Mead, the Colorado River and Mt. Charleston) and has a tourist industry that pumps $14 billion into the economy. With no state income tax and a phenomenal housing market (half of all new homes sell for under $100,000), new residents feel they've hit the jackpot!

As for great places to live, we favored Henderson. Now the fastest-growing city in Nevada, families have discovered excellent health care, award-wining parks and recreation and schools (opened 26 news schools in two years,

with another eight in the plans). Economic growth is also tremendous (Lake Las Vegas, a $3.5 billion master-planned resort, recreation and residential community is in progress). But the ace in the hole is the spectacular views. The "night lights" from Las Vegas playing shadow games on the mountains add to the sweet dreams.

Possible drawbacks: Since 1988 there have been two major industrial accidents in Henderson. And, the Nevada Test Site (underground nuclear weapons testing) is 65 miles away. Initially we were torn about including Henderson but ultimately felt the risk-awareness level was so high among residents, manufacturers and the government, and the safeguards so improved in the past decade, places with less obvious risks (and less government control) could actually pose more danger. • The desert climate is totally unique. Winters drop down into the 20s, summers sizzle with continuous 100-plus days. Some love the variety, others yearn for a "normal" place.

"You can quote me on that"

"Henderson is clean, friendly and growing so fast because it has everything to offer. I think the schools are excellent, we love our house, and coming from New York it is wonderful not paying any income tax."—N.W.

Real Estate

Market overview: Local realtors report that Henderson is a buyer's market. Because Las Vegas offers a variety of jobs, many out-of-town buyers are attracted to this fast-growing suburb. A slow market in neighboring California and general uncertainty about the economy has affected the appreciation (little or none) in the last year. Land prices on undeveloped lots are high. Lake Las Vegas, a new planned community, sells lakeside and lakeview lots from $210,000 to $1.2 million.

What houses look like: There are many styles and price ranges. Construction is mostly frame and stucco, and concrete block wall. Most homes are 10 yrs. or newer. Lots avg. 1/3 acre. Landscaping is cactus, palm trees, cottonwood, and nurtured pines and lawns. Sundecks are scarce (too hot!). A popular style originating here is the Southwestern, featuring vaulted ceilings, recessed shelving and interior open balconies overlooking living rooms.

Starter homes: $65,000-$100,000. Usually older tract homes on 60 x 100 lots, 2-3BR/1-2BA, living room, kitchen. Look in the Townside, Highland Hills, and Summerfield neighborhoods.

Trade-ups: $110,000-$200,000 buys 3BR/2-3BA, separate living room and dining room, family room, fireplace, kitchen and 2-car garage. Lots up to ½ acre. Occasionally, you'll find an inground pool. Look in Mission Hills, and areas known only as Sections 19 and 27. Most are less than 10 years old. The Southwestern style is prevalent. Both 1-story and 2-story homes are available.

Luxury homes: $300,000-$600,000, featuring ½-acre lots, 3-4BR/2-3BA, garden tubs, upgraded tiles and flooring, 2-car garage. Extras include pool, spa and jacuzzi, a courtyard entry w/fountain, and more. Exteriors are contemporary, Tudor or rambling ranches. Calico Ridge, Quail Ridge, and The Fountains are neighborhoods to see.

Rental market: There are adequate rentals available for around $460/mo. for 1BR; $550/mo. for 2BR; and $615/mo. for 3BR. A 2BR/2½BA condo rents for $650/mo. A 3BR/3BA SFH is $800/mo.

Great neighborhoods: Many families move to Highland Hills because of the well-kept homes and scenic landscaping. Section 19 offers newer homes, larger lots and spectacular views. Both neighborhoods are a walk to elementary schools. Many new developments still have unpaved roads.

Nearby areas to consider: Boulder City, 10 miles south, is much smaller and practices growth control. Gambling is not allowed. The homes are more expensive. The average list price for a single family home in Boulder City is $220,000.

What Things Cost

Runzheimer's Living Cost Index: Avg. annual costs for family of 4 with household income of $50,000: $47,200 (4.6% below avg. city).

ACCRA's national comparisons: Overall living costs in the Las Vegas metro area are 8.4% above the national avg. Health care and housing are what tip the scales (23.9% and 16.3% above avg. respectively). Utilities are 16% *below* avg.

Utilities: Phone: Hookup: $27.90 Service: $6.08, w/$3.30 subscriber surcharge, for local calls. The local calling area includes Henderson, Blue Diamond, Boulder City, Las Vegas and northern Las Vegas. Electricity: Avg. $61/mo. Gas: Avg. $28/mo. Garbage pickup: $8.21/mo.

Kid care: Avg. $70/wk. for infants; $65/wk. for toddlers; $45-$55/wk. for older kids. Many licensed preschools are full and have waiting lists. However there is an adequate number of licensed in-home care facilities available. **Pediatric visit:** $50-$55.

The Tax Ax

Sales tax: 7%.

Property tax: There are eight different tax rates in Henderson starting at $2.1737 per $100 of assessed value, and topping at $2.8840 per $100 of assessed value. The assessment is 35% of the appraised value. The formula on a $100,000 at the lowest tax rate would be: $35,000 divided by 100 = 350 x $2.1737, which results in $760 of taxes.

State income tax: None.

Climate

Elevation 2,000'	Avg. High/Low	Avg. Rain (Inches)	Avg. Snow (Inches)	Avg. Days Rain	Avg. % Humidity
Jan.	56/33	.5	--	3	29
April	78/50	.3	--	2	15
July	104/75	.4	--	3	14
Oct.	81/53	.2	--	2	19
YEAR	79/52	3.6	2	23	20

# of days 32° or below: 41	# of days 90° or above: 132

In this semi-arid climate, the seasons are well-defined. Summer days are hot and dry (low humidity makes it bearable), with chilly evenings. When tropical air moves in, watch out for the monsoons. Winters are sunny, mild and pleasant, with daytime temps near 60. Snow is rare and melts quickly.

Earning a Living

Economic outlook: The Las Vegas economy and that of the surrounding communities continued to advance last year, supported by the impressive 31% growth in the number of new firms in the area over the last five years. Las Vegas leads the nation in the creation of new jobs for the 4th year running, with unemployment remaining stable at 5.5%. Job growth leaders were retail, wholesale, finance, insurance, real estate, government, services and manufacturing positions. Spurring on the economic growth are the strong revenues from retail sales. The influx of new residents (avg. 5,000/mo.) continues to sustain a strong construction industry. Tourism remains the number-one industry, however, with several new casinos opening recently. More than 20 million tourists contributed $14 billion in revenues to the economy. Gaming-related activities continued to make strong gains in both revenue and development of the "mega" hotel-casinos (MGM Grand, Silver Canyon and Riviera Hotel). Hotel construction has slowed after the phenomenal rate of the past 2 years, but it is anticipated that renewed building growth will continue. The demand for goods and services has brought about numerous new retail outlets. Wal-Mart, the largest retailer in the U.S., opened 2 stores in 1991, joining other major newcomers such as T.J. Maxx. The military impact through Nellis Air Force Base and the Nevada Test Site (more than 20,000 employees) has had an economic impact of more than $1 billion. Motion pictures and commercials, relatively new to the Las Vegas area, produced 126 projects bringing in $49.3 million.

Where the jobs are: Construction of Lake Las Vegas, a year-round extended-stay resort vacation complex, will create 25,000 new jobs and generate a recurring tax revenue of approximately $144 million annually. Car Country International will be a planned, theme automotive community with 20 auto sales dealerships totalling over 200,000 sq ft., a hotel/casino/conference center, a town center, and associated retail/commercial companies. Construction of this facility is expected to create more than 3,000 new jobs. Apex, an industrial site northeast of Las Vegas, will be the largest industrial park in Clark County. The site will be developed over the next 15 years, creating as many as 2,500 new jobs.

Business opportunities: In the last year Henderson has experienced a 19% growth rate. The community can use small home and business services such as auto repair, body shops, and medical offices. Businesses specializing in recreational activities are enjoying success.

Making the Grade

Public education overview: Henderson is part of the Clark County School District, the 14th largest in the nation. It educates more than 60% of the student population in the state. Henderson has 13 elementary, 4 middle schools, and 2 high schools. The district's magnet school, Southern Nevada Vocational Technical Center, offers an array of occupational and educational programs. In 1992 Henderson had 8 National Merit semifinalists from Greenvalley High School alone. SAT scores have been above the national average. Parent involvement runs very high with a strong PTA. A former president of National PTA and a member on The President's Advisory Council on Education is from this area. The district has a project designed to coordinate dropout prevention strategies with programs for at-risk students. Approximately 2/3 of the district's graduates go on to post-secondary education. The state has a $550 million annual budget going to education. Due to a drop in state revenues from tourism, funding will be a big challenge in the near future.

Class size: High School-28:1, Elementary-25:1.

Help for working parents: The city's Parks and Recreation Dept. runs an after-school program in the city's elementary schools called Safekey. Rates vary; discounts for siblings.

School year: Last week in Aug. to the first week of June. Children must be 5 by Sept. 30 to enroll in kindergarten.

Special education/gifted programs: Children identified as special education students have an I.E.P. (individualized educational program) developed for them. When possible, children are mainstreamed with support services in the classroom. Henderson has special schools for the blind, deaf, and mentally retarded. Gifted and talented students are tested before being enrolled in GATE (gifted and talented education program). A Henderson G&T class recently won a contest for its entry in the Secret Witness Crime Free Program.

Nearby colleges/universities: The University of Nevada Las Vegas specializes in computer science and engineering. Its Hotel Administration program is one of the best in the nation. Future plans include a school of law and expansion in master's and doctoral programs. Community College of Southern Nevada is a multi-campus institution with a site in Henderson. The college offers programs centering around business, industry and health care. Another school located is Clark County Community College, in North Las Vegas.

Medical Care

Hospitals/medical centers: The opening of St. Rose Dominican Hospital is a tremendous boost for local health care. This state-of-the-art 4-story facility is now considered the most modern in southern Nevada. It offers labor/delivery suites, laser surgery, 24-hour emergency and extensive outpatient services. Green Valley Medical Center is an acute care, comprehensive medical care facility offering 24-hour emergency and outpatient services: physical therapy, radiology, and respiratory therapy.
Specialized care: Nathan Adelson Hospice (speciaized care for the terminally ill—only 12 such hospices in the nation); Children's Hospital, staffed by specialists providing neonatal services and health care for children with special needs.

Crime & Safety

The Henderson City Police Dept. employs 100 officers with an average of 10 on duty per shift. The force anticipates having to hire more officers in the near future because of an 11% population influx each year. The avg. response time for emergency calls is between 5-7 min. Most responses involve theft of property. Domestic disturbances can be a problem. Las Vegas is a 24-hour town and many couples work late shifts. Police surmise that this creates stressful situations. The community has more than 200 neighborhood watch groups. The group also has a program that marks property with I.D. numbers to discourage theft. All the elementary schools have a DARE program, with 2 officers working full-time on the project.

CommunityLife

Much of Henderson's volunteer efforts revolve around vocal homeowners associations and the city's Citizen's Advisory Council. These dedicated volunteers act as a liaison between the city and residents. In addition, the Henderson Chamber of Commerce sponsors an annual week-long event, Industrial Days. Activities include a talent contest, chili cook-off, softball tournament, classic car show, street dancing and a parade. Community participation runs very high. This year's theme is a celebration of Christopher Columbus. Another volunteer effort involves the community's business population. Local employers work closely with the area's high schools in a match-up program. Students are paired with potential employers and participate in day-long visits to local companies. Each year, 65-70 employers work with approximately 130 students in this mutually beneficial program.

Let the Good Times Roll

Family fun: Henderson has an award-winning Parks and Recreation Dept., which operates 3 centers (youth, civic, and recreational). The Silver Springs Recreation Center features tennis courts, an outdoor pool and amphitheater, and a 1-mile lighted rim trail built for cycling. Youth sports programs include baseball, soccer and basketball. Lake Mead National Recreation Area, a 10-minute drive, offers 6 marinas, and great striped bass fishing. Also only a 10-minute drive away is Hoover Dam, the largest dam in the Western Hemisphere. Nearby Mt. Charleston offers a cool respite from the summer heat. Visitors enjoy hiking, picnicking and camping in summer and skiing in the winter. Wet-n-Wild, a 20-acre water theme park is only 20 min. away in downtown Las Vegas. Cathedral Gorge (120 mi.) is known for its eroded cliffs and spires—great for hikers. An hour north is the Valley of Fire, known for ancient Indian markings found on the rocks. Hiking and camping facilities are available.
Sports: Las Vegas is known as the boxing capital of the world. The city's premier boxing facilities are the sites of many world championship titles. Las Vegas has many championship golf courses. The city hosts the PGA's Seniors Classic, Ladies PGA International, and the Las Vegas Invitational. Also, the minor league basketball Las Vegas Stars play at Cashman Field. UNLV's Runnin' Rebels play at the Thomas and Mack Center (Rebels were the NCAA National Champs in the '89-'90 season and have had consecutive NCAA tournament appearances since 1983).
Arts & entertainment: Shakespeare in the Park is a National Awards for Parks and Recreation winner. The Clark County Heritage Museum features authentic Western and Indian relics. Las Vegas provides opportunities for residents interested in theater, opera, ballet and symphony: the Las Vegas Symphony Orchestra performs 12 concerts a year. The Nevada Dance Co. performs on the UNLV campus from Oct.-May; The Opus Dance Company was formed by Las Vegas dancers and choreographers who wanted to retain their classical skills. The Nevada Opera Co. performs at UNLV; The Charles Vander Masters Series runs from Oct.-April, attracting international artists such as the Vienna Boys Choir and The Russian Ballet.
Annual events: Henderson Expo (Oct.); Helldorado Days, a rodeo and chili cook-off, (May); Harvest Festival (late Oct.); North Las Vegas Balloon Races (late Oct.); The National Finals Rodeo, "The Super Bowl of Rodeos" and the Cowboy Christmas Show (Dec.).

The Environment

The Community Awareness and Emergency Response Program works to reduce the number of accidental chemical spills or releases, and keep the community informed about current emergency response techniques. Of the EPA's four prime pollutants with guidelines, Henderson meets the requirements. However, Las Vegas does not. Measures have been taken to lower the levels. Because there are a number of chemical companies located in the Henderson industrial park, the EPA monitors Henderson for ammonia and chlorine even though there are no specific guidelines for these chemicals. Consistently, the measurements are barely discernible on reading instruments. The county is planning an $8 milllion recycling facility.

In and Around Town

Roads and interstates: I-15 (east-west); US 95 (north-south) and US 93 (south).
Closest airports: McCarron International Airport is 12 mi. from Henderson and a 45 min. drive. North Las Vegas Air Terminal is 45 min. away.
Public transportation: Las Vegas Transit provides limited bus service throughout the city. Interstate passenger service is provided by LTR Bus Lines.
Avg. commute: The avg. commute to downtown Las Vegas takes 40 min. in rush hour.

What Every Resident Knows

Desert life means being at one with nature, ready or not! Tarantulas, scorpions and rattlesnakes are long-time residents and not any happier about people than people are about them. Believe it or not, bites are rare. • Newcomers are equally surprised by the large number of wild mules. Many are the offspring of those that were left behind by early settlers and miners. Every year the state rounds them up, and for a nominal fee you can adopt one. Lots of residents are doing just that. • In Henderson the roadrunner is not just the pesky cartoon character that says "Beep! Beep!" These little critters are a common sight in many front yards.

FYI

Henderson Chamber of Commerce
100 E. Lake Meade Drive
Henderson NV 89015
702-565-8951

Las Vegas Convention and Visitors Authority
3150 Paradise Road
Las Vegas, NV 89109
702-892-0711

Henderson Home News
2 Commerce Center Drive
Henderson, NV 89014
702-564-1881

Coldwell Banker/Gargis Assoc.
160 E. Horizon Drive
Henderson, NV 89015
702-564-6969
Kristine "K.C." Barker, Rel. Dir.

Century 21/Henderson Realty
18 Water Street
Henderson, NV 89015
702-564-2515
Doris Johnson, Realtor

Nevada Power
227 Water Street
Henderson, NV 89015
702-367-5555

Southwest Gas Corp.
P.O. Box 98512
Las Vegas, NV 89193-8512
702-565-8941

CENTEL
702-877-7400 (Call collect)

Henderson Economic Development
240 Water Street
Henderson, NV 89015
702-565-2409

Small Business Development Center
UNLV, Box 456011
4505 South Maryland Parkway
Las Vegas, NV 89154

School district: 702-799-5011
Property tax assessor:
702-455-3883
Interfaith Council: 702-564-4571
Physician's referral: 702-564-4508
Day-care referral: 702-734-0504

Reno, Nevada

Area Snapshot

Local population: 136,630
County: Washoe   **Population:** 256,640
U.S. region: Southwest
Closest metro area: Sacramento, Calif. (140 mi. southwest)
Median housing price: $110,000
Avg. household income: $35,500
Best reasons to live here: Strong job possibilities, affordable housing, no state income tax, endless outdoor recreation, good schools, exciting entertainment and events, four diverse seasons, fabulous scenery.

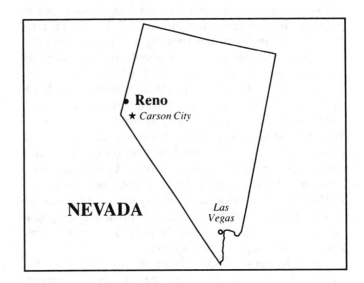

Fabulous Features

It's hard to think of Reno as a place to earn a living, especially if your only association with this spellbinding region is the entertainment and recreation. But 150,000 in the labor force prove it's possible to concentrate on something other than gambling and golf.

The transition from play days to pay days is made easier by the fact that Nevada is in a state of unparalleled job growth (it leads the nation for the past three years). In particular, the Reno/Sparks/Lake Tahoe area has been dealt a great hand! Business growth was up 20 percent last year, with a record 42 companies moving in. Recent newcomers include Porsche Motors, Ralston Purina and R.R. Donnelly.

Of course, with more than 7 million tourists a year being lured to the tables and slopes, this $2.5 billion visitor industry is a perennial winner. It's a safe bet you'll also love the no income tax rule, the educational opportunities (University of Nevada is here, along with a school district that has one of the highest ratios of computers to students in the nation) and the low crime (tough anti-drug programs).

Real estate is another wild card. Gorgeous custom built homes from $100s-$160s are cropping up, with a jewel of a planned community in the works. When completed, the Double Diamond Ranch will offer 4,000 new homes, five schools and commercial developments.

The real riches, of course, are the glimmering alpine lakes and tantalizing views of the Sierra Nevadas. There's everything from hang gliding to horseback riding, but most especially skiing (25 exceptional ski resorts within 90 minutes). Culture, top name entertainment and special events are wonderful year-round fixtures as well (Reno has its own ballet, opera and philharmonic). Perhaps Reno is the 1990s answer to "How the West Was Won."

Possible drawbacks: "On the road again" will be your theme song. Life in the desert means getting accustomed to driving long stretches of road at high speeds in order to get anywhere. • Need to be lulled to sleep by the crashing surf? Better buy a video or look elsewhere.

"You can quote me on that"

"Living here is like stepping back in time when neighbors cared about each other. We also love the incredible views of the Sierra mountains on one side and the desert on the other."—D.R.

Real Estate

Market overview: The market is well balanced between buyers and sellers and has shown steady growth. Resale inventory is up 5%-10% over past few years; residents are trading up or custom building. Spec builders are everywhere, putting up lovely homes in the $110,000-$160,000 range. Resales priced right sell in less than two months. With low property taxes to boot and many new manufacturers relocating, activity is brisk.

What houses look like: Ranches are the most popular style, usually wood or w/vinyl siding. Cathedral ceilings and master suites becoming more common. Many houses have great rooms—combination living, dining and family room. Usually no basement, but w/2-car garages. Garden tubs popular, pools not (pool season is only 3 months). Emphasis is on larger living spaces.

Starter homes: $90,000 buys an older 1000 sq. ft., 3BR/2BA "fix up" w/2-car garage, no basement. $110,000 could buy a newer, larger (1000-2000 sq. ft.) 3BR/2BA on a 60 x 100 lot.

Trade ups: $125,000 buys a newer home in a newer subdivision (new northwest Reno, East Sparks, Spanish Springs [outside city])—1800 sq. ft., 3-4BR/2BA, 2-car garage on a 60-80 x 100 lot. $150,000 buys a 3-4BR/2BA home w/2 car-garage on a 80 x 100 lot, with upgraded kitchen appliances, some parquet wood entryways.

Luxury homes: $200,000 buys a 2000 sq. ft, 3BR/2BA home w/2-car garage on a 80-90 x 100 lot: formal living and dining rooms, in established area, older renovated all-brick home. $500,000 buys a luxury home in a new subdivision: custom built, 3-5BR/2-3BA, 2500 sq. ft. and ½ acre (1-2 acres if in outlying areas). Nice neighborhoods include Caughlin Ranch and Lake-ridge, and southwest suburban areas.

Rental market: SFHs are scarce and very expensive—minimum of $800/mo. There are plenty of apartments, ranging from $450-$650/mo., but the majority are 2BR/1BA. Quite a few condos—range from $450 and up for a 2BR.

Great neighborhoods: Northwest and southeast Reno (Donner Springs area), and Sparks all offer good residential communities. There are lots of SFH with choices of old and new, lots of starter homes and very good school systems.

Nearby areas to consider: Carson City, 30 mi. south of Reno, is the capital of Nevada and smaller (less crowded) than Reno, with good schools, nice residential areas, and lots of government jobs. Fernley is a very small (pop. 5,000), quaint town 30 mi. east.

What Things Cost

Runzheimer's Living Cost Index: Avg. annual costs for family of 4 with household income of $50,000: $49,033 (1.9% below avg. city).

ACCRA's national comparisons: Overall living costs are 8.4% above avg., primarily because of housing and health care costs (23-25% above avg.). Groceries and transportation are 2.7% above avg. Utilitiy costs are 15.4% below avg.

Utilities: Phone: $13.58/mo. (unlimited local calls). Installation: $45. Electric: $65-$85 (winter), as high as $130 (summer). Gas: Avg. $30/mo. Water: Avg. $29/mo.

Kid care: Day care avg. $95-$110/wk for infants, $85/wk for toddlers. Working parents have not had problems finding licensed day care within 2-5 mi. of home unless they're far north of the city (Stead, Cold Springs). However, the centers that offer academics often have waiting lists. **Pediatric visit:** $65-$75.

The Tax Ax

Sales tax: 7%.

Property tax: Homes are assessed every 5 years at 35% of value and taxed at $3.1542/$100 assessed value. Example: $100,000, assessed at $35,000, pays $1,104 annual taxes.

State income tax: None.

Climate

Elevation 4,500'	Avg. High/Low	Avg. Rain (Inches)	Avg. Snow (Inches)	Avg. Days Rain	Avg. % Humidity
Jan.	45/18	.6	6.2	4	54
April	64/30	.3	1.5	3	34
July	91/47	.3	--	3	21
Oct.	70/31	.4	.3	3	30
YEAR	67/32	4.6	25.9	39	36
# of days 32° or below: 187			# of days 90° or above: 47		

Very dry year-round. Temperatures vary but are rarely extreme due to protection of surrounding mountain ranges. Although snowfall accumulates (26 inches a year), the Sierra Nevadas take the brunt of any major storm systems.

Earning a Living

Economic outlook: Emerging as an expanding warehousing, manufacturing and distribution center, Reno's prime west coast location ensures success on many economic fronts. The area's future is strongly tied to the booming Nevada economy—state led nation in job growth (spurred by fast-growing manufacturing sector), during past 3 years. Corporation for Enterprise Development in Washington, D.C. ranked Nevada 2nd nationally in economic performance and 11th in both business vitality and development capacity. Business growth up 20% in 1990. The number of companies moving into the Reno region reached a record of 42. They created 1,635 new jobs.

Where the jobs are: Employment growth in the manufacturing area is expected to increase at a faster pace than in previous years, mostly in the durable goods category. Now totaling 389 (including General Motors, Porsche, Ralston Purina, R.R. Donnelly, J.C. Penney and K-Mart), manufacturing firms employ 8,788 people. Recently relocated companies include Citation/Caliber Medical (medical instruments), Duraline, Inc. (plastic conduit pipe), Empire Brushes (brooms and brushes) Fullerton Design/Zip Nut (aeorspace fasteners), and Transkrit Corp (business forms printer). Transportation, communications, public utilities positions all grew strongly. Major communications/data centers are America West Airlines, J.C. Penney, National Data, Pacific Telesis, Spiegel, USAir and Western Union. Tourism is also an important industry: gaming and recreation employ more than 21% of the county's 145,000 workforce. Tourism is expected to boom, with completion of the new bowling stadium, Galena Ski resort (expected to create 1,500 jobs and boost the local economy by $140 million), Sierra Reflections conference center, Montreaux Wellness Center, and restoration of the Mapes Hotel (hotel and boutiques will employ approx. 400 people.) Retail trade received a major boost with the opening of the Sparks Factory Outlet Mall.

Business opportunities: Gaming and service sector has driven the economy for the past 30 years, and they continue to do so. The entertainment sector is still growing—5 hotel expansions were slated for 1992, 6 more for '93. Businesses that service hotels, casinos, etc. are profitable. Warehousing is 2nd largest area industry. Reno has no corporate tax and no state income tax. Getting permits for smaller companies is easy; harder for larger manufacturing companies that will have an impact on the environment.

Making the Grade

Public education overview: The Washoe County School District serves more than 40,000 students with 50 elementary, 10 middle, and 9 high schools. District also operates Glenn Hare Occupational Center, an alternative high school and a school for the severely handicapped. Annual dropout rate is 6.1%, one of the lowest in the state. The District has a variance policy, under which parents can request to send a child to school other than the local one—requests are routinely granted if there is room. Washoe HS is the alternative HS, with a flexible schedule and individualized teaching. The school district has strong support from business and professional community. All of middle schools (grades 7-8) are close to full implementation of Carnegie Commission recommendations: flexible scheduling, teaching by multidisciplinary teams, use of adviser/advisee progams & thematic units. School libraries are part of county library system, so public can use them, too. The district has been growing at a 4-5% rate annually. Washoe County residents pas-sed a $155 million bond issue in Sept. 1992. ACT ('91-'92) test scores: composite county avg 21.0; state, 21.1; nat'l, 20.6. 50% of high school students go on to college.

Class size: 22:1.

Help for working parents: Before- and after-school day-care is available at about 2/3 of elementary schools, generally from 6:30 a.m. to 6 p.m. Cost is $3-$4/day. Some have breakfast programs.

Blue Ribbon School Awards: Proctor Hug High School ('86-'87).

School year: From wk. before Labor Day through 2nd wk. of June. Children must be 5 on or before Sept. 30 to enter kindergarten. Starting in '93-'94 school year, three elementary schools will be on year-round calendars (60 days in, 20 days off).

Special education/gifted programs: Mainstreaming is emphasized for those with learning disabilities, although special resource programs are available at almost every school. There are self-contained classrooms, where students who need full-time services stay in same classroom. Other kids get hour or two of special services, rest of time in regular classrooms. IEPs for each handicapped student. Gifted and talented program is available throughout the school system.

Nearby colleges/universities: Univ. Nevada/Reno offers degrees in 72 baccalaureate, 28 doctoral, and 67 other graduate programs. National Judicial College; Truckee Meadows Community College; Western Nevada Community College; Sierra Nevada College.

Medical Care

Hospitals/medical centers: Sparks Family Hospital (comprehensive medical care specializing in diabetes, pediatrics and in-patient rehabilitation services); St Mary's Hospital (acute, comprehensive medical care, specializing in maternity, cardiac surgery, home care, rehabilitation and chemical dependency); Washoe Medical Center (comprehensive medical care, specializing in rehabilitation, psychiatric, chemical dependency, trauma unit, renal dialysis, Women's and Family Center, Washoe Pregnancy center).

Specialized care: Veterans Administration Medical Center (nursing home care unit, psychiatric unit, alcohol drug treatment, medical surgical); Nevada Mental Health Institute; HCA Truckee Meadows (alcohol and drug abuse).

Crime & Safety

As a convention and entertainment center, Reno attracts more than 7 million visitors annually. Consequently, the police department is intricately committed to the special needs of the community, for a healthy tourist industry is dependent on low crime. Violent crime is low. Residential and retail burglaries are vigilantly kept under control by an interconnecting net of neighborhood watch groups. In addition, a private security staff is employed by several of the larger businesses, assisting the police department in preventive safety programs. Secondary schools are involved in the DARE program, and officers are assigned to schools to monitor its implementation. Reno police department (290 on force) started using communityoriented policing philosophy in 1987, which holds that community should have input and help identify problems to which police should respond, rather than police deciding themselves what problems to address. Representatives from 100-200 departments from around the country have come to Reno to see how its program works.

Community Life

Residents of Reno—"the biggest little city in the world"—love to celebrate. Community life therefore revolves around a busy social calendar, one in which all age groups can find something to participate. Reno is known throughout the region for its heart and community spirit. When a need arises, many community groups make a combined effort to fill that need, whether it be replenishing the Food Bank or helping a family in trouble.

Let the Good Times Roll

Family fun: When you hear "shushing," don't be quiet. Move aside for skiers. The nation's largest concentration of ski resorts—16 alpine and 9 cross-country w/avg. snowfall of 25 ft./season—are all located within 90 min. Downtown Reno has the River Walk and Amphitheater, which has scheduled concerts and other performances. The area also has the Fleischmann Planetarium; Great Basin Adventure, a children's theme park; Liberty Belle's Slot Machine Collection; the National Automobile Museum; the Pioneer Theatre Auditorium: the Wild Island water theme park; Sierra Safari Zoo; and Nevada Historical Society Museum. The Nevada State Museum has natural history exhibits; the Nevada State Railroad Museum has vintage railcars and offers train rides on summer weekends. Nearby parks feature swimming, camping, hiking and fishing. Fishing, boating, waterskiing, hiking, camping and swimming can be found at Pyramid Lake and a number of other streams and lakes. Within an easy day's drive are a wealth of federal parks and forests—Sheldon Natl. Wildlife Refuge, Fallon Natl. Wildlife Refuge, Humboldt Natl. Forest, Toiyabe Natl. Forest. In Calif.: Eldorado and Tahoe Natl Forests, Lassen Volcanic Natl. Pk., Desolation Valley Wilderness, Yosemite Natl. Pk. Reno has golf clubs, (20 courses available) tennis clubs, horseback riding stables, and a variety of cold-weather sports: cross-country skiing, downhill skiing, ice skating, and snowmobiling.

Sports: There are no professional major league teams in the area. Univ. of Nevada Wolfpack play all intercollegiate sports. Reno Silver Sox are minor league affiliates of the Seattle Mariners. Professional boxing matches are held at the convention center.

Arts & entertainment: Performance spaces in Reno include Pioneer Center for the Performing Arts, Reno Little Theater, the 12,000-seat Lawlor Events Center, Sierra Arts Center, Church Fine Arts Complex, Redfield Theatre and Nightingale Concert Hall. Reno has the Philharmonic Orchestra; Reno Chamber Orchestra; Nevada Opera Association; the Nevada Festival Ballet; and the Reno Little Theater. The Nevada Museum of Art is Nevada's largest art museum.

Annual events: Winter Carnival (Feb.); Reno International Jazz Festival (March); Festival Reno (June); Reno Rodeo and Parade (June); Reno Jumping Horse Classic and El Dorado Grand Prix Jumping (June); Reno Towne Faire (July); Great Reno Balloon Race (Aug.); Nevada State Fair (Aug.); Coors International Bicycle Classic (Aug.).

The Environment

Five consecutive years of below-normal precipitation make water conservation a must in Truckee Meadows. Westpac Utilities, the main water purveyor for the area, has joined with other government agencies and business organizations to form the Drought Busters, a water conservation coalition. The Desert Research Institute's ongoing cloud seeding program has successfully increased precipitation in the Tahoe Truckee Basin. A proposed 35-mile pipeline from Honey Lake (to be completed in two years) will help ease the water shortage. The new environmental committee has achieved success over the past year in encouraging use of scheduled weekly recycling efforts. Residents as well as several leading hotels and businesses are active in recycling paper, cardboard, bottles, and cans. Other efforts: to protect air quality, oxygenated fuels are used during winter; spring clean-up of parks and wildlife areas are part of an active calendar.

In and Around Town

Roads and interstates: I-80 (east-west) and U.S. Highway 395 (north-south). U.S. 50 (east-west) and U.S. 95 (north-south) are within 30 miles.

Closest airports: Reno Cannon International Airport (4 mi. from downtown); Reno Stead Airport (general aviation reliever airport)

Public transportation: Citifare is the public transit system operated by the Regional Transportation Commission (RTC). It provides service to the community with 26 individual routes and 63 vehicles. The RTC also operates Citilift, a para-transit service with 36 vehicles providing door-to-door service for the disabled and those with special transportation needs.

Avg. commute: 20-25 min.

What Every Resident Knows

Reno is no place for couch potatoes. The great outdoors beckons and all people talk about is what they've just done or what they plan to do next. • Anything goes, as is evidenced by the fact that one of the hottest events of the year (literally) is a giant 50s revival called Hot August Nights. Held for four days, people come from all over the country to show off vintage cars, attend the prom at the convention center (yes, it still helps if you have a date, but at least now you won't have a curfew), and hop and bop 'til they drop. They sure know how to throw a party here!

FYI

**Greater Reno-Sparks
Chamber of Commerce**
P.O. Box 3499
Reno, NV 89505
702-786-3030

**Reno/Sparks Convention
& Visitors Authority**
P.O. Box 837
Reno, NV 89504
702-827-7643

Reno Gazette-Journal
955 Kuenzli Lane
Reno, NV 89502
702-788-6200

Sparks Tribune
1002 C Street
Sparks, NV 89431
702-358-8061

**Coldwell Banker Plummer
& Associates**
290 E. Moana Lane, Suite 1
Reno, NV 89502
702-689-8228
Lornie B. Wagner

Sierra Pacific Power Co.
(electric, water, and gas)
6100 Neil Road
Reno, NV 89502
702-689-4444

Nevada Bell
1450 Vassar Street
Reno, NV 89510
702-333-4811 (Call collect)

**Economic Development
of Western Nevada**
5190 Neil Road
Reno, NV 89502
702-829-3700

Small Business Development Center
Mail Stop 032
College of Business Administration
Reno, NV 89557-0016
702-784-1717

School district: 702-348-0200
Property tax assessor:
702-328-2510
Newcomer's Club: 702-322-4797
Physician's referral: 702-825-0278
Day-care referral: 702-328-2300

Morristown, New Jersey

Area Snapshot

Local population: 19,189
County: Morris   **Population:** 419,000
U.S. region: Northeast/central New Jersey
Closest metro areas: New York City (30 mi. southeast)
Median housing price: $223,491
Avg. household income: $52,478
Best reasons to live here: Prosperous, fast-growing county, New England-style charm, voted New Jersey's best town, wonderful parks, ethnic and cultural diversity, progressive schools and medical care, excellent transportation, super shopping, historic area.

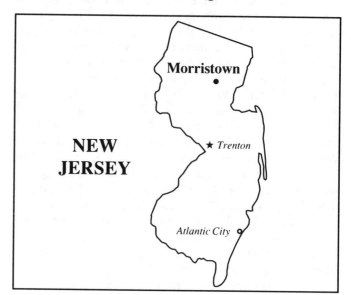

Fabulous Features

You've seen the funny signs that say, "General Washington slept here," but in Morristown, it's no joke! Just 30 miles northwest of New York City, amid rolling hills and lakes, is the historic Jacob Ford Mansion, Washington's winter headquarters during the Revolutionary War. In fact, Morris County is surrounded by historical landmarks.

But it is the *future* of this area that grabbed us. Morris County is the third fastest-growing county in the New York, New Jersey, Connecticut region because many multinational firms have world headquarters or major operations along the I-287 corporate corridor. Among the Fortune 500 companies are AT&T/Bell Labs, Nabisco and Warner-Lambert.

With a large presence of foreign labor, the Morristown schools offer strong foreign language programs (Russian, Japanese, Italian and others) and an exceptional high school (career center, TV studio, radio station, computer labs and 27 athletic programs).

The town itself is a mix of wonderful antique shops and nouveau restaurants, of charming tree-lined streets with stately, old homes and high-rise condominiums and a resident base more akin to the United Nations than a small town. It's why in a recent *New Jersey Magazine* reader's poll, Morristown tied for best town in the state. And if it's true that history repeats itself, perhaps it will also be the home of a future chief commanding officer!

Possible drawbacks: The New York/New Jersey region is still reeling from the recession, job losses and a flat real estate market, so inventory is limited. New construction also slowed and what does sell is usually at asking price. • Although improvements along Routes 80 and 24 and I-287 will help, there will still be congestion in town (75,000 people a day come for the hospital, government offices and major employers. • Unaccustomed drivers should never travel without a co-pilot. New Jersey's on/off ramps take getting used to.

"You can quote me on that"

"We moved back to Morristown from Pittsburgh. We left in the first place because of my husband's company. When he told me we were moving again I thought 'Now where?' When he told me we were going back to Morristown I was the first one packing, with my kids right behind me!"—R.R.

Real Estate

Market overview: Plain and simple, because it's a seller's market, people are staying put, reducing inventory. With so few homes to choose from, sellers are getting close to their asking price. New construction is expected to pick up with condos making a slow comeback (still not as popular as single family homes). Realtors hope that the recession has bottomed out and the next 12-18 months will be more active.

What houses look like: Colonials (4BR/2 1/2BA) are predominant here. Many are all-brick or brick with wood shingles, stone or slate. Popular features include gourmet kitchens, vaulted ceilings, skylights, BAs w/jacuzzis, and garden tubs. Most newer homes have great rooms—combination living/dining/den. Decks, garages, fireplaces and basements are common.

Starter homes: $175,000-$230,000. At the low end, you'll get 3BR/1 1/2BA, 1-car garage, no central air, on 1/3 acre. $230,000 buys a split level or older colonial w/3-4BR/2BA, 1-car garage, central air, combo living/dining room and fireplace.

Trade-ups: For $250,000 you get an older 3-4BR/2BA, 1-2-car garage, family room on 1/3 acre. For $350,000, you get a 4BR, 2 1/2BA, 2+ fireplaces, updated kitchen and BAs, skylights, gourmet kitchen, family room, and 2-car garage.

Luxury homes: Range from $650,000-$1 million. The low end buys 1 acre or more, 4-5BR/3-3 1/2BA, 2-3-car garage, jacuzzi, skylights, custom deck, fireplaces, formal living/dining room, gourmet kitchen, ceramic tile or polished hardwood floors.

Rental market: SFHs are rare. When available, a 4BR/2 1/2BA runs $2,300/mo. A very small house might rent for $1,400/mo. Few co-ops.

Great neighborhoods: Morristownship is in the Morristown school district, though a separate municipality. This multi-ethnic community has its own radio station, swimming pool, and beautiful parks. Morris Plains students go to one of the top high schools in the nation. It's family-oriented and convenient to shopping.

Nearby areas to consider: Randolph is country-like and only 15 minutes away. The schools are great, it has all the metropolitan conveniences, there are lots of young families—but taxes are high. Madison is 5 minutes away with a good school district, convenient shopping, beautiful parks and recreation. Homes are more expensive but the taxes are lower. Roxbury, Flanders and Jefferson Township are a little farther west and seem to give a lot for the money.

What Things Cost

Runzheimer's Living Cost Index: Avg. annual costs for family of 4 with household income of $50,000: $56,655 (13.3% above avg. city).
ACCRA's national comparisons: Not available.
Utilities: Phone: $11/mo. Installations: Avg. $42. Gas: Avg. $20-$30/mo. (summer), $230/mo. (winter). Electric: Avg. $113/mo. with a high of $200/mo. in summer.
Kid care: Licensed day care for infants is pretty limited. Most centers only accept children from 18 mo. to 5 yrs. Prices avg. $445/mo. **Pediatric visit:** $50.

The Tax Ax

Sales tax: 6% (clothing, food and professional services exempt).
Property tax: Morristown's current millage rate is $2.10 per $100 of assessed value. For example, a home assessed at $200,000 would pay $4,200/yr. Generally, homes are assessed at 90.75% of the home's market value.
State income tax: Tax rates range from 2%-7%. For example, taxable income of $40,000-$75,000 would be $1,025 plus 6.5% of excess over $40,000 (filing single). Married filing jointly with incomes between $50,000-$70,000 would pay $1,150 plus 3.5% of excess over $50,000.

Climate

Elevation 400'	Avg. High/Low	Avg. Rain (Inches)	Avg. Snow (Inches)	Avg. Days Rain	Avg. % Humidity
Jan.	36/18	2.8	9	8	60
April	61/38	4.3	1	11	47
July	84/60	4.3	--	10	53
Oct.	65/41	3.8	.1	8	54
YEAR	61/39	46.4	36	112	55
# of days 32° or below:136			# of days 90° or above: 14		

This area is typical of continental climates, with four changable seasons and a wide range of temperatures throughout the year. Moderated somewhat by the Atlantic Ocean, extreme hot and cold weather is rare. When it does occur, it doesn't stay long. Count on an avg. 13 snowfalls in winter.

Earning a Living

Economic outlook: Morris County remains one of the few economic bright spots in the New York metropolitan area, as is indicated by the fact that close to 15% of all Fortune 500 companies are headquartered and/or have major corporate/distribution facilities here. All told, more than 10,000 businesses have Morris County addresses (there are more than 60 industry/office parks). Unemployment remains at 5.8%, the low end of the national average, in part because of the area's central location off the I-287 corporate corridor. And now with its announced expansion (completed in 1994-95), the prospects are even brighter because it will spur development in the northern part of the county while attracting a new labor force from Rockland County, New York (they'll now have direct access to Morris County employers). The recent expansion of Route 24 (east-west corridor) into the I-87 will also make companies more accessible. It's why companies such as Six Flags/Great Adventure and Days Inn moved their headquarters here and why American Home Products recently announced plans to close its Manhattan headquarters and move to Madison. The hope is that the continued growth will reduce the office vacancy rate (now at 25%, but down from the past 2 years) while increasing the corporate tax base.

Where the jobs are: One reason that Morris County has been somewhat insulated from the region's weak economy is the large number of multinational companies headquartered here. Their bread and butter is across the ocean (Europe and Asia), not across the Hudson River. In the retail sector, the growth of discount outlets has revitalized an otherwise lackluster period. BJ's (warehouse) opened in western Morris County and is looking for a second site. Macy's and I. Magnin opened a clearance outlet at the International Trade Center (Mt. Olive) that is going gangbusters. Packaged goods manufacturers and high-tech firms, including AT&T, Nabisco, Warner-Lambert, Sandoz (pharmaceuticals) and Picatinny Arsenal (weapons research), continue to expand.

Business opportunities: In general, thriving small businesses are the ones providing support services to major corporations that have downsized or eliminated departments. Printing and graphics companies, mailing houses and advertising agencies are busy. And with an affluent buying audience, retailers with high-end fashions and giftware should also do well.

Making the Grade

Public education overview: Education expenditure per pupil per year is $9,625. And the results show that the investment is worth it—85% of the 1990 senior class is enrolled in college, a good percentage in Ivy League schools. In 1991, there were 23 National Merit Scholars, and 4 National Merit Scholarship winners. The college preparation in this progressive school district is superb. Because of the multi-ethnic, multi-cultural nature of the population, the foreign language programs (including Russian, Japanese, Italian and more) in the high school are particularly strong. The athletic program is also impressive, with more than 100 co-curricular and athletic programs offered to students. The high school has a series of peer leadership programs, the only school in the county offering such a program. The district's only middle school (Frelinghuysen Junior School) is currently crowded, and an addition to the building is being considered.

Class size: 20:1 (elementary).

Help for working parents: Each elementary school offers before- and after-school programs (from 7 a.m. to 6:30 p.m.) for $270/mo.

Blue Ribbon School Awards: Delbarton School ('83-'84).

School year: Begins after Labor Day and ends mid-June. Children must be 5 on or before Oct. 31 to enter kindergarten.

Special education/gifted programs: There are special classes for gifted students in grades 3-12. Morris High School offers 11 advanced placement courses, and enriched studies programs in art, music and more. The Special Education Lafayette Learning Center serves the district, helping students from grades 2-12 who demonstrate learning, behavioral or emotional difficulties to such a degree that they cannot be maintained in their home school.

Nearby colleges/universities: In the Morris County area: College of St. Elizabeth, a private 4-yr. women's college; County College of Morris, a 2-yr. school; Drew University, liberal arts, theological school and graduate school; Fairleigh Dickinson University, the state's largest private university offering nearly 100 majors; Centenary College at Hackettstown, a 4-yr. school; Upsala College in Sussex, a 4-yr. liberal arts college; Sussex County Community College, a 2-yr. college. In addition, Princeton, Rutgers and a number of schools in New York City are also a short distance away.

Medical Care

Hospitals/medical centers: Its central location and proximity to the metropolitan area gives Morristown residents a wide choice of medical care. Local medical centers with a variety of specialties are: Morristown Memorial Hospital (pediatrics, obstetrics-gynecology, heart disease and oncology); St. Clare's Hospital (pediatrics, radiation therapy, women's center); Dover General (internal medicine, burn center, cancer treatment). Morristown Memorial Hospital is a major teaching hospital and regional referral center. It offers facilities for treating cardiovascular disease, including open heart surgery and ambulatory surgery. In addition, the hospital offers neonatal and pediatric special care units.

Specialized care: St. Clare's-Riverside Medical Center (Alcohol Abuse).

Crime & Safety

An effective police force and a small-sized area make Morristown such a safe and secure place. Although there are 75,000 people coming into town each day, as well as a number of restaurants and bars that draw crowds in the evening, residents are comfortable walking downtown at night. The police have a visible presence, patrolling by foot, motorcycle and car—response time is avg. 1 min. There are some drug problems and instances of domestic crimes in the low-income public housing areas. But there's been a slight decrease in larcencies from the previous year. There are also very active community watch programs. DARE is active and residents are familiar with the DARE officer, who drives a cadillac bearing the sign: "This car was seized from a drug dealer, thank you very much."

Community Life

As Morris County encompasses a large area, the community life of this region is held together more by topics and issues rather than physical places. Also, the county regards itself as a separate entity, not a bedroom community for New York City. While many residents do work and commute to New York City, Philadelphia and Trenton, people spoke of the relieved feeling of coming home to Morris County. The much-awaited "First Night" New Year's Celebration in Morristown will see plenty of community spirit.

Let the Good Times Roll

Family fun: The Morris County Park Commission has preserved more than 10,000 acres of land for the recreational and educational needs of its residents. There are more than 24 town parks and facilities, the largest being Mahlon Dickerson Reservation and Lewis Morris Park. Seasonal activities include swimming, boating hiking, golf, bicycling, camping, ice skating, sledding, picnicking and horseback riding. There are farming and milling demonstrations, year-round ice skating instruction, hockey, horticultural and education classes, a trail for the blind, and two parcourse fitness trails, one at Lewis Morris Park, the other at the Tracton Line recreation area. The Frelinghuysen Arboretum attracts many, as will the planned 8.5-mile bikeway across Washington Township at the foot of Schooley's Mtn. Morristown National Historical Park is the site of the winter encampments of George Washington and his Continental Army. Favorite museums for the kids (and adults) include the Morris Museum and the Museum of Early Trades and Crafts in Madison.

Sports: The New Jersey Meadowlands is home to the New Jersey Devils (NHL), the Jets Giants (NFL) and the New Jersey Nets (NBA). The New York Yankees and New York Mets are the Major League Baseball teams in the area.

Arts & entertainment: Headquarters Plaza Hotel is a center for a lot of activity. There are many restaurants as well as a spa and a 10-plex movie theater. The Paper Mill Playhouse in Millburn, just 30 min. away, features a variety of productions including ballet (Nutcracker Suite performed by the N.J. Ballet), opera, children's programs and concerts. The Morris Choral Society is an organization of amateur singers and the Masterwork Chorus has 200 singers with David Randolph as the conductor. This group has performed at Carnegie Hall. There is so much going on here that Historic Morristown, Inc., issues a monthly calendar of activities.

Annual events: "First Night," a New Year's town celebration is a new festival started in 1992. The Morris County Arts Council and Morris Museum sponsor a wide range of events throughout the year. In April, 1993, a new festival, "Arts Aurora" will be presented. Intended for children, it will be an all-day entertainment and hands-on arts festival. In addition, the Winter Film Festival has been a popular area attraction, as well as the summer Geraldo Farms New Jersey Symphony Orchestra Lawn Concert.

The Environment

Morristown's plethora of environmental programs, proves it is very aware of the ecology. One of only two cities in New Jersey that has been certified by Keep America Beautiful, Morristown has an annual Litter Pick-Up Day and numerous clean-up programs. The Schools Committee Project teaches environmental curriculum within the schools, running seminars (sponsored by Warner-Lambert). A new improved recycling program was initiated. The Clean Community committee, a volunteer group, conducts its own waterway audit, and acts as a liaison in helping the Environmental Prosecutor on legal infractions. The Upper Raritan River Water Association effectively ensures clean water for the community. The Whippany, Passaic and Raritan Rivers are still polluted, however.

In and Around Town

Roads and interstates: I-287, 80 (east-west), 280, 78; Routes 46, 202, 206; Highways 10, 15, 23, 24, 53. Interstate 287 is being expanded north to the Thruway and connects with the Garden State Pkwy, as does 80. Highway 24 is currently being connected to 287.
Closest airports: Morristown Airport. Newark Airport is less than 1 hr. away.
Public transportation: New Jersey Transit provides bus and rail service. Several bus lines go to Port Authority (1½ hrs.) in Manhattan. Morristown has an electric train that goes to Newark and Hoboken, called the Morristown Lines. Morris County Rides is a nonprofit ride-sharing service that matches carpoolers.
Avg. commute: 20-25 min. within Morris County.

What Every Resident Knows

In the late 1800s, many of the nation's business and financial leaders, such as Charles Mellon, built large country estates in Morris County. By 1900 it was claimed that more millionaires lived within a 1-mile radius of the Morristown Green than elsewhere in the world. • It might help having that kind of wealth today, because Morris County residents are so close to phenomenal shopping. The upscale Short Hills Mall, Livingston Mall and Somerset Mall will capture your imagination if not your wallet. • The hottest topic currently (and may be for some time) concerns the need for a new Morris County jail. The need exists, but NIMBY (not in my backyard).

FYI

Morristown County Chamber of Commerce
10 Park Avenue
Morristown, NJ 07960
201-539-3882

Morris County Daily Record
P.O. Box 217
Parsippany, NJ 07054
201-428-4444

Newark Star Ledger
1 Star Ledger Plaza
Newark, NJ 07102
800-242-0850

Coldwell Banker/Schlott Realty
211 South Street
Morristown, NJ 07960
201-267-8990
Phyllis Lunetta

Public Service Gas & Electric
80 Park Plaza
Newark, NJ 07101
201-538-7000

Jersey Central Power & Light
800-452-9155

New Jersey Bell
800-755-1080

Morris Area Development Group
10 Park Avenue
Morristown, NJ 07960
201-530-8270

School district: 201-292-2000
Property tax assessor:
201-292-6667
Newcomer's Club: 201-292-8384
Physician's referral: 800-447-3337
Day-care referral: 201-539-9514

Albuquerque, New Mexico

Area Snapshot

Local population: 384,736
County: Bernalillo   **Population:** 480,577
U.S. region: Southwestern U.S.
Closest metro area: Santa Fe (61 mi. north)
Median housing price: $90,700
Avg. household income: $33,617
Best reasons to live here: Promising job growth, low taxes and living costs, pleasant, year-round climate, rich ethnic/cultural diversity, abundant recreation, excellent schools and universities, fast-growing research/medical center, plentiful water supply, scenic wonders.

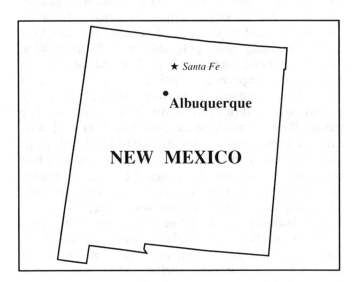

Fabulous Features

You may not be able to spell it, you may even have a hard time saying it, but once you see Albuquerque, you'll simply never forget it! This "Land of Enchantment" is nestled beneath the spectacular Sandia Mountains adjoining the famed Rio Grande Valley. The panoramic views, sunny climate and abundant fresh air have been the region's snake charm for thousands of years.

But there's nothing deceiving about Albuquerque. True to its Mexican, Spanish and Indian heritage, there is a spirit of cooperation that unified this city long before it started growing at twice the rate of the nation. In fact, it was the hard-working, highly educated work force (more Ph.D.s per capita than any other city) that convinced Martin Marietta, Metropolitan Life and General Mills to open facilities here. It's also why dozens of others, including Motorola and J.C. Penney Credit, have announced expansions (8,000-plus new jobs).

On the homefront, realtors have been punching overtime cards, showing off new construc-

tion in the city and adjacent Rio Rancho (the fastest growing "micropolitan" area in the U.S.). The price is right (*Kiplingers Personal Finance* magazine said the Albuquerque area has the most affordable housing in the U.S.), and so is the exquisite architecture.

Even better are the amenities: phenomenal recreation (from skiing the Sandias to camping in state parks), excellent educational opportunities (La Cueva High was named best in the state) and extensive art and culture. It's all so *magnifico!*

Possible drawbacks: As anyone over 30 remembers, New Mexico was the country's guinea pig for testing nuclear energy. Today, it is still the U.S. nuclear capital. Residents have grown up with this, but say that strenuous government controls reduce serious risks. • Personnel directors claim there are hundreds of applicants for most job openings. With unemployment at 6%-7%, if you come without a job offer, you might add to the statistics.

"You can quote me on that"

"We're thoroughly enjoying this very friendly community and a house that was more affordable and larger than we could have bought back home. The best part is the great weather. We ski in winter and swim in summer. We also love the convenience of the two big malls, and there are so many things for the kids to do."—M.B.

Real Estate

Market overview: *Kiplinger's Personal Finance* magazine rated Albuquerque the most affordable housing market in the U.S., based on the fact that overall housing costs only take a 17% share of a family's income (compared to 28% nationally). It also showed appreciation going strong at a rate of 7.4%. Albuquerque is a balanced market. Property priced right and in good condition is selling like hot cakes. Resales average around $100,000 and new construction ranges from $100,000-$150,000. Supported by lower interest rates, new construction has risen nearly 25% and is expected to remain strong. Townhouses are popular, ranging from $75,000-$200,000. Patio homes are the same range.

What houses look like: Naturally, the predominant architectural style is Southwestern. However, you'll also find Victorians, California ranches, colonials and contemporaries. Most are frame stucco (brick is expensive). Most homes under $150,000 are 1-level. Interior trends include gourmet kitchens, family rooms and elegant master suites. Pools and fireplaces are popular.

Starter homes: $75,000 might buy an older home with a 1-car garage, 3BR/1 3/4BA, 1100-1200 sq. ft. $110,000 could buy a house with 1500-1700 sq. ft., 2-car garage, 3BR/1½BA, fireplace. Homes in this range are generally 30-50 years old.

Trade-ups: For $150,000, you can buy a home 5-10 years old with 1800-2000 sq. ft., possibly a split-level, 2-car garage, 3-4BR/2-2½BA, living and dining room combination, family room, and fireplace in the northeast.

Luxury homes: $300,000 buys 2500-3000 sq. ft. on an 80 x 100 lot with 4BR/3BA, fireplace, family room and large kitchen. For $500,000, you get 5000 sq. ft., 4BR/3BA, 3-car garage, gourmet kitchen, elegant master suite, formal living room and dining room, and indoor pool,. This might include 3-4 acres in Placitas, Cedarcrest and Edgewood.

Rental market: Single family homes are hard to find—there's a 98% occupancy rate. Where available, they're $700-$1,500/mo. for a 3BR/1½BA. Apartments rent for $350-$500/mo.

Great neighborhoods: The west side is ideal for families. The homes are newer and affordable. Neighborhoods like Taylor Ranch offer good schools and convenient shopping. Cedarcrest and Edgewood are nice, with slightly older, smaller homes.

Nearby areas to consider: Rio Rancho (20 min. northwest) is one of the fastest-growing suburbs in the U.S. Prices are very low, starting at $40,000, up to the low $100s. Children attend Albuquerque schools.

What Things Cost

Runzheimer's Living Cost Index: Avg. annual costs for family of 4 with household income of $50,000: $47,655 (4.7% below avg. city).

ACCRA's national comparisons: Overall living costs are .4% below the national avg. The only categories above avg. are health care (6.1%) and goods and services (1.8%). Housing is avg., and utilities and groceries are 2.2% and 6% below avg.

Utilities: Phone: $18.08/mo. unlimited local calls; Hookup: $45.15. Electric: Avg. $31/mo. (majority use for cooking). Gas: Avg. $48/mo. ($60 in winter). Water, sewer and trash: Runs $35/mo.

Kid care: Avg. costs for day care for infants (under 18 mo.): $340/mo.; toddlers and older: $325.50/mo. Childcare is quite accessible, with more than 20 private contractors. **Pediatric visit:** $40 avg.

The Tax Ax

Sales tax: 5.8%.

Property tax: To calculate, take one-third of the home's market value (equals the assessed rate) and multiply by the current millage rate (36.588-37.791). For example, a $100,000 home would run $1,220/yr.

State income tax: Tax rates from 2.4% to 8.5% (for taxable incomes over $64,000). For example, if married filing jointly with taxable income of $40,000, you'd pay $1,864/yr.

Climate

Elevation 5,300'	Avg. High/Low	Avg. Rain (Inches)	Avg. Snow (Inches)	Avg. Days Rain	Avg. % Humidity
Jan.	47/24	.9	2.4	3	37
April	70/41	.5	.5	3	17
July	92/65	1.4	--	9	28
Oct.	72/45	.8	--	5	29
YEAR	70/44	6.8	11	55	28

# of days 32° or below: 121	# of days 90° or above: 61

People assume it's hot 365 days a year. Far from it. Many days are sunny and hot, but dry and bearable because of the altitude; temperatures rarely top 100 in the summer. But with arctic air intrusions, winters can be chilly, although temperatures rarely drop below zero. Snowfall is light (less than a foot), although the mountains get much more. And 50% of the rainfall occurs between July and Sept.

Earning a Living

Economic outlook: Albuquerque is the economic and geographic center of New Mexico. Its strong economy is bolstered by a combination of manufacturing (GE, Honeywell, Intel), business service (Baxter Health Care Corp., Pioneer Teletechnologies, Metropolitan Life) and scientific research.(Sandia National Laboratory and Kirtland Air Force Base). The labs, in turn, are supported by a network of national high-tech suppliers and consultants (General Dynamics, RCA, Rockwell). Albuquerque combines a skilled labor force with low labor costs (the state ranked 4th in the nation for lowest overall labor costs). New Mexico is a "labor peace" state; of the nearly 700 manufacturing plants in and around Albuquerque, only three have organized workers. There have been no major work stoppages in recent years. There is an abundance of affordable, developed and undeveloped, industrial-zoned land. In addition, New Mexico has one of the most favorable tax rates in the country (2nd-lowest property tax and 14th lowest income tax). The recent arrivals of General Mills, Martin Marietta, CS Manufacturing and Fusion, Inc., and expansion announcements by existing firms such as Bueno Foods, Intel and Motorola are fueling the growth.

Where the jobs are: More than 700 manufacturing firms are located in Albuquerque, producing everything from food products and electronic components to industrial heaters. Tourism is a growing industry—more than 6 million tourists visited Albuquerque last year. And, each year, nearly 200,000 delegates attend conventions in this convention city of the Southwest. A recent expansion at Intel (a Fortune 200 company specializing in the production of electronics) will bring total employment to approximately 2,000 when fully staffed. Signetics Corp. announced early this year that it would shift work to its Albuquerque plant, the most modern of the company's three chip-fabrication facilities. This move may add 120 workers. Honeywell added 80 new jobs in the first half of 1992 to its plant. Other local companies that have expanded include: Martin Marietta; Motorola; Siognetics; Honeywell Controls; and Citicorp Credit. By the end of 1992, Albuquerque had 4,100 new jobs from companies that relocated or expanded in the area in the past 2 years. Unemployment stood at 5.3% for 1991.

Business opportunities: It appears that high-tech suppliers and consultants will rule the economic roost for some time. The number of R&D firms continues to grow. A major shortcoming for the area is the lack of an exclusive resort hotel.

Making the Grade

Public education overview: The Albuquerque Public School System is one of the largest in the nation, with 11 high schools, 23 middle schools, 79 elementary schools and 6 alternative schools. Schools are dispersed widely over the city, Bernalillo County and a portion of neighboring Sandoval County. Per pupil expenditure for the 1991-92 school year was $3,767. In order to meet the demands of a community with a variety of special needs, many of the schools have developed individual programs, including year-round education and magnet schools. The Community School, Freedom High School, Porvenir, and School on Wheels offer high school programs to students who prefer less structure. There are 20 schools that are either presently on a year-round schedule or will be within the next 2 years. Albuquerque Public Schools has a number-1 ranking among the 50 largest school districts for SAT scores. Students ranked 6th for avg. ACT scores among the same 50 districts. La Cueva High School was named best high school in New Mexico by *Redbook* magazine. Seniors receive $4 million in annual scholarships, gifted students have access to seminars, mentorships and internships, and 84% of the teachers hold advanced degrees.

Class size: 22:1.

Help for working parents: Before- and after-school extended-care programs are available at more than 60 schools. Fees vary.

Blue Ribbon School Awards: Since its inception in 1983, 17 public schools in Albuquerque have been named Blue Ribbon Schools (the most in any U.S. district). The most recent recognition was earned by McKinley Middle School ('88-'89).

School year: Starts before Labor Day (mid-Aug.) and ends late May. Children must be 5 on or before Sept. 1 to enter kindergarten.

Special education/gifted programs: Students in special education are integrated into the regular program whenever appropriate, but half-day and full-day resource pullouts are also available. Approximately 15% of students are in the special education program, which has attracted families to the community. Gifted students are eligible for special pull-out and research programs as well.

Nearby colleges/universities: University of New Mexico (25,000 students) brings much to the community in terms of culture, sports, performing arts, and extensive continuing education. It is one of the top research and scientific development centers in the country. Other schools include: College of Santa Fe; St. John's College; Chapman College; National College; and Parks College.

Medical Care

Hospitals/medical centers: Overall quality of medical care in Albuquerque is excellent. Comprehensive medical care ranges from teaching hospitals to private clinics. University Hospital (comprehensive medical care center, trauma and burn centers, high-risk pregnancy care); Presbyterian Hospital (specializing in cardiac care, neonatology and women's diseases); Lovelace Medical Center (specializing in diabetes); St Joseph's Medical Center (specializing in cancer care); Northside Presbyterian; and Kaseman Presbyterian Hospitals (comprehensive medical care).

Specialized care: St Joseph's Rehabilitation Center (head and motor injuries); Healthsouth Rehabilitation Center (victims of catastrophic illnesses); Heights Psychiatric Hospital; University of New Mexico's Children's Psychiatric Hospital; and Children's Hospital of New Mexico.

Crime & Safety

There are 1,800 Neighborhood Watch block captains assigned throughout Albuquerque. The Children's Crime Prevention Program is very popular and has been effective in helping elementary children understand the role of the police and of the importance of personal and property safety. A program designed to educate the students on what the justice system is and how it operates is aimed at the middle and senior-level high school students. There is also a DARE program, particularly targeted for 5th graders. While violent crime is low (down 10% since 1990), drugs remain a problem, due to drug offenses and drug-related crimes, which rose 8% over the last 2 years. Residential burglary also remains high.

Community Life

Integration is a key to the community life of Albuquerque. Park your prejudices elsewhere because everyone gets involved in a variety of cultural and social activities. People enthusiastically share backgrounds, ideas and customs and volunteer in one of the many festivals. These celebrations reflect a wide diversion of backgrounds, and the community joins together to enjoy them all. The International Balloon Festival, for example, is a colorful event that gets much of the community involved in preparation. The traditional New Mexico State Fair is an event that few residents pass up, or cease to talk about each year.

Let the Good Times Roll

Family fun: Albuquerque's mild climate makes outdoor recreation a delight year-round. There are more than 200 neighborhood parks, 3 major bikeways and 20 community centers. In the nearby Sandia Mountains there is hiking, camping and horseback riding. In additon, Albuquerque is convenient to national forests, grasslands and national wildlife refuges, including Apache, Cibola, Gila, Lincoln, Carson, Coronado and Santa Fe National Forests, and Kiowa National Grasslands. Streams, irrigation ditches, and the City of Albuquerque Fishing Lagoon are stocked with trout each winter. From Thanksgiving to Easter, there is enough snow at the higher elevations for downhill and cross-country skiing. Museums and attractions include: Albuquerque Museum; Coronado Monument; Geology Museum (UNM); Albuquerque's Children's Museum; Indian Pueblo Cultural Center; International Balloon Museum; Museum of Natural History; National Atomic Museum; University Fine Art Museum; New Mexico State Fairgrounds; the Rio Grande Nature Center; Rio Grande Zoo; Maxwell Museum of Anthropology; American International Rattlesnake Museum; Cliff's Amusement Park; and Old Town, the historic Spanish center of the town.

Sports: For the spectator, sports opportunities abound: Take in the Albuquerque Dukes Baseball Team (AAA minor league, top LA Dodgers farm team) or the New Mexico Chiles (pro soccer). The University of New Mexico offers 22 varsity sports in the Western Athletic Conference. Spectators can also enjoy quarter horse and thoroughbred racing at the fairgrounds from Jan. through June.

Arts & entertainment: The array of culture impresses even the skeptics. Albuquerque has several theatrical companies including an excellent children's theater. Other offerings include: the New Mexico Symphony Orchestra; Albuquerque Philharmonic Orchestra; Chamber Orchestra of Albuquerque; Albuquerque Ballet Company; Bill Evans Dance Company; and Opera Southwest. There are more than 100 art galleries displaying original works, ranging from traditional to contemporary.

Annual events: New Mexico State Fair, the nation's 3rd largest (Sept.); Rio Grande Arts and Crafts Festival (March); Great Rio Grande Raft Race (May); International Balloon Fiesta (Oct.); Southwest Arts and Crafts Festival (Nov.) New Mexico Arts and Crafts Fair (June); Ducke City Marathon (Oct.); Sunwest Bank/Charley Pride Senior Golf Classic (Aug.).

The Environment

Albuquerque's plentiful water supply is from deep wells, which pump water from the Rio Grande Basin. A recent report estimates that the volume of recoverable fresh goundwater in storage makes Albuquerque better situated with respect to water supply than any large city in the Southwest. The Albuquerque municipal water system is generally recognized as one of the country's most technologically advanced. Albuquerque is the nuclear capital of the U.S., with much of the nation's nuclear research conducted here, as 40% of the uranium reserve is found in deposits 70 mi. west. Air quality is very good and has consistently remained below EPA ozone guideline standards.

In and Around Town

Roads and interstates: I-25 (north-south), I-40 (east-west); Hwy. 85, (north-south); 66 (east-west).
Closest airport: Albuquerque International Airport.
Public transportation: Suntran, the city's bus system, provides more than 30 routes and 107 buses throughout Albuquerque.
Avg. commute: 20-30 minutes.

What Every Resident Knows

The city was named for the Duke of Alburquerque, Viceroy of New Spain. The first "r" was eventually dropped because the name was already difficult enough to spell without it. • The problem with New Mexico is that there are too many Americans who don't realize it is part of the U.S.. One resident traveling in the Midwest was told, "You speak English so well for a foreigner." Another was trying to book airline reservations back home and was connected with the international desk. • Over a third of the state's population lives in Albuquerque. And, in fact, the county is so big, it is almost as large as the state of Rhode Island. • Shouts of "Water! Water!" indicate that a tourist or newcomer has just tasted his or her first chili peppers, a common ingredient in many dishes.

FYI

Greater Albuquerque Chamber of Commerce
P.O. Box 25100
Albuquerque, NM 87125
505-764-3700

Albuquerque Convention and Visitors Bureau
121 Tijeras NE, 1st Floor
Albuquerque, NM 87102
800-284-2282

Albuquerque Journal and Albuquerque Tribune
7777 Jefferson NE
Albuquerque, NM 87109
505-823-7777

Small Business Development Center
525 Buena Vista SE
Albuquerque, NM 87106
505-224-4246

Coldwell Banker/The Real Estate Center
8205 Spain, Suite 106
Albuquerque, NM 87109
505-821-8700
Connie Ryan, Broker

Small Business Development Center
525 Buena Vista SE
Albuquerque, NM 87106
505-224-4246

The Gas Company of New Mexico
723 Silver SW
Albuquerque, NM 87103
505-880-7460

Public Service Company of New Mexico
414 Silver SW
Albuquerque, NM 87102
505-761-5700

U.S. West Communications
505-245-6800 (Call collect)

Albuquerque Economic Development, Inc.
851 University Blvd SE, Suite 203
Albuquerque, NM 87106
505-246-6200

School district: 505-842-8211
Property tax assessor:
505-768-4040
Newcomer's Club:
505-888-4331
Interfaith Council: 505-255-1509
Physician's referral: 505-764-9494
Day-care referral: 505-293-6614

Huntington, New York (Long Island)

Area Snapshot

Local population: 18,180
County: Suffolk   **Population:** 1,324,944
U.S. region: Northeastern U.S./tip of southeastern New York
Closest metro area: New York City, 40 mi. west
Median housing price: $268,300
Avg. household income: $62,121
Best reasons to live here: Sophisticated suburb, active cultural scene, good schools, proximity to beaches, scenic woods and rolling hills, very involved, safe community, access to the Big Apple and its 1,001 things to do.

Fabulous Features

Once upon a time there was a small village that bordered the glistening Long Island Sound. With its glorious beaches and woodlands, quiet surroundings and cultural awareness, it was the idyllic retreat for bedraggled city folks.

Although the population has grown measurably, the charm of Huntington remains largely unchanged. Families who would otherwise find the suburbs bland, are delighted by this community's warmth and vitality. Tree-lined streets showcase old brick Tudors, the downtown is brimming with quaint restaurants, shopping and art cinemas. The cultural arena is a fine mosaic of exhibits, concerts, theater and community events and the school district is progressive. From the Woodhull Early Childhood Center (kindergartners are in their own nurturing environment) to award-winning music programs (Huntington High School Band has been the Long Island champ for three out of the past four years), residents put their money where there kids are (expenditures are $9,300 per student, almost double the national average).

Another reason Huntington is the "smart" choice is because of its proximity to the largest corporate corridor development on Long Island.

Since 1980, nearby Melville has built 7 million square feet of office space, and is home to the regional head-quarters of Chase Manhattan and Chemical Banks, Newsday, Estee Lauder, several retail chains and dozens of high-tech, communica-tions and manufacturing firms.

Residents who work on the island covet their shorter-than-average commute, which leaves more time for Huntington's annual Family Festival, the Hecksher Art Museum, sailing the harbor, oil painting classes at the community visual-arts school...

Possible drawbacks: Living costs and taxes make Suffolk County one of the most expensive places to raise a family. Local property taxes shot up 178% between 1980 to 1990 (although recently reduced). On the other hand, the median household income is one of the highest in the country. • With an unemployment rate that fluctuates between 8% to 9% (Long Island has lost an estimated 100,000 jobs in the past two years), coupled with high living costs, this is no place to come without a high-paying job! • The population density of Long Island is never more evident than when driving on the Long island Expressway ("world's largest parking lot"). The 58-minute train ride to and from Manhattan is a saner way to go.

Real Estate

Market overview: The spring of 1991 brought a sharp reduction of inventory, reflecting lower taxes. Homes that had been on the market for some time are being sold. Current inventory is stable, and there are still lots of potential buyers, consequently the current trend of peaks and valleys is expected to continue. House values have remained fairly stable (depreciated only slightly). Anything selling for $175,000-$250,000 goes quickly because there is limited inventory in that price range.

What houses look like: Huntington's tree-lined streets feature frame houses, natural cedar shakes and brick accents. Colonials and ranches are the most popular styles. In the village, homes are 75+ years old on small lots. Outside the village are newer homes—30+ years on ½-1-acre lots. The village has a sewer system, other areas have cesspools. Most homes also have garages, basements and updated kitchens and BAs. Bleached oak floors are favored. Although many homes have pools, everyone enjoys the beaches (5 min. away).

Starter homes: Avg. $200,000, and are popular in the Village area. A 2-3BR/1½BA Cape Cod or ranch on a 50 x 100 lot (possible w/1-car garage) begins in the $150s.

Trade-ups: Look in Centerport and Hillside for larger homes. $200,000 can buy a 3-4BR/2-2 1/2BA on 1/3 acre. $300,000 can buy as much as an acre with 3-4BR/2-2 1/2BA w/larger rooms. Larger, newer homes closer to the water sell in the $400s.

Luxury homes: Incorporated villages within the area have either 1- or 2-acre zoning, with their own private police force, private beaches and private trash pick-up. There are no commercial properties. Prices are $300,000-$800,000 for non-waterfronts, and $900,000-$2 million for waterfront location.

Rental market: It's a tight market for SFHs but there are some 4BR/2 1/2BA for $2,200-$2,500/mo. 1-2BR condos run $1,000-$1,500/mo., and apartments from $700-$900/mo.

Great neighborhoods: Larger, luxury homes are in Lloyd Neck, Lloyd Bay, and Cold Spring Harbor. These have private beaches and mooring (for boaters). The Parkways and access to LIRR Huntington Station stop are nearby.

Nearby areas to consider: Cold Spring Harbor, Centerport, and Greenlawn are all within Huntington Township and all offer similar amenities—scenic beauty, parks, recreation, lots of history, great schools and culture. Northport has more affordable homes although they will be somewhat smaller. These areas are convenient to the Parkway and to the Huntington Station commuter line.

What Things Cost

Runzheimer's Living Cost Index: Avg. annual costs for family of 4 with household income of $50,000: $64,784 (29.6% above the avg. city).

ACCRA's national comparisons: The most expensive place to raise a family of 4 is Long Island (Nassau/Suffolk Counties). Overall living costs are 49.5% above the national avg. Housing and utilities are more than 200% above. Groceries and transportation are about 20% above. Health care is 30% above and goods and services 20.7% above.

Utilities: Phone: Hookup: $55. Budget service: $15/mo. Electric: Avg. $90/mo. w/low of $65 and high of $125. Gas: For cooking and hot water: $50-$85/mo., more ($130) if gas used for heating.

Kid care: Licensed day-care avg. $168/wk. for infants, $156/wk. for toddlers. Certified day care for children from 6 wks. to 14 yrs. is provided in 14 licensed day-care centers. Waiting lists depend on the schedule requested. **Pediatric visit:** $60.

The Tax Ax

Sales tax: 8.5% (food, prescriptions and professional services exempt).

Property tax: $119.754 per $100 of assessed value plus $507 for garbage pick-up. Assessed value varies depending on age of house. A $200,000, 35-yr.-old home on 1/3 acre might be $5,000-$5,500.

State income tax: Residents pay a graduated rate on taxable income ranging from 4% to 7.875%. The highest rate is for income over $13,000 (single return) or $26,000 (married filing jointly). No credit for personal exemptions, only dependent exemptions.

Climate

Elevation 100'	Avg. High/Low	Avg. Rain (Inches)	Avg. Snow (Inches)	Avg. Days Rain	Avg. % Humidity
Jan.	40/23	3.8	7	9	57
April	57/40	3.7	1	10	64
July	83/65	3.6	--	9	52
Oct.	63/49	3.3	T	8	54
YEAR	61/48	40.5	30	113	55
# of days 32° or below: 95			# of days 90° or above: 10		

Long Island's 4 seasons are distinct, with frequent cold fronts resulting in cool, damp weather, particularly in winter. Spring and summer are pleasant and sunny. Fall is beautiful (gorgeous foliage), mostly cool and sunny for days at a time.

Earning a Living

Economic outlook: Growth remains static, with unemployment up to 6%, and a reported overall loss of 51,000 jobs on Long Island for 1992. Yet, new office buildings continue to be constructed, there remains a highly skilled work force and industry has generally remained innovative. The manufacture of aircraft, spacecraft and component parts, electronic equipment, pharmaceuticals, office supplies, printing, and lithographing are among the major industries employing thousands. Thousands more are employed in various service industries, such as utilities, government, transportation, home repair, offices and a food service industry.

Where the jobs are: Service industries have led the surge in Long Island's economy over the last 10 years, with 70,000 new jobs, and wholesale and retail operations adding 52,00 new workers. Eating and drinking establishments and food stores were the leaders in the retail sector, adding 10,00 and 6,000 jobs respectively. Gains in finance, insurance, real estate, and construction numbered 14,000 jobs apiece, and transportation and public utilities increased by 8,000. In Suffolk County, most jobs are in wholesale and retail trade, which employ over 301,000. The service industries employ the second highest, at 279,000. In addition, more than 1,000 Long Island firms are engaged in high-tech related fields. Suffolk County is the leading agricultural county. New and rapidly expanding agricultural industries include thoroughbred horse breeding and training. Wine-making is another growth industry. Tourist-related industries continue to boom, employing more than 94,000. Suffolk and Nassau Counties attracted more than 24 million visitors last year with an estimated economic impact of $7 billion. Companies that have shown a strong boost in their profits over the last 18 months and anticipate expansion and creation of new jobs include ILC Industries (producer of micro electronic products) and LNR Communications (telecom equipment manufacturer). Other expansions include Dowling College, which announced plans in 1992 to build a $34.5 million National Aviation & Transportation Center at Brookhaven Airport.

Business opportunities: As a center of technological excellence, Long Island's immediate outlook for economic growth continues to be in the high-tech fields. Ties between high-tech industries and academic and research institutions strengthen. In addition, communication to government agencies on technical matters continues to expand. Manufacturing has become increasingly specialized on Long Island.

Making the Grade

Public education overview: Within Huntington Township are 8 school districts. Per student expenditure is $9,310. All kindergarten students in the district attend the Woodhull Early Childhood Center, a full-day program. All pupils learn to use computers beginning in the primary level. There's a strong foreign language program, at the secondary level, with 6 languages, including Chinese, for students to choose from. District has a K-12 writing program that has received national recognition; students write often, with real audiences and real purposes in mind. The district has a strong music program, and from the junior high level virtually everyone is involved in either band, orchestra or choir. Nearly 80% of high school seniors go on to college. For the past 2 years, 40% of state aid for the schools has been cut. This is happening all over the state, with Long Island schools hit hardest. Huntington is not the only school experiencing cutbacks and reacting to difficult economic times, however, they are making every effort to reduce expenses without eliminating programs in education.

Class size: 20:1.

Help for working parents: There are no before-school programs. After-school childcare is provided by SCOPE (Suffolk County Organization for Professional Education) at Woodhull Early Childhood Center. Children (K-6) are bused in, and the program runs from 2 p.m.-6 p.m. Registration is $25, and daily rates vary.

School year: Starts after Labor Day and ends the 3rd week in June. Children must be 5 on or before Dec. 1 to enter kindergarten

Special education/gifted programs: SEARCH (Scholastic Enrichment And Resource program for Children in Huntington) is the gifted-and-talented program in each elementary school, offering differentiated curriculum in science, social science and liberal arts. For children who need special education, programs range from mainstreaming with help from aides, to separate facilities to 12-month programs.

Nearby colleges/universities: Four-year and graduate schools are: Hofstra University (Hempstead); strong liberal arts program; SUNY at Stony Brook; NY Institute Technology (Old Westbury-Central Islip); Long Island University (3 campuses: C.W. Post, Brookville, Southampton); Dowling College (Oakdale). Also nearby is Suffolk Community College.

Medical Care

Hospitals/medical centers: Brookhaven Memorial Hospital Medical Center (comprehensive health center specializing in day surgery, radiology, cardiology); Brunswick Hospital Center (acute medical care and rehabilitation); Central Suffolk Hospital (renal dialysis center, ambulatory surgery, pediatric rehabilitation center, emergency, acute, pediatric, maternal and geriatric care); Community Hospital of Western Suffolk (psychiatric care, maternal medical-surgical, pediatric); Good Samaritan Hospital (chronic renal dialysis center, diagnostic and therapeutic facilities, pediatric clinical center, hospicare program, comprehensive medical care); Huntington Hospital (nuclear medicine, coronary care, maternity, radiology); Mather Memorial (emergency care); St. John's Episcopal Hospital (coronary care, outpatient services); University Hospital Health Sciences Center (broad, comprehensive medical care, specializing in cardiology, renal dialysis, high-risk obstetrics).

Specialized care: Sagamore Children's Psychiatric Center, South Oaks Hospital (psychiatric and substance abuse); St. Charles Hospital and Rehabilitation Center; Veterans Administration Medical Center.

Crime & Safety

Huntington is a safe community, as police and residents work together through neighborhood watch programs, DARE programs and more. Any crime seems to be the result of the warm-weather lure of beaches and bars, which results in some alcohol-related disturbances and property crime. Violent crime is minimal although residential burglary grew by 7% since 1990. Drug-related crimes have shown a 5% increase. There are no gangs in the area. The county-run police dept. is short-staffed because of budget cuts.

Community Life

Although Huntington has no official status, residents call the community a village. The sense of a small, private area, where neighbors pitch in and participate and/or celebrate any number of village events, truly typifies the community life. For example, the high school Key Club, a community service club, has 200 active members. Last year, it raised $2,000 for cancer research. There are nearly 80 cultural organizations, including the Huntington Arts Council helps embody this concept of "cultural identity" by helping to unify the spirit and direction of community life.

Let the Good Times Roll

Family fun: The Huntington area abounds with parks and beaches along Long Island Sound, providing a wide range of recreational activities. Other nearby beaches include a short 20-minute trip to the South Shore Atlantic Ocean beaches of Long Island, such as Jones Beach and Smith Point County Park, Wildwood State Park, and Robert Moses State Park. The 2 major parks, Dix Hills and Crab Meadow Parks offer golf courses, an ice rink, 2 swimming beaches, and picnic, hiking, and barbecue facilities. A summer arts and crafts program is held through the Dept of Parks and Recreation annually for children. The Heckscher Museum is the only art museum on Long Island with exhibitions and collections covering 500 years of Western art; There are a number of historic homes to tour, including Conklin House, Kissam House and Coindre Hall. Nearby trips include the Vanderbilt Planetarium, New York Science Laboratory, Walt Whitman's birthplace, and the Eisenhower Puppet Theatre. In addition, there's auto racing at Riverhead, Westhampton and Bridgehampton Raceways, and horse racing at Aqueduct Race Track, Belmont Park Race Track and Roosevelt Raceway.

Sports: You'll have a ball following all the New York area sports teams. There's the New York Jets and Giants (NFL), New York Islanders and Rangers (NHL), the New York Yankees and Mets (Major League baseball), and the New York Knicks (NBA) In addition, C.W. Post College and State University of New York (SUNY) at Stony Brook offer collegiate sports.

Arts & entertainment: It's not enough that Huntington is a short drive from the world capital of culture. This community has plenty of first-class art and entertainment itself: including the Long Island Philharmonic Orchestra, Island Lyric Opera, Nassau Pops Symphony Orchestra, Huntington Choral Society, and National Grand Opera. The Tilles Center for the Performing Arts offers a wide range of performances. Numerous local dance and theater groups abound. Kids for Kids Productions are especially designed for younger children, but are equally enjoyed by all ages. A wonderful place for live concerts year round is IMAC, with top-name jazz, rock and other musical performances. Galleries and art workshops, sponsored in large part by the Huntington Arts Council, display a wide range of artistic expression.

Annual events: Heckscher Park Summer Arts Festival, 6 weeks of dance, drama and musical presentations; Village Green Arts Festival (June); Bach Aria Festival in Stony Brook (June).

The Environment

Recycling is strenuously encouraged in Huntington. Carters bring garbage to the Resource Recovery Plant, and residents can take advantage of a weekly curbside pickup. There is also a Household Hazardous Waste Facility, where residents may bring toxic wastes. Environmental education is emphasized in the schools. A Conservation Board, comprised of volunteers and funded by the state, presents school programs and curriculum on environmental education. Air quality is monitored by the State, and while acceptable, has exceeded the ozone standard on 7 occasions the past year. Water studies are continuously being performed, and no definite link has so far been connected to the high incidences of cancer. Water quality is sampled for shellfishing and bathing. If water quality does not meet acceptable standards, beaches are closed.

In and Around Town

Roads and interstates: I-495, state highways 25 and 27 (east-west); Routes 110, 97, 83 and 46 (north-south).

Closest airport(s): JFK International Airport and La Guardia Airport (25 mi. away). Private and municipal airports: Long Island MacArthur Airport, Brookhaven Airport, East Hampton Airport, Republic Airport and Suffolk County Airport.

Public transportation: Long Island Railroad (commuter lines within Long Island to Manhattan): Suffolk County Transit System operates 39 county-supported bus routes. Huntington Area Rapid Transit System (HART) operates 15 buses, only within the Town of Huntington and to and from major mall and shopping center sites.

Avg. commute: 15-35 min. to other communities on the Island. 60-75 min. to Manhattan.

What Every Resident Knows

Huntington residents are notorious activists when it comes to local issues. There is always something in the works to fight for or against. Whether opposing a proposed public parking garage in the shopping area or worrying about the number of bars and discos coming in, Huntington residents fight long and hard. • In 1966, a group of Huntington women got together in support of residents serving in Vietnam. In 1972, they planted 41 cherry trees on the Village Green as a memorial to the residents who died or were missing in action. The 20th anniversary of the planting was celebrated on Arbor Day, April 24, 1992, and all the trees are now in bloom.

FYI

Huntington Township Chamber of Commerce
151 West Carver Street
Huntington, NY 11743
516-423-6100

Long Island Convention & Visitors Bureau
Nassau Veterans Memorial Coliseum
1255 Hempstead Turnpike
Uniondale, NY 11553
516-794-4222

Newsday
235 Pinelawn Road
Melville, NY 11747
516-454-2000

New York Times
800-631-2500

Daniel Gale Agency
408 Ft. Salonga Road (25A)
Northport, NY 11768
516-754-1300
Carol Kelly, Relocation Director

Coldwell Banker/Schlott
82 Main Street
Huntington, NY 11743
516-673-6800
Mary Rice, Manager

**Long Island Lighting Co.
(LILCO: gas and electric)**
175 East Old Country Road
Hicksville, NY 11801
516-427-4000

New York Telephone
516-890-1350 (Call collect)

Small Business Administration
35 Pinelawn Road, Suite 207 W
Melville, NY 11747
516-454-0750

Suffolk County Dept. of Economic Development
H. Lee Dennison Building
Hauppauge, NY 11788
516-853-4800

School district: 516-673-2038
Property tax assessor:
516-351-3226
Newcomer's Club: 516-421-3035
Physician's referral: 516-351-2236
Day-care Referral: 516-462-0444

Greensboro, North Carolina

Area Snapshot

Local population: 196,000
County: Guilford   **Population:** 348,000
U.S. region: East Coast/central N.C.
Closest metro areas: Winston-Salem (30 mi. west), Raleigh (75 mi. east), Charlotte (90 mi. south), Durham (55 mi. east)
Median housing price: $77,600
Avg. household income: $46,678
Best reasons to live here: A National Civics League "All American City," delightful year-round climate, affordable real estate, fast-growing economy, excellent schools, accessible roadways, central to mountains and beaches.

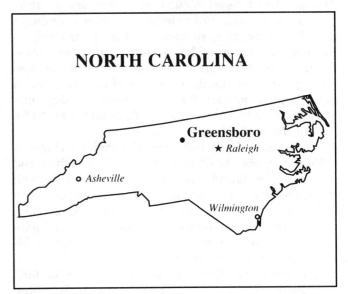

Fabulous Features

They say only hindsight is 20-20, but Greensboro's foresight has been just as clear. In the heart of the Piedmont Triad region is this quiet, unassuming city with steely determination. Intent on guaranteeing the population boom wouldn't backfire (it grew by 26% between 1980-1990), its "Greensboro Visions," a braintrust of government and business leaders, developed strategic plans for schools, housing and more.

Creative problem-solving was one reason the National Civic League designated Greensboro as an "All American City" last year (hundreds competed for the honor). Another was the economy, which politely bowed out of the recession. The area was too busy welcoming American Express, Sears, AT&T, Volvo and others, paving the way for 225,000 new jobs.

The real estate market has also been in an enviable position. New construction accomodated the growth without driving resale prices up. Buyers can choose from super starters ($55,000-$75,000), terrific trade-ups ($85,000-$110,000) or luxury homes ($200,000-plus).

Another wise decision? Merging the region's school districts. Now, millions of dollars in cost consolidations will allow for sharing the best ideas from each (Greensboro schools have an excellent reputation for foreign language, global studies, magnet schools and incentive programs). Add to that the five colleges and universities in the area, the unbelievable recreation (skiing, mountain climbing and boating are a few minutes to a few hours away) to the always delightful climate (one season is prettier than the next). Now you understand why Greensboro's future is so bright!

Possible drawbacks: Ever had a party where no one showed up? That's how it feels at the gorgeous, new Piedmont Triad International Airport. Because of limited direct flights out of Greensboro, many still drive to Charlotte or Raleigh to make better connections. • Rapid growth has its downside in the form of higher crime. Overall rates jumped 17% in one year. Ad hoc committees have offered solutions, and it's helped. Crime dropped by 6% in the first half of 1992, but authorities are still on alert.

"You can quote me on that"

"We've told so many family and friends about Greensboro, if they all come we might open up our own real estate agency. This was the best move we could have made."—Y.K.

Real Estate

Market Overview: With resale inventory up 15%-20%, buyers can afford to be choosy! The abundance of sellers is because so many people are trading up (taking advantage of low interest rates) or transferring out of the area. New construction is also picking up with the development of subdivisions in price ranges perfect for young families—$80,000-$90,000 for a brand-new home! Approximately 10%-15% of the buyers are from out-of-town.

What houses look like: The Greensboro Home is a 2-story brick traditional. But some ranches and capes can be found. Contemporaries don't do well here, and if it's a Victorian you're looking for it will be quite a search. Cathedral ceilings, master BAs, garden tubs, jacuzzis, and fireplaces are very popular. Kitchens are large and airy, and white cabinets and great rooms are the latest.

Starter homes: Range between $60,000-$100,000. A typical starter home is a 3BR ranch, w/dining room, eat-in-kitchen, family room, cathedral ceilings, skylight in bathroom and 1-car garage on a 60 x 100 lot. Check out High Point.

Trade-ups: Prices are from $100,000-$250,000. $150,000 buys 1/4 acre w/an older (20-50 yrs.) 4BR/2BA, fireplace, 2-car garage, formal living and dining rooms, and large kitchen. For $250,000 you can find a 4BR/2 1/2BA, 3000 sq. ft. w/playroom, fireplaces, formal living and dining, ceramic-tile BAs w/jacuzzi, modern kitchens and hardwood floors.

Luxury homes: Range from $300,000-$1 million. For the mid-range, you'll find an elegant, brand-new, 4000 sq. ft. 5BR/2 1/2-3BA. It might include a horse farm w/2-4 acres, fireplaces in living room and study, cathedral ceilings, and garden tub. Adams Farm and the Cardinal area are beautiful.

Rental market: Single family homes are available but limited and require a minimum 1-year lease. A 3BR/1 1/2-2BA can cost $1,000-$1,500/mo. 2BR apartments are $450-$650/mo.; 3BRs are $600-$800/mo. Townhomes are $700-$1,000/mo. Look at River Hills.

Great neighborhoods: River Hills is ideal for young families w/housing in the $100,000 range. It's scenic, convenient to shopping and has excellent schools. Hickory Woods is a nice residential area with good schools, convenient (15 mins.) to anything, w/housing ranging from $100,000-$150,000.

Nearby areas to consider: Kernersville, 15 minutes west, is a more rural, family-oriented community, with good schools. Houses are a little more affordable ($90,000-$125,000), taxes are lower and you can get more land for your money.

What Things Cost

Runzheimer's Living Cost Index: Avg. annual costs for family of 4 with household income of $50,000: $48,378 (3.3% below avg. city).

ACCRA's national comparisons: Overall living costs are 5.6% below the natioal avg., with the biggest savings in health care costs (12% below). In every category measured, costs are less than the national avg. Groceries are 8% below; housing and transportation are 4%-5% below.

Utilities: Phone: Unlimited calling $12/month. Hookup: Avg. $43. Electric: Avg. $118/mo., in winter, $140/mo., and $80-$100/mo. in summer. Gas is not widely available.

Kid care: Avg. $75/wk. for infants to 18 mo.; $68/wk. to 5 yrs. **Pediatric visit:** Avg. $50.

The Tax Ax

Sales tax: 6% (prescriptions and professional services exempt).

Property tax: Current millage rates wn/city limits: 1.3233 per $100 of assessed value. Outside city limits, the rate is .5960 per $100, plus a county school tax of .0385. At this rate, a $100,000 would pay $1,163/yr.

State income tax: 6%-7.75% depending on number of exemptions. State also allows $2,000 personal exemptions ($5,000 if married filing jointly). If married filing jointly with taxable income over $21,250, taxes will be $1,275, plus 7.75% on income above that.

Climate

Elevation 840'	Avg. High/Low	Avg. Rain (Inches)	Avg. Snow (Inches)	Avg. Days Rain	Avg. % Humidity
Jan.	49/29	2.9	3.1	9	58
April	71/46	3.2	T	9	48
July	88/67	4.4	--	12	60
Oct.	71/47	2.9	--	7	55
YEAR	69/47	40.5	8.9	111	55
# of days 32° or below: 85			# of days 90° or above: 37		

Greensboro has a nearly ideal climate with mild temperatures year-round and evenly distributed precipitation. Occasionally winter storms develop southwest of the area, which deposit large amounts of snow, but it only remains for a few days. Spring and summer thunderstorms are frequent, but most days are pleasant with low humidity. Fall is magnificent—sunny, dry and with beautiful foliage.

Earning a Living

Economic outlook: Greensboro's sound economy is very much the product of its central geographic position within the Piedmont Triad, a region anchored by the cities of Greensboro, Winston-Salem and High Point. The towns and communities of the Triad are physically close and economically interdependent in many ways. Manufacturing is the traditional cornerstone of the Piedmont economy, employing 30% of the labor force. Textile manufacturing employs the single largest group of industrial workers. Furniture and tobacco manufacturing are also major players. A broad range of other production industries, from chemicals to printing and publishing round out the manufacturing base. Greensboro's excellent access to major highways, railways and the presence of many trucking firms make it a major distribution center. A low unemployment rate of 5.5% also reflects the economic impact of its numerous industrial parks. The Greensboro area has more than 47 industrial parks, with additional parks under development.

Where the jobs are: As the service sector has expanded over the last 5 years, Greensboro is freed from its reliance on furniture, textiles and tobacco. Sears, American Express, AT&T and USAir are now among the largest employers, along with customer service, telecatalog ordering centers and credit-card processing. Tourism, the state's 3rd-largest industry, is vital to Greensboro, as it brought more than $500 million to Guilford County in 1991. Wholesale and retail trade continue to play an important economic role, employing nearly 26% of the county's workers, in over 3,500 businesses. Retail sales in Guilford County for 1991 were nearly $5.5 billion, with sales in the city of Greensboro accounting for 73% of that figure. The home furnishings industry also adds to the area's economic health. Despite some layoffs in 1990, 225,000 new jobs were created in 1991, and more are expected for 1992. Over the last year, AT&T added 800 manufacturing jobs when it moved to the area.

Business opportunities: Small electronics and plastics parts firms are most needed and are currently experiencing strong growth. Support services are also an expanding area. There is currently not an oversupply of any type of small business. As Mack Williams, Senior Economic Development Officer of the Greensboro Chamber of Commerce, says, "Any small business can do well in Greensboro if it combines the right product with the right service at the right price."

Making the Grade

Public education overview: The citizens of Guilford County voted to consolidate the area school systems, effective July 1993, which may result in an initial tax increase for some, since the 3 systems were taxed differently. The overall feeling was that consolidation will result in cost-containment and the ability to maintain successful programs, such as Spanish Immersion in the elementary schools, and LEAP (Learning Expectations and Achievement Program), enrichment and help for remedial students in grades K-5. Greensboro schools are very progressive; they implemented a magnet-school approach a few years ago, that is proving successful and has earned more than $6 million in federal support. Parents may choose to send their child to a regular school assignment or apply to one of 9 elementary magnet schools such as: Acceleration and Enrichment Center, Cultural Arts & Foreign Language, Global Studies and Year Round School. High school students outscore their counterparts throughout the state on SATs; 76% go on to higher education, and graduating seniors annually earn more than $2.5 million in scholarships and financial aid. Community involvement is strong, as shown by extensive volunteer activity.

Class size: 21:1.

Help for working parents: There are on-site after-school programs, and the YMCA also coordinates programs with schools at 8-10 sites.

School year: Last wk. in Aug. through first wk. in June. Children must be 5 on or before Oct. 16 to enter kindergarten.

Special education/gifted programs: Gateway Education Center is a facility for severe and profoundly handicapped adolescents up to age 22 (can attend from as early as 6 wks. old). McIver, a school for the mentally handicapped, is known nationwide for its excellent programs and success.

Nearby colleges/universities: The University of North Carolina at Greensboro (10,688 students); North Carolina Agricultural & Technical State University (5,991 students); Guilford College, (1,734 students) is a private liberal arts school; Greensboro College, (968 students), is affiliated with Methodist Church; Bennett College, (549 women) also affiliated with Methodist Church, is a private liberal arts school. Winston-Salem State University, High Point College, John Wesley College (High Point), Wake Forest University (Winston-Salem), North Carolina School of the Arts (Winston-Salem), and Salem College.

Medical Care

Hospitals/medical centers: Greensboro offers the most up-to-date medical advancements in 4 nonprofit hospitals. In a recent survey by *Health* magazine, Greensboro ranked in the top 10 healthiest cities in the U.S. The Guilford County Health Dept. has been recognized by the U.S. Dept of Health and Human Services for promoting healthy environments in day-care. Greensboro Hospital is slated to become one of the state's first free-standing women's and infant's hospitals. The Moses H. Cone Hospital, a teaching hospital, is expanding to offer ambulatory surgery center. It specializes in cardiac care and neonatology. Other area hospitals include: Wesley Long Community Hospital; L. Richardson Hospital; Women's Hospital of Greensboro; North Carolina Baptist Hospital; and Bowman Gray School of Medicine.

Specialized care: Greensboro Diabetes Self-care Center and Hospice; Charter Hospital of Greensboro (emotional problems and addictive diseases)

Crime & Safety

As in most metropolitan areas, crime is present and on the rise. Here it's up 17% from 1991 to 1992, with the greatest problem drug-related crime and domestic violence. The police have implemented community awareness programs, curbing crime somewhat. Although residents are aware of the underlying problems, they still feel relatively secure. People still flock to downtown at night for entertainment, and children roam relatively freely around their neighborhoods.

Community Life

Residents are brought together by school-related community projects. One school raised $10,000 in pennies for St. Jude's Research Hospital. Another volunteer program is the Lunch Buddies, through which people from the community can be buddies with schoolkids during lunch time. Other volunteers help as tutors, classroom aides, and as members of advisory councils. "Partnerships in Education-Adopt a School" allows businesses to contribute to schools by providing occupational information, educational incentives, classroom assistance, fund raising support, and building improvements. Other fund raising festivities draw residents together as well. The Friday at Five series, run by the Old Greensborough Preservation Society, helps raise money for preservation.

Let the Good Times Roll

Family fun: Greensboro has a Natural Science Center, which includes a barnyard zoo, interactive exhibits, mineral and gem collections, a tidal pool, and a planetarium. The city also has a Historical Museum that includes an extensive exhibit of the city's most famous author, O. Henry. The park system includes more than 3,000 acres of parks, including the 1,006-acre Bryan Park Complex on the shore of Lake Townsend, 2 18-hole golf courses, a wildlife sanctuary, and an 11-field soccer complex. Emerald Pointe is a 45-acre water theme park. The Greensboro Coliseum Complex, with a 16,800-seat arena, hosts concerts, shows, and fairs. Within a short drive are beautiful state parks, whitewater rivers and wilderness. There are many municipal golf courses in the area, and North Carolina is known as a mecca for that sport. Ski centers two hours west in the Blue Ridge Mountains, and the famous Blue Ridge Parkway (cars) and Appalachian Trail (hikers) travel the crest of those mountains, too. North Carolina beaches are 4 hours east. Bicycling is extremely popular, and Greensboro hosts the Carolina Cup Bicycle Festival with world-class racers from around the world. Greensboro's J. Spencer Love Tennis Center is home to the North Carolina Tennis Hall of Fame and hosts national tennis championships on its 13 courts.

Sports: Baseball fans can watch minor-league action with the Greensboro Hornets, the Winston-Salem Spirits, and the Burlington Indians. There's also pro indoor soccer, pro basketball (in Charlotte), and pro hockey (Greensboro and Winston-Salem).

Arts & entertainment: The Piedmont Triad has a wealth of artistic offerings: the North Carolina Dance Theater; the Eastern Music Festival; High Point's Shakespeare Festival; the North Carolina Black Repertory Company. Greensboro and Winston-Salem have symphonies, and Greensboro also has a concert band, 3 vocal ensembles, and the Greensboro Opera Company. Each community has outdoor concerts in the summer, such as High Point's Pops in the Park, Winston-Salem's Music at Sunset, and Greensboro's Music for a Sunday Evening in the Park. The Civic Ballet Theatre also calls Greensboro home.

Annual events: Greensboro African-American Arts Festival (Feb.); Memorial Day Weekend Bluegrass Festival (May); Winston-Salem Tanglewood Steeplechase (May); Greensboro Jazzfest (June); Greensboro Fun Fourth (July); Greensboro City Stage Celebration (Oct.); Greensboro Marathon (Nov.); Greensboro Festival of Lights (Dec.).

The Environment

Air and water quality are quite good and monitored throughout the year for EPA guidelines. Greensboro receives its water from a series of stream-fed lakes north of the city. The city currently has a safe yield of 37 million gallons per day and uses an avg. of about 25 million gallons. Greensboro has a strict watershed protection ordinance that is a model for the state in working to ensure that the water supply lasts well into the 21st century. Greensboro's 2 waste-water treatment plants have a daily capacity of 36 million gallons. Currently, they are treating about 23 million gallons of waste water a day. These facilities should also be adequate into the 21st century.

In and Around Town

Roads and interstates: I-85 (north-south); I-40 (east-west); U.S. 29, U.S. 220 (north-south); U.S. 421 (east-west); NC68, NC22.
Closest airport: Piedmont Triad International Airport (10 mi. west of downtown Greensboro).
Public transportation: Duke Transit Co., a subsidiary of Duke Power Co. operates the many routes of the city's bus system.
Avg. commute: 15-20 min.

What Every Resident Knows

Come April and October, hotels and restaurants are filled to the rafters. That's when 50,000 buyers and sellers from around the world converge for the International Home Furnishings Market in nearby High Point. • If someone asks you to order from the Irving Park Deli, or the IPD, don't bother looking it up in the phone book. The name of the place is really Cellar Anton's and its been in the Anton family for years. It's also been a fixture in Irving Park for so many years, the nickname took on a life of its own. • Would you buy a product called Vicks Magic Croup Salve? Didn't think so. What about Vicks VapoRub? It was developed right here by Lunceford Richardson, owner of Porter Drug Store. • Thirty-two years ago, four young black students launched the national drive for integrated lunch counters at Woolworths, making Greensboro the birthplace of the sit-in.

FYI

Greensboro Chamber of Commerce
125 South Elm Street, Suite 100
Greensboro, NC 27401
919-275-8675

Greensboro Convention and Visitors Bureau
317 S. Green Street
Greensboro, NC 27401
1-800-344-2282

Greensboro News & Record
P.O. Box 20848
Greensboro, NC 27420
919-373-7000

Coldwell Banker/Jim Joyner & Assoc.
1400 Battleground Ave., Suite 164
Greensboro, NC 27408
919-275-7202
Jim Joyner, President, Connie
Hillis, Realtor Assoc.

Duke Power Company
201 North Church Street
Greensboro, NC 27402
919-378-9451

Piedmont Natural Gas Company
806 Greenvalley Road
Greensboro, NC 27402
919-378-1845

Southern Bell
800-767-2355

Economic Development Division
Greensboro Area Chamber of Commerce
125 South Elm Street, Suite 100
Greensboro, NC 27401
919-275-8675

Center of Entrepreneurship (Small Business Incubator)
2007 Yanceville Street
Greensboro, NC 27405
919-379-5001

School district: 919-370-8307
Property tax assessor: 919-373-3362
Newcomer's Club: 919-288-7056
Welcome Wagon: 919-282-5554
Piedmont Interfaith Council: 919-274-6051
Physician's referral: 919-379-4000
Day-care referral: 919-378-7700

Raleigh, North Carolina

Area Snapshot

Local population: 207,951
County: Wake   **Population:** 423,380
U.S. region: Southeast
Closest metro areas: Durham (23 mi. north), Greensboro (78 mi. northwest), Charlotte (123 mi. southwest)
Median housing price: $125,000
Median household income: $44,302
Best reasons to live here: World-renowned research center, outstanding medical care, endless recreation, low unemployment, low crime, superb educational institutions, beautiful communities, affordable real estate, ideal climate.

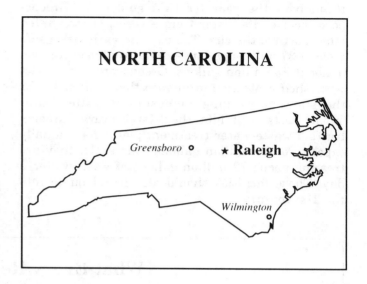

Fabulous Features

Life in the Raleigh/Durham area is like a beloved Christmas carol. There are three major state universities, two internationally acclaimed teaching hospitals, one world-renowned research park and a partridge in a pear tree (OK, robins in a dogwood tree).

Seriously, with the University of North Carolina (Chapel Hill), Duke University (Durham), North Carolina State (Raleigh), Duke University Medical Center, UNC Hospital, and Research Triangle Park (largest in the U.S.) here, opportunities reproduce as fast as rabbits.

Residents also spoke of the genuine friendliness of people, the easy manner in which business is conducted and the slow pace of life. They also boast about the infinite cultural activities (symphony, opera, ballet and theater tickets are affordable) and wonderful family recreation. Raleigh's nickname is the "city within a park" (it owns 3,600 acres of parkland and lakes), but it could also be the U.S. soccer capital (6,000 kids and grownups play in leagues at the new 21-field soccer center).

Everyone's a winner when they buy local real estate. Raleigh is in the top 20 housing markets (*U.S. News and World Report*) because of the wide range of prices ($65,000-$500,000) and neighborhoods (from Victorian era to new planned communities, the houses are simply gorgeous). And although there are more Ph.D.s per capita here, you don't need one to tell you this is a *smart* place to live!

Possible drawbacks: Wake County has grown so fast, the infrastructure is only now catching up. Six new schools just opened. The roads are being widened, but when the growing pains will stop is anyone's guess. The ones who are most concerned are the newcomers! They'd hate growth to ruin this wonderful area! • Raleigh/Durham became a major hub for American Airlines, growing from 100 to 5,000 employees in five years. So when rumors persist that the hub is not yet profitable, it sends a communal chill through the region. If American pulled out, the loss would be devestating.

"You can quote me on that"

"I moved here from New York about six years ago and it's a totally different way of life. It's not as pressured, there are not as many demands on you...and if you can't get it done today, tomorrow's OK, too!"—C.B.

Real Estate

Market overview: The real estate market is strong and healthy. Although houses aren't given away, it's a buyer's market. There has been a lot of new home construction, which competes with the resales. There are about 6,000 homes for sale at any one time, including townhomes, fortunately, there continues to be a lot of corporate relocation. Since population has been growing at a high rate, home prices have been appreciating at about 5% a year.

What houses look like: Transitional 2-story homes (high ceilings, 2-story foyers, open interiors, skylights) and ranches are popular, but you can find almost any style. Inside the Beltway (the interstate and federal highways that circle the city) are older neighborhoods, such as Oakwood, which has many Victorian style homes. Farther out where most of the recent development is, a 10-year-old house is considered "old." Here you will find the transitional and expansive ranches. Brick is a popular exterior. Homes have decks, European kitchens, master suites & BAs, jacuzzis and split plans.

Starter homes: Prices range from $65,000-$85,000 for a 3/BR/1-2/BA, living room, eat-in kitchen, 1200 sq. ft., fireplace, central air, on 1/3 acre. Areas include Knightdale, Broadlands and Heddingham.

Trade-ups: Expect to pay $125,000-$200,000 for a 3-4/BR,/2/BA, living room, family room, upgraded kitchens and BAs, 1/2 acre, 2500 sq. ft. Houses in planned developments may have sports club memberships—pool, tennis, clubhouse. Areas include Greystone, Windham and Lochmere.

Luxury homes: $250,000-$750,000 buys a 3000-6000 sq. ft 4/BR/ 2 1/2BA, family room, den, utility, living room, dining room, master suite, gourmet kitchen, neighborhood pools and clubs. Areas include River Oaks and Sheffield Manor

Rental market: SFHs (3BR/2BA) are $650-$900/mo. The market is tight because of the college population. Apts. and condos (2BR/2BA) are $450-$600/mo.

Great neighborhoods: North Raleigh features newer homes in a variety of prices and proximity to the airport and Research Triangle Park. Exclusive developments include Swans Mill and Bent Tree, where prices range from $350,000-$400,000. Cary, to the south, is the hottest area, with an excellent school system, new residential developments and proximity to Research Triangle.

Nearby areas to consider: Wake Forest, 12 mi. north, is more rural, but growing fast. Housing prices are lower. Chapel Hill, 23 mi. northwest, is a beautiful college town with good schools but higher prices.

What Things Cost

Runzheimer's Living Cost Index: Avg. annual costs for family of 4 with household income of $50,000: $50,182 (.4% above avg. city).

ACCRA's national comparisons: Overall living costs are 3.3% below the national avg. Utilities are the only category above avg. at 5.7%. Housing is avg. Health care is 5% below, goods and services are 6.1% below and groceries are 3% below.

Utilities: Phone: Avg. $20/mo. Hookup: $42.75. Electricity: Avg. $185/mo. on budget plan. Gas: Avg.s $47/mo., higher in winter.

Kid care: Avg. for day-care centers or at-home care: $50-$100/wk. for full-time (5 full days) and $30-$75 for part-time. **Pediatric Visit:** $36, $41 for new patients.

The Tax Ax

Sales tax: 6%.

Property tax: For Wake County: Tax rate 88 cents per $100 of assessed or declared value. Raleigh: Tax rate is .775 cents per $100 of assessed or declared value. Thus, in Wake County, taxes on a $150,000 house are $1,320; in Raleigh, they'd be $1,162.50.

State income tax: 6%-7.75% depending on the number of exemptions. State allows $2,000 personal exemptions ($5,000 married filing jointly). If married filing jointly with taxable income over $21,250, taxes are $1,275, plus 7.75% on income above that.

Climate

Elevation 430'	Avg. High/Low	Avg. Rain (Inches)	Avg. Snow (Inches)	Avg. Days Rain	Avg. % Humidity
Jan.	51/30	3	2.5	9	56
April	72/47	3.1	--	9	46
July	88/67	5.1	--	12	61
Oct.	72/48	2.8	--	7	54
YEAR	70/48	41.8	7.3	111	54
# of days 32° or below: 81			# of days 90° or above: 23		

Residents swear by the weather here, rather than at it. Protected by the Appalachian Mountains from bitterly cold southeast winds, and by the Atlantic Ocean from intense summer heat, the year-round climate is delightfully mild, with very few extremes. Precipitation is also evenly distributed throughout the year. Snowfall is light.

Earning a Living

Economic outlook: Home of the state capital and a high-tech business center, Raleigh has an unemployment rate of only 4.2%. The major employment center is the Research Triangle Park, with more than 50 corporations and governmental agencies specializing in microelectronics, telecommunications, chemicals, biotechnology, pharmaceuticals, and environmental health sciences. Research Triangle Park has 34,000 scientists, technicians, and support personnel. More than 90% of these companies expanded dramatically since opening.

Where the jobs are: Businesses continue to relocate to Raleigh, current businesses are expanding, and population growth is projected at 25% through the 1990s. Total employment has increased by 12,300 jobs to 439,000—with 7,000 more jobs projected, reflecting the continued economic health of the region. American Airlines recently opened a 2,100-employee regional reservations center, and has seen total employment in the Triangle area jump to more than 5,000, creating an annual payroll of nearly $150 million. Glaxo recently opened a $350-million research and development center at its Triangle Park headquarters. Reichhold Chemicals built a $50-million laboratory. Other major companies that have expanded and anticipate continued job growth are Ericsson GE Mobile Communications, Deere, Dupont Electronics and N.C. Farm Bureau. New companies moving into Raleigh over the last year include Builder's Square, Food-4-Less, Penn Life, Seer Technology and Upside Publishing. Announced expansions include Bristol-Myers Squibb, Fujitsu, and Ashton Mortgage.

Business opportunities: Raleigh is within a day's trucking distance of 60% of the U.S. population. The work force is highly educated, as this is one of the top college areas in the country. The development and expansion of Research Triangle Park has brought not only research, but businesses that feed off that research. There are also organizations that help businesses get started—from site selection to relocation assistance to job training. In addition, the Raleigh area places special emphasis on attracting manufacturing businesses, offering special financing, constructing special access roads and extending utilities to new sites at no cost. High-tech, biotechnology, robotics, advanced materials businesses will find the educated employees they need. Retailing has shown a steady increase since the mid-'80s and construction is healthy, too. Government and private industry have added 3 million sq. ft. of office, museum, and display space downtown in the last 2 years.

Making the Grade

Public education overview: Raleigh's well-educated population (more Ph.D.s per capita than anywhere in the world) demands quality education for its children. And that's exactly what it gets from a very progressive system, where kindergarten is a full-day program and children learn on a year-round basis (9 wks. on/3 wks. off). The Wake County School System (2nd largest in N.C.) adopted a "school of choice" program that allows students to attend their neighborhood school or one of the following magnet schools: Gifted and Talented, International Studies, Extended Day, Year-Round, or Classical Studies. Of the 1991 graduates, 82% pursued higher education. Students received $5.7 million in academic scholarships ($540,000 in athletic scholarships). The system boasted 48 National Merit semifinalists, the largest number of any state public school system. SAT scores topped national avgs. with 75% taking SATs as compared to 42% nationwide. With projected growth at more than 40,000 students during the 1990s, total enrollment by 2000 is projected at 105,000. The Wake County school system is meeting its needs with a long-range building program.

Class size: 24:1.

Help for working parents: After-school care 'til 6 p.m. is available at 17 elementary schools—3 offer extended-day educational program with certified instructors from 7 a.m.-6 p.m. All elementary schools offer early arrival programs starting at 7 a.m.

Blue Ribbon School Awards: William G. Enloe High School ('82-'83), Needham Broughton High School ('83-'84).

School year: Last wk. in Aug. to 1st wk. in June or year-round elementary school runs 45 days in class/15 days break. To enter kindergarten, children must be 5 on or before Oct. 16.

Special education/gifted programs: There are 10,000 gifted students out of 71,000 (close to 15% of the school!) There are gifted programs in 89 out of 91 schools. Wake County School System boasts one of the best special education programs in the state because they work in conjunction with the universities and state-funded centers. Many families move here *because* of this. Programs are for children 3-21, including visually-impaired, hearing impaired, learning disabled, emotionally and behaviorally handicapped, language impaired and others.

Nearby colleges/universities: North Carolina State University; St. Augustine's College; Shaw University; Meredith College, Wake Technical Community College; North Carolina at Chapel Hill and Duke University in Durham.

Medical Care

Hospitals/medical centers: The university medical centers, University of North Carolina at Chapel Hill and Duke University in Durham are among the nation's best. Physicians trained at these universities are likely to set up practice here. Duke University Medical Center is one of the finest and most respected medical schools, teaching and research hospitals in the country. Its Heart Center boasts one of the largest cardiac groups in the country, performing major cardiac surgery. Duke has a cancer center, AIDS center and Alzheimer's research center, and a world-renowned diet center as well. University of North Carolina Medical Center is known for its treatment of cystic fibrosis as well as a comprehensive transplant program for heart, lung, liver, and kidney. Raleigh Community Hospital offers general medical and surgical services. Rex Hospital is known for cancer care, obstetrics, same-day surgery and a wellness center.
Specialized care: The Lenox Baker Children's Hospital, Dorothea Dix Hospital (comprehensive psychiatric hospital); HCA Holly Hill Hospital (mental health).

Crime & Safety

Generally, there's a feeling of safety here. You can walk downtown at night, and residents know which areas to avoid. The crime index for Raleigh is the lowest in the area (Charlotte, Durham, Greensboro). Murders have decreased by 22%, but there's been an increase of aggravated assault and robbery, all drug-related. The city has taken an aggressive stand against drugs with 4 programs that target drug buyers, gets the community involved and educate children and adults. C.O.P.E. (Community Oriented Police Enforcement) opens up communication between police and residents and businesses.

Community Life

Raleigh is indeed a "pitch-in" city. Residents volunteer in soup kitchens, help to spruce up the entrances to the city, and roll up their sleeves to remove asphalt from the original brick streets downtown. Tutors work with schoolchildren struggling with math, or with adults learning to read. Stream Watch participants clear streams of refuse. Thousands pitched in to make the U.S. Olympic Festival held in Raleigh in 1987 the most successful on record. The city recently sponsored a New Year's Eve party for families called, "First Night Celebration" in downtown Raleigh which met with tremendous success.

Let the Good Times Roll

Family fun: Looking for something to do? Go to the park—your choice of 250 parks, to be exact. And you can count on more recreational options that just walking the dog. With 3,600 acres, 23 community centers and 900 acres of lakes, Raleigh has indeed earned the nicknamed "city within a park." Outdoor activities range from traditional picnicking, paddleboating and playgrounds to swimming lessons, adult and kid softball leagues, jogging and fitness trails, tennis complexes, bicycle motocross tracks, an 18-hole Frisbee golf course, volleyball, soccer leagues (Capital Area Soccer League has 6,000 players—children to adults) and more. Or take a trip to nearby Falls Lake and Jordan Lake, for skiing, swimming, boating, sailing, fishing. Raleigh's Durant Nature Park at Hemlock Bluffs is great for bird watchers. Umstead State Park is 5,200 acres with boating, fishing, camping, hiking, and picnicking. Raleigh is an hour away from North Carolina Zoological Park in Asheboro, a natural habitat zoo.
Sports: Raleigh is a mecca for sports fans—especially college basketball fans. The University of North Carolina, N.C. State, Duke, and N.C. Central play home games here. The Durham Bulls and Carolina Mudcats (minor-league baseball), the Raleigh-Durham Skyhawks (football), Raleigh IceCaps (minor league hockey), and Raleigh Edge (professional tennis) offer great spectator action!
Arts & entertainment: The North Carolina Symphony performs a full schedule of classical, pops, and children's concerts at the refurbished Raleigh Memorial Auditorium, and. moves outdoors in summer for a series of open-air concerts. The Raleigh Civic Symphony, the Chamber Music Guild, the North Carolina Bach Festival, and the National Opera Company offer more musical entertainment. The Smith Center in Chapel Hill and the Carter-Finley Stadium in Raleigh host big-name rockers. Duke's American Dance Festival performs each summer. Playmakers Repertory Company is a regional professional theater. Duke's Broadway preview series brings New York's next big hits. The North Carolina Museum of Art is noted for its collection, and all-day family festivals, special children's programs, and popular movie series.
Annual events: Antique Extravaganza (Jan.); Run for the Roses (Feb.); Spring Herb and Lamb Day (May); Tarheel Regatta, (June); Farmers Market Festival (July); "Hot Hoops" Basketball Tournament (Aug.); Pops in the Park, Artsplosure Jazz and Heritage Music Festival (Sept.); North Carolina State Fair (Oct.).

The Environment

Wake County is a relatively healthy place to live, with clean air and clean water. Industrial pollution is low, as most of the industry is new and have high-tech "clean" factories. Raleigh has a curbside recycling program and recycling drop-off locations The North Carolina Steel Recycling Partnership was formed in 1992 by the steel industry to heighten public awareness of increasing the amount of steel recycled across the state. Its goal is to recycle all steel, including 1 billion cans used in the state annually. Water comes from Falls Lake, which originates from the Neuse River. One reason water quality is good because there is little heavy industry as compared to other areas of the state. Raleigh's planning for the future to assure adequate water supply by expanding the water treatment plant.

In and Around Town

Roads and interstates: I-40 (north-south); U.S. 64 (east-west); Highways 1 and 70.
Closest airport: The Raleigh-Durham International Airport is located 15 mi. from downtown, and is a hub for American Airlines.
Public transportation: The city-owned Capital Area Transit provides extensive bus service, and Raleigh Trolley provides light rail service to the city.
Avg. commute: 20-25 min. from either the city or outlying areas or suburbs. Easy access to downtown areas, Research Triangle Park, or airport.

What Every Resident Knows

Wouldn't you be proud if your kids developed real manners? Living in Raleigh will do the trick. Raleigh was named the "Most Polite City in the Country-1992" by Marjabelle Young Stewart—a noted etiquette expert—who has been compiling this list for the past 16 years. In no time, your little ones will be saying "Yes ma'am, or no sir" instead of, "Why the heck should I brush my teeth?" • All that polite talk can take time, which is why you should never do your food shopping when you're in a hurry. Between the friendly neighbors you bump into and the considerate clerks at the checkout, you'll need extra time to let everyone know how you're doing, how you like it, etc. • Before you start your furniture shopping, remember that High Point is a 1½-hr. drive. Prices don't get any better than direct from the furniture capital of the world!

FYI

Raleigh Chamber of Commerce
800 South Falisbury Street
Raleigh, NC 27601
919-664-7000

Raleigh Convention & Visitor's Bureau
225 Hillsborough Street, Suite 400
Raleigh, NC 27603
800-849-8499; 919-834-5900

The News and Observer
215 S. McDowell
Raleigh, NC 27602
919-829-4500

Southern Bell Telephone Co.
800-767-2355

Russell Gay & Associates/Century 21
5909 Falls of Neuse Road
Raleigh, NC 27609
919-872-5100
Myra Little, Relocation Director

Carolina Power & Light Co.
411 Fayetteville Street
Raleigh, NC 27601
919-783-5400

Public Service Co. Of N.C.
1720 Hillsborough Street
Raleigh, NC 27605
919-833-6641

Economic Development Department
c/o Raleigh Chamber of Commerce
919-664-7040

Small Business Development Center
4509 Creedmoore Rd., Suite 201
Raleigh, NC 27612
919-571-4154

School district: 919-850-1600
Property tax assessor:
919-856-5400
Newcomers' Club: 919-847-7185
Welcome Wagon: 919-755-5405
N.C. Council of Churches:
919-828-6501
Physician's referral: 919-821-2227
Day-care referral: 919-571-1420

Wilmington, North Carolina

Area Snapshot

Local population: 60,131
County: New Hanover   **Population:** 123,211
U.S. region: Southeastern North Carolina
Closest metro area: Raleigh (123 mi. northwest)
Median housing price: $102,000
Avg. household income: $33,649
Best reasons to live here: Charming, progressive Southern city, waterfront living, diverse business base with great growth potential (Hollywood South), affordable housing and living costs, fabulous recreation, mild year-round climate, respected schools and hospitals.

Fabulous Features

Ever dreamt of being a Hollywood extra? Would you settle for a *Wilmington* extra? In the past 10 years, 54 major motion pictures, made-for-TV movies and commercials have been shot in this impressive port city at the southeastern tip of North Carolina (it's now a $250 million local industry).

Lower production costs and a gleaming oceanfront location have been the main attractions, but the stars haven't had a corner on the market! Since 1970, the population has jumped nearly 25 percent (for every 100 who move out, 170 move in according to a Ryder Truck rental survey)! Not wanting to miss out on the favorable climate (economic and otherwise) or the perfect tee (there are a dozen courses and several beautiful golf communities), Fortune 500 companies such as General Electric, Corning Glass Works, DuPont and Hoecht-Celenese have opened major facilities (Corning is doubling its operation to become the world's largest pro-ducer of micro-optic fiber).

The housing market is a buyer's dream. Inventory is plentiful (nearly a 25 percent jump in new construction), with average prices in the $125,000 to $150,000 range. The New Hanover County schools are on the leading edge (two elementary schools are starting full-year schedules). And as home to the University of North Carolina at Wilmington (one of the leading marine biology programs) and the respected New Hanover Regional Medical Center, education and health care are nothing to sneeze at.

But Wilmington really shines on the outside! Nestled between the Cape Fear River and the Atlantic Ocean, the warm-water beaches are the only ticket you need to windsurf, sail, fish, scuba dive or just plain float. Exciting theater and cultural opportunities share the spotlight with more than 50 different arts organizations sponsoring events. Hollywood isn't the only place where they shout, "action!"

Possible drawbacks: The Carolina Power and Light nuclear power plant is 20 mi. south and has made headlines due to a maintenance backlog. The company shut down the problem areas and subsequently began a three-year upgrade plan. Given that nuclear power is now one of the most heavily regulated industries, the risk factor has been significantly reduced.

"You can quote me on that"

"We're water lovers and enjoy fishing and just plain being by the water. We were tired of the cold winters in Philadelphia and wanted to escape without going as far south as Florida."—F.S.

Real Estate

Market overview: Easterners love that they can move south without being "burned," either by over-built real estate or the oppressive sun. They also love the variety of prices, styles and choices among resales or new construction (a 20%-25% increase in building permits helps). Sellers anxious to trade up are happy to be able to sell in usually fewer than 60 days. Much is available in the $125,000 range—new 3BRs in great developments).

What houses look like: This is the land of choices! Everything from ranches, capes, Victorians, colonials and contemporaries are here. Brick with vinyl siding is popular on older homes. Newer homes show stucco and even Southwestern-style decor. Interiors feature great rooms with fireplaces, sunrooms and garden tubs. Ceramic tile and hardwood floors are the most requested feature; 2-car garages are common, but with mild weather, they're more like storage warehouses. Due to high water levels, basements are rare so FROGs are in demand (finished room over garage).

Starter homes: Prices start at $65,000, but there's more to show for $85,000. That buys 1200-1500 sq. ft. on close to ½ acre, 3BR/2BA w/1-car garage. Look at Fawn Creek, Ivy Woods and Kings Grant.

Trade-ups: Starting at $110,000, you'll get a larger 3BR/2BA. At $150,000, the possibilities open up. You'll get 2000 sq. ft. (new homes are somewhat smaller) on ½-acre, including 2-car garage, 3-4BR/2BA. $200,000 buys a large 4BR/2½BA w/master suite and study, fireplace and a minimum ½-acre. Woodberry Forest, Echo Farms (golf-course community) and Brittany Woods are beautiful.

Luxury homes: $300,000+ buys waterfront property with 3000 sq. ft. (4BR (large)/2½BA). New on the ocean starts at a half million. Look at Masonboro Harbour, Landfall and Shinn Point.

Rental market: Affordable SFH rentals are available, but don't hesitate or they'll be gone. A 3BR/1½BA ranges from $450-$1,000/mo. Condos are more readily available with a 3BR/1½ BA renting for $475-$800/mo. (co-ops on the beach cost same). 3BR apartments rent for $500/mo. and up.

Great neighborhoods: Stratford Place is a lovely residential area for homes in the under $100,000 range. It's new, offers good values and is close to shopping.

Nearby areas to consider: Castle Hayne (20 mi. north) is a charming, rural and tranquil area seeing a lot of growth. South is the Brunswick area, with great golfing, beaches and casual lifestyles. Private schools in Wilmington have many children from these communities.

What Things Cost

Runzheimer's Living Cost Index: Avg. annual costs for family of 4 with household income of $50,000: $46,636 (6.7% below avg. city).
ACCRA's national comparisons: Not available.
Utilities: Phone: $13/mo. (unlimited). Installations avg. $43. Electric: Avg. $146/mo. ($84/mo. in winter, $200/mo. in summer). Water/sewer/trash has 2-month minimum of $57 (recyclers get $3 discount). Most homes are all electric.
Kid care: Avg. cost for day care is $69/wk. infants, $64/wk. for 18 mo.-4 years. Most centers charge avg. $30 enrollment fee (sibling discounts available). Some now offer swing shifts (2 p.m.-midnight). **Pediatric visit:** $35 avg.

The Tax Ax

Sales tax: 6% (professional services, prescriptions exempt).
Property tax: Current combined city and county millage rate is $1.17 per $100 of value. Taxes on a $100,000 house would be an estimated $1,100/yr.
State income tax: 6%-7.75% depending on number of exemptions. State also allows $2,000 personal exemptions ($5,000 if married filing jointly). If married filing jointly with taxable income over $21,250, taxes will be $1,275, plus 7.75% on income above that.

Climate

Elevation 30'	Avg. High/Low	Avg. Rain (Inches)	Avg. Snow (Inches)	Avg. Days Rain	Avg. % Humidity
Jan.	57/36	3.2	.3	11	57
April	74/52	2.9	--	8	48
July	89/72	8.3	--	13	64
Oct.	75/55	3.3	--	7	57
YEAR	74/54	53.4	1.6	116	57

# of days 32° or below: 27	# of days 90° or above: 46

The Atlantic Ocean and the Gulf Stream wields a heavy influence on Wilmington's weather. High humidity and 50 inches of rain per year are the drawbacks; mild winters and springs are the good news. Although there can be polar cold fronts, snow rarely accumulates. Summers bring warm days and mild nights, and several tropical storms.

Earning a Living

Economic outlook: Wilmington's growing economy is what the "New South" is excited about. Tourism increased 12.5% from 1989-1991 (generated nearly $400 million in 1991), real estate sales by 14%, and retail sales by 6.9%. In addition, Wilmington has attracted giants like General Electric, DuPont, Corning, and Hoecht-Celenese, as well as smaller high-tech firms such as Applied Analytical, R & E Electronics, and Sunbrokers. Firms are attracted because of a high degree of accessibility. I-40 connects Wilmington with the Research Triangle (Raleigh, Durham and Chapel Hill). Coupled with the highway network and the resources at the State Port, Wilmington possesses an excellent transportation and distribution center. Wilmington is the 3rd-largest film production facility outside of Hollywood. Since 1983, more than 50 new companies, including Carolco Film Studios and several large European firms have established operations here. Production and operating costs are lower here. Film studios and associated production firms employ an estimated 500 people full-time and have contributed an average of $133 million annually to the local economy since 1985. Several home grown firms are now million-dollar businesses including South Atlantic Services, Miller Building Corp., and Dorothy's Ruffled Originals.

Where the jobs are: The region's economic diversity contributes to its stability, with many sectors prospering. Health care has played an increasingly important role in the area. New Hanover Regional Medical Center's annual payroll is more than $80 million, employs 2,400 people and generates 17% of all the jobs in New Hanover County (and now Cape Fear Memorial Hospital is involved in an $8.5 million expansion to keep pace with growth). Corning Glass Works is doubling its Wilmington facility and adding 300 employees to become the world's largest producer of micro-optic fiber. Other companies planning or in the process of upgrading include E.I DuPont de Nemours & Co. (producing polyester and other fibers), General Electric Company (producing jet engine parts and nuclear fuel) and Federal Paper Board Co. (produces paper). The current 6% unemployment rate is projected to decline within the next 12-18 months.

Business opportunities: People within a 50-mile radius come to Wilmington for virtually all of their needs: health care, education, recreation and culture and shopping. With the promising population growth, that presents great opportunities for service/support businesses (ditto for the film production industry).

Making the Grade

Public education overview: The New Hanover County School System earns top marks. It was one of 14 in North Carolina to score above avg. on the State Education's Report Card (1990-'91), and California Aptitude Test scores are in the top 10% of the state. College-bound students received $4.2 million in scholarships/aid last year with 86% of seniors attending college. Innovative programs include extraordinary reading and math incentive efforts (Overnight School Read-In, Reading Run Night with Parents, Turn Off the TV Week, Drop Everything and Read (DEAR), Math Superstars, Math-Bowl and MathCounts). The district is also a model for arts education. Different cultures are studied through dance and drama. "Best Foot Forward," an annual student talent show, is a major fund raiser. The Chamber of Commerce's Education Council sponsors mini-grants through area businesses for special projects. Cape Fear Careers is an awareness and development program for 8-12 grades offering on-the-job-mentors, field trips, speakers, etc. A community resource file includes 200 businesses that share their expertise in the classroom. Last year, Blair and Howe Elementary Schools implemented voluntary, year-round education (from July-June with long intercessions). Also scheduled are $43 million of planned improvements.

Class size: 18:1 (K-3 teachers have an assistant).

Help for working parents: The YMCA offers "Prime Time After-School Child Care" for grades K-5 (sports, homework help, etc.) at many grade schools (costs based on ability to pay). The YWCA after-school program is "Funsters Camp" (K-5) and "Teen Leadership Camp" (middle school program). Bus service is available.

Blue Ribbon School Awards: John T. Hoggard High School ('90-'91).

School year: Last wk. in Aug. through first wk. in June. Children must be 5 on or before Oct. 16 to enter kindergarten.

Special education/gifted programs: The district's Exceptional Children Department coordinates programs for handicapped, emotionally disturbed, learning disabled, and visual/speech impaired students. It also oversees academically gifted and talented (including advanced placement) programs.

Nearby colleges/universities: University of North Carolina at Wilmington (excellent marine biology program, MBA program through Cameron School of Business Admin.); Cape Fear Community College. (High school students can enroll for college credit at both.)

Medical Care

Hospitals/medical centers: Health care surpasses many regions twice its size. New Hanover Regional Medical Center is now the hub for medical services in southeastern North Carolina, operating one of 8 regional trauma centers in the state (tied in to Vita-Link, a 24-hour mobile intensive care unit). Other specialties include: the Coastal Heart Center, neonatal intensive care, Sleep Disorders Center and Medical Mall for outpatient services. Cape Fear Memorial Hospital offers comprehensive services including ambulatory, medical and surgical units. A current $8.5 million expansion will provide for new programs in radiology and obstetrics/gynecology. In addition, there are numerous immediate care facilities.

Specialized care: Southeastern Mental Health Center; Wilmington Treatment Center (substance abuse).

Crime & Safety

Oh the times they are a changin'. To figure out if an area is safe today you have to know about the level of stranger-to-stranger crimes. According to the Wilmington Police, the rate here is very low. However, it does have its share of property and drug-related crime. To stem the tide, the police instituted "Community Wellness," a coordination of resources to heal troubled neighborhoods. In high-risk areas, it sets up Neighborhood Area Base Stations (NABS). Semi-annual questionnaires ask residents for ideas and to grade police protection. (The police chief even has a listed phone number). This has all contributed to a tremendous vote of confidence for the department and, more important, a reduction in crime.

Community Life

There is a long history of devotion to the arts in Wilmington. Pick up the paper and you'll invariably read about an upcoming event or restoration to a historic site (the $5 million renovation of Thalian Hall and $4 million expansion of the Cape Fear Museum were truly a source of community pride). Recent efforts include the Emerging Artists Program, and several arts education initiatives. The Park District also offers art and music appreciation (the Goodtimers Band had seniors make their instruments). A wonderful grassroots volunteer effort is the new Hospitality House. Funded solely through donations, it offers food, shelter and compassion for families visiting hospital patients.

Let the Good Times Roll

Family fun: The year-round mild climate and coastal location guarantee that life in the great outdoors is just what the doctor ordered! The "River to the Sea" Bikeway was recently completed. This 8-mile stretch between the historic riverfront and Wrightsville Beach is already a popular bike and hike trail. Camping is super, with more than 20 public and private sites along the Cape Fear Coast. Horseback riding is on the comeback trail, with many new stables and saddle clubs opening. The warm waters of Wrightsville Beach, Carolina Beach, Kure Beach and the South Brunswick Islands are the ideal place for boating, fishing, sailing, windsurfing and of course, swimming. Jet skis and catamarans, as well as scuba diving and boat charters, are also popular. Golf rivals water sports as a favorite local pastime, and area courses are both challenging and in good supply (you can "swing" almost all year). A regional golf classic is held each spring and fall. Other family entertainment includes Moore's Creek National Battlefield (Revolutionary War), the Aquarium at Fort Fisher, Chandler's Wharf, Fort Fisher State Historic Site (Civil War site) and the Tote-Em In Zoo. The Parks and Recreation Dept. maintains more than 500 acres of local parks with everything-you-could-want facilities, and sponsors youth leagues for baseball, soccer and volleyball. After-school and summer camp programs are extensive.

Sports: The University of North Carolina at Wilmington Seahawks are in strong intercollegiate conferences for baseball and basketball. Students participate in 16 different competitive sports.

Arts & entertainment: The newly restored Thalian Hall (originally built in 1855 as the city hall and a cultural center) continues to serve as Wilmington's cultural center. More than 35 area arts and civic organizations use the facility to host events, including exciting musical, theatrical and dance performances, on as many as 300 nights a year. These include the North Carolina Symphony, Playwrights Production Company, Opera House Theater Company, Wilmington Choral Society, Wilmington Symphony Orchestra and stage productions from the Tapestry Theater Co.

Annual events: The North Carolina Azalea Festival, Wilmington's most popular event, (April); Riverfest Celebration (Oct.); Holiday Flotilla at Wrightsville Beach, kicks off holiday festivities (Nov.); North Carolina Jazz Festival (Jan.); New Hanover County Fair (Oct.); Popular Grove Peanut Festival (March).

The Environment

North Carolina claims to be one of the cleanest states because of a lack of concentrated industries. Water quality meets or exceeds EPA standards (Cape Fear River is the source) and available supply is not an issue. Air quality is also good because sea breezes move pollutants offshore (reduces smog), and auto emissions are manageable. Recycling efforts are extensive. The one caution is Carolina Power and Light's nuclear power plant, which is now refurbishing the generators after a serious maintenance backlog. The plant's impact on the environment is constantly monitored.

In and Around Town

Roads and interstates: I-85, I-95, I-40, U.S. Highway 74, Northern Outer Loop (connecting I-421 with I-17.
Closest airport: New Hanover International Airport (recently completed $23 million renovation) has direct flights to Atlanta, Baltimore and Philadelphia. Most connections are through Charlotte or Raleigh.
Public transportation: Wilmington Transit Authority runs 6 routes weekdays and Saturday from 5:30 a.m. to 8 p.m.
Avg. commute: 20-25 min. into downtown (no rush hour).

What Every Resident Knows

What do the movies "Terminator 2," "Sleeping with the Enemy," "Ramblin' Rose" and even "Teenage Mutant Ninja Turtles" have in common? All or part of them were filmed at Carolco Studios in Wilmington. • In this 250-year old city, preservation is a serious matter. The historic Thalian Hall (Wilmington's Great White Way since the mid-19th century) underwent a $5 million facelift so it remains the center of theatrical performances into the 21st century. • Residents are waging a battle in Raleigh over the Fort Fisher State Historical site. Seems water is encroaching on the sights of many Civil War battles and they want to build a retaining wall to prevent further damage. State regulators say it can't be done safely so it can't be done at all. Petitions are flying!

FYI

Greater Wilmington Chamber of Commerce
P.O. Box 330
Wilmington, NC 28402
919-762-2611

Cape Fear Coast Convention and Visitors Bureau
24 N. 3rd Street
Wilmington, NC 28401
800-222-4757

Star News (daily)
1003 S. 17th Street
Wilmington, NC 28401
919-343-2000

Wilmington Journal (weekly)
412 S. 7th Street
Wilmington, NC 28401
919-762-5502

Southern Bell
800-767-2355

Century 21/Gardner Real Estate
1401 S. 39th Street
Wilmington, NC 28403
919-392-1380
Sally Fulks, Relocation Director

Carolina Power & Light Co.
401 N. Front Street
Wilmington, NC 28401
919-762-8701

North Carolina Natural Gas
1321 S. 10th Street
Wilmington, NC 28401
919-763-3305

Committee of 100 (Industrial Devl.)
508 Market Street
Wilmington, NC 28401
919-763-8414

Small Business Development Center
Cape Fear Community College
411 N. Front Street
Wilmington, NC 28401
919-343-0481

Downtown Area Revitalization Effort (D.A.R.E.)
201 N. Front Street
Wilmington, NC 28401
919-763-7349

School district: 919-763-5431
Property tax assessor:
919-341-7136
Newcomer's Club: 919-343-0782
North Carolina Council of Churches: 919-828-6501
Physician's referral: 919-452-8381 (Ask-A-Nurse)
Day-care referral: 919-799-4140

Blue Ash, Ohio *(Greater Cincinnati)*

Area Snapshot

Local population: 11,923
County: Hamilton   **Population:** 866,228
U.S. region: Midwest/Southwest Ohio
Closest metro area: Cincinnati (12 mi. southwest)
Median housing price: $105,000
Median household income: $55,696
Best reasons to live here: Accomplished city government, great parks and recreation, outstanding schools and higher education, exceptional low-cost health care, endless diversions, booming business environment, easy access to Cincinnati.

Fabulous Features

The people of Blue Ash know how to paint their town, and what a colorful canvas it is! The city makes a splash with exciting celebrations—Springfest, Holidayfest, and the grand-daddy of extravaganzas—the Taste of Blue Ash (over three days, the eating and entertainment jubilee attracts much of Southwest Ohio).

The Sycamore Schools serve up a first-rate education. Considered one of the top 10 districts in the state, it gets straight A's for academics, athletics and achievements. It has instituted primary (K-4), intermediate (5-6), junior (7-8) and senior (9-12) high schools. The end result is top-performing students (half the 8th grade class is eligible to take the SATs).

Procter & Gamble, Johnson & Johnson's Ethicon Endo-Surgery, Merrell Dow, Hewlett-Packard and numerous other corporations have created "Management Mile" along Reed Hartman Highway (modern office parks surrounded by lakes and trees). Others commute to Greater Cincinnati, home to numerous Fortune 500 regional and national offices (International Paper, Fidelity Investments, Star-Kist Foods and Xerox Corp. are "copying" the trend by opening branch operations here).

City Council administrators boast that Blue Ash's success as the consummate "live, work and play" hometown was all part of a master plan. And to keep the city humming, they recently revitalized the downtown and built a gorgeous Towne Square where families gather for concerts and events. They even erected a life-sized bronze statue (23 ft. high) of a family of four alongside a tree—a blue ash, we hope.

Possible drawbacks: Newer homes in the $200,000 and under range are scarce (ditto with SFH rentals). • Many residents want Blue Ash Municipal Airport *and* its planes to go up, up and away—or at least to another part of town! In its current location, it is a possible noise, pollution and safety hazard. Talks of moving the facility remain stalled. • Blue Ash's daytime population soars from 12,000 to 70,000. The good news is that they all pay a 1% earnings tax to Blue Ash, for an annual $11.5 million to city coffers. The bad news is how many workers come and go at the same time.

"You can quote me on that"

"Cincinnati is one of the most overlooked cities in the American cityscape. It offers so much in the way of culture, beauty and sports, with a truly vital downtown. The skyline is absolutely breathtaking, yet it still has an intimate, hometown feel."—J.W.

Real Estate

Market overview: Homes in Blue Ash are so desirable, they're like Hondas. They sell themselves! Unlike Hondas, there won't be very many new models...unless the city changes the zoning laws or annexes more land. Retirees and corporate transfers leaving the area will keep the resale market in play. Although the homes are spacious and well built, there is very little to look at in the $200,000-and-under range. Easterners who've looked in other outlying suburbs are quite surprised by the high prices and property taxes. What makes the decision easier are the neighborhoods (most properties are on woodsy half-acre lots), the size of homes (3000 sq. ft.), and the proximity to major employers (a "rough" commute takes 25 min.)

What houses look like: The "Cincinnati" home is a traditional 2-story brick box—not an architect's dream, but a sturdy abode. Many of the newer homes (5-15 years) are "transitionals"—great rooms instead of formal living rooms and dens, 1st-floor master BR suites (gives a feeling of a sprawling ranch-style home, with bedrooms upstairs for kids), deluxe kitchens and "glamour" baths. Many show cedar trim, cathedral ceilings and 2-story foyers.

Starter homes: Realtors tell us that if a house in Blue Ash's Ravenwood section goes on the market in the $125,000-$150,000 range, it'll be snatched up before the "For Sale" sign hits the ground. These small 3-4BR/2BA 2-story houses are 15-20 years old and offer great values for the money.

Trade-ups: You'll spend $200,000-$250,000 for a starter home. This includes a large, formal 4BR/2½BA colonial (2800-3600 sq. ft.) in Peppermill or Sycamore Trace.

Luxury homes: Homes built around the Blue Ash Golf Course start at $275,000 and go up to $500,000. Generally 3000-3600 sq. ft., they offer 3-car garages, finished basements, 4-5BR/2½BA, screened porches, decks, and large, designer kitchens. Homes avg. 5-15 years old.

Rental market: You need the luck of the Irish to find a house for rent, paying $1,600/mo for it. You'll have better luck with condos and apartments: 2BR/2BA units go for $550-$650/mo.

Great neighborhoods: Fox Chase, Chimney Hill, Carpenter's Run, Legends of Carpenter's Run, Tangleridge and Tiffany Ridge.

Nearby areas to consider: Loveland and West Chester are outlying areas starting to develop quickly. Homes are less expensive, and new construction is everywhere. Although they're out of the Sycamore school district, the Loveland and Lakota (West Chester) schools are quite good.

What Things Cost

Runzheimer's Living Cost Index: Avg. annual costs for family of 4 with household income of $50,000: $49,303 (1.4% below avg.).

ACCRA's national comparisons: Overall living costs for the Cincinnati MSA are 7.1% above the national avg., with housing the main offender (13.4% above). Utilities and health care are 2.8% below. Transportation and goods and services avg. 8%-10% above.

Utilities: Phone: Avg. $20/mo. Installation: $30. Gas and electric are billed together. Summer avg. is $220/mo.; winter, $180/mo.

Kid care: There are ample licensed day-care facilities as well as licensed day-care homes. Avg. cost is $94/wk. for infants, $78/wk. for preschoolers. **Pediatric visit:** $35-$45.

The Tax Ax

Sales tax: 5.5%.

Property tax: As a rule, taxes avg. 1%-1.5% of a home's selling price. For example, a house valued at $250,000 would run $3,750/yr. (estimated).

State income tax: For married taxpayers filing jointly, Ohio has a graduated tax liability based on federally adjusted gross income minus $670 per personal exemption. The rate for income over $20,000 up to $40,000 is 4.46%. From $41,000-$80,000 is 5.2% The cap is 6.9% for income over $100,000.

Note: Blue Ash imposes a 1% local earnings tax on both residents and nonresidents. Residents who pay an earnings tax to Cincinnati receive a credit toward the Blue Ash tax.

Climate

Elevation 700'	Avg. High/Low	Avg. Rain (Inches)	Avg. Snow (Inches)	Avg. Days Rain	Avg. % Humidity
Jan.	40/24	2.6	7.9	10	68
April	66/45	3.9	.5	13	54
July	87/66	4	--	10	57
Oct.	69/47	2.2	.1	9	55
YEAR	65/45	37.5	25	126	60
# of days 32° or below: 98			# of days 90° or above: 28		

Cincinnati's continental climate brings wide but short-lived temperature swings, particularly from Nov. to May. Compared to other Midwest cities, winters are considered mild (annual snowfall is generally lighter). Fall is delightfully warm and sunny, while summers can be hot and humid.

Earning a Living

Economic outlook: After an unprecedented growth spurt between 1984 and 1990 (24,000 new jobs were created), Greater Cincinnati is now experiencing a '90s-style reality check (negative job growth in 1991, and the current unemployment rate is 5.8%). But not to worry. They call this the "Blue Chip" region because with a broad economic base of industry, they're like a solid portfolio—managing to stay even, if not slightly ahead. Cincinnati has been ranked first among 24 major U.S. cities for economic vitality since 1985 (Grant Thornton Index) and 7th in Cushman & Wakefield's top 10 cities for locating a business. Here's why: Despite the grim national economy, in the first 6 months of 1992, there was more than $60 million in investments committed to the region by Fortune 500 companies. Fidelity Investments, Xerox Corp., International Paper, and Star-Kist Foods are just some of the companies who've announced they're moving in or building out. Other locally based firms, including Chiquita Brands International, General Electric Aircraft Engines and E.W. Scripps, are forging ahead. In light of the area's central location, excellent transportation (there's more barge traffic than through the Panama Canal, and the international airport is one of the fastest-growing in the country), low energy costs, ample water supply and high quality of life, Greater Cincinnati is still very much like a preferred stock.

Where the jobs are: Two of Blue Ash's leading employers recently experienced expansions. Johnson & Johnson's Ethicon Endo-Surgerys almost doubled its employment from 900 to 1,600 while Procter & Gamble hired an additional 800 employees, for a total 3,000. Other major employers in Blue Ash include Merrell Dow Chemical, Masco Industries, Belcan Engineering, Warner Cable Communications and Raymond Walters College (branch of University of Cincinnati).

Business opportunities: Light manufacturing, warehouse and retail concerns continue to be the most coveted commodities in Blue Ash's business parks. However, tax incentives and real estate abatements aren't in the cards (anything that can potentially affect the school budget is political suicide). In spite of this and limited land availability, 50 to 100 new businesses open every year, adding to the 1,800 existing businesses with Blue Ash addresses. The big draw is the burgeoning daytime population of 70,000. That's enough to keep retail, dining and service businesses flourishing. Hotel and residence chains have also keyed in on the opportunities, with close to 1,100 rooms and suites.

Making the Grade

Public education overview: Ask families why they moved here and there's a universal response: "Sycamore Schools!" The district is recognized as one of the top 10 in Ohio for both academic and extracurricular achievements. Sycamore High students have access to so many advanced placement courses, many earn enough credits to enter as college sophomores. The junior high has the highest number of students eligible for the Midwest Talent Search (50% of its 8th-graders take the SATs), 70% are involved in athletic programs, and the school consistently wins first prize in numerous academic and art contests. Three things make this district tick—tremendous community support (a local club raises $125,000 a year for cultural events), endless parental participation, and a zealous effort to maintain an optimum budget (the city nixes tax incentives to businesses because it reduces school funds). Every year there's a 20% turnover due to all the corporate transfers, so there's a buddy system (old hands show new kids the ropes) and even an "International Mom's Club" (helps acclimate all the foreign families). Although there's an emphasis on global education, the community focus is also strong. The high school opens for continuing education classes, cultural programs, etc. The district is also affiliated with the Joint Vocational District, offering 100 free courses.

Class size: 20:1 (K-4), 23:1 (5-8).

Help for working parents: The YMCA operates a latchkey program at each Sycamore Elementary School from 7 a.m. to 6 p.m. ($95-$140/wk.).

Blue Ribbon School Awards: Sycamore Junior High ('86-'87).

School year: First week of Sept. through the first week of June. Children must be 5 on or before Sept. 30 to enter kindergarten (testing for early entrance is possible).

Special education/gifted programs: The Hamilton County Office of Education offers a complete range of programs for the physically handicapped, hearing and visually impaired, and those with behavioral or developmental problems. Academically gifted students participate in special math and language arts programs. Selected 5th graders work on critical thinking and creative problemsolving. High School Advanced Placement programs are extensive.

Nearby colleges/universities: University of Cincinnati; University of Cincinnati's Raymond Walters College; Xavier University, Hebrew Union College-Jewish Institute of Religion; Miami University.

Medical Care

Hospitals/medical centers: Greater Cincinnati boasts one of the nation's most advanced health care systems (20 acute-care hospitals) as well as one of the most cost-efficient (compared to 18 other comparably sized metro areas, it ranks first for low-cost medical care). The University of Cincinnati's Medical Center is one of the biggest teaching/research/ treatment hospitals in the U.S., with three colleges and numerous specialty centers. It offers a Level I trauma center and Air Care, the first 24-hour emergency service in the tri-state area. Bethesda North (Montgomery) serves Blue Ash with urgent care and extensive outpatient services.

Specialized care: World-renowned Children's Hospital Medical Center and Shriner's Burns Institute bring patients and physicians from around the world. Barrett Cancer Center at University Hospital is nationally recognized.

Crime & Safety

Blue Ash's 12-point crime prevention efforts are so effective (ranked first in the state), you can feel safe walking at midnight or jogging at 5 a.m. Overall crimes per capita in Greater Cincinnati are exceedingly low (ranked 7th lowest in the U.S. for metro areas with 1 million-plus population). And while most cities have a DARE program today, Blue Ash now has DARE graduates (6th graders complete a 17-week drug abuse awareness program and earn their degrees). It also has a cooperative program with 23 other communities to combat drug trafficking. The fire department has significantly reduced the number of Blue Ash homes going up in smoke by distributing free smoke detectors to residents.

Community Life

For a city of 12,000, Blue Ash leaves most communities in the dust when it comes to showing residents one great time. The city sponsors so many multiday extravaganzas and "fests," you'll be wondering how you existed on such a meager social life before you moved here. There's a huge 4th of July party, the Taste of Blue Ash, Springfest, free concerts and films, a Holidayfest and much more. To commemorate its 200th birthday, there was a yearlong Bicentennial Bash, culminating with the burial of a time capsule. Should you happen to be living here when it's opened July 4, 2041, don't forget where you first heard about it!

Let the Good Times Roll

Family fun: Blue Ash's Parks and Recreation Department offers several hundred classes, programs, events and leagues throughout the year. There are Tuesday Concerts in the Park, Friday Evenings on the Square, Movies in the Park, numerous special events, etc. The Summer Artventure Camp and Camp Blue Fish have imaginative theme weeks for kids 4-14. The city's anchor facility, a gorgeous, modern Recreation Center, features an outdoor Olympic-size pool with a 150-ft. double-twist tube slide, a championship-level 18-hole golf course (rated by *Golf Digest* as one of the top municipal courses in the country), and the Blue Ash Sports Center (lighted baseball, soccer and softball fields). The Crosley Field is an exact replica of the Cincinnati Reds' old playing field. The city also boasts the Blue Ash Nature Park, Blue Ash Towne Square and Bicentennial Veterans Memorial Park. A major renovation to the Recreation Center will include a gym and a zero-depth children's pool with aquatic play structures. Annual Family memberships are only $40/yr. Minutes away is the Kings Island Amusement Park, a 1,600-acre theme park.

Sports: Cincinnati sports fans are in a league of their own! They cheer for the Champion Cincinnati Reds (baseball's oldest team), the Bengals (NFL), the Cyclones (minor league hockey), and even the Rockers (arena football). Numerous pro events come to the Jack Nicklaus Sports Complex, including men's ATP tennis and LPGA tournaments.

Arts & entertainment: The wonderful Blue Ash Symphony presents joyous family concerts during the year—a tremendous achievement for a city this size. For children there is also ARTrageous and a city-sponsored performing arts series at Raymond Walters College. Cincinnati offers the Cincinnati Art Museum, Contemporary Art Museum, Natural History Museum, Children's Discovery Center, plus fascinating archaeological sites like the Serpentine Wall and Ft. Ancient Indian Burial Grounds. Recently there was a major commitment to build the Ohio Center for the Arts—a multimillion-dollar arts and theater complex.

Annual events: The Taste of Blue Ash (sample dozens of restaurants, stars and entertainment, and art, late Sept.); Blue Ash Dash (bike race, Aug.); Springfest (4-day extravaganza with 5K run, concerts, antique cars and parade, Memorial Day weekend); Crosley Old Timers Baseball Game (legendary greats, Aug.); "Oktoberfest Zinzinnati" (second only to the Munich original); Cincinnati's Riverfest (one of the best fireworks displays in the country, Labor Day weekend).

The Environment

All eyes are on Cincinnati as it unveils the world's first granular activated carbon water treatment facility. The $60 million state-of-the-art plant (3½ years in the making) will systematically remove all organic contaminants, making the area's drinking water some of the purest, best-tasting in the world (supply has never been a problem). Air quality could use similar help. While one or two "bad" days here would be considered "good" days in Los Angeles, Hamilton County does not meet EPA standards for ozone attainment. The suburban areas, however, are much cleaner than the industrialized valley. In addition, Blue Ash's residential and light industrial parks are well separated.

In and Around Town

Roads and interstates: I-75, I-71, I-275, Cross County Highway.
Closest airports: Cincinnati-Northern Kentucky International Airport (35 min.), Blue Ash Airport (small commuter planes only).
Public transportation: Queen City Metro provides bus service between Blue Ash and downtown Cincinnati as well as to many suburban communities.
Avg. commute: 20 min. (to downtown Cincinnati). Thanks to the excellent highway system, it's just as easy to commute to Cincinnati as it is to travel locally on Reed Hartman Highway.

What Every Resident Knows

The city doesn't roll up the sidewalks at night because there aren't all that many. You'll find beautiful bike trails, but the "Big Wheels" set mostly rides in the streets or special trails. • Better not fake calling in sick. Since the hospitals are internationally known for having developed the oral polio vaccine, the Heimlich Maneuver, laser surgery, the heart-lung machine and other medical miracles, they'll find the cure for what ails you. • Blue ash trees are more like endangered species. Disease has wiped out all but 50. • It's not politics as usual here. Government runs smoothly, the 7 City Council Administrators actually like one another, and the same basic leadership has been in place for 20 years. You know what they say about not fixing what ain't broke!

FYI

Greater Cincinnati Chamber of Commerce (Northeast Branch)
9545 Kenwood Road, Suite 103
Blue Ash, OH 45242
513-891-8833

City of Blue Ash (Relocation info.)
4343 Cooper Road
Blue Ash, OH 45242
513-745-8500

Sycamore Messenger
8160 Corporate Park Dr., Suite 100
Cincinnati, OH 45242
513-489-6397

Northeast Suburban Life (weekly)
9121 Union Cemetery Road
Cincinnati, OH 45249
513-683-5115

Cincinnati Enquirer
213 Elm Street
Cincinnati, OH 45202
513-721-2700

West Shell Realtors
9600 Montgomery
Cincinnati, OH 45242
513-891-8500
Carolyn Lowitz, Bobbie Gold

Sibcy-Cline Realty, Inc.
4770 Cornell Road
Cincinnati, OH 45241
513-489-0066
Mary Bokon, Vice President, Sales

Cincinnati Gas & Electric
4th & Main Streets
Cincinnati, OH 45201
513-651-4466

Cincinnati Bell
201 E. 4th Street
Cincinnati, OH 45202
513-397-9900

School districts: 513-791-4848 (Sycamore), 513-771-8560 (Princeton). Contact Child Advocacy Center for special ed. programs, 513-381-2500
Property tax assessor: 513-632-8212
Northeast Welcomers: 513-247-0001
Interfaith Council: Contact the city for list of churches/synagogues.
Physician's referral: 513-745-1111 (Bethesda Hospital's Ask-a-Nurse).
Day-care referral: 513-891-1723

Bend, Oregon

Area Snapshot

Local population: 20,469
County: Deschutes　　**Population:** 74,958
U.S. region: Pacific Northwest/central Oregon
Closest metro areas: Eugene (126 mi. west), Portland (131 mi. northwest)
Median housing price: $92,000
Avg. household income: $30,859
Best reasons to live here: Scenic beauty on a grand scale, year-round recreation paradise, low crime, clean environment, strong buyer's market, growing economy, mild climate.

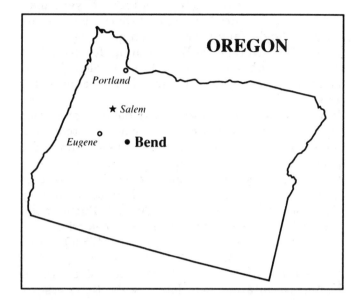

Fabulous Features

Small-town living has taken a bad rap over the years, mostly from big-city folks who think people shrivel up without steady diets of culture and cuisine. But in majestic Bend, nestled at the base of the Cascade Mountain Range, residents are thriving on steady diets of outrageous fun. Even through July you can ski Mt. Bachelor, rock climb at Crooked River Canyon, mountain bike through Swampy Lakes, salmon fish at Lake Chinook, river raft down the Deschutes. And then on Sunday's...

Of course, Mondays through Fridays aren't bad either. To start, the Bend-LaPine schools are brimming with outstanding teachers. Over the years, several have been recognized as Oregon's Teacher of the Year (one went on to win National Teacher of the Year). With beautiful new schools, strong ties to businesses and numerous program innovations, Bend proves that big cities didn't corner the market on quality education.

Speaking of the market, local realtors are busy as beavers since *U.S. News and World Report* discovered Bend was one of the 10 most desirable places to live (April 1990). That started an almost 7-percent increase a year in population (the county population zoomed by 170 percent between 1970-1990), and a boom in housing starts (an average of 250 residential building permits are issued each year, a phenomenal rate for a small town). And the word is, out-of-town buyers are like owls—wide eyed and always saying, "ooooh." The gorgeous new properties on 1-plus acres that sell for a song ($160,000 and up) are what gets 'em thinking.

What gets the checkbooks out are the convenient neighborhoods (this is a real "walk to" community—walk to schools, shopping, the parks, even work), perpetual sunshine (highest average of sunny days in Oregon), and the breathtaking scenery (a daily dose of mountain views, rivers, and frosted forests may be the only supplement you need). Add to that the progressive new City Commission, exciting growth in retail and high-tech firms and it's unlikely you'll see any shriveling here.

Possible drawbacks: Snow drifts melt. People drifts tend to linger. And unfortunately, job growth hasn't kept pace with the growing population (7-percent unemployment). Come with a job or business and you've got it made. • Here's a stock tip. Buy Kleenex. Frigid winters and high pollen counts in spring and summer have many residents never leaving home without it.

Real Estate

Market overview: It's turning into a buyer's market here. Prices are holding and there's more availability. Single family houses comprise 95% of the sales. The average SFH is selling for $105,319. Many new subdivisions have been developed in the last year. The avg. time a house is on the market is 143 days.

What houses look like: Most homes have wood exteriors, with stucco or brick more limited. Contemporary designs with vaulted, open ceilings are popular; 2-stories are the most common. Older houses (50-80 yrs.) downtown are chalets or cottage types, w/hardwood floors and detailed trimming. Expensive homes in exclusive Awbrey Butte neighborhood have tiled entries, brass and oak trim.

Starter homes: Prices begin at $75,000, and homes include 2BR/1½BA, and 1-car garage. Most are 1-story and built closely together. Most starter homes are in areas with lots of kids. Exteriors are made with wood siding and nicely landscaped. New homes are in "walk-in" condition. Check out Colvin Estates, Avelon Estates, Tamarack Park, East Brook Estates and Aspen Heights.

Trade-ups: $90,000-$150,000 buys a newer 3BR/2½BA, 1600 sq. ft., w/master suite and family room. These homes are found in Homestead, Pine Brook, Pauline Estates, and Starwood.

Luxury homes: For $250,000-$400,000, you get 3-4BR/2BA, 2200-3000 sq. ft, 2-3-car garage, scenic views, and large lot. Smaller homes come with multiple acreage. Homes feature open spaces and upscale decor, hardwood floors, plush carpeting, and tile and marble accents. Other extras include jacuzzis and skylights. Look at Broken Top, a new development w/homes at about $450,000.

Rental market: Apartments are rented before the newspaper hits the stand. 2BR/1BA go for $450-$550/mo., 3BR for $650-$725/mo., not including utilities. When available, SFHs are the same rates.

Great neighborhoods: Middle-class neighborhoods favored by families with kids (close to parks and schools) include Tanglewood, Tamarack Park, Tillicum, Homestead, and Deschutes River Woods. Although there are new subdivisions in Bend, there is an Urban Growth Boundary, which limits new construction.

Nearby areas to consider: Redmond, 16 mi. north, has a higher tax rate, but more affordable homes than Bend (new homes for as little as $53,000), and is showing strong industrial growth in its economy. Schools are also good. Sisters is a picture-postcard town. Houses are slightly more expensive. Children attend good schools.

What Things Cost

Runzheimer's Living Cost Index: Avg. annual costs for family of 4 with household income of $50,000: $48,146 (3.7% below avg. city).

ACCRA's national comparisons: Overall living costs are 6.1% above avg., with housing the culprit at 40.8% above avg. Health care costs are 6.8% above avg., and all other costs are below: Utilities (18%), groceries, transportation and goods and services 2%-3% below.

Utilities: Phone: Hookup: $12; Service: $17/mo. Gas: $63/mo. for 3BR. Electric: $50-$70/mo. in summer, $85-$150/mo. in winter, for 3BR on avg.

Kid care: Full-time at day-care center: $145-$150/wk.; at-home care: $115-$120/wk. There are 17 childcare centers, but only 1 takes infants and toddlers (2½ years and older). There are 250-300 non-licensed home providers. **Pediatric visit:** $50-$65.

The Tax Ax

Sales tax: None.

Property tax: $17.415 per $1,000 assessed valuation, which is 100% of market value. For example, property tax on a $60,000 house is $1,045.

State income tax: Married filing jointly pay $620 on the first $10,000 of taxable income and 9% on anything above that. For example, $25,000 of taxable income would be liable for $1,970 in state taxes.

Climate

Elevation 3,600'	Avg. High/Low	Avg. Rain (Inches)	Avg. Snow (Inches)	Avg. Days Rain	Avg. % Humidity
Jan.	41/21	.8	12.3	8	68
April	57/28	.3	2.3	8	35
July	82/44	.3	--	5	21
Oct.	63/31	.7	.2	8	37
YEAR	60/31	7.5	40.2	110	42
# of days 32° or below: 196			# of days 90° or above: 13		

In Oregon's interior section, temperature ranges are quite varied within 24-hour periods. Daytime temps are mostly mild, but evenings get downright chilly. Spring and fall are dry and sunny. Winters see an average 40" of snow. Rainfall is moderate with the Cascade Mountains squeezing out moisture from Pacific storm systems.

Earning a Living

Economic outlook: Central Oregon continues to make a slow recovery from the recession, although the unemployment rate has risen to 7.2%. This is not so much from job losses as much as newcomers who aren't employed yet. The greatest boost to the economy is coming from motor home, R&D, custom window and doors and recreation equipment industries. The lumber industry is depressed (massive layoffs have occurred), but this area is better off than most because the emphasis is on producing wood products, not harvesting timber. A new City Commission is in place that is very pro-growth. Aggressive action to recruit more industry will eventually create the needed jobs.

Where the jobs are: The primary industries are wood products, agriculture, and tourism and recreation. The top 10 employers are Bend Millwork Systems; St. Charles Medical Center; Bend/LaPine School District; Bright Wood Corp.; Mt. Bachelor Ski Area; Sunriver Resort/Properties; Warm Springs Tribal Govt.; State of Oregon; Clear Pine Mouldings, Inc.; and Deschutes County. Although Bend is a lumber-producing area, more than 80% of jobs are in retail and services. Lake-tronics (electronics) has opened a manufacturing facility. Grow Tools (manufacturer of environmental controls for greenhouses) is planning to relocate to Bend in the next few months, adding another 100 jobs (management, clerical, technical).

Business opportunities: Bend is a major resort area, with three year-round destination resorts nearby and others planned. In addition, there are several ski resorts. Businesses that serve the tourist industry, as well as restaurants, sporting goods and other specialty stores should do well, especially with the population growth. Also, with many retirees moving here, services for seniors are needed. The Central Oregon Economic Development Council, Inc., has targeted information technologies, communications equipment, medical instruments, environmental sciences, aviation/aerospace and recreational equipment as industries to bring to the area. To improve access, the region's major airport (in Redmond), is undergoing extensive expansion.

"You can quote me on that"

"Bend is the most beautiful part of the country. Particularly at night, when you're on Mt. Bachelor, looking down and seeing the lights twinkling, you think they are stars. It's a homey, happy place."—B.P.

Making the Grade

Public education overview: Bend's excellent academic reputation is based on its philosophy that the curriculum meet the needs of all students, and that parental and community support is required for success. For example, the Student Discount Program for Academic Achievement is a community effort by the Bend-LaPine Schools and participating businesses to recognize and reward academic effort by students in grades 6-12. The high school Century Club is a business partnership between students and the Chamber of Commerce. Students receive credit and payment for working for local companies. District teachers have received awards such as national and state Teacher of the Year and the prestigious Milken Award for excellence in teaching. Two new elementary and 1 junior high school are under construction. Elementary school classes are large, 25-30 students per class, and the upper grades have 30-35 students per class.

Class size: 35:1.

Help for working parents: There is no formal early drop-off program, although private day-care centers coordinate with parents' needs. There is a "child-time after school" program, sponsored by the Parks and Recreation Dept., which supervises children up to 6 p.m.

Blue Ribbon School Awards: North Bend High School ('86-'87).

School year: Starts around Labor Day and ends early June. Children must be 5 before Sept. 1 to enter kindergarten.

Special education/gifted programs: Mainstreaming special education children is emphasized through pull-out programs and special tutoring one-on-one programs. The Educational Resource Center serves learning-disabled students who can be mainstreamed into regular classes. There are specialized facilities for the more handicapped, such as Larsen Learning Center for emotional and more severe physical handicaps, and Cascade Child Center for emotionally disturbed children. The Talented and Gifted (TAG) program offers opportunities for children in grades K-12 in reading/English and mathematics in their home schools, as well as self-contained TAG classrooms (located at Bear Creek Elementary for grades 4-5, and Cascade Junior High for grade 6). The schools have an Early Intervention program to assist families with children with developmental problems (infancy to 5).

Nearby colleges/universities: Central Oregon Community College (offers some 4-yr. programming); The University of Oregon in Eugene is a 2½ hr. drive through a mountain pass.

Medical Care

Hospitals/medical centers: Top-notch professionals and superb facilities are the hallmark of Bend's health care system. St. Charles Medical Center (181 beds) offers 145 physicians in specialties such as radiation, oncology, neurology, neurosurgery, open-heart surgery, radiology, urology, pathology, emergency medicine, rehabilitative medicine, family practice, cardiology, dermatology, orthopedics, psychiatry and men's and women's health services. A new trauma center and upgraded intensive care unit have recently been completed.

Specialized care: Central Oregon Family Support Program relieves stress faced by families who have a member with developmental disabilities; Children's Dental Clinic; Healthy Start Prenatal Service; WIC (health/nutrition program for pregnant women); Rimrock Trails Adolescent Treatment Center (substance abuse); Ponderosa Treatment Center (alcohol and drug dependency). St. Charles Medical Center has a pediatric physiatrician, a relatively new type of specialist who works with children needing physical rehabilitation.

Crime & Safety

Bend has a low crime rate for a city its size. While arrests on minor crimes were up 14% and on major crime 22%, this reflects the growth of the general urban community. The Bend Police Department is a full-service department with 37 officers. Policemen-on-the-beat are becoming a common sight. Community lectures and programs on security, residential theft prevention and personal assault prevention are given regularly by the staff. Police also work with schoolchildren on safety issues. The community supports the police, and city government is very responsive, voting for funding to provide needed equipment and crime prevention programs.

Community Life

In addition to the Salvation Army and Red Cross, Bend also has: Bend Aid, an assistance program for low-income working families; St. Vincent de Paul Community Service Center, emergency services for local disaster; Family Kitchen, food and shelter for the homeless; COBRA (Central Oregon Battering and Rape Alliance) shelter and support groups for women and children; COCAAN (Central Oregon Community Action Agency Network) shelter for the unemployed; and Together for Children, a 9-month educational program designed to help inform care givers about the special needs of children up to 3 yrs. Many parents volunteer at the local schools.

Let the Good Times Roll

Family fun: Within a short drive are a variety of outdoor environments. Lava Butte (Lava Lands Visitor Center) is a unique volcanic cone with a paved road to the top providing an outstanding view of the Cascades. Deschutes Historical Center, Pine Mountain Observatory, Reindeer Ranch, and Sunriver Nature Center are also of interest. There are 25 developed city parks and overnight camping at Tumalo State and La Pine State Parks. To the west of Bend are the Cascade Mountains—the Three Sisters peaks are about 40 miles distant. The Pacific Crest National Scenic Trail (footpath running from Mexico to Canada) passes through the area, with many opportunities for hiking. To the east is the high desert region, the beautiful, arid region between the Cascades and the Rockies. Crater Lake National Park is only about 2½ hours south, and Mt. Hood is about the same distance north. The area enjoys one of longest ski seasons in North America. Mt. Bachelor is rated one of 5 best U.S. ski areas by *Snow Country Magazine.*

Sports: Professional sports are represented by the Bend Rockies (baseball), an A farm team of the brand-new National League Colorado Rockies. They play from June-Sept. at the Vince Genna Stadium.

Arts & entertainment: The Community Theater of the Cascades, and the Magic Circle Theater provide plays and entertainment year-round. Concerts are held outdoors at Drake Park during good weather. The Deschutes Historical Center features permanent exhibits on logging and pioneering, and a one-room schoolhouse. The High Desert Museum, near the Deschutes National Forest, is a combination natural and cultural museum featuring Native American artifacts and exhibits, live animal presentations and living history presentations. The Cascade Festival of Music is a summer festival that includes jazz and classical music.

Annual events: Oregon Winter Special and Junior Championship Olympics (March); Riverhouse Golf Tournament (May); Cascade Festival of Music-Summer Concerts Series (June); Bend Summer Festival (July); Cascade Children's Festival (July); Halloween Ghost Train and Oktoberfest (Oct.); Christmas Parade Weekend (Dec.); Pole, Pedal, Paddle race (May).

"You can quote me on that"

"I've been very happy in Bend. It's so much less hectic and down to earth than California. I love getting involved in all the outdoor recreation"— A.S.

The Environment

Bend's unparalleled scenic beauty in large part reflects the city's commitment to environmental concerns. Bend municipal water is of exceptional quality, for example. It exceeds EPA standards in all categories. Air quality, however, is close to nonattainment because of woodburning stoves and carbon monoxide emissions from cars. The community has a citizen-based clean air committee focusing on the problem. A new transportation corridor currently on the drawing board may lessen the problem. Bend Recycling is in charge of a voluntary monthly curbside recycling program. Area residents are asked to recycle newspaper, milk jugs, glass, tin cans and cardboard. They have received numerous certificates of achievement from the state for their educational programs.

In and Around Town

Roads and interstates: U.S. 97 runs north-south; U.S. 20 runs east-west.
Closest airports: Bend Municipal Airport (5.5 mi. northeast); Redmond Municipal Airport (16 mi. north); and Sunriver Resort Airport (17 mi. south).
Public transportation: Bus system is available for senior citizens. Bend is beginning to think about expanding the system.
Avg. commute: 20 min.

What Every Resident Knows

If you thought walking and chewing gum at the same time was tough, you'll really be impressed with the tots in Bend. They learn to walk and ski at the same time! Why waste all those good years in the playpen when it could be happy trails? • The biggest gripe about newcomers is they botch the pronunciation of Oregon. To be accepted with open arms, say *ory-gun.* • Forget McDonalds. Move to Bend and you'll be feasting on "buffalo burgers." This, after all, was where the recipe was perfected.
• Most outsiders think that the whole state of Oregon is deluged with rain. Due to its high desert location, Bend enjoys sunshine and dry spells year-round.

FYI

Bend Chamber of Commerce
63085 N. Hwy. 97
Bend, OR 97701
503-382-3221

The Bulletin
1526 NW Hill Street
Bend, OR 97701
503-382-1811

*The Small Town Observer
P.O. Box 324
Bend, OR 97709
800-535-8853

Economic Development Council
63085 N. Highway 97, #105
Bend, OR 97701
503-388-3236

Linda Blankenship Real Estate Co.
2106 NE Fourth Street
Bend, OR 97701
503-388-2236
Natalka Merrill

Pacific Power and Light
P.O. Box 1209
Bend, OR 97709
503-382-1011

Cascade Natural Gas Co.
P.O. Box 5399
Bend, OR 97708
503-382-6464

U.S. West Communications
503-382-3494

School district: 503-385-5201
Property tax assessor:
503-388-6508
Newcomer's Club: 503-382-4289
Interfaith Council: 503-548-6246
Day-care referral: 503-385-6753

*Excellent quarterly publication about relocating to Bend and other small towns in the U.S.

Eugene, Oregon

Area Snapshot

Local population: 117,155
County: Lane   **Population:** 282,912
U.S. region: Center of Western Oregon
Closest metro area: Portland (100 mi. south)
Median housing price: $82,894
Avg. household income: $22,972
Best reasons to live here: Delightful year-round climate, attractive, affordable housing, outstanding recreation, excellent schools and health care, close proximity to the ocean and mountains, many growing industries, laid back lifestyle, popular college town.

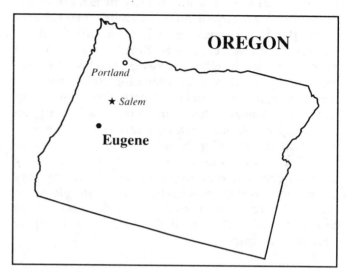

Fabulous Features

Eugene's past is characteristic of a favorite relative who has seen hard times but managed to bounce back. For generations, lumber was the life support of the city, only to become the industry that environmentalists beat to a pulp. The '90s have been kinder and gentler to this pristine Willamette Valley, thanks to a newly diversified economy and residents who cried, "This place is too nice to write off!" With a moderate year-round climate and lush surroundings, the city is owned by former fast-trackers who needed resuscitation.

With the Pacific Ocean an hour to the west, the Cascade Mountains an hour to the east, the outdoor action "de-hypers" everyone. Stress relief also comes from moderate living costs. Spiraling housing prices of the '80s are now in line with other parts of Oregon, with super contemporary homes from the $90s to the $150s (spend $200+, but only if you must).

And as a progressive college town, public education takes a back seat to nothing! The schools consistently earn top grades (three President's Awards for Excellence and numerous state honors for teachers and principals) and are best known for multi-cultural innovations (elementary schools have Japanese, French and Spanish immersion programs).

Success in recruiting food packaging, computers/software and medical equipment manufacturers has painted a bright picture for the economy (the $18.3 million dollar expansion of Mahlon Sweet Airport will be another huge boost). With low violent crime, excellent health care (Eugene was identified as one of the 10 best cities in which to get sick) and phenomenal recreation (fishing, white-water rafting and skiing are great diversions), Eugene is like that resiliant uncle who's on the comback trail, big time!

Possible drawbacks: Eugene isn't likely to win a clean air award in the near future. Between winter air inversions, particle build-up from wood-burning stoves and veneer drying, some days don't meet EPA standards. • The job market is highly competitive, and even with the growing business base, those who come without a job could find that they are the only ones reviewing their resumes.

"You can quote me on that"

"We enjoy a very friendly and diverse community. The schools here are very good. Best of all we're only an hour away from the ocean and an hour from the mountains."—P.Y.

Real Estate

Market overview: Eugene has been declared a buyer's market after many years of seller's reaping giant profits from California's "equity immigrants" (house-rich Californians came and bought anything with a front door, driving prices way up and inventory way down). What changed the picture was the Savings and Loan crisis, which affected both the mortgage market and commercial loans. New construction has slowed and makes up 20% of total inventory. Still, housing prices and property taxes are low enough to entice out-of-town buyers.

What houses look like: Newer homes are spacious and airy with skylights, windows, and lots of natural woods. Contemporary and ranch styles are predominant. Newer houses also show island kitchens opening out into the family room with a breakfast bar. Master suites with jacuzzi and garden tubs are popular.

Starter homes: Resales 10 years old can go for $70,000, and offer 3BR, 1½BA (few 2BA), family rooms, 1-car garage or car port. Older homes have more costly electric ceiling heat. $80,000 buys a 3BR/2BA resale. Many starter homes are in Lynnbrook II, a large development in the north.

Trade-ups: These range from the $90s-$150s. At the lower end, you get 1100 sq. ft., 3BR/2BA, 2-car garage, vaulted ceilings and skylights. $125,000 buys a new home with 1800 sq. ft., a 65 x 100 lot, 3BR/2BA, family room, 2-car garage, master BR and formal living and dining room. For $150,000, you get a new energy-efficient home, with as much as 1800 sq. ft. on a 70 x 100 lot, 3BR, 2BA, 2-car garage with jacuzzi, master suite and cathedral ceilings. Look at River Hills and West Springfield.

Luxury homes: For $200,000, you get a large resale or a new home with 2-3 skylights, fireplace, 2400 sq. ft., 4BR/3BA, extra-large den, 2-car garage, hardwood floors, and jacuzzi. $400,000 buys a luxurious new custom-built home with custom kitchen, fireplace, exercise room, tile floors, jacuzzi, skylights, 4BR/3BA on ½-¾ acre. Large lots are hard to find. Somerset Hills is a desirable location.

Rental market: Single-family homes are tough to find because the rental vacancy is less than 1%. 2-3BR apartments are available for $350-$1,000/mo.

Great neighborhoods: The Hills area attracts families—it's very affordable, and stays cool in the summer. School districts are said to be outstanding.

Nearby areas to consider: Cottage Grove (20 mi. south), is affordable for young families, with good schools and a small-town atmosphere. Springfield (5 min. from downtown) is an ideal commute. Schools are great, and nice residential areas are affordable.

What Things Cost

Runzheimer's Living Cost Index: Avg. annual costs for family of 4 with household income of $50,000: $49,971 (.1% below avg. city).

ACCRA's national comparisons: Overall living costs are .3% above national avg. You'll save money on utilities (30% below avg.) and groceries (8.5% below avg.), but housing and health care (15.5% and 22.6% above avg. respectively) take a bigger bite out of the budget. Goods and services are an estimated 1% above avg.

Utilities: Phone: Installation $12-$25. $20/mo. plus long-distance. Electric: Avg. $90/mo. Gas: Avg. $45-$50/mo. Water: Avg. $67/mo.

Kid care: Day-care avg. $285/mo. for toddlers, $405/mo. for infants. In-home care tends to be less expensive, and many sources are available through day-care referral assistance. **Pediatric visit:** $60.

The Tax Ax

Sales tax: None.

Property tax: Ranges from $10-$27 per $1,000 of assessed value depending on the district. In 1990, the state passed Ballot Measure 5, which will phase in property tax reductions; by 1993, taxes will not exceed $15 per $1,000 of assessed value.

State income tax: Married couples filing jointly pay $620 on the first $10,000 and 9% on anything above. For example $15,000 of taxable income would be $620 plus 9% on the additional $5,000 ($450) for a total of $1,070.

Climate

Elevation 420'	Avg. High/Low	Avg. Rain (Inches)	Avg. Snow (Inches)	Avg. Days Rain	Avg. % Humidity
Jan.	46/33	7.1	4.7	16	80
April	61/39	2.3	--	13	57
July	83/51	.3	--	2	37
Oct.	64/42	4	--	11	63
YEAR	63/42	41	7.2	100	60
# of days 32° or below: 55			# of days 90° or above: 14		

Although located in a river valley 50 miles east of the Pacific Ocean, Eugene still has a marine climate. Summer temperatures rarely exceed 90 (days are fairly dry) and there is seldom bitterly cold weather (Cascade Mountains block Arctic air masses). The mountains get ample rain and snow, but Eugene, at a much lower elevation, misses any extreme downpours.

Earning a Living

Economic outlook: While traditionally a lumber and agricultural-based economy, Eugene has enjoyed more diversity, which has served to stabilize the economy and help it to grow at a moderate rate. Further growth is expected from the food pro-ducts, printing and publishing, computer software development, electronics, equipment manufacturing and metal fabrication industries. Eugene's unemployment rate has held in the 5 1/2% range during 1991, reinforcing local confidence. In the past five years within the Willamette Valley, Kyotaru has built a food packaging and international distribution facility; Molecular Probes, the largest biotechnology company in the state, has expanded 3 times; Computer Memory Disk, manufacturer and supplier of hard disks, has completed a $3.4 million expansion; Mitsubishi Steel has completed its $55 million silicon wafer manufacturing plant expansion; Hewlett-Packard added a $100 million clean room; Willamette Industries has completed a $60 million plant upgrade; OREMET has implemented a $25 million plant upgrade; and Oregon Freeze Dry has undergone an $11 million expansion.

Where the jobs are: Forest products account for 80% of exports in Lane County, the country's lumber capital. The industry will continue to play a significant role in the area's economy, as more than 60 firms produce secondary wood products. But the numbers employed in this industry are down, reflecting continued expansion in other industries. More than 30 food processing companies have relocated here to take advantage of fresh local products. Continued aggressive expansion and diversification is expected with the construction of Riverfront Research Park, a 67-acre site adjacent to the University of Oregon campus. This area will be zoned for research and development, data processing, computer software development and other hi-tech businesses. Software is expected to be the industry of the future in Eugene. There are currently more than 130 such companies in the area. The $18.3 million expansion of Mahlon Sweet airport is also expected to give the economy a boost.

Business opportunities: The Eugene Area Chamber of Commerce, working with the Business Assistance Team, provides information and assistance to new or relocating small businesses. With so many new companies relocating or expanding, there is a need for service/support businesses, such as data processing, advertising and marketing and even messenger services.

Making the Grade

Public education overview: The Midwestern Research Institute ranked Oregon fifth in the nation for its quality of education in public schools and for the fact that students consistently rate second in the nation in SAT scores (Eugene's students consistently rate above the state average). Three President's Awards for excellence have been awarded within the district. Per student expenditure is approximately $5,200. Students have achieved mean scores in the upper 70th percentile nationally in all grade levels and subjects, and 83% of graduates go to college or post-graduate education. Teacher and staff awards include: Principal of the Year award from the Oregon Association of Secondary School Administrators; Foreign Language Teacher of the Year in Oregon; Community Educator of the Year; The district has a Multicultural Educational Specialist who provides training for teachers in a multicultural perspective. There are programs offered in grades K-5 for French, Spanish and Japanese bilingual education. Several schools, from elementary to high school offer language immersion programs. International High School has 2 campuses here, accredited by the renowned Swiss International Baccalaureate program. Students specialize in at least 1 foreign language while studying the histories and cultures of other nations. Arts-In-Education Program brings visual artists, performers and writers to elementary, middle and high schools.

Class size: 22:1 elementary; 30:1 high school.

Help for working parents: Creative Care, the largest latchkey program in the state, provides before- and after-school care for elementary children and, in some schools, all-day care for kindergarten.

Blue Ribbon School Awards: Monroe Middle School ('83-'84), Marist High School ('84-'85).

School year: Begins after Labor Day and ends the middle of June. Children must be 5 on or before Sept. 1 to enter kindergarten.

Special education/gifted programs: Talented and Gifted program offers attention to identified students through high school, providing activities matching each student's level of learning. There are special education programs for a variety of levels. The district is also piloting 2 integrated kindergartens that mainstream special education children into the classroom setting.

Nearby colleges/universities: The University of Oregon and Oregon State University (Corvallis) are Oregon's major research institutions and anchor the state's Southern Williamette Research Corridor. Lane Community College was rated among the top five community colleges.

Medical Care

Hospitals/medical centers: Sacred Heart General Hospital has a cancer care unit and a heart center equipped with the latest medical technology. McKenzie-Willamette Hospital is a full-care facility and provides pulmonary care, cardiology, oncology, vascular and neurosurgery. Eugene Clinic and Hospital provides acute, comprehensive medical care.

Specialized care: Eugene Hearing and Speech Center (offers diagnostic testing and therapy for hearing and/or speech disorders); Oregon Heart Center and Oregon Rehabilitation Center (associated with Sacred Heart General Hospital); Sacred Heart Adolescent Recovery Program—regional center for education, prevention and treatment of adolescent chemical dependency.

Crime & Safety

The metropolitan area is covered by city, county and state law enforcement agencies. The crime rate is below the national average, especially for crimes against persons. Violent crime is slim (2 homicides a year on average). This is because of an innovative police force and active neighborhood associations. However, property crimes are slightly higher than average. The Police Dept. has nationally recognized programs in community policing efforts, such as the Community Response Team, made up of uniformed police officers, mental health professionals, drug treatment people and the Parks & Recreation Dept. There's a high-profile bicycle patrol team and some foot patrols. The high schools have uniformed officers for youth relations. Eugene has an active Block Home program—safe havens for children walking to and from school.

Community Life

Eugene is a place with a lot of things going for it, and the residents take pride in its beauty, its variety, and its relaxed setting. This pride particularly comes out in the community spirit of Eugene. The residents appreciate the tempo of their city so much, they host The Eugene Celebration—a three-day festival, each September. Families love the unique fun: bed races and typewriter throws are favorites. The local Rotary Clubs host the annual Duck Race, where 30,000 rubber ducks are released in a river. There's a mad scramble to catch them as they cross the finish line. The proceeds go to such causes as the prevention of child abuse. The Lions Club and a number of other civic groups host fund raisers throughout the year.

Let the Good Times Roll

Family fun: Eugene's 50 developed parks covering 1,600 acres contain picnic areas, open play spaces, jogging trails, bike paths, 4 community centers, 2 senior centers, 1 outdoor pool, 2 indoor pools, 8 wading pools, an outdoor amphitheater, 19 athletic fields and 22 tennis courts. There are more than 60 miles of bike paths, 11 golf courses, bowling alleys and a roller skating rink. The Kidsports program organizes athletic activities for youngsters interested in after-school training and competition. Each year, 10,000 kids participate in volleyball, basketball, soccer, football, baseball, tennis and softball. The white water of the McKenzie River or the Willamette River provide excellent fishing, rafting and canoeing. Numerous local streams and lakes offer some of the finest sports fishing in the Northwest. At Fern Ridge Lake, 12 miles west of Eugene, you can swim, sail and water-ski. Hiking trails and a backpacking area are found along the ridgelines of the city and in the nearby Cascade Mountains. Just 90 minutes away, hiking, camping and picnicking abound in the Willamette and Siuslaw National Forests. Museums include: Willamette Science and Technology Center; University of Oregon Art Museum; University of Oregon Natural History Museum; Lane County Historical Museum; Maude Kerns Art Center; Oregon Aviation and Space Museum; Siuslaw Pioneer Museum.

Sports: Hayward Field hosts national and international track and field events. World-class track and field events reflect the many professional track and field athletes who reside in the Eugene area. Civic Stadium is home to the Eugene Emeralds, a Class-A pro baseball team. There's also a semi-professional ice hockey team, the Eugene Blues.

Arts & entertainment: Hult Center of the Performing Arts, a 2,500-seat civic center complex; Silva Concert Hall, featuring the Eugene Symphony, the Eugene Ballet Company and Eugene Opera Company; Autzen Stadium seats 40,000 for city sports and cultural events, including the Eugene Concert Choir, Eugene Festival of Musical Theatre, Oregon Bach Festival, Oregon Children's Choir; Eugene Jazz Co.; Actors Cabaret/Mainstage Theatre; University Theatre; Lane Community Center for the Performing Arts; Cottage Theatre, Inc.; and Very Little Theatre.

Annual events: Eugene Oktoberfest (Sept.); Oregon Bach Festival, attracts 30,000 participants (June); Eugene Celebration (Sept.); Lane County Fair (Aug.); Doll and Toy Festival (Nov.); Eugene Pro Rodeo (Sept.); Mid-Winter Square & Round Dance Festival (Jan.).

The Environment

Oregonians pride themselves on their environment. Clean air and clean water are an integral part of their lives and outlook. Recycling is encouraged, with regular weekly pickups. There are relatively low acid levels in the rainfall. Sewage treatment is an important concern. The Metropolitan Waste-water Management Commission, an intergovernmental agency, has constructed a sewage facility to serve the Eugene-Springfield metropolitan area. The air quality can be poor for anyone with respiratory problems. Eugene is in a valley, and air, with industrial pollutants, can get trapped here. Natural allergans, pollens, spores and molds can also make things very uncomfortable for those with allergy problems.

In and Around Town

Roads and interstates: I-5 (north-south). State Highways 58 and 99 connect with the Eugene metropolitan areas. State Highway 126 provides convenient access west to the coast and east to the mountains and Central Oregon.

Closest airport: Mahlon Sweet Airport (9 miles northwest of the city).

Public transportation: The Lane Transit District provides scheduled bus service for the Eugene/Springfield metropolitan service area.

Avg. commute: 20-25 min.

What Every Resident Knows

Get your running shoes ready. Eugene is known as the "running capital of the world," not just for the great races but also for famous residents, track stars Mary Slaney and Alberto Salazar. In fact, some say this was where the term "weekend warrior" came into being. For years, the amateur athletes, joggers, bikers and hikers have been taking over the town trying to stay in shape. • Wearing jeans to the opera or a fine restaurant is no big deal. With a large mix of hippies, yuppies, "dinks" (dual income, no kids) and retirees, being laid-back and unpretentious are the unwritten laws. What you wear is strictly up to you. People are just glad you came.

FYI

Eugene Area Chamber of Commerce
1401 Willamette Street
P.O. Box 1107
Eugene, OR 97440
503-484-1314

Eugene/Springfield Convention & Visitors Bureau
305 W. 7th Avenue
Eugene, OR 97401
503-484-5307

Eugene/Springfield Metropolitan Partnership Inc.
P.O. Box 10398
Eugene, OR 97440
503-686-2741

The Register-Guard
975 High Street
Eugene, OR 97401
503-485-1234

Breeden Brothers Realty Co.
366 East 40th Street
Eugene, OR 97405
503-686-9431
David C. McJunkin, Sales Associate

Keystone Real Estate
1501 N. 18th Street
Suite 100
Springfield, OR 97477
503-746-1233
Susan Rasmussen, Owner

Northwest Natural Gas Co.
790 Goodpasture Island Road
Eugene, OR 97401
503-342-3661

U.S. West Communications
272 Country Club Road
Eugene, OR 97401
503-484-7770

Eugene Water and Electric Board
P.O. Box 10148
Eugene, OR 97440
503-484-2411

Small Business Development Center
Lane Community College
1059 Willamette Street
Eugene, OR 97401
503-726-2255

School district: 503-687-3123
Property tax assessor: 503-687-4170
Newcomer's Club: 503-744-0936
Physician's referral: 503-686-7000
Day care referral: 503-726-3954

Milwaukie, Oregon (Portland)

Area Snapshot

Local population: 18,830
County: Clackamas **Population:** 279,500
U.S. region: Pacific Northwest
Closest metro area: Portland (Borders on the south)
Median housing price: $97,400
Avg. household income: $30,111
Best reasons to live here: Clean environment, good schools, scenic beauty, abundance of health care services, variety of cultural and visual arts, growing economy, excellent transportation.

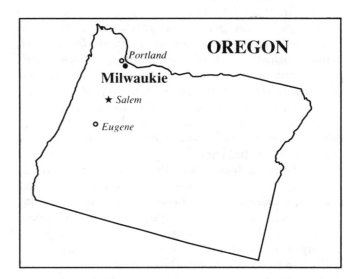

Fabulous Features

Whatever happened to the kids from high school who defied the dress code and organized sit-ins? You'll probably find them in Portland (only now they own restaurants, program computers and have families). No fools were they to settle where it was tranquil but cosmopolitan, clean but prosperous, gorgeous but affordable.

Above all, this area guarantees vigorous, year-round recreation or your money back! In spite of the population boom, (the county grew 27.3% in 10 years), Portland is still one of the best areas of the country to work and play. Rapid growth in high technology, international trade, retail (10 malls opened in 1990), and film/TV production (600 commercials have been filmed here) are propelling the economy.

When it's T.G.I.F., head 80 miles to the ocean or 70 miles to Mount Hood (the only year-round skiing in the U.S.). Or, stay and windsurf on the Columbia River Gorge, hike the wilderness in Forest Park, attend the Oregon Symphony, or root for the champion Trail Blazers!

As for where to hang your gear, a special "family" town is the Milwaukie-Gladstone area.

It's an older, revitalized community with award-winning schools (emphasis on science and technology). The district sends the most students to the Odyssey of the Mind competition than any other in the U.S. And SAT scores are 17 points higher than the state average.

Housing is eclectic and reasonable (from $60,000-$250,000+) and the commute to Portland is more a joy ride (20 min.). Today's Portland is much like the anti-establishment crowd that converged here. Smart but feisty!

Possible drawbacks: FBI statistics show rising crime (murder up 61% last year). Police say rates are still well below the national average. Levels of concern vary depending on where you moved from. • Oregon's Measure 5 (property taxes shall not exceed $15 per $1,000 assessed value), will reduce school-directed dollars in 1993. The fallout is anyone's guess. • The rain in Spain is at least seasonal. Here, the gray skies and drizzle are like a boomerang (just when you think they're gone, they're back)!

"You can quote me on that"

"We moved here from California and really enjoy the area. The clean air and invigorating environment has meant a lot to our active family. We love being outdoors. We also found the people to be very friendly and interested in any type of family activities. That's probably why our transition was a smooth one."—J.C.

Real Estate

Market overview: Realtors are accustomed to buyers in shock ("I can't believe I'm going to have a mortgage!"), but getting great values softens the blow. SFHs are appreciating at about 5% a year, unlike other areas of the country. There aren't many new homes (40-50 built per year) as Milwaukie is well-developed. But plenty of new construction is going up outside city limits. There was a push to incorporate these areas, but it hasn't happened. Custom-built homes and developments are being constructed rapidly.

What houses look like: Pre-1975 homes tend to be bungalows and ranches with single-car garages. Post-1975 homes are split-levels (called tri-levels), Victorians, saltboxes, and gables, with traditional floor plans. In newer homes, jacuzzis are popular, as are European kitchens, decks, and master BR suites. Exteriors are mostly cedar and other wood. Lots tend to be small (greater Portland area is trying to increase density to decrease sprawl). Due to hilly topography, homes may be on slopes and have little yard space.

Starter homes: For $50s-$80s, you can get a resale requiring work, 1000 sq. ft. ranch, 2-3BR/1BA, a 50 x 100 lot, with or without basement. Exteriors are pine or clapboard.

Trade-ups: $80s-$120s will buy an older 1200-1700 sq. ft. home with 3BR, 2BA, 2-car garage, family room, and 80 x 120 lot. Exteriors are almost always wood—pine or cedar are common.

Luxury homes: In the $125s-$250s, you'll find 2200+ sq. ft., 2-stories, 1 or more fireplaces, master BR suites and 2-3BRs, 2 or 3-car garages, jacuzzis, modern kitchens, dens and extra rooms. Exteriors tend to be stone facade or oak. Contemporary designs tend to be cedar.

Rental market: 3BR/2BA SFHs are available for $900/mo. 2-3BR apts. with great amenities go for $500-600/mo. Condo rentals are scarce.

Great neighborhoods: Sunnyside (east of Clackamas Town Center) is very popular for trade-ups. The Alder Crest Road appeals to affluent buyers. Westwood and Lake Road areas are family-oriented neighborhoods with top-quality homes. Hawthorne is a small, off-beat neighborhood filled with shops and older, charming and affordable homes.

Nearby areas to consider: Oregon City in the Willamette Valley is the state's farming region with many developments and a wide-open feeling. Vancouver, the metro area in Washington state just across the Columbia River, has lower land prices and property taxes. Gladstone has a number of pre-1900 Victorian homes.

What Things Cost

Runzheimer's Living Cost Index: Avg. annual costs for family of 4 with household income of $50,000: $52,218 (4.4% above avg.).

ACCRA's national comparisons: Overall living costs in the Portland metro are 8.1% above the national avg. because of housing and health care, (an estimated 32.5% and 25.9% above the national avg. respectively). On the other hand, utilities are 28% below the national avg. Food as well as goods and services are slightly above avg. (1%-3%).

Utilities: Phone: Unlimited flat rate: $22.50; $12 hookup. Gas and electric: $90/mo. (Jan.); $55/mo. (April); $70/mo. (July); $55/mo. (Oct.).

Kid care: Day-care centers: $165/wk. At-home day care: $100/wk. Day care is widely available.

Pediatric visit: $35-$40.

The Tax Ax

Sales tax: None.

Property tax: In November 1990, Oregon passed Measure 5, which will phase in property tax reductions so that by 1993 property taxes will not exceed $15 per $1,000 of assessed value. On a $100,000 home, taxes would be $1,500.

State income tax: Married filing jointly pay $620 on the first $10,000 of taxable income and 9% on anything above that. For example, $25,000 of taxable income would be liable for $1,970 in state taxes ($620 on the first $10,000 + 9% of balance.)

Climate

Elevation 20'	Avg. High/Low	Avg. Rain (Inches)	Avg. Snow (Inches)	Avg. Days Rain	Avg. % Humidity
Jan.	44/33	5.5	4	18	76
April	60/41	2.2	--	14	55
July	79/55	.5	--	3	45
Oct.	63/45	3.6	--	13	64
YEAR	62/44	30.9	7.2	151	60

# of days 32° or below: 43	# of days 90° or above: 10

The Portland area has a mild climate with comfortable humidity. The annual average precipitation of about 38 inches is high, but not as wet as the Cascades. However, an avg. 165 days a year have some precipitation, and 220 days are "cloudy."

Earning a Living

Economic outlook: The boom years of 1989-1991 are over (35,000 jobs a year were added), but the area is still enjoying a boomlet (7,000-10,000 jobs a year) of growth. Unemployment in July 1992 was 6.4%, up from 4.9% a year before, but still more than a point below national rates. High-tech, health services and medical technology, and trucking are the big growth areas. It's also helpful having a varied economy, not dependent on one major employer or sector.

Where the jobs are: Manufacturing is soft, reflecting the national economy, with little or no net job growth. Construction and services have contributed most to the job increases. Recent construction projects have included the $85 million Oregon Convention Center, the three-block downtown mixed-use (retail and office space) area, a museum complex for the Oregon Museum of Science and Industry, 6-8 new hotels built with more on the way. Business services (accounting, legal, and data processing) remain strong. Also health services are growing as hospitals continue to expand. Freightliner Trucking is undergoing an $8 million expansion of its R&D offices (adding 100 jobs). Nike will be adding another 500-1,000 jobs and Delta Airlines added 85,000 sq. ft to their cargo warehouse, doubling its capacity at the airport. National retailers are entering the area, including Tandy (opening an electronics superstore) as are national supermarkets and discounters.

Business opportunities: The tax situation is favorable for business, and utilities are plentiful and affordable. Workers in the area are generally well-educated, with almost half having a college education. In urban areas, office and factory space have low vacancy rates, with more availability in the suburbs. More than 6 million sq. ft. of retail space has been added since 1988. Portland is a transportation hub as well as a seaport. This is a good place for computer-related businesses, as there are a number of computer software (Central Point Software is one well-known firm) and hardware companies in the area, and a large number of very small businesses serving the computer industry. The permit process for building is streamlined—no variances are required, no planning board presentations—and it only takes a couple of weeks instead of several months. Quality of life is the main reason people come to the Portland area to start businesses. However, because it is a relatively small area, it's best to make a product here (like Nike) and market it elsewhere.

Making the Grade

Public education overview: The Oregon Educational Act for the 21st Century is changing school systems across the state. Its goals are to produce the best-educated citizens in the nation by 2000, and to develop a work force equal to any in the world by 2010. It also promotes accountability of school systems to the community. The North Clackamas School district (13,000 students in Milwaukie and outlying areas) is excellent. Their Character Education program is a model for other districts: teaches children integrity, patriotism, honesty, and other important social character traits. Sabin Occupational Skills Center provides students innovative training through state-of-the-art technology, and partnerships with business and industry. SAT scores are 17 points higher than the Oregon average, which is highest in nation. The district has qualified more Talented and Gifted teams to the international Odyssey of the Mind competition than any other district in the country. Science programs and teachers have received national honors. Grades K-3 will be shifting to "nongraded primary program," which allow students to learn at their own pace.

Class size: 25:1.

Help for working parents: Three elementary schools provide after-school care up to 6 p.m. In the rest of the district, after-school activities and/or day-care centers with transportation are available.

Blue Ribbon School Awards: Clackamas High School ('83-'84), McLoughlin Junior High School ('83-'84), Rex Putnam High School ('84-'85), Wilbur Rowe Junior High ('86-'87).

School year: Starts around Labor Day and ends mid-June. Children must be 5 by Sept. 1 to enter kindergarten.

Special education/gifted programs: Project Challenge and Project Advance let high school students earn college credit. The district is developing magnet programs/schools for math, science, language, arts, and technical education. Children with disabilities are mainstreamed as much as possible.

Nearby colleges/universities: Portland State University; Oregon Health Sciences University; Marylhurst College; Mt. Hood Community College; Clackamas Community College; Portland Community College; Lewis & Clark College; University of Portland; Reed College; and Pacific Northwest College of Art.

Medical Care

Hospitals/medical centers: University Hospital, Emanuel Hospital and Health Center, Kaiser Sunnyside Medical Center, St. Vincent Medical Center, and Providence Milwaukie Hospital have good reputations. Kaiser Sunnyside Medical Center focuses on neurology and neurosurgery. Emanuel Hospital and Health Center has a noted children's hospital. Providence Milwaukie Hospital is a full-service hospital, with modern diagnostics, community outreach, a new maternity-obstetrics unit, and a large pediatric department.

Specialized care: Pacific Crest Rehabilitation (older patient care); and Doernbecher Children's Hospital.

Crime & Safety

Major crimes (robberies, rapes) have remained constant for the last several years (20 robberies/year, 3-4 rapes/year). Burglaries have been trending down for the last 5 years. But car break-ins are up. Other problems typical for a big-city suburb include criminal mischief (graffiti, knocking over signs, etc.) and some gang activity. The police department has instituted a DARE program in cooperation with the schools, helps set up neighborhood watch programs, and helps businesses with burglary and shoplifting prevention. The department, which has increased by only two officers in the last decade (about 24 officers on the streets), also communicates actively with other area departments on gang and other criminal activities. There has been an 8% growth in personal aggravated assault. Police offer detection and prevention programs for schools, home and businesses. Residents feel safe, as the crime rate for property damage and personal assault is still below the national average for major metropolitan areas.

Community Life

There's a major effort to revitalize downtown Main Street, which fell into disuse when malls began to take shoppers out to the suburbs. The Milwaukie Downtown Development Association has been instrumental in bringing in a number of new merchants, and the Association sponsors festivals to promote the area, including a square dance festival, a bike rodeo and safety day, and the Share the Light Festival in December. The Milwaukie Center provides services to older people, and more than 500 volunteers help run the programs. Down to Earth Day is in May, and local Scout groups and service clubs clean up the downtown area.

Let the Good Times Roll

Family fun: Portland's mild climate insures year-round leisure activities, such as snow skiing, water-skiing, golfing, wind surfing, fishing, hiking, hunting, camping, sailing, running, and mountain climbing. The Portland metropolitan area has 37,000 acres of parks. Forest Park, Mill Ends Park, and Washington Park are among the most popular. Downtown Portland has the Carousel Courtyard, Carousel Museum and Carousel Children's Theater. East of Portland lies the Columbia River Gorge National Scenic Area, with the spectacular Multnomah Falls. Columbia River Gorge is also known as the wind-surfing capital of the world. Mt. Hood and the Pacific Ocean are within 75 miles of Portland. There are many miles of riverfront activities and beaches, 20 golf courses, 15 tennis courts, 17 downhill and cross-country skiing areas in the Portland area. Just a couple of hours away is whale-watching along the Pacific Coast and Mt. St. Helen's National Volcanic Monument.

Sports: Portland is home to: the Trailblazers, one of the premier National Basketball Association teams; the Winter Hawks of the Western Hockey League; and the Beavers baseball team, minor league affiliate of the Minnesota Twins. There's the Portland 200 Indy car race in June, bicycle races at Portland International Raceway, thoroughbred racing from October to April at Portland Meadows. Portland State University Vikings play football at Portland Civic Stadium. In addition, there's the Fred Meyer Challenge (professional golf tournament), the Cascade Run-Off 15-k race (June) and the Portland Marathon (Sept.)

Arts & entertainment: Portland is home to about 150 nonprofit arts organizations. The Portland Center For The Performing Arts is home to many of Portland's performing arts groups, including the nationally acclaimed Oregon Symphony and The Portland Opera Association. Portland's premier dance group is The Oregon Ballet Theatre, and the dramatic arts is represented by the new Rose Theatre, The Musical Co., The Storefront Theatre, Oregon Shakespeare Festival Portland, and The Music Theatre of Oregon. In Milwaukie, there's the Milwaukie Historical Museum.

Annual events: Ashland Shakespeare Festival (Feb.); Milwaukie Festival Daze (June); Clackamas County Fair (Aug.); Portland Rose Festival (June); Mt. Hood Festival of Jazz (Aug.); Artquake (Sept.); Waterfront Classics (classical music concerts in Sept.); Harvest Festival (Nov.); and the Holiday Parade of Ships (Dec.).

The Environment

The greater Portland area has a very clean environment that does not adversely affect outdoor activities during the year. Combine a mild, year-round climate (less need for heat and air-conditioning) with the fact that most local industries run on electricity generated by nearby mountain streams, and you have virtually no smog to damage the high air quality. Environmentalists agree that the quality of the air and water is high. Their concerns are to maintain that level of quality, despite the growth in industrial processing. As for Milwaukie's well water, several years ago higher-than-normal levels of contaminants were found in some wells. But since the city built treatment plants 3 years ago, the water quality is very good. Milwaukie has weekly curbside recycling of glass, metal, and newspaper, and picks up lawn debris for compost.

In and Around Town

Roads and interstates: The major north/south route is I-5, which skirts the west side of Portland metro area. Take I-84 for points east; U.S. 26 for points east and west. I-205 cuts off from I-5, providing access to east side of metro area.
Closest airports: Portland International Airport is 20 min. away.
Public transportation: TRI-MET system serves the three counties surrounding Portland with extensive bus service; most routes operate from 5:30 a.m. to 9 p.m., some to 12:30 a.m., and some all night. Also, MAX, a light-rail system, runs every 15 min. from downtown Portland east to the suburb of Gresham.
Avg. commute: 20-25 min.

What Every Resident Knows

Willamette (as in the river and the famous agricultural valley) is pronounced will-AM-ette, not will-a-METTE. • Milwaukie has some of the best salmon fishing in Oregon right in its front yard. People come from all over the world to fish the Willamette and Clackamas rivers during the spring salmon run—50-pound Chinook salmon are common. For whatever reason, the fish seem willing to take the bait here. • Milwaukie had the first municipal electric service west of the Mississippi River. • Guess where people like to shop in Portland? At the Portland International Airport! Seems their 3-year old Oregon Marketplace is a major attraction in the main terminal. Nike, Hanna Anderson and other state-made products are featured.

FYI

Portland Oregon Visitors Assoc.
26 SW Salmon Street
Portland, OR 97204
503-275-9750

North Clackamas Chamber of Commerce
15010 Southeast McLoughlin Blvd.
Milwaukie, OR 97267
503-654-7777

Milwaukie Downtown Development Association
10952 SE 21st Avenue, Suite 5
Milwaukie, OR 97222
503-653-0378

The Oregonian
1320 SW Broadway
Portland, OR 97201
503-221-8240

Pacific Real Estate
1522 Southwest Sunset Blvd.
Portland, OR 97201
503-245-1111
Jeffrey Geisler

REMAX Preferred Realtors
10121 SE Sunnyside Road
Clackamas, OR 97015
503-659-1550
Bob Hennessy

Portland General Electric
121 SW Salmon Street
Portland, OR 97204
503-228-6322

Northwest Natural Gas
220 NW Second Avenue
Portland, OR 97207
503-226-4211

Pacific Northwest Bell
P.O. Box 3881
Portland, OR 97251
503-242-7428

Small Business Development Center
7616 SE Harmony Road
Milwaukie, OR 97222
503-656-4447

School district: 503-653-3600
Property tax assessor: 503-655-8671
Welcome Wagon: 503-659-4273
Interfaith Council: 503-221-1054
Physician's referral: 503-682-1846
Day-care referral: 503-659-5832; 503-655-7826

Bucks County, Pa. *(Philadelphia)*

Area Snapshot

Local population: 61,077
County: Bucks   **Population:** 500,000
U.S. region: Northeast U.S./Southeast Penn.
Closest metro areas: Philadelphia (25 mi. south); Trenton (15 mi. east); Princeton (40 mi. northeast); New York (95 mi. northeast)
Median housing price: $154,600
Avg. household income: $43,347
Best reasons to live here: Pleasant rural environment, central to urban areas and mountains, fast-growing communities, vibrant culture, history and the arts, strong buyer's market, progressive schools, excellent recreation.

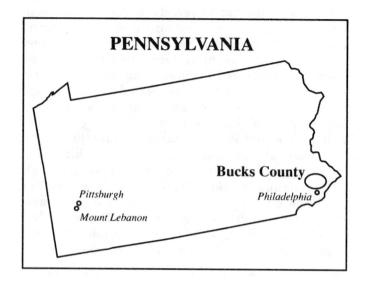

Fabulous Features

Bucks County was always the quaint place to stop en route to somewhere else. Today, it's less a pit stop and more a permanent stay. Runaway living costs and a near-death economy in the Northeast have sent thousands of families scurrying. Their only request? To be close enough to visit Mom but far enough away to start over. It's why the county grew by close to 100,000 ('80-'89), and a projected 100,000 more are expected by the year 2000.

Much of the growth is in the county's lower and mid-sections because of the rural, charming surroundings and easy access to Philadelphia, Trenton and Princeton. And with the most available acreage in the area, there's been a boom in retail, office and industrial parks. This is helping to "buck" the trend of residents working outside the county (50 percent do now).

Another plus is the excellent Council Rock schools (Northampton, Newtown, Upper Makefield and Wrightstown townships). This fast-growing district has one of the highest expenditures per pupil in Pennsylvania ($5,234), with an ideal teacher-student ratio (avg. 16:1).

Desirable homes in a buyer's market (prices are down 20% since 1989) is another attention-getter. For the Northeast there are excellent values. Families moving in are discovering an added bonus: thousands of things to see and do, from the historical to the hysterical (skiing, camping and other year-round recreation). As they say, "It's Bucks or bust!"

Possible drawbacks: The highways, interior roadways and bridges that were quaint in the '70s are inadequate in the '90s. The Newtown bypass to I-95 has brought some relief, but not enough. Unfortunately, with every bridge that's demolished to make way for a highway, a cherished piece of history is lost. • With so little industry in the Council Rock district, the burden for education funding is on homeowners. And with the state slashing budgets, property increase notices will likely be staple items in the mailbox.

"You can quote me on that"

"This part of Bucks County is so rural and friendly, yet we're close to Philadelphia. I love the fact that kids play out in the fresh air all year long. Where we came from, kids hung out at home waiting for somebody to arrange a play date."—G.H.

Real Estate

Market overview: Yes, housing prices are still relatively high, although they have dropped an average of 20%-25% since the peak period ('86-'87). With interest rates down, demand has picked up; and real estate activity in '92 has been superior to '90-'91. If buyer confidence levels and employment stabilization improves, the market should become stronger. In the meantime, it's very much a buyer's market. The past year has seen no appreciation at all. The last six months has seen new construction starting a slow pick-up.

What houses look like: Colonials are predominant, though there are a variety of splits, capes, contemporaries, ranches and bi-levels. Most homes are between $170,000-$250,000, w/aluminum siding exteriors. More expensive homes are usually brick or stone, w/cedar siding. Avg. lot size is 80 x 100. Newer homes have 2 stories, large foyers and fireplaces. Master suites are large, other BRs are smaller. Nearly 75% of the houses have basements.

Starter homes: $150,000-$200,000. The low end buys a 3BR/1BA, older home (20-30 years), ranch style on a 100 x 200 lot, fireplace in living room and possibly a garage.

Trade-ups: $200,000-$275,000. $225,000 buys a 4BR/2 1/2BA, colonial w/2-car garage, basement, family room w/fireplace, about 10 years old on an 80 x 100 lot. At the higher end, you get a 4BR/2 1/2BA w/2-3-car garage on 1 acre.

Luxury homes: $500,000-$800,000. You'll see magnificent colonials w/4-5BR/3BA, sitting room off the master BR w/fireplace, all-stone front with cedar siding, 3-car garage, large family room w/fireplace, large working kitchen, on 3 acres, possibly more.

Rental market: Single family homes are difficult to find; rents are $1,100-$1,2000/mo. for a 3BR. Townhomes are available for $800-$900/mo. for a 2-3BR/1 1/2BA.

Great neighborhoods: Newtown Borough, a 300-year-old community, has houses of all ages, ranging from $160,000-$600,000. In Northampton, there is Windmill Village and Hillcrest Shires for older homes from $175,000-$230,000 w/large lots and scenic surroundings.

Nearby areas to consider: Newtown Village, Northampton and Upper Makefield offer homes ($250,000 and up) of all ages, with lots of land and minutes from shopping in Newtown. Children attend the excellent Council Rock school system.

What Things Cost

Runzheimer's Living Cost Index: Avg. annual costs for family of 4 with household income of $50,000: $55,348 (10.7% above avg. city).

ACCRA's national comparisons: Overall living costs in the metro area are 30.7% above national avg. Utility costs are 92.5% above avg., housing is 42.4% above and health care is 31.8% above. You don't even get a break with groceries (close to 20% above). Compared to other East-Coast cities (Boston and New York), living costs are more affordable.

Utilities: Phone: Hookup: $40; $8.35-$12.60/mo. Gas: Avg. $100/mo. for 3BR/2BA. Electric: Avg. $75/mo. Water: Min. $50/quarter.

Kid care: Childcare availability is not a problem. The Public Information office at City Hall has a directory of licensed providers. Cost for infants (6 wks.-18 mo.): $528/mo.; Toddlers (18 mo.-3 yrs.): $494/mo.; Preschoolers: $455/mo. **Pediatric visit:** $35-$50.

The Tax Ax

Sales tax: 6%.

Property tax: To calculate taxes, take the millage rate times the assessment divided by 1,000. (Bucks County assessments are .052 of home value.) For example, a $200,000 home would be assessed at $10,400. If the millage rate were 311.45 (Northampton) taxes would be approximately $3,114. (Millage rate in Newtown: 306.854; Upper Makefield: 307.40.)

State income tax: Pennsylvania has a flat 2.8% tax on all taxable income. There are no exemptions.

Climate

Elevation 75'	Avg. High/Low	Avg. Rain (Inches)	Avg. Snow (Inches)	Avg. Days Rain	Avg. % Humidity
Jan.	40/24	2.2	6.3	9	60
April	64/42	3.3	.2	11	49
July	87/67	4.1	--	9	54
Oct.	68/47	2.5	.1	7	53
YEAR	64/45	39.9	22	110	55
# of days 32° or below: 101		# of days 90° or above: 19			

Four distinct seasons are modified by the proximity to the Atlantic Ocean and the Appalachian Mountains. Extremely high or low temperatures are rare. Snow falls an avg. 6 times a year. Summer thunderstorms and high winds are common (it's also when most of the rainfall occurs).

Earning a Living

Economic outlook: Bucks County's unique geographic location puts it into an excellent position for economic growth and expansion. The center point for Boston to Washington and, also locally, Princeton to Philadelphia, the county's growth potential is now just being realized. For example, it's the last suburban Philadelphia county to enter the office and research market. The extensive highway system, including the Pennsylvania Turnpike-Northeast Extension, traverses the county. New business centers are being built, such as Floral Vale Professional Park, or the Quakertown Interchange Business Center, which provide office space for such expanding companies as AM Communications and Southland Corp. Bristol Township Industrial Park is a new 2 million sq. ft. development. The county continues to maintain a strong industrial base, with more than 2,000 manufacturing facilities. Although more than 50% of the county's work force is employed outside the county, the professional, high-tech labor force is being absorbed by Bucks County's expanding economic base. A growing number of advanced technology, biomedical and pharmaceutical companies are relocating or expanding here. Unemployment stands at 6.2%.

Where the jobs are: A number of manufacturing and advanced technology firms are in the midst of expansion, including: White Engineering Surfaces Corporation, a medium sized advanced technology firm; Thermocouple Technology Inc.; Aim Electronics, Inc.; Marketing Technologies, Inc.; and Compu-Craft Fabricators (CCF).

Business opportunities: The Chamber of Commerce and the Bucks County Industrial Development Corporation (BCIDC) provide assistance and information to entrepreneurs. The BCIDC offers loan information, seminars and industrial and office park information. The BCIDC also produces guides, which include school district, tax, and demographic information, an industrial directory and a membership directory. In addition, the Bensalem Township Economic Development Corporation promotes the economic and general welfare of the township by securing new business and assisting the growth and expansion of existing firms. The Delaware Entrepreneurs' Forum held its annual Venture Idea Fair in Wilmington in May 1992. This fair is for early-stage startups with proprietary products or specialized service.

Making the Grade

Public education overview: There are many good schools in the area, but we were impressed with the Council Rock district, comprised of 5 municipalities: Newtown Borough and the townships of Newtown, Northampton, Upper Makefield and Wrightstown. The financial support is among the highest in the state (per-pupil expenditure is $5,234). Students scored above average to well above average on SATs when compared nationally, the district placed 11 finalists, 11 semifinalists and 19 commendations in the 1992 National Merit Scholarship Program, and 82% of graduates went on to higher education (has been as high as 89%). Council Rock High School in Newtown offers a broad curriculum with academically challenging programs. Middle Bucks Area Vocational-Technical School serves Council Rock. Students spend a half-day learning a vocation, the other half at their high school. Seniors can take courses at Bucks County Community College's BCCC High School Enrichment Program. Within the past 3 years, 2 new elementary schools have been opened, as well as 2 new additions to existing schools. A new elementary in Newtown is expected to open in Sept. 1994.
Class size: 16:1.

Help for working parents: Children's Learning Center provides morning (7 a.m. for breakfast and activities) and after-school care (to 6 p.m.) at 3 elementary schools, $210/mo. per child.

Blue Ribbon School Awards: Buckingham Elementary School ('85-'86).

School year: Begins after Labor Day through 3rd week of June. Children must be 5 on or before Sept. 1 to enter kindergarten.

Special education/gifted programs: The exceptional youngster's needs are met within the normal school environment to the greatest extent possible. A variety of special evaluative and educational services are available through the Dept. of Special Services: educational diagnostics, psychological evaluation, gifted support, emotional support and lifeskills support programs. Additional services such as speech, language, vision, hearing, and physical and occupational therapies are available through the Special Services Office. There are some high school programs for gifted students.

Nearby colleges/universities: Bucks County Community College; Delaware Valley College of Science and Agriculture are local. In the region are some of the most outstanding colleges in the East: Princeton University (New Jersey); University of Pennsylvania, Thomas Jefferson University and LaSalle University (all in Philadelphia).

Medical Care

Hospitals/medical centers: Major medical centers, offering acute, comprehensive medical care in the vicinity: Lower Bucks Hospital (Bristol); Saint Mary Hospital (Langhorne); Delaware Valley Medical Center (Langhorne); Medical College Hospitals, one of the Delaware Valley's largest hospital systems (the Bucks County Campus is in Warminster); and Mercer Medical Center (Trenton), a state-of-the-art regional comprehensive care center. **Specialized care:** Livengrin Foundation (alcohol and chemical dependency); Good Friends, Inc. (alcohol and chemical dependency); Booth Maternity Center; Children's Heart Hospital; and Fox Chase Cancer Center.

Crime & Safety

Neighbors watch out for neighbors (if a strange car is seen in an area *twice* in a short period of time, people call the police); the police department is well-staffed, well-educated and involved within the community. Each municipality has its own police force. That's resulted in low crime, especially violent crime. Overall, the area is extraordinarily safe, and the residents are law-abiding. There are not a lot of access routes that encourage crime.

Community Life

Many residents express their community spirit through the Bucks County Opportunity Council, a nonprofit organization that helps low-income residents. The Doylestown Golf Classic (Sept.) is one event that draws lots of participation; it raised $25,000-$30,000 in 1992 for Project Self Sufficiency. This project provides vocational, educational, housing and child care assistance so that people can get back on their feet. Corporate sponsorship and admissions are what brings the money together as well as help from 25-30 volunteers to put this event together. Another event, Secretary's Day Luncheon, also raises funds for the project. Notable area bosses pay for lunch and serve their secretaries. In 1992 this event raised $8,000. The Village Fair is an annual May fund raiser at and for the Doylestown Hospital. Rides, games, foods and entertainment are provided by hospital volunteers who are comprised of community members as well as staff. Finally, there's Neat Day (Northampton), on which the boy scouts and girl scouts clean up the streets and pick up litter.

Let the Good Times Roll

Family fun: Bucks County maintains 8,500 acres of state parks and more than 4,000 acres of game preserves. In addition there are 14 county parks and 4 noted historic properties—which means endless opportunities for boating, fishing, swimming, picnicking, hunting, camping and more. There are plenty of outlets for golf fans, via public courses and country clubs. For children: there's Discovery Zone in Bensalem (tunnels, roller slide, obstacle courses and more); Marty's Circus of Fun in Bensalem (miniature golf course, batting cages, etc.); Quarry Valley Farm in Lahaska (working farm with petting zoo, pony rides and hayloft); and Sesame Place in Langhorne, a unique family playpark for kids 3-13 with appearances and live entertainment by the Sesame Street characters. In addition, you can't get away from history in this area. The Artists Colony of New Hope is an unspoiled cultural center with quaint shops, historic buildings and the Bucks County Playhouse. Washington Crossing Historic Park offers outdoor enjoyment as well as an 18th-century farm. Delaware Canal State Park features an historic path along the 60-mile Delaware Canal. Embark on an 11-mile excursion to see the countryside and canal life as it was 150 years ago by a mule-drawn barge. The New Hope Ivyland Railroad (circa 1891) offers scenic trips to Buckingham Valley on an authentic steam locomotive. Take a narrated tour of Memorial Building in Washington Crossing, where the "Betsy Ross" flag with 13 stars is exhibited. For outdoor action, Belle Mountain Ski Area and Lake Afton are great for avid skiers and ice skaters. Peace Valley reservoir offers sailing.

Sports: Veteran's Stadium in South Philadelphia presents plenty of sports action: the Eagles, for football; the Phillies, for baseball. And at the Spectrum, there's hockey (the Flyers) and basketball (the 76ers). Presently under construction is the Spectrum II.

Arts & entertainment: Bucks County Playhouse in New Hope is a nationally recognized theatre and cultural center. Located in Washington Crossing is the Bucks County Symphony Orchestra, which performs several concerts during the year. The Mercer Museum, built in 1916, houses one of the world's first great collections of artifacts, "Tools of the Nation Maker." A rare exhibit or unusual display awaits the visitor at every turn.

Annual events: Southampton Days Country Fair (June); Strawberry Festival (May). Candlelight Dinner Dance (Fallsington) on the grounds of the historic 1790 Stagecoach Tavern (June); Bucks County Wine and Food Festival (Nov.).

The Environment

Bucks county is part of the Philadelphia Consolidated Metropolital Statistical Area (CMSA), which the EPA has designated as a severe nonattainment area for air quality. Air pollution is centered mainly in Philadelphia and Camden. Contributing factors are the older industry along the Delaware River and the rush hours. The air and water quality in Bucks is better because the winds push pollution away. Environmental safety is a concern of Bucks County with Waste Management, Inc., one of the world's largest environmental services, here. Recycling is available on a scheduled weekly basis. To make the greatest use of landfilled waste, the Pennsbury Power Plant collects methane gas produced by decomposed waste and turns it into useful energy.

In and Around Town

Roads and interstates: I-95, U.S. Routes 1, 13.
Closest airports: Philadelphia International Airport (off I-95) is 35-45 min. from Bucks County. Newark International Airport (in N.J.) is an hour away. Mercer County Airport, Buehl and Doylestown airports supplement local air taxi and charter services. Northeast Philadelphia Airport offers air taxi, corporate and charter service.
Public transportation: Southeastern Pennsylvania Transportation Authority provides public bus and commuter rail routes connecting the entire region.
Avg. commute: 20-40 min. A good majority of the commuters are driving to Princeton (25 min.) and Philadelphia (35 min.).

What Every Resident Knows

Popular bumper sticker seen around the area: "Preserve Our Farm Land—We Can't Eat Townhouses." The area is not as anti-development as that may sound; the real natives just want to save the rural surroundings and maintain open space. As far as development, they look at "controlled growth." • In Middletown Township is Styers Apple Orchard. During the fall the parking lots are packed with buses for field trips and people picking up homebaked pies (you cannot get a parking spot close enough). The aroma is fantastic.

FYI

Central Bucks Chamber of Commerce
Fidelity Bank Building
115 West Court Street
Doylestown, PA 18901
215-348-3913

Bucks County Tourist Commission
P.O. Box 912
Doylestown, PA 18901
215-345-4552

Bucks County Courier Times
88400 Route 13
Levittown, PA 19057
215-949-4000

Intelligencer/Record
333 No. Broad Street
Doylestown, PA 18901
215-345-3000

Realty World/The Market Place
240 Taylorsville Road
Yardley, PA 19067
215-493-3373
Donald Schulte, MaryAnn Pazdan

Philadelphia Electric Company
400 Park Avenue
Warminster, PA 18974
215-672-8141

Bell of Pennsylvania
400 Cherry Street
Norristown, PA 19401
215-590-6500

Bucks County Industrial Development Corp.
Small Business Development
2 E. Court Street
Doylestown, PA 18901
215-348-9031

School district: 215-355-9901
(Council Rock)
Property tax assessor:
215-860-9801
Newcomer's Club: 215-848-3723
Interfaith Council: 215-855-8241
Physician's referral: 215-243-2584
Day-care referral: 215-493-8048

Mt. Lebanon, Pennsylvania (Pittsburgh)

Area Snapshot

Local population: 33,362
County: Allegheny   **Population:** 1,336,449
U.S. region: Southwestern Pennsylvania
Closest metro area: Pittsburgh (13 mi. north)
Median housing price: $72,700
Avg. household income: $47,251
Best reasons to live here: One of the most livable areas of the country, low living costs, outstanding medical care, excellent schools, clean environment, low crime, expanding business sector, wonderful variety of culture and recreation.

Fabulous Features

Parents of preschoolers know, "It's a beautiful day in the neighborhood." What they don't know is that for 23 years, Fred Rogers has been singing the praises of the city where his show is taped. Pittsburgh.

Surprised? Don't be. Images of steel mills and soot disappeared 30 years ago. Today's Allegheny region delivers a one-two punch—great opportunities and easy-on-the-heart lifestyles. In fact, the only sparks flying are from the sizzling economy! Pittsburgh is the largest research and development center in the U.S. (more than 100 university/corporate centers including Carnegie Mellon), the fourth-largest concentration of Fortune 500 companies (plus 90 U.S. headquarters of overseas firms), 31 colleges and universities, 700 high-tech firms and one of the most internationally acclaimed medical communities (55 hospitals and the best teaching and transplant facilities in the world).

But the ticket to the future is the new Midfield/Terminal, the $690 million airport that will insure Pittsburgh's place in the sun into the next century. Back on the ground, there are some of the most livable, lovable communities in the Northeast (magazines trip over each other to see who can give higher accolades).

Take Mount Lebanon, an exceptional suburb with a do-or-die spirit. It's got the best high school in Pennsylvania (*Redbook* magazine), a well-run city government with an A-1 bond rating, and very inviting neighborhoods (homes range from $60,000-$250,000+). It's all a quick "pitt" stop from the excitement: the world-renowned Pittsburgh Symphony, Ballet and Opera, the champion Pirates, Penguins and Steelers, even super skiing (downhill racing is less than hour away). Mr. Rogers was right. It's a beautiful day in these neighborhoods, indeed!

Possible drawbacks: Without an industrial base, tax revenues are the burden of Mt. Lebanon homeowners. But while taxes are higher, the schools and services are so great, its worth every penny. • This is an older, established community with traditional (often small) homes. If contemporary architecture is your thing, there's little to buy. • Scared of tunnels? They're everywhere, and one of the oldest goes from Mt. Lebanon to Pittsburgh. Maybe there's a support group...

"You can quote me on that"

"We moved to the Pittsburgh area from Maryland, and the area is very affordable. Mt. Lebanon is family-oriented, and it offers a lot. We're very happy here—it's just a great place to raise a family."—J.M.

Real Estate

Market overview: Whatever the market, Mt. Lebanon holds its own. The desirable schools and amenities are so great, residents move up but not out. The area is almost totally built up, so there is little new SFH construction. That has helped home appreciation keep a steady 3%-5% a year. Even when interest rates went through the roof in the late 1970s and early 1980s, these homes held their value. There are about 250-300 SFHs on the market at any one time.

What houses look like: More than half the homes are 2-story, Tudors or colonials, with usable 3rd floors, as well. Brick or stone exteriors are common on older homes. Frame houses, including ranches and colonials, tend to be about 30-40 years old, and there are some contemporaries, about 10-15 years old. In most cases, the interiors are traditional—formal living and dining rooms, den, 3BR on 2nd floor, perhaps 2BR on 3rd floor. Masters are found in newer, more expensive homes.

Starter homes: $60,000 buys a 2-story w/2-3BR in Aliquippa and Beaver Falls. Up to $120,000 gets a 3BR/1 1/2BA, 2-story, 1-car garage, 1000-1200 sq. ft., 50 x 120 lot, and possibly a den or enclosed a porch added. Sunset Hills is popular with young families (affordable, smaller homes).

Trade-ups: $75,000-$80,000 buys a 3-4BR, 2-story ranch in Center Hopewell and Brighton. For the $120s-$200s, you'll get 3-5BR, at least 2BA, 2-3 story, 1-2-car garage, family room, fireplace, 1300-2000 sq. ft., 60 x 130 lot, master BR w/BA, and maybe an updated kitchen and BAs. Areas to look are Seminole Hills, and Mission Hills.

Luxury homes: Deluxe homes start at $150,000 for a 3-4BR, 2-story ranch in Center, Hopewell and Brighton. In the $200s-$500s+, you'll get a 3-5BR/2-3BA, 2-3 story, 2-3-car garage, European kitchen, deck, master BR w/BA. Look at Virginia Manor.

Rental market: Very few SFHs but where available, a 3BR/2BA goes for $1,000-$1,200/mo. Apts. go for $400-$800/mo. Condos start at $500/mo.

Great neighborhoods: Mission Hills and Hoodridge are close to the city with older and more expensive homes. Oxford Park has newer homes, and young families like the excellent Hoover Elementary School Brighton Township, Cedar Ridge and Kane Hts.

Nearby areas to consider: Upper St. Clair has newer homes, larger lots, and mid to high prices. Bethel Park offers mid-range prices, good schools, recreational facilities and transportation.

What Things Cost

Runzheimer's Living Cost Index: Avg. annual costs for family of 4 with household income of $50,000: $53,204 (6.4% above avg. city).

ACCRA's national comparisons: Not available.

Utilities: Phone: $40 hookup charge. Four different packages, one being $20/mo. w/unlimited local and suburban Pittsburgh calls. Call waiting: $3.20/mo., touchtone is $1/mo. more. Gas and electric: $100/mo. (Jan.); $65/mo. (April); $75/mo. (July); $60/mo. (Oct.).

Kid care: Day-care centers charge $165/wk. At-home day care costs $100-$125/wk. Preschool and infant care is readily available through an extensive childcare network offered through the YMCA.

Pediatric visit: $50-$60.

The Tax Ax

Sales tax: State sales tax is 6%. Food, medicine and clothing are exempt. There is a local wage tax of 2.875% for city residents, 1% for suburban residents.

Property tax: Local property taxes are calculated by multiplying ¼ of the assessment value of the house times the millage rate (163.75). Property tax for a $100,000 home would be ($25,000 x 163.75) $4,094 per year.

State income tax: Pennsylvania has a flat income tax rate of 2.8% of gross income. There are no exemptions.

Climate

Elevation 760'	Avg. High/Low	Avg. Rain (Inches)	Avg. Snow (Inches)	Avg. Days Rain	Avg. % Humidity
Jan.	37/24	1.6	13	13	66
April	63/42	3.2	1.5	14	50
July	84/65	3.8	--	11	53
Oct.	66/45	2.5	.2	10	54
YEAR	62/44	31	46	138	57
# of days 32° or below: 97			# of days 90° or above: 16		

A continental climate is like continental cuisine. It's a little bit of everything. Polar air masses from Canada influence cold fronts in winter. Warm air from the south brings in the warmest of summer days (although humidity is relatively mild). Rainfall is evenly distributed throughout the year. Snow will blanket the ground about 35 days between November and March.

Earning a Living

Economic outlook: The region is doing everything possible to stave off the recession. With a new, highly diversified economic base, it will very likely succeed. Although unemployment is up to 6%, there is job growth across the board. As one of largest R&D centers in nation (more than 100 university and corporate centers), this is a leading center for software engineering, robotics, artificial intelligence, advanced materials, and biomedicine. Carnegie Mellon and the University of Pittsburgh partnered with Westinghouse Electric to build a supercomputing center, and with the Urban Redevelopment Authority to build an advanced technology park. Another draw is Carnegie Mellon's Software Engineering Institute, financed by a $103 million grant from the Defense Dept. Pittsburgh is a headquarters city. More than 90 firms, many of them Fortune 500 companies, are here. The new $690 million airport opened on Oct. 1, 1992. Pittsburgh's central location and its strong transportation system (air, land, rail and water) all add to its economic strength.

Where the jobs are: Nonmanufacturing industries are now the biggest employers (85% of region's jobs), gaining 104,400 jobs from 1980-1991 (manufacturing lost 133,800 in the same period). Employment in the service sector has grown fastest—a 30% increase 1980-1991. There are more than 700 advanced technology companies in the region. By the year 2000, Pittsburgh High Technology Council predicts the high-tech work force will double to more than 150,000. The new airport will also spin off new jobs, from construction, transportation, and distribution to airline (food, fueling, baggage and freight) and passenger services (restaurants, shops, etc.) Companies on the grow include: Sony; Genesis Plastics; Dormont Manufacturing; ITEC coal processing; Koppel Steel; SMS Engineers; Conrail transportation center; and Sysco food distribution.

Business opportunities: Light manufacturing is dovetailing the high-tech industry growth. New companies are typically small, employing 250 or less. Many manufacture metal, plastic or electronic components. A multitude of financing plans are available. Because of the large number of corporate headquarters, opportunities for business support services—law, finance, accounting, and communications are strong. There is continued need for medical care support staff.

Making the Grade

Public education overview: Mt. Lebanon schools are a mutual admiration society. The teachers commend the student body and parents for their achievements. In turn, the community lavishes praise on the faculty and staff for their dedication and innovativeness. In the mid-'80s, an integrated math curriculum was introduced to 7-12-graders, making math more concept-oriented. Math scores on standardized tests have risen dramatically. In 1991, SAT scores (math 533, verbal 475) exceeded state average by 132, and the national average by 112. The Class of 1992 had more National Merit semifinalists (16-14 became finalists) than any other Western Pennsylvania school, public or private. In the Mt. Lebanon district, with a budget of approximately $40 million, the expenditures per pupil are $7,913—almost double the national avg.! The district has its own fine arts building, with theater, art studios and dance studio. The high school graduation rate is 99.7%, and 90% go on to college. The high school was cited as one of 42 "overall excellent" schools in the nation by *Redbook* (April 1992). Special programs in foreign exchange, fine arts, drama, math and science result in the district schools winning awards and recognition in many areas.

Class size: 20:1.

Help for working parents: The extended day program operates in 6 elementary schools, offering supervision from 7 a.m. until 6:30 p.m.

Blue Ribbon School Awards: Mt. Lebanon Junior High School ('90-'91), Mt. Lebanon Senior High School ('83-'84, '90-'91).

School year: Begins immediately after Labor Day and runs through the 3rd week of June. Children must be 5 before Jan. 31 to start kindergarten.

Special education/gifted programs: In 1991, the state-mandated Instructional Support Program was implemented in 2 elementary schools to help students with academic or life-skills difficulties; students receive help in academics and self-esteem. Disabled students receive support in classrooms or supplemental assistance through a resource program. Physical/occupational therapy are offered.

Nearby colleges/universities: Carnegie Mellon University (business, economics, computer science, robotics, and international relations); University of Pittsburgh (medicine, biotechnology, and transplant surgery); Duquesne University (law, business, religion); Robert Morris College (business); Chatham College (women's liberal arts college); Community College of Allegheny County (4 campuses, 160 programs).

Medical Care

Hospitals/medical centers: Pittsburgh's medical care facilities are internationally renowned for innovative research and state-of-the-art care. Some of the facilities include Presbyterian University Hospital (the world's leader in organ transplants; the world's top surgeons practice and research here); St. Francis Medical Center (cardiology, oncology, laser surgery); Allegheny General Hospital (organ transplants, cardiology); Forbes Health System; Pittsburgh Mercy Health System; West Penn Hospital; Montefiore Hospital; Children's Hospital of Pittsburgh; and the Pittsburgh Cancer Institute. St. Clair Hospital in Mt. Lebanon is a general acute care hospital. Its Family Center is one of top hospitals in infant deliveries. Pittsburgh Emergency Medical Services is the leading pre-admission emergency system in the state.

Specialized care: St. Clair's Healthy Hearts (cardiac rehabilitation) and Second Wind (pulmonary rehabilitation), Allegheny General's Neuropsychiatric Institute, and the Burn Trauma Center at West Penn Hospital are some specialized care services.

Crime & Safety

Most communities would swap crime statistics with Mt. Lebanon in a minute because their rates are so low. The major crimes reported are burglaries (60 in 1991) and theft (130 in 1991) actually down 25% from a decade ago, although present levels are one-quarter of what they were a deade ago. The police department's award-winning Crime Prevention Unit sets up neighborhood watch programs, and provides home security checks to alert residents of how they can protect themselves. It runs programs in the schools, from safe walking and saying no to strangers in elementary school to drug and alcohol education in junior high and high school. The unit also target special self-protection programs for the elderly and women.

Community Life

PTA meetings and school-sponsored events are so well-attended, people show up early to get good seats. Ditto for high school sports and theatrical productions. Plain and simple, the schools are the lifeblood of the community. Other organizations that attract involvement are the South Hills Art League, Friends of the Library, Adult Interest Center, and Business and Professional Women. Residents volunteer at St. Clair Hospital, and the Democratic and Republican committees and the League of Women Voters are all active.

Let the Good Times Roll

Family fun: Mt. Lebanon Park includes the Recreation Center, an Olympic-sized pool (there is also an indoor pool at the high school), a full-size indoor ice-skating rink (the Penguins practice there), and a 15-court Tennis Center that hosts the National Amateur Clay Court Championships and the West Penn Tennis Tournament. Pittsburgh has its natural habitat zoo, the Pittsburgh Aviary (world's largest zoo for birds), Buhl Science Center and planetarium. There are 10 ski centers in the Pittsburgh area, three within 45 min. of downtown. Carnegie Museum of Natural History houses most complete dinosaur collection in the world. Bicycling is popular in the area, and there are several miles of bike paths in Highland, Schenley, North, and South parks. Boating is also popular (Allegheny County has one of the highest concentrations of pleasure craft in the nation) on the Monongahela, Allegheny, and Ohio rivers, and the many lakes in the region. There are a number of state parks for camping, hiking, and picnicking near Pittsburgh. And the huge Allegheny National Forest offers hiking and back-country camping less than 2 hrs. away. Amish Country in New Wilmington is less than 60 miles away.

Sports: Pittsburgh has a tradition of championship teams. The Pirates, perennial leaders of the National League Eastern Division, play at Three Rivers Stadium. The Steelers, who were the class of the National Football League in the 1970s, are again becoming a power. And the National Hockey League Penguins have won 2 league championships in a row. Each year, Pittsburgh hosts the Vintage Grand Prix.

Arts & entertainment: With the help of the city's strong corporate and university infrastructure, a vibrant performing and visual arts community is an integral part of Pittsburgh's life. More than 200 nonprofit arts organizations call Pittsburgh home, including The Pittsburgh Symphony, Pittsburgh Opera, Pittsburgh Ballet Theater, Pittsburgh Public Theater and The Pittsburgh Civic Light Opera. Performing arts facilities include Heinz Hall, The Syria Mosque, The Carnegie Music Hall, and The Benedum Center For The Performing Arts. The region also maintains about 100 art galleries, museums and landmarks.

Annual events: Pittsburgh Marathon (May); Three Rivers Regatta (Aug.); Pittsburgh Folk Festival (May); Mellon Jazz Festival (June); Three Rivers Arts Festival (June); Pittsburgh Vintage Grand Prix (July); In Mt. Lebanon: Fourth of July celebration and fireworks.

The Environment

Greater Pittsburgh is clean and safe because of a strong emphasis on health, safety, and environmental quality. Through responsible handling of waste, water supplies meet EPA standards. A $2.5 million water treatment plant is currently being built to ensure high-quality water reserves. 87% of Allegheny County gets its water from the rivers. Water contaminants, which a decade ago were a cause of concern, have been cleaned up considerably. Steel recycling has extended the life of the nation's landfills by several years. Mt. Lebanon has curbside pickup of recyclables: glass, cans, clear plastic, and leaf wastes.

In and Around Town

Roads and interstates: East-West: I-70, I-76, I-80, and I-376. North-South: I-79, I-579, I-279.
Closest airport: Greater Pittsburgh International Airport (16 mi.). This brand-new facility, which offers 100 shopping outlets, features "people movers" that take you straight from the parking lot to the terminal of your choice.
Public transportation: The Port Authority Transit operates more than 160 buses and light rail routes.
Avg. commute: 20 min. during rush hour; 10 min. at other times.

What Every Resident Knows

Summer block parties are very big in most "Lebo" neighborhoods. Streets are roped off, kids can ride their bikes, and parents can relax and catch up with each other amidst the karaoke music, covered dishes and beer. • You're pretty certain to meet the namesakes of the local businesses: Walt owns Walt's Tavern, Sonny owns Sonny's Shoe Repair, and the Rubinsteins own Ruby's. However, there's no Dante at Dante's. • At the high school, if it sounds like someone is asking for an autograph, they're most likely asking for Otto Graf—the high school principal. • Mt. Lebanon residents have Pittsburgh addresses.

FYI

Greater Pittsburgh Chamber of Commerce
Three Gateway Center
Pittsburgh, PA 15222
412-392-4510

Pittsburgh Press
34 Blvd. of Allies
Pittsburgh, PA 15230
412-263-1121

Coldwell Banker
1107 Broad Head Road
Monaca, PA 15061
412-728-4509
Eileen Baker

RE/MAX CSI
1720 Washington Road
Pittsburgh, PA 15241
800-537-2434
Bonnie Olenn

Uptown Mt. Lebanon Economic Development Corporation
710 Washington Road
Mt. Lebanon, PA 15228
412-344-7623

Bell of Pennsylvania
P.O. Box 1676
Pittsburgh, PA 15255
412-497-7000 (call collect)
1-800-660-2215 (in-state only)

Duquesne Light
301 Grant Street
Pittsburgh, PA 15222
412-393-7100

Columbia Gas of Western Pennsylvania
650 Washington Road
Mt. Lebanon, PA 15228
412-344-9800

University of Pittsburgh Small Business Development Center
208 Bellefield Avenue
Pittsburgh, PA 15219
412-648-1544

School district: 412-344-2076
Property tax assessor: 412-343-3405
Newcomer's Club: 412-561-8278
Interfaith council: 412-833-6177
Physician's referral: 412-359-3027 or 412-572-6560 (St. Clair Community Health Information Center)
Day-care referral: 1-800-392-3131 (in-state); 412-392-3131 (out-of-state)

Charleston, South Carolina

Area Snapshot

Local population: 506,875
Counties: Charleston, Dorchester, Berkeley
Population: 506,875
U.S. region: Southern Central Coast
Closest metro areas: Savannah, Ga. (105 mi. south), Columbia, S.C. (114 mi. north)
Median housing price: $80,600
Avg. household income: $33,539
Best reasons to live here: Charming Southern city, exciting history, Atlantic coast is your backyard, great climate, affordable real estate, favorable economy, growing population, exciting recreation and culture, good schools.

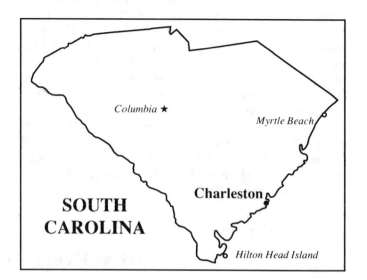

Fabulous Features

C is for *charm* in this picturesque, coastal city, with its narrow cobblestone streets, horse-drawn carriages and antebellum homes. *H* is for the rich *history* of this colonial port. As the first U.S. city to serve as a model for preservation, there are 1,000 homes, gardens and buildings, circa 1670 to the 1840s. *A* is for *Armed Forces*. Close to 50,000 residents are employed by the Navy, Air Force and Coast Guard, pouring $4.5 billion into the local economy.

R is for *religious freedom* in this, the "Holy City." Charleston's founding constitution guaranteed religious choice, and the city is the home of the oldest existing reform Jewish congregation. *L* is for *luxury homes* at affordable prices. *E* is for the burgeoning *economy* that helped Charleston "dance" past the recession. Tourism brings in $850 million, the Port of Charleston is at 100 percent capacity, and construction is booming. *S* is for the delightful *seasons,* with average daily temperatures ranging from 54 to 75. It's also for the progressive *schools*, making great headway after decades of inadequate funding. *T* is for the *tax bite,* which is more like a whimper. South Carolina's per-capita tax burden is the 41st lowest in the U.S. *O* is for the *ocean* breezes that await you on the 75 miles of unspoiled Atlantic beaches.

N is for all the *new businesses* moving in. In 1991 *Inc.* magazine rated it 7th in the country for the most new business starts between 1988 and 1990. Put it all together and what do you have? One fabulous place to call home!

Possible drawbacks: As a coastal city, Charleston has a limited number of bridges and public transportation options. • The majority of funding for education comes through property taxes. With such a heavy population of retirees and transient employees, mention an increase and stand back for the uproar. Fortunately, the new school superintendent has made it a top priority to look for alternative financial support. • Living in a low-lying area means being on standby to batten down the hatches during hurricane season.

"You can quote me on that"

"I was sick about leaving Texas even though my husband got transferred to a wonderful job in Charleston. But as a young mother, I really appreciate the wonderful parks and recreation for even a 2-year old. We never run out of places to go or things to do."—P.L.S.

Real Estate

Market overview: What's your pleasure? Antebellum mansions, beachfront property, luxury townhouses or beautiful new single-family houses? The Trident region has it all, but shop carefully, each area is unique. James Island and West Ashley are mostly older homes on or near laid-back Folly Beach. Mount Pleasant is where young professionals head, Summerville (Dorchester County) attracts the military, and Goose Creek (Berkeley County) is a rural area with nice starter homes. Overall, there is much to choose from in the under-$100,000 range (in this active market, houses sell in less than 90 days). Condos and townhouses are available but limited. Most people look for SFHs. Avg. carrying charges (principal and interest) are $669/mo.

What houses look like: New colonials and capes are popular inland, with contemporaries found on the beachfront. Older resales are mostly 3BR/2BA (1400 sq. ft.) homes with garages. Don't expect to find basements. The alternative is a FROG (finished room over garage). Exteriors are mostly brick, wood and vinyl siding. Interiors show cathedral ceilings, wraparound porches and gracious master suites. With the ocean near, buyers look for decks and screened-in porches, but not pools.

Starter homes: $70,000-$90,000 buys 3BR/2BA either new or resale (5-10 years old). Lot sizes avg. 70 x 100 to 100 x 100. Land values are high, and property size is less a priority. West Ashley and James Island offer older homes close to downtown.

Trade-ups: $120,000-$200,000 buys a new 3-4BR/2BA colonial or cape with 2-car garage, extra ½ bath, and dining room. Developments may offer tennis, pools and hiker/biker trails.

Luxury homes: Prices range from $225,000-$600,000. At $200,000 you get a new 2-story, 4BR/2½-3BA home (3000-4000 sq. ft.) with high ceilings and traditional layouts; many have pools/tennis.

Rental market: Where available, 3BR houses in good school areas avg. $700-$850/mo. Townhouse apartments and condos (very limited) avg. $600/mo.

Great neighborhoods: Dunes West and Brickyard in Mount Pleasant are beautiful new developments with homes from $145,000 to $750,000. The Crown Point section has more modest homes, but all have access to the excellent schools. The Crowfield Plantation (Goose Creek) is a lovely planned community with townhouses, SFHs, a lake, an 18-hole golf course, and homes from $75,000-$500,000.

Nearby areas to consider: Now that the new bridge and I-526 are open, Daniel Island and Cainhoy will see a tremendous boom in population and new construction.

What Things Cost

Runzheimer's Living Cost Index: Avg. annual costs for family of 4 with household income of $50,000: $47,567 (4.9% below avg. city).

ACCRA's national comparisons: Overall living costs are comparable to the national avg. Utilities and groceries are the best buy (11% and 8% below avg. respectively). Health care costs run 3% above avg. Housing costs are 1.6% above avg.

Utilities: Phone: $20/mo. Installations: Avg. $44. Gas and electric: Avg. $91/mo.

Kid care: Day-care costs: $50-$100/wk. **Pediatric visit:** Avg. $45.

The Tax Ax

Sales tax: 6% (Charleston); 5% (Dorchester and Berkeley).

Property tax: To estimate taxes, multiply the home value times 4% (provided you own and occupy it) and multiply again by the current millage rate. 1991 rates in Charleston County avg. .2800. Thus, tax on a $100,000 home would run approximately $1,100/yr.

State income tax: Federal taxable income over $10,350 is taxed at 7%.

Climate

Elevation 40'	Avg. High/Low	Avg. Rain (Inches)	Avg. Snow (Inches)	Avg. Days Rain	Avg. % Humidity
Jan.	60/37	2.9	--	10	56
April	76/53	3	--	8	50
July	89/71	8.2	--	14	64
Oct.	77/55	3.1	--	6	56
YEAR	75/51	52.1	.6	115	56

# of days 32° or below: 35	# of days 90° or above: 48

With the exception of the warm, humid summer days, Charleston is pleasant, mild and sunny. Ocean breezes moderate the climate, almost guaranteeing that temperatures will get neither too hot or too cold. Most rainfall is in the summer, which is followed by hurricane season. Snowfall amounts to a light dusting (.5 in. annually).

"You can quote me on that"

"My husband is in the military, so I know all about moving, and Charleston is as wonderful a place as you could hope for. I hope we get to stay."—J.H.

Earning a Living

Economic outlook: Talk about turning lemons into lemonade. The massive rebuilding after Hurricane Hugo poured millions of insurance dollars into construction and retailing. Unemployment is still high for the area (6% compared to the usually steady 4%), with layoffs mostly military (civilian labor force at the naval shipyards went from 8,000 to 5,700 in 6 months). Considering that the armed forces are one of the three engines that drive the economy, it hurts. However, the other two, the port and tourism, are going gangbusters. The Trident region expects 5 million visitors this year, topping previous records, and the port, the second largest in the South, is at capacity and expanding. The population boom (steady 2%-3%/yr.) and the high number of companies moving here have brightened up the region tremendously. Last year 10 new manufacturers, including Dynapower, AGFA Photo and CIGNA Insurance's General Graphics (printing and publishing division), relocated or announced plans to do so. When the new plants are complete, there will be an added 750 jobs and $150 million in capital investments. Commercial construction and banking are experiencing serious slowdowns.

Where the jobs are: The military is still the region's largest employer, and with the recent announcement that the new C17s are coming here, it means the Air Force base has been taken off the "closing" list (a real stay of execution). On the civilian side, manufacturing continues to be an important force. DuPont, Amoco and Exxon Chemical have been here for decades (Exxon recently expanded). Other fast-developing firms include George J. Meyer Manufacturing (high-speed beverage packager), DRW Machines, and MDT Corp. (medical diagnostic equipment). A sixth TV station (Channel 36) will soon be broadcasting from the area. In addition, the health care industry is projected to grow by 10% annually, making it the fastest-growing local sector. Currently 15,000 people are employed by the hospitals and medical companies.

Business opportunities: Convincing businesses to relocate here is like taking candy from a baby. With the low tax structure (South Carolina is ranked 41st in the U.S. for lowest per-capita tax burden), access to one of the fastest-growing ports on the Atlantic coast, not to mention the fabulous golfing (executives come for the tour and are sold by the 4th tee), *Inc.* magazine rated Charleston 7th for most new business starts (1988-1990). In spite of the recession, the Trident region is outperforming state and national activity.

Making the Grade

Public education overview: Trident area schools are expanding at a rapid rate and appear to be managing the growth. New school buildings and improvements of older facilities are almost standard operating procedure. An aggressive new state superintendent is committed to putting to rest old myths about public schools in the South. Although the number of disadvantaged children is high across the state, Charleston area schools are starting to build excellent performance records. Test scores of college-bound students are very competitive (all the high schools now have advanced placement courses), and while an average of only 50% of students go on to 4-year colleges, many are accepted at Ivy League schools and other prestigious institutions. Charleston County has a magnet school system, Berkeley County has a very successful Partners in Education Program, and Dorchester County has a high number of schools that have received state grants for the greatest test score increases. One possible drawback is that with the area being so transient (military and corporate transfers), many teachers stay a few years and leave. The bottom line, is Trident area schools can hold their own in terms of nationally accepted standards (or better). Parents should not feel it imperative to enroll their children in private school.

Class size: 19:1 (avg.).

Help for working parents: In Charleston County, 20 grade schools offer extended day programs (both tutorial and activities) in cooperation with the YWCA.

School year: Day after Labor Day through mid-June. Berkeley and Dorchester Counties start the last week of Aug. Children must be age 5 on or before Nov. 1 to be enrolled in kindergarten.

Special education/gifted programs: Special education programs include LIT (Low Incidence Team) for hearing-impaired and handicapped students (starting from preschool). There are also programs for students with more complex needs (excellent program for autistic children). Gifted students have access to SAIL (Students Actively Involved in Learning) from grades 1-10 and advanced placement courses for college credit in grades 11 and 12.

Nearby colleges/universities: Charleston Southern University and College of Charleston (4-year colleges offering both bachelor's and advanced degree programs); The Citadel (Military College of South Carolina); Johnson and Wales University (fine Culinary arts and degrees in hospitality management); Medical University of South Carolina and Trident Technical College.

Medical Care

Hospitals/medical centers: Four major joint-accredited hospitals are within an 8-block radius of downtown Charleston. The Medical University of South Carolina Med Center is the state's largest teaching center (they have 6 different medical colleges) and has a highly respected heart and kidney transplant program. It is the only tertiary care and Level I trauma center in the area. Charleston Memorial, St. Francis Xavier, Roper Hospital and VA Medical Center are also downtown. Trident Regional Naval Hospital is a private facility in Charleston, specializing in coronary care.

Specialized care: Charter Hospital specializes in psychiatric care, and Fenwick Hall Hospital offers drug and alcohol rehabilitation. Hospice of Charleston offers long-term care for terminally ill patients. There is also a Ronald McDonald House.

Crime & Safety

Charleston is as safe a place to live as any area this size. In fact, there's less crime today than 20 years ago, because public safety awareness has become a top priority. Charleston proper actually has the highest ratio of police for every 10,000 citizens of any city in the U.S. At present the major crime problems are larceny and theft, a result of a growing population. Violent crime is rare. When asked about fear of walking the streets at night, residents responded, "What are you talking about?" That's the answer you hope to hear!

Community Life

Four years ago, the city wanted to create gathering places for residents to mingle and started biweekly farmers' markets (May-Oct.). They set up sidewalk cafés, and now hundreds of people come to buy produce from local truck farmers, order dinner from restaurants, or just socialize with coffee and pastry. Christmas in Charleston is also a delight. There are 140 different events, but every year, families look forward to guessing how Santa will drop in (literally) at King St. Square. Last year he arrived by helicopter; next year it could bungee jumping! Some say the reason Charleston is such a close-knit community is its history. Dating back from the American Revolution to Hurricane Hugo, helping hands are never far away.

Let the Good Times Roll

Family fun: All the waterways and barrier islands surrounding Charleston make it ideal for sailing and freshwater fishing. Lakes Marion and Moultrie (Berkeley County) are great spots. Edisto Beach State Park is the perfect place for camping and water sports (it's one of the most popular on the coast); James Island County Park is another. Favorite stops for kids are the waterfront park at the foot of Vendue Range (there are huge water sprays to cool off in) and boat rides through Cape Romain National Wildlife Refuge (an exciting, real wilderness experience). Boating on the Intercoastal Waterway, hiking through the Francis Marion National Forest and biking through Magnolia Plantation Gardens (the oldest in the U.S.) or Palmetto Island County Park make for glorious days. If golf is your game, there are dozens of courses (many championship ones) in the area, including several designed by Gary Player, Jack Nicklaus and Tom Fazio (check out Kiawah Island). The Wild Dunes course is ranked 34th best in the world.

Sports: Sports fanatics will definitely want to hook up to cable TV. The most live action here is from the Charleston Rainbows (minor league team of the San Diego Padres) and collegiate sports. A gorgeous new coliseum, which will likely attract a professional hockey team, is under construction in North Charleston.

Arts & entertainment: The Charleston Area Arts Council and the Charleston Cultural Affairs Committee have done a wonderful job of bringing music, theater and art to the region. They boast their own symphony orchestra, a community repertory theater, ballet and recital groups. Historic museums continue to fascinate people, including the Gibbes Museum of Art (it offers a splendid showcase of American art and Southern history as well as one of the finest collections of miniatures in the world), the Charleston Museum (the oldest in North America, with a wonderful "Discover Me" room for children), and Patriot's Point (world's largest maritime and naval museum). Dock Street Theater, one of America's first playhouses, offers delightful free performances.

Annual events: Spoleto International Arts Festival USA (celebration of music and art, attracts thousands from around the world May-June); Lowcountry Oyster Festival (Feb.); Southeastern Wildlife Exposition (Feb.); House and Garden Candlelight Tours (Sept.-Oct.); Plantation Days (Nov.); Greek Spring Festival (May), downtown Charleston.

The Environment

Air and water quality are considered excellent, with a good distance between the industrial and residential areas keeping pollution at a minimum. Air quality meets both EPA standards and Clean Air Act requirements. Ocean sea breezes contribute to clean air as well. Charleston's drinking water comes from the Edisto River, and daily samples are tested for bacteria and other pollutants and then certified by the Department of Health and Environmental Control. The Clean City Commission sponsors neighborhood cleanups and citywide drives. At least 2,000 people pitch in to pitch out. (See pages 56-57 for information on EPA Findings on lead levels in Charleston's water.)

In and Around Town

Roads and interstates: I-26, I-95, I-526, U.S. Highway 17, U.S. 52, U.S. 78 and 178.
Closes airport: Charleston International Airport (8 mi. from downtown).
Public transportation: Charleston's bus service is a public utility and is operated by SCE & G (local gas company). Routes are throughout the city and to the barrier islands.
Avg. commute: 10-30 min. from outlying suburbs.

What Every Resident Knows

The Charleston dance was born on King Street by the Jenkins Orphanage Band (it eventually gained worldwide fame). Blacks and whites immediately took to the simple step, but had no idea it would ever come to symbolize America's swinging years. • Natives cherish their marshes and take exception when newcomers compare them to cornfields. "They change colors with each season, they attract wildlife, and if you live on one, you can be sure of privacy (nobody can build a house too close)," said a marsh enthusiast. • Bring your green thumb to South Carolina. The mild four seasons are ideal for planting perennials, annuals and edibles. • The Palmetto State is horse country. In Charleston, the Plantation at Stono Ferry has polo and steeplechasing. Giddyap!

FYI

Charleston Trident Chamber of Commerce
P.O. Box 975
Charleston, SC 29402
803-577-2510

Charleston Convention & Visitor's Bureau
P.O. Box 975
Charleston, SC 29402
803-853-8000

Charleston Post & Courier
134 Columbus Street
Charleston, SC 29403
803-722-2223

Hamrick-Carter Real Estate, Inc.
1118 Savannah Highway
Charleston, SC 29407
803-571-1655
Betty Carter, Broker

Century 21-Limerick East, Inc.
389 Johnnie Dodds Blvd., Suite 103
Mount Pleasant, SC 29464
800-531-6030
Shirley Gilbert, Broker

Prudential Carolinas Realty
342 E. Bay Street
Charleston, SC 29401
800-334-0171
Doris Pack, Relocation Specialist

South Carolina Electric & Gas Co.
P.O. Box 760
Charleston, SC 29402
803-554-7234

Southern Bell Telephone Co.
800-336-0014

Small Business Development Center
Trident Technical College, Palmer Campus, P.O. Box 20339
Charleston, SC 29413
803-727-2020

Trident Economic Development Authority
P.O. Box 975
Charleston, SC 29402
803-577-2519

School districts: 803-724-7733 (Charleston), 803-723-4627 (Berkeley), 803-873-2901 (Dorchester II)
Property tax assessor: 803-723-6718
Welcome Wagon: 803-763-0632
Interfaith Council: 803-766-2815
Physician's referral: 803-577-1163
Job service: 803-792-7040

Columbia, South Carolina

Area Snapshot

Local population: 472,000
Counties: Richland, Fairfield, Newberry and Lexington   **Population:** 527,000
U.S. region: Southeast coast, central S.C.
Closest metro areas: Charlotte (100 mi. north), Atlanta (200 mi. west)
Median housing price: $88,090
Avg. household income: $30,000
Best reasons to live here: In the top 10 U.S. housing markets, abundant higher education, affordable living costs, pleasant climate, growing and diverse population, recession-proof economy, award-winning schools, great recreation.

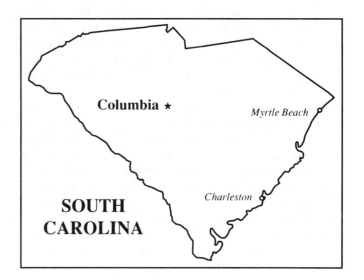

Fabulous Features

Many states in the nation have a city of Columbia, but none could be finer than the one in Carolina in the '90s. As with the ancient pyramids that were towers of power, this unpretentious river region is forging ahead, thanks to a solid foundation.

As the state capital, the home of both the University of South Carolina and Fort Jackson (the top U.S. army installation in the world), Columbia has been bestowed with several recession-proof legs to stand on. That's why in the past four years, more than 32,000 private sector jobs were created and $1 billion in capital investments were made, no small thanks to the fact that compared to 180 other U.S. markets, it ranked second-lowest in building costs.

Columbia also looks great in a comparison of 100 housing markets. *U.S. News and World Report* rated it 9th due to great values (the $60,000-$150,000 range is very impressive) and diversity (everything from pleasing starter homes to luxury lakefront property). An honorable mention goes to all the attractive family-style communities and conscientious neighborhood associations within the Columbia metro (Newberry, Fairfield, Richland and Lexington counties). Regardless of where you drop anchor, you'll be within 20 minutes of downtown and within hours of the beaches and mountains.

But the river runs deep here, too. Glistening waterways, including the 520-mile shoreline of Lake Murray, give water sports enthusiasts a year-round subscription to fun.

Another thing we learned was how terrific the educational opportunities are. There are 10 colleges and universities including the main campus of USC (its master's of international business program is ranked among the nation's top). And thanks to landmark education reform, public schools in the area offer award-winning scholastic programs, many of which are models for the country (vocational, special education and gifted programs have earned national recognition). As with the pyramids, it seems the strong get stronger.

Possible drawbacks: Columbia's climate is a good news/bad news scenario. The good news is that most of the year is mild (enough to golf in January). The bad news is that August's 100-degree days will have you dreaming of Alaskan cruises. • As progressive as this city is, some of the news stories will seem shockingly back-wards. A man on trial for videotaping the rape of his wife was found not guilty. Isolated in-cident, perhaps, but some say South Carolina has some catching up to do.

Real Estate

Market overview: Somewhat of a buyer's market, with inventory at highest in 2 years. Most activity can be found in the $75,000-$100,000 range. The market is stable, though there are slightly more houses than buyers. Steady growth in the past 2 years is expected to continue. Out-of-town buyers comprise 35% of the market.

What houses look like: Predominant style is 2-story brick; there are also country, contemporary, Victorians, ranches and capes. If house has a garage, it's probably a double. Almost no basements. In newer homes, palladium windows, cathedral ceilings and skylights are common. Homes above $100,000, especially older ones, feature formal living/dining rooms. Avg. lot size is 1/3 acre, perhaps less in $75,000-$100,000 range. Spacious master suites in houses $100,000 and above. Screened porches are popular.

Starter homes: $75,000 buys a 1300-1500 sq. ft., 3BR/2BA home on 1/3 acre w/great room and fireplace, but no garage or basement. $100,000 buys a 1300-1700 sq. ft. 3BR/2BA w/formal living and dining rooms, fireplace, possibly a single garage, 1/3 acre (and no basement). Starter homes tend to be 10-year-old, smaller houses.

Trade-ups: $125,000-$175,000. $150,000 buys a newer 2000 sq. ft, 3-4BR/2-2½BA on 1/3+ acre in nice area w/2-car garage, fireplace, formal living room and dining room.

Luxury homes: $250,000-$400,000. $300,000 buys a 10-20 yr. old, 3700-4200 sq. ft., 4-5BR/3-4BA home in a country club community w/2-car garage, room for an office, screened-in porches, pool, fireplaces, jacuzzi and spacious master suites.

Rental market: SFHs easy to find, from $600-$900/mo. for a 3BR/2BA. Apartment complexes are numerous; 2BR is $275-$450/mo.

Great neighborhoods: The Summit is a planned community on the northeast side of Columbia that offers bike trails, a rec center, scenic beauty and tennis. Houses range from $75,000-$300,000. Quill Valley Harbison is ideal for starter-home families ($80,000-$120,000)—lots of trees, bike trails, walking trails, and great schools of its own.

Nearby areas to consider: Lexington connects to Lake Murray (not directly on it), with good schools, convenient to shopping (15 min. to downtown). Camden, founded in 1762 has lots of older homes, good schools, and is 30 min. away. Other fast-growing communities are Chapin and Blythwood. Both have good schools and easy access to interstate.

What Things Cost

Runzheimer's Living Cost Index: Avg. annual costs for family of 4 with household income of $50,000: $47,242 (5.5% below avg. city).

ACCRA's national comparisons: Overall living costs are 6.8% below the national avg. Utilities and transportation are approximately 14% below avg. Health care and groceries are 7% below avg. Housing costs are 0.4% above avg.

Utilities: Phone: $16.90/mo. (unlimited local calls). Installation: Avg. $44. Electric: $47-$50 to $87-$90/mo. Gas: Avg. $21-$27/mo.

Kid care: Available care for infants 6 wks.-18 mo., not extensive but can be found. Avg. costs $75/wk. for infants, $50/wk. for age 2+. Hours are 6:30 a.m.-6:30 p.m. but there is a late shift at some centers from midnight to 8 a.m. **Pediatric visit:** $40.

The Tax Ax

Sales tax: 5% (prescriptions, professional services, medical supplies exempt if physician-prescribed).

Property tax: There are 20+ tax districts in the area with varying rates. In the city, the current millage rate is .3136.

State income tax: Federal taxable income over $10,350 is taxed at 7%.

Climate

Elevation 260'	Avg. High/Low	Avg. Rain (Inches)	Avg. Snow (Inches)	Avg. Days Rain	Avg. % Humidity
Jan.	57/34	3.4	.3	9	55
April	77/51	3.5	--	8	43
July	92/70	5.7	--	12	56
Oct.	77/51	2.6	--	6	50
YEAR	75/52	46.2	1.7	109	52
# of days 32° or below: 62			# of days 90° or above: 86		

Protected from cold air masses by the mountains to the west and intense heat by the Atlantic Ocean to the east, seasons vary, and there are rarely extremes. Rain is evenly distributed (lots of thunderstorms in spring/summer) and snow occurs 2 days a year. Fall and spring are sunny and warm.

> **"You can quote me on that"**
> *"Living costs are so reasonable, and there is so much to do. We won't have to work until we're 100 to enjoy a great life."—F.F.*

Earning a Living

Economic outlook: Anchored by its status as the state's capital, and backed by the economic solidity of the University of South Carolina (one of the area's largest employers), state government and Fort Jackson (largest U.S. Army installation in the world), Columbia's economy is virtually recession-proof. Thanks in large part to its revitalized downtown and the expansion of health care treatment and research centers and nationlly recognized educational institutions, Columbia has earned some very impressive rankings. A Chase Econometrics study named Columbia the 16th fastest-growing employment center in the country. In 1989, *Inc.* magazine named it the 20th fastest-growing U.S. metropolitan area for new business.

Where the jobs are: Officials from local chambers of commerce, businesses and government agencies have taken aggressive steps to ensure a proactive business climate. Those efforts are paying off. Over the past four years, more than 32,000 new private-sector jobs were created in the four-county region. Local industry announced more than $1 billion in capital investments last year. Columbia's diverse economic base includes 32 Fortune 500 and 14 Fortune 100 companies. The area is also a center for service-oriented companies dealing in finance, insurance, computers, telecommunications and real estate. Fort Jackson has a yearly economic impact on the area in excess of $400 million. Over the past 4 years, new industrial facilities were announced by Mack Trucks, Pirelli Cable Corp, Golden State Foods, RiteAid, NAPA Genuine Parts, Dana Corp, Federal Paper Board and Hon Office Furniture. Major industrial expansions have been made by Michelin Tire, Westinghouse Electric, NCR, Whirlpool and Square D Corp. Columbia has 2nd-lowest building costs of 180 major U.S. cities. Development along the metro area's riverfront, the Congaree Vista, is expected to incorporate office and retail space, residential developments, recreational facilities and an arts and entertainment district. A substantial number of new jobs (nearly 1,200) are expected upon completion of the project. BMW's move into the Spartanburg area in June 1992, is expected to create an additional 2,000 jobs.

Business opportunities: The rosiest outlook for new businesses is in the service sector. Businesses involved in some way with the university or government sector are faring the best. Paper, computer applications and dry cleaning firms have shown the greatest growth. Because of recent consolidation of banks within North and South Carolina, banking jobs are declining.

Making the Grade

Public education overview: Columbia has 9 school districts within its boundaries, but Richland County District 2 is on the cutting edge of innovation: 75% of graduating seniors plan to pur-sue post-high school education; 8 of 14 schools have been named model schools in the nation by the U.S. Dept. of Education. Three new schools opened since 1990, and the district anticipates the need for 5 more within the next 8 years to meet population growth. There are numerous special programs. The district has had strong emphasis on music and fine arts—its orchestra was the first in South Carolina invited to perform in Carnegie Hall.

Class size: 21:1.

Help for working parents: 3 elementary schools in Richland County District 2 offer after-school enrichment care activities (nominal charge to cover operating expenses).

Blue Ribbon School Awards: Clifdale Elementary ('85-'86), Dent Middle School ('84-'85), Irmo High School and Spring Valley High School ('82-'83), Joseph Keels Elementary ('85-'86), Dreher High School ('88-'89), E.L. Wright Middle School ('83-'84), Lonnie B. Nelson Elementary ('87-'88), Richland Northeast High School ('84-'85), Satchel Ford Elementary Schools ('87-'88).

School year: Last wk. of Aug. through 1st wk. of June. Children must be 5 on or before Nov. 1 to enter kindergarten.

Special education/gifted programs: The 1984 Education Improvement Act for South Carolina required schools to implement programs for gifted and talented students (as well as other educational reforms). ALERT (Active Learning Experiences in Resourceful Thinking), for grades 2-12, is designed to increase learning through innovative experiments and field studies. Children with mental, physical and emotional handicaps are mainstreamed into the regular school environment to the extent possible.

Nearby colleges/universities: 10 institutions of higher learning, including the main campus of the Univ. of South Carolina (25,500+ students). USC's master's of international business program is ranked No. 1 in the country. The university is a major resource for high-tech research and development firms due to its $30 million Swearingen Engineering Center. Other schools: Midlands Technical College; Benedict College; Columbia College; Columbia Bible College and Seminary; Allen University; Newberry College; Lutheran Theological Southern Seminary.

Medical Care

Hospitals/medical centers: Baptist Medical Center (433 beds; specializing in cancer treatment, neonatology and women's health); Fairfield Memorial Hospital; Lexington Medical Center (240 beds; specializing in women's obstetrical and gynecological comprehensive health care, trauma center); Newberry County Memorial Hospital (102 beds); Providence Hospital (191 beds; facilities for diagnostic and radiation care, emergency unit); Richland Regional Medical Center (536 beds; specializing in internal medicine, rehabilitative therapy, cardiac care, cancer therapy); Women's Hospital of Lexington.

Specialized care: Charter Rivers Hospital (substance abuse); Children's Hospital at Richland Memorial; (internal and rehabilitative therapy for infants and children); Dorn Veterans Hospital; Hall Psychiatric Institute (emotionally handicapped); Health South Rehabilitation Center (stroke and spinal cord injuries); South Carolina State Hospital (psychiatric).

Crime & Safety

Crime is down 6% in Columbia because of programs such as community-based policing (officers walk the beat in higher crime areas), and lower mortgage rates are offered to officers who move into the city (as opposed to living in the suburbs). The Crime Prevention Unit has a mechanical McGruff that speaks to children at day-care, schools and community groups. Numerous other programs: Stranger Danger & Latch Key Kids programs (grades K-5), personal safety for women; neighborhood watch programs; residential and commercial crime surveys.

Community Life

Columbia is alive with history, and remembering the past through the celebration of the present is a special part of its community life. The old and the new (energetic, growing economy) blend together to make Columbia's community life distinctively Southern and yet uniquely its own. Volunteers are active in organizations such as Boy Scouts, Salvation Army and the Red Cross. But what makes the community come to life are such organizations as the Columbia Action Council, which organizes and sponsors the city's many festivals and parades. With a volunteer base of 2,500, it puts on a variety of events—something for everyone to participate in. Mayfest, the largest festival in South Carolina, is the most important event.

Let the Good Times Roll

Family fun: A trip to Riverbanks Zoo, home to more than 1,000 animals, is always popular with both young and old. Congaree Swamp National Monument, Columbia's Riverfront Park and Historic Columbia Canal are also major local attractions. Sesquicentennial State Park and Peachtree Rock Preserve offer swimming, picnicking, hiking and boating. Columbia boasts a wide variety of parks and county athletic facilities. In Richland County alone, there are 11 county parks, 3 swimming pools and 3 tennis centers. There are 21 golf courses plus hundreds of baseball, softball, basketball, flag football and volleyball teams for all ages. The recreational opportunities of Lake Murray (78 sq. mi. of water, 500 mi. of shoreline) attract visitors from all over the state. Sidney Park, located in the heart of Columbia's Congaree Vista, features a 4-acre manmade lake, island stage and a multipurpose amphitheater.

Sports: The Columbia Mets are the New York Mets' Class A affiliate. The Persimmon Hill Golf Club has an 18-hole championship golf course open to the public. The Univ. of South Carolina Gamecocks play to capacity crowds at William Brice Stadium. New to Columbia are the Cougars, members of the infant Professional Sports Football League. In the winter, Gamecock and Lady Gamecock basketball teams play in the 12,000-seat Carolina Coliseum.

Arts & entertainment: Columbia has more than 60 cultural organizations that present more than 700 events a year. It supports 12 live theater groups, including Town Theatre, the oldest continuously operating theatre in the U.S. Columbia is home to the $15 million Koger Center for the Arts at the Univ. of South Carolina, which in turn houses the South Carolina Philharmonic Orchestra, Columbia City Ballet, Columbia Lyric Opera, and the Univ. of South Carolina Symphony, chamber orchestra and concert choir. The city's 12 art and history museums include the South Carolina State Museum, the Columbia Museum of Art and USC's McKissick Museum (natural history).

Annual events: Mayfest is the city's largest festival—3 days of music, cultural events, arts and crafts, food and other family-oriented activities. Autumnfest and St. Patrick's Day are also among the most celebrated of the nearly 2 dozen festivals held annually in and around Columbia. Others include Taste of Columbia (April); Festival of Heritage (Sept.); South Carolina State Fair (Oct.); Autumnfest (Sept.).

The Environment

Air and water quality are monitored several times a year and do not exceed Federal standards. Smog and air pollution are minimal. Environmental risks in the area remain negligible, reflecting the expansion of high-tech and light industry, as well as environmental awareness and pride in maintaining the riverfront area free of pollution. The environmental issues are part of the school curriculum, and community participation is encouraged. There is scheduled curbside recycling. The City of Columbia Sanitation Dept provides trash pick-up twice weekly and other curbside trash once a week.

In and Around Town

Roads and interstates: 120, 126, 177; U.S. Hwy 321, 378.
Closest airport: Columbia Metropolitan Airport.
Public transportation: Local buses are provided by South Carolina Electric and Gas Co., and operate more than 30 separate routes, covering nearly 370 mi.
Avg. commute: 20-40 min. (Columbia is fairly spread out and the commute will vary depending on time of day and traffic).

What Every Resident Knows

Everything is just peachy in South Carolina. As the nation's largest peach producer east of the Mississipi, you'll be trying peaches in everything from pie to pot roast. Don't knock it 'til you try it.
• During the Revolutionary War, dozens of battles and skirmishes were fought here. During the Civil War, Columbia was burned to the ground by General Sherman. But like the watch, Columbia has taken a lickin' and keeps on tickin' (many streets are named in honor of war heroes). • April showers bring May flowers, but nobody's figured out what the intense thunderstorms bring (other than frightened kids). That and the inevitable spring-time tornado watches keep folks glued to the radio.

FYI

Greater Columbia Chamber of Commerce
930 Richland Street
Columbia, SC 29202
803-733-1110

Greater Columbia Convention & Visitors Bureau
P. O. Box 15
Columbia, SC 29202
803-254-0479

Economic Development Inc.
P.O. Box 1149
Columbia, SC 29202
803-737-0888

Small Business Development
1710 College Street
Columbia, SC 29208
803-777-4907

The State (daily)
P.O. Box 1333
Columbia, SC 29202
803-771-8380

Coldwell Banker Jenkins & Gallup Realtors
2926 Devine Street
Columbia, SC 29205
803-733-3650
Ann Duggan, Relocations

South Carolina Electric & Gas
1400 Lady Street
Columbia, SC 29201
803-799-9000

Southern Bell
400 Laurel Street
Columbia, SC 29201
800-336-0014

School district: 803-733-6000
Property tax assessor: 803-748-4900
Newcomer's Club: 803-699-0881
Interfaith Council: A list of churches and synagogues can be obtained from the Chamber of Commerce.
Physician's referral: 803-765-1498, 800-254-2288
Day-care referral: 803-735-7000

Greenville, South Carolina

Area Snapshot

Local population: 250,000
Counties: Greenville   **Population:** 333,000
U.S. region: Northwest South Carolina (Piedmont Region)
Closest metro areas: Charlotte (90 mi. north); Atlanta (140 mi. south)
Median housing price: $83,800
Avg. household income: $34,000
Best reasons to live here: Affordable living, low taxes, country's second best housing market, fast-growing job market, mountain views, pleasant climate, great education, growing cultural arena, environmentally sound.

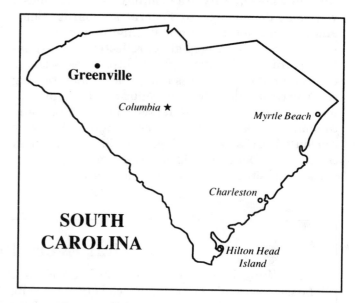

Fabulous Features

If you knew Greenville, like we knew Greenville, oh, oh, oh what a place! The mountain scenery, fresh air and rushing streams are the greatest possible wake-up call, inviting you to infinite possibilities.

The economy has been been zooming past the rest of the state and much of the country. Unemployment has held at a steady 3% thanks to a record-breaking $1.3 billion spending spree on capital investments. That doesn't include a new $300 million BMW plant being built next to the regional airport (2,000 jobs will open up). More than 7,500 jobs were added last year due to the relocation or expansion of foreign interests (Hitachi, Adidas, and 158 others).

Greenville was just identified as the second-best housing market in the country by *U.S. News and World Report* because of a great inventory of reasonably priced homes in the midst of "Beauty and the Boom" (wait 'til you see what's under $100,000)!

Education is also first-rate: Southside High School is the only one in the state (and one of 70 in the U.S.) to have the prestigious International Baccalaureate Program (the study of global affairs), and Hillcrest High just moved into a new $20 million dollar facility.

Residents roll out the green carpet for great recreation (golfing, hiking and horseback riding). And with the new $42 million Peace Center for the Performing Arts, your calendar will be filled. Peace is an appropriate name, because this is a community in accord. Race relations are enviable (there is minority representation on every elected body). One newcomer said, "We moved here and friends are "green" with envy!"

Possible drawbacks: Many older residents are resisting tax hikes to improve roads, libraries, and a much needed civic center. It's a constant battle between them and the newcomers who want beautiful, new facilities. • The start of the Appalachias is 20 miles, but good snow skiing is still a 90-minute drive. At least the views are fabulous.

"You can quote me on that"

"Coming from New York, my husband and I were shocked to see just how much more we could get here. It's not just lower-priced houses, it's taxes, day-care costs, entertainment and especially eating out. We also love the weather and how much there is to do."—J.P.

Real Estate

Market overview: It's a buyer's market all right! In one recent month, there were 2,258 houses listed in the area and only 342 were sold. With average homes prices in the $90,000 range, out-of-town buyers are delighted with prices and selection. As for new construction, there has been tremendous growth in the eastside area, the northeast (Greer) and southeast (Mauldin and Simpsonville). New homes start at $125,000. Many are in magnificent country club communities with lavish amenities.

What houses look like: Residential areas are colorful, lined with red maple and dogwood trees. And with diverse housing styles, neighborhoods are filled with brick and vinyl ranches, Victorians and contemporaries. Homes are well insulated—they stay cool in summer and warm in winter. Interiors show jacuzzis, fireplaces, cathedral ceilings, gourmet kitchens, hardwood floors and decking. Many newer homes also show great rooms instead of formal living and dining areas. The latest status symbol is a triple-trace ceiling (three-border molding set-in lighting)—say goodbye to ordinary molding.

Starter homes: $50,000 to $70,000 will buy a 3BR/1½BA home (1200 sq. ft.) on 80 x 100 lot in Simpsonville and Mauldin. Newer homes include a fireplace, carport or 1-car garage and possibly a great room. Basements aren't part of the deal.

Trade-ups: From $85,000-$175,000, newer, larger homes (1700-1900 sq. ft.) are on the market by the dozens. Homes are mostly 3BR/2BA, possibly with a basement. Look at Lake Forest and Botany Woods.

Luxury homes: $200,000+ buys a large, new 4BR/3½BA all-brick home (2000-4200 sq. ft.) with 9' ceilings, oak-paneled den or great room w/fireplace, master suite, 2-car garage on a ½-1 acre lot. $500,000 buys a 5BR executive home, usually more traditional (formal living and dining areas). Botany Woods, Thornblade and Middlecreek are desirable.

Rental market: With homes so affordable, SFH rentals are tight. Even condo rentals are scarce. Where available, condos rent for $400-$600/mo. Houses start at $550/mo up to $750+.

Great neighborhoods: Families are heading northeast to Del Norte and Merrifield Park, where housing prices and taxes are lower, and the neighborhoods are convenient to schools and shopping. They're also more rural.

Nearby areas to consider: Greer (between Greenville and Spartanburg) is a fast-growing community with excellent schools (Buena Vista Elementary earned a Blue Ribbon Award and Riverside High was named best in the state by *Redbook*. Housing prices are in all ranges.

What Things Cost

Runzheimer's Living Cost Index: Avg. annual costs for family of four with household income of $50,000: $46,627 (6.8% below avg. city).

ACCRA's national comparisons: Overall living costs are 5.5% below the national avg. Health care costs represent the greatest savings at 25% below. Housing costs are an estimated 7% below, groceries and transportation are about 6% below and goods and services are about 4% below. Utilities are the only category above avg. (4.3%).

Utilities: Phone: $17/mo. (unlimited). Installations avg. $44. Gas: Ranges from $11/mo. to $25/mo. Electric: Avg. $60/mo. w/high of $80/mo. (summer).

Kid care: Day care is widely available, but the sooner you register, the better. The best centers can have waiting lists from two months to a year. Costs avg. $52/wk. for infants and $45/wk. for 18 mo. and older. **Pediatric visit:** $35-$40.

The Tax Ax

Sales tax: 5% (professional services and non-prepared food are exempt).

Property tax: To calculate taxes, take appraised value times 4% to get assessment. Multiply times the current millage rate (range from 98.0-337.10 depending on district). For example, a $100,000 home ($100,000 X 4% = $4,000 X 200 millage) would be $800/yr.

State income tax: Federal taxable income over $10,350 is taxed at 7%.

Climate

Elevation 900'	Avg. High/Low	Avg. Rain (Inches)	Avg. Snow (Inches)	Avg. Days Rain	Avg. % Humidity
Jan.	52/33	3.8	1.9	11	56
April	72/50	4.3	--	9	47
July	88/69	4.2	--	12	58
Oct.	72/51	3.2	--	7	53
YEAR	71/51	46.9	6.1	116	54
# of days 32° or below: 68			# of days 90° or above: 52		

Year-round conditions are mild and mostly pleasant, with evening temperatures dropping by as much as 20 even in the middle of summer (attributed to the higher elevations). Winters are also mild, but with the start of the Appalachian Mountains 20 miles west, polar air masses are weakened and bring light snowfalls. Summer days are often hot and humid, although they rarely exceed 100. Thunderstorms accompany many heavy rainfalls.

251

Earning a Living

Economic outlook: Textile and apparel manufacturing originally put Greenville on the map, and while they still have a big impact on the economy, there are a lot more eggs in the basket now. The tremendous growth in the past several years is mostly attributed to new industries relocating here. Greenville now has the greatest concentration of engineering firms in the Southeast, and the most engineers per capita in the U.S. Local products now include computer components, machine tools, contact lens solutions, pharmaceuticals, food items, electronic devices and polyester film, to name a few. Greenville is also one of the leading counties in the state in the number of new jobs created as well as investments in expansions. 1989 was a record-breaking year with $601 million in capital investments. Investment figures for 1990 totaled nearly $680 million and created 2,500 jobs. Having also built up the largest chamber of commerce membership in South Carolina (3,000 members) and nabbed the site of the new $300 million BMW auto plant, the outlook is downright peachy!

Where the jobs are: The largest employers in the county are the Greenville County School District (6,000), the Greenville Hospital System (5,539) and Michelin North America (4,200). Since the late 1970s, the county's unemployment rate has been consistently lower than state and national figures (just under 3%). Much of this is attributed to the high concentration of foreign-owned firms with interests here, such as Hitachi Ltd., Adidas and Simons-Eastern Services. They've created more than 7,500 jobs in the past year. Recent expansions include Bowater Inc., a major paper manufacturer, and Hitachi Electronic Devices which recently completed a $150 million plant near Mauldin (will employ 300 workers). Construction of Mita Industries' new $50 million copier facility will create 60 jobs and Zett Corporation is building a $2 million golf and baseball manufacturing plant to employ 100-150 people. But the biggest news you "auto" know is about BMW's first U.S plant, being built adjacent to the Greenville/Spartanburg airport (will employ 2,000 workers). The only concern is that the UAW will try to unionize the plant (Greenville is a non-union town).

Business opportunities: The Greater Greenville Chamber of Commerce provides assistance to entrepreneurs interested in business startups. Its "Opportunity Greenville" program helps newcomers understand government regulations, the local economy and other important information about the area.

Making the Grade

Public education overview: Students attending Greenville County schools are getting a state-of-the-art education. The largest district in the state (104 schools), and one of the most prestigious, it owns the Roper Mountain Science Center. This magnificent facility offers science-enrichment classes, nature exhibits, an observatory, planetarium and arboretum. At Brushy Creek Elementary, an interactive multi-media network links classrooms to information from around the world. But the greatest accomplishment is having only one of 70 schools in the country with an International Baccalaureate Program (Southside High). Ivy League colleges have been so impressed with the grasp students have of global affairs, they often start them as sophomores. Other recognition has come from the Kennedy Center for the district's support of the arts. Pelham Road Elementary won state Teacher of the Year (5th time) and 11 elementary schools earned the Palmetto Award (state recognition for excellence). High school students consistently outscore other districts in the state on SATs, and 76% of graduating seniors attend college.
Class size: 18:1.

Help for working parents: After-school extended day programs are available at some schools and at four YMCA's. After-school transportation is provided to day-care drop offs when not available on-site. Some schools also have breakfast programs.

Blue Ribbon School Awards: League Middle School ('82-'83), Spartanburg High School ('82-'83, '88-'89), Clifdale Elementary School-Spartanburg ('89-'90).

School year: Starts mid-Aug. through first week of June. Children must be 5 on or before Nov. 1 to enter kindergarten.

Special education/gifted programs: The Fine Arts Center is the state's only public fine arts magnet high school and is available to 10th-12th grade students who want to pursue visual, literary and performing arts (they travel between here and "home" school). Governor's School for the Arts at Furman University is an honors summer program for artistically talented juniors and seniors (nominated by their school). Camperdown Academy and Meyer Center for Special Children are nonprofit schools for the learning disabled, handicapped and emotionally at-risk.

Nearby colleges/universities: Furman University, Clemson University; Bob Jones University, Greenville Technical College; North Greenville College; and University Center.

Medical Care

Hospitals/medical centers: Greenville Memorial Hospital is a well-respected teaching hospital with a Level I trauma center. It also offers diagnostic services, outpatient surgery, an optical surgery center and comprehensive cardiac care (including pediatric). St. Francis Hospital offers the area's only women's hospital (including cancer care, a vitality center and inpatient rehabilitation). The Children's Hospital offers a pediatric ICU, pediatric chemotherapy and oncology, and will soon open a pediatric emergency program. Greenville General Hospital offers a Center for Intensive Pain Management.

Specialized care: Roger Peace Rehabilitation Hospital (for brain and spinal cord injuries); Marshall Pickens Hospital (psychiatric care for children, adults); North Greenville Hospital (substance abuse); Shriner's Hospital for Crippled Children

Crime & Safety

A few years ago, the Greenville police flew in a consultant to get advice on managing a growing drug problem. After careful analysis, he congratulated them and implied that if every city was in such good shape, he'd be out of work. It's indicative of the pro-active attitude of the force. When there was suddenly a noted increase in drug-related crimes (mostly burglaries), police were right on top of it before it could become unmanageable. In truth, relative to the size of the county and how fast the area is growing, crime is low. There are no gangs or graffiti, and a lot of people still leave keys in the car. The widespread concern is that with other cities losing the battle, it could happen here. Excellent crime prevention programs (Stranger Danger, Housewise/Steetwise and DARE) and 40+ active neighborhood watch groups are making a difference.

Community Life

Volunteerism is not just an extracurricular activity during the holidays, it's a way of life year-round. Such organizations as Project Host (soup kitchen), Place of Hope (help for substance abusers), and Habitat for Humanity (build homes for the needy) are manned by a continual roster of volunteers— young and old (scouts, 4-H clubs and YMCA Indian Guides and Princesses) who pitch in. Personal involvement is the reason that many annual events are such big successes. From hot-air ballooning festivals to the city-wide New Year's Eve family fireworks display and party, Greenville residents spoke of giving small tokens and getting huge returns.

Let the Good Times Roll

Family fun: The Greenville Recreation Dept. promotes the theme "Life. Be In It." And it certainly does its share to make an active lifestyle enjoyable. The city operates 37 parks (420 acres) offering everything from grass volleyball courts to bike trails to mini-golf. Five community centers provide great programs and leisure activities year-round. (In tandem with the county, they offer extensive programs for handicapped children and adults). The athletic department is busy organizing sports leagues, including four major annual tennis tournaments ("You'd think it was Wimbledon!"). Brushy Creek Park, on Greenville's east side has the beautiful new Pavilion with an Olympic-sized skating rink and indoor tennis. Reedy River Historic Park, Paris Mountain State Park and at least six other state parks are within a short drive for hiking, biking, swimming and picnicking. Other popular hot spots are the Greenville Zoo, the Roper Mountain Science Center (the new T.C. Hooper Planetarium is out of this world) and Cowpens National Battleground. Horseback riding is also a favorite pastime at J&J Stables or Riverbend Park.

Sports: Greenville is the home of the country's largest membership amateur swimming organization—S.A.I.L. (youngsters receive training in team and individual skills for a series of organized competitive meets each summer.). The exciting Greenville Braves (the Atlanta Braves' class AA minor league team) play at Municipal Stadium, and the Greenville Spinners (Global Basketball Association) play at Greenville Memorial Auditorium.

Arts and entertainment: Don't let anyone tell you small cities are synonymous with cultural deprivation. They haven't seen Greenville's new $42 million Peace Center for the Performing Arts, home to the Greenville Symphony, the Greenville Ballet, the Greenville Savoyards (musicians), the Warehouse Theater and the Heritage Chamber Players. Local colleges and universities present exciting performances as does the popular Theater on the Green. The Greenville Museum of Art and the Bob Jones University Art Gallery offer revolving and permanent exhibits.

Annual events: Downtown Alive (Metropolitan Arts Council presents music and dance in spring); Music on the Mountain (free outdoor concerts May-Sept.); Freedom Weekend Aloft (largest hot-air balloon festival east of the Mississippi July 4th weekend); Fall for Greenville (food festival, Oct.); First Night Greenville (New Year's Eve celebration and fireworks); South Carolina Peach Festival (entertainment, antique car show in summer).

The Environment

Greenville prides itself on its ability to keep the city clean from top to bottom. Water quality is excellent (and many say great-tasting) and although air quality approached EPA limits three times in the past four years, it has never exceeded the guidelines (most cities would be thrilled with that record). The biggest environmental challenge is that the sewage treatment facility is approaching capacity and a task force is now investigating alternative methods. Recycling is big business (the state is the largest plastic recycling producer in the world because of Wellman Industries and other area firms), with a weekly curbside pick up effort that has gotten tremendous response.

In and Around Town

Roads and interstates: I-85, I-385, I-185.
Closest airport: Greenville-Spartanburg Airport.
Public transportation: Greenville Transit Authority provides a range of intercity routes. Downtown trolleys operate weekdays during business hours.
Avg. commute: 20-25 min. from outlying communities to downtown.

What Every Resident Knows

What newcomers quickly learn about true, Southern living is that charity and volunteerism are not something to squeeze in when time permits. You simply do it, like breathing. In fact, families taking responsibility for each other goes back to pre-Civil War days. • A world renowned conductor from the Soviet Union recently moved here with his family. They spoke no English and couldn't answer questions at the many press conferences about why they chose Greenville. Shortly afterwards on a sunny, winter day, they were sitting on a bench on Main Street, taking in the sights and sounds. They were beaming from ear to ear. Their expressions were enough of an answer. • In the new globe of the planet produced by Replogle, a dot was created for Greenville. Seems students in Asia, Latin America and many other countries will be learning a lot more about this up and coming "international" city.

FYI

Greater Greenville Chamber of Commerce
P.O. Box 10048
Greenville, SC 29603
803-242-1050

Greater Greenville Convention & Visitor's Bureau
P.O. Box 10527
Greenville, SC. 29601
803-233-0461

The Greenville News/Piedmont
P.O. Box 1688
Greenville, SC 29602
803-298-4110

Century 21/Bryan Realty
700 E. North Street, Suite 5
Greenville, SC 29601
803-233-2121
Hubert McLeod, Relocation Coord.

Piedmont Natural Gas
P.O. Box 1905
Greenville, SC 29602
803-232-5141

Duke Power
325 West McBee Avenue
Greenville, SC 29601
803-242-3261

City of Greenville Economic Development
P.O. Box 2207
Greenville, SC 29602
803-467-4401

Small Business Development Center
P.O. Box 5616, Station B
Greenville, SC 29606-5606
803-271-4259

Southern Bell
800-336-0014

School district: 803-241-3100
Property tax assessor:
803-467-7100
Welcome Wagon: 803-244-6329
Interfaith Council: Contact Chamber of Commerce
Physician's referral: 803-233-7999 (Ask-A-Nurse); 803-242-7949 (Greenville County Medical Society)
Day-care referral: 803-859-4727, 803-455-8320

Nashville, Tennessee

Area Snapshot

Local population: 510,784 (Metro: 985,026)
County: Davidson
U.S. region: Southeastern U.S./Middle Tennessee
Closest metro areas: Knoxville (178 mi. east), Memphis (210 mi. west)
Median housing price: $89,200
Median household income: $28,687
Best reasons to live here: Big-city living in a country setting, affordable housing, mild year-round climate, clean environment, thriving job market, great entertainment, excellent school system, abundance of colleges and medical care, outdoor recreation, racial harmony.

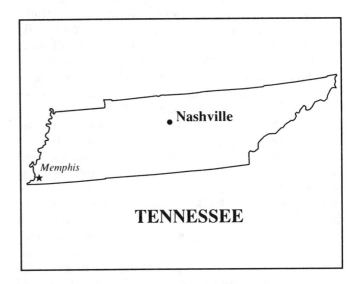

TENNESSEE

Fabulous Features

If you are raising a family in a city where it's getting harder to face the music, Nashville will put more than a song in your heart. It will put extra money in your pocket. The overall tax burden and living costs are lower than in any other major city in the country. Housing prices add to the good news. The extensive inventory and quality of construction for homes in the $100,000 range will make you pinch yourself.

But not only can you afford the keys to the door, you can keep up with mortgage payments, because employment opportunities are outstanding (in the past two years there was a net gain of 13,000 jobs). Corporate relocation has been exceeding expectations. Last year, 37 companies moved here, such as Bankers Trust and Lockheed support systems. It's why *Kiplinger's Personal Finance Magazine* recently identified Nashville as one of 15 "supercities"—one of the best places to look for work, own a business and enjoy a high quality of life.

Nashville has a highly rated school system (8 Blue Ribbon schools), outstanding health care (Vanderbilt University Medical Center is world-renowned), and no fewer than 16 colleges and universities (only New York City has more). Add to that the beautiful rolling hills, a sparkling clean environment (newcomers say the first thing they notice is how nice the air smells), incredibly easy access (30 minutes is a *long* commute), and fantastic family entertainment and recreation. As they say in Music City USA... "and the beat goes on."

Possible drawbacks: The tranquillity has a downside in the form of a time warp. While the rest of the country is getting the latest movies, fashions and restaurant chains, Nashville is playing catch-up. The only thing that starts here is music, but man cannot live on brass alone. • Compared to other cities this size, an 8.25% local sales tax is quite high. We've heard of cities wanting to compete with the big boys, but not usually in this category. • Like heading to the beaches? Better gas up the car. The closest one is in the Florida Panhandle, 5½ hours by car.

"You can quote me on that"

"We love the easy pace and laid-back attitudes. Kids grow up slowly. They're not under the gun to compete at everything, and honestly, they're just not exposed to bad influences as much as other cities. The other thing we like is, people always seem to be in a good mood. It must be all the sunshine and fresh air."—D.B.

Real Estate

Market overview: Nashville's realty market is like a tennis match (look one way, then the other). In the '70s, there was record-breaking activity. By the '80s, the recession and a deeply overbuilt market had realtors talking to each other. Now in the last half of '92, it's been the best selling period in 19 years (building permits up 48%). Homes are spacious for the price (the under-$125,000 market is unbelievable), and property taxes are low. Nashville is also condo country. A tremendous glut plus foreclosures dropped prices substantially (consider resale values before you buy). Avg. carrying charges on SFHs (principal/interest) run $613/mo.

What houses look like: Contemporary styles were the rage through the '80s, with vinyl the siding of choice. Brick is making a comeback (some subdivisions require homes to be a minimum 40% brick). Capes and colonials with cathedral ceilings, large eat-in kitchens, and formal living/dining rooms are most popular. Decks and patios are widely available, fireplaces are not.

Starter homes: Prices range from $70,000-$90,000 for a 3BR/2BA house on a 1/4 acre that's anywhere from 10-50 years old. Many are split levels and capes. Basements and garages are rare. Harpeth Woods and Poplar Ridge are great places to look.

Trade-ups: Prices range from $100,000-$140,000 for 5-10 year old 3BR/2BA homes (1200-1800 sq. ft.) with 2-car garage. Charming colonials and capes with an extra ½BA, wooded views, huge master BR suites on 1/4-acre lots are what you'll see.

Luxury homes: Expect to pay between $200,000-$250,000 for spacious 4BR/2½ BA homes (2200-2800 + sq. ft.) on a 1-acre lot with 2-car garage. Many are custom-built colonials with 17 ft. ceilings, huge master suites, walk-in closets, jacuzzi tubs, extra baths and lots of built-ins. Look at Belle Meade, Green Hills, Brentwood and the lakes area.

Rental market: With everything gone condo or co-op, rentals are very tight. Where available, 2BR units rent for an avg. $444/mo.

Great neighborhoods: Ransom Place is a great new area, with homes priced from $95,000-$125,000 (commute is 10 min.). Homes in the Hearthstone section (also close to downtown) start at $150,000.

Nearby areas to consider: Brentwood (15 min. south of downtown) is an exceptional bedroom community with excellent schools, exciting real estate and growing light industry. It was recently named a model city in President Bush's Take Pride in America program. Bellevue offers beautiful new homes in the low $100s, and Rutherford County offers many new homes in the $80s.

What Things Cost

Runzheimer's Living Cost Index: Avg. annual costs for family of 4 with household income of $50,000: $46,540 (6.9% below avg. city).

ACCRA's national comparisons: In every category, Nashville's living costs are below the national avg. (overall costs are 6.4% below). The big savings are in health care (avg. 15½% below), housing (10% below), utilities (9% below), food and goods and services (avg. 4% below).

Utilities: Phone: $19/mo. Installations range from $42-$63. Total energy costs avg. $99-$150/mo. Water costs seem high due to lack of population density (less people per sq. mile to foot the bills). Avg. water/sewer bill: $50-65/mo.

Kid care: Avg. weekly care for infants run $65-$85/wk. (toddler care runs $45-$70/wk.) Licensed care is widely available (Department of Human Resources issues a directory of facilities—see FYI).

Pediatric visit: Avg. $45.

The Tax Ax

Sales tax: 8.25% (prescriptions, professional services exempt).

Property tax: Assessed at 25% of home's appraised value multiplied by county tax rate of $3.64. A $100,000 home would run $910/yr. Brentwood tax rate is $3.80

State income tax: None.

Climate

Elevation 590'	Avg. High/Low	Avg. Rain (Inches)	Avg. Snow (Inches)	Avg. Days Rain	Avg. % Humidity
Jan.	48/29	4.4	4.3	10	66
April	71/49	4.1	.1	11	53
July	90/69	3.8	--	10	59
Oct.	73/49	2.2	--	7	55
YEAR	70/49	44.8	11.7	115	59
# of days 32° or below: 74			# of days 90° or above: 38		

One day is lovelier than the next, with avg. daily temps in the 60s. Each season is well defined, and there are rarely extremes. Two big selling points are lots of year-round sunshine and relatively low humidity (very moderate compared to other cities located east of the Mississippi River). Thunderstorms are the worst offenders (late March through Sept.).

Earning a Living

Economic outlook: The best thing to say about the '80s is they're over. Nashville is still smarting from its "boom and bust" reputation (out-of-control spec building resulted in Nashville being ranked second in personal bankruptcies in 1990). Careful planning has paved the way for a resounding comeback. For the first time, Nashville is the fastest-growing city area in the state, and has just overtaken Memphis as the largest metro area in the state (projections call for 16% growth by the year 2000). Of all money raised in U.S. initial stock offerings in 1991, 10% was for Nashville-based companies (many in the health care field). In fact, there have been so many corporate expansions, relocations and start-ups, competing cities are singing the blues. The Nissan plant is the largest single Japanese investment outside their country (the plant recently hired 1,600 people to gear up for the new Altima car). GM's Saturn Plant (Spring Hill, 35 mi.) is rapidly expanding production now that they're selling 7% of all small cars sold in the U.S. Nashville's American Airlines hub is now their third largest *and* the fastest-growing. Keep in mind that Nashville is also considered the "Third Coast" (after New York and Los Angeles), with a $2-billion-a-year record-producing, movie and commercial-production industry. Adding to the diversity and economic well-being are the health care industry ($1.2 billion in annual revenues), tourism and educational industries.

Where the jobs are: During the past year, 37 companies have moved here, creating 4,300 jobs. Bridgestone/Firestone Tires, Bankers Trust (service center), Lockheed International (mail-processing division) and OrNda Health Corp (third largest hospital management company) are just some of the major firms that relocated here. Unemployment levels have been below state and national levels for the past 20 years. All told, there was a net increase of 13,700 jobs in the past 2 years. Residential construction has regained momentum, and publishing continues to grow (*USA Today* regional plant and religious publishers employ 14,000 people).

Business opportunities: *Kiplinger's Personal Finance Magazine* says Nashville is one of 15 "Supercities" (Nov. 1991). Because of low personal and corporate taxes, commercial space and the population boom, it's an ideal city for job hunting, launching or relocating a business. At the moment, specialty retail stores and restaurants are making a big splash. Shoney's, PoFolks, Cracker Barrel and O'Charley's are successful franchises that started here.

Making the Grade

Public education overview: Nashville has class, with 121 public schools and 50 private schools. The Metro School System has made tremendous strides in the past 10 years and is recognized for academic achievements and program initiatives. Eight area schools have earned Blue Ribbon awards, and last year 80 elementary and middle schools reached exemplary status according to the Tennessee Department of Education. More than 1,600 high school students take college-level courses, and 400 seniors earn $5.4 million in college scholarships (SAT scores avg. 25-38 points above the national). The district has also made remarkable progress with programs for at-risk children, with the first locally funded early childhood education program, and one of the state's top dropout prevention programs. The district's 3 magnet schools and Excel, a K-8 enrichment program, contribute to the number of students participating in the Distinguished Scholars Program for high school grads. And the Metro school system is among 6 in the country selected to pilot the College Board Equity Agenda, a project that will increase the number of minority students enrolled in college prep courses and attempt to get 100% of the freshman class completing Algebra I.

Class size: 18.5: 1 (avg.).

Help for working parents: 46 schools have before- and after-care programs for grades K-6. (most are run in cooperation with the YMCA).

Blue Ribbon School Awards: Hillsboro High School ('86-'87), Dodson Elementary ('87-'88), Eakin Elementary School ('85-'86), Lakeview Elementary ('88-'89), Glencliff High School ('88-'89), Andrew Jackson Elementary School ('90-'91), Head Middle School ('89-'90), Meigs Magnet School ('89-'90).

School year: Last week of Aug. through mid-June. Children must be 5 on or before Sept. 30 to enter kindergarten.

Special education/gifted programs: There's a tremendous range of programs for autistic, emotionally disturbed, learning disabled, mentally retarded, multihandicapped and other impaired students. Encore, Excel and Advanced Placement are the gifted programs available from kindergarten on.

Nearby colleges/universities: Nashville boasts 16 colleges and universities, 2 law schools and 2 medical schools (second only to New York City); including the prestigious Vanderbilt University, Fisk University (private liberal arts college), Tennessee State University (7,000 students), Middle Tennessee State (15,000 students-Murfreesboro), plus 5 junior colleges.

Medical Care

Hospitals/medical centers: With 15 hospitals and 118 clinics, health care is Nashville's 2nd-largest employer. Vanderbilt University Hospital is one of the most respected research facilities in the country. It offers 86 specialty clinics and a Children's Hospital. Baptist Hospital (the largest non-profit health care center in mid-Tennessee) has a laser surgery center (first in the U.S.), the Institute of Reconstructive surgery, a heart center and a full-service fitness center. Centennial Medical Center offers 24-hour emergency, a transplant center, diabetes treatment and a research center.

Specialized care: Cumberland Hall offers acute psychiatric care, and Luton Community Mental Health Center treats residents on an outpatient basis. The New Horizons of Tennessee offers drug and alcohol rehabilitation. A Ronald McDonald House is centrally located.

Crime & Safety

Nashville has always been considered one of the safest cities in the South (it has the 8th-lowest crime rate for cities with 250,000+ people), but a growing population has brought its share of crime. Auto theft, up 20% over the previous year, is the culprit. On the other hand, violent crimes are way down (homicide by 10.5%, rape by 7.9%), attributed in part to a highly progressive new police chief. Determined undercover detectives working area high schools have also substantially cut drug activity. Overall, people had high praises for the quality of police efforts. Said one longtime resident, "The only people who shouldn't feel safe here are the criminals."

Community Life

With the last incident of civil unrest almost 30 years ago, Nashville has been a model of racial harmony. In fact, in the midst of the recent Los Angeles riots, 2 young black brothers were discovered missing. Thousands of residents, black and white, joined the search party until they were found (tragically, they had fallen into the Cumberland River). But people of all backgrounds coming to the rescue has never been big news. When Meharry Medical College, a historic black medical school, was in serious financial trouble, it was merged with a city hospital ready to close due to lack of doctors. The school and hospital were saved, another example of this solution-hungry city at work.

Let the Good Times Roll

Family fun: With delightful year-round weather, Nashvillians put their 30,000 acres of man-made lakes to good use. Fishing, boating and waterskiing are 10 minutes from town. For those who like excitement in a confined area, the city's computer-operated Wave County Pool at Two Rivers Park is open all summer. You can keep your feet on the ground at its 18-hole championship golf course, lighted tennis courts and recreation center. The Centennial Sportsplex is a phenomenal city treasure. It's a gorgeous new multipurpose facility with an Olympic-sized pool, ice rink and fitness center. Its tennis center has a 2,000-seat stadium and is starting to attract major events. Nearby is the Radnor Lake State Natural Area, a protected wildlife sanctuary, perfect for hiking and biking. The Nashville Zoo, the Davy Crockett State Park and Grassmere Wildlife Park are other exciting outings. By far the biggest attractions are the Grand Ole Opry and Opryland Park, a nothing-else-like-it musical show park with exciting rides (eat lunch *after* you go on the Grizzly River Rampage), top-name entertainment and more.

Sports: You'll keep your eye on the ball with the Nashville Sounds, the Cincinnati Reds' AAA farm team, which plays at Herschel Greer Stadium (one of the nicest AAA stadiums in the country), and the Nashville Knights (Eastern Hockey League), play to sell-out crowds. The Vanderbilt Commodores compete in the exciting Southeastern Conference.

Arts & entertainment: Opryland USA, home to the Grand Ole Opry, theme park and world-famous Music Row. brings the best sounds around (the Bluebird Cafe and 328 Performance Hall are the "hot" clubs). Cultural offerings are not overshadowed, with the Tennessee Performing Arts Center, the first state-funded fine arts forum in the U.S., offering Broadway and original productions. It is also home to the Nashville Symphony, Ballet, Opera and Tennessee Repertory Theater. The Parthenon (built as the world's only full-scale replica of the original Athen's Parthenon) is Nashville's most visible art museum. Other museums include the Van Vecten Gallery (with permanent Renoir and Picasso exhibits), Cumberland Science Museum and Tennessee State Museum (with many art programs directed to children).

Annual events: Iroquois Steeplechase (50,000 spectators come out for the oldest, richest steeplechasing event in the U.S. in May); International Country Music Fan Fair (Tennessee State Fairgrounds and Opryland, June); Kidsfest at Opryland (Aug.); and Nashville Country Holidays (Dec.).

The Environment

Long gone are Nashville's black smoke factories. Air quality is excellent, thanks to an abundance of light manufacturing and service industries and an innovative thermal transfer plant. Nashville burns its garbage for energy, heating and cooling commercial buildings throughout downtown (everyone comments on how fresh the air smells). Water quality is crystal-clear out of the tap (the Cumberland River is the main source, providing ample supply). Recycling efforts are growing, with curbside pickups, community compost heaps and an annual drive to collect phone books. When the area landfill closes in 1994, the city will pay for out-of-county disposal.

In and Around Town

Roads and interstates: I-440, I-65, I-265, I-24, and I-40. Nashville is one of 6 U.S. cities that has 3 interstate highways intersecting the city. I-840 is under construction.

Closest airport: Nashville International Airport (8 mi. east of downtown), with 658 daily arrivals and departures. Direct flights to London's Stansted airport will soon be available.

Public transportation: Metro Transit Authority provides bus service throughout the entire metro area.

Avg. commute: 10-30 min.

What Every Resident Knows

In 1975 Phil Bredesen and his wife looked for a city that would be a great place to raise kids and start a business. All roads pointed to Nashville, and they've been happy here ever since. In turn, the city has been just as happy with them, enough to elect Mr. Bredesen mayor in 1991! • Nashville International Airport gets a workout on weekends, with people thinking nothing of heading to New York, Atlanta and Chicago for shopping and theater excursions. There are so many Nashvillians carrying Marshall Field's and Bloomingdale's shopping bags, tourists think the stores are here! • They don't call this Music City USA for nothing. Maybe you won't be hanging out with Garth Brooks every night, but you can go "clubbing." More than a dozen clubs feature live performances of both Grand Ole stars and up-and-comers!

FYI

Nashville Area Chamber of Commerce
161 Fourth Avenue North
Nashville, TN 37219
615-259-4755

Nashville Convention & Visitor's Bureau
161 Fourth Avenue North
Nashville, TN 37219
615-259-4700

The Tennessean and Nashville Banner (dailies)
1100 Broadway
Nashville, TN 37202
615-254-1031

First Realty Group Inc.
3343 Perimeter Hill Drive, Ste. 121
Nashville, TN 37211
615-833-4466
John Duval

Shirley Zeitlan & Co. Realtors
278 Franklin Rd., Suite 140
Brentwood, TN 32027
615-371-0185
Patty Carter, Managing Broker

Nashville Electric Service
1214 Church Street
Nashville, TN 37246-0001
615-259-3555

Nashville Gas Company
665 Mainstream Drive
Nashville, TN 37228
615-734-0665

South Central Bell Telephone
800-557-6500

Small Business Development Center
Tennessee State University
10th & Charlotte Avenue No.
Nashville, TN 37203
615-251-1178

School district: 615-259-8400
Property tax assessor: 615-741-2837
Welcome Wagon: 615-883-9521
New Neighbors League: 615-662-1488
Conference for Christians and Jews: 615-327-1755
Physician's referral: 615-327-1236
Day-care referral: 615-741-0290

Austin, Texas

Area Snapshot

Local population: 465,622
County: Travis   **Population:** 576,407
U.S. region: Central Texas (Texas Hill Country)
Closest metro area: San Antonio (75 mi. south)
Median housing price: $101,000
Avg. household income: $51,513
Best reasons to live here: Phenomenal job and business growth, highly educated population, wonderful schools, exciting family recreation, very affordable housing, beautiful lakes and hills, no state income tax, mild winters.

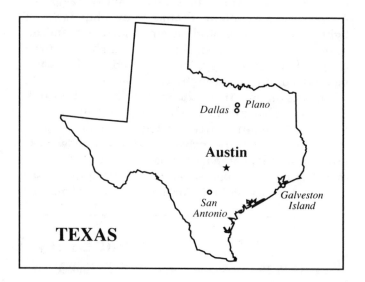

Fabulous Features

To live deep in the heart of Texas Hill Country is to have the privilege of nature's grandeur at your doorstep. The first things that strike newcomers are the sparkling lakes and sloping terrain (this is no Texas dust bowl). The eclectic man-made skyline is impressive but not the one residents hold dear. And yet this is as much a corporate, political and educational arena as the largest cities in the country. As the Texas capital, the home of the University of Texas, and headquarters for scores of growing high-tech firms, there is more "intelligence" here than at the CIA.

People spoke of the liberal attitudes and cutting-edge technology but also of the innate ability to get back to basics. When year-round sunshine and fabulous outdoor recreation calls, you answer. The great indoors is just as promising, with continuous live entertainment, performing arts and great activities for the family.

Housing prices are up but well within reach (under $100,000 buys a brand-new showplace), the schools are exceptional, and the job market is as hot as a pistol. Austin's thriving economy and low living costs spell R-E-L-I-E-F to newcomers fleeing the job-ravaged north. And accolades rattle off like a movie critic's review: "A Top 10 All-American City," says the National Civic League; "Top 10 Cities to Live," says *Money* magazine; "One of 4 Greenest and Cleanest Cities," says *New Woman* magazine; "One of the 10 Best Family Cities," says *Parenting* magazine.

Possible drawbacks: Summer months are hot and humid. • Statistically speaking, crime is Austin's Achilles heel. While it's still a safe place to live, an increase in personal and property crime has heightened awareness. People lock doors, avoid certain parts of town, and teach children not to take chances. This is hardly news for big-city folks, but a difficult fact of life for this once small, peaceful town. • Direct flights to New York and California are limited, making air travel out of Austin an all-day affair.

"You can quote me on that"

"When IBM transferred my husband to Austin, at first I said no way. I thought it would be a small, boring town. He came down a few months ahead of us and would call every night with something new he discovered. We're here two years and we absolutely love it. There are so many great things to do as a family. My son begged not to go away to camp because he was afraid he'd miss something."—B.J.

Real Estate

Market overview: In the late '80s, the oil crunch and savings and loans debacle whipped through the state like a Texas tornado. A once-booming real estate market suffered sky-high interest rates, foreclosures and a shutdown of new construction. The past two years have seen a remarkable recovery. Housing prices are up 14% but still go like hotcakes (avg. listing is on the market 51 days). The rebound caught builders off guard, resulting in a labor shortage (why resales are still popular). Avg. carrying charges on SFHs range from $585-$740.

What houses look like: Austin's neighborhoods are in natural, parklike settings. Homeowners are militant about landscaping, but anxious to conserve water. Hearty native plants and grass are used that require little moisture. Houses range from capes to contemporaries, with some English Tudors. Because of the hilly terrain, there are no basements. Exteriors are brick, native stone and wood frame.

Starter homes: Prices start at $50,000, with the avg. first home in the $60s-$70s. This buys a modest 3BR/2BA (1500 sq. ft.) house in a lovely older neighborhood (under 10 years).

Trade-ups: Prices start in the $80s for new homes, with the avg. ranging from the $90s-$120s. This buys a larger 3BR/2BA (1800-2000 sq. ft.) with 2-car garage in the northwest such as the Round Rock area, Brushy Creek, Cat Hollow area, Anderson Mill West. To the south is Shady Hollow. Avg. lot size is ¼ acre.

Luxury homes: Prices range from $150,000-$200,000 for new 4BR/2BA (2000 sq. ft.) homes. Most are 2-story brick and stone with large island kitchens, sprawling floor plans, upstairs den, fireplace, decking and fencing, some landscaping. Homeowners pay for tennis, pools and clubhouse.

Rental market: Inventory is tight (95% occupancy), but with more new construction, listings should increase. A 3BR/2BA home rents for $1,000+; 2BR apartments and condos range from $700-$1,000 (duplexes rent for $500+).

Great neighborhoods: Major growth is running north and south along the I-35 corridor. Most new home buyers (75%) have an Austin address; others settle in Round Rock, Georgetown and Leander Park. River Place, Long Canyon and Oak Hill are great new devlopments offering parks, golf courses and excellent amenities.

Nearby areas to consider: Pflugerville, a fast-growing rural community, has Victorian-style architecture and a renovated town square. Young families are attracted by the schools and affordable homes. Avg. commute is 20-30 min.

What Things Cost

Runzheimer's Living Cost Index: Avg. annual costs for family of 4 with household income of $50,000: $48,576 (2.9% below avg. city).

ACCRA's national comparisons: Housing runs more than 20% below avg., health care 12% below and utilities 6% below (city-owned). Goods/services are below the avg. (4%); food costs are on par.

Utilities: Phone: $13.85/mo. Gas and electric: Avg. $125-$150 (summer); $150-$200 (winter).

Kid care: The Austin metro has more than 700 registered family home providers ($55-$75/wk.); 300+ licensed day-care centers ($80-$100/wk.). Child Care Management System subsidizes day-care costs based on income. **Pediatric visit**: Avg. $25-$35.

The Tax Ax

Sales tax: 8% (food and medicine are exempt).

Property tax: Currently assessed at a rate of $2.63 per $100 of value. Estimated annual taxes on a $75,000 home would be $1,000. A $150,000 home pays $2,000; a $250,000 home, almost $3,000/yr.

State income tax: None.

Climate

Elevation 550'	Avg. High/Low	Avg. Rain (Inches)	Avg. Snow (Inches)	Avg. Days Rain	Avg. % Humidity
Jan.	60/50	1.8	--	8	71
April	79/69	3.5	--	7	65
July	95/85	1.9	--	5	62
Oct.	81/70	3.0	--	6	65
YEAR	79/68	32	--	--	--

# of days 32° or below: 24	# of days 90° or above: 114

Austin's temperate climate means lots of warm, sunny days and only a few dozen chilly ones (snow is rare). Summer humidity is something to reckon with, although it's more comfortable than the Gulf area. The best way to cool off is to head for the Texas hills, where the lakes and rivers bring relief.

> ### "You can quote me on that"
> *"When my kid brother lost his job, I begged him to check out Austin. It took a year to convince him, and now he's sorry he waited. He and his wife both found jobs and bought a house twice the size of the one they had and for half the price."—T.D.*

Earning a Living

Economic outlook: Once upon a time, Austin was a government town. If you worked, it was for the city, the county or the state (this is the Texas capital), the IRS regional office, or Bergstrom Air Force Base. While these remain the largest employers (over 80,000 workers), they're by no means the only show in town. There are 7 major sectors supporting the local economy, and all have grown dramatically (70% of the labor market set record high levels of employment since 1990). These include high-tech manufacturing (grown to over 400 firms), service industries (business and personal services increased by 8%), government, research and development, real estate and finance, retail and wholesale, and small business (employs 50% of the entire work force). The tremendous diversity accounts for the low unemployment rate (4.5%) and the Chamber's optimism regarding job growth. There's a projected increase of 26,200 new jobs between 1991 and 1992 (a 6.9% jump). Wages are also up (3.9% between '91-'92). As a true measure of success, while the state experienced a 2.7% decline in job growth during the '80s, Austin had a 36% increase. By 1991 over $800 million of industry construction projects had been completed. Everything is coming up roses here (yellow, of course).

Where the jobs are: It's more than sweet talk when the "M&Ms" of Austin announce plans for ongoing expansion. Motorola, IBM and 3M are Austin's 3 largest private-sector employers, and are all increasing their facilities and number of employees (Motorola added 2,440 new jobs in 1991). Other recent corporate expansions were at SM Long Distance, Radian Corp., Trimble Navigation, Austin Diagnostic Clinic and Golfsmith. In addition, 24 companies announced plans to come to Austin, including Apple Computer Customer Service, American Airlines Reservations and Tadpole Technologies.

Business opportunities: The entrepreneurial spirit is alive and well (many of today's computer industry stars got their big break in Austin). For the 2nd consecutive year, *INC.* ranked Austin the #1 city in the U.S. for new business starts. *Fortune* rates it as one of the top 10 cities for business (Oct. '91). High-tech entrepreneurs will find enormous support through The Greater Austin Technology Incubator (joint effort of the university, Chamber and city, which provides capital and staff to qualified technology-based startups), the University of Texas Center for Technology Ventures (help with patents and marketing strategies), and a think tank called IC2 (promotes innovations via seminars).

Making the Grade

Public education overview: In a town where 31% of all adults have had 16+ years of schooling (Austin has the most educated population in the country), you can bet public education is a top priority. For the past 5 years, students in the Austin Independent School District (AISD) ranked first among urban schools in Texas on mandatory graduation tests and also consistently rank above the national average on SATs. The science curriculum at the magnet high school has been ranked at the top as well. Success is attributed to innovative programs such as the Austin Adopt-A-School (more than 1,300 partnerships with local business have contributed $9 million to schools) and ESP (Employers Support Parents). This new program urges companies to give parents time off for school activities, assists with childcare referrals, etc. In addition, IBM chose Austin as the site for its "Project A+" program, designed to make it a world-class school district by the year 2000.

Class size: 23:1.

Help for working parents: Nearly every elementary campus is set up for early drop-off and after-school programs. The YMCA and Extend-A-Care run many of the programs, and prices are on a sliding scale.

Blue Ribbon School Awards: Canyon Vista Middle School ('90-'91), Hill Country Middle School ('90-'91), Westlake High School ('88-'89), Forest Trail Elementary ('89-'90). Stephen F. Austin High School has also been recognized.

School year: Last week of Aug. to first week of June. Children must be 5 on or before Sept. 1 to enter kindergarten.

Special education/gifted programs: "Aim High" is one of the most innovative gifted programs for elementary grades in the South, focusing on learning how to think rather than being a consumer of information. Middle and high schools offer extensive honors programs. There are more than 20 special education services, such as Content Mastery Centers and Vocational Adjustment Coordination.

Nearby colleges/universities: University of Texas (50,000 students and more than 270 degree programs); St. Edward's University (small private college and new training camp for the Dallas Cowboys); Southwest Texas State University-San Marcos (20,000 students, 130 undergraduate and 40 postgraduate programs); Southwestern University-Georgetown, (small private liberal arts college); Austin Community College (one of the largest in the country); and Huston-Tillotson College (black private liberal arts college).

Medical Care

Hospitals/medical centers: Brackenridge Hospital is the 24-hour city-owned regional trauma center and is affiliated with the Children's Hospital of Austin (the only specialized facility in the region). St. David's Health Care System offers state-of-the-art cardiology services, a Women's Health Resource Center, and centers for diabetes and *in vitro* fertilization. Seton Medical Center, a large regional facility, offers heart and transplant centers and a critically ill newborn program. Other hospitals: Central Texas Medical Center, Georgetown Hospital, and Round Rock Hospital (has a new Family Birthing Center).

Specialized care: Austin Diagnostic Clinic, Seton Northwest Health Plaza (sports-related injuries, radiation therapy and same-day surgery); and Rehabilitation Hospital of Austin (in/outpatient services for pain, pediatrics and injuries).

Crime & Safety

Austin is ranked 14th in the nation for crimes per capita, but statistics don't tell the whole story. While there have been some highly publicized crimes of late, Austin is still ranked 49th out of 50 cities for crimes against persons (only 7.14 per 100,000 people). What skews the numbers is that even the smallest crime is recorded (most cities don't do that). Also, there is a disproportionately high automobile ownership, thus a high rate of car theft. People take precautions but rarely feel threatened. Neighborhood Watch programs (some have over 600 volunteers), the Mayor's Gang Task Force and the DARE programs have tremendous support in the community.

Community Life

Each year the National Civic League nominates 10 cities for their "All American City" award. In 1991 Austin was so named for its ability to resolve community problems by getting government, business and individuals to work together. A recent example of the caring spirit was the discovery that the famed Treaty Oak (the 500-year-old tree where Stephen F. Austin signed a peace treaty with the Indians) had been poisoned with a potent herbicide. Arborists applied charcoal treatments, soil replacement and microbes injections. Residents brought giant screens for shade and came with prayers, flowers—even chicken soup. The tree was saved and stands as a living tribute to goodwill.

Let the Good Times Roll

Family fun: "Free Admission" are the two most famous words in the Austin language. In this "Jewel of Texas Hill Country," there are more than 12,000 acres of parks and recreation facilities and some of the most sparkling lakes in the South. Town Lake Hike & Bike Trail is a spectacular 5-mile stretch looping the Colorado River. Highland Lakes is the largest concentration of freshwater lakes in Texas (more than 700 mi. of shoreline). Fishing (the bass are so big, you won't have to lie), waterskiing and windsurfing are great. Cool off by sailing Lake Travis, rafting on the Gaudalupe River, or jumping into the spring-fed pool at Zilker Park or the blue Barton Springs (always a cool 68). There are 18 private and public golf courses (the rolling greens and waterfalls are super) and more than 200 tennis courts (every "Grand Slam" surface is here). Must-do's are the Austin Symphony's Instrumental Petting Zoo (musical instruments dangle on ropes so kids can "fiddle" around), the Austin Children's Museum, Austin Nature Center and the Jourdan/Bachman Pioneer Farm. For the children, check out Schlitterbahn Waterpark (New Braunfels), Sea World (San Antonio) and Fiesta Texas (San Antonio's newest theme park).

Sports: Pro football fans, feast your eyes on this mighty catch: the Dallas Cowboys training camp is here after 27 years in California. Professional and Amateur sports are big business, too. Look for the Liberty Mutual Legends of Golf tournament, the Austin American-Statesman Capital 10K Race (largest in the U.S.), and the annual Rowing Club Regatta. University of Texas Longhorns teams add to the excitement.

Arts & entertainment: To start, this is the *real* musical capital of the country (with more than 100 clubs, there are more live performances on a given night than in any other U.S. city). From Bach to rock, the beat goes on down Sixth Street (Historic Entertainment District). Other offerings include Ballet Austin, the Paramount Theater for Performing Arts and dozens of museums, galleries and live theater.

Annual events: Captial 10K race (30,000 athletes compete in April); Austin Aqua Festival (30th year of 70 bands and 40 water/land events over 3 weekends in July); Texas Food and Wine Festival (spring); The Austin Chronicle and BMI Music sponsor the annual Southwest Music & Media Conference (300 bands and 2,000 industry biggies join together for a 4-day music marathon in March).

The Environment

Austin was the *only* U.S. city to receive an award at the recent Earth Summit in Rio de Janeiro. It was cited for its innovative "Green Builder" program, which requires home builders to install solar heating, use environmentally sound materials, etc. Air and water quality are excellent (the city was recently ranked #1 for best-tasting water in the state). The strong environmental stand is attributed to the fact that the city owns and operates the entire infrastructure: electric, water, sewers, waste—even the airport. When there's finger pointing, it points to *them*.

In and Around Town

Roads and interstates: I-35, Texas 71. A $230 million improvement project is under way at the Loop 1 and U.S. Highway 183 interchange.
Closest airport: Robert Mueller Municipal Airport (Austin), served by 9 airlines.
Public transportation: Capital Metro serves 120,000 riders daily, with express routes and park-and-ride facilities. The Business District has over 2,000 daily riders on trolleys.
Avg. commute: 30 min. (rush hour).

What Every Resident Knows

Who needs Batman? Every summer the Congress Avenue Bridge converts to a "hangout" for 750,000 Mexican bats. Observing is a time-honored event. • If you're a betting man or woman, lottery fever has struck Texas. Plus, the first pari-mutuel license in the state has been approved, making way for a $50 million race track in adjacent Hays County. • The "A" in Austin could be for allergies. Many newcomers develop reactions to cedar wood and other airborne substances. • Austin has become the "Ellis Island" of Texas, attracting newcomers from around the world, and with that, great cultural and ethnic diversity. • Overheard at the Austin airport, "This is the one city I've lived in that I can't wait to get back to, and I just came from a Caribbean cruise."

FYI

The Greater Austin Chamber of Commerce
P.O. Box 1967
Austin, TX 78767
512-478-9383

Convention & Visitor's Bureau
800-888-8AUS

Austin American-Statesman
P.O. Box 670
Austin, TX 78767-0670
512-445-4040

Coldwell Banker/Richard Smith Realtors
907 Ranch Road 620 S., Suite 102
Austin, TX 78734
800-531-7667
Peg Boone

The Prudential Owens Realty
3303 Northland Drive, Suite 100
Austin, TX 78731
800-866-6125
Jean Winslett

Southwestern Bell
P.O. Box 1329
Austin, TX 78767
512-870-5150

Southern Union Gas
P.O. Box 1268
Austin, TX 78785
512-477-6461

Austin Electric Utility Dept. (city owned)
721 Barton Springs Road
Austin, TX 78704
512-322-6300

Austin Independent School District
1111 W. 6th Street
Austin, TX 78703
512-499-1700

Small Bus. Development Center
2211 S. IH-35, Suite 103
Austin, TX 78741
512-326-2256

Southeast Business Incubator
2020 E. St. Elmo Road, Suite 100
Austin, TX 78744
512-462-9444

Property tax assessor: 512-473-9473
Newcomer's Club: 512-328-4417
Area Conference of Churches: 512-472-7627
Physician's referral: 512-458-1121 (Travis County Medical Society)
Job search: 512-469-6381 ("Key To The City" helps newcomers with job search)
Day-care referral: 512-454-1194

Galveston Island, Texas

Area Snapshot

Local population: 59,070
County: Galveston   **Population:** 217,399
U.S. region: Central Southern tip of Texas
Closest metro areas: Houston (50 mi. northwest)
Median housing price: $62,600
Avg. household income: $22,053
Best reasons to live here: Coastal island with glorious scenery, sunny, semi-tropical climate, most affordable housing market in U.S., tremendous ethnic diversity, close-knit community, good schools, excellent medical care, active historic preservation efforts.

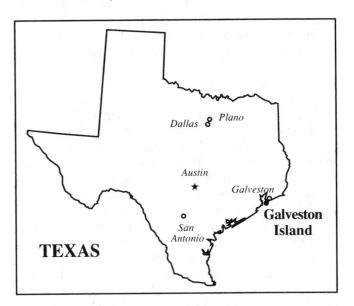

Fabulous Features

Ever vacation in a picturesque beach resort and wonder what it's like to live there? If you're ready to take the plunge, may we suggest Galveston Island? This sparkling Gulf Coast city is on the cutting edge! A truly heterogeneous community (middle school students represent 26 races and nationalities), newcomers marvel that "harmony" is more than a cliché. From organizing the annual Victorian Christmas celebration (attracts 90,000) to school tutoring by FRIENDS (Fantastic, Resourceful, Interested in Education, Note-worthy Dedicated Seniors), volunteers make the city hum.

Residents have time to give, because the average commute is a cakewalk (35 minutes to Houston) and most aren't working several jobs to keep up with the Joneses. There's no state income tax, Galveston is the most affordable housing market in the country relative to income levels (so says Prudential Realty), and living costs are 10% below average. And here's a place where 32 miles of sandy beaches, the charming historic district and Victorian ar-

chitecture are the natural backdrop at no extra charge!

As for jobs, the growing visitor industry (6 million tourists a year), the recent $168 million expansion of University of Texas Medical Branch and the new Moody Gardens Convention Center are pumping millions of dollars into the economy and creating hundreds of jobs.

There's no waiting for first-rate medical care (the state's oldest, most prestigious medical school is here, with 7 hospitals and 90 clinics) or educational opportunities (no other Texas city has branches of both the University of Texas and Texas A&M). No wonder so many have discovered that a "short" stay in Galveston Island can last a lifetime!

Possible drawbacks: Galveston is part of an 8-county region that doesn't meet EPA smog standards. Although most of the bad ozone days are in Central Houston and Texas City, Galveston has 3-4 bad days a year. • High humidity and the threat of hurricanes are reminders that Gulf Coast living has its hazards.

"You can quote me on that"

"We relocated here from Oklahoma City for my husband's position at UTMB. We fit right in here—my husband loves to fish and I love to swim. Just being near the water attracted me. There's everything from theater to outdoor concerts. When we got here we found the public school system surpassed the one we left behind—and it had an excellent reputation."—M.H.

Real Estate

Market overview: The Galveston area was identified as the most affordable housing market in the country, compared to 219 markets in a Prudential Realty survey. There are even large Victorians for as low as $100,000. Based on the low home prices and the higher than average annual household incomes, here you can buy a beautiful house and still have money left to redecorate. The low interest rates are a plus, too. And the banks seem to be more "user-friendly," arranging loans quickly.

What houses look like: Victorians are popular, but all types can be found. The Victorians are found in the two historical areas, East End and Silk Stocking. Beach fronts and resort homes are also popular. Split levels are few, but traditional styles such as colonials are plentiful. Older houses usually do not have garages but offer formal living and dining areas. A restored Victorian in top shape can go for as much as $300,000, but a "handyman's special," can be snatched up for $100,000.

Starter homes: From the $30s-$50s. At the low end, you'll get a 2-3BR/1BA that needs work. $50,000 buys a newer home with 3BR, 1 1/2BA, 1500-1700 sq. ft. with a garage.

Trade-ups: $70,000 buys an older 3BR/2BA that may have a garage, 1500-1700 sq. ft. $100,000 buys a 3BR/2BA, 10 years old, w/2-car garage, living and dining rooms (combination), den, and 2000 sq. ft.

Luxury homes: $175,000-$500,000. $180,000 buys a 4BR/2 1/2BA, 2800 sq. ft., formal living and dining rooms, 2-car garage, fireplace, pool, large country kitchen. $300,000, buys a renovated Victorian in mint condition or a brand-new contemporary on the water as large as 3000 sq. ft.

Rental market: Single family homes for rent are few because of the transient nature of the population. The good news is that they're often vacated quickly, too. A 3BR house will rent for $650-$1,000/mo. There are some condominiums.

Great neighborhoods: East End Historical District has an excellent school system, with restoration of the area offering beauty and history. The Silk Stocking Historical District also offers good schools. There are many young families. Cedar Lawn has been beautifully renovated, offers scenic beauty and older homes that have larger rooms. Its affordability attracts young families.

Nearby areas to consider: Clear Lake, Friendswood and Dickinson are all located northwest of Galveston Island, roughly a 30-minute commute, and offer newer houses and proximity to Houston. They are all small towns with tight communities, offering good public school systems.

What Things Cost

Runzheimer's Living Cost Index: Avg. annual costs for family of four with household income of $50,000: $44,905 (10.2% below avg. city).

ACCRA's national comparisons: Not available. However, we note that relative to the higher cost of living in Houston (50 mi.), particularly for housing, the Galveston area is very reasonable.

Utilities: Gas: Avg. $55/winter; as low as $11/summer. Electric: Avg. $55; as high as $303/summer. Phone: Hook-up and installation $38.35 with proof of prior service. Jacks start at $60 for the first, $35 for additional. Water: $45-55/mo., includes sewer and garbage.

Kid care: Day care runs about $85/wk. for infants, $55/wk. for toddlers, and includes hot lunch, breakfast and 2 snacks. Many institutional day-care centers have lengthy waiting lists. There are many registered home providers, however, and they are less expensive. **Pediatric visit:** $36.

The Tax Ax

Sales tax: 7.75% (prescriptions, food and water exempt).

Property tax: There is no state property tax. However, there are county, school district and special amenity taxes that vary widely, depending on the district.

State income tax: None.

Climate

Elevation 10'	Avg. High/Low	Avg. Rain (Inches)	Avg. Snow (Inches)	Avg. Days Rain	Avg. % Humidity
Jan.	59/48	3	.1	10	77
April	73/65	2.6	--	6	75
July	87/79	4.4	--	9	70
Oct.	78/68	2.8	--	6	65
YEAR	75/65	42.2	.3	96	72
# of days 32° or below: 4			# of days 90° or above: 35		

The island's weather is heavily influenced by the maritime tropical air. This means that there are rarely extreme temperatures. But you can't get away from the high humidity in spring and summer, and hurricane season. Particularly after Hugo and Andrew, people recognize the risks.

Earning a Living

Economic outlook: Galveston has a multi-faceted economic base, covering a wide range of industries, from tourism to medical technology, engineering, electronics and aeronautical research (Houston is home to the National Aeronautics and Space Administration (NASA) and its many related industries). Sales tax receipts for 1991 continued to be up substantially over the previous year, largely attributable to Galveston's growing visitor industry, which has had a $300 billion annual impact on the economy. Unemployment for the county remains high at 10.1%, reflecting the higher proportion of civilian labor force and the greater flux of potential employees just recently out of school.

Where the jobs are: The area's largest employer is the University of Texas Medical Branch (employs 8,500). Other major employers include the Port Facilities, Texas A&M Campus, Galveston College, and the tourist industry (hotel and motel management and related services). The American National Insurance Company continues to be the backbone of the local economy with an annual payroll of over $30 million and a work force of 1,400 employees. Continued construction has boosted the economy, with a $150 million, 142-acre Moody Gardens complex being built, which includes a convention center and the world's largest theater screen and only three dimensional IMAX theater in the world. Tatsumi, an international warehousing, terminal and transportation company, purchased the Todd Fabricating Plant and has announced plans for improvement and expansion.

Business opportunities: Biomedical research is one of the key industries being pursued. Also, spin-off businesses abound in Galveston, particularly related to Texas Copper Corp. The University of Texas Medical Branch has increased purchases from Galveston businesses, reflecting the recent completion of UTMB's recent $168.1 million expansion program. Any business that serves the needs of Galveston Island's transitional population (students, health care workers) would be welcomed. Also, a spokesperson from the Galveston Economic Development Corp. suggested that they are actively seeking motion picture industries (low production costs and an available supply of labor makes this appealing). A new trade agreement with Mexico should also open up import/export opportunities. Any business requiring large manufacturing facilities should probably not look to Galveston Island—space is scarce, thus expensive.

Making the Grade

Public education overview: Galveston Island School District is making headway with innovative programs and creative solutions to accommodate the diverse student body (26 different ethnic backgrounds in the middle school). To accommodate the growing number of Spanish-speaking children, English as a Second Language (ESL) is provided at several elementary schools. GISD is in the middle of a 5-year Strategic Planning Effort to improve educational programs and business operations in the school district. All schools are well-maintained, fully equipped and air-conditioned. The Computer Literacy Program and Computer Labs begin in grades 5-6. Nearly 60% go on to college, many to prestigious universities, such as Harvard, Yale, Georgetown and Princeton. Some innovative help from outsiders includes the Gold Card Incentive Program (in conjunction with the Chamber of Commerce), which provides "Gold Card" gift and discount incentives from numerous community businesses to students who excel academically. FRIENDS (Fantastic, Resourceful, Interested in Education, Noteworthy Dedicated Seniors) lets senior volunteers enjoy free admittance to school sports and functions in honor of their exemplary service to students and teachers.

Class size: 18:1.

Help for working parents: Parents can drop off children at school at 7:30 a.m. (breakfast is offered for free or nominal charge). The YMCA offers after-school day care (until 5:30 p.m.) on site at the elementary schools ($100 per month). Several private day-care facilities offer pick-up and after-school care as well.

School year: Begins third week in Aug. through last week in May. Children must be 5 on or before Sept. 1 to enter kindergarten (which is a full-day program).

Special education/gifted programs: The school district's special education services include: individualized programs; multidisciplinary teaming; mainstreaming support; child-centered education; teacher and parent training; and life skills, community-based training. Special Activities in Gifted Education (SAGE) enrichment program is for academically gifted students (K-12). Banks Special Learning Center is a multi-handicapped facility.

Nearby colleges/universities: Galveston College, a two-year school; Texas A&M University at Galveston; University of Texas Medical Branch; College of the Mainland (15 mi.); University of Houston-Clear Lake (35 mi.).

Medical Care

Hospitals/medical centers: The University of Texas Medical Branch (UTMB), the state's oldest medical school, has seven hospitals with more than 80 specialty clinics, 850 beds and 590 doctors. UTMB is the only multi-categorical health referral center in Texas, and one of the principal medical centers in the Southwest for patient care, research and medical education. St. Mary's Hospital, the oldest private hospital in the state, has 271 beds and 190 doctors. The Emergency Medical Service provides ambulance service for the island.

Specialized care: Shriners Burn Center is a world-renowned research and treatment center operated by the Shriners of North America. Moody State School is for children with Cerebral Palsy.

Crime & Safety

The crime level here is typical for a tourist town and urban area. The majority of crimes are assaults and property crimes—thefts, burglaries and motor vehicle theft. Most crime is narcotic or inter-gang-related. Galveston Island has a big-city atmosphere—with some big-city problems. In efforts to reduce the crime rate, police have initiated active neighborhood crime watch programs in which parents, children and the schools are involved. There's Community Policing and Safe Play—police volunteer in sports-oriented activities during their off-duty time. Overall, residents feel safe but understand that growth has its good and bad points.

Community Life

Dickens on The Strand, a Victorian Christmas celebration that is a fund raiser for the Historical Foundation, attracts 70,000 to 90,000 visitors a year. And 4,000 residents volunteer to work during the two-day celebration. Citizens also get involved in Clean Galveston, organizing community clean-ups. Volunteer turn-out is in the hundreds. Seaman's Center is a volunteer-run program that provides transportation around town, recreation and food for sailors that come into the area. And, finally, Elissa, a sailing ship from 1877, is maintained by 200 volunteers and is open for people to tour. The volunteers actually sail the ship on special occasions.

Let the Good Times Roll

Family fun: Beach fun abounds for sun-lovers. Galveston Island State Park, a beautiful 2,000-acre tract from Galveston Bay to the Gulf of Mexico, is a family favorite for swimming, bird-watching and camping. Apffel Park is a sandy beach ideal for boat launching, surf fishing and dining. Palm Beach at Moody Gardens is a great way for a family to discover a tropical paradise, featuring the whitest sand and cleanest waters you've ever seen. Stewart Beach Park, the principal beach park of Galveston, is a family recreation area with a new pavilion, mini-golf, water slides and bumper boats.

Sports: Galveston Junior College has the White Caps baseball team, and the only college team around.

Arts & entertainment: Bishop's Palace is ranked among the top 100 homes in the country for its architectural significance; Galveston Arts Center schedules exhibitions, works of major artists in all media, in three galleries that are free to the public. It also offers morning drop-in art classes for kids; The Galveston County Historical Museum is located in the restored 1919 City National Bank Building on Market Street. It features fascinating exhibits of history specific to Galveston County; The Galveston Island Trolley is a fixed-rail streetcar system with four turn-of-the-century operating cars along a 4.7 mile route from 21st Street to Seawall to the Strand. Moody Garden and other attractions are along the way; The Grand 1894 Opera House is magnificently restored and ranked among the nation's finest historical restoration. It serves as a showcase for outstanding live entertainment, classic films and special events; The Railroad Museum is the Southwest's largest train museum with more than 40 railway cars displayed; Strand Street Theatre is the county's only professional repertory company. Presentations include musicals, comedy, drama and classical works; The Upper Deck Theatre is a renowned community college theater offers five productions annually, ranging from musicals to comedy to mystery.

Annual events: Mardi Gras features 20 masquerade balls, parades, hundreds of private parties, sporting events and art shows during this two-week celebration (mid-Feb.); Jazz Festival, with street musicians, dinner cruises, renowned jazz headliners at the Grand Opera house and more (Nov.); Dickens on the Strand is a weekend salute to Charles Dickens and Galveston's Victorian heritage. Participants dress in period costumes (Dec.)

The Environment

Galveston is undergoing a beach replenishment project that will enhance the beaches as well as create more jobs. The Marine Spill Response Center selected Galveston as the site for a major installation of oil spill equipment. Galveston Island, as well, is assisting in devising new efforts to control the problem. Water quality, for both beach and bayside, is continuously monitored to protect the native marine life. As a consequence, shellfish and oysters are no longer harvested commercially. Air quality in Galveston proper is good (see page 57 for updates on air quality reports), and recycling is actively encouraged. The industrial waste and sewage disposal facility across from Galveston Island has been a growing concern among residents, who want to ensure that it is properly maintained and not leaking hazardous elements into the water.

In and Around Town

Roads and interstates: I-45; Highways 6, 3 and 146. The island is connected with the mainland by the Galveston causeway and the San Luis Pass-Vacek Bridge, along with the Texas Highway Dept. free ferry service to Port Bolivar Peninsula.
Closest airports: Scholes Field, Galveston; Houston Intercontinental Airport: 84 mi.; Hobby Airport: 44 mi. (Houston).
Public transportation: City bus service is run by Island Transit. Transportation Enterprises has bus service to Houston and connecting cities.
Avg. commute: 20-25 min.

What Every Resident Knows

The Island's best-kept secret: The ferry at Bolivar offers a free, 24-hour, seven-day-a-week tour. It's one of the nicest ways to see the island and watch the sun set. • Gaido's Restaurant is one of the most famous seafood restaurants around and it's only known locally by islanders. It's famous for its pecan pie—islanders say it's the best in the country. • Other best-kept restaurant secrets include Sonny's (hamburgers), DiBella's (Italian) and El Nopalito and the Original Mexican Cafe (Mexican). • Garten Verein is an old German dance hall built in the 1880s, and the Galveston Symphony presents evenings with Strauss there.

FYI

The Galveston Chamber of Commerce
2106 Seawall Blvd.
Galveston, TX 77550
409-763-5326

Galveston Convention & Visitor's Bureau
2106 Seawall Boulevard
Galveston, TX 77550
800-351-4237

The Galveston Daily News
P.O. Box 628
Galveston, TX 77553
409-744-3611

The House Company
2615 Broadway
Galveston Island, TX 77550
409-763-8030
Carolyn Clyburn, Owner/Broker

Southern Union Gas
910 25th Street
Galveston, TX 77550
409-763-8551

Houston Light & Power Co.
2116 Church Street
Galveston, TX 77553
409-763-1111

Southwestern Bell
409-942-8677

The Galveston Economic Development Corp.
P.O. Box 8029
Galveston, TX 77553
409-762-8355

Small Business Development Center
5001 Avenue U
Galveston, TX 77550
409-740-7380

School district: 409-765-9366
Property tax assessor: 800-252-9121
Physician's referral: 409-762-5000

Plano, Texas (Dallas)

Area Snapshot

Local population: 137,000
County: Collin   **Population:** 264,036
U.S. region: Southern U.S./northern Texas
Closest metro areas: Dallas (20 mi. south), Fort Worth (45 mi. southwest)
Median housing price: $113,000
Avg. household income: $62,997
Best reasons to live here: Work-hard/play-hard attitude, award-winning schools, booming local economy, pleasant year-round climate, affordable housing, no state income tax, ethnic diversity.

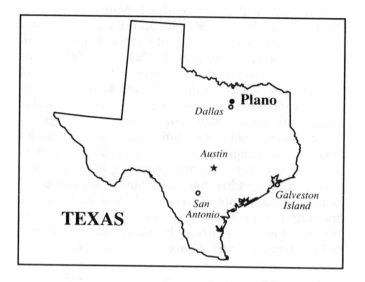

Fabulous Features

Returning to Plano after a long absence is like going to a class reunion and not recognizing anyone. This once-sleepy bedroom community has undergone such a metamorphosis, residents are tongue-tied when asked, "What's new?"

For starters, there's been a 78% population increase in just 10 years. For another, it's enjoyed a veritable business bonanza since J.C. Penney, EDS, Frito-Lay, Inc., and dozens of corporations settled here. Plano has a new $19-million civic center, a new 38-acre health care complex with a children's hospital, and a record 31,000 students attending 39 schools (most are state-of-the-art). The city also leads the state in housing starts (7,000 lots approved for construction in one recent three-month period).

If bigger isn't necessarily better, here's a place where Texas-sized gains have enhanced the quality of life. Ask parents the best thing about Plano and the response is more like a mantra: "Schoooools." The district has the highest SATs in the country for its size, 6,000 computers network for global study and any academic, cultural, social and recreational opportunity you can think of (the district's 20-acre science learning center is the wave of the future)!

Plano offers great recreational outlets (summer camps and sports leagues are so important, parents sign up for carpools before closing on the house). And what a house you can buy! Spend $80,000 or $800,000 and get a beautiful, new home in a family-planned development. The Plano experience is much like its annual Balloon Festival. Full of high spirits—and that's not hot air!

Possible drawbacks: Most residents brag about the quality of education in Plano schools, but in the same breath lament about the Olympic-style competition that comes with it. Peer pressure is tremendous and although many agreed that awareness among parents had lightened things up, this is a tough place to send a tender child. • Too many fans of "Dallas" come here expecting to buy homes with property like Southfork. Most new homes are on 1/5 acre—so close, neighbors can open their windows and practically shake hands.

"You can quote me on that"

"Coming from Colorado, I'm thrilled with the warm climate. No more scraping ice from my car before I can get anywhere in the winters. There's lots of recreation here and the community is not only family-oriented but very friendly."—C.B.

Real Estate

Market overview: Buyers are playing the game, "Name That Price." And if it's low enough, they say yes. Massive new construction has made it a buyers' market—more than 4,000 lots were approved for building in 1992 alone. That's hurting resales and real estate values. In the spring of '90, prices bottomed out. Since then homes have appreciated at around 2% annually. High-end buyers from the '80s who bought during a time of high interest and inflation are now losing money due to low interest and low inflation. The avg. price for a new home is between $200,000-$250,000.

What houses look like: Ranches here are called single-stories. New construction offers 2-stories. It's not the place to move if you've got your heart set on a Victorian. Most exteriors are all brick. Formal living rooms and dining rooms are common as are master suites. Interiors are bright, spacious and feature high ceilings, fireplaces of marble or brick and gourmet kitchens. Houses do not have basements. All have 2-3-car garages. Out-of-town buyers are impressed by the size of the house but disappointed in property size (avg. lot is 1/5 acre).

Starter homes: $50,000-$60,000. A higher-priced starter might have 3BR/2BA, in-ground pool, a fireplace on 1/5 acre—in excellent condition. Look in West Plano, High Place and Briarmeade.

Trade-ups: $60,000-$200,000. For $100,000, you can buy a 3BR/2BA 2 fireplaces, 2-car garage, in a nice subdivision. At the high end, you get a 3-4BR/2½BA, w/2 fireplaces, 2-3-car garage, in mint condition.

Luxury homes: Homes start at $250,000 and go as high as $2 million. $300,000 buys a 4-5BR/3-4BA, 2 living areas, 3-car garage, 3 fireplaces, large elegant master suites, ½-¾ acre lot, large, airy gourmet kitchen. $500K buys 1/2 acre or if you go to outlying areas, 3-4 acres w/5BR/4BA, 2 living areas, den, 3-car garages. Check out Pittman Creek, Deerfield, Forest Creek and Willowbend.

Rental market: Single family homes are scarce since the prices are so low. Available rentals go for $900-$4,000/mo.

Great neighborhoods: Family-oriented Willow Bend offers good schools, shopping convenience and accessible public transportation.

Nearby areas to consider: To the South of Plano is North Dallas with great schools (part of the Plano school system), and very affordable housing (though taxes are a drop more than Plano.) Richardson is an older community with lovely neighborhoods and excellent schools.

What Things Cost

Runzheimer's Living Cost Index: Avg. annual costs for family of 4 with household income of $50,000: $48,155 (3.7% below avg. city).

ACCRA's national comparisons: Overall living costs in the Dallas metro area are 5.9% above the national avg., with utilities and health care costs 20.9% and 12% above avg. respectively. Housing is almost 6% above avg. and transportation 8.2% above. Groceries are slightly below.

Utilities: Phone: $22/mo. (call waiting not available yet). Hookup: Avg. $41. Gas: $20-$25/mo. summer; up to $125/mo. winter. Electric: $75/mo. (April); up to $275/mo. (summer avg.).

Kid care: Licensed day care: $76/wk. (toddlers) to $100/wk. (infants). Private licensed home care for children over 18 mo. is readily available. Infant care is harder to find and there are waiting lists, approx. 60 days. **Pediatric visit:** $73 avg.

The Tax Ax

Sales tax: 8.25% (medical services and food are exempt).

Property tax: Exemptions for disabled and senior citizens. The new tax rate is $2.32995 per $100 of 100% assessed value (market value). The taxes on a $150,000 home, for example, would be $3494.93.

State income tax: None.

Climate

Elevation 550'	Avg. High/Low	Avg. Rain (Inches)	Avg. Snow (Inches)	Avg. Days Rain	Avg. % Humidity
Jan.	56/34	1.6	1.6	6	61
April	76/54	4.3	--	8	59
July	96/74	1.8	--	5	50
Oct.	79/56	2.7	--	5	54
YEAR	77/54	32	3.5	77	57
# of days 32° or below: 41			# of days 90° or above: 102		

The only thing consistent about the weather is that it changes constantly. Winters are mild, with an occasional cold snap (every few years a snowstorm hits and people go berserk). Summers are hot and dry with some humidity. Fall is bliss, with constant warmth and sunshine. Spring is the rainy season, and flash flooding or even tornadoes can occur.

Earning a Living

Economic outlook: Plano is sittin' pretty! The local economy is based on research and development and manufacturing in the fields of computer technology, data processing and telecommunications. Research in the areas of radar and the exploration and production of oil and natural gas contributes to a significant portion of the prosperity. Publishing and printing, banking, government employment, insurance, real estate and diverse midsize manufacturing (Packaging Corp. of America and Laminator) offer a wide variety of opportunities. The city has a strong retail, wholesale and service industry base. With its educated, professional work force (60,000 or nearly half the population), Plano's economic expansion has been intimately woven into the growth of the telecommunications industry. Fortune 500 companies as well as business newcomers are drawn to Plano's qualified work force, fast-paced commercial development, and the city's prime location in relation to the Dallas-area Metroplex. Unemployment is relatively high (6.5%), but it is consistently below the state and national avg., with total employment expected to grow by 80% by the year 2000.

Where the jobs are: Plano is on the wave of the future. People commute to work in a complex of telecommunications manufacturing plants that began in another suburb, Richardson (MCI Labs, Bell Labs, No. Tel, Rockwell), and pushed its way into Plano. Legacy Park is a huge office development that houses one of the world's largest data processing centers and the national headquarters of 4 major corporations: Frito-Lay, Inc., the Electronic Data Systems Corporation (15,000 employees), Murata Business Systems, and the J.C. Penney Company, Inc. With new technology, new capital investment, new specialties and new medical facilities, Plano is on the cutting edge of a burgeoning health care industry. Baylor Health Care System, Continental Medical Systems, Presbyterian and Children's Healthcare Center and Presbyterian Hospital all are expanding or moving to Plano. Medical personnel and technicians continue to be in demand.

Business opportunities: Industrial and commercial development within the past 15 years has created a very sound, balanced economy. While a substantial economic base has been built on manufacturing and agriculture, retail and commercial development has made an increasing contribution to Plano's economic growth. Retail sales growth is expected at 7.6%. The Chamber of Commerce offers information and assistance for entrepreneurs.

Making the Grade

Public education overview: The district professes to have the highest SAT scores in the nation among districts of comparable size. In 1992, 53 students were named as National Merit Semi-finalists, and 86% of Plano's students go on to college. The district has more than 6,000 computers for student use. Computer education starts with the "Writing to Read Lab" in kindergarten and continues through high school where computers are regularly used in classroom instruction. The district now has 2 elementary schools going full year, causing a major controversy among parents who don't want their schools to be next. In 1990 Plano passed a bond issue to build new schools with little difficulty, suggesting strong community support. A Worldclassroom and online computer telecommunications network provides opportunity for students to gain a global perspective. There's an after-school reading program for students grades 1-12 who are having reading difficulties. The district also provides an after-school math clinic for elementary and middle school students. The Science Learning Center is an onsite indoor and outdoor learning center for all grades. The outdoor center includes a 20-acre wooded area and creek used by students and teachers for the study of environmental awareness. Back in the early '80s there were a number of student suicides. Today the district's teen support programs serve as models for other schools.

Class size: 21:1 (to 4th grade).

Help for working parents: The local YMCA runs an after-school program in many of the elementary schools, from 3 p.m. to 6:30 p.m.

Blue Ribbon School Awards: H.B. Carlisle Elementary ('87-'88), Dooley Elementary ('89-'90), Schimelpfenig Middle School ('88-'89), Wilson Middle School ('88-'89), Plano Senior High ('84-'85).

School year: Starts mid-Aug. and runs through 3rd wk. in May. Children must be 5 on or before Sept. 1 to enter kindergarten.

Special education/gifted programs: Students with special needs go to neighborhood schools and are mainstreamed with support services. Students who need very specialized attention may go to individual cluster sites. Gifted students are identified twice a year and become eligible for enrichment and honors programs. Senior high students are eligible "Mind Journeys," independent projects that include several seminars and field trips.

Nearby colleges/universities: Collin County Community College (fastest-growing community college in the nation); University of Texas; and Southern Methodist University.

Medical Care

Hospitals/medical centers: In addition to the extensive and excellent medical centers located in nearby Dallas, Plano offers a strong selection of diverse medical specialties. HCA Medical Center is a 254-bed general acute-care medical and surgical hospital. Specialties include open-heart surgery, neonatal, pediatric intensive care, neurological intensive care and oncology. Presbyterian and Children's Healthcare Center is a 120-bed facility offering programs and services designed for care for the entire family. Specialties include general medical and surgical services, critical care and diagnostic facilities, and child development. Baylor Health Care System has planned a hospital in Plano, in addition to an already-existing medical plaza.

Specialized care: Plano Rehabilitation Hospital provides rehabilitative services for individuals who have suffered disabling accidents or illnesses. Texas Back Institute, North Texas Regional Cancer Center and Texas Heart Group offer specialized services. HCA Willow Park Hospital (76 beds) and Charter Hospital (116 beds) treat psychiatric and substance abuse disorders.

Crime & Safety

Plano has the lowest crime rate in Texas for cities with a population over 50,000. This is attributed to a very cooperative neighborhood crime watch network. More than 160 citizen volunteer groups help the police prevent and solve crimes. Most crimes involve theft or vandalism. There has been a slight increase in theft calls, attributed to population growth. Calls are still below the federal avg. for a city of its size. In 1991 the police introduced the DARE program to Plano's elementary schools.

Community Life

Community spirit is centered around the town's 2 high school football teams. There is a friendly rivalry between East and West High Schools. According to locals, game attendance is around 60,000. This is because Plano has always had a winning team, and one of the two teams usually ends up in the state finals. Long after your children finish high school you'll still be attending games. Volunteering is also a major way of life. Companies in the area encourage employees to become involved in charitable causes. One of the city's largest fund raisers is "The Weekend to Wipe Out Cancer." VIP (Volunteers in Plano) help in day-to-day city operations. Volunteers work for various city government agencies such as Parks and Recreation and Public works.

Let the Good Times Roll

Family fun: Plano has 2,624 acres of parks. There are 6 Hike and Bike Trails, 4 recreation centers, 3 public pools, a tennis center and a municipal golf course. Plano's newest recreation center features 6 racquet ball courts, 2 squash courts, weight and exercise rooms, 2 gymnasiums, and an elevated running track. The town also offers a very complete summer recreation program for all ages, from pre-schoolers to senior citizens. The Parks and Recreation Dept. has won national awards for Plano's parks. A favorite tourist attraction located in Plano is Fairview Farms, featuring live farm animals, a farmers market, a general store, musical performances and hayrides. In nearby Dallas the family can visit the Dallas Zoo. If you want to take an hour ride you can visit Six Flags Over Texas in Arlington. If you want to sail, water-ski or camp you can do so at nearby Lake Lavon, Lake Lewisville and Lake Ray Roberts—all less than an hour away.

Sports: Pro sports include: the Dallas Cowboys (NFL) at Texas Stadium; the Dallas Mavericks (NBA) at Reunion Arena; the Texas Rangers (Major League Baseball) at Arlington Stadium; the Dallas Sidekick (soccer), Reunion Arena. Dallas also hosts the Mobil Cotton Bowl Classic college football game and the Byron Nelson Golf Classic in the fall.

Arts & entertainment: Plano does not have to rely on nearby Dallas for arts and entertainment. The new ArtCentre is located downtown, and the Plano Repertory Theater is right behind it. The Cultural Arts Council Of Plano has numerous member organizations: Plano Repertory Theatre; Civic Chorus; Dance Consortium; Plano Dance Theatre; Plano Community Band; Connemara Conservancy; and The Younger Generation. Of special note is the "On My Own Time" art exhibition, which displays works of art created by employees from the business community. In Dallas, The Arts District features: the Morton H. Meyerson Symphony Center, hosting many performing groups; Dallas Museum of Art known for pre-Columbian art, but also American and European masters; and the Eugene McDermott Concert Hall, permanent home of the Dallas Symphony Orchestra. Also in Dallas: The Dallas Opera performs at the Centrum.

Annual events: Fourth of July Parade and Star Spangled Fourth Of July features live entertainment, parachuting and fireworks; The Plano Balloon Festival attracts more than 300,000 with live entertainment, arts & crafts, food and hot-air balloons (last weekend in Sept.); Dickens Downtown Christmas features tree-lighting and holiday singing (mid-Dec.).

The Environment

Plano is totally committed to the Clean Texas 2,000 campaign, which has encouraged Texans throughout the state to recycle and compost. The Legislature has set a goal of reducing waste sent to landfills by 40% by 1995. Plano has established a 1992 Keep Plano Beautiful campaign. A Glad Bag-a-thon was held in April where more than 1,100 volunteers collected 1,000 bags of litter and debris in the annual city-wide cleanup. Community pride has made the Keep Plano Beautiful program a major success. Water quality is in complete compliance with E.P.A. guidelines. The air quality has been affected by the community's proximity to Dallas. It has experienced some ozone problems due to auto emissions. As a result Plano is planning more in-depth regulations of auto emission controls.

In and Around Town

Roads and interstates: U.S. 75 (becomes I-45); I-635, state highways 190, 121, 5; Dallas North Tollway.
Closest airports: Dallas/Ft Worth International (40 min. southwest); Love Field in Dallas (30 min. south); Addison Airport (20 min. south); Airpark Airport (serves corporate and private aircraft); and McKinney Airport (15 mi.).
Public transportation: Dallas Area Rapid Transit (DART) provides commuter 45 min. express service between Plano and downtown Dallas. DART also provides cross-town service in Plano.
Avg. commute: 25-30 min.

What Every Resident Knows

Each year the rivalry between Plano Sr. High (PSH) and Plano East Sr. High (PESH) culminates on the football field when East meets West. The PSH Wildcats battle it out with the PESH Panthers to see who will be the town's champs. The week before the big game the town takes on a festive look. Streamers, panther's eyes and wildcat paw prints are plastered everywhere. Tickets to the game are like gold and are not sold until the day of the game. That morning people line up in the dark with their lawn chairs and coolers to wait for the box office to open. • At one time or another, Plano has been home to some pretty famous people—Boz Scaggs, Tommy Lee Jones, and many of the Dallas Cowboys. • For the last two years Plano has hosted the Mrs. U.S.A pageant. This year's winner is homegrown—Mrs. Debra Williams, wife of Herb Williams (a star of the NBA's Dallas Mavericks).

FYI

Plano Chamber of Commerce
P.O. Drawer 940287
Plano, TX 75094-0287
214-424-7547

Plano Convention and Visitors Bureau
P.O. Box 860358
Plano, TX 75086
214-422-0297

Dallas Morning News
P.O. Box 655237
Dallas, TX 75265
214-977-8937

Plano Star Courier
P.O. Box 860248
Plano, TX 75086
214-424-6565

Century 21 Elite
2301 Coit Road, Suite B
Plano, TX 75075
Steve Miller
214-964-0021

TU Electric
1130 E. 15th Street
Plano, TX 75074
214-554-1414

Lone Star Gas Co.
P.O. Box 308
Plano, TX 75074
214-423-2043

Plano Economic Development Board
4975 Preston Park Blvd.
Plano, TX 75093
214-985-4380

Small Business Development Center
P.O. Box 860358
Plano, TX 75086-0358
214-578-7115

City Of Plano
Plano City Hall
1520 Avenue K
Plano, TX 75074
214-424-6531

School district: 214-881-8100
Property tax assessor: 214-578-7110
Community Connection: 214-881-0520
Welcome Wagon: 214-578-6306
Ministerial Alliance: 214-867-6510
Physician's referral: 214-596-6800
Day-care referral: 214-422-1850

Provo, Utah

Area Snapshot

Local population: 80,300
County: Utah   **Population:** 257,000
U.S. region: Western U.S.
Closest metro area: Salt Lake City (44 mi. south)
Median housing price: $72,000
Avg. household income: $30,000
Best reasons to live here: Fabulous mountain scenery, perfect year-round climate for outdoor enthusiasts, unbelievable recreation, wholesome family community, friendly people, tremendous economic growth, affordable living costs, beautiful neighborhoods and homes.

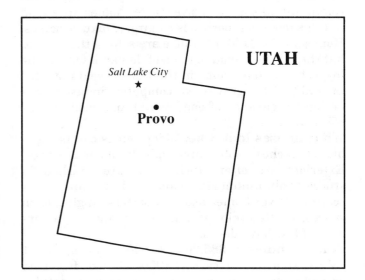

Fabulous Features

Who says beauty and brains don't mix? Not anyone who's ever been to Provo! Situated at the foot of the majestic Wasatch Mountain Range and overlooking freshwater Utah Lake, Provo is at the epicenter of some of the earth's most varied landscapes and colors. Gold-streaked canyons, turquoise streams and green forests are centuries-old wonders that await.

Once a poor farming community colonized by founding Mormon Brigham Young, Provo is now a booming business community that's out-producing some of the biggest cities in the country. Since 1991, it has earned: "America's Most Livable Metropolitan Area" and first in U.S. job growth at 7.3% (*Money*), "Most Livable City under 100,000" (National Conference of Mayors), "Third high-tech cluster in U.S." (*Fortune*). From Los Angeles to Japan, journalists have been descending, trying to solve the mystery of what makes Provo run.

It's simple. Take a group of hard-working people with irrefutable ethics, mingle them with intelligently managed powerhouses like WordPerfect Corp., and other software manufacturers (a combined $1.1 billion in sales), throw in low living costs and taxes, new homes under $100,000, low crime (60% below other comparably sized regions), a clean, healthy environment (Utah is tied with Minnesota as the #1 healthiest state), good schools, a pleasant year-round climate and the *piece de resistance*, some of the most exciting recreation in the world (you haven't lived until you've skied at Snowbird). *Voilà!* The Provo puzzle is solved. When the quality of life is as high as the city (4500 feet), you've got a winner!

Possible drawbacks: The idea of moving to a sheltered city with strong family values can be very appealing. However, lifestyles can also be restrictive. The few liquor stores in town are state-owned and only fine restaurants will serve liquor on request. • One thing newcomers found unnerving was constantly being asked if they were Mormon. The ground doesn't open up if you answer no, but it does take getting used to.

"You can quote me on that"

"Provo is clean and beautiful. We love the variety of weather and the lack of traffic. If you go to Salt Lake City, a 45 mile drive takes 45 minutes. It's a pleasure."—A.J.

Real Estate

Market overview: Provo is a very heterogeneous community. Less expensive starter homes are found in the same neighborhoods as larger, luxury homes. Homes in the $120,000 range are selling the fastest, but there aren't enough to meet demand. One of the biggest building booms in the last 15 years started in 1990. (The growth of computer industry has brought thousands of employees.) Appreciation was 8% in 1992.

What houses look like: Older homes can be ramblers (ranches), split entry, split levels or 2-stories. Exteriors are often brick, some are finished in stucco or aluminum siding and are beautifully landscaped. Newer homes feature dormers, angles, open spaces, vaulted ceilings, and arched and circle windows. Most have decks.

Starter homes: $85,000-$95,000 buys a 3BR/1 1/2BA w/garage or carport (900-1200 sq. ft.). Lots are smaller to cut down on watering desert-dry ground. Most have basements. Look in the southeast and southwest.

Trade-ups: Prices range from $129,000-$250,000 for 4-5BR/2-3BA, 2-car garage, fireplace, central air, elegant kitchen, jacuzzi, 1800-2000 sq. ft. w/finished basement. A lot of ramblers (ranch-style) with 3BR/2BA on the 1st floor, more BRs/BAs in basement.

Luxury homes: There's a wide selection of new homes in the $250,000-$500,000 range that are 4000-6000 sq. ft. Interiors feature vaulted ceilings, large formal living room and dining room, open kitchen, large master suite w/jacuzzi and a game room. Tennis courts and 3-car garage are common. Look in Sherwood Hills, Indian Hills, River Bottom and Grandview.

Rental market: Rental houses are difficult to find because of high number of married students at Brigham Young. Where available, 2BR/1BA fourplexes go for $400-$800/mo., 3BR/2BA homes for $650/mo. Best time to look is spring (graduates move out).

Great neighborhoods: East Bench, Bretton and Riverbottom are very exclusive communities with homes in the $250,000-$800,000 range. Homes closer to downtown are less costly.

Nearby areas to consider: Pleasant Grove, Alpine, Springville, Mapleton, Spanish Folk are surrounding communities within 5-10 min. that offer affordable housing and that allow horses (Provo residential areas do not). If you're interested in having horses, these are the places to move to.

What Things Cost

Runzheimer's Living Cost Index: Avg. annual costs for family of 4 with household income of $50,000: $46,443 (7.1% below avg. city).

ACCRA's national comparisons: Overall living costs are 5.3% below the national avg. Housing and utilities offer the most savings (13% below avg.). Groceries and health care are an estimated 2%-3% below avg., and goods and services are 4.2% below avg. Only transportation was above avg. (4.6%).

Utilities: Phone: Hookup: $18.75; $15/mo. for unlimited local calls. Electric: $85/mo. (Jan.); $66/mo. (April); $93/mo. (July); $67/mo. (Oct.). Gas: $91/mo. (high); $12.88/mo. (low); Avg. $38/mo.

Kid care: Infant cost $75/wk.; toddlers $60/wk.; 3yrs+ $50/wk. There are many home day-care providers at less expensive rates. Licensed toddler child care is widely available. Infant child care is available, but 6-wk. waiting lists are common.

The Tax Ax

Sales tax: 6.25% (medicine exempt). Fast food is taxed an extra 1%, w/proceeds going to the Recreational Tourism fund.

Property tax: 6.7% of market value times millage rate (.014444) per $1,000 of value. Avg. tax on a $150,000 home would be $1,250.

State income tax: State tax rate starts at 2.55% for joint and individual returns and tops at 7.2%. The top rate kicks in at a taxable income of $7,500. 50% of federal income tax is deductible on the state return.

Climate

Elevation 4,550'	Avg. High/Low	Avg. Rain (Inches)	Avg. Snow (Inches)	Avg. Days Rain	Avg. % Humidity
Jan.	37/18	.1	15	4	66
April	62/35	1.4	7	8	37
July	93/59	.7	--	4	18
Oct.	66/37	.9	3	--	37
YEAR	64/37	8.7	65	66	40

# of days 32° or below: 135   # of days 90° or above: 53

Located in the intermountain region at 4500 feet, Provo fends off massive rainfall (less than 20"/yr.), but guarantees 65" of snowfall (there's always some on the ground). Winters are long and cold but sunny. Summers are hot but bearable (very low humidity and pleasant cool nights).

Earning a Living

Economic outlook: Vitality is the operative word. What with a highly educated and youthful work force (avg. age of Provo residents is 21.5), the health of the software industry here and the expansion of many existing industries, Provo promises to continue to provide a stable economy in an area seemingly unaffected by recession. Although Provo has had a good growth in retail (most recently Walmart and Phar-mor), it seems there's more success with expanding and developing existing companies, which keeps residents working (a low 4% unemployment has remained the same for the past couple of years). There is, however, an overabundance of professionals (Brigham Young University feeds into the educated labor supply). Provo, set in the midst of an area that boasts the 3rd-largest high-tech industry in the country, is home to major software companies, WordPerfect and Novell. Each have over $600 million in sales. WordPerfect employs 3,000 people, mostly as programmers and in customer service. Novell is also a large employer and has plans to expand and add 1,500 employees in the next 2 years.

Where the jobs are: East Bay Business Center houses 24 businesses—plus a 27-hole municipal golf course (city-owned, govt.-operated), and is anchored by Novell (software manufacturer), NuSkin (complete hair/skin care line and Dynix (automated library software). The Downtown Business District is home to all financial institutions, government offices, and county office buildings—there are more than 600 businesses here. Because of tremendous growth in the past 2 years, there is a newly opened industrial park—Riverwoods Business & Research Park—with more than 120 acres, and including businesses such as Novell, BYU credit union, Word Perfect, and Dynix. Nearly 40% of Riverwoods is dedicated to "green space," because companies want employees to be in nice surroundings. Other major employers in the area: Brigham Young University; Geneva Steel; Alpine School District; Utah Valley Regional Medical Center; Sears Telecatalog Center. There are few jobs available in health-related fields.

Business opportunities: Small software companies are actively encouraged to come to Provo—by the big software companies, no less, because of the support services they would provide. If you have good software ideas—please come! There is also a growing need for stores that specialize in outdoor recreation. This community loves outdoor recreation. Elegant gourmet restaurants are also needed. The area is saturated with boutiques and gift stores.

Making the Grade

Public education overview: The Provo school system is proof that dedicated teachers, strong parental involvement and a community that values education can overcome low budgets and achieve genuine success stories. Teachers are paid average salaries, school facilities are old, but nearly 95% of all high school students go on to higher education, 80% attend college, and Provo schools rate very high on standard national exams. The district develops its own curriculum, with involvement from parents. Some examples are: a reading program that combines whole language with strong phonics, with a goal of having 95% of all 3rd-graders reading on or above grade level; a strong AP program for high school students (85% passed the AP exam with a score of 3 or higher); and a character education program teaching responsibility and accountability. Utah is an equalized education state, so each district receives the same amount of tax dollars to educate each child ($1,409). Experts attribute Provo's success to strong values and widespread support of education. The district has been nominated in prior years for the Governors Project (16 districts nationwide explore reform in schools).

Class size: 26:1.

Help for working parents: The district just received a grant to help set up a Latch Key program. There are many outside after-school programs, including church-sponsored activities.

Blue Ribbon School Awards: Timpview High School ('83-'84).

School year: Starts first week of Sept. and ends mid-June. Children must be 5 on or before Sept. 1 to enter kindergarten.

Special education/gifted programs: There are no special programs for gifted students because the district doesn't believe in "elitist" groups. Learning disabled students are in resource centers in neighborhood schools and mainstreamed when possible. Even mentally and physically handicapped students are being integrated into district schools. The philosophy is that students benefit from a shared environment.

Nearby colleges/universities: Brigham Young University (30,000+ students, one of the largest private universities in the U.S.); Utah Valley Community College (2 campuses and offers 2-year associate degrees).

Medical Care

Hospitals/medical centers: Utah Valley Regional Medical Center is a 409-bed facility, with a staff of 400, and is the busiest emergency center. It also acts as a referral center to other nearby hospitals, and is considered a full-service hospital, known for oncology, newborn intensive care, intensive/coronary, open heart surgery, rehab center, and its wellness center. It's an IHC (Intermountain Health Care) facility, a regional health care provider. IHC was given the Health Care Forum/Witt Award, the health care industry's most prestigious honor, in recognition of quality health care. The Primary Children's Medical Center, in Salt Lake City (45 min. away), is also part of IHC.

Specialized care: Utah Valley Medical Center has a phone information line for parents to call in regarding behavioral-developmental concerns. Handicapped facilities and services include Kids on the Move, in Orem, which is a center for developmentally delayed children.

Crime & Safety

Crime is an estimated 64% below other regions. There's an avg. of 1 homicide a year in Provo. Other crimes such as theft, shoplifting, bicycles, car strips, and some robberies occur, but not with such great frequency. Rapes however have increased by 20% over last year. Police are working hard to increase awareness of the problem and teach defense methods. There are several school programs including Officer Friendly, who speaks to grades K-3 about personal safety, and McGruff (the crime-fighting dog) speaks at schools about bicycle safety and pedestrian safety. Residents are active in neighborhood watch programs. Most people claim they feel safer here than in most places.

Community Life

Because the church is so important to most residents here, most of the social activities and get-togethers are organized under their auspices. There is also a very active United Way. In addition, there are many unique efforts that promote a good quality of life. When newcomers move into a neighborhood, neighbors drop in immediately bringing food and offering services. The same is done when someone is in the hospital. The residents are very community oriented; anything that will bring people together becomes a top priority.

Let the Good Times Roll

Family fun: When you see what's here, you'll never stay inside. There's an incredible variety of recreation because of Provo's fantastic location at the foot of the Wasatch Mountain Range. Provo has 18 city parks and 1 state park—Utah Lake State Park, the east shore of Utah's largest natural freshwater lake. It's perfect for great river and lake-front water play, including fishing, swimming, water-skiing, power boating and ice skating in winter. There's also snowmobiling and sledding. Speaking of snow, Utah boasts the "greatest snow on earth." Provo is an hour's drive from a number of major ski resorts: Brighton, Alta, Park West, Snowbird, Deer Valley, Solitude, and Sundance (owned and operated by Robert Redford) which has one of the state's most popular summer outdoor theaters. The resort and the National Forest surrounding it offer numerous hiking, horse and mountain biking trails, a very popular activity. Seven Peaks Resort Center offers a water park, 18 hole golf course and ice skating.

Sports: Brigham Young University is known for its basketball, football, golf and baseball teams. BYU sports teams are called the Cougars.

Arts & entertainment: Brigham Young University hosts a variety of theater events, concerts, sports, dance and arts. McCurdy Historical Doll Museum is an award-winning museum, with more than 3,000 dolls. Provo LDS Tabernacle hosts internationally known performers. The Utah Valley Symphony is a 90-member community orchestra. Sundance Resort sponsors a children's summer theater and the Sundance Summer Theater. For other cultural opportunities, Salt Lake City is a 45-min. drive.

Annual events: America's Freedom Festival is a 3-week celebration with parades, speech and essay contests, concerts, sporting events, National Bluegrass and Fiddlers Festival, hot air balloon festival, Downtown Fair, Awards Gala and Mayor's Ball, and Stadium of Fire in BYU's Cougar Stadium presented by Alan Osmond (June-July); World Folkfest in nearby Springville is the largest folk festival in North America attracting dancers from 13 countries (late Aug.); Children's Celebration of the Arts is a free arts and crafts day for children designed for hands-on experience and entertainment (July); Strawberry Days in nearby Pleasant Grove features sporting events, parades, and a rodeo (June).

The Environment

Provo's water quality is good, but there is concern about the air quality. Geneva Steel (formerly U.S. Steel) contributes to the problem as does a high concentration of cars. Additionally, Provo's valley location causes temperature inversions and poor air quality in winter. When this happens, outside activities can be canceled (3-4 times a year) as it can pose risks to young children, the elderly and those with respiratory problems. As for recycling, there are numerous programs.

In and Around Town

Roads and interstates: I-15 north-south and U.S. 50, 89, 91, and 189.
Closest airport: Salt Lake International Airport (40 mi.).
Public transportation: Utah Transit Authority provides daily mass transit service to both Provo/Orem and the Salt Lake/Ogden areas.
Avg. commute: Salt Lake City (45 min.).

What Every Resident Knows

What people want to know is, "Will we feel welcome if we're not affiliated with the Church of the Latter Day Saints (Mormon faith)?" Welcome yes. Comfortable? That depends if by nature you are conservative, deeply family-oriented and think a clean, wholesome environment is the only way to fly. As for being "accepted," LDS families are very friendly but do stick together (so much of their time is spent at church). • Provo has some interesting variations on "fast foods." Locals dip their French fries in "fry sauce"—a special blend of mayonnaise and ketchup. Another favorite is the scone—fried bread batter dipped in honey butter. Bon appetit. • Yes, the Osmonds still live here, right on Osmond Drive, of course.

FYI

Provo Chamber of Commerce
51 S. University Avenue
Provo, UT 84601
801-379-2555

Utah County Travel Council
51 South University
Provo, UT 84606
801-370-8393

The Daily Herald
1555 North 200 West
Provo, UT 84604
801-373-5103

Coldwell Banker/John West Realty
455 N. University Avenue
Suite 201
Provo, UT 84601
801-377-8140
Gary Tate

Provo City Power
251 W. 800 North
Provo, UT 84601
801-379-6800

U.S. West Communications
75 E. 100 North Street
Provo, UT 84601
801-377-9200

Provo City Dept. of Economic Development
152 West Center Street
P.O. Box 1849
Provo, UT 84603
801-379-6160

UVEDA—Utah Valley Economic Dev. Admin.
100 East Center Street
Suite 2500
Provo, UT 84601
801-370-8100

Small Business Development Center
790 Tanner Building
Brigham Young University
Provo, UT 84602
801-378-4022

School district: 801-374-4933
Property tax assessor: 801-370-8280
Physician's referral: 801-377-8488
Day-care referral: 801-374-7800

Chesapeake, Virginia

Area Snapshot

Local population: 157,669
County: None   **Population:** 1.3 million (Norfolk/Virginia Beach/Newport News)
U.S. Region: Eastern U.S./southeastern Va.
Closest metro areas: Norfolk (5 mi. northwest)
Median housing price: $98,000
Avg. household income: $37,270
Best reasons to live here: Fast-growing coastal region, affordable housing, exciting economic growth, progressive schools, abundant recreation and culture, very low crime, great community spirit, beautiful, historic area.

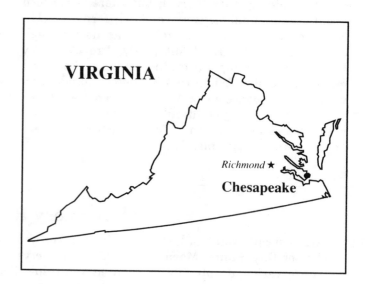

Fabulous Features

From Bangor to Bakersfield, cities create catchy slogans. Chesapeake says it's "a city that's good for life." Nice concept if you can get it! Upon investigation, we discovered truth in advertising! Chesapeake *is* one of those special cities where you could live from cradle to grave and not feel like you missed a thing. Situated in the heart of the dynamic Hampton Roads region (Norfolk/Virginia Beach/Newport News), residents are a short drive away from the Atlantic Ocean and hundreds of cultural, historic and "*fun*-omenal" activities (Colonial Williamsburg, the Virginia Air and Space Center and Busch Gardens).

While the leisure suits you fine (a wilderness park has families camping, canoeing and horseback riding), the opportunities for advancement will really dress up your life! Because of excellent transportation (air, rail, interstates and the world's largest natural harbor) and its central location, Chesapeake, according to *The Wall Street Journal*, will experience some of the greatest job growth in the coming years—24 companies recently expanded or moved in (in-cluding Volvo Penta North America headquarters), and 12 new industrial areas are on the drawing board.

With companies from more than 30 countries here, Chesapeake's neighborhoods are like global villages. The common bond is the love of high-quality construction and great value (custom homes in the $100,000-$150,000 range).

Regardless of nationality, everyone appreciates security (crime stats rank it the safest city in Virginia) and great education. There's a planetarium, an FM radio station in the high school and even a money-back guarantee that students who graduate are proficient in work skills. So the advertising is right: Whether you're 8 or 80, there is something to do, to see or to be in Chesapeake!

Possible drawbacks: Managing growth keeps city officials busy (population is expected to reach 205,000 by 2000). Adequate water supply and roads are a concern, but long-term plans should eventually catch up. • High humidity in summer discourages the use of the expression, "no sweat."

"You can quote me on that"

"We have nice shops, good libraries, excellent golf courses, great seafood—and you thought we were just some hick town!"—M.G.

Real Estate

Market overview: Chesapeake is a buyer's market that is currently very active. Since the Hampton Roads area is so heavily military, there are always residents who are being transferred out, and who have to sell quickly. Those transferring *in* have their pick of a large variety of homes. New construction is strong (1,206 single family home permits in 1991). Homes have appreciated 2%-3%/yr.

What houses look like: Most homes are either ranches or 2-story colonials. Exterior construction is usually brick or vinyl, and occasionally drivitte (similar to stucco). Homes built in the more rural areas are on 3-acre sites. Trees native to the area are oak, pine and gum. Typical shrubbery includes boxwood and azaleas, for which the area is famous.

Starter homes: Prices are $75,000-$90,000 for a basic 3BR/2BA ranch. Houses are between 1400-1600 sq. ft. Most come with a 1-car garage. Look at Fentress Gardens and Homemont.

Trade ups: For a little more money you can get a lot more home; 2-story colonials and custom ranches can be bought for $100,000-$150,000. These homes are between 1600-2100 sq. ft. and are on lots that are 12000-15000 sq. ft. Typical features include crown molding, custom cabinets, skylights, fireplaces and ceramic tile floors in the BAs. Wellington, Etheridge Woods and Tunsridge Station are popular.

Luxury homes: These homes start at $200,000 and go up to $400,000. Most have been built on 3-acre sites and are 3000-5000 sq. ft., 2-story colonials w/4-6BR/3-4BA, with inground pool, jacuzzi, hot tub, formal living and dining rooms, gourmet kitchen and deck. These beautiful homes are in Chesapeake Colony Estates, Woodwards Mill and Caroon Farms.

Rental market: The rental market is stable with year-round availability. A 2BR/1BA apartment in a nice neighborhood rents for $525/mo. SFH rentals are hard to find; the average cost is $625/mo.

Great neighborhoods: The Great Bridge and Western Branch areas are in high demand.

Nearby areas to consider: Virginia Beach borders Chesapeake and is desirable because it is near the ocean. Oceanfront and bayfront property is available (15%-25% more). Suffolk, another independent city, borders Chesapeake on the south. Housing costs are about 5%-10% less. You get a better buy on land and larger lots. Suffolk, a fast-growing residential area, has its own school system.

What Things Cost

Runzheimer's Living Cost Index: Avg. annual costs for family of 4 with household income of $50,000: $48,912 (2.2% below avg. city).
ACCRA's national comparisons: Not available.
Utilities: Phone: Hookup: $38.50. Service: $17.09 for local calls. Electricity: $15 connection charge; $120/mo. avg. for 1500-sq. ft. w/central air, electric dryer/hot water heater. Sewer and Water: $30 bimonthly. Gas: Avg. $45mo.
Kid care: Avg. $100/wk. for infants, $90/wk. for toddlers. In areas such as Greenbriar, Great Bridge, and Western Branch, there are enough daycare centers. In more rural sections, there are not enough centers, and those that are there have waiting lists, although the Hampton Roads Planning Council is active in recruiting more centers.
Pediatric visit: $35-$45.

The Tax Ax

Sales tax: 4.5%.
Property tax: Property taxes are based on 100% fair market value, plus an extra $1.31 per $100 of value for mosquito-control areas. A home valued at $100,000 would pay an estimated $1,310/yr.
State income tax: Virginia residents pay $720 on the first $17,000 of taxable income and 5.3% on anything over that amount.

Climate

Elevation 25'	Avg. High/Low	Avg. Rain (Inches)	Avg. Snow (Inches)	Avg. Days Rain	Avg. % Humidity
Jan.	49/32	3.1	3	9	59
April	68/48	2.7	1	10	50
July	87/70	5.7	--	11	60
Oct.	70/53	3.1	--	8	60
YEAR	68/51	44	7.4	114	58
# of days 32° or below:55			# of days 90° or above: 37		

With the Atlantic Ocean as your next-door neighbor, ocean breezes are constant companions. Rarely is there extreme hot or cold weather for any significant period of time. Snowfall occurs once or twice a season but doesn't stick. High humidity and frequent rainy days describe much of the summer, although evenings are delightfully cool. Fall and spring are gorgeous.

Earning a Living

Economic outlook: Chesapeake's exciting growth can be attributed to three key ingredients. First, it has a very experienced labor pool because of the experienced military personnel in the area. Secondly, its location is midpoint on the East Coast and close to the largest, deepest ice-free port in the U.S. And finally, the quality of life meets companies' expectations for their employees. Chesapeake is currently experiencing an annual job-growth rate of 2%-3%. The current rate of unemployment (Aug. 1992) is 6%, up from about 4% in previous years because of the recession. Retail sales were essentially flat from 1990-1991, although the number of establishments has been rising, and national retailers such as Montgomery Ward and Wal-Mart have recently entered the area.

Where the jobs are: Chesapeake continues to lure businesses, and to diversify its economic base away from the military and government. A major employer is HFC (Household Finance Co.) with 750 employees at the regional processing center. It will soon move its Credit Card Division here, bringing 1,200 new jobs. Q.V.C. T.V. has moved some of its telecommunications operations to the area, and employs 850 people. Norfolk is home to the world's largest naval base. As a result, many defense contractors have set up shop here. Volvo North America (the marine engineering division) recently moved here. Loral Training (military training systems) opened in 1992, with 100 employees. A number of Japanese firms have recently moved in. Sumitomo Machinery Corp., a subsidiary of the Sumitomo Group, owns a 220,000 sq. ft. facility that currently employs 200, but plans to expand in the future. Mitsubishi Kasci moved here in 1988 and opened 2 product plants, with plans for more expansion. On the down side, Norfolk Steel Division closed, costing 220 jobs, although a group of investors was looking into reopening the plant. The Bendix Corporation laid off 1/3 of its 200 employees. The military and government are downsizing, and a few thousand jobs have been lost in those areas.

Business opportunities: Chesapeake still offers reasonably priced land opportunities, and its highly educated, growing population makes it a good place to own a business. A recent target marketing study by Old Dominion University identified several occupations and businesses needed in the Hampton Roads area: commercial printing industry, machine tools and metal cutting, shipbuilding and repair, surgical and medical instruments. Retailing has been strong, and two new regional malls have opened in the last two years.

Making the Grade

Public education overview: The Chesapeake school district has grown from a small country system to a miniature "big city" district during the last 30 years. Along the way it has acquired many attractive "extras" not normally found in a school system. The first that bears mentioning is the district planetarium, where each month a new program on space exploration is featured. These programs are geared for all grade levels, and at night the planetarium is used for adult education. The district also owns a student-operated television station and FM radio station. The district does not track students after graduation but estimates that 60%-70% go on to higher education. It also offers a "warranty" on each graduate. If an employer finds that a graduate is deficient in a basic area, the school will retrain the graduate through its adult education program at no charge to the graduate or the business. Avg. SAT scores are 393 for verbal and 430 for math. The biggest challenge facing this district is the tremendous influx of new students (estimated at 800 a year). A bond referendum to build new schools is anticipated in the near future. In 1989-90 the district's gifted and talented students won the international "Odyssey of the Mind" competition.

Class size: 25:1.

Help for working parents: The district does not run a before- or after-school program, but will provide bus transportation after school to a childcare center.

School year: Starts after Labor Day and ends 3rd week in June. Starting with 1993-94 school year, children must be 5 years old by Sept. 30 to enroll in kindergarten.

Special education/gifted programs: When possible, students are mainstreamed, with support services in the regular classroom. There are self-contained classrooms for those who require more individualized attention. The Kirk Cohen Center is for students who need intensive help and very special equipment. The district runs a gifted and talented program for students in grades 4-12 year-round. The program places special emphasis on deductive reasoning skills. Students in grades 5-6 are bused to a special laboratory school for half-day.

Nearby colleges/universities: The College of William and Mary, Williamsburg; Virginia Wesleyan College; Norfolk State University; Hampton University; and Tidewater Community College.

Medical Care

Hospitals/medical centers: Chesapeake General Hospital is a 210-bed facility, offering cardiac care, geriatrics, obstetrics, pediatrics, and general emergency care. It recently completed a $30 million expansion—on emergency, x-ray and outpatient surgery facilities, and added a cardiac catheterization lab, MRI suite and ambulatory diagnostic center. Its Mom's Mobile Unit offers free home visits to first-time mothers and first-time breastfeeding mothers. Riverside Regional Medical Center offers comprehensive health care as well as a drug overdose center, diabetes center, kidney dialysis services and open-heart surgery. Sentara Norfolk General, a 644-bed facility, is the largest area hospital, with dialysis, neonatal ICU, open-heart surgery, major trauma, drug overdose and diabetes care.
Specialized care: The Harbors, a chemical dependency recovery program, w/locations in Norfolk, Portsmouth, and Virginia Beach; Tidewater Psychiatric, inpatient substance abuse counseling; New Beginnings and Serenity Lodge for drug treatment; Norfolk State University has a sports injury clinic.

Crime & Safety

Annual statistics gathered by the FBI show that Chesapeake is among the top 20 safest communities of comparable size in the country. From 1990-1991, incidents in all categories except robbery declined. Chesapeake is serviced by its own police dept., comprised of 5 precincts and 282 officers. It is a highly visible police force on the streets, and 27 new officers will be hired soon. The highest incidence of crime involves personal property, usually in the form of theft or vandalism. The homicide rate is very low. Avg. response time for police calls varies because the area is 360 sq. mi. Numerous neighborhood watch groups help keep the crime rate down. The police run a successful DARE program in all of Chesapeake's elementary schools.

Community Life

This city has a strong sense of civic and community involvement. Attendance is very high at meetings for local government and community projects. One upcoming project that has drawn lots of volunteers is the city's 30th anniversary celebration, beginning in Jan. 1993. "Friends of the Library," a group that raises funds for the library system, attracts hundreds of volunteers each year. "Paint Your Heart Out, Chesapeake" is a program sponsored by the Rotary, involving 700-800 volunteers who paint, repair, and beautify the homes of elderly residents.

Let the Good Times Roll

Family fun: Chesapeake's Park and Recreation Dept. calls the Northwest River Park its "jewel in the crown." This beautiful 763-acre park is located on the scenic Northwest River. It features equestrian and camping facilities, nature trails, fishing, canoeing and paddleboating. The park is open year-round for community use, and a year-round leisure program for kids and adults offers more than 400 programs including ballet, karate, dog obedience and more. An athletic program attracts more than 20% of Chesapeake's school children with programs like football and cheerleading. In 1992, the *Virginia Pilot* cited the P&R Dept. for "Outstanding Contributions to the Community." For swimming, boating and fishing, Virginia Beach is only 25 minutes away. The Intercoastal Waterway (running from Maine to Florida) passes through Chesapeake, and provides plenty of boating opportunities. Colonial Williamsburg and Busch Gardens are a 1-hour drive. Snow skiing, mountain climbing and hiking are a 4-hour drive to Shenandoah National Park and the Blue Ridge Mountains. The Great Dismal Swamp National Wildlife Refuge is less than an hour's drive west of Chesapeake.
Sports: The area has an identity crisis when it comes to pro sports. Residents are fans of numerous pro teams mainly because no teams are based nearby. One team that seems to be picking up a local following is the NBA's Charlotte Hornets, in Charlotte, N.C. Locals follow college football and are loyal to Norfolk State University's Spartans and Old Dominion University's Monarchs. Another big attraction is auto racing at the Richmond Speedway.
Arts & entertainment: Most cultural events are held at the Chrysler Hall in neighboring Norfolk. National and international artists, including The Virginia Symphony, perform concerts, opera, and ballet here. The Virginia Opera performs at the Center Theater in Norfolk. The Chrysler Museum (also in Norfolk) features numerous art collections. Local museums include the Virginia Air and Space Center, the National Americana Museum, the Peninsula Fine Arts Museum and the U.S. Army Transportation Museum.
Annual events: Chesapeake Jubilee, at the Chesapeake City Park (3rd weekend in May); Trailathon Fall Festival Weekend (3rd weekend in Sept.); Christmas Parade, a nighttime affair (Dec.).

The Environment

Air quality readings for the city of Chesapeake are monitored at a site in Suffolk. Therefore, the site readings are not always an accurate reflection of what is happening in Chesapeake. Readings for the area place Chesapeake in "marginal attainment," primarily due to auto emissions. The water supply for the city is obtained from the Northwest River and supplemented by buying from Norfolk and Portsmouth. In order to meet the increasing demands for water, the city is developing an aquifer storage and recovery system that will store water underground. The city has a curbside recycling program sponsored by the Southeastern Public Service Authority. It recycles glass, aluminum, tin, and paper. The city also has an interesting landscape ordinance designed to beautify the area, affecting new commercial and industrial developments.

In and Around Town

Roads and interstates: The New Beltway includes I-664, I-464 and J-64; circling Hampton, Newport News, Chesapeake, Virginia Beach, and Norfolk. Other major roads: U.S. 58, 13, 168 & 17.

Closest airports: Williamsburg International Airport in Newport News (about 45 min. north via the James River crossings);, Norfolk International Airport in Norfolk (25 min. north); regional South Norfolk Airport in northern Chesapeake; and the regional Chesapeake Portsmouth Airport in western Chesapeake.

Public transportation: Local bus service is provided by Tidewater Regional Transit. Most buses start running by 6 a.m. and stop between 6 p.m. and 7 p.m.. A few run as late as 11 p.m.-midnight.

Avg. commute: 30 min. from Chesapeake to Norfolk and across the James River to Newport News and Hampton.

What Every Resident Knows

If you ask Chesapeake residents where they're from, the answer would be "Hickory." "Great Bridge." "Western Branch." "Deep Creek." "Greenbriar." But never Chesapeake! They use neighborhood names because Chesapeake has been in existence for only 30 years. The boroughs have been around since before the Civil War. • Good Italian restaurants are in short supply as is evident by the fact that pizza is often prepared with American cheese. *Mama mia!*

FYI

Hampton Roads Chamber of Commerce
400 Volvo Parkway
Chesapeake, VA 23320
804-547-2118

Norfolk Convention and Visitors Bureau
236 East Plume Street
Norfolk, VA 23510
804-441-5266

Virginia Pilot and Ledger-Star
150 West Brambleton Avenue
Norfolk, VA 23510
800-446-2004

RE/MAX Advantage Real Estate
100 Volvo Parkway, Ste. 100
Chesapeake, VA. 23320
800-543-3886
Willie Colston, Ralph Cates, Realtors

Regal Realty
303 Effingham Street
Portsmouth, VA 23704
804-397-8588
Gary Frye

Virginia Power
P.O. Box 1446
Chesapeake, VA 23327
804-857-7701

Virginia Natural Gas
5100 East Virginia Beach Blvd.
Norfolk, VA 23502
804-466-5550

C&P Telephone
P.O. Box 27783
Richmond, VA 23272-7783
804-455-2100

Chesapeake Economic Development
860 Greenbriar Circle
Greenbriar Tower I, Suite 304
Chesapeake, VA 23320-2624
804-523-1100

Public Information Office-City of Chesapeake
306 Cedar Road
City Hall Building
Chesapeake, VA 23320
804-547-6241

School district: 804-547-0153
Property tax assessor: 804-547-6235
Greetings to You: 804-547-3850
Clergy Association: 804-547-0356
Physician's referral: 804-547-7800
Day-care referral: 804-627-3993

Reston, Virginia *(Washington, D.C.)*

Area Snapshot

Local population: 53,800
County: Fairfax   **Population:** 754,000
U.S. region: Mid-Atlantic/East Coast
Closest metro area: Washington, D.C. (18 mi. east)
Median housing price: $183,000
Avg. household income: $60,000
Best reasons to live here: Successful planned community, a "city in the country," educated, ethnically diverse population, beautiful new town center, excellent schools, attractive park settings, proximity to Washington, D.C., and its vast, historic, cultural offerings.

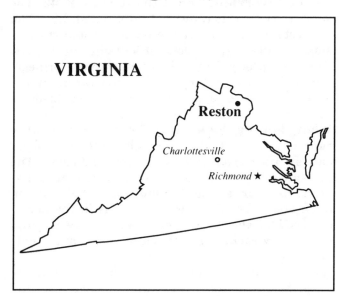

Fabulous Features

Thirty years ago, Robert E. Simon had a vision about building a community perfectly suited to living, working and enjoying leisure time to the fullest. He was so sure people would respond, he sold Carnegie Hall to raise the money! And the "Reston" they say, is history.

Today's community *is* a dream-come-true. Located in lush western Fairfax County (one of four "megacounties" in the U.S.), Reston is now the second-largest business center in Virginia, home to Unisys (formerly Sperry Rand), Apple Computers, NASA, U.S. Sprint, Rolls Royce and the CIA. All told, 2,100 companies employ 34,000 people (25% bike or hike to work).

Initially attracted by the proximity to Washington, D.C., and Dulles International Airport, residents are more enamored of Reston's home front advantage—its natural charm and serenity (wooded areas camouflage shopping centers), thoughtfully laid-out neighborhoods (home designs and amenities are gorgeous) and the cultural and recreational outlets (dozens of enjoyable things to see and do in 11 square miles)! Spend the day at the dazzling, new Town Center for fine dining, shopping and family entertainment. Go bass fishing on Lake Audubon. Then head home on bike or foot through 50-miles of pathways.

Choose from luxury townhouses overlooking Lake Ann to patio homes on the greens to a designer showcase in a park setting. Prices start at $60,000, average $350,000 and don't stop until they hit $1 million. Reston's finishing touches are low crime, excellent schools (the Fairfax County district is one of the most prestigious in the East) and a diverse ethnic population. If ever there was an urban, suburban, countrified life rolled into one, *Robert E. Simon's TOwN* is it.

Possible drawbacks: You need deep pockets to live comfortably in northern Virginia. Overall living costs are 11%-17% higher than the national average. Housing is the biggest culprit (prices are 35% higher than average). • Commuting to D.C. by car can mean 1-1½ hours of pounding the steering wheel (with high summer humidity, commuting is hardly a joy.) Fortunately, public transportation is!

"You can quote me on that"

"This town makes you feel like you live way out in the country, but the reality is you're only 20 minutes from D.C."—C.S.

Real Estate

Market overview: Forget the summer of '42! The summer of '92 was the year that counted. It's when real estate came out of the doldrums and the bus stopped, discharging lots of out-of-town buyers. Prices are pretty firm with not much room for negotiation because of large reductions taken in the past. The rate of appreciation is around 2%-3% a year.

What houses look like: Reston has it all—ranches, Cape Cods, colonials, and split-foyer entries. The town is filled with trees and parks. The community is only 25 years old, so homes are fairly new. Exterior sidings include vinyl, aluminum, brick and cedar. New construction is in the northern section, known as Northpoint. Here you'll find lots of new condominiums, patio homes and single family homes.

Starter homes: Small single family homes range in price from $99s-$150s. These homes usually feature 3BR and 1½BA. A townhouse in this price range buys a lot more—3 or 4BR and 2 or 3BA. You can find these values in Sawyer's Cluster, Tanner's Cluster and Golf Course Island.

Trade-ups: From $200,000 to $300,000 gets a 4BR/2½BA colonial with separate living and dining rooms, large master BR with garden BA (sunken tub, jacuzzi), and a basement. Check out Hunters Woods, Old Brookville, Old Bayberry and Post Oak.

Luxury homes: The luxury showplaces start at $300,000 and go to $650,000, with a few over $1 million (usually waterfront property). These spectacular homes feature multi-level decks, walk-out master BR balconies, brick fronts, screened porches, and sometimes swimming pools. These homes can be found in Carisbrooke, Northpoint, Woodstock and Woodstone.

Rental market: Rentals are widely available. Agents say you'll need no more than 30 days to find suitable accomodations. A 1BR condo is $650/mo. 3BR/1½BA townhouses go for $850-$1,000. SFH will rent for $1,200.

Great neighborhoods: You can't go wrong in any of 19 developments. Two favorites are Old Brookville (distinct New England flavor) and Hemingway (proximity to the lake). Both areas are considered upscale.

Nearby areas to consider: Herndon is a fast-growing community with a small-town feel. It's very historic and charming, but with a lot of new construction. Shopping centers are within walking distance for Herndon residents.

What Things Cost

Runzheimer's Living Cost Index: Avg. annual costs for family of 4 with household income of $50,000: $58,974 (17.9% above avg. city).

ACCRA's national comparisons: Overall living costs in the Washington, D.C., metro area are 11% above avg. The trouble spot is housing (35% above avg.). Utilities, transportation and health care range 10% to 14% above avg. However, food is only 1.7% above avg. and goods and services are actually 3% below avg.

Utilities: Phone: Installation: $39; service: $9/mo. Electric: Avg. for 3BR: $160/mo. (Jan.), $135/mo. (April), $110/mo. (July); Gas: Avg. $50/mo.

Kid care: There are many full-day childcare programs in the area, with some taking 6-week old babies. Day care is readily available, but to get the closest location to your home, register early. Prices range from $100-$150/wk. Infant care is higher.

Pediatric visit: $45-$50.

The Tax Ax

Sales tax: 4.5%.

Property tax: Fairfax County basic rate: 1.16% of the assessed value. Reston residents pay an additional 6¢ per $100 of assessed value, plus $300 annual Homeowners Association dues.

State income tax: Pay $720 on the first $17,000 of taxable income and 5.3% on anything in excess of that.

Climate

Elevation 100'	Avg. High/Low	Avg. Rain (Inches)	Avg. Snow (Inches)	Avg. Days Rain	Avg. % Humidity
Jan.	41/23	2	6.2	8	60
April	65/41	2.9	.1	9	47
July	86/64	4.1	--	10	56
Oct.	68/44	2.7	.1	7	56
YEAR	65/43	36.6	23.1	105	56

# of days 32° or below: 117	# of days 90° or above: 28

Reston enjoys all four seasons with a climate that is best described as mild. Located halfway between New York and Florida, winters aren't as frigid and summers aren't as oppressive. Spring and autumn are wonderfully warm and sunny. Late spring/early summer gets the lion's share of rain and thunderstorms. Ice storms are common in winter, but crippling snow storms only blow in every few years.

Earning a Living

Economic outlook: Reston has emerged as a major business center within the Washington D.C., area and is the second-largest business center in Virginia. There are more than 1,700 businesses, associations, and government agencies (including the CIA) employing more than 34,000 people. Business picks up 27% of the tax base. Reston has a 15% office vacancy rate, while the avg. for the state of Virginia is 20%. The major growth area for industry has been in high technology, primarily telecommunications. The area has become a magnet for many corporate headquarters, because of five major assets: it's located in the Eastern time zone, has international accessibility, a great quality of life, a very good public and private school system, and is close to the federal government. Making their home in Reston are Rolls Royce, Molson Brewery U.S.A., and Lafarge Corp. Other major employers are Unisys, US Sprint, General Electric, Grumman Space Station Program Support, Computer Associates, and Boeing Technical Management Information Systems.

Where the jobs are: The federal government is the largest employer in Reston, with the U.S. Geological Survey employing more than 3,000. Mobil Oil and NASA's space station project have also become major employers. AMSC (American Satellite Corp.) announced that it will be coming to Reston in the Spring of '93, bringing 1,000 new jobs. DYNCORP, a company specializing in professional services in management and engineering, has been expanding dramatically. This is an employee-owned company with 60% of the shares held by the employees. On the down side, Systems Center, a company that specializes in software, recently laid off 200 employees. In nearby Manassas, IBM, going through a corporation-wide restructuring, also laid off hundreds.

Business opportunities: Reston has experienced tremendous growth in the last 8 to 10 years. The number of businesses occupying space in the central business district increased 312% during the 1980s. At this time, the area could use a mid-sized accounting firm and a decent-sized ad agency. Local in-town shoppers could use more retail shops and dining spots. Don't come if you're thinking of opening a commercial real estate business—small ventures have gone under lately with only the big ones surviving. The only tax advantages offered in Reston are for light manufacturing companies, which the area is trying to attract.

Making the Grade

Public education overview: Fairfax County Public Schools serve Reston and are nationally acclaimed as models of excellence. As Mary Futrell (past president of the National Education Association, the nation's largest teachers' union) said, "Other districts around the nation have learned something from Fairfax County." Success is due in part to a pay-for-performance program (outstanding teacher performance is rewarded with a monetary bonus). In addition, the sheer size (it's the 10th-largest school system in the nation), ample funding and innovation have allowed the system to offer top-quality programs, a full array of support services and an extensive extracurricular programs. Fairfax County students score significantly higher than state and national averages on achievement tests (on the SAT tests, students avg. 36 points higher on verbal, 44 points higher on math). More than 90% of the 1989 high school graduates are attending post-secondary institutions, and almost 71% are attending four-year colleges and universities. Within Reston are 7 elementary schools, 2 middle schools and 2 high schools (students who are eligible can attend Jefferson High School for Science and Technology). The district was recently given the A+ Award, from Secretary of Education, for the district's libraries and Media Center.

Class size: 26:1.

Help for working parents: The School Age Child Care program (SACC) in elementary schools is run by the County Office for Children. Hours of operation are 7 a.m. to 6 p.m.

School year: Starts after Labor Day and ends the third week in June. A child must be 5 on or before Sept. 30 to enter kindergarten.

Special education/gifted programs: Approximately 12,000 students receive special education programs that are highly touted on the national level. There are 13 distinct programs offered to students 2-21 with support services provided in regular classrooms when possible. Gifted students can attend a special magnet school or special classes within a home-based school.

Nearby colleges/universities: George Mason University; Northern Virginia Community College. Universities serving in metropolitan Washington D.C. are: American University, Catholic University, George Washington University, Howard University, Gallaudet College, Georgetown University, Marymount College, University of Virginia, Virginia Polytechnic Institute and State University.

Medical Care

Hospitals/medical centers: HCA Reston Hospital Center is a full-care, 127-bed facility. It offers "specialized centers of excellence," such as state-of-the-art cardiac care, maternity, a critical care center, a comprehensive diagnostic radiology dept., and 24-hour emergency services. Fairfax Hospital specializes in nuclear medicine and psychiatry. Fair Oaks Hospital has coronary care, maternal and child health care. Loudon Hospital Center offers diagnostic imaging and cardiopulmonary care.

Specialized care: The Loudon Hospital Center recently opened the Loudon Cancer Care Center. With Washington, D.C., and Bethesda, Md., so close, Reston residents also have access to world-famous Walter Reed Hospital

Crime & Safety

Fairfax County police patrol Reston with a local police substation and 60 officers. Most of the crime involves personal property (mailbox smashing and auto tampering head the list). Low crime is attributed to the area's affluence, active neighborhood watch groups and, in no small way, to the Fairfax police. This was one of the first 10 departments in the country to meet the rigid standards of the National Commission on Accreditation for Law Enforcement Agencies, Inc. Roughly two-thirds of the officers are assigned to regular patrol duty and are active in community programs such as the Crime Solver's program, home and business security programs and children's safety programs.

Community Life

Families devote ample time and energy to supporting school activities and local sporting events. There are youth clubs for baseball, basketball, soccer, football and cheerleading. Many residents volunteer for the Reston Association, either working at the Nature Center or serving on advisory committees helping to form policies. The Reston Community Center is the primary facility for cultural, educational, civic and recreational events. Residents are so supportive, they voted to tax themselves to pay for its operation.

"You can quote me on that"

"We came from a large city and were concerned we'd feel confined in a suburb, but if anything, we feel freer in Reston. You don't mind running errands because it's so nice to be outside."—K.Y.

Let the Good Times Roll

Family fun: The entire community looks like one huge park. Reston's four lakes are surrounded by residential homes where residents enjoy the abundant fishing. There are more than 50 miles of jogging and walking paths along with a 71-acre Nature Center. In the summer, residents use 16 association swimming pools and 46 tennis courts. There is one public golf course and driving range. The Reston Association provides many summer programs to children of all ages. Hug-a-Tree for ages 3-4 years, Day Camp environment studies for ages 5-12 years, and outdoor adventures are just a few of the offerings. Great Falls National Park in McLean is known for its scenic views of the Potomac River. Lake Fairfax Park offers paddle-boating, fishing, camping and a golf course. Shenandoah National Park, Skyline Drive, and Luray Caverns are about 2 hours to the west. Kings Dominion Family Fun Park is an hour and a half away. Mt. Vernon, home of George Washington, is an easy drive, as are a number of Civil War battlefields. Of course, there is nearby Washington, D.C., packed with endless sightseeing and events.

Sports: The Washington Redskins are perennial powers in the National Football League (they've won four Super Bowls). At the Capitol Center (Landover, Md.) you can catch the Capitol Bullets of the National Basketball Association, and the Washington Capitols, one of the better teams in the National Hockey League. And American League baseball action, with the Baltimore Orioles, is nearby, too.

Arts & entertainment: The Reston Community Center is home to many cultural events. Residents can enjoy performances given by the Young Actors Theater, Dance Theater Expression, Reston Chorale, and professional touring companies. The Reston Art Gallery showcases work of area artists and also produces a weekly cable television show focusing on the arts. In nearby Fairfax is Wolf Trap Farm Park for the Performing Arts, the Wolf Trap Opera, and the Fairfax Symphony Orchestra. In Washington, D.C., is the Kennedy Center. Other museums include the National Museum of American Art, National Museum of African Art, National Portrait Gallery, Renwick Gallery, National Gallery of Art and the Smithsonian Institute.

Annual events: Reston Festival at the Lake (weekend before Memorial Day); Youth Triathalon (summer); Adult Triathlon (second weekend in Sept.); and October Fest (Oct.).

The Environment

Reston is an ecologically conscious community. Area residents work with the Reston Association on policy development that will maintain the area's good environmental quality. It is extremely clean, with no industrial pollution and no heavy industry. The biggest source of pollution is from cars. Occasionally in the summer, ozone levels exceed EPA standards, but the problem lasts for only hours. There are no landfills in Reston, although there are in Fairfax and Lorton. The community participates in recycling.

In and Around Town

Roads and interstates: I-495, I-66, I-95, Rt. 7 (Leesburg Pike) and Dulles Toll Road (Rt. 267).
Closest airports: Washington Dulles International Airport (5 mi.), Washington National Airport (14 mi.).
Public transportation: Reston Internal Bus System (RIBS) provides service in and around Reston. Washington Metrobus Service provides Reston with continuous service throughout the metropolitan area during peak periods and weekends.
Avg. commute: At the peak of rush hour, it can take as long as 60 min. to get to Washington, D.C.

What Every Resident Knows

Robert E. Simon's dream was to build a community that had it all. Back in the early '60s, he bought the Sunset Hills Farm in Fairfax Co. and proceeded to make his dream come true by building a well-planned community on this site. Although financial difficulties forced him to sell his new community, the town bears his name today: Reston stands for Robert E. Simon's Town. • The Reston Town Center is the place to be for seasonal celebrations—from Easter egg hunts to lawn chair concerts in summer to Halloween costume contests to Christmas caroling and parades. Even after 30 years, nobody seems to "reston" their laurels here!

FYI

Reston Association
1930 Isaac-Newton Square
Reston, VA 22090
703-437-9580
(Manages town's wildlife, recreation and outdoor programs and facilities. All residents are members.)

The Washington Post
1150 15th Street, NW
Washington, DC 20071
202-334-6100

Reston Times (daily)
1760 Reston Parkway, Suite 107
Reston, VA 22090
703-437-5400

Reston Land Corp.
11911 Freedom Drive, Suite 300
Reston, VA 22090
703-742-6400

Virginia Power Co.
171 Elden Street
Herndon, VA 22070
703-437-8800

C and P Telephone Co.
P.O. Box 27783
Richmond, VA 23272
703-876-7000

Washington Gas Co.
6801 Industrial Road
Springfield, VA 22151
703-750-1000

Reston Visitors Center
11450 Baron Cameron Avenue
Reston, VA 22090
703-471-7030

Prudential Preferred Properties
11400 Commerce Park Drive
Reston, VA 22091-1505
703-620-0700
Anita Cebulash, Managing Broker

ERA/5 Star Realty
1801 Reston Parkway
Reston, VA 22090
703-471-7220
Mary O'Brien, Relocation Director

George Mason University Small Business Development Center
4260 Chain Bridge Road, Suite A1
Fairfax, VA 22030
703-993-2130

School district: 703-246-2502
Property tax assessor: Fairfax Co.
703-222-8234
Interfaith council: 703-476-6452
Physician's referral: 703-845-4848
Day-care referral: 703-359-5860

Richmond, Virginia

Area Snapshot

Local population: 203,056
County: Chesterfield   **Population:** 209,274
(693,517 in 3 county metro area)
U.S. region: East coast, central Virginia
Closest metro areas: Norfolk (93 mi. southeast), Washington D.C. (109 mi. north)
Median housing price: $112,657
Avg. household income: $64,549
Best reasons to live here: Fast-growing metro area, booming business, great recreation, diverse housing, award-winning schools, excellent medical care, easy pace, historic state capital, 1½ hours to mountains and beaches.

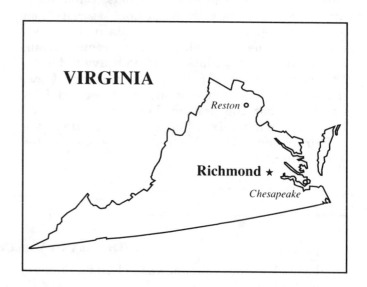

VIRGINIA

Reston ○

Richmond ★

Chesapeake

Fabulous Features

Unlike the new, monotonous "microwave" towns that have popped up across the country, metropolitan Richmond is a living, breathing American History book. At every turn is a reminder of a rich past ("Give me liberty or give me death"), *and* signs of a bright future.

Virginia's largest financial and corporate center has seen more than 2,000 companies relocate or expand here in the past 10 years, including 14 Fortune 500 companies. Just as promising, Richmond incorporates three of the fastest-growing counties in the state (Chesterfield, Hanover and Henrico). Projections indicate that between 1990 and the year 2000, the population will increase by 110,000.

Richmond's big draw is its "Cuburban" life—part country, part urban, part suburban. Head in any direction and you'll see all three landscapes intermingled with graceful, historic charm. Real estate options are as vast as the James River. Choose from 100-year old farm houses to contemporary masterpieces that cap-

ture the imagination but not the pocketbook (prices start at $60,000; average $150,000.)

But man does not live on backyards alone. From Shenandoah National Park and the Blue Ridge Mountains to the symphony and ballet, from sightseeing to science museums, from bike racing to baseball—active, healthy lifestyles are as natural as the hickory trees (rated one of the healthiest place to live in the U.S. by *Health* magazine). Take a look at Richmond and make a little history of your own!

Possible drawbacks: Richmond's "Civil War" battles aren't over. It's grappling with drug-related crimes, a result of its location off I-95 (midway between Miami and New York) and the ease in which guns are purchased (no waiting period). Task forces are taking dead-aim at the problems, which overshadow an otherwise tranquil, deeply committed family community. • You'll need more than a cool mint julip in summer. Heat, humidity and occasional poor air quality can get the better of you.

"You can quote me on that"

"Coming from a large city like Chicago, I was surprised to see how family oriented Richmond really is. The school systems are great and the city offers every type of recreation and entertainment you can think of. Most importantly, we have a wonderful community life here. I don't think there is anything lacking here."—M.L.

Real Estate

Market overview: After years of sellers calling the shots, the tables have turned. Home appreciation, while historically higher, has been flat in the past couple of years. (Richmond is finally feeling the effects of the recession.) In addition, a lot of older residents are retiring out of Richmond and moving farther south, making this a buyer's market. New families appreciate the variety of styles and the wide range of prices. New construction is limited and expensive. Custom-built homes on 1/3-½ acre (3000-3500 sq. ft.) go for $250,000-$350,000. There are also a number of planned communities, for anywhere from $90,000-$1 million.

What houses look like: Brick ranches, 2-story colonials and contemporaries are found with much of the architecture influenced by historical Williamsburg. Styles are conservative, with brick or vinyl siding. Virginians spend time over meals, reflected in the big, gourmet kitchens and large dining rooms. And family-oriented Virginian homes have formal living rooms. Master suites, tile floors and polished hardwood floors are popular.

Starter homes: $50,000-$100,000 for a 3BR/1-2BA, 1/3 acre, garage, new or resale. The farther outside the city, the more you'll get—20 min. away, $60,000 buys 1/3 acre, 3BR/1-1½BA, w/garage.

Trade-ups: $100,000-$150,000, with $100,000 buying a 3BR/1½-2BA, 1000 sq. ft., w/garage on the east side. At the higher end, you get a 4BR/2½BA, w/garage, pool, on 1-2 acres, about 15-20 min. from city, in a subdivision like Hanover.

Luxury homes: For $300,000 you can buy a 4-5BR/3-3½BA (2 master suites instead of 1), all-brick house, on 4 acres, 2-car garage, newer house. Look at Rivers Bend.

Rental market: It's difficult to find home rentals when purchase prices are so low. There are no co-ops, and condos aren't popular with families, as they often only have 2BR.

Great neighborhoods: Hanover, Rivers Bend and Woodlake all offer affordable family neighborhoods and good school systems. Windsor Farms uses Richmond public schools and is conveniently within city limits—close to stores and activities.

Nearby areas to consider: Windham is a planned community located in the western corridor of Henrico County. It boasts excellent schools, a golf course, private clubhouse and great community activities. New homes are available for as little as $90,000 and for as much as $1 million. Salisbury, in West Chesterfield, is one of the area's oldest communities and home of the prestigious Salisbury Country Club on Lake Salisbury.

What Things Cost

Runzheimer's Living Cost Index: Avg. annual costs for family of 4 with household income of $50,000: $48,243 (4.5% below avg. city).

ACCRA's national comparisons: Not available.

Utilities: Phone: Hookup: $38.50. Gas: $100/mo. (winter); $16/mo. summer; avg. $600/yr. Electric: $100-$225/mo. depending on usage. Water: billed every two months, roughly $55-$65.

Kid care: Day care in Richmond avg. $110/wk. for infants (formula & diapers not included). Toddlers avg. $80/wk. Infant care in Richmond is tough to find and the majority of day-care centers only take children 2 and up. **Pediatric visit:** $40.

The Tax Ax

Sales tax: 4.5%.

Property tax: For the city of Richmond, the tax rate is $1.45 per $100 of assessed property value. Thus, tax on a $100,000 home would be $1,450/yr. For Chesterfield County, it's $1.09 per $100 assessed value, and for Henrico County, it's 98¢ per $100 assessed value.

State income tax: Residents pay $720 on the first $17,000 and 5.3% on anything above that amount.

Climate

Elevation 150'	Avg. High/Low	Avg. Rain (Inches)	Avg. Snow (Inches)	Avg. Days Rain	Avg. % Humidity
Jan.	47/28	2.4	5	9	57
April	70/45	2.8	.1	9	45
July	88/68	5.6	0	11	57
Oct.	71/47	2.9	14.1	7	53
YEAR	69/47	41.2	14.1	110	53
# of days 32° or below: 86			# of days 90° or above: 45		

This region has a modified continental climate. Winters are generally mild (snow lasts a day or two), while summers can be hot and humid (yes, temperatures can go over 100), in part because of the Chesapeake Bay and the Atlantic Ocean. The fall is dry, sunny and delightfully warm.

Earning a Living

Economic outlook: Richmond is Virginia's largest financial, manufacturing, and distribution center, with more than 28,000 businesses operating in the area, and a labor supply of 475,500. Reflecting business expansion, the labor force has grown at an annual rate of 3.0%. However, 14,000 new workers enter the labor pool each year, outpacing the growing job market, resulting in an economic growth of 2% and an unemployment rate of 6.6%—which is still below the national unemployment rate for the year. The economy is diverse and relatively stable, with a skilled labor pool and lots of state employees (Richmond is the state capital). As a distribution center, Richmond is in an ideal location, at the crossroads of two major highways, I-95 and I-64.

Where the jobs are: While government, manufacturing and services are more or less equally divided, the service industry has grown by 60% the last 10 years. Nonagricultural employment has grown by 26%. Nonmanufacturing, with 401,500 employees, has also boomed, particularly in the areas of finance, insurance, and real estate. This growth has been fed by office expansion and construction of new facilities. Over the past 10 years, 2,186 companies have relocated and/or expanded in the Richmond area, creating 33,425 new jobs and investing $4.5 billion into the economy. Richmond is headquarters for more than 35 major corporations, including 14 Fortune Industrial 500 or Service 500 companies, with annual revenues exceeding $130 million. Other major business areas include fabricated rubber and metal products, (E.R. Carpenter Co., Inc., Safetex, Alfa-Laval Thermal Co., and Naito America) distribution (Mazda Motors of America, Inc., Stanley Hardware, Circuit City Distribution Center) and Customer Service. (General Electric Lighting, Time-Life Books, J.C. Penney Co., Inc.). Tobacco, food processing, chemicals, printing/publishing, and paper are the area's largest industries.

Business opportunities: Opportunities exist in a variety of areas, including printing and publishing, the emerging biotech industry, financial, and governmental services—such as data collection, accounting, legal, etc. There is ample land and space for light and heavy industry. In the three surrounding counties, 60% of the land is undeveloped, and plants and factories are welcome. As the number of new workers is outpacing the job market, there is a ready supply of labor for a new business. But anyone considering starting a small business should be aware that there is competition in every area.

Making the Grade

Public education overview: Richmond-area residents are served by 4 public school systems. Chesterfield School District is the area's largest (and the state's 3rd largest), the fastest-growing and very progressive. A 2-tier kindergarten program allows children who are ready to get a head start on learning. The Whole Language Reading Program (kindergarten through middle school) furthers reading skills and emphasizes literature. The percentage of graduating seniors who go on to further education is 82%. A program in the middle school identifies at-risk students (those who might drop out) and works with them to increase their chances of graduating. The district is also exploring the possibility of creating a math/science high school. Emphasis is on global education throughout the school system beginning at elementary through high school. High schools are internationalizing the curriculum through foreign language seminars and courses in Japanese, Russian, French, German, Spanish and Latin.

Class size: 23:1.

Help for working parents: YMCA offers before- and after-school day care for 14 elementary schools and 3 middle schools. The programs are at the YMCA, churches or school sites.

Blue Ribbon School Awards: Hermitage High School ('83-'84); Brookland Middle School ('84-'85); R.C. Longan Elementary ('85-'86); Dooley School ('86-'87); Mills E. Godwin High ('88-'89).

School year: Begins after Labor Day through middle of June. Children must be 5 on or before Dec. 31 to enter kindergarten (full day).

Special education/gifted programs: All schools have gifted and special education programs. Chesterfield County offers extensive programs for physically and mentally handicapped students.

Nearby colleges/universities: There are 12 colleges and universities in greater Richmond: Virginia Commonwealth University (VCU) is the largest public, urban doctoral-granting institution in the state. It includes the Medical College of Virginia and the School of the Arts; The University of Richmond (Henrico) offers liberal arts, professional and occupational programs. Other nearby institutions: Virginia State University in Petersburg; Virginia Union University in Northside Richmond; Randolph-Macon College in Ashland. John Tyler (Chesterfield) and J. Sargeant Reynolds (Henrico) offer associate degrees.

Medical Care

Hospitals/medical centers: Richmond was rated the "Healthiest City in the U.S." (*Health* magazine, March 1988). Major hospitals include: Medical College of Virginia (4th largest medical center in the U.S.), a teaching hospital; Chippenham Medical Center, an acute-care facility and a 113-bed psychiatric unit; Richmond Memorial, a general care facility of 920 beds and 1,800 employees; St. Mary's Hospital, a general-care facility specializing in long-term care of 401 beds and a staff of 1,200; Johnston-Willis Hospital, specializing in general medical and surgical services and Metropolitan a general, acute and psychiatric facility with 180 beds.

Specialized care: Children's Hospital treats children from infancy to age 21 with 36 beds and staff of 135; Richmond Eye and Ear Hospital specializes in surgery; Psychiatric Institute of Richmond has 84 beds, and Sheltering Arms, a physical rehabilitation facility.

Crime & Safety

Crime in the city of Richmond is considerably higher than the surrounding counties (specifically, drug-related murder and violent crime). The Governor has initiated various multi-jurisdictional task forces to fight violent crime and illegal firearms. The city manager unveiled the Urban Violence Strategy Plan in Sept. 1990, which outlines a series of short- and long-term strategies to achieve five goals: create a feeling of safety throughout the city, reduce street-level drug sales, mobilize community resources to fight violence, increase local government responsiveness to citizen safety and well-being, and lower the violence in the city. Already, a reduction in homicide and violent crime has been seen. The change is attributed to the efforts of the police and community, which includes expanded foot patrol beats, housing community patrols, and police field offices.

Community Life

The spirit of volunteerism is strong in Richmond, whether preserving the garden of a national landmark, or participating in a Parks and Recreation baseball game. The United Way Information Referral Center has been established to help direct people into areas where their services could best be utilized. Richmond is a big club and organization town. Richmond residents are also known for their love of fun and flamboyance—from the Jaycees' downhill ski races to the Big Brothers/Big Sisters annual "rubber ducky" races.

Let the Good Times Roll

Family fun: Outdoor recreation flourishes, as the area abounds with lakes for swimming, fishing, water-skiing, and wind surfing. Several state parks are open to campers. The James River and Chesapeake Bay are a boater's dream. Nearby Shenandoah National Park in the Blue Ridge Mountains features close to 500 miles of hiking and biking trails, including nearly 100 miles of the famous Appalachian Trail. Major local parks are Byrd, Byron and Forest Hill Parks. The James River Parks preserve plant and wildlife habitats and offer easy access to the river for fishing and canoeing. In Chesterfield County, the 1,800-acre Pocahontas State Park features a nature center, trails, and camping in natural surroundings. The Park and Recreation Dept. sponsors programs, such as Indian lore, canoe trips, fossil and archaeological digs, wildflower and bird walks, crafts and day camps. Fascinating historical sites and museums include: Richmond Children's Museum; Science Museum of Virginia (a hands-on science center); Virginia Museum of Fine Arts; Confederate Museum; Civil War Battlefields; Valentine-Wickham House and Plantation Row (historic buildings); St. John's Church (site of Patrick Henry's famous "Give me Liberty or Give me Death" speech); Edgar Allen Poe Museum; Hollywood Cemetery (burial site of two U.S. presidents and 18,000 Confederate soldiers) Nearby is Kings Dominion for family fun.

Sports: Plenty of action here: There's the AAA Richmond Braves (baseball); ECHL Richmond Renegades (hockey—AA); and the Richmond International Raceway (car racing). In Sept. the Crestar Bank PGA Tournament draws pros and spectators. Richmond is the headquarters for the Tour du Pont, the nation's largest bicycle race held in May.

Arts & entertainment: Residents fill their calendars with the following offerings: Richmond Symphony and Sinfonia performances; Richmond Ballet; Virginia Opera; Theatre IV (2nd-largest U.S. touring theater for young audiences); Theatre Virginia (professional theatre); Richmond Jazz Society; Richmond "Pops" Band; Monument Brass Quintet; and live performances throughout the year at the Richmond Coliseum, Richmond Mosque, and Carpenter Center for Performing Arts.

Annual events: Henricus Day, historical reenactments (Sept. 15); June Jubilee, with arts and music; Garden Week, historical homes and gardens tours (April); The Big Gig, local guests and musicians at city parks and theaters (July); International Food Festival (Sept.); Richmond Children's Festival, a weekend of music, art and storytelling (Oct.).

The Environment

Water and air quality are among the best in the state. Those with respiratory problems should be aware, however, that Richmond's hot and humid summers can cause some distress. The city is profuse with flowers and pollen counts can be high. Richmond has a wide variety of recycling programs, including a weekly pick-up. It is one of the few programs in the state that has a pre-sorted drink carton pick-up. There is also a curbside and drop-off program for yard waste composting, which serves more than 57,000 homes. Richmond has initiated a "Leave it on the Lawn" Program for grass clippings, in an effort to keep biodegradable organic elements in the soil.

In and Around Town

Roads and interstates: I-64 (east to Norfolk, west to St. Louis, Mo.); I-85 (north to Richmond, south to Charlotte, N.C. and Atlanta, Ga.); I-95 (north to Maine, south to Florida); I-195, 295, and SR 288 (beltways for the Richmond area).
Closest airport: Richmond International Airport, 10 min. east of downtown Richmond off I-64.
Public transportation: GRTC is the Richmond area municipal bus system. GRTC also operates trackless trolley cars, which are free to the public. Parking shuttles are also available.
Avg. commute: 20-25 min.

What Every Resident Knows

The nation's first canned beer and aluminum foil wrap were produced in Richmond. • Famous residents include Patrick Henry (he gave his famous "Give me liberty or give me death" speech in Richmond), John Wilkes Booth, Warren Beatty, Pocahontas, Shirley MacLaine, Edgar Allen Poe, Robert E. Lee, and Arthur Ashe. • Richmond takes great pride in its historic homes—tours are a must! • Another must-see is the historic Monument Avenue, probably one of the country's most awesome boulevards.

FYI

Metro Richmond Chamber of Commerce
P.O. Box 12280
Richmond, VA 23241
804-648-1234

Metro Richmond Convention & Visitors
300 East Main Street
Richmond, VA 23219
804-782-2777

Richmond Free Press
P.O. Box 27709
Richmond, VA 23261
804-644-0496

Richmond Times-Dispatch
333 E. Grace Street
Richmond, VA 23219
804-649-6000

Around The James
(Rental/Relocation Specialists)
3212 Skipwith Road, Suite 212
Richmond, VA 23294
804-346-4911 or 800-899-1285

ReMax Metro Realtors
7201 Glen Forest Drive, Suite 100
Richmond, VA 23226
804-288-1556
Mary Dean

Commonwealth Gas
22 South Sycamore
Petersburg, VA 23803
800-543-8911

Virginia Power Co.
P.O. Box 26543
Richmond, VA 23290
804-756-2010

Chesapeake & Potomac Telephone
P.O. Box 27783
Richmond, VA 23272
804-954-6222

Metro Economic Development Council
201 E. Franklin Street
Richmond, VA 23219
804-643-3227

Small Business Development Center
403 E. Grace Street
Richmond, VA 23219
804-648-7838

School districts: Chesterfield: 804-748-1405, Hanover: 804-752-6000, Henrico: 804-226-3727, Richmond: 804-780-7710
Property tax assessor: 804-780-5605
Newcomer's Club: 804-932-3572
Interfaith Council: 804-359-5661
Day-care referral: 804-271-6221

Burlington, Vermont

Area Snapshot

Local population: 38,492
County: Chittenden   **Population:** 135,000
U.S. region: Northeast
Closest metro area: Montreal, Canada (65 mi. north)
Median housing price: $120,000
Average household income: $40,000
Best reasons to live here: Glorious Lake Champlain area, Vermont's only economic bright spot, cosmopolitan college town, excellent schools, super year-round recreation, clean, safe environment, friendly, laid-back community.

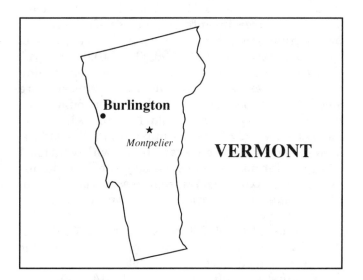

Fabulous Features

National trends suggest there's been a mass exodus South from the Northeast because of brutally cold winters and an equally chilly economy. But the statistics overlook the millions of hearty souls who couldn't be *paid* to live in Florida or other "hot" cities. Greater Burlington is the perfect example. This scintillating oasis on the eastern shore of Lake Champlain is enjoying a renaissance because it appeals to people who thrive in a robust climate. It was no aberration when Burlington was named "Most Livable Small City in America" (U.S. Conference of Mayors, 1988) and recently rated one of the top five cities in the country to grow a business (*Inc.* magazine, June '91).

This is a super place to live *and* work. In fact, dozens of companies have seen the light after studying the record growth at General Electric and long-time neighbor, IBM. Digital Equipment Corp., Rossignol Skis and Ben and Jerry's Ice Cream, are a few of the companies prospering in the area. Burlington also snared more than 200 insurance companies and trade sector businesses that, in turn, spawned new support businesses (5,300 jobs were created from 1988-

1990). With a state-of-the-art telecommunications network, a "bull's eye" location (dead center between Boston, New York and Montreal) and a highly educated labor force (home of the University of Vermont), Burlington's only uphill challenges are the slopes! Stowe, Sugarbush and many other world-class ski areas are less than an hour away, with the entire region a winter wonderland (sailing, leaf-peeping and apple-picking are the beginning of outdoor diversions).

Real estate is another wonder to behold. Inventory of new homes and resales is in great supply at starter-home prices. Award-winning schools (recently earned Vermont's teacher and principal of the year) and low crime (one of the lowest murder rates in the country) are the icing on the lake. You can't help but have a warm feeling about this place!

Possible drawbacks: Frosty the Snowman spends a lot of time in the front yard. The 30-year avg. for annual snowfall is 78". • State aid to Burlington schools has declined, forcing local schools taxes to almost double in one year. For now, they've averted budget cuts.

"You can quote me on that"

"We are so impressed with the schools. Education is very important here, maybe because of the university influence. Whatever it is, it works!"—A.S.

Real Estate

Market overview: It's a buyer's market, mainly because new business has flooded into the area. There is a large inventory of homes—homeowners are upgrading and first-time buyers are very active. The most activity is in the $90,000-$110,000 range.

What houses look like: A wide variety, including ranches, capes, Victorians and splits. Majority are wood frame/wood sided. Brick isn't popular (too expensive); vinyl siding on older homes. All houses have basements. Fireplaces in homes for $140,000+. Newer homes feature elegant baths with whirlpool tubs. Starter homes tend to be 20 yrs. old; trade-ups around 10; luxury homes from new to 100 yrs. old. Many beautiful Victorian homes on the Lake in excellent condition.

Starter homes: $90,000 buys a small (1000 sq. ft.) 3BR/1BA ranch with basement and single-car garage on a good-sized 80 x 100 lot.

Trade-ups: $140,000 buys a 4BR/2-3BA, 1500-1600 sq. ft. home with 2-car garage (possibly) and fireplace (probably) on a 80 x 100 lot. This house could be as new as 5 years, as old as 45 depending on its location. A larger house—3-4BR, 2000-2500 sq. ft., w/hardwood floors, upgraded kitchen (cherry wood cabinets, kitchen island) and 2-car garage on ½ acre lot—costs from $150,000 to $175,000.

Luxury homes: $300,000 buys 3000 sq. ft., 4BR/3BA brand-new colonial or contemporary home with 2-car garage, basement, family room and fireplace. $500,000 buys brand-new 5BR/3BA, 4000 sq. ft. house with in-ground pool, gourmet kitchen, master suite, massive walk-in closets, 2-car garage, view of lake, large lot. In the country, this price could include as much as 10 acres of land.

Rental market: Quite a few single family homes available for rent—avg. $800/mo. for a 3BR/1-2BA. Condominiums and townhouses (no co-ops) are both popular and avg. $700/mo. for 2BR. Rents start at $500/mo. for 3BR mobile homes.

Great neighborhoods: The new North End is scenic, "treesy," convenient to shopping and family-oriented. It offers both older and newer homes at affordable prices. The school system is great.

Nearby areas to consider: Essex, 10-15 min. east, offers nice residential areas (homes avg. $140,000-$200,000), shopping and recreation for the whole family and some of the best schools in Vermont. Colchester, 5 min. away, has its own good school system, is convenient to shopping, lots of new parks, lots of recreation and housing in variety of price ranges (Avg. $125,000-$165,000).

What Things Cost

Runzheimer's Living Cost Index: Avg. annual costs for family of 4 with household income of $50,000: $50,640 (1.3% above avg. city).

ACCRA's national comparisons: Not available.

Utilities: Phone: $25/mo. (includes $9.45 of local calls); Installation: $33. Electric: Avg. $40/mo. Gas: Avg. $60-66/mo. Water: Avg. $25-30/mo.

Kid care: Available for kids 6 wk. to 10-yrs. old, from 6:30 a.m. to 6 p.m. Average cost for infants: $95/wk.; for 2+ yrs. old: $85/wk.

Pediatric visit: $55.

The Tax Ax

Sales tax: 5% (packing and manufacturing equipment exempt).

Property tax: $1.67 per $100 of assessed value. For example, a house assessed at $100,000 would pay $1,670.

State income tax: Taxable income under $10,000 taxed at 5.5%; anything over that is taxed on a scale that slides up to 8.25%.

Climate

Elevation 330'	Avg. High/Low	Avg. Rain (Inches)	Avg. Snow (Inches)	Avg. Days Rain	Avg. % Humidity
Jan.	26/8	.9	19.1	9	64
April	53/33	2.2	3.6	11	53
July	81/59	3.5	--	12	54
Oct.	59/39	2.7	.3	11	63
YEAR	54/35	24.6	79	130	60

# of days 32° or below: 160	# of days 90° or above: 9

Baby, it's cold out here. And snowy. Because of its proximity to the polar air masses that shoot down from Canada, winters in Burlington are frigid: an average of 160 days are below freezing. Summers and autumn make up for the tough times: July and August are warm and pleasant, the evenings nice and cool. Fall is gorgeous: dry, sunny and with magnificent foliage.

> **"You can quote me on that"**
> *"There are five seasons here. Winter, spring, summer, fall and mud!"—C.C.*

Earning a Living

Economic outlook: As the financial center of the region, Burlington has taken a balanced, progressive approach toward business. Home to stable employers (IBM and General Electric), its recession has been kinder and gentler than the rest of New England's. Burlington sits in the middle of a geographic circle containing 80 million potential customers in top markets—Boston, New York, Toronto and Montreal. The 1988 Free Trade Agreement between U.S. and Canada has enhanced that position, prompting many Canadian companies to look southward for a foothold in lucrative U.S. market. Vermont remains an enviable place to do business. The Lake Champlain region is the banking hub of Vermont.

Where the jobs are: 43 high-growth companies, 35 new companies and 5,300 new jobs were created between 1988-1990. Burlington has attracted so many new companies to the area that the June, 1991, *Inc* magazine named it one of top five cities in the country in which to grow a successful business. As a result, Burlington has become a mecca for entrepreneurs and growing companies. Workers are employed by more than 300 manufacturers. Chief industries include printing, woodworking, electronics, manufacturing of complex instruments, high-temperature wire, strip casting, silicone chips and computer assembly. Burlington attracted more than 8 million tourists, with a $1.35 billion impact on the local economy, in 1991. Vermont ranks near the top in terms of percentage of its labor force employed in high technology industries and in the growth of high-tech employment. Since spring 1992, several new companies have relocated here: Burton Snowboards selected Burlington for its new headquarters location; KoBel, a subsidiary of KoPak, moved into the area in May, ready to print specialized pressure sensitive labels. Rhino Foods, a specialty dessert manufacturer, has also expanded, seeing a three-fold increase in sales volume in the past year with a work force that grew from 15 to 50.

Business opportunities: The Greater Burlington Industrial Corporation supplies statistical market data for new companies. Community Economic and Development Office is part of a progressive city agency's strategy to attract quality manufacturing jobs, upgrade the work force through training programs, keep the downtown vital and encourage entrepreneurs by creating a network of "incubator spaces" for fledgling companies. The Blue Chip Enterprise Initiative is a program designed to help small businesses by forming a networking alliance to share strategies for success.

Making the Grade

Public education overview: District's greatest attributes: 1) Diversity of curriculum; 2) National/state recognition: In 1991, it received 3 major state awards (for high school, Lawrence Barnes Elementary School and Burlington Technical Center, located on high school campus); 3) Uniqueness of curriculum: it has the only performing arts program in the state. Technical center offers programs such as aircraft technology, computer-assisted designing and drafting. Advanced placement available for high school students gifted in biology, physics, history, math or foreign languages; 4) 55% of high school grads go to college. 98% go to college or are successful in landing a job; 5) Test scores worth bragging about: Combined SATs (920) are above state and national averages. 6) Drop-out rate only 6%; absenteeism low. Due to recession, Burlington's share of state aid has declined. Last year, the school tax rate went up 7.78%. Its challenge is to improve levels of academia and pilot more programs with less money. No budget cuts yet, though positions recently vacant have not been filled.

Class size: 21:1.

Help for working parents: No organized programs to aid working parents, though a good variety of after-school sports and actitivies.

Blue Ribbon School Awards: Mater Christi Elementary School ('89-'90), South Burlington High School ('84-'85), South Burlington Middle School ('86-'87).

School year: Starts after Labor Day and ends mid-June. Children must be 5 on or before Sept. 1 to enter kindergarten.

Special education/gifted programs: Extensive special education programs, but goal is to mainstream learning disabled children. Children with extensive special needs have individual classes but are mainstreamed where possible. No gifted programs, but there are accelerated programs where high school students take courses at the University and middle school children take high school-level courses. A new preschool program called "Success By Six" for 4-5-year-olds offers family visits, educational and recreational programs, teaches socialization skills, parenting workshops and links up families with local pediatricians.

Nearby colleges/universities: University of Vermont is recognized as a top school, has a medical center and is a teaching college. Trinity College is one of the top 10 small women's colleges in U.S. and offers an extensive liberal arts program. Also: St. Michaels (in bordering town of Winooski); Burlington College; Champlain College.

Medical Care

Hospitals/medical centers: Medical Center Hospital of Vermont (full-service teaching hospital affiliated with Univ. of Vermont's College of Medicine) is a referral center for the area. It specializes in state-of-the-art cardiology services, radiology, kidney dialysis and transplant, rehabilitation, occupational and physical therapy. Fanny Allen Hospital provides acute-care, 24-hr. emergency care, a full range of inpatient and outpatient preventative care, diagnostic treatment and surgical services (specializing in internal medicine, oncology, orthopoedics and obstetrics/gynecology). Also: Copley Hospital (specializing in orthopoedics), Northwestern Medical Center, Porter Medical Center, Central Vermont Hospital.

Specialized care: Ronald McDonald House, Visiting Nurse Assoc. Emergency Response Center (hospice programs for the elderly); Vermont/New Hampshire Regional Blood Center; Immediate Care Health Center: urgent care, family practice, occupational health.

Crime and Safety

Burlington is considered very safe, with a low rate of crime and one of the lowest rates of murder in the nation (20 last year). Community-based policing began in 1991 (as part of the DARE program). There's a successful program that permanently assigns each area a single officer who is solely responsible for complaints and problems in that area. Crime Stoppers is also active—people call in to report any drug-related activity and the collected information is investigated by a special drug unit. The community is concerned about drugs, although not a major problem, but they believe these programs will lessen future problems.

Community Life

Tree Planting Day: sponsored by the city, community volunteers get together each year and plant trees (many trees have died from Dutch Elm Disease). Thousands of trees have been planted in the past 10 years. GreenUp Day (annually in May, statewide): volunteers clean up town, waterfront and riverfront; city supplies garbage bags and picks up litter. Project Home (funded both privately and by the United Way of Burlington, run primarily by volunteers: matches volunteers with elderly or disabled adults in the community. Care and assistance—from simple companionship to shopping, cleaning and more extensive aid—help many avoid institutionalization or nursing home care.

Let the Good Times Roll

Family fun: How sweet it is here! Ben & Jerry's: 30-min. tour of Vermont's finest all-natural ice cream factory. Kamp Kill Kare State Park: boat rentals, launch, ferry to Burton Island. Sand Bar State Park: swimming beach, boat rentals. Chapters Bookstore Cafe: books on anything and everything plus cafe (soups, sandwichs, pastries). Ethan Allan Park: historic site with views of Green Mountains, Adirondacks and Lake Champlain, picnic area, hiking, biking trails. Leddy Park: Burlington's largest, most heavily used facility features 1800' of beach, indoor ice rink, 4 lighted tennis courts, lighted ball field, soccer, natural areas, trails and playground. Oak Ledge Park: 2500' of lakefront, picnic shelter, beach, bath house, tennis courts, ball fields and trails. Battery Park: historic park, view of Lake Champlain and Adirondacks, promenade, playground, band shell for summer concerts. Other attractions: Univ. of Vermont Dairy Farm; Ethan Allen Homestead; Discovery Museum; Green Mt. Audubon Nature Center; Pine Ridge Adventure Center. The area is a skier's paradise with excellent skiing at Bolton Valley Ski Resort, Middlebury College Snow Bowl, Bread Loaf, Sugarbush, Smuggler's Notch, Jay Peak, Stark Farm Ski Touring Center, Catamount Family Center and Sherman Hollow Cross-Country Skiing Center. Fishing, camping, swimming, boating and marinas available at Lake Champlain and numerous other state parks and rivers.

Sports: College sports teams include University of Vermont (Catamounts): doesn't play football but has hockey, basketball, soccer, baseball and track; St. Michael's College, Champlain College, Middlebury and Trinity College. Residents support the Montreal teams. Boston Red Sox and Yankee rooters form a solid percentage of sports fans.

Arts & entertainment: The Discover Museum—"place for kids and the kid in you"—features hands-on science and nature workshops and native wildlife learning center. Robert Hall Fleming Museum houses one of New England's finest art museums with collections of American and European art. Shelburne Farms: 1,000-acre national historic property. Flynn Theater (presents musical and dramatic works), Vermont Ballet, Vermont Symphony Orchestra. Discover Jazz is an annual salute to jazz. Champlain Shakespeare Festival presents classical works.

Annual events: Fine Wine & Food Festival (Sept.); First Night (Dec. 31); Sugar on Snow Festival (March/April); Arts Alive (June); Vermont Reggae Festival (July); Champlain Valley Fair Week (Aug.).

The Environment

Burlington residents pride themselves on their clean air and green environment. Spared from the pollution of heavy industrial waste firms, Vermont's water and air quality is excellent. It strongly endorses environmental efforts through state legislation. Act 250, passed in 1970, protects air and water quality, promotes soil conservation, and preserves wildlife habitats and scenic, archaeological, and historic sites. Scenic, uncluttered roadways are a key reason visitors flock to Vermont. Roadways remain clean as a result of state laws that prohibit off-premise signs and restrict the size, height and distance of on-premise signs. There are weekly scheduled curbside recycling pickups.

In and Around Town

Roads and interstates: I-89, I-91, U.S. 2.
Closest airport: Burlington International Airport.
Public transportation: Chittenden County Transit Authority has 9 inter-city and local bus routes connecting Burlington and South Burlington, Shelburne, Essex and Winooski.
Avg. commute: 20-45 min.; people commute to Burlington from a wide range of outlying areas—in both Vt. and N.Y. border towns.

What Every Resident Knows

One of the most popular current bumper stickers says "Don't Mall Williston." Seems some residents of this fast-growing Burlington suburb are perturbed at the growing number of shopping malls and the commercialization of what was once a quiet, rural place. • Hot-dog lovers are in luck: Lois' Hot Dogs are an institution (or could put you in one if you overdo it). Look for her famous cart on Church Street. • You've heard of the Loch Ness Monster, but Burlington has the "Champ"—the Champlain monster. Rumor has it that it's been photographed and looks like a dinosaur with a head the size of a horse. There are actually state laws protecting the monster from harm.

FYI

Lake Champlain Regional Chamber of Commerce
P.O. Box 453
209 Battery Street
Burlington, VT 05402
802-863-3489

Convention & Visitor's Bureau:
P.O. Box 453
Burlington, VT 05402
802-863-3489

Vermont Times Publishing
P.O. Box 940
Shelburne, VT 05482
802-985-2400

Small Business Development Center
Greater Burlington Industrial Corp.
7 Burlington Square
P.O. Box 786
Burlington, VT 05402
802-862-5726

Century 21/Ray Ploof
1993 Williston Road
South Burlington, VT 05403
802-862-6433
Steve Abair

Coldwell Banker Hicock & Boardman
346 Shelburne Road
Burlington, VT 05402
802-863-1500
Kent Smalling

Burlington Electric Co.
585 Pine Street
Burlington, VT 05401
802-658-0300

Vermont Gas Systems
P.O. Box 467
Burlington, VT 05402
802-863-4511

New England Telephone
800 Hinesburg Road
Burlington, VT 05402
802-658-7200

Burlington Economic Development
c/o City Hall
Room 32
Burlington, VT 05401
802-658-9300

School district: 802-864-8474
Property tax assessor: 802-865-7111
Newcomer's Club: No longer exists
Interfaith Council: Chamber of Commerce will provide a listing of churches and synagogues.
Physician's referral: 413-445-5631
Day-care referral: 802-863-2331

Kent, Washington (Seattle)

Area Snapshot

Local population: 37,400
County: King   **Population:** 1,460,000
U.S. region: Northwest
Closest metro areas: Seattle (10 mi. north), Tacoma (12 mi. southwest)
Median housing price: $127,500
Avg. household income: $23,778
Best reasons to live here: Central to Seattle and Tacoma, some of the most affordable housing in the area, excellent schools, family-oriented, access to major highways, award-winning parks and recreation.

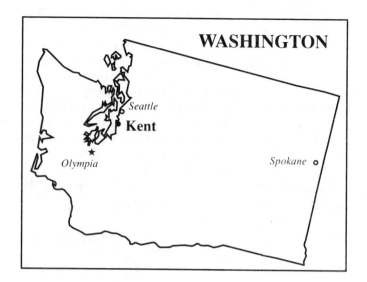

Fabulous Features

Greater Seattle may get 38 inches of rain every year, but that doesn't explain how the region has virtually stolen the *thunder* from dozens of major cities. Back in the '80s, while the "pack" was arguing over who was more centrally located, Seattle was quietly capitalizing on its exclusive Pacific Coast setting, getting a huge jump on penetrating the lucrative global economy (it's the closest mainland port to Asia, equi-distant to London and Toyko, and has first crack at Alaska's gold and oil and the fish-full Pacific).

As home to Boeing (100,000-plus employees within 30 miles), Nintendo, Microsoft and dozens of major aerospace, high-tech and biotech giants, the competition pleaded "no contest" when *Fortune* magazine ranked Seattle as the number-one city for business in the country (Nov. 1992). Who else could boast of a decade that resulted in a 22-percent increase in population, a 40-percent jump in employment and 119-percent leap in personal income?

Ironically, the bait that lured fast-track, Armani-suit types by the thousands was the promise of decent weekends. Between the vast natural resources (Mt. Rainier, the Cascade Mountains and Olympic Peninsula), the exciting sports action (professional and NCAA), the cultural offerings (theater, art, dance and opera) and the "like totally hip" attitudes, it's really possible to get a life!

As for where to hang out, we liked Kent, a fast-growing community with strong family ties. Centrally located between Seattle and Tacoma, they boast award-winning parks, affordable real estate (beautiful choices for well under $200,000, a veritable steal in these parts), many Blue Ribbon schools (75 percent of parents said they chose Kent because of the district) and loads of family fun (from concert series to annual ballooning festivals). If you'd like living on the edge (of the country, that is), there's nothing like greater Seattle.

Possible drawbacks: King County is struggling with traffic (it has the fourth worst traffic mess in the U.S.). Even in Kent, the daytime population soars from 40,000 to 160,000 and city services can only try to catch up. It's tough because of a recent budget shortfall (sales tax revenue down), but local leaders are working hard to turn things around. • Unless you're coming from New York or San Francisco, Seattle's high living costs may scare you (overall costs are 18 percent above the national average.) Shooting for one of those high paying jobs should help.

Real Estate

Market overview: Kent is strictly a buyer's market due to a large inventory of resales and new construction. It's getting harder to get building permits; some areas have experienced building moratoriums. Developers with permits are going ahead while they can. Starter homes havn't suffered any depreciation and sell fast; in the last year, $150,000+ homes have depreciated 10% and are slow to sell.

What houses look like: 2-story traditional, w/ living and dining rooms, kitchen and family room on 1st floor, 3-4BR/1BA upstairs and 2-car garage, is most common. Avg. lot is 8000 sq. ft. Homes landscaped with evergreens, azaleas, and rhododendrons.

Starter homes: Ranging from $110,000 and $125,000, starter homes are usually 1-story and called "ramblers." They feature a living roon, dining area, kitchen, 3BR/1BA, and 2-car garage. Lot size approx. 80 x 100. New construction is available in the Elk Run area. Older homes can be found in the Glen Carin neighborhood.

Trade-ups: Ranging from $150,000 to $175,000, avg. home is 1800-2000 sq. ft., 3-4BR/1½BA and 2-car garage on ¼ acre. Styles include 2-story traditional, split entry and tri-level, some w/deck or patio. Older homes found in Misty Meadows and Seven Oaks. New construction at Crown Royale.

Luxury homes: Range from $175,000-$250,000. Avg. is 2000-2500 sq. ft. on a lot slightly smaller than an acre, w/living and dining rooms, den, bonus room (large room above garage), kitchen w/pantry, 4BR, patio. BAs have double vanities and jacuzzi or soaking tub. Windows are larger; many homes have skylights. Most of these are newer homes located in the Shadow Run and Crafton areas.

Rental market: SFH rentals are scarce. A 3BR home rents for $700/mo.; 4BR home, $800/mo. There are many 1-2BR/1-2BA apartments renting for $525-$650/mo. Condos are neither popular nor plentiful, although the city council is investigating the possibility of converting rental apts into condos.

Great neighborhoods: Seven Oaks and North Peak Crest are great areas because of the many quiet cul-de-sacs and good neighborhood schools.

Nearby areas to consider: Federal Way (8 mi. southwest) is more developed and lies directly on I-5, offering easy access to Seattle and Tacoma. It has terrific shopping. Housing values are comparable to Kent; some homes boast views of Puget Sound. Auburn (6 mi. south) has a more rural atmosphere, is not nearly as developed as Kent, and has a small, close-knit school system.

What Things Cost

Runzheimer's Living Cost Index: Avg. annual costs for family of 4 with household income of $50,000: $54,694 (9.4% above avg. city).

ACCRA's national comparisons: Overall living costs in the Seattle area are 17.8% above avg., with major influence of housing (55% above avg.) and health care (32.8% above avg.) Groceries and transportation are 11% above, utilities 37% below.

Utilities: Phone: $14.25/mo. Installation: $31. Electric: $5 hookup charge; $64/mo. Water: City of Kent, avg. $35/mo.

Kid Care: Average cost for weekly childcare: $120-infant, $97-toddler, $84-preschool. The area has numerous childcare centers, but there are waiting lists for children under 2. **Pediatric visit:** $50-$60.

The Tax Ax

Sales tax: 8.2%.

Property tax: $13.87 per $1,000 of assessed value of home (includes state and local levies). Homes are assessed at 100% of market value. So taxes on a $125,000 house, for example, would be $1,733.75.

State income tax: None.

Climate

Elevation 400'	Avg. High/Low	Avg. Rain (Inches)	Avg. Snow (Inches)	Avg. Days Rain	Avg. % Humidity
Jan.	45/35	3.4	3.7	18	74
April	59/42	2.5	T	14	58
July	76/56	.7	--	5	48
Oct.	62/47	3.9	T	14	68
YEAR	60/45	38	7.9	156	62

# of days 32° or below: 16	# of days 90° or above: 2

The Puget Sound brings cloud covers and wet weather year-round, though heavy downpours are rare. The Cascade and Olympic mountains protect from cold Canadian air masses, making for mild winters with minimum snowfall. Summers are mostly dry and sunny.

"You can quote me on that"

"Everyone is from somewhere else, so they understand how it feels to be new in town. We felt more welcomed here in a month than we did after two years in Maryland."—B.G.

Earning a Living

Economic outlook: The reason for this area's tremendous economic growth in recent years can be summed up in one word: *Location*, mid-way between the deepwater ports of Seattle and Tacoma. A major international trade program is being developed by the Chamber of Commerce to attract Pacific Rim companies. Over last few years, Kent has realized 6% job growth per year; current projections over the next 3 years are 2%/yr. The current unemployment rate in King County is 4.9% (state: 6.9%). *Fortune* (Nov. 1992) rated Seattle the top city for doing business in the U.S. From 1985-1990, more than 270,000 jobs were created. Boeing and aerospace are the major employers, but other industries include computer software, biotechnology, tourism, international trade and natural resources. High-tech businesses are sprouting. Computer software, led by Microsoft, is a major part of the economy, so programming and analysis services are important. Fred Hutchinson Cancer Research Ctr. is the largest recipient of NIH grants, helping to fuel biotech companies. Washington Technology Center and Univ. of Washington are major research centers. Seattle is the 3rd largest apparel design center in the country.

Where the jobs are: Boeing is the major private employer in the area and state, with facilities in every major city here. It presently employs some 99,000 people. The Aerospace Div., located in the Kent Valley, is responsible for over 11,000 jobs. In 1990 the company announced its intention to trim employment—it has been realizing a 6% rate of attrition each year due to retirements and consolidation. Aerospace in general is not growing right now, due in part to cutbacks in federal defense spending. However, Boeing is the strongest commercial airline manufacturer in the U.S., and will soon be producing its much-anticipated Boeing 777. Other major employers in the area include Heath Tecna Aerospace Co. (1,000 emp.), Food Services of America (375), and Continental Mills Co. (525). A regional justice center planned for the area will create 750 new jobs, bringing with it the need for lawyers and bail bondsmen. There are more than 2,000 businesses in Kent; many are warehouses employing 50 people or less.

Business opportunities: Kent is a good place for small businesses because it is less expensive than Seattle. The city charges $75/yr. for a business license, but there are no business or occupation taxes. 80% of all the small businesses in the area provide services/products to local big companies.

Making the Grade

Public education overview: This district educates more than 23,000 students in 24 elementary schools, 5 junior highs, and 3 high schools. One alternative high school serves students who have not been successful in a regular school setting. The district's greatest attribute is the impressive involvement from parents and community: There are more than 35 standing committees and 27 active PTAs. In a local survey, 77.5% said they moved to Kent so they could be part of the school system. SAT scores are above state and national avg. (math: 498, English: 429). 50% of grads go on to post-secondary education. In 1990, a $105 million bond issue was passed to buy land and build 6 new schools. It is expected that another bond issue will be needed by 1994.

Class size: 26-1 (grades 1-3); 29-1 (grades 4-9); 31-1 (grades 10-12).

Help for working parents: Five of 24 elementary schools have a before- and after-school program, 3 run by YMCA, 2 by Parks and Rec. Dept.

Blue Ribbon School Awards: Meridian Junior High, Kentridge High ('84-'85), Lake Youngs Elementary ('85-'86), Kent Junior High ('88-'89), Pine Tree Elementary ('89-'90).

School year: 1st wk. Sept. to mid-June. Children must be 5 by Aug. 31 to enter kindergarten.

Special education/gifted programs: The district follows federal guidelines for its special education program. Children are mainstreamed when possible with support services coming to the regular classroom. Seven other school districts bus children to Kent for special education services. There are 6 sites for the elementary gifted and talented, a self-contained program, with children bused to the site. All 3rd graders are tested for eligibility; currently a waiting list to get in. The program offers more enriched studies, particularly in science. In junior high, 2 periods blocked together for gifted students. Emphasis is placed on Social Studies and Language Arts. In high school, gifted students are offered Advanced Placement courses and computer programming.

Nearby colleges/universities Highline Community College, with 8,400 students, has a marine technology facility. Green River Community College (7,500 students). Other schools include: Valley College, Renton Vocational Technical Institute, Cornish College of the Arts, University of Washington, Seattle University, Seattle Pacific University, Pacific Lutheran University and the University of Puget Sound.

Medical Care

Hospitals/medical centers: Auburn General Hospital, 149-bed community hospital in Auburn. Valley Medical Center (Renton) is largest medical complex in south King County. Kent Medical Center, a professional corporation with 30 physicians, operates 3 clinics. Chec Medical Center runs a clinic in Kent for emergency, preventive and occupational/industrial medical care. In Seattle, Swedish Hospital Medical Center is Washington's largest health care facility, specializing in medical, surgical and diagnostic services. Univ. of Washington Medical Center (UWMC) is a research hospital with a bone and joint center, cancer center, cardiology and cardiac surgery, fertility and endocrine center, high-risk maternity and newborn intensive care. Children's Hospital and Medical Center, the center for pediatric medicine in Pacific Northwest, has a national reputation in cardiac surgery, infectious diseases, and birth defects.

Specialized care: Fred Hutchinson Cancer Research Center; Northwest Kidney Center; Northwest Hospital Center for Medical Rehabilitation (inpatient hospice); CPC Fairfax Hospital in Kirkland (psychiatric disorders); CareUnit Hospital of Kirkland (chemical dependency); Schick Shadel Hospital in Seattle (chemical dependency); Ballard Hospital in Seattle (weight/eating disorders).

Crime & Safety

Residents are aware of increasing crime rates as population has grown (assaults, burglaries, and auto thefts were the most reported crimes) but still feel it's a safe community. Unfortunately, due to budgetary problems, the police force has actually decreased in size—presently 82 officers on the force. Recent measures to promote crime prevention include neighborhood block watches (a plainclothes, proactive group that targets gangs and drugs) and a DARE program in the elementary schools.

Community Life

Two years ago, 2 area residents, heavily involved in the Foster Care program, opened a clinic for crack babies. The community rallied to their side, and the Pediatric Interim Care Center was born. Financial aid, local volunteers, even baby showers have been part of the support network that continues to make this project work. Anything to do with family life gets support. Parent volunteers are heavily involved with their local schools through PTA work and committees, Little League, soccer, football and other sports.

Let the Good Times Roll

Family fun: Kent is a family fun paradise surrounded by open spaces. Beautiful Mt. Rainier is only 45 min. away. Almost the entire Cascade Range is National Forest land, open for backcountry camping, hiking, and horseback riding (w/ski resorts in winter). The Pacific Crest National Scenic Trail, a continuous hiking trail running down the West Coast, is only 45 mi. east. There are 7 National Wilderness Areas within a day's drive. Kent also borders Puget Sound, "the boating capital of the world." Only 15 min. away, joined by a system of locks to Puget Sound, is Lake Wash-ington. Closer to Kent are Lake Sammamish and 3 state parks. Surrounding Puget Sound are 6 more state parks. Families can take advantage of the Woodland Park Zoo, Seattle Aquarium, and Univ. of Washington Arboretum. Historical attractions include the Klondike Gold Rush National Historical Park and Pioneer Square. In Tacoma: Washington State Historical Society, Point Defiance Zoo and Aquarium and Historic Fort Nisqually.

Sports: The Seattle Seahawks play NFL football at the Kingdome; the Seattle Supersonics play NBA basketball at the Seattle Center Coliseum, and the Seattle Mariners play American League baseball at the Kingdome. Minor league baseball is played by the Pacific Coast League Tacoma Tigers and Northwest League Everett Giants. Univ. of Washington Huskies are one of the top-rated college football teams in the nation. The Seattle Thunderbirds play ice hockey in the WHL.

Arts & entertainment: The Seattle Center Opera House is home to the Pacific Northwest Ballet, the Seattle Opera and the Seattle Symphony. Meany Hall for the Performing Arts, located on the Univ. of Washington campus, hosts many international artists. The Seattle Repertory Theatre performs in the Bagley Wright Theatre in the Seattle Center. The Northwest Chamber Orchestra performs in area theaters. Other performing arts groups include the Empty Space Theatre, the Intiman Theatre, and the Seattle Group Theatre. Seattle museums include the Seattle Arts Museum, Henry Art Gallery, Burke Museum, Museum of History and Industry, the Children's Museum, and the Pacific Science Center.

Annual events: Kids Arts Day (March); Folklife Festival (Seattle/May); Kent Saturday Market (Sats., May-Oct); Seafair International Festival (Seattle/July); Kent Summer Concert Series (July-Aug.); Kent International Balloon Classic (3rd wkend July); Canterbury Faire (3rd wknd. Aug.); Winter Festival Parade (Dec.).

The Environment

The city's water supply comes from groundwater. A brand-new $5 million water treatment plant has opened to treat the city's two new wells. The State Dept. for Social and Health Services certifies that Kent water quality meets or exceeds the states standards. Air quality is acceptable as far as national EPA standards go, but the valley does have a problem with lingering smoke from woodstoves and fireplaces. The air quality is better up in the hills. The Trojan Nuclear Power Plant is located in Chelais, Wash., more than 100 mi. away. Kent has a voluntary curbside recycling program. Two times/mo., the city collects recycled glass, newspaper, wastepaper, tin, plastic, cardboard and aluminum.

In and Around Town

Roads and interstates: I-5, I-405, Rte. 167, Hwy 18, and the Valley Freeway.

Closest airport: Seattle Tacoma International Airport, 20 min. south of downtown Seattle, 12 min. north of Kent.

Public transportation: Metro Bus System serving Seattle and East King County provides express routes during morning and evening rush hours. Strategically placed free parking is provided for bus riders. Kent currently has no in-town public transportation system, but the municipalities in the Kent Valley are looking into a commuter rail system to ease traffic congestion. (Kent has 2 rail lines that run through town.)

Avg. commute: 35-50 min. to Seattle or Tacoma.

What Every Resident Knows

Seattle is in the Pacific Time Zone, but there's also a Boeing Time Zone. That's when you set your watch to the three times a day when they change shifts. At 6 a.m.-8 a.m., 2 p.m.-3:30 p.m. and midnight, the freeways are packed with Boeing workers. • Kent's name derived from the local hop farmers who hoped success would rub off if they used the same name and coat of arms as Kent, England, home of the largest hop crop in Europe. As any beer drinker can tell you, next to water and yeast, hop is the most important ingredient in a good brew. • Seattle is famous for a lot of things, but the latest is the introduction of "grunge" rock and roll. If you're not familiar with the likes of Nirvana and Pearl Jam, ask the nearest teenager.

FYI

Kent Chamber of Commerce
P.O. Box 128
Kent, WA 98035
206-854-1770

Seattle-King County Visitors Bureau
520 Pike Street, Suite 1300
Seattle, WA 98101
206-461-5840

Valley Daily News
P.O. Box 130
Kent, WA 98035-0130
206-872-6600

RE/Max Richards Real Estate
20920 108th Avenue SE
Kent, WA 98031
800-669-9196, 206-852-4037
Carol Glidewell

Puget Sound Power and Light Co.
400 W. Gowe Street, Suite 100
Kent, WA 98032
206-255-9344

Washington Natural Gas
P.O. Box 1869
Seattle, WA 98111
206-464-1999

U.S. West Communications
206-251-9191 (Call collect)

Economic Development Council
701 Fifth Avenue
Seattle, WA 98104
206-386-5040

Washington State Business Assistance Center
919 Lakeridge Way SW
Olympia, WA 98504-2516
206-664-9501

School district: 206-852-9550
Property tax assessor:
206-296-5145
Newcomer's Club: 206-630-0177 or 206-622-6348
Interfaith Council: 206-630-5868
Physician's referral: 206-641-4319
Day-care referral: 206-852-1908

Spokane, Washington

Area Snapshot

Local population: 178,500
County: Spokane   **Population:** 366,000
U.S. region: Inland northwest/eastern Washington
Closest metro areas: Seattle (278 mi. west), Portland (348 mi. southwest)
Median housing price: $66,900
Avg. household income: $30,108
Best reasons to live here: Fast-growing economy, strong job possibilities, affordable housing, no state income tax, immaculate region, minimal traffic, vast recreation, innovative schools, four distinct, pleasant seasons.

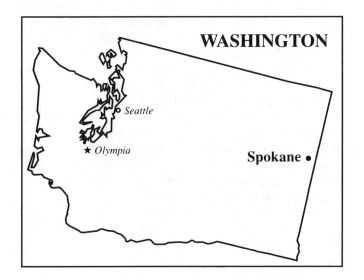

Fabulous Features

New residents marvel that the pristine Spokane region was here all along. They compare the discovery to falling in love with the boy next door, the one with the gentle qualities and upstanding values. Spokane was simply overshadowed by the adulation of its northwest teammates (Denver and Seattle), but even small dogs have their day!

Although the county population only rose by 20,000 in the '80s, major momentum is expected in the '90s. Boeing moved here in 1990 and has already announced an $11 million expansion. The Spokane Industrial Park (4.1 million sq. ft.) is now the largest in the Northwest and still growing. A once dormant downtown (it took a long nap after the 1974 World's Fair) is booming (and looking forward to the Research and Technology Institute). Retail sales, construction and real estate are having their best years ever (realtors reported a $441 million listing volume in 1991).

But what's exciting is not the sudden popularity or vast natural resources, it's the commitment to preserve ideals. Spokane is wooing corporations, but only those that will contribute to the quality of life. It's worked hard to create a well-balanced school system (47% of the high school's honor roll are athletes), a safe community, and a place where families thrive (the annual Bloomsday Run attracts 59,000 grownups and kids).

Add the wonderful year-round weather (lots of mild, sunny days) and recreation (skiing, mountain climbing and fishing are first rate) and you'll see why giving the boy next door a second look can be a winning move!

Possible drawbacks: Looking for a place so far away the in-laws will only write? Trips to the West Coast take five hours through the mountains and commuter flights are costly. Isolation can be a nuisance. • Air quality in the fall is not always favorable. Strong winds cause mini-dust storms and air inversions cause particles to linger. Those with allergies or asthma feel it. • There's no state income tax, but cheapskates still bristle at the 8% sales tax.

"You can quote me on that"

"Coming from Michigan I'm thrilled with the four seasons and the dry climate. The warm, friendly atmosphere and all of the outdoor activity for families give it a strong family orientation. It's a wonderful place. We're here to stay!"—B.M.

Real Estate

Market overview: In this market, sellers have the edge! A well-priced home in mint condition sells within 7-14 days. Resale inventory is down by almost 50% compared to the go-go years in the mid-'80s. New construction has slowed and builders only build when they have a paying customer. With many companies relocating from California, buyers are flooding the market. What's more, according to a recent home affordability index, Spokane is ranked 31st out of 219.

What houses look like: Split-levels are most popular in the $85,000-$125,000 range. Ranches, capes and 3-4 level homes are available. Most exteriors are wood or wood/vinyl siding. There's very little brick (too expensive). Popular features are cathedral ceilings, skylights, tile and hardwood floors, jacuzzis, and fireplaces. Pools are not in demand (season too short).

Starter homes: For $55,000, you'll get a 10-year-old handyman special (2BR/1BA w/garage). For $75,000 you can buy 1000 sq. ft., w/garage (2-3BR/1½BA). Shadle Park on the north side is nice, but really there are no "bad" neighborhoods.

Trade-ups: Prices range from the $90s-$130s. At the low end, you'll find a new 1000-1200 sq. ft. home on a 50-60 x 100 lot (3BR/1½BA), with unfinished basement; $130,000 buys a larger 3BR/2BA w/master suite, 2-car garage, finished basement, fireplace (1500-2000 sq. ft., on 80 x 100 lot). Ponderosa, surrounded by pine trees, is lovely.

Luxury homes: For $200,000, you can buy a 3BR/3BA resale in mint condition with family room, rec room, finished basement, formal dining and living rooms, and large country kitchen (2000-4000 sq. ft.). At the high end, $400,000 buys a new 3-5BR/3BA in South Hill, with jacuzzi, walk-in closets, 2-3 fireplaces, formal living and dining rooms on a ½ acre. Check out Belleterre (fabulous views).

Rental market: SFH rentals are scarce and expensive. A $60,000 house rents for $600/mo. There are no co-ops.

Great neighborhoods: The north end of Spokane is ideal with good schools and top-quality homes. Downtown Spokane is a short commute although taxes are a little higher.

Nearby areas to consider: Deer Park (15-20 mi. north) has good schools, a slower pace and a convenient commute. Cheney (20 mi. west) is a college town (Eastern Washington Univ.) with nice residential areas.

What Things Cost

Runzheimer's Living Cost Index: Avg. annual costs for family of 4 with household income of $50,000: $47,773 (4.5% below avg. city).

ACCRA's national comparisons: Overall living costs are 1% below national avg. The saving grace are utilities (a whopping 35% below avg.), the sticks in the mud are housing (12.9% above avg.) and health care (21.9% above avg.). Food and goods and services are slightly below avg. (1%-2%).

Utilities: Phone: Hookup ranges from $31-$43. Service: Avg. $16/mo. Electric: $125/mo. Gas: Avg. $20-$40/mo. in summer; as high as $120/mo. in winter.

Kid care: Day-care avg. is $75/wk. for infants/toddlers. Infant care, though, is difficult to find; families are advised to get on waiting lists 6 months before the baby is born. **Pediatric Visit:** $50.

The Tax Ax

Sales tax: 8% (food, prescriptions, professional services exempt).

Property tax: Ranges, depending on the area and whether there's a school district, from $11-$20 per $1,000 of assessed value. On a $100,000 home, for example, the tax may be $15.50 per $1,000 value, or $1,550 per year.

State income tax: None.

Climate

Elevation 2,360'	Avg. High/Low	Avg. Rain (Inches)	Avg. Snow (Inches)	Avg. Days Rain	Avg. % Humidity
Jan.	31/20	1.9	18.3	9	77
April	57/35	1.1	.6	9	44
July	84/55	.4	--	4	25
Oct.	58/38	1.4	.5	8	49
YEAR	57/37	12.1	53.1	97	51
# of days 32° or below: 141			# of days 90° or above: 16		

Situated between the Rocky Mountains to the east and the Cascade range to the west, Spokane misses out on much of the precipitation, although it does get its share of cloud covers and rain. Summers are warm and dry and temperatures rarely go above 90. Winters get cold, but are still considered moderate if you come from the Midwest.

Earning a Living

Economic outlook: Spokane, the largest city between Seattle and Minneapolis, is at the economic center of a dynamic and growing region. It serves as a distribution center for the entire region, and connects the area's manufacturers to their markets via I-90. It also protects its growing economy through a supportive business climate, from pro-development public policies to major private sector initiatives. The work force is highly educated, and the cost of living, wage rates, turnover and absenteeism are well below national averages. Cheap, abundant hydroelectric power is a treasured resource. It's the force that brought the aluminum industry here from the East, and the power that's helped the regional mining and timber industries to flourish over the years.

Where the jobs are: There are more than 500 manufacturing firms, 700 wholesale companies, 2,000 retail stores and 4,000 businesses in the service, construction, transportation and utility areas. Spokane's current unemployment rate is over 6%. The largest employers include: the State of Washington (6,500 employees); Fairchild Air Force Base (5,200); and the U.S. Government (4,200). Systems analysts, engineers and data processor professionals have shown the greatest percentage growth in employment over the last 10 years, rising by 23%. Annual wages paid in 1990 were in excess of $3 billion. The economy has greatly diversified in the last decade, resulting in less reliance upon natural resource industries such as mining, timber and agriculture. Washington is the world's largest producer of apples. Tourism is the 4th-largest industry in the state. Conventions are a major boost to Spokane's economy, supported by the Riverpark Convention Center. Construction of a $45 million arena south of the old Spokane Coliseum, starting in spring 1993, is also expected to boost the economy and generate new jobs. Other new jobs coming to the area are Powers Candy and Nut Co., Costco Wholesale Corp., Spokane Community College, Gonzaga University, Alloy Trailers, and Aladdin Steel Products, Inc.

Business opportunities: Spokane is actively recruiting high-tech and light manufacturing businesses in the following areas: electronics, aerospace, environmental and biomedical products. Service companies, such as bank credit card and data information companies, are also needed. (A significant number of military personnel who want to work part-time in data entry is a plus for small-business employers.)

Making the Grade

Public education overview: Spokane County has 14 public school districts, and, because of equitable funding, all have a high level of quality. The Mead School District, north of Spokane, is one example. It requires exceptional credentials for its teachers—72 of 86 teachers hold master's degrees. Elementary schools have extensive before-school programs in music and after-school sports programs (soccer, basketball, volleyball, track, softball, and tennis) so that children can participate in both. The high school athletics program is impressive: 47% of the honor roll is made up of athletes, and 76% of the student body participates in athletics. The Creative Writing Program at the high school is particularly strong, staffed by noted authors and the recipients of numerous awards. School buildings are up-to-date and offer state-of-the-art equipment. Several elementary schools have been built or renovated recently. There's active community involvement, with focus groups looking at specific school issues.

Class size: 27.1 (average).

Help for working parents: Community use of schools is well-established throughout the area and allows adults and youngsters access to school facilities before, during and after class hours. Grades 1-6 have a before- and after-school program (6 a.m.-6 p.m.), sponsored by the PTO and run by the YMCA.

School year: Begins after Labor Day and ends mid-June. Children must be 5 on or before Sept. 1 to enter kindergarten.

Special education/gifted programs: The philosophy is that all kids have talent. A three-level program allows children to explore their abilities because of greater flexibility in the curriculum. Special education students are mainstreamed to the extent possible; the district works with handicapped students from birth to age 21.

Nearby colleges/universities: Washington State University (17,000+ students), a multi-campus university with a central campus in Pullman (south) and a branch in Spokane; Eastern Washington University (8,000 students), located 16 mi. west of Spokane in Cheney; Spokane Community College; Spokane Falls Community College; Gonzaga University, a liberal arts school; and Whitworth College, a Presbyterian liberal arts college. Downtown Spokane will be the location of a 50-acre campus known as the Spokane Intercollegiate Research and Technology Institute at Riverpoint (SIRTI).

Medical Care

Hospitals/medical centers: Spokane offers some of the finest quality medical care in the region, with 7 general hospitals and 7 specialized hospitals. Medical specialties are heart surgery, orthopedics, cancer treatment, kidney treatment, radiation therapy and eye surgery. Hospitals include: Sacred Heart Medical Center (a comprehensive health center specializing in open-heart surgery); Deaconess Medical Center (cancer and kidney dialysis); Holy Family Hospital (lung transplants); St. Luke's Hospital (cancer treatment and open-heart surgery); and Valley Hospital and Medical Center (comprehensive health care center specializing in neonatal care and cancer treatment).

Specialized care: Shriners Children's Hospital (specializing in treatment of disabling children's diseases); Veteran's Administration Medical Center; Mountainview Hospital (treatment center for alcoholism and other substance abuse); and Interlake Hospital (state hospital for severely developmentally disabled).

Crime & Safety

Spokane's crime rate is 50% less than other cities the same size (burglaries have decreased by 33% from 1991 to 1992). The relative safety is attributed to its stand-alone location (it's inland and not close to any other large city) and the fact that the residents are involved in community policing. There are almost 2,000 Block Watch programs involving 50,000 residents), as well as strong DARE and COPY Kids (Community Opportunity Program for Youth) programs. This success is attributed to the activities of the property recovery unit and community awareness. Another plus is that the ethnically diverse population lives together rather than in separate neighborhoods.

Community Life

Life in Spokane very much includes the great outdoors, so exchange your second TV for a good pair of cross-country skis. The annual May Bloomsday Run, for example, calls on more than 50,000 adults and 9,000 youngsters (Junior Bloomsday Run) to participate, in addition to countless Spokane residents who support the event in other ways. Participation is also evident in the arts. The Spokane Children's Theatre is always on the lookout for local acting, directing and writing talent.

Let the Good Times Roll

Family fun: Spokane County is located in the center of a vast recreational area surrounded by 12 national parks including Coulee Dam National Area, Mt. Rainier, North Cascades and Glacier National Parks. The city and county operate more than 80 parks and 1,600 miles of maintained trails for biking, walking and cross-country skiing. Riverfront Park is 100 acres of hiking and picnicking, and includes: the Lilac Bowl Amphitheatre (seats 30,000), for outdoor concerts and theatrical performances; Clocktower (a concert stage); the five-story high Imax Theatre; and the Gondola Sky-Ride. Other parks include Finch Arboretum, Manito Park (noted for its 18th-century gardens), Mt. Spokane State Park, Spokane Falls and Riverside State Park. There are also 76 freshwater lakes within a 50-mile radius. Most offer excellent fishing, boating, swimming, camping and water-skiing. Cross-country skiing, snowmobiling white-water rafting and horse back riding are also popular. Indian Canyon Golf Course is one of 30 excellent golf courses. Other attractions include: Silverwood, an Old West theme park; Grand Coulee Dam; Turnbull National Wildlife Refuge; Walk in the Wild Zoo, a children's petting zoo; Fairchild A.F.B. Heritage Museum (Air Force memorabilia museum); Cheney Cowles Memorial Museum; and the Museum of Native American Cultures.

Sports: Catch semi-pro sports action with the Spokane Chiefs Hockey, and the Spokane Indians Baseball. The $50,000 Rainier Lilac Golf Open is held in July, and is one of the Northwest's top golf events. Youth and adult sports programs run year-round in the Spokane area, including baseball, basketball, football, hockey, soccer, softball and volleyball leagues. Fun runs are very big (from 2 miles to marathons).

Arts and entertainment: The Spokane Opera House is host to the area's biggest cultural events—Broadway shows on regional tour, and the Spokane Symphony, to name a couple. The Metropolitan Performing Arts Center features ballets, concerts and the Spokane Symphony. For plays, check out the Spokane Civic Theatre, the Coeur d'Alene Summer Theater (summer musicals), the Centre Theatre Group, the Spokane Children's Theatre, and the Spokane Interplayers Ensemble. Riverfront Park offers music festivals throughout the summer.

Annual events: Wampum Auction (April); Spokane Lilac Festival (May); ArtFest (May); Washington Trust Cycling Classic (Aug.); Spokane Interstate Fair (Sept.); Northwest Bach Festival (Jan.); Bloomsday Run (May).

The Environment

A clean environment is Spokane's hallmark. Determination is strongest in protecting one of its greatest resources—natural wildlife—as it is estimated that one of every 3 Washingtonians hunt or fish. Spokane is also blessed with a never-ending supply of fresh water (most is non-fluoridated). The drinking water comes from the Spokane Aquifer, which is fed by the clean Lake Coeur d'Alene, in Idaho. There is little concern for depleting the water supply source, and water quality is sampled every 3 months. Recycling is encouraged, with weekly scheduled pick-ups. A concern is whether a new trash incinerator is safely burning tires. Two major tire dumps were recently closed.

In and Around Town

Roads and interstates: I-90 (east-west); State Highways 290 and 10 (east-west; 395,195 and 2 (north-south).

Closest airports: Spokane International Airport (7 mi. west). Felts Field, (5.5 mi. northeast), Deer Park Airport (24 mi. north) and Mead (10 mi. northeast) can accommodate private aircraft, charters and helicopters.

Public transportation: Spokane Transit Authority operates a public bus system with more than 33 routes to all parts of the city. In addition, the Authority operates 11 park-and-ride lots around the city.

Avg. commute: 20-25 min.

What Every Resident Knows

The name Spokane is an old Indian name meaning "Children of the Sun." The city started as a fur trading center along the Spokan River and the town name originally was spelled without the final "e." Thus, Spokane rhymes with man, not mane. • Father's Day was founded in Spokane in 1910 by Sonora Smart Dodd, and President Woodrow Wilson proclaimed Father's Day as a national day of observance in 1916. • The Pend Oreille River flowing in Spokane County is one of the few rivers in North America that flows north. • Famous residents include Nez Perce warrior Chief Joseph, Bing Crosby, actress Dyan Cannon, and Redskins quarterback Mark Rypien.

FYI

Spokane Area Chamber of Commerce
W. 1020 Riverside Avenue
Spokane, WA 99201
509-624-1393

Spokane Regional Convention and Visitors Bureau
W. 926 Sprague, Suite 180
Spokane, WA 99204
509-747-3230

Spokesman-Review Chronicle
Box 2160
Spokane, WA 99201
800-338-8801

Spokane Area Economic Development Council
N 221 Wall, Suite 300
Spokane, WA 99201
509-624-9285

Coldwell Banker Columbia Realty
North 10015 Division
Suite 100
Spokane, WA 99218
509-467-9000
Guy Carrado

Century 21/Crane
East 12213 Broadway
Spokane, WA 99206
509-927-2121
Andrea Butterfield

Washington Water Power
(Gas & Electric)
1411 East Mission
Spokane, WA 99252-0001
509-489-0500

U.S. West Communications
P.O. Box 12480
Seattle, WA 98191
509-838-6636

Small Business Development Center
West 601 First Avenue
Spokane, WA 99204-0399
509-456-2781

School districts: Mead Schools: 509-468-3000; District #81: 509-353-3767, District #56: 509-922-6740
Property tax assessor: 509-456-3696
Newcomer's Club: 509-624-1661
Physician's referral: 509-455-3131 (Sacred Heart Hospital)

Fast Facts

Location	Local Population	Median Housing	Best Reasons to Live Here
Albuquerque, N.M. (p. 185)	384,736	$90,700	Promising job growth, low taxes and living costs, pleasant, year-round climate, rich ethnic/cultural diversity, abundant recreation, excellent schools and universities, fast-growing research/medical center, plentiful water supply, scenic wonders.
Arkadelphia, Ark. (p. 75)	10,018	$70,000	Small, friendly college town, great scenic beauty and natural resources, outstanding school system, growing industry, affordable housing and taxes, great recreation, very safe community.
Aurora, Colo. (Denver) (p.100)	222,000	$85,932	300 days of sunshine and an equally bright economic outlook, phenomenal recreation and family fun, top-rated Cherry Creek school district, excellent medical care, great neighborhoods, new airport and major league baseball team creating positive momentum.
Austin, Texas (p. 260)	465,622	$101,000	Phenonmenal job and business growth, highly educated population, wonderful schools, exciting family recreation, very affordable housing, beautiful lakes and hills, no state income tax, mild winters.
Bend, Ore. (p. 215)	20,469	$92,000	Scenic beauty on a grand scale, year-round recreation paradise, low crime, clean environment, strong buyer's market, growing economy, mild climate.
Blue Ash, Ohio (Greater Cincinati) (p. 210)	11,923	$105,000	Accomplished city government, great parks and recreation, outstanding schools and higher education, exceptional low-cost health care, endless diversions, booming business environment, easy access to Cincinnati.
Boise, Idaho (p. 125)	125,738	$92,896	Sparkling clean mountain town, some of the best recreation in the West, very diversified business base, affordable housing and taxes, friendly people and low crime.
Bucks County, Pa. (Philadelphia) (p. 230)	61,077	$154,600	Pleasant rural environment, central to urban areas and mountains, fast-growing communities, vibrant culture, history and the arts, strong buyer's market, progressive schools, excellent recreation.
Buffalo Grove, Ill. (Greater Chicago) (p. 130)	36,427	$160,023	Impressive school districts, excellent parks and recreation system, all "young family" neighborhoods, convenient access to the "golden career corridor," major shopping in every direction, low crime.

50 Fabulous Places to Raise Your Family

Location	Local Population	Median Housing	Best Reasons to Live Here
Burlington, Vt. (p. 295)	38,492	$120,000	Glorious Lake Champlain area, Vermont's only economic bright spot, cosmopolitan college town, excellent schools, super year-round recreation, clean, safe environment, friendly, laid-back community.
Charleston, S.C. (p. 240)	506,875	$80,600	Charming Southern city, exciting history, Atlantic coast is your backyard, great climate, affordable real estate, favorable economy, growing population, exciting recreation and culture, good schools.
Chesapeake, Va. (p. 280)	157,669	$98,000	Fast-growing coastal region, affordable housing, exciting economic growth, progressive schools, abundant recreation and culture, very low crime, great community spirit, beautiful, historic area.
Columbia, Mo. (p. 165)	68,600	$80,900	One of the nicest small metro areas in the country, highly educated population, award-winning schools, outstanding medical care, affordable housing, abundant green space, booming job market, great college town.
Columbia, S.C. (p. 245)	472,000	$88,090	In the top 10 U.S. housing markets, abundant higher education, affordable living costs, pleasant climate, growing and diverse population, recession-proof economy, award-winning schools, great recreation.
Coral Springs, Fla. (p. 105)	83,000	$105,100	One of the most successful planned communities in the U.S., fabulous neighborhoods, award-winning parks, endless family recreation and events, best public schools in the country, no state income tax.
Eden Prairie, Minn. (Minneapolis) (p. 160)	39,311	$142,000	Beautiful lakefront city, low crime, outstanding health care and public schools, very committed to family recreation and the arts, stable job market, phenomenal shopping, friendly people.
Eugene, Ore. (p. 220)	117,155	$82,894	Delightful year-round climate, attractive, affordable housing, outstanding recreation, excellent schools and health care, proximity to the ocean and mountains, many growing industries, laid back lifestyle, popular college town.
Fayetteville, Ark. (p. 80)	42,099	$75,000	Breathtaking Ozark Mountain country, delightful 4 seasons, very affordable housing and taxes, strong employment possibilities, fabulous outdoor recreation, good school system, laid-back college town.

Location	Local Population	Median Housing	Best Reasons to Live Here
Fort Myers, Fla. (p. 110)	45,206	$70,100	Subtropical climate and one of the "hottest" job markets in the country, real estate in all price ranges, greatly improved school system, gorgeous Gulf Coast beaches, no state income tax.
Fountain Hills, Ariz. (Greater Phoenix) (p. 65)	10,030	$115,000	Spectacular mountain views, wonderfully diverse housing market, small, family-oriented community, abundant recreation, good schools, access to Maricopa County's booming job market, endless sunshine and clean, dry air.
Gaithersburg, Md. (Washington, D.C.) (p. 155)	43,732	$155,000	Good schools, growing business base, low crime, relatively affordable housing, abundant recreation facilities, beautiful planned community, residents have strong voice in city government.
Galveston Island, Texas (p. 265)	59,070	$62,600	Coastal island with glorious scenery, sunny, semi-tropical climate, most affordable housing market in U.S., tremendous ethnic diversity, close-knit community, good schools, excellent medical care, active historic preservation efforts.
Greensboro, N.C. (p. 195)	196,000	$77,600	A National Civics League "All American City," delightful year-round climate, affordable real estate, fast-growing economy, excellent schools, accessible roadways, central to mountains and beaches.
Greenville, S.C. (p. 250)	250,000	$83,800	Affordable living, low taxes, country's second best housing market, fast-growing job market, mountain views, pleasant climate, great education, growing cultural arena, environmentally sound.
Henderson, Nev. (Las Vegas) (p. 170)	83,913	$100,700	Fastest-growing city in Nevada, excellent job prospects, breathtaking mountain scenery, fabulous culture and recreation, dry desert climate, no state income tax, beautiful new homes, first-rate medical care, central to the "Best of the West."
Huntington, New York (Long Island) (p. 190)	18,180	$268,300	Sophisticated suburb, active cultural scene, good schools, proximity to beaches, scenic woods and rolling hills, very involved, safe community, access to the Big Apple and its 1,001 things to do.
Indianapolis, Ind. (p. 140)	741,952	$84,100	Rapidly growing economy, good job prospects, affordable housing and living costs, outstanding medical, clean environment, low crime, great sports, recreation, culture, innovative schools, exceptional higher education, very family-oriented.

50 Fabulous Places to Raise Your Family

Location	Local Population	Median Housing	Best Reasons to Live Here
Lexington, Ky. (p. 150)	225,366	$73,900	Beautiful horse farm country, delightful year-round climate, historic college town, low crime, range of housing options, strong public school system, abundant recreation, low unemployment, taxes.
Kent, Wash. (p. 300)	37,400	$127,500	Central to Seattle and Tacoma, some of the most affordable housing in the area, excellent schools, family-oriented, access to major highways, award-winning parks and recreation.
Mt. Lebanon, Pa. (p. 235)	33,362	$72,700	One of the most livable areas of the country, low living costs, outstanding medical care, excellent schools, clean environment, low crime, expanding business sector, wonderful variety of culture and recreation.
Morristown, N.J. (p. 180)	19,189	$223,491	Prosperous, fast-growing county, New England-style charm, voted New Jersey's best town, wonderful parks, ethnic and cultural diversity, progressive schools and medical care, excellent transportation, super shopping, historic area.
Milwaukie, Ore. (Portland) (p. 225)	18,830	$97,400	Clean environment, thriving job market, great entertainment, good schools, scenic beauty, abundance of health care services, variety of cultural and visual arts, growing economy, excellent transportation.
Nashville, Tenn. (p. 255)	510,784	$89,200	Big-city living in a country setting, affordable housing, mild year-round climate, clean environment, thriving job market, great entertainment, excellent school system, abundance of colleges and medical care, outdoor recreation, racial harmony.
Overland Park, Kan. (p. 145)	111,790	$125,700	Fastest-growing county in Kansas, stable economy, low unemployment, superb public schools, affordable housing and beautiful new subdivisions, excellent health care, great roads/transportation.
Plano, Texas (Dallas) (p. 270)	137,000	$113,000	Work-hard/play-hard attitude, award -winning schools, booming local economy, pleasant year-round climate, affordable housing, no state income tax, ethnic diversity.
Provo, Utah (p. 275)	80,300	$72,000	Fabulous moutain scenery, perfect year-round climate for outdoor enthusiasts, unbelievable recreation, wholesome family community, friendly people, tremendous ecomonic growth, affordable living costs, beautiful neighborhoods and homes.

Location	Local Population	Median Housing	Best Reasons to Live Here
Raleigh, N.C. (p. 200)	207,951	$125,000	World-renowned research center, outstanding medical care, endless recreation, low unemployment, low crime, superb educational institutions, beautiful communities, affordable real estate, ideal climate.
Reno, Nev. (p. 175)	136,630	$110,000	Strong job possibilities, affordable housing, no state income tax, endless outdoor recreation, good schools, exciting entertainment and events, four diverse seasons, fabulous scenery.
Reston, Va. (Washington, D.C.) (p. 285)	53,800	$183,000	Successful planned community, a "city in the country," educated, ethnically diverse population, beautiful new town center, excellent schools, attractive park settings, proximity to Washington, D.C., and its vast, historic, cultural offerings.
Richmond, Va. (p. 290)	203,056	$112,657	Fast-growing metro area, booming business, great recreation, diverse housing, award-winning schools, excellent medical care, easy pace, historic state capital, 1½ hours to mountains and beaches.
Roswell, Ga. (Atlanta) (p. 120)	47,923	$148,000	Vibrant regional economy, historic, fast-growing community, great neighborhoods and schools, award-winning parks, wonderful year-round climate, fantastic diversions for kids, excellent transportation.
Sacramento, Calif. (p. 85)	385,127	$135,000	One of California's fastest-growing and most affordable big cities, stable economy with good job growth, vast choice of housing and neighborhoods, rural, rolling hills and rivers, great recreation, pleasant Mediterranean climate, excellent transportation.
Spokane, Wash. (p. 305)	178,500	$66,900	Fast-growing economy, strong job possibilities, affordable housing, no state income tax, immaculate region, minimal traffic, vast recreation, innovative schools, four distinct, pleasant seasons.
Tampa, Fla. (p. 115)	288,565	$72,500	Semi-tropical climate, fabulous recreation on the Gulf of Mexico, vast corporate relocations and expansions, low living costs, no state income tax, good schools and health care, affordable housing.

50 Fabulous Places to Raise Your Family

Location	Local Population	Median Housing	Best Reasons to Live Here
Tuscon, Ariz. (p. 70)	419,100	$80,000	Breathtaking mountain scenery, dry, sunny climate, one of the fastest-growing job markets in the U.S., diversified housing market, abundant culture and recreation, excellent medical care, nationally recognized public schools.
Valencia, Calif. (p. 90)	160,000	$230,000	A gorgeous master-planned community, one of the best commutes to Los Angeles, low crime, ample recreation, choice homes and schools, great climate without the smog, wonderful mountain views.
Vestavia Hills, Ala. (Birmingham) (p. 60)	19,749	$105,000	Lush, green streetscapes, outstanding public schools, access to a fast-growing job market, very low crime and pollution, great recreation and culture, easy accessibility to business and shopping, tremendous community spirit.
Vista, Calif. (p. 95)	76,000	$186,000	Absolute perfect climate, dynamic job and business growth, rated best high school in California, wonderful recreation and fun, solid community spirit, best of San Diego 45 minutes away.
Wheaton, Ill. (Greater Chicago) (p. 135)	51,464	$148,700	Historic community with traditional values, one of the fastest-growing regions in Illinois, outstanding schools and local universities, beautiful neighborhoods in parklike settings, convenient commute to booming Research and Development Corridor, phenomenal shopping, low crime.
Wilmington, N.C. ((p. 205)	60,131	$102,000	Charming, progressive Southern city, waterfront living, diverse business base with great growth potential (Hollywood South), affordable housing and living costs, fabulous recreation, mild year-round climate, respected schools and hospitals.

Index

About the Authors

The coauthors of two other bestselling relocation guides combine their unique backgrounds and expertise to produce this valuable and long-awaited relocation guide for families: Lee Rosenberg, as a Certified Financial Planner, has successfully guided hundreds of clients through retirement planning and relocation issues. Saralee H. Rosenberg adds personal experience to the mix, having relocated a dozen times and counting.

As the co-founder of ARS Financial Services, Inc., Lee Rosenberg brings more than 17 years of solid financial management experience to his company. Mr. Rosenberg is a Registered Representative of Cadaret Grant, Inc. (member firm of the National Association of Securities Dealers).

With his expertise in the areas of investments, estate and retirement planning, Mr. Rosenberg has been interviewed extensively by the New York media. He has appeared on Fox 5's "Good Day New York," WABC TV's "Eyewitness News," WABC, WOR, WMCA, WEVD Radio, and the ABC Radio Network. He has also been frequently quoted in New York's *Newsday* and *The Daily News*.

On the national scene, Mr. Rosenberg has appeared on CNN, CNBC, and been featured in *Money* magazine and *The Wall Street Journal*. He has also been a guest on hundreds of local television and radio talk shows throughout the country.

He recently served as the Chairman of the Long Island Society of the Institute of Certified Financial Planners and is listed in *Who's Who of Financial Planning* (1989-1993). He is also a recognized member of the International Association of Financial Planners and the International Association of Registered Financial Planners.

Mr. Rosenberg is a well-known public speaker and guest lecturer, conducting financial planning seminars at local colleges, libraries, banks and Fortune 500 companies throughout the tri-state area. He is a graduate of Brooklyn College and the College for Financial Planning.

Saralee H. Rosenberg is a former sales and marketing executive with more than 12 years of corporate communications experience. She has previously been published in *The New York Times* and numerous other magazines and newspapers. Ms. Rosenberg holds a degree in telecommunications from Indiana University, Bloomington, and is a Chicago native.

Lee and Saralee Rosenberg are also the coauthors of *Destination Florida: The Guide to a Successful Relocation* and *50 Fabulous Places to Retire in America*. The Rosenbergs live in Baldwin Harbor, N.Y., with their three children. If you would like to correspond with them, write to the Rosenbergs at 125 Franklin Ave., Suite 6, Valley Stream, N.Y. 11580.

NCK

LBC

NCR